PRISONERS' RIGHTS SOURCEBOOK

Theory • Litigation • Practice

CRIMINAL LAW SERIES

Searches & Seizures, Arrests and Confessions
By William E. Ringel

Eye-Witness Identification: Legal and
Practical Problems
By Nathan R. Sobel

New York Criminal Practice Under the CPL
By Robert M. Pitler

PRISONERS' RIGHTS SOURCEBOOK

Theory • Litigation • Practice

Edited and Compiled by

Michele G. Hermann

and

Marilyn G. Haft

Clark Boardman Company, Ltd.
New York, New York
1973

TO ROBERT AND WOBIE

LIST OF CONTRIBUTORS

Stanley A. Bass
Phyllis J. Baunauch
Haywood Burns
Nancy Crisman
Martin Erdmann
Howard L. Feinstein
W. Anthony Fitch
David Fogel
David F. Greenberg
Richard C. Hand
William E. Hellerstein
Robert Hermann
Philip J. Hirschkop
Hillel Hoffman
Hon. William Wayne Justice
Hon. Robert W. Kastenmeier
Edward I. Koren
Richard R. Korn

Robert B. McKay
Michael Millemann
Tom Murton
Robert Plotkin
Monroe E. Price
David Rothenberg
David J. Rothman
Herman Schwartz
Barbara Shapiro
James D. Silbert
Richard Singer
Martin Sostre
Alan Sussman
Julian Tepper
William Bennett Turner
Donald Wallace
Hon. Jack B. Weinstein

ABOUT THE EDITORS

Michele G. Hermann is currently serving as Federal Criminal Trial Attorney for The Legal Aid Society of New York City. In addition she is an Adjunct Professor at New York University School of Law and serves with Ms. Haft as Co-Director of the Women's Prison Clinical Program there. Prior to her current position with The Legal Aid Society Ms. Hermann was Associate Director of the American Civil Liberties Union Foundation National Prisoners' Rights Project. Additionally, she and Ms. Haft co-chaired a series of Practising Law Institute Seminars on Prisoners' Rights Litigation across the country. She has also served as a *Pro Se* Law Clerk for the Second Circuit Court of Appeals. Ms. Hermann received her B.A. degree from Bryn Mawr College and her J.D. degree from Yale University.

Marilyn G. Haft has served for the past two-and-a-half years as Staff Counsel with The National Office of The American Civil Liberties Union. In this position she has participated in litigation in general civil rights and civil liberties cases on the federal and state levels and has specialized in women's rights in prison. She is currently Director of the ACLU National Litigation Project on Sexual Privacy. In addition Ms. Haft is an Adjunct Professor at New York University School of Law and serves with Ms. Hermann as Co-Director of the Women's Prison Clinical Program there. She and Ms. Hermann have co-chaired a series of Practising Law Institute Seminars on Prisoners' Rights Litigation across the country. She serves as Co-Chairperson of the Subcommittee on Corrections, New York State Committee of the United States Commission on Civil Rights. Ms. Haft received her J.D. degree from New York University.

FOREWORD

ROBERT B. McKAY *

Inmates of American penal institutions and members of the general public may not agree on many things. But, for rather different reasons, both groups would like to see prisons disappear. There is in both cases a self-interest motivation that prompts the wish. Inmates are likely to believe that if there were no jails or prisons, they would be free of restraint on their liberty. The self-interest wish that I attribute to the general public is less obvious and perhaps almost entirely unconscious. The public does not want to do away with jails and prisons, but does want those institutions to be out of sight and out of mind. The thought is that "they"—institutions and inmates—should be someone else's responsibility. "We" should not be troubled with having to know how society punishes those who overstep the rules.

Plainly, this out-of-sight, out-of-mind locution has not worked. In a society in which crime and law and order are topics very much at the epicenter of social and political discussion, it is not possible to conceal our penal institutions and their manifest failures. After decades of public neglect, the correction system has secured a measure of attention as part of the overall problem of the criminal justice system. Tragic episodes like Attica have the dramatic power to focus public attention for a time; and other jail breaks, prison riots, and inmate strikes have kept the prison issue alive in the mind of the public.

It is, however, one thing to observe that the issue is not dead and quite another to determine whether it is alive and well. Efforts to arouse the public to a need for action do not provide assurance of thoughtful or constructive reaction. Prison unrest breeds as many demands for increased security and harsh treatment as it does for reexamination of the premises of detention and amelioration of brutalizing conditions. Without perceptive guidance, the spotlight of publicity may as easily lead to destructive change as to improvement.

* Dean and Professor of Law, New York University School of Law; Chairman, New York City Board of Corrections; Chairman, Citizens' Union; Chairman, New York State Special Commission on Attica (McKay Commission); B.S. University of Kansas; J.D. Yale University.

At this crucial point in the reordering of attitudes about the correction system and the criminal justice system as a whole, it is vital that the animus of change be humanitarian rather than vengeful. Fortunately, a society that heeds its humanitarian instincts will also be a society that better serves its understandable concern for self-preservation from the inroads of a feared rise in criminality. Let me explain.

I begin with the premise, unchallenged I believe, that most American jails and prisons brutalize and degrade their inhabitants. The dispute relates only to the question whether that is a proper sanction to be imposed upon those who have offended against society. There are those who argue that harsh treatment is necessary as punishment or to deter others from similar offenses, or both. Without for the moment dealing with the inadequacy of these theories of detention, let me state my simple thesis in favor of more humanitarian conditions and improved programs in penal institutions. Whether an individual is moved by humanitarian considerations (which I hope is true of most) or whether he is motivated by personal fear of a breakdown in law and order, the result should be the same. The humanitarian is unwilling to tolerate the brutalizing of his fellow human being, no matter what the offense. The person who fears an upsurge in crime must be made to understand that the present detention practices necessarily enlarge the number of ex-offenders who will return to a life of crime because of their prison-fed hostility to society; their failure to learn alternative skills; and the unwillingness of the public to permit employment of the meagre skills available to the inmate upon release.

There is nothing mysterious or complex about the above argument. The logic seems to me overwhelming; but somehow this obvious (to me) truth has not yet won the day. Accordingly, I welcome the reasoned discourse in this *Prisoners' Rights Sourcebook;* the calm, dispassionate analysis of the serious problems of the prison society; and the statement of techniques for calling these issues to public attention. With the increasing visibility of the problems of detention much has been written on particular aspects of the correction system. This *Sourcebook,* however, is unique in providing an overview of all the complex, interrelated issues, from a history of prisons in the United States, through the problems of detention, to hopeful suggestions for improvement.

One of the most interesting aspects of the *Sourcebook* is the emphasis on litigation as a means of improving prison conditions. Until recent years the courts, like the public, had not discovered the prisons, believing it wiser (easier?) to leave the final determination of prison matters to the administrators of those institutions. This view, curiously inverted from general judicial willingness to scrutinize other aspects of government, has now been largely overcome. But it remains true that places of detention yield less readily to change by judicial mandate than probably any other institution in our society. Jails and prisons are often still closed to the public and the press, and this is the last significant bastion of individual censorship and denial of privacy. The judiciary, particularly federal courts, have brought about change, but mostly episodic because of the limited intervention that is possible. The experience has often been that change required in a particular instance is denied general application despite apparent identity of subsequent cases. Unless and until courts become virtual receivers of individual jails and prisons, accepting responsibility for ongoing operations, it is unlikely that courts can do more than prod the conscience and, more hopefully, call to the attention of concerned members of the public and individual legislators the need for more regular scrutiny and general reform.

The *Sourcebook* is important also for demonstrating once more another point that seems hard to get across. Even if there is fairly general acceptance of the proposition that prisons are a failure, there is no general agreement about the reasons for failure or even the purposes of a system of detention. Various reasons are given in justification for confinement, including rehabilitation of the inmates, deterrence from future criminal activities, punishment, and isolation of the crime-prone from the opportunity to commit offenses. But our present places of confinement do not educate, do not rehabilitate, and do not train realistically for employment after release. We know—at least we should know—that the prison experience has not been a significant deterrent to criminal action by present prison inmates (most of whom are repeaters) or to those on the outside (as the rate of crime escalates). On the other hand, prisons do some things exceedingly well: They *do* punish; and, in the very act of degrading their charges, prisons wreak the vengeance that society apparently demands. We know also that the prisons teach that human life and human dignity are of small worth, thus encouraging inmates on release to respond in kind, repaying in crime and violence—and revenge—the tender mercies to which their keepers subjected them.

The crisis of our prison system is at last visible, and the moment of truth is near. Decision is in the balance. The *Sourcebook* should be studied by all who want to make sure the decision is reasoned and sensible.

March 1973

EDITORS' PREFACE

The aim of this *Sourcebook* is an ambitious one. We have attempted to compile a comprehensive collection of articles by persons who are active in the prisoners' rights field, encompassing legal, historical, sociological, and political perspectives. The *Sourcebook* is not a casebook which reprints and analyzes the major and significant cases. Nor is it a manual of litigation, although it contains some chapters which do engage in traditional case discussions and others which detail litigation techniques. These contributions are written by some of the leading attorneys in the prisoners' rights field today. Other, broader articles have been contributed not only by lawyers but also by judges, state attorneys general, correctional administrators, prisoners, ex-offenders, sociologists, legislators, and historians.

It is important to note that many of the discussions contained herein, particularly in the legal areas, concentrate on the favorable decisions in the prisoners' rights area and do not extensively cite or analyze the many cases where the prisoner has not prevailed.

Rather than commencing with a discussion of the many rights currently enjoyed or sought by prisoners, the *Sourcebook* starts with a section designed to give a broader background to the general prison area. These articles discuss the historical roots and development of our nation's prisons, give a perspective on the new political and racial consciousness found in many of today's prisons, and set forth the typical experiences in the criminal conviction process which often lay the foundation for the outrage and resentment exhibited by so many prisoners.

The second section of the *Sourcebook* is primarily legal in scope. It contains a series of articles which discuss both the substantive and procedural aspects of litigating prisoners' rights suits, with sample pleadings in the appendix to aid the litigator. The first chapter elaborates the wide range of rights sought to be protected by the First Amendment: religion, reading, writing, mail, press access, political organization, and personal expression. The following chapters detail the due process requirements of discipline in prison and discuss challenges to conditions in prisons and in jails housing pretrial detainees which may constitute cruel and unusual punishment in violation of the Eighth Amendment. The chapter on jails also includes a description of a pending challenge to the money bail system as a denial of equal protection.

The subsequent chapters consider the right to medical treatment, and the nascent right to rehabilitative services, with the correlative right not to be rehabilitated.

The next substantive discussion in the *Sourcebook* deals with parole, a topic which may appear to be outside prison concerns. Parole, however, determines the length of time the prisoner spends behind bars and is therefore of primary concern to inmates. Civil disabilities is another subject which does not constitute a purely in-prison problem, but which is vital to the lives of inmates. This chapter discusses statutory bars to prisoners' civil suits and statutory forfeiture of rights by ex-offenders, with particular emphasis on employment problems.

The treatment of procedural aspects of prisoners' rights litigation begins with a discussion of the jurisdictional problems of such suits. That article is followed by a comprehensive discussion of trial preparation and strategies and an article on the pitfalls of emergency litigation. An analysis of remedies available in prisoners' rights suits is next, and the section concludes with a discussion on alternatives to lawsuits and the limits of litigation.

The third section in the *Sourcebook* deals with problems of special groups in prison: women, juveniles, Spanish-speaking inmates, and the criminally insane. The chapter on women in prison describes an innovation program now going on in a New York penitentiary for females.

The fourth and final section in the *Sourcebook* deals with trends for the future in prisoners' rights. These articles are predominantly theoretical, and many are pessimistic in their perceptions of the future. In the prison administrator's view of reform, a director of a corrections department sets forth some hopeful views, which are then disputed by a leading social scientist. A United States Congressman discusses the role of the legislator in reform, followed by a brief discussion of areas where legislatures can best act.

The chapters on the courts and reform contain two thoughtful expositions by federal judges on judicial administrative reforms in the area of prisoners' rights and pro se prisoners' suits generally.

The discussions of trends in inmate self-help include an article describing successful experiments where prison administrators have fostered inmate autonomy and self-government within institutions and a description of the functions of an ex-offender organization.

The book concludes with a comprehensive chapter summarizing new trends in prison and parole and an article on alternatives to today's prisons.

We hope that the *Sourcebook* will be useful to the many people who are interested in prisoners' rights. It is aimed primarily at the legal community, but it should be of interest to prisoners, concerned community groups, penologists, social scientists, and prison administrators.

We would like to express our appreciation to all the contributors, not only for the fine quality of work presented but for their unfailing cooperation, which we know was motivated by a very deep, shared concern for the plight of prisons and prisoners in our country.

Michele G. Hermann

March, 1973

Marilyn G. Haft

SPECIAL EDITORS' NOTE

After the manuscript for this book was printed, the U.S. Supreme Court handed down two important decisions that have substantial impact on the law in the prisoners' rights area. One relates to the necessity for exhaustion of state remedies before suing in federal court, the other to the right to counsel at parole revocation hearings.

In Preiser v. Rodriguez, — U.S. — (May 9, 1973) the Supreme Court held that when a state prisoner challenges in federal court "the very fact or duration of his physical imprisonment" and seeks release as a remedy, he must be regarded as suing for a writ of habeas corpus and is required to exhaust his state remedies pursuant to 28 USC §2254. While this decision will certainly have an impact on prisoners' rights suits that challenge deprivation of good time for punitive confinement, it should not broadly affect most prison suits, despite some sweeping dicta. There are, of course, a number of questions left open by this case, particularly regarding its application where a prisoner complaint seeking release from confinement is coupled with a request for damages or an allegation of unconstitutional treatment that seeks injunctive relief. While there is still immediate federal jurisdiction to hear the latter claims under §1983, controversy still undoubtedly arises over whether such suits must be heard at once, or whether they may be held in abeyance pending exhaustion of state remedies in the habeas corpus action. Federal courts may be reluctant to act on suits which will be determined by state courts. It must be hoped, however, that they will not refuse immediate action to stop prison practices that infringe constitutional rights where confinement has been used as a punishment.

The second case, Gagnon v. Scarpelli, — U.S. — (May 16, 1973) holds that there is no right to assigned counsel in parole or probation revocation hearings where the violation is a conviction for another crime or where the charges have been admitted. The Court indicates that the right to counsel in revocation hearings will be determined on a case-by-case basis, with a presumption that counsel should be assigned where the parolee or probationer can colorably claim either that he has not committed a violation or that there are substantial factors which mitigate the offense. In all cases where a request for counsel is refused, reasons for this action must be given.

Besides these two Supreme Court cases which will await further interpretation, there have also been a number of lower court decisions in the prisoners' rights area since this book went to press. It must be noted that the law in this field is extremely volatile, as it is undergoing rapid development and frequent change.

M. G. H.

May, 1973   **M. G. H.**

TABLE OF CONTENTS

FOREWORD   ix
Robert B. McKay

EDITORS' PREFACE   xiii

SECTION I   PRISONERS AND THE IMPRISONED

Chapter 1   HISTORY

History of Prisons, Asylums, and Other Decaying Institutions   5
David J. Rothman

Chapter 2   THE NEW BREED

The Black Prisoner as Victim   25
Haywood Burns

The New Prisoner   35
Martin Sostre

Chapter 3   THE CRIMINAL JUSTICE SYSTEM

An Indictment by an Inmate   49
Donald Wallace

An Answer by a Lawyer   57
Martin Erdmann

SECTION II   LITIGATING THE RIGHTS OF PRISONERS

Chapter 4   THE FIRST AMENDMENT

First Amendment Rights   67
Stanley A. Bass

Chapter 5   DISCIPLINE AND DUE PROCESS

Due Process Behind the Walls   79
  Michael Millemann

Chapter 6   PRISON CONDITIONS

Challenging Conditions in Prisons Which Violate the Eighth
  Amendment   113
  William Bennett Turner

Chapter 7   PRETRIAL CONDITIONS

Improving Conditions in Pretrial Detention Facilities   125
  Stanley A. Bass

Money Bail as a Denial of Equal Protection (Bellamy Brief)   133

Chapter 8   MEDICAL TREATMENT

The Right to Medical Treatment   165
  Edward I. Koren

Chapter 9   REHABILITATION

The Coming Right to Rehabilitation   189
  Richard Singer

Chapter 10   PAROLE

Problems in Parole   201
  Herman Schwartz

Chapter 11   CIVIL DISABILITIES

Attacking Barriers to Employment: The Former Offender's
  Dilemma   217
  Julian Tepper and Howard Feinstein

SECTION III   PROCEDURAL ASPECTS OF
              PRISONERS' RIGHTS LITIGATION

Chapter 12   JURISDICTION

Federal Jurisdiction and Practice in Prisoner Cases   243
  William Bennett Turner

Chapter 13   TECHNIQUES OF LITIGATION

Litigating an Affirmative Prisoners' Rights Action   255
    Philip J. Hirschkop, Nancy Crisman, and
    Michael Millemann

Crisis Litigation: Problems and Suggestions   287
    William E. Hellerstein and Barbara Shapiro

Chapter 14   REMEDIES

Enforcing Prisoners' Rights: Remedying the Remedies   317
    Richard C. Hand and Robert Plotkin

Chapter 15   ALTERNATIVES TO LITIGATION

The Limits of Litigating—Alternatives to a Lawsuit   331
    Hillel Hoffman

        SECTION IV   THE PROBLEMS OF SPECIAL
                      GROUPS IN PRISON

Chapter 16   WOMEN AS PRISONERS

Women in Prison   341
    Marilyn G. Haft

Chapter 17   JUVENILES AS PRISONERS

The Rights of Juveniles Confined in Training Schools   357
    James D. Silbert and Alan Sussman

Chapter 18   SPANISH-SPEAKING PRISONERS

The Problems of Spanish-Speaking Prisoners   385
    Marilyn G. Haft

Cruz Complaint   388

Chapter 19   THE CRIMINALLY INSANE

The Rights of the Criminally Insane   405
    Monroe E. Price

SECTION V   FUTURE TRENDS

Chapter 20   ADMINISTRATORS AND REFORM

Corrections in the Year 2000—Some Directions   423
    David Fogel

The Prisoners of Affirmation: Correctional **Administrators**
  as Reformers   437
    Richard R. Korn

Chapter 21   LEGISLATORS AND REFORM

The Legislator and the Legislature: Their Roles in Prison
  Reform   455
    Hon. Robert W. Kastenmeier

An Introduction to Prison Reform Legislation   463
    W. Anthony Fitch and Julian Tepper

Chapter 22   COURTS AND REFORM

Administrative Reform and the Courts   501
    Hon. Jack B. Weinstein

Prisoners' Litigation in the Federal Courts   515
    Hon. William W. Justice

Chapter 23   PRISONERS AND REFORM

Organizing to Help the Ex-Offender   533
    David Rothenberg

Shared Decision-Making in Prison Management: A Survey
  of Demonstrations Involving the Inmate in Participatory
  Government   541
    Tom Murton and Phyllis J. Baunach

Chapter 24   THE FUTURE

New Trends in Prison and Parole   577
    Robert Plotkin

Chapter 25   ALTERNATIVES TO PRISON

Guideposts for Prison Reformers Lost in the Woods of
  Litigation   595
    David F. Greenberg

APPENDIX A

A-1   Complaint (*Clutchette v. Procunier*)   609

A-2   Sample Complaint in a §1983 Action
       (*Oliver v. Schoonfield*)   616

A-3   Form: Notice to Members of Class of
       Commencement of a §1983 Class Action
       (*Collins v. Schoonfield*)   626

A-4   Sample Interrogatories Propounded by
       Plaintiffs in a §1983 Class Action
       Challenging the Constitutionality of
       Jail Conditions (*Collins v. Schoonfield*)   628

A-5   Sample Interrogatories Propounded by
       Plaintiff in a §1983 Class Action
       Challenging the Constitutionality of
       Prison Conditions (*Stinnie v. Gregory*)   642

A-6   Sample Interrogatories Propounded by
       Plaintiffs in a §1983 Class Action
       Challenging Violation of First
       Amendment Rights in Prison
       (*Arey v. Oliver*)   652

A-7   Form: Request for Production of
       Documents (*Collins v. Schoonfield*)   658

A-8   Sample Deposition of a Friendly Expert
       Witness (*Collins v. Schoonfield*)   661

A-9   Sample Deposition of a Hostile Witness
       (Tombs Case—Manhattan House of
       Detention for Men) (*Rhem v. McGrath*)   675

A-10   Enforcement of a Favorable Decision by a
       Finding of Contempt: The Contempt
       Opinion in *Landman v. Royster*   680

A-11   Forms: Pro Se Actions of Prisoners
       (Jailhouse Lawyer's Manual)   691

A-12   Constitutional Arguments Against Pretrial
       Detention of the Poor: An In-Depth Study
       of the Impact of the Bail System on the

Outcome of a Criminal Case (*Bellamy v. Judges and Justices of New York, etc.*)   719

A-13   Model Regulations for Classification and Discipline at Correctional Institutions   741

APPENDIX B   List of The Fortune Society   753

BIBLIOGRAPHY   769

TABLE OF CASES   777

GENERAL INDEX   799

SECTION II
PRISONS AND THE IMPRISONED

CHAPTER 1
HISTORY

EDITORS' INTRODUCTION

Chief Justice Burger has called the prisons of this country "a national disgrace." Where did these prisons come from, from whom did we inherit these decaying theories and edifices of shame? These are questions that have not only gone unanswered in today's study of prisons, but too often have gone unasked.

The following article not only summarizes the history of institutions but also goes on to reflect the author's growing disillusionment with "an experiment that didn't work," and concludes with a plea and an affirmative program for decarceration. An historical treatment of prisons probably should stop at the present, with the self-spoken admonitions against repeating disastrous errors of the past, but it would have been a mistake to deprive the readers of the fruits of a truly creative and thoughtful analysis of the future.

HISTORY OF PRISONS, ASYLUMS, AND OTHER DECAYING INSTITUTIONS

DAVID J. ROTHMAN *

    Over the course of the past several decades, without clear theoretical justification or even a high degree of self-consciousness, we have been completing a revolution in the treatment of the insane, the criminal, the orphaned, the delinquent, and the poor. Whereas once we relied almost exclusively upon incarceration to treat or punish these classes of people, we now frame and administer many programs that maintain them within the community or at least remove them as quickly as possible from institutions. Policy makers in each of these areas interpret their own measures as specific responses to internal developments—an advance in drug therapy or a dissatisfaction with prevailing penitentiary conditions—not as part of a general anti-institutional movement. But such a movement exists, and it must be seen in a comprehensive way if it is ever to be understood.

    The basic statistics are, themselves, most striking. Since 1955 the annual number of inmates in the nation's mental hospitals has been falling. New York institutions, for example, held 93,000 patients in 1955; in 1966, their number dropped to 82,765, and in 1970 to 64,239. A similar decline has occurred in correctional institutions. In 1940, 131.7 prisoners per 100,000 of the population served time in federal or state penitentiaries; in 1965, the number fell to 109.6 per 100,000, and this without a concomitant drop in the number of crimes committed or criminals convicted. Dramatic changes have also affected the young. The orphan asylum has almost disappeared, and the juvenile correction center has also declined in use. As for the poor, the almshouse or traditional poorhouse is no longer a specter in their lives.

    Obviously, no one would be foolish enough to predict that

---

* Professor of History, Columbia University; author, Discovery of the Asylum (Little, Brown & Co. 1971); member, Committee for the Study of Incarceration; Ph.D. Harvard University.

within the next twenty or thirty years incarcerating institutions will disappear. Some 400,000 adults and juveniles remain in correctional institutions, and a similar number fill mental hospitals. Nevertheless, when our current practices are viewed within historical perspective, the degree to which we have moved away from the incarcerative mode of coping with these social problems is clear enough. We are witnessing nothing less than the end of one era in social reform and the beginning of another.

The Movement for Incarceration

Institutionalization of "problem people" in the United States originated in the opening decades of the 19th century. Prior to that, colonial communities, particularly the more settled ones along the seaboard, relied upon very different mechanisms of control. Their level of expectations was very low; they did not expect to eliminate poverty or to reform the criminal. Rather, the colonists devoted their energies to differentiating carefully between neighbor and stranger. Typically, they provided assistance to the resident within his household or that of a friend—and they banished the troublesome outsider. A neighbor's poverty was not suspect—clergymen, after all, preached regularly on the virtue of charity, making little effort to distinguish the worthy from the unworthy poor. Local ne'er-do-wells were fined or whipped or shamed before their neighbors through such devices as the stocks. Outsiders on the other hand, whether honest and poor or petty criminals, were sent on their way as quickly as possible, often with a whipping to insure their continuing absence.

When these responses proved inadequate, as they often did—residents might not correct their ways or strangers might persist in returning—the community had recourse to the gallows. The frequency with which 18th-century magistrates sentenced offenders to capital punishment testified to the fragility of the system. But almost nowhere did the colonists incarcerate the deviant or the dependent. Jails held only prisoners awaiting trial, not those convicted of a crime; and the few towns that erected almshouses used them only in exceptional cases—for the sailor so ill that he could not be moved, or the resident so incapacitated that no neighbor would care for him.

Beginning in the 1820's the perspective on both poverty and crime underwent a major shift. The relatively passive attitudes of the 18th century gave way to a new, energetic program, as Americans became convinced that poverty and crime, as well as insanity and delinquency, could be eliminated from the New World. Crime, it was decided, did not reflect the innate depravity of man but the temptations at loose in the society. Insanity was not the work of the devil, but the product of a deleterious environment. Poverty was not inevitable, but rather reflected the inadequacies of existing social arrangements. These interpretations revealed not only an Enlightenment optimism about the perfectability of human nature, but a nagging fear that American society, with its unprecedented geographic and social mobility, was so open and fragmented that stability and cohesion could not be maintained unless reforms were instituted. An odd marriage of ideas occurred in the young republic. The optimism of an environmentalist doctrine joined a basic concern that American society was in a state of imbalance —though the majority were coping well enough, a minority seemed unable to confront the challenges of American life. The result was a widespread belief that insanity could be cured in the New World because its causes were rooted in a social order that encouraged limitless ambition and disrespect for traditional opinions and practices. The criminal, too, could be reformed, once he was removed from a setting in which gambling halls and dens of iniquity corrupted him. Poverty would also be eliminated as soon as the poor were taught to resist the temptations at loose in a free community.

Starting from these premises, reformers moved quickly and enthusiastically to a new program: the construction of asylums—new "environments"—for the deviant and dependent. Between 1820 and 1840 penitentiaries spread throughout the country, and the states constructed insane asylums. Concomitantly, they built orphan asylums, houses of refuge (for juvenile delinquents), and almshouses. The walls that surrounded these structures were intended not only to confine the deviant and dependent but also to exclude the community—for, in origin, incarceration was a semi-utopian venture. Superintendents aimed to establish a corruption-free environment which would compensate for the irregularities and temptations existing in the larger, more turbulent society. Thus the bywords of all Jacksonian institutions became order and routine, discipline and regularity, steady work and steady habits. The inmates would be provided with a new spiritual armor, so that upon release they would go forth shielded from temptations and corruptions.

Models of Reform

In fact, the initial organization of the asylums closely approximated the reformers' designs. The institutions consistently isolated the inmates from the community. Wardens sharply limited the number of letters and visits a prisoner could receive and prohibited the circulation of periodicals and newspapers. Insane asylum superintendents instructed relatives to remove the sick patient from the family and bring him to the institution as soon after the onset of the disease as possible, and then not to visit or to write him frequently. Many child-care institutions insisted that the parents abdicate all rights to their children.

The asylums' internal organization put a premium on bell-ringing punctuality and a precise routine. Regimentation became the standard style of prison life in the popular Auburn plan, where the inmates remained isolated in individual cells during the night and worked in congregate shops during the day. Convicts did not walk from place to place, but went in lock step, a curious American invention that combined a march and shuffle. A military precision marked other aspects of their lives. At the sound of a morning bell, keepers opened the cells, prisoners stepped onto the deck, lock-stepped into the yard, washed their pails and utensils, marched to breakfast, and then, when the bell rang, stood, and marched to the workshops where they remained till the next signal. The new world set before the insane was similar in many respects. The essential ingredient in "moral treatment" was to bring discipline and regularity into chaotic lives without exciting frenetic reactions. In the well-ordered asylum, declared Isaac Ray, a prominent 19th-century psychiatrist, "quiet, silence, regular routine, would take the place of restlessness, noise, and fitful activity." One of his colleagues noted that in the asylum "the hours for rising, dressing, and washing, for meals, labor, occupation, amusement . . . should be regulated by the most *perfect precision.*" This style reappeared in the first houses of refuge. One official boasted that "a month's stay in the company with boys accustomed to systematic discipline and obedience, with a sense that there is no escape from order and regularity, generally converts the most wayward into good pupils." And a visitor to a Long Island orphan asylum was struck by the military exercises that the children followed, ostensibly "as a useful means of forming habits of order." She added that it was supposed to be "beautiful to see them pray; for at the first tip of the whistle, they all dropped to their knees. . . . Everything moves by machinery."

Under these routines American asylums became world famous as models of progressive social reform. Tocqueville and Beaumont and a host of European visitors traveled here to examine our penitentiaries, and the verdicts were almost always favorable. Americans themselves were not reluctant to boast of the glories of their insane asylums or of their almshouses. The reformers' rhetoric and these accolades from distinguished visitors sanctioned the new program, and few contemporaries objected to it. On the contrary, incarceration became the first resort as psychiatrists rushed to put patients behind walls, and judges, with little hesitation, meted out long sentences for convicted criminals. Legislators kept commitment laws as simple as possible, reluctant to erect legal barriers between the insane and the asylum, or between the delinquent and the reformatory. With the promise of rehabilitation by incarceration so grand, safeguards were clearly irrelevant.

From Rehabilitation to Custody

Unfortunately, the promise turned out to be hollow, and by 1870 the asylums exhibited all their modern ills. They were overcrowded and in sad disrepair, without internal discipline, disorderly, enervating, monotonous, and cruel. Their preoccupation was with custody and security, not rehabilitation. And yet they lasted, maintaining through the 19th century their monopoly over corrections and treatment.

Both the failure and the persistence of the asylums had common causes. The environmental theories of the founders helped at once to promote and disguise the shift from rehabilitation to custody. Superintendent after superintendent succumbed to the notion that in administering a holding operation he was still promoting rehabilitation. The first proponents had so enthusiastically praised the benefits of incarceration that their successors could smugly assume that just keeping the inmates behind walls accomplished much good. Regardless of the degree of overcrowding, or the extent of corruption, or the absence of supervision, officials could still self-righteously declare that institutionalization was therapeutic.

Another critical element in both the asylums' failure and

persistence was the ethnic and class composition of the inmates. By 1870, and increasingly thereafter, the lower classes and the immigrants filled the penitentiaries and mental hospitals. First it was the Irish, then the Eastern Europeans, and later the Blacks. Incarceration thus became identified in the public mind as the particular fate of the ousider. To the middle and upper classes, the inmate was an outcast even before entering his ward or cell. Since institutionalization served marginal people, the conditions could be no worse than the inmates. In essence, the promise of reform had built up the asylums and the functionalism of custody perpetuated them.

The New Reform Movement

The Progressive era marked a dividing point in public policy, giving the initial thrust to new, non-institutional programs. Change was uneven and selective, affecting some areas more quickly than others. Nevertheless, between 1890 and 1920 care and correction of the deviant and dependent began to shift away from incarceration. The changes were most popular and complete where citizens' suspicions and fears were least intense. The first caretaker institutions to decline in importance were orphan asylums, replaced by foster homes and liberalized adoption proceedings.

New Deal legislation furthered these trends. The Social Security Act of 1935 eliminated incarceration for other segments of the poor, keeping the aged and the able-bodied unemployed out of the almshouse.

In the first decades of the 20th century, state mental hospitals also began to decline in importance. Between 1920 and 1940, out-patient facilities for the mentally ill—caring for the patient during the day and returning him home at night—opened in several metropolitan centers. In the post-World War II period the program grew increasingly popular, particularly after the passage of the Community Mental Health Act of 1963, under which the federal government matches state funds for constructing community mental health facilities. As a result, institutionalization in large state mental hospitals has steadily dropped, so that patients discharged now outnumber patients admitted. Indeed, the principles of anti-institutionalism are now so widely accepted that the mental health literature is beginning to focus on the administrative question of how best to convert custodial institutions into community outpatient centers.

The Decline of the Prison

Although prison walls still impose themselves massively upon the public eye, in this field too we have decreased our reliance upon incarceration. Correctional institutions have lost their 19th-century monopoly. Since 1961 the percentage of the population in prisons has declined annually. The most important procedure effecting this change is probation. In 1965, 53 per cent of all offenders were out in the community under the periodic supervision of a probation officer. By 1975, according to the estimates of an advisory committee to the President's Commission on Law Enforcement and the Administration of Justice, the proportion will rise to 58 per cent. The most dramatic increases have been among juvenile offenders. In 1965 only 18 per cent of convicted delinquents served in correctional institutions, while 64 per cent were on probation. Among adult offenders, 39 per cent of those convicted of a crime were institutionalized, while 49 per cent (including, to be sure, misdemeanants) were on probation.

The other major alternative to prolonged incarceration is parole, whereby a convict having completed some fraction of his sentence is discharged from prison and obliged to report regularly to a corrections officer. Although the idea of parole is not new—it was advocated by many prison experts as early as the 1870's—it has been extensively used only in the post-1930 period. Reliance on parole, it is true, varies enormously from state to state. In New Hampshire and Washington, practically every convict leaves the state prison before completing his formal sentence; in Oklahoma, Wyoming, and South Dakota, less than 20 per cent of the inmates enjoy this privilege. Still, by 1965, 18 per cent of all juvenile delinquents and 12 per cent of adult offenders were on parole. Among all convicts serving in American prisons in 1964, fully 65 per cent won release under this program.

Several states are also experimenting with new programs to decrease the distance between correction programs and the community. The publicity given these procedures to date outweighs their actual importance, but they all look to the same anti-institutional goal. One such effort is work-release, whereby the offender leaves the prison in the morning, works at his job in the community, and then returns to confinement at night. One warden regards this innovation as "revolutionary, not evolutionary. It's going to change," he predicts, "about all of penology." For the moment, however, work release has been authorized in some twenty-four states and for the federal corrections systems.

Important programs operate in Wisconsin, California, Minnesota, and North Carolina; in Wisconsin, for example, it affected 30 per cent of the misdemeanants in 1956, and 48 per cent in 1964. And, at present, some 5 per cent of all federal offenders come under it. But the scope of work-release is limited, typically not covering those convicted of crimes of violence or of a morals charge, or those believed to be part of an organized crime syndicate. Some preliminary evaluations also suggest that the arrangement is expensive and cumbersome to administer. Nevertheless, some states are trying to extend the program to cover felons, and they also report a significant drop in such incarceration-related costs as welfare payments to convicts' families.

Legal Reform

Public interest law firms and reform organizations have launched major campaigns to extend legal protections to prison inmates and to reduce the disabilities convicts suffer after release. As a result of these efforts, lower courts have ruled that solitary confinement for juveniles violates their constitutional right against cruel and unusual punishment. They have also extended this reasoning to prohibit the use of "strip cells," in which the convict must crouch naked in a space so designed that he can neither stand nor sit down. Recent state penal codes have begun to expand convicts' procedural rights, and the courts, most notably and recently in Landman v. Royster (333 F. Supp. 621 (E.D. Va. 1971)), have also insisted on expanding the prerogatives and protection due the convict. In Landman, the federal district court forbade the Virginia state penitentiary system from any longer imposing a bread and water diet, from using chains or tape or tear gas except in an immediate emergency, from using physical force as a punishment; it also demanded minimum due process protections before a convict lost "good time" (that would shorten his sentence), or suffered any deprivation of his normal prison privileges (such as loss of exercise or communication with other inmates). Suits now pending are also contesting the constitutionality of prohibiting ex-convicts from obtaining trucker's or chauffer's licenses and the restrictions on parolees' rights of association and travel. Thus, one detects not only a closing of the gap between the legal rights of citizens and those of inmates, but the beginnings of a series of changes that will make the prison system as we know it increasingly unworkable.

There is little debate among all lawyers active in the prisoners' rights movement that melioration of the condition for inmates now serving in state penitentiaries is essentially humane. Implications for the moment aside, there is a basic need to make sure that convicts are not arbitrarily disciplined and cruelly punished, that they have the right to communicate with their lawyers in confidentiality, that they have freedom of religion, that they are not penalized for holding political views. Our humanity as a society is at stake—brutal punishments and senseless retributions within the prison system affect us all. But the prisoners' rights movement is not just concerned with benevolence, with minimal inmate protections. Rather, two divergent strategies dictate this approach.

For some, the movement is the way to make our penitentiaries truly rehabilitative. If due process changes are affected, if prisoners are respected as persons, then the penitentiaries will accomplish what they are supposed to do: to prepare inmates to return to society as law-abiding citizens. Or, to turn this point around as one activist lawyer has done: "Only with the abandonment of the concepts of retribution and deterrence in favor of modern theories of rehabilitation, will physical punishments be abandoned in our prisons and rights of prisoners be allowed to emerge." In both formulations the goal of rehabilitation is bound up with prisoners' rights. The two go together. If we are to rehabilitate, we must give rights. If we give rights, we will promote rehabilitation.

Many proponents of prisoners' rights, however, subscribe to a very different definition of ends. They share a crisis strategy, convinced that the implementation of prisoners' rights would necessarily upset the balance of power within the institutions, and lead ultimately to making the prison as we know it now more or less inoperative. These lawyers often nervously debate the wisdom of due process changes within penitentiaries. Their most acute fear is that such changes might possibly do little more than legitimate existing institutions. They worry that once some small degree of free speech and religious freedom exists in the prison, then judges and lawyers may believe that prisons are reformed, genuinely rehabilitative places, and consequently, they will relax and allow incarcerating institutions to do business as usual. Responding to this anxiety, many advocates of the movement take a counter position, insisting that due process changes are really not minimal. They do not believe that one can talk meaningfully of civil rights within a prison setting. Rather, they contend that once a guard is forced to answer to the inmate for the reasons for his discipline, once a prisoner cannot be punished at will or subjected to discretionary abuse, then the prison system will be unable to function. Persuaded that terror and arbitrariness are at the root of the penitentiary organization, these proponents insist that due process protections are really a major step in the direction of decarceration. Prisoners' rights will not legitimate penitentiaries. To the contrary, they will help to eradicate them.

The fundamental divergence over ultimate goals has the gravest implications for activists. What actions properly accompany a prisoners' rights movement? For the one school, it would seem vital to educate and persuade citizens and legislators alike to improve our penal institutions, to bring them to the point where rehabilitation is achieved. No sums should be spared in this effort. Investments in building bigger and better prisons, in upgrading the staff, in improving lighting and ventilation, in bringing in more teachers, in building more classrooms, in designing vocational training programs, are all appropriate and useful. Moreover, the next steps in litigation are clear: it is time to fight for conjugal visiting, better classification schemes, in effect to move the right-to-treatment doctrine into the prison field. The crisis school, however, would argue for a markedly different strategy. This is not the time to invest in prisons. Funds should be expended in very different ways, with priority going to experiments with work-release, parole, halfway houses, and other measures which have decarceration as their goal. While they do not wish to abandon those inmates now incarcerated to a hellish existence, they are persuaded that now is the moment to innovate decarcerating responses to crime.

The two strategies are not easily reconciled. One cannot promise to compromise by moving ahead on all fronts. At stake is whether we keep alive the notion of rehabilitative institutions or once and for all try to ring the bell on incarceration and move as quickly as possible to decarcerating programs. To minimize the clash here, to try and split the difference, is to take a shortsighted and ultimately self-defeating stance.

At the very least, both those who subscribe to concepts of rehabilitation within institutions and those who would employ crisis strategies to empty them are under a heavy obligation, one that they have not altogether faced up to, to devote much more direct and systematic attention to the decarceration issue. Those who would use right to treatment as a way of emptying asylums must confront *all* the implications of their decision. It is hardly enough to work for the release of inmates and let the matter go at that. What about society's welfare and the interests of the patient under the new arrangements? What kinds of programs would win community support for decarceration? And it is not altogether clear whether some alternatives to confinement do not have serious drawbacks of their own. Boardinghouse arrangements for ex-mental patients, for example, may promote worse cruelties than state hospitals; keepers who lock their charges in all day may allow them even less comfort, exercise, and nutrition than badly managed institutions. To allow, through inaction and inattention, a casual and unregulated boardinghouse system of care to replace the asylum is not an obvious advance in social progress. So, too, even those who retain a belief in the rehabilitative potential of asylums and prisons ought to be hesitant and unsure enough about their position to scrutinize alternatives, indeed to fund them as a first priority. Given new modes of thinking and the long record of failure with institutions, decarceration deserves its turn at the center of policy thinking and implementation.

The Lesson of Attica

Perhaps the most compelling reason for experimenting with anti-institutional programs is that the penitentiary has actually lost much, if not all, of its legitimacy in our society. It is not just academic students of criminal incarceration who despair of the penal system. Those in charge of the prisons, from wardens and corrections commissioners to state legislators, also share an incredibly high degree of self-doubt, ambivalence, dismay, and even guilt over prison operations. They are no longer secure in what they are doing. The depth and impact of these attitudes emerged with striking clarity and force in the recent events at Attica. Given the history of prison administration in this country, what is surprising and unusual about this revolt is not that it was suppressed harshly, but that several days were spent in negotiation. Attica was not our first prison riot; all through the 1920's and 1930's bloody revolts broke out, only to be repressed immediately, even at the cost of some hostages' lives. Why was Attica different? Why were negotiators flown in, an ad hoc committee formed, proposals and counterproposals exchanged? Why did this prison riot come to resemble so closely the student uprising and the university administration's response at Columbia in 1968?

The most obvious answer, that many hostages' lives were at stake, is altogether inadequate. It is a clear rule of prison guard life, one that is conveyed immediately to recruits, that guards are not ransomable. Should one or more of them be taken hostage, no bargain will be struck for their release. The maxim is not as cold-hearted as one might first think. On the contrary, it assumes that once convicts understand that guards are not ransomable, they will have no reason—except for pure revenge—to take them as hostages. And, in fact, events have usually borne out the shrewdness of this calculation: for all the brutality of the prison system, guards have not often been the victims of the prisoners' anger or desperation. Then why did not officials in New York stand by this rule, move in quickly at Attica to regain control, and rationalize the entire operation as necessary to protect guards' lives everywhere?

The failure to act immediately and with confidence points directly to the prison's loss of legitimacy. Both the inmates and their keepers shared an attitude that Attica was in a fundamental way out of step with American society. Most of the convicts' demands were not obviously unreasonable in the light of public opinion today: better pay for their work, better communication with their families, rights to law books and counsel. Most citizens were probably surprised to learn that these privileges were not already established. Commissioner Oswald himself had promised Attica inmates just before the riot that these changes were long overdue and would soon be enacted. How could he then act with sure and fast resolve to repress harshly a revolt when many of its aims were conceded to be sensible and appropriate and long overdue? It is one thing to sacrific guards' lives for a system that has a sense of its own purpose; it is quite another to sacrifice them when the system is full of self-doubts. So Oswald negotiated, brought in outsiders, and tried to bargain. In the end it did not work, perhaps because not enough time was allowed, perhaps because compromise is impossible in such a charged situation. The revolt was suppressed, with a rage and force that in part reflects the urge to obliterate the questions and the ambivalence. Still, from Attica we have learned that we cannot administer penal institutions that we no longer believe in.

From Attica we have also learned how impossible it is to administer existing prisons when inmates withhold their compliance. The internal organization of penitentiaries today is an irrational mix of old rules, some relaxed, others enforced. Whereas once all prisoners spent their time isolated in a cell, now they mingle freely in the yard, communicate with each other, and move about. As a result, the cooperation of hundreds of prisoners is necessary to the smooth running of the institution. The ratio of guards to inmates is generally low; officers are able to prevent mass break-outs but are not able to prevent takeovers. As events at Attica demonstrated clearly, a group acting in concert has great power to disrupt the normal routine. Moreover, the likelihood of similar actions recurring seems very high. For one, prisoners are certain to sense the steady loss of legitimacy of incarcerating institutions in our society. For another, the convicts in state institutions are bound to be more homogeneous in terms of class (lower), color (Black), crime (violent), and politics (radical). As White embezzlers or Blacks guilty of property offenses increasingly go out on probation or enter minimum-security prison farms, the possibilities for uprisings by those remaining in penitentiaries increases. To be sure, the state might respond to this crisis by building bigger and internally more secure prisons; we do have the managerial ability to structure settings where twenty guards can keep 1,000 men captive. But this response will probably not get very far. The courts, given their due process inclinations, will not allow such prisons, and wardens do not seem to have the inclination to administer them.

A New Calculus

The implication of this state of affairs makes clear that we must experiment with alternatives. Incarceration is at once inhumane by current standards, destructive of inmates, incredibly expensive, and increasingly losing its legitimacy. Our institutions of incarceration are 19th-century anachronisms, out of step with the other American institutions of the 1970's. This marked discrepancy among our social institutions cannot continue for very long without provoking crises more disastrous than Attica. It is time for a new calculus and a new strategy.

There are several general guidelines that may help to structure a consideration of decarceration. First, one ought not to get caught in the "hard core" argument trap. Because each of us can imagine some person who should be incarcerated is no reason to use his case as a means of legitimizing all incarceration. Often in discussions of decarceration a critic will devote all his remarks to describing one case that simply had to be put away— as if thereby he has weakened a decarceration argument. But there is no need to be caught in a one hundred per cent decarceration position. The alternative is to see how many persons now in institutions could be let out without worrying as yet about eradication of confinement for every inmate. Second, one must be acutely sensitive to the problems of coordinating strategies. Decarceration may heighten community risks. Probably the increase would not be great. Overprediction of dangerousness is so rampant in the present system that major efforts at decarceration, whether for the criminal, the mentally ill, or the juvenile, might well have minimal effects. Still, the public must be reassured, and meaningfully so. One cannot move in compartmentalized ways in this area. Coordinated programs that link, for example, crime insurance with improved prevention techniques to a substantial increase in probation, stand a much better chance of successful implementation.

Third, it is useful to remember that incarceration is incredibly expensive. It costs $10,000 a year to maintain one youngster in New York's juvenile institutions—this exclusive of construction costs. Reform here will probably be less costly in economic terms than maintaining the old system. In other words, there is considerable room for maneuvering. Fiscal conservatism and decarceration are not at odds, as those familiar with developments in California are learning. Finally, the defects of older solutions ought to spur on the most imaginative thinking. The field is wide open for innovative suggestions, for experimentation. No matter how badly we fare, the programs we pass on to the next generation cannot be any worse than the legacy we have received.

As for specifics, the suggestions that follow should be taken as nothing more than some examples as to the variety of programs that will be necessary to move to decarceration. There may not be a single legal doctrine around which this goal will be accomplished; perhaps no one constitutional provision that will operate in this area the way right to privacy does in abortion and birth control. Indeed, the courts may well be ancillary institutions so far as this movement is concerned, with attention better devoted to the legislature.

Advocates of decarceration in the criminal field urge first a massive increase in the use of probation, with a willingness to tolerate many more failures than we do now. (Scandinavians, for example, will try probation three or four or five times before turning to incarceration.) They look to a dramatic reduction in sentence length, conscious of the fact that Europeans are astonished at the ease and frequency with which our courts mete out fifteen to twenty year sentences. Concomitantly, an end to discretionary parole, allowing release after a fraction of the sentence has been served on an automatic basis, would work to this end too. Proponents also urge the decriminalization of many acts, especially in the case of victimless crimes (drunkenness, sexual and drug offenses). The free distribution of heroin, not just for maintenance (which would keep an addict from suffering withdrawal symptoms) but for pleasure (allowing him the drug at will) might also be part of this program. They are conscious of the ethical and political problems: would such a measure attract more people to heroin? Is it a form of race suicide or a new way to control the black ghetto? But they are persuaded that the saving of lives through a reduction of death from overdoses, contaminated drugs, drug-related illnesses like hepatitis, and deaths occurring in the commission of crimes, might more than offset the risks. This measure alone would drastically reduce prison populations at least by a third, perhaps by as much as half, and it might also notably increase safety on the streets.

In return for raising by some degree community risks, decarceration proponents urge extensive and state funded crime insurance (a step that is being accomplished in a few areas), as well as increased efforts at prevention of crimes. At the moment, the American criminal system seems to rely more on the symbolic and harsh punishment of a few (on a theory of general deterrence) rather than upon a system of wider enforcement with lower penalties. Under the second strategy, the major deterrent to crime would not be incarceration but the increased likelihood of being apprehended. And in an area such as tax evasion, wider enforcement with lower penalties would not even have any of the potential disadvantages that putting more policemen of the street might entail.

As for prisons, and the hard core that remains there, one might experiment with turning their administration over to the private sector, letting entrepreneurs compete for housing the incarcerated. Under this scheme, the state would direct some convicted criminals that they owe three years of incarceration, give him a credit of, say, $18,000, and then allow him to pass his time in an institution of his choosing. This model follows on the lines of state tuition grants, where the student selects his college, and to some degree, on the nursing home system under Medicare.

It abandons the idea of rehabilitation completely. Confinement would serve the purpose of prevention, and to some extent, of retribution.

Juvenile confinements might be reduced in the same way —families compensated to keep at home children that they now give away, foster homes well reimbursed where child abuse is incontrovertible. Proponents would want to move juvenile proceedings into the criminal area. Persuaded that the state cannot deliver on its promise to rehabilitate, they would be far less willing to tolerate intervention. Where the issues at stake seem to demand state response, it would be best to give defendants all the protections inherent in the criminal law system. Implicit here too is an attack on such statutes as wayward minors, habitually disobedient, persons in need of supervision, and the like. In the juvenile area, as in other instances, the community would be compensated, through insurance schemes and enforcement techniques, thereby increasing its tolerance for deviant behavior.

The point of these examples is not to promote the merits of one specific proposal or another, nor to provoke a debate on the efficacy of one alternative or another. Rather, they are intended to illustrate that the sums now expended on incarceration might well be used in more productive ways. The implications of a recognition that incarceration cannot accomplish the heady goals that many observers have set for it should encourage and stimulate, and fund, innovations. House confinement (with working hours excepted), greater use of fines, still more liberalized bail procedures, more punishment by stigma without institutionalization, these all suggest themselves as possibilities also worth considering. There are implications in this field for behavior modification techniques using chemotherapy or surgery. It is not out of the question that one might in the end prefer simple, straightforward, and ineffective incarceration to the potentially efficient engineering of biochemists and surgeons. Advances neither in decarceration nor behavior modification are so well defined as to allow one at this juncture to draw up a balance sheet. But the time to make the accounting may not be very far away.

Furthermore, the proposals enumerated here demonstrate that decarceration is a large order. One cannot operate in one isolated area of the criminal justice system; probably not through the courts alone could one hope to accomplish this end. And one cannot rely just upon constitutional privileges to make the case. Civil liberties are at issue, but so is the larger question of social organization and social planning. Still, the very grandiose nature of the task at hand ought not to inhibit action. The implications of this analysis warrant immediate consideration. A commitment to the goal of decarceration would mean, first, a thorough reexamination of litigation projects in light of this ultimate aim. Strategies that might be counterproductive to it would be discouraged. Second, the rhetoric in public pronouncements and legal actions would change even where the substance would not. Rather than being a minor or unimportant shift, this might stand as the beginning of public reeducation.

There is no magical plan for prison reform that can promise to reduce the number of criminals or the number of crimes. We know of no correction system that can deliver on such a promise. But that is no reason to continue to suffer our present arrangements. If we scale down our expectations and rely upon such basic standards as human decency and economic costs, we will be in a better position to consider the merits of innovation and decarceration.

CHAPTER 2
THE NEW BREED

EDITORS' INTRODUCTION

An enormous change in the attitudes and expectations of the men and women in prison has taken place during the past decade. There is a new breed of prisoner today: self-aware, militant, and outspoken. The first of the two articles in this chapter deals with the Black prisoner as the victim of racism, and stresses the vital position of Blacks in the forefront of the prisoners' rights movement.

THE BLACK PRISONER AS VICTIM *

HAYWOOD BURNS **

"The degree of civilization in a society can be judged by entering its prisons."
Dostoevsky—*The House of The Dead*

"Don't be shocked when I say I was in prison. You're still in prison. That's what America means: prison."
El-Haj Malik Shabazz (*Malcolm X*)

Many have often agreed with Dostoevsky that the degree of civilization of a nation can be judged by its prisons. Measured by this standard, this country falls far short of the mark. Coast to coast, with too few exceptions, America's jails and prisons are crumbling, inadequate structures, understaffed overcrowded, unfit for human habitation. They are, in fact, a national disgrace.

There are, of course, reasons why individuals are still being housed in jails built at the time of the American Revolution, thrown with two other persons into cells built for one person, subjected to indignities and humiliations from insufficiently trained, insensitive prison guards. These reasons basically add up to a lack of caring on the part of the public. Prisoners are part of America's invisible population. They are shunted off behind the gray stone walls where they can be more readily forgotten or ignored, making it easier to pretend that many of the serious social problems they represent do not exist. But beyond apathy, there is vengeance. For those who are apt to think about prisoners

* Reprinted from The Black Law Journal, Vol. No. 2, 1971.

** Director, National Conference of Black Lawyers; Adjunct Professor, New York University Law School; Staff Attorney, NAACP Legal Defense Fund; A.B. Harvard; LL.B. Yale University Law School.

at all are more apt to have a negative or antagonistic attitude toward them, often with the hostility born of the vindictive desire to punish other human beings because they are evil, and because of their "crimes against society." [1] It is the prevalence of attitudes such as these that is largely responsible for the pittance of our national wealth that is allocated to corrections. Perhaps even more telling, however, is the way in which the money that is available is spent. Ninety-five per cent of the country's entire correction effort is spent on holding people in (and down)—on custodial costs: walls, bars, guards—with only the remaining meager five per cent to cover rehabilitation efforts: education, job training and health services. [2]

From penal institutions of every size and description across the country come reports of corrections officers who overstep their authority, misuse their power, and often in the most vicious and wanton fashion inflict summary punishment upon inmates who are in their charge. [3]

These problems—inadequate facilities, inequitable bail, unfair administrative procedures, physical and psychological brutality—make up the lot of thousands of men and women caged behind American bars. For the Black prisoner, however, there is a peculiar racial dimension to these problems. To understand the Black prisoner's plight, it is necessary to look beyond the general surveys and critiques of American prison conditions and view his situation through the prism of race.

In the first instance it is important to note that non-Whites make up a disproportionate number of the nation's prison population. In California over forty per cent. [4] In New York, more than seventy per cent. [5] Thus the described burdens of an oppressive prison system are disproportionately borne by non-Whites. This is likewise true of the victims of the money-bail system. Under this system it is the poor who are sentenced by their poverty to long terms in jail awaiting trial though convicted of no crime. Again, a disproportionate number of the poor are non-White. On the other hand, those who administer the prison system, who are responsible for the custody, care and rehabilitation of inmates are disproportionately White. In New York, for example, it is reported that despite the fact that close to some three-fourths of the prisoners are non-White, some ninety-eight per cent of the corrections officials over them are White. [6]

For the Black prisoner the general problems of lack of administrative fairness and brutality are compounded by the racism rampant in many penal institutions. Complete racial segregation within prison systems is less widespread than it used to be,[7] but reports of systematic discrimination persist—especially with regard to exclusion of Blacks from certain preferred prison work assignments and programs. Further, the personal racism—conscious or unconscious—of prison authorities works to the distinct disadvantage of Blacks enmeshed in prison administrative proceedings. This is particularly true where the decision-maker is not required to articulate the grounds of his decision or is free to exercise a series of options without close detailed standards as to their exercise. Much racism can be cloaked behind the rubric of "administrative discretion." It is particularly hard for black inmates who are outspoken and who refuse to adopt the proper degree of servility expected of them when they are placed in the position of having prison officials make decisions about them that will ultimately affect their lives. The indeterminate sentence especially as employed in California is supposed to be a progressive bit of penology. It is often in fact a dangerous weapon in the hands of hostile guards who are always capable of imagining, provoking, or exaggerating some or other prison infraction until the incident becomes the basis in whole or in part for the prolongation of a one year to life sentence, on the ground that the inmate is "not ready" yet. It is all the more dangerous when the guard in question is actuated by racial animus.[8]

The brutality problem has racial vectors, not only because of the extent to which a guards' racism may stimulate him to act out his antipathy to Blacks violently, but because the racism can become so pervasive that racist guards and racist White prisoners team up in their attacks upon the non-White prisoners. The fact that one is guard and the other is prisoner makes no difference. They have found common ground; in a microcosm of much in the larger society, they are bound together only by the whiteness of their skin and the depth of their anti-Black feeling. That is enough. They attack.[9]

Apart from the racism that he finds in the prisons, the situation of the Black prisoner must be viewed differently from that of others because of the role that racism has played in getting so many Blacks into jail in the first place. The Kerner Commission told the nation something most Blacks have known for a long time —America is a country permeated by racism.[10] The law like other institutions has not been able to escape this racism. Rather than transcend the racism of the society, the law, like other institutions, often reflects it. In fact, the law has been the vehicle by which the generalized racism in the society has been made particular and converted into the policies and standards of social control that govern our lives. In this kind of social context, "antisocial" acts by Blacks otherwise denominated as criminal, may be signs of health or at least signs of life. They may be acts of self-preservation, evidences of a refusal to acquiesce in a system which by calculation and design is bent on the destruction of non-White peoples and which, daily, accomplishes that mission. This is not to over-romanticize Black prisoners to say that every Black man and woman in prison is necessarily a race hero—but many are. That there are not even more Blacks behind bars may often be no more than an indication of lives of "getting by," made up of a string of bitter accommodations and stale compromises with oppression. Our American history begins with our capture and imprisonment in the bacaroons—the fetid slave pens erected on the coast of West Africa to hold Blacks until their imprisonment as cargo in the dark holds of the slave ships which would carry them (those who lived) to imprisonment in the American social system of slavery. Our struggle through slavery, Jim Crow, discrimination, and modern racism has been for liberation from these prisons. Every major social indicator reflects that we still have not made it. Regardless of which side of the bars you are on, if you are Black and American you are, as Malcolm said, in prison—the prison of racism, the prison of exploitation, the prison of governmental repression. Some victims are just more obvious than others. We are all victims.

A significant development in recent times has been the increased awareness on the part of Black prisoners of the nature and extent of their victimization. A growing political awareness in the prisons has fomented an acute social analysis that is often unrivaled among so-called "free" Blacks walking around outside the prison walls. Though a great number of Black prisoners have arrived at their political conclusions through independent study and informal group discussion, the politicalization of the Black prisoner has also been aided greatly by the organized efforts of the Nation of Islam (Black Muslims) and more recently, the Black Panther Party. As prisoners become more and more conscious of the social and political ramifications of their situation and are able to exchange destructive negative self images for new senses of dignity and pride, they become less willing to accept passively the dehumanizing conditions of American prisons as an immutable given. Responses have come in various forms. In the past year major jail or prison rebellions have flared in almost every part of the country. There has been as well an upsurge in litigation on prison conditions and prisoners' rights, as inmates, sometimes on their own and sometimes through efforts of civil rights and civil liberties organizations, turn to the courts seeking vindication.[11]

Great attempts at self-help are being made through the organization of Black groups within the prisons. Afro-American societies springing up at various institutions engage in a wide range of programs, from studying Black history and culture to carrying out political activity directed at their grievances. A survey of activity within the nation's prisons reveals that Black prisoners are not only men and women on the move, but increasingly they are moving from a basis of group solidarity with concerted action.

Prisoners are being aided now by support groups on the outside which, through a variety of techniques, address different aspects of the prisoner's dilemma. There are those, for example, who concentrate on alleviating the prolonged pretrial incarceration by providing bail for the indigent accused from a revolving bail fund. A pool of money is raised from which bail for individual prisoners is posted. When the bail is returned, the money goes back into the pool to bail other prisoners out. Simultaneously attempts are constantly being made to increase the size of the pool. The revolving bail fund approach has been pioneered by the Womens' Bail Fund of New York City in efforts to assist inmates in New York's Women's House of Detention—most of whom are Black and Puerto Rican.

Other outside groups concentrate on helping inmates who are serving sentences. They may even form an outside organization which becomes an adjunct of a group already existing in the prison. These outside support groups are limited according to the latitude permitted them by the various prison authorities, but they attempt to form a communications link with those on the inside. They visit the inmates, hold classes for them, contact and assist inmates' families, carry out tasks for inmates in the outside world that imprisonment makes impossible, and attempt to inform others about the realities of prison life. One group that has achieved a notable degree of success in using this approach is a Black organization in Rhode Island, affiliated with the Afro-American Society in the Rhode Island state prison.

Still other groups focus their energies on assisting the man or woman just coming out of prison. For many ex-prisoners this is a critical period. If he or she can be assured of some assistance in finding a job, food, clothes and shelter, as well as sensitive, sympathetic, supportive people, the adjustment to the outside world is less difficult and the chances of returning to prison less great. This has been one of the major thrusts of the Fortune Society, an East Coast based group that has been in operation for a little more than three years. The work of the Fortune Society is directed and carried out largely by ex-inmates.

Present outside efforts in assisting the imprisoned are far from adequate—especially the Black prisoner, whose problems are, after all, special. The Black community cannot afford to share the distance and the hostility which much of the dominant society reserves for those in prison. We must not be in a position of having others define for us who our friends and who our enemies are, which *persona* is *non grata*. Some of the finest talent of an oppressed people is always to be found in the prisons of the oppressor. For the strength of our community we must redeem from human waste as many of our imprisoned brothers and sisters as possible. We must address the problems of the American penal system because of the historic threat it has represented and continues to represent to significant portions of our youth. The fight for the humanity and dignity of those of us who are behind bars is part and parcel of our overall fight for liberation. For we—those on both sides of the wall—are the common victims of a social system that demands of us to be less than we are. Any quest for Black justice is incomplete that does not include within its scheme the Black prisoner. We must not take the judgment of a criminal society as to who the real criminals are. Black voices from within the prison walls are growing louder now, as brothers and sisters, despite cruel hands that would twist and maim, are straightening themselves out, wending their way to health, strength and eventually, power—power with which to confront the afflictions of prison life and beyond, the larger injustices of America. The voices are calling to us for help. It is a call which, in this uncivilized land, must not go unheeded.

Footnotes

1 See K. Menninger, The Crime of Punishment, at 3–15 (The Viking Press, New York, 1969).

2 R. Clark, Crime in America, at 213 (1970). See also President's Commission on Law Enforcement and the Administration of Justice: The Challenge of Crime in a Free Society (1968).

3 See G. Jackson, Soledad Brother (1970); Etheridge Knight, Black Voices From

Prison (1970); Prisoners' Solidarity Day Committee, "Prisoners Call Out: Freedom" (1971), detailing the experiences of Black inmates in Auburn Prison (New York) who charge that they have been the victims of a campaign of systematic brutality following their participation in a Black Solidarity Day demonstration within the prison in November, 1970. Former Attorney General Ramsey Clark details an extreme example as revealed by the 1966 investigations of the Cummins and Tucker prison farms in Arkansas: "Allegations, at least partially verified and largely credible, included the murder of inmates, brutal beatings and shootings. Shallow graves with broken bodies were uncovered. Food unfit to eat was regularly served. Forced homosexuality was openly tolerated. Extortion of money by wardens and sexual favors from families of inmates to protect their helpless prisoner relatives from physical injury or death were alleged. Torture devices included such bizarre items as the 'Tucker telephone,' components of which were an old telephone, wiring and a heavy battery. After an inmate was stripped, one wire was fastened to his penis, the other to a wrist or ankle, and electric shocks were sent through his body until he was unconscious." Clark, note 2, supra, at 213.

4 Ridenour, "What Is a Political Prisoner," 1 Black L.J. 17 (1971).

5 Sostre v. Rockefeller, 312 F. Supp. 863, 877–878 (1970).

6 Id.

7 See Washington v. Lee, 263 F. Supp. 327, 331 (M.D. Ala. 1966).

8 See Mitford, "Kind and Usual Punishment in California," The Atlantic, vol. 227, p. 45 (March 1971).

9 See Jackson, note 3, supra. For a varied and provocative description of Black prison life as seen through the eyes of several Black prisoners, see The Black Scholar (April–May 1971).

10 Report of the National Advisory Commission on Civil Disorders, at 10 (Bantam Books, Inc., New York, 1968).

11 Though many organizations have taken an interest in litigating questions of prisoners' rights, some of the most important work in this field is currently being done by lawyers in the Corrections Project of the NAACP Legal Defense and Education Fund, under the direction of Stanley Bass, Esq., 10 Columbus Circle, New York, New York 10019.

EDITORS' INTRODUCTION

The rage and bitterness which constitute the prevalent mood of those men and women who are incarcerated in our nation's prisons may come as a shock to the attorney who becomes involved in prisoners' rights issues for the first time. Increased militancy and politization are not, of course, limited to the prisoners of our country. They are widely present in many and varied groups which perceive themselves to be oppressed. The prisoner as a client will, more often than not, take an active, militant posture in directing the course of a lawsuit which determines his fate in prison. This, too, is a spreading trend in which clients—both individuals and groups—are seeking to exercise a direct control over legal matters which concern them.

Martin Sostre, in writing about Black prisoners in the following article, expresses views which may strike many as extreme in their political and racial tenor. These views, however, are an accurate reflection of the feelings of a large number of the Black and Spanish-speaking prisoners of today. As such, they should be considered by those involved in the field of prisoners' rights, not only on the question of their inherent validity, but also as an aid to understanding the men and women with whom they will be dealing. This book would not be complete or honest if it failed to include the voice of the militant prisoner.

THE NEW PRISONER

MARTIN SOSTRE *

Listen, pig, are you really that naive to believe you can fool and pacify us with nightly bribes of ten-cent candy bars and cookie "snacks" while caging us like animals in your inhuman steel cages; by removing the wire screen from the visiting room but replacing it with the three-foot wide table thrust between our mothers, wives, children and loved ones to maintain your inhuman separation; by changing the color of our uniforms from gray to green (and those of our jailers) while exploiting our slave labor for pennies a day; by establishing a phony "furlough program" which is programmed to exclude from eligibility 1690 prisoners out of 1700; [1] by passing a token "equalization bill"; by ripping off our earned "good time" with the device of "conditional release," which forces us to do over again on parole "good time" already earned? After Attika?! Well dream on, pig, until the next rude awakening overtakes you.

Your widely-publicized "prison reform" programs are a smoke screen not only to cover up the greatest domestic massacre in a century, but to conceal your current repressive pacification program consisting of the post-Attika multi-million dollar appropriation for guns, gas, chemical sprays, for training killers on their effective use, construction of additional gun towers and assault tunnels within your prison camps from which to shoot us down, building and reinforcing "special treatment housing" or "maxi-maxi" units (euphemisms for solitary confinement torture chambers), etc., and they will have the same successes as your "Vietnamization Program" in Vietnam upon which they are patterned. Indeed, as in Vietnam, your repressive prison pacification program, *sub nom* "prison reform," has already proven counter-productive in that it has set in motion dynamic revolutionary forces that will effect the overthrow of your racist capitalist system.

---

* This 50-year-old Black Puerto Rican prisoner is considered to be one of the foremost "political prisoners" in the nation. He is currently serving a forty-one year sentence for an alleged sale of a $15 "bag" of heroin in 1967. He has spent over twenty years in prison, seven of them (so far) in solitary confinement. He has been responsible for litigating a number of major issues in the prisoners' rights area.

Are you so spiritually dead and blind that you fail to perceive the cause, effect and consequences of your repressive acts? Are you so hung up on the repressive-genocidal aspect of your technology that you still refuse to believe that your perverse technology cannot prevail over human spirit?

If Attika fell to us in a matter of hours despite its being your most secure maximum-security prison-fortress equipped with your latest repressive technology, so shall fall all your fortresses, inside and out. Revolutionary spirit conquers all obstacles.

Every one of your prison camps has now become a revolutionary training camp feeding trained revolutionary cadres to each revolutionary "foco" in the ghetto. The recruits are the thousands of Black militants and revolutionaries framed and kidnapped from the ghettos in your desperate effort to put down the spreading Black Rebellion. While on the surface it appears you've cooled the ghettos, all you've done was remove the dynamic elements, dumped us in your prison camps where our diverse ideologies and experience cross-fertilized, hardened and embittered us in your dehumanizing cages by abuse, breaking up our families, etc., to then return us to the ghettos as fully-hardened revolutionary cadres. Your oppressive mentality blinds you to these clear facts.

Do you not see that we've converted your prison camps into revolutionary training camps for cadres of the Black liberation struggle? More important, your prisons have become ideological crucibles and battle grounds. Soon you shall reap the harvest.

The above capsulizes the ideology of thousands of Black revolutionaries being repressed in your prison camps. Although expressed in many ways—rhetorically and organizationally through the many militant and revolutionary prisoners' groups formed in every prison in the U.S.—the basic ideology is the same: using our time in prison to get it together for our return to the ghetto.

While I speak only for prison camps in New York State— and I've been tortured in the major ones: Sing Sing, Clinton, Attika, Green Haven, Wallkill, and Auburn—I have compared notes with many out-of-state prisoners serving time in New York prison camps and found that the identical ideological situation exists in out-of-state prisons.

We are all political prisoners regardless of the crimes invoked by white racist oppressors to legitimize their kidnapping us from the ghettos and torturing us in their cages. You don't believe it? Well, what crimes did our forebears commit when they were kidnapped from Africa, imprisoned aboard slave ships and brought to Amerika where their labor was exploited for 350 years? Didn't you legalize these crimes against Black people and codify them in your slave codes? Didn't you legitimize your genocidal slaughter of the Amerikan Indians and theft of their land by legislating Indian laws and the Homestead Act? Were not these crimes politically motivated and formed the very foundation of United States Capitalism? And are you not now the benefactor of this loot and enjoying a standard of living many times higher than your kin in Europe, South Africa and Australia?

Yet, after our forebears were forced to build for you the richest country in the world with their blood and slave labor, the descendants of those who inherited the blood-stained loot have deluded themselves in the belief that they are the guardians of "law and order," that their victims must recognize them as such, acquiesce in their oppression, and relinquish all claims to their stolen heritage!

The consequences of this self-delusion shall soon bear bitter fruit, as surely as the invasion of Vietnam effected the present ignoble defeat at the hands of the heroic Vietnamese people. The delusion of the oppressor will be submerged by the reality of the struggle waged by the oppressed.

So continue pursuing your Eichmann-like repressive policies which your sadistic racist torturers are seeking to enforce. Never will they succeed in breaking our spirit to resist injustices; or convince us that they are the lawful authority—nay, their very outlaw acts remove all doubt (if it ever existed) that they are the outlaws, since they violate not only the laws of humanity but the constitutional and statutory laws they are duty-bound to uphold.

The McKay Report whitewashing the Attika Massacre is a case in point of the people's support of the oppression. Its statement in regard to the taking of hostages that "the holding of human lives for ransom is wrong and only leads to more violence and to a backlash that makes change more difficult," evokes sardonic smiles when read by us, the real hostages whose human lives are being held for exploitative ransom—as were the human lives of our forebears—solely because we are Black. Or does the dictum that holding hostages leads to more violence, apply only when Blacks hold white hostages and not when Black hostages are held by whites?

But if your dictum has universal validity, does it not then follow that the rising tide of Black rebellion in Amerika by your 25 million Black hostages is the natural legacy of the "wrong" which you state "only leads to more violence?"

Despite your self-delusion that you can pervert reality with lies, the fact is that "when everything has failed" (as it already has, since we cannot get justice from our oppressors)—"when a person is pressed to the wall" (as we already are)—"the taking of hostages may be the only way of reaching the outside world"—as Bill Kunstler correctly observed. The reality is that we politically-aware prisoners, whom you cannot deceive into believing the lie that you are the guardians and dispensers of law and justice, shall continue to employ all means necessary to free ourselves from your genocidal white racist oppression.

Hostage-taking is to us as legitimate a means of struggle as was your seizure of agents of the Crown during the Amerikan Revolutionary War, and the seizure of British tea during the Boston Tea Party. We, and not our oppressors, are the sole deciders of what means to employ in our liberation struggle.

The Attika Rebellion not only was the direct consequence of your systematic denial of our basic human rights, but of your adamant refusal to accord us the civilized treatment ordered by federal courts in *Sostre v. McGinnis*,[2] *Sostre v. Rockefeller*,[3] *Sostre v. Otis*,[4] and in many other decisions.

Despite this fact being common knowledge to thousands of lawyers, judges, legislators, administrators and ordinary "people" familiar with the sweeping prison reforms ordered by federal courts in the *Sostre v. Rockefeller* and *Sostre v. Otis* decisions, and the millions of words written on the causes of Attika, why hasn't this fact—the obdurate refusal of outlaw state officials to obey federal court orders—been exposed? It is due to the white racist conspiracy of silence inherent in oppressive-racist Amerika when the victims of white atrocities are Black.

When the 28 Attika Reform Demands presented to and accepted by Commissioner Russell Oswald on September 12, 1971 are viewed against the background of *Sostre v. Rockefeller*,[5] *Sostre v. Otis*,[6] and other directives, it becomes clear that your refusal to comply with the directives of the courts and implement the reforms resulted in the Attika Rebellion fifteen months later. The following facts represent irrefutable evidence that, had the provisions of the federal court mandates been complied with, and had other legitimate grievances brought to your attention by us prior to September 1971 been redressed, not one person would have died or been injured on September 9–13, 1971.

The first three of the 28 Attika Reform Demands dealt solely with procedures to be adopted after the anticipated agreement between the state officials and rebelling prisoners, and the return of prisoners to their cells. These three demands seek the provision of food, water and shelter (necessities of life which even animals in the zoo receive as a matter of course), an Observers Committee to monitor this operation, complete administrative and legal amnesty for the rebels, etc.

Reform Demand No. 4 sought "the application of the New York State Minimum Wage Law Standards to all work done by inmates. Every effort will be made to make the records of payment available to inmates." This grievance (and many others) was brought to the attention of your prison officials on at least four occasions. Each time it was rebuffed and repressed—usually with force.

The first time it was presented was in July 1970 when slaves in the Attika Metal Shop presented their demand for a minimum wage. You responded out of your usual "gorilla" bag by throwing into solitary confinement the representatives presenting the grievance. Having no outlet for this legitimate grievance, and having it compounded by your additional injustice of punishing our representatives, we responded with a work strike in the Metal Shop. Warden Mancusi and Commissioner Oswald reacted by confining to solitary confinement all the leaders. In July and August 1970 the strike leaders were transferred to Auburn and other prison camps throughout the state.

Seeking to pacify with crumbs the spreading prisoner discontent with the five to thirty cents per day slave wage of New York State prisons, you then raised prison wages to twenty-five cents for the lowest job category, and up to one dollar per day for the highest. But you immediately raised the already outrageously high commissary prices—e.g., we are forced to pay 40¢ for a two-pound box of sugar while outside you pay 59¢ for a five-pound bag—and cancelled out the few pennies raise in our slave wages.

The second time this grievance was brought to your attention was on November 4, 1970 during the Black Solidarity Day rebellion in Auburn Prison. In fact, it was the same militant leaders of the Attika Metal Shop strike that were transferred to Auburn Prison who led the Solidarity Day rebellion at Auburn.

The third time the unredressed slave labor grievance was presented to you was in July 1971 when the Attika Liberation Faction sent Oswald a list of grievances including the demand for higher wages. As usual, they were rebuffed.

The fourth time this labor grievance was brought to Oswald's attention was in July, 1971 when prisoners in Green Haven presented to Warden Zelker and Oswald their list of grievances in the form of 13 Prisoners' Demands, headed by the demand for a Prisoners' Labor Union. The following is a copy of the Prisoners' Demands:

"PRISONERS' DEMANDS

"Attention:

"We the inmates of Green Haven Prison demand . . .

"1. That there be set up an Inmate Labor Union free from the creation of, and the control, by the State or any correctional agency thereof, that administers to the prisoners. But instead however, a private organization whose main concern is the welfare of the prisoners. To be headed by dedicated lawyers, whom we will choose, to act as President, Vice President, Treasurer, and people from organizations in our communities to serve on the Board of Directors of such a Union.

"2. We demand that when a person is released on Conditional Release, all institutional holds be resolved. Conditional Release is time earned by inmates, therefore, he should not be held as if on parole. The present guidelines of Conditional Release is illegal and it's a form of chattel or indenture servitude.

"3. We demand that there be a review board set up to bring about the release of those adults who have served ten (10) and more years for a crime that has been long atoned for.

"4. We demand a complete revision of the New York State sentencing statutes—everyone sentenced under the old Penal Law (pre-1967) be recalled before court for re-sentencing under the new law.

"5. We demand that there be an 'Inmate Law Office' where we can set up inmate lawyers to study, prepare and review each inmate's case, who so wishes, and perfect appeals, legal briefs and all forms of writs and petitions in order to present our grievances and other important issues before the courts and other municipal bodies.

"6. We demand that all inmates be allowed to correspond with whomever wishes to write him. The correspondent should be left up to the corresponding parties . . . not by the institutional administrators. We further demand to be allowed to order and receive any periodicals, books, newspapers, magazines or literature that we would normally be able to read if we were free men.

"7. We demand that all inmates have religious and political freedom . . . that any religious and political books published in the U.S.A. be allowed to enter the prisons, so that prisoners can learn and get about to up-lift their wretched souls.

"8. We demand a well balanced, wholesome and nutritious diet. That the F.D.A. inspect all penal institutions to enforce cleanliness and diets.

"9. We demand proper medical attention both by the prison hospital and dental department. We demand that the dental department use and administer novacain for all filling of teeth.

"10. We demand an immediate end to cruel and inhuman treatment and brutality by prison officials.

"11. We demand that we be able to obtain personal typewriters, to be kept in our persons, in order to help us prepare ourselves for society and in order to prepare legal material for the courts in our legal efforts.

"12. We demand that Deputy Superintendent H. Sawner and his Gestapo agents be removed from their positions and jobs because of the use of cruel and inhuman treatment issued out to prisoners.

"13. Last, we demand to be treated like MEN . . ."

On August 18, 1971 Earl Smoake, one of the militant representatives of Green Haven, wrote to Zelker and Oswald asking to discuss with them the Prisoners' Labor Union and the other twelve grievances set forth above. He received no reply.

However, when on August 23, 1971 Earl Smoake discussed the organization of the Labor Union in a meeting with his fellow prisoners in the prison yard, he was thrown in solitary confinement.

Thus Oswald was presented with the labor grievance on at least four occasions prior to the Attika Rebellion. He ignored them and used force to repress our legitimate desire to receive some of the fruits of our labor and end the inhuman and unconstitutional treatment of prisoners in the prison-fortresses of New York State.

Reform demand No. 6 of the Attika rebels demanded that the state "allow all New York State prisoners to be politically active without intimidation or reprisal." Why should it have been necessary to demand the right to exercise constitutionally protected political rights without intimidation or reprisal when the federal court thirteen months earlier in *Sostre v. Rockefeller,*[7] had already enjoined the Commissioner of Correction and Warden Mancusi of Attika "from punishing Sostre for having in his possession political literature and for setting forth his political views or in writing." [8] The answer is clear: your prison officials disregarded the court's mandate and continued to punish us for exercising our political beliefs.

The same applies to Reform Demand No. 7 which seeks the allowance of "true religious freedom." Were not prison officials ordered by the federal courts in *Sostre v. McGinnis,*[9] to permit the exercise of the First Amendment right to worship? Why then should prisoners still have to demand the exercise of this "preferred right" seven years later? The pleadings of the case prove that *Sostre v. McGinnis* was the result of a six-year spiritual, physical and legal struggle led by three determined prisoners. The struggle commenced in Clinton Prison during 1958 when we first sued in Plattsburgh Supreme Court via writ of mandamus seeking the exercise of religious freedom.[10]

The spiritual and physical aspect of the struggle involved years of torture in solitary confinement, beatings, tear gassings while locked in cages, bread and water diets, and many other barbarities inflicted by the state to break our spirit, health and resoluteness, and coerce other prisoners from joining our ranks. But far from breaking our spirit in the solitary confinement dungeons of Clinton and Attika Prisons, these dungeons became the "foco" of rebellion which spread to every prison in the state and involved hundreds of prisoners. The story of the spread of the struggle, how the problem became so serious that the state Attorney General was forced to set up a special bureau to handle the scores of Muslim complaints flooding the courts, and how the Muslim struggle evolved into the revolutionary struggle which led to the Attika Rebellion, is detailed in my forthcoming book.

It took six years of suffering and litigation to get the *Sostre v. McGinnis* [11] ruling in 1964. I personally spent five years in solitary confinement struggling, and had my sentence not expired in September, 1964 while in Attika solitary confinement, I probably would have spent many more years under torture. The 1964 ruling of the Second Circuit Court [12] remanded the case to state court [13] where it was stalled through *Bryant v. Wilkins,*[14] and *SaMarion v.*

McGinnis,[15] to demand No. 7 of the Attika Demands to "allow true religious freedom"—seven more years! Thus the struggle to exercise a First Amendment "preferred" right took from 1958 till 1971, thirteen years of torture, suffering and death at the hands of those who recognize no law except that of force, violence and murder.

Demands Nos. 8, 9, 17 and 25 of the Attika rebels seeking the end of arbitrary censorship of literature and correspondence, the employment of Black and Spanish-speaking officers, and the end of unlimited punishment in solitary confinement were already ordered by the U.S. District Court (Constance Baker Motley, J.) sixteen months earlier in *Sostre v. Rockefeller.*[16]

The very fact we have to demand "rehabilitation" from those whose primary function is the rehabilitation of prisoners, and food and medical treatment—basic necessities of life recognized by all civilized beings—makes manifest the type of individuals into whose care the "People of the State of New York" have thrown us.

Our claim that your prison officials are the real outlaws and we prisoners the victims is supported by the holding of the U.S. District Court in *Sostre v. Rockefeller,*[17] where the court stated:

"It is not the function of our prison system to make prisoners conform in their political thought and belief to ideas acceptable to their jailers. On the other hand, one function is to try to rehabilitate the lawbreaker by convincing him of the validity of our legal system. There is little chance that such an objective will be achieved if prisoners are entrusted to those who likewise break the law by denying prisoners their basic constitutional rights. This Court holds that Sostre's confinement to punitive segregation for the letters he wrote and for refusal to answer questions about a political organization, and his subsequent punishment for mere possession of political literature, were unreasonable punishments and violated his First Amendment right to freedom of political expression." [18]

The Attika Rebellion was the result of recognition, after decades of painful exhaustion of all peaceful means of obtaining redress, of the impossibility of obtaining justice within the "legal" framework of an oppressive racist society which was founded on the most heinous injustices: murder, robbery, slavery. The ghetto rebellions were the result of a reaching of the same conclusion by the oppressed masses after centuries of civil rights struggle and court litigations, such as the 1954 *Brown* [19] school integration decision, which after a twenty-year struggle for implementation was nullified by anti-busing legislation. The rising tide of revolutionary guerrilla struggle throughout the world is likewise due to the failure of all other means to redress injustices heaped on the oppressed.

Attika defrocked the outlaws who were passing themselves off as lawful authorities.

The reality of what must be done has been made manifest through the process of elimination of "legal" remedies. No longer shall we waste time and suffer prolonged needless punishment and injustices litigating civil rights cases in your oppressive courts as we did in the 1950's and 60's. From now on we shall respond to oppressive violence with revolutionary violence. Many of us will die in the struggle, but so will many of you. Even in the Attika Massacre where we had no weapons and all the advantage was with you, the death ratio was less than 3-to-1 with eleven of your mercenaries going to hell with us. What the ratio will be in circumstances more favorable to us than those of Attika (which amounted to shooting fish in a barrel) when we obtain firepower we leave up to your imagination.

Gone forever is our naivete of the 1960's which deceived us to regard as militant the "we want" programs we followed, which in reality were the product of 400 years of slave mentality, in which the foolish slaves begged their master to grant them freedom, justice, equality, fertile land, etc. We've been saying "we want" this and "we want" that for 400 years, but the truth of the matter is that those who have been robbed of their freedom and heritage obtain justice only by using all means necessary in the struggle against their oppressor.

Little did you imagine that the very dungeons used to torture us where you forced us to sleep naked on the cold concrete floor with windows opened to give us pneumonia, on bread and water diet, and with a five-gallon paint bucket for a toilet, would become the crucibles from which evolved the new hardened prisoner and the Vanguard revolutionary ideology which has now spread throughout New York State prisons and into the ghettos.

The Vanguard revolutionary ideology formulated by the survivors of your torture dungeons is reflected in the following program:

PROGRAM OF BLACK
VANGUARD FOR LIBERATION

WHY WE FIGHT, OUR
AIMS AND OBJECTIVES

1. Since our heritage of 350 years of Black slave labor was stolen and invested in the development of this continent of North America by our oppressors, our aim is to recover this stolen heritage by liberating, through revolutionary armed struggle and all means necessary, a portion of this developed land from our oppressor's control. We shall establish our Black independent nation on this liberated territory which is ours by right of our labor invested in its development, our blood shed in its behalf, and by right of birth and history.

2. Our armed struggle for liberation, like that in Africa, Asia and South America, is a just struggle. We seek not to steal someone else's land property, but to recover our stolen heritage, the product of 350 years of Black slave labor stolen from our ancestors and employed by our oppressors to make the U.S. the richest country in the world.

3. We fight for the liberation of Black people held captive in ghetto-colonies inside the United States by the white racist oppressor. By liberation we mean complete freedom from the physical, political, social and economic control of the white racist U.S. government, and the establishment of our own independent Black nation.

4. Since our struggle for liberation in America is a part of the world revolutionary struggle for liberation against the common U.S. enemy and its allies, we will use the same means employed by all oppressed peoples to liberate themselves: guerrilla warfare first and foremost.

5. As a first step towards nationhood, we must obtain revolutionary bases from which to operate. We must seize areas in urban and rural Black communities from the control of the oppressor. From these liberated and expanding areas we will wage our war of liberation.

6. Our independent Black nation will be a Socialist nation based on the principle that people, and not property, are the most precious of all possessions. Having freed ourselves from 400 years

of genocidal white racist capitalism, we are not about to imitate our white oppressors by establishing a Black capitalist nation.

Does not the Vanguard program differ from the "we want" programs of the Panthers and the Muslims like day does from night? Don't you wish we had remained mentally dead and in the "we want" trick bag while believing all the while we had the "key" to the problem of our oppression? It's too late now, for once mental chains are broken there is no return to the *status quo ante.*

We the new politically-aware prisoners will soon galvanize the revolutionary struggle in Amerika to its new phase that will hasten the overthrow of your exploitative racist society, recover the product of our stolen slave labor which you now enjoy, and obtain revolutionary justice for all oppressed people.

Footnotes

[1] See N.Y. Corr. Law, §§851–854.

[2] 334 F.2d 906 (2d Cir. 1964).

[3] 312 F. Supp. 863 (S.D.N.Y. 1970).

[4] 330 F. Supp. 941 (S.D.N.Y. 1971).

[5] Note 3, supra.

[6] Note 4, supra.

[7] Note 3, supra.

[8] Id. at 885.

[9] Note 2, supra.

[10] See Pierce v. LaVallee, 293 F.2d 233 (2d Cir. 1961).

[11] Note 2, supra.

[12] Note 2, supra.

[13] Case was remanded to the federal district court which took no action pending the outcome of state court proceedings. SaMarion v. McGinnis, 253 F. Supp. 738 (W.D.N.Y. 1966).

[14] 45 Misc.2d 923, 258 N.Y.S.2d 455 (Sup. Ct. Wyo. County 1965), rev'd 24 A.D.2d 1077, 265 N.Y.S.2d 995 (4th Dept. 1965).

[15] 55 Misc.2d 59, 284 N.Y.S.2d 504 (Sup. Ct. Erie County 1967), cert. denied 392 U.S. 944 (1968) (see also SaMarion v. McGinnis, 35 A.D.2d 684, 314 N.Y.S.2d 715 (4th Dept. 1970)).

[16] Note 3, supra.

[17] Id.

[18] Id. at 863.

[19] Brown v. Bd. of Education, 347 U.S. 483 (1954).

CHAPTER 3
THE CRIMINAL JUSTICE SYSTEM

EDITORS' INTRODUCTION

The crisis in our criminal courts, particularly in urban areas, is well known across the nation. Insufficient funds, judges, prosecutors, defense lawyers, court personnel and courtroom space have so eroded our criminal justice system that in many areas it has virtually ceased to function. The first of the following articles tells of the chaos and injustice observed in the system by a former inmate and is responded to with a defense of a legal aid organization operating in the same system.

These discussions are particularly important for a full understanding of the prisoners' rights field, because only by comprehending the experiences of the inmate in the conviction process can one appreciate the frustration, bitterness, and hostility which all prisoners seem to share.

AN INDICTMENT BY AN INMATE

DONALD WALLACE *

I am not now, nor have I ever been one of "the silent majority." If I step on some toes, it is purely intentional, and hopefully will prick the consciences of some of those who are in a position to make incalculable corrections in the criminal justice system. I am not one of the apathetic few who couldn't care less about the functions of our courts, and our laws. I believe in a government of the people, by the people, and for the people . . . but for *all* the people. Our laws, as written, are an aesthetic piece of art. When put into practice, no finer instrument exists to protect one hundred per cent of the citizenry of our nation—as well as any visitors to its shores.

Forgive the bit of personal history inserted at this juncture, but I feel it's an absolute necessity to make you, the reader, realize that my views on criminal justice are derived from my having personally known almost 100,000 men who had been convicted of crimes against society—as was I. In 1956, I was convicted of murder, second degree, and robbery, second degree, upon my own plea of guilty to both crimes, and sentenced to concurrent terms of twenty years to natural life, and seven and one-half years to fifteen years by Judge Carmine J. Marasco.

The primary operation of the criminal justice system in New York is largely viewed by those unfortunate enough to have been adjudged guilty as a pact previously arrived at by the judge, prosecuting attorney, and defendant's Legal Aid attorney or 18-B assigned counsel. To a large degree, there is merit to this assumption. Because of the heavy case load in our courts, the backlog of the court calendars, etc., cases are discussed in the courtrooms before the accused is brought before the presiding justice. This in itself is contrary to the statutory mandate, "No further proceedings must take place, in a court of law, where a felony is charged,

---

* Mr. Wallace was released from prison in 1973 after serving 14½ years on a second degree murder conviction. He is founder and Executive Director of the Federation for Legal Assistance and Defense, a newly founded organization seeking to provide quality legal assistance for the poor.

without the defendant's presence in that courtroom." Any colloquy held pertaining to that defendant, at which he is not present, is thereby an illegal part of his trial. It isn't done that way, however. Our present presiding justices very rarely, if ever, correct their own mistakes.

As a result of the callous attitudes of many of our jurists, they've earned for themselves, their colleagues, the district attorney's staff, and the court-appointed lawyers, an infamous pseudonym—"the injustice practitioners." How deserving they are of such a name is a matter for conjecture. Yet on a purely personal basis I'd have to agree that it fits like the proverbial glove. Too many injustices are perpetrated in the name of justice for all of it to be unintentional. Justice is not justice unless tempered by mercy.

The protective mantle of the court is not placed about the shoulders of the accused, and all his rights are not protected by the court, as our statutes say they should be. The presumption of innocence until proven guilty has become a myth in our courtrooms. Defendants are now presumed guilty until or unless they conclusively establish their innocence, a task made more difficult by the impoverished status of ninety per cent of those accused of felonious crimes. These men and women do not have the wherewithal to pay for investigative services or to ask witnesses to take time off from their work to testify in their behalf. Too many motions made in their behalf to assert constitutionally guaranteed rights are arbitrarily and contumaciously denied by judges who merely want a disposition, whether fairly attained with proper protections or not.

"Power corrupts, and absolute power corrupts absolutely." The function of a judge is to act as an arbiter or referee between two opposing lawyers, one representing the People, the other, the defendant. Too many judges align themselves with the prosecution when plea bargaining is going on, with a subtle threat to the defendant, not in the spoken words, which will be recorded in the transcribed minutes, but with a stern, menacing look and a tonal inflection that brooks no misunderstanding by the accused. Another coercive tactic used to induce defendant to accept a plea rather than go to trial is to take him over to the court building almost daily, without once allowing him to enter the courtroom. To have him sit on a steel bench in the crowded detention cells behind the courtrooms for six or seven hours, with only a bologna sandwich on hard bread for lunch, is to make him more amenable to an offer by wearing down his resistance.

A plea for sympathy, or leniency? I hope not. Many of us were guilty, to some degree, of the crime or crimes we were charged with, and we expected to be punished—but legally and in accordance with the law. We did not expect to be indicted for crimes greater than those we had actually committed, or to have a judge turn a deaf ear to our layman's terms of explanation, or to have our lawyers told, "Shut up and sit down," and see them meekly accept such an admonishment. An accused person is involved. Rightly or wrongly, he expects his counsel to be fighting his toughest fight for him and to be as involved as he, the defendant is. The passive acceptance of a judge's order takes the heart out of the accused. Whatever hope he may have had of winning at trial is dashed out of him.

For many years, a particularly callous judge would signal with a pencil to his court stenographer: when he reversed the pencil and tapped his bench top with the eraser, the stenotypist would only go through the motions of striking the keys of his machine. Overt threats were issued by this judge but never appeared in the transcribed minutes, though courtroom observers had sworn they were shocked at the abuse of judicial demeanor. It was a common occurrence in this courtroom for the judge to condemn an accused long before any facts had been proven. Complaints lodged against this judge and his courtroom tactics, tantrums, and illegal shenanigans brought no relief on appellate review. "Justice" became a dirty word to anyone unfortunate enough to appear before this man. Today in this particular county, it seems that several other justices are attempting to emulate this notorious judge.

True justice should not be meted out like a pittance, nor have to be sued for. This latter course was adopted by myself and six other detainees as a class action representing almost 1,500 inmates at the Brooklyn House of Detention for Men, filed in June of 1972. This suit seeks federal injunctive relief against six justices to restrain them from perpetrating further violations of federal and state statutes and the constitutional rights of the plaintiffs.

Our laws were created to serve as a guide for self-government and determination by the individual states. But no state statute is to be enacted that would abridge or circumvent a constitutional guaranty. Our state laws were thus created with uniformity in mind, so that all might be governed equally. Not so in this county, where justice is administered at the whim and caprice of the particular jurist. The king's ransoms asked in lieu of bail are unbelievable when comparison is made with other New York State counties.

The news media are forever shrieking that our courts are mollycoddling men accused of crimes against society, that the judges are too lenient in sentencing, etc. This is insignificant, if true, when placed in conjunction with the abuse and abrogation of the rights of these same accused men that occurs daily in the courts.

In layman's terms, defendants play the game and know the penalty for getting caught. If they are availed of their rights as cited under New York and federal statutes, they have no recourse but to hope for the best plea their attorneys can bargain for in good faith. If convicted in accordance with the law, this individual harbors no animosity towards society, the court, the prosecutor, or his particular attorney. His anger is directed inward towards himself for a host of reasons—most prominently for getting caught. Hence, the name "penitentiary" is apropos, for the defendant does become penitent at some point during his incarceration. I know! I've been that route, lived it, and elicited the views from many others who were similarly situated.

The public, too, is not truly concerned about how a man accused of a crime is placed in prison. This also is callousness. As a productive and rehabilitated member of society, citizen, and taxpayer today, I am concerned about how my money is being spent to pay the salaries of judges, assistant district attorneys, court clerks, Legal Aid attorneys, and other assigned counsel, who are taking shortcuts, abridging the law, and unconstitutionally depriving a segment of society of rights that are supposed to be inalienable. This is a larger crime than any other—with the possible exception of treason.

Many of the wrongs perpetrated against an accused while he is being prosecuted can be laid directly at the feet of his court-appointed attorney. Most men do not know what rights they are entitled to. Their attorneys can claim no such ignorance. If a criminal lawyer is not a fighter, then he is nothing. For the most part, the Legal Aid Society is laden with non-fighters.

Thus far, I've made every attempt to stay away from the issue of race, creed, or ethnic background. Yet today approximately eighty-seven per cent of those arrested and charged with a crime are Black or Puerto Rican. These people are not getting adequate representation from their court-assigned lawyers, nor are they being tried by a jury of their peers. Most of the crimes they are accused of are crimes against others of their own race. Are they judged by predominantly Black and Puerto Rican citizens? No! The jury box is laden with lily-white residents of Hollis, Queens; Roslyn, L.I.; Westchester County; and Bensonhurst. These people live in well police-patrolled neighborhoods and do not have the least conception of the difference in the quality of police service rendered them and the abusive service tendered in the "jungle"—East New York, Brownsville, Bedford-Stuyvesant, Williamsburgh, and the Bushwick sections of Brooklyn.

Is it justice to try a man accused of a crime committed in the ghettos, against another of his race, by a stacked jury of Whites, when that jury can neither identify with the neighborhood, its conditions, or the victim of the crime? I think not. And this is the first flaw in our criminal justice system. The courts, more so than anyone else, are well aware of what constitutes a trial "by a jury of one's peers" and totally disregard this primary prerequisite.

From arrest to culmination of trial, the records are fraught with errors committed by judges, prosecutors, and attorneys, all of whom know better yet still stubbornly refuse to correct an error committed by themselves, or by fellow officers of the court. Even the appellate courts contribute to the grievousness of the errors by not ordering their correction when they are brought to the courts' attention on a prejudgment appeal. This is a senseless waste of our tax dollars and manpower, and contributes greatly to the backlog of cases and the slow administration of justice by the higher courts.

Defendants in criminal litigation often wonder why justice cannot be expedited as swiftly as their arrest and detention. They do not wish to supplant the supervisory power of the administrative judges; they merely want exactly what the law stipulates is their right. In New York the appellate court is empowered to censure a county court judge, assistant district attorney, or attorney at law, but it is almost a hard-and-fast rule that they do not, except in a few widely-publicized cases. This is of no assistance to the average defendant, who is Black or Puerto Rican and has less than a high-school formal education.

If due process of law is continually denied Black and Puerto Rican defendants in criminal proceedings, an increase in court personnel may alleviate the backlog of cases on the court calendars but will do nothing to correct the many injustices emanating from these selfsame courtrooms.

In many instances, a defendant loses his right to correct an error in a coram nobis action because his attorney did not take a timely exception to a certain ruling or make an objection to a blatant and obvious error. To cite inadequate or incompetent counsel is frowned upon and occurs only rarely. Where higher courts have held that errors of law or proceedings do exist, the lower courts have shunned the responsibility for correcting the errors until mandated to do so.

Thus far we have presumed that each of the defendants was guilty to some degree. The system must be far more traumatizing for the man who is innocent of any wrongdoing whatsoever. He is forever disillusioned about justice being meted out fairly and impartially. He is detained on unreasonably high bail or none at all, depending on the charge he is arraigned upon. He is subject to life in a house of detention, where brutalization is the rule, where the food is garbage, where filth abounds in the visitors' sign-in room and increases throughout the institution, where rats and roaches thrive, where even the correctional officers complain of working in such an atmosphere, and where the riot squad, commonly known as the "Goon Squad," periodically goes on head-whipping excursions. Is it any wonder that riots are so prevalent in our institutions?

You, the reader, are not stupid. You, of course, realize that many a totally innocent man will grab at any plea, allowing the conviction if it will take him to freedom and permit him to rejoin his family and loved ones, regardless of the resultant felony conviction on his record. Think how much more aware of this the district attorney's office and staff are.

The New York State Department of Correction has aligned itself with "the injustice practitioners" by making its House of Detention a living hell—pestilence-ridden and conducive to plea acceptance. The fact that ghetto products are guilty of near poverty and cannot afford the exorbitant bails set makes them fair game within this dehumanization factory.

With all these named horrors, you might well ask, Where does the strength and determination to persevere in the face of such adversity come from? From our loved ones who suffer the anguish of the damned in the name of love, from the communities in Brooklyn that are finally awakening to the maltreatment being suffered by other human beings who are not all guilty as charged.

The dissatisfaction does not end there. Our federal laws state that no organization or company shall hold an exclusive monopoly upon a product or service rendered. Yet the Legal Aid Society is a monopolizing agency in the State of New York, with a token offering of Blacks within its ranks. If an accused wants representation by counsel and can't afford one of his own selection, he has to accept Legal Aid assistance. The Black and Puerto Rican people of Kings County are even now attempting to establish an organization comprised of attorneys who will fight diligently for their clients and be dedicated to the premise that the poor are entitled to the very best defense possible. These lawyers will not be intimidated by judges or the bar associations, because they will have the full support of all of the Black, Puerto Rican, and fair-minded White people in the City of New York.

If justice were functioning as it is supposed to, there would be no need for some citizens to sue for what was promised them almost two hundred years ago. This is what it's all about—the campus disturbances, demonstrations in the streets, etc. The older generation keeps asking that cooler heads prevail, promising that things will get better, just be patient. Patience is a virtue the luxury of which one innocent of a crime, yet incarcerated, cannot afford. The cost is too great. It is virtually impossible for him to even recover from the debts incurred, with no chance of suing for false arrest because he would have to prove that his misarrest was deliberate, if he could afford an attorney to sue the city.

Enforce the laws already on the books. Is that too much to ask? The younger generation is sick and tired of having words written and spoken, with no teeth in them. If you were accused and saw your Legal Aid attorney on only two occasions, once immediately before conference for plea bargaining, and another time three or four days before your trial was to begin, I'm certain you would know the frustration and futility that most indigent Black and Puerto Rican defendants now feel.

Most letters to such attorneys elicit no response, and the attorneys are averse to all paperwork, i.e., motions, unless they can make the motions en masse. This same do-nothing legal representative takes great umbrage at his client's audacity in instituting a motion in his own behalf. Why? Partially because it calls attention on the court record to the glaring fact that the representation being given is lacklustre and shoddy. Should a reversal later ensue, appertaining to a point raised or an error aptly brought to the court's attention, it would bring home with an undeniable clarity that the defendant was not given adequate representation by his counsel.

To further compound the fiction that all are afforded competent counsel and given a fair trial, a letter is mailed back to the accused detainee, who filed his own motion papers, stating that no pro se applications are entertained by the courts and that the motion is being forwarded to the assigned counsel of record. Many of these motions are immediately disposed of by that assigned counsel—in the nearest wastebasket. Were such destruction a jailable offense, many attorneys would now inhabit cells adjoining those of their former clients.

The most painful thing to accept, however, is that the courts compound this error—knowing full well that the attorneys very rarely follow up on motions their clients ask be submitted. Most attorneys have monumental egos and are convinced that they know the best defense for an accused. Nevertheless, should his defense prove ineffective, an attorney will still be going home nightly to the loving arms of his wife and children, while his convicted client faces four walls and visits through wire, steel, and half-inch-thick glass. Therefore, the man facing the time should have a great deal to say about the type of defense he would like to have presented in his behalf.

Our Pledge of Allegiance seems to have no meaning for Blacks or Puerto Ricans today. They realize that the words "with liberty and justice for all" are hollow as applied to them. It isn't disrespect that makes Black athletes and schoolchildren refuse to sing our national anthem. One has to feel the truth and beauty of the words in order to sing it with soul, as we have been credited with doing with our own music. We balk at the word "justice." In the very strictest sense of the word, the minority is served by justice, for the rich are in the minority and they are the only recipients of it.

I'm certain many of those who feel threatened by my words can offer opposing arguments in refutation of some of the allegations contained herein that would convince others of similar stature. But that's not where it's at. You'd better try justifying it to the Black and Puerto Rican populace who will have to help you defend this country if it is ever invaded by a foreign power. Put your own house in order, and practice what you preach.

AN ANSWER BY A LAWYER

MARTIN ERDMANN *

Dear Mr. Wallace:

Winners enjoy an overview not granted to losers. While your constituents deplore the rape of their rights by biased judges, others delight in the knowledge that they owe their liberty to just such bias, which, in their cases, resulted in reversible error or the alienation of increasingly sensitive jurors. Fortunately for such victors and those to come, the ratio of bias to brains among the judiciary remains impressively great.

So far as guilty defendants are concerned, the most disastrous state of affairs imaginable would be the existence of an intelligent and dispassionate judiciary. Luckily for them there is no immediate cause for alarm.

It is precisely this same absence of overview which leads you, I think, to suggest in your article that client satisfaction may be more important than either professional integrity or skill. You don't say it in so many words, but it's implicit in the substance of your plaint. What you are saying, if I read you rightly, is that guilty defendants don't mind losing as long as their procedural and substantive rights remain intact, and that these rights include an attorney who will, within the canon of ethics, comply with any and all wishes of the client.

It's a loser's point of view in more ways than one. The name of the game is winning. No trial lawyer worth his salt ever really believes he is going to lose a case once the trial begins. Nonetheless, the loser's point of view is dangerous because it is superficially attractive, particularly for a lawyer associated with the Legal Aid Society.

Can you guess why it is attractive? I'll tell you: because assigned counsel and, more particularly, lawyers associated with the Legal Aid Society, are hassled by their clients from the inception of a case past its conclusion. At times, when tired, it is tempting for the attorney to please them rather than to serve their best interests.

What is the cause of the hostility, Mr. Wallace? Let me set

---

* Attorney-in-Charge, Legal Aid Society, New York City; A.B. Dartmouth College; LL.B. Yale University Law School.

down the reasons as I see them and then discuss whether they are valid. (For convenience sake, I shall first illustrate and then discuss the reasons for what I choose to call preassignment hostility. I shall then follow a similar course with what I choose to term postassignment hostility.)

1. I am frightened, bewildered and indigent. I cannot choose my defender at this crucial juncture of my life. I must accept the assignment of counsel.

2. The Legal Aid lawyer is "free." Whoever heard of anything good being "free"?

3. Not only is the lawyer "free," he is also paid by the same hand that pays the police, the district attorneys and, in some cases, the judge. Obviously, he is simply another member of the same establishment, concerned only with putting a veneer of legality on my foreordained conviction.

4. As further proof that my lawyer is a member of the establishment, consider the token number of Blacks on the Legal Aid staff and the virtual absence of lawyers of Spanish ethnic background.

5. I spoke to some fellow prisoners last night who were down from Attica. They told me they had been represented by Legal Aid and had been coerced into "copping out"; they said they had been innocent and/or could have beaten the case.

6. Some of the inmates told me that Legal Aid lawyers got paid $50 for a plea of guilty and only $25 for an acquittal.

Of course, the indigent defendant is unhappy that he has no say as to who will defend him at this critical time. Nobody is comfortable about putting his life in the hands of a "free" unknown quantity, yet the same thing will happen to him in the field of medicine should he develop a serious illness. Curiously, his reaction will *not* be the same in the latter instance. Perhaps that is because the layman knows that he has no knowledge of medicine but believes he has some knowledge of the law. Whatever the reason, the fact remains that he will receive the same kind of service from the Legal Aid Society as he will receive from the staff of a large, well-run hospital, that is to say, service ranging from the superb to the pedestrian.

The Legal Aid Society is not part of the "establishment," nor are its lawyers. The Legal Aid Society is a private organization with a strong defense-oriented Board of Directors which is under contract with the City of New York to furnish defender services. It has never been subjected to political pressures. If objective proof of its independence is needed, I call your attention to the fact that there is presently pending before the state courts a suit naming all the judges of the New York Criminal Courts, all the justices of the New York Supreme Court, as well as the district attorney of New York County, as defendants in a lawsuit to have the present bail system declared unconstitutional. Another Legal Aid suit has been filed in the federal District Court of the Eastern District of New York naming the Commissioner of Correction and the Administrative Judge of the Kings County Court as defendants in an action to compel the prompt production of prisoners in the Supreme Court, Kings County. A third suit by the Legal Aid Society names the Commissioner of Correction and the Mayor of the City of New York as defendants in an action to close down the "Tombs" for overcrowding and unsanitary conditions and is presently pending in the federal District Court for the Southern District of New York.

It is true that there are but a handful of Black lawyers and almost no lawyers of Spanish ethnic origin on our staff. In 1971–72, following an intensive recruitment drive in law schools throughout the country, over three thousand potential applicants were interviewed; six Black lawyers and one lawyer of Spanish ethnic origin applied for positions on the staff. All were hired. Unfortunately, we cannot begin to meet the starting salary offered by the federal government or private industry, and thus we often lose in the employment competition.

Lawyers associated with the Legal Aid Society, with few exceptions, do not "coerce" pleas. Indeed, most bemoan the fact that so few cases go to trial. This is not to say that coercive factors do not exist in the system; they do. Every defendant knows, or must be made to know, that a sentence following a conviction is, in most cases, harsher than the sentence following plea. The strength of the district attorney's case, if in fact it is strong, is also a coercive factor. Any lawyer who fails to assess frankly the strength or weakness of the prosecutor's case and who fails forcefully to convey that assessment to his client is guilty of abdicating his responsibility.

I suppose it is human nature, once a plea has been entered

and sentence imposed, to dream of what might have been had there been a trial instead of a plea of guilty; to smell victory instead of defeat; to seek to lay the blame of pleading guilty on other heads. Courage is cheap when danger is past.

Lawyers associated with the Legal Aid Society are paid salaries. They are not paid for pleas, acquittals, or convictions. The tired rumor that we are paid $50 for a plea of guilty and $25 for an acquittal was initiated over thirty years ago by members of the private bar who were frightened by the threatened encroachment of the Legal Aid Society upon their private hunting preserves.

So much for preassignment hostility—which is real, and the reasons for it—which are fantasy.

Let me address myself now to postassignment hostility and its attendant reasons. This is a more serious problem, if only because the entire configuration of the attorney-client relationship is in issue.

1. I'm charged with robbery. I didn't do it. It's a case of mistaken identity. I don't know where I was at the time. I have no witnesses. My lawyer only spent twenty minutes with me. I wanted to talk longer. How can he be ready for trial after only spending twenty minutes with me?

2. One of my buddies in prison told me about five motions that my lawyer should make. I asked my lawyer to make them. He said he wouldn't—that they had no merit. I want them made. What kind of a lawyer is he?

3. We're going to trial tomorrow. I asked my lawyer if he believed my story. He said "No." I want a lawyer who believes in me. How can he defend me if he doesn't believe my story?

4. We started picking the jury today. One of the prospective jurors is the wife of a patrolman. I told my lawyer to kick her off. He refused. I'm being railroaded.

5. The evidence started today. On several occasions the judge shouted at my lawyer and told him to sit down and keep quiet. Each time my lawyer meekly apologized and sat down. I want a fighting lawyer. I don't want him.

6. Today the district attorney asked a question of

a witness which I didn't want answered. My lawyer objected very quietly and the judge said, "Overruled." After the answer, which hurt, my lawyer said, so low you could hardly hear him, "I move for a mistrial." The judge said, "Denied." I told my lawyer to get on his feet and argue, argue, argue. He didn't. I think he and the district attorney are in cahoots.

In discussing the reasons for postassignment hostility it will facilitate matters if you will assume that I am the lawyer who represents the complaining client above.

I go to the city prison to interview him and four others. Clearly there is nothing I can learn from him about the case. I spend about fifteen minutes with him and get up to see another client. He wants to keep talking. Time must be allocated in every busy profession in terms of what can be accomplished. Not everyone is entitled to equal time. I leave him.

Two weeks elapse. I receive a message from my client. "I want the following five motions made." I tell him the motions are without merit. He insists. I refuse. I have ten valid motions to make for six other clients. I cannot sacrifice their rights simply to make him happy.

The trial date approaches. My client asks if I believe his story. I don't. Should I lie to him and make him feel good? It is not just a question of personal integrity. If I say I believe him, he may be led to believe he can also persuade a jury. This may cause him to reject a plea which otherwise he might decide to accept. I tell him the truth. He says he doesn't want me for a lawyer; he wants a lawyer who trusts him. "How can you defend me if you don't believe me?" he says. I try to explain that my belief or disbelief is immaterial: it's the jury's belief or disbelief that counts. I strive to assure him that I can sell his case with all the fervor of a real estate salesman selling underwater land. He remains dubious.

The trial commences. We begin to select a jury. One of the prospective jurors is the wife of a patrolman. I like the way she answers questions. I know that the most damaging evidence in the case will come from a detective. Patrolmen have no excess of love for detectives. My client instructs me to get rid of her. I refuse.

Testimony begins. The judge may be a seemingly benign old man with a heart of broken razor blades, or a bellowing bigot. In each case I will be deferential and awkwardly apologetic when brought to heel; in the first case because the jury has been at least temporarily persuaded that the judge is a kindly old duffer; in the second because I want to capitalize on the nastiness which the jury sense. My client mutters to me, "I want a lawyer who is a fighter."

The case is going badly. I realize that it is a case that can only be lost. The district attorney asks a highly improper question. Meekly, I object. "Overruled, sit down," trumpets the judge. The answer is horrendously prejudicial. Almost inaudibly I move for a mistrial. "Denied," says the judge. "Aren't you going to argue the point," whispers my client, "Are you selling me down the river?" Argue—and maybe persuade the judge to rule corectly? Never.

My client is convicted. He fires me. He wins the appeal. "See," he says when we meet at a later date.

There you have it, Mr. Wallace. Had I spent thirty hours with my client; had I made five meritless motions; had I expressed my undying belief in my client's story; had I challenged the patrolman's wife; had I fought with the judge and alienated the jury; had I argued with logic and passion for a mistrial, had the motion been granted and a new trial ordered, then my client, according to your tenets, would be happy—doing twenty years—instead of being faced with more generous options.

That, you see, is what I fear if inmates' attitudes are accepted as valid criteria of a lawyer's performance. Once lawyers seek the approbation of clients at the expense of professional skills and integrity, then, and then only, will you truly be able to complain that you are being sold down the river.

One final word. Lawyers are in part responsible for their clients' lack of confidence. They tend to be arrogant in their expertise and disdain an explanation of their actions or nonactions. They forget (if they ever realized) that their clients are sentient human beings; that it is their liberty and not their lawyers' liberty which is at stake; and that they are entitled to participate in and understand any action or non-action which affects or may affect their case. There may have been a time when it sufficed for lawyers to look down their noses and say to clients, "Mother knows best." Those times are past. Even mother is not the word it used to be.

SECTION III
LITIGATING THE RIGHTS OF PRISONERS

CHAPTER 4
THE FIRST AMENDMENT

EDITORS' INTRODUCTION

The First Amendment freedoms have always enjoyed a pre-ferred position in constitutional jurisprudence. The spectrum of rights encompassed under freedom of speech, association, and religion is broad indeed, and courts have been more willing to protect these rights on behalf of prisoners than to enforce other constitutional protections in prisons. Thus, the case law in this area is developing rapidly. This is particularly important because the First Amendment may hold the keys to opening our prisons to public scrutiny and end the pattern of unexamined discretion, which has given rise to so many prison problems.

FIRST AMENDMENT RIGHTS

STANLEY A. BASS *

The rights of prisoners in the United States have received increasing recognition in the past several years. Particularly in the First Amendment area, courts have been willing to closely scrutinize prison regulations and to require prison officials to demonstrate clearly their asserted need for restrictions which limit freedom of religion and expression, the right to read, to petition for redress of grievances, and to peaceably assemble and organize.

The principal Supreme Court effort in this constitutionally "preferred" area has involved freedom of religion. In 1964, the Court, in a per curiam opinion, held that a civil rights complaint of religious discrimination, filed by a Black Muslim prisoner in Illinois, stated a claim upon which relief could be granted.[1] More recently, in another per curiam opinion, the Court held that a similar complaint, filed by a Buddhist prisoner in Texas, was sufficient to withstand a motion to dismiss.[2] In the same Term, the Court, again per curiam, narrowly construed a federal parole condition forbidding "association" with ex-convicts so as to permit incidental contacts between ex-convicts in the course of work on a legitimate job for a common employer.[3] Although that decision was expressly premised on a nonconstitutional ground, one could raise a constitutional "freedom of association" argument in cases challenging similar parole restrictions on the state level.

The lower federal courts, in a growing number of cases, have articulated a two-step analysis of prisoners' First Amendment rights. In order to limit such freedoms, the state has the burden of showing: (1) that the regulation is required by a compelling state interest and (2) that the method chosen to limit the right is the least restrictive means of serving that interest.[4] Absent such a particularized showing, prison officials' reliance upon generalizations or speculative fears have been judicially overruled.[5]

---

* Staff Attorney, NAACP Legal Defense Fund; former Community Legal Counsel, Chicago; former Director, Council of Civil Legal Aid Service, Cook County Jail, Illinois. A.B. College of the City of New York; J.D. University of Chicago.

Specific Problem Areas

Mail Communication

Many prison administrators continue to characterize a prisoner's use of the mails as a "privilege," in justification of a host of restrictions which they place upon that avenue of expression. However, the Supreme Court has held that communication by mail is a *right* protected by the First Amendment,[6] which, lower courts have repeatedly stated, is not lost by virtue of imprisonment.[7]

At a minimum, prison officials may not refuse to deliver mail, either to or from a prisoner, and may not delete the contents of letters with approved correspondents, absent a showing of "clear and present danger." [8]

A requirement that letters be written in English (or American) effectively forecloses communications by non-English-speaking prisoners, and can be attacked on both equal protection and First Amendment grounds.[9]

Many states have a variety of constitutionally vague and overbroad mail regulations which forbid prisoners, at the risk of punishment, from "magnifying grievances" or discussing "prison gossip," the names of correctional employees, "improper" business, "offensive" subjects, or "objectionable" matters. Challenges to such limitations have succeeded.[10]

Moreover, in view of the obvious chilling effect upon free communication, which is caused by official reading of inmate mail, such indirect means of censorship have been restrained as well, although some courts have predicated the relief granted upon the alternative due process right of effective access to courts.[11]

Other courts have recently ordered the virtual abolition of mail censorship.[12]

Prison officials, of course, have the responsibility for preventing the introduction of contrabrand into the prison. This state interest can be satisfied by techniques less onerous than censorship or reading of incoming mail. For example, letters might be subjected to manual or fluorscope inspection without opening them.[13] Alternatively, mail could be opened but not read, with the inmate being present as a prophylactic measure.[14]

Some jailers have asserted the need to read inmate mail in order to detect possible "escape plots." However, this notion is extremely speculative. Moreover, it is severely undermined by the general practice of permitting unmonitored personal interviews, at which time the most seditious plans imaginable might be discussed undetected.[15] In addition, where the indigent's inability to hire an attorney to make the trip to a distant prison for a personal interview effectively precludes him from enjoying any kind of confidential attorney-client relationship, serious due process and equal protection problems arise.[16]

In another First Amendment area, the right to petition for redress of grievances was given effective recognition in a First Circuit case, where the court upheld the right of inmates to write letters to the press about grievances.[17] At a time when prison conditions, rehabilitation, crime control, and expenditure of tax dollars are all matters of great public concern, press access to prisons is an important method for serving the public's right to know about the operation of its criminal justice system. Accordingly, some courts have followed up by holding that prisoners are also entitled to have personal interviews with the press.[18]

The prisoner's attorney in these cases should attempt to build a factual record, which shows: (1) that the inmate's vital need to communicate is abridged by the challenged regulation; (2) that the state's legitimate interests can be served by feasible, less drastic alternatives; and (3) that the institution's restriction adversely affects the potentialities of rehabilitation. Also, since the practices in other jurisdictions are of "substantial probative value,"[19] it is often helpful to bring to the court's attention the increasing number of correctional systems which have abandoned the type of restriction challenged at bar. Comparative data might be obtained from such organizations as The National Prison Project,[20] the Center for Correctional Law,[21] or the Prison Law Reporter.[22]

Visitation

Prison officials have traditionally considered visitation, like mail communication, to be a "privilege" which they are free to limit as they please. However, the courts have begun to recognize that the constitutionally protected First Amendment right to freedom of association has some vitality in prison.[23]

It may not be long before conjugal visits are held to be constitutionally guaranteed. The deprivation of heterosexual relations is arguably dehumanizing, anti-rehabilitative, violative of basic rights to privacy and human decency, and may also constitute an impairment of the obligation of contracts (in the case of married prisoners).[24] This basic denial, coupled with the problem of homosexual attacks in prison, cries out for some type of solution, although the most immediate response might be a legislative or administrative authorization of furloughs, work-release programs, or conjugal visits. Conceivably, individual relief of vacating a sentence of imprisonment might be obtained from a sympathetic state court judge.

Receipt of Literature

It is now well established that a citizen's right to read [25] also applies to prisoners, who are entitled to receive material that does not present a "clear and present danger" to the institution.[26] Moreover, if prisons intend to censor reading material, they are required, by due process, to give the inmate notice and an opportunity to be heard in connection with such censorship.[27]

A "prohibited source" rule, which allows prisoners to receive only those publications sent directly from the publisher, would seem to be an overbroad restraint upon constitutionally protected rights. Prison officials have available less onerous alternative methods for preventing the introduction of contrabrand into the prison. To bar entirely the gift of any used books from persons other than publishers would bear too heavily upon the fundamental right to read and would also discriminate against the poor.[28] The general inadequacy of most prison libraries, especially the law libraries, underscores the need of prisoners to receive books from persons who are willing to provide them.

Prisoners' Writings

Prisoners have been permitted to prepare diaries, memoirs, or manuscripts so long as such preparation does not conflict with orderly and reasonable prison administration.[29] Whether or not such material may also be circulated or published is an unresolved question.[30]

In one case prisoners complained that their newspaper, *Vibrations,* was arbitrarily shut down by prison officials.[31] Relying upon an earlier decision,[32] the prisoners argued that, once officials establish a forum of communication, they may not interfere with protected speech without demonstrating an overriding state interest. The Court of Appeals reversed and vacated the District Court's dismissal of the complaint without reaching the merits of the difficult censorship issue.

In another area, a District Court [33] refused to dismiss a complaint which had alleged that prison officials punished the prisoner for wearing a peace symbol and otherwise expressing his political views, and for bringing a complaint in federal court.

Counsel representing prisoners in these cases should utilize the favorable doctrines articulated in analogous First Amendment cases. Particular emphasis should be placed here, as in the mail censorship area, upon three primary factors: (1) the inmate's vital need to communicate; (2) the officials' ability to resort to less restrictive alternatives in order to satisfy legitimate state interests; and (3) the adverse effects which the challenged penal restraints have upon the rehabilitative process.

Religious Freedom

Most of the relevant cases in this field have resulted from the persistent, and finally successful, efforts of the Black Muslims.[34] It is now well settled that prisoners are entitled to gather for religious services, to consult members of their faith, to possess religious books like the *Koran* and *Message to the Blackman in America*, to subscribe to religious literature, including *Muhammad Speaks*, to wear unobtrusive religious medals and other symbols and to have a special diet prepared as required by their religion.[35]

Political Activity

As the courts continue to recognize that prisoners ought to retain many fundamental rights enjoyed by free citizens, which do not substantially interfere with orderly institutional functions, the validity of such efforts as voting, unionizing, and other forms of organizational activity is raised. Judicial development in these relatively new areas has been sparse.

Voting

The California Supreme Court has narrowly construed the state's "infamous crime" disenfranchisement provision and applied it only to ex-convicts who had been convicted of offenses involving "moral corruption" or "dishonesty." [36] There, a former draft law violator was held entitled to vote because his offense was not "infamous." If this rationale is adopted as a due process or equal protection analysis, many other groups would be able to avoid state statutory or state constitutional disenfranchisement, based upon conviction of an arguably noninfamous crime. The entire area of civil disabilities imposed upon ex-convicts now seems ripe for litigation.[37]

The problem of providing appropriate machinery to enable these prisoners to vote who are not statutorily disenfranchised (such as pretrial detainees, convicted misdemeanants, and civil committees) has recently been before the Supreme Court twice. In 1969,[38] the Court reserved decision on the basic question whether pretrial detainees could constitutionally be prevented from voting, since it concluded that the inmates in that case, who were denied absentee ballots (a "convenient" method of voting), had not been absolutely denied the *right* to vote where alternative methods of voting were theoretically available, such as temporary release from prison or establishing a polling booth at the jail. Four years later,[39] the Court remanded, for the convening of a three-judge district court, a similar case brought by Pennsylvania prisoners who had alleged that they sought and were refused any of the alternatives discussed. The issue of unconstitutional denial of the right to vote was there found to be substantial and not foreclosed by the Court's previous decision.[40]

Unionizing

The recent efforts of American prisoners to organize into labor unions has begun to generate some discussion, though little case law.[41]

In one recent case, the Second Circuit avoided decision on whether New York State prisoners were entitled to form a labor union.[42] Instead, the court merely acted to protect the prisoners' right to communicate effectively with counsel, in order that the issue could then be adequately presented to a state administrative agency for its decision on the basic issue. In contrast, a Michigan District Court, in a questionable abstention ruling, declined to grant similar protective collateral relief to prisoners whose ability to present the underlying issue to state tribunals was allegedly being impaired by prison officials.[43]

It would seem that the Second Circuit acted correctly in protecting the federal due process right to effective assistance of counsel. This right was particularly essential in order to allow plaintiffs properly to present to a state agency the state law issue of the propriety of inmate unionization.

Thus federal litigation can be useful in the first stage of any inmate union movement in order to fend off unreasonable official interference with the prisoners' ability to present their case to the appropriate state administrative body. However, until First Amendment rights of peaceable assembly inside prisons are further developed, it may be difficult to establish now, as a constitutional matter, the right to organize a union. Moreover, where state labor laws are susceptible to a possible construction which might avoid the constitutional issue, federal courts will probably abstain.[44]

In counselling prisoner groups interested in organizational activities, attorneys might bear in mind the practicality of choosing titles and objectives that would minimize the potential opposition from the administration. Thus, a "student union" might obtain initial acceptance, while an avowed pro-strike labor union would be fought tooth and nail from the outset.

However, if litigation ensues on the merits, counsel should adduce comparative data to show that prison labor unions are able to function elsewhere, as in Sweden and Germany, without causing unmanageable problems. It would be advisable, in the initial cases in this area, for the prisoners' attorney to rely extensively upon expert testimony.

Conclusion

The First Amendment area presents a number of issues which are ripe for litigation. Since these rights enjoy a "preferred" status of protection by the courts, this type of lawsuit has unusual prospects of success. The lawyer will often find that less complex factual issues are involved and that there is a substantial body of favorable case law upon which to rely.

Footnotes

[1] Cooper v. Pate, 378 U.S. 546 (1964).

[2] Cruz v. Beto, 405 U.S. 319 (1972).

[3] Arciniega v. Freeman, 404 U.S. 4 (1971).

[4] See Jackson v. Godwin, 400 F.2d 529, 541 (5th Cir. 1968); Barnett v. Rodgers, 410 F.2d 995 (D.C. Cir. 1969); Long v. Parker, 390 F.2d 816 (3d Cir. 1968); Rowland v. Jones, 452 F.2d 1005 (8th Cir. 1971); Brown v. Peyton, 437 F.2d 1228 (4th Cir. 1971); Hoggro v. Pontesso, 456 F.2d 917 (10th Cir. 1972); Goodwin v. Oswald, 462 F.2d 1237, 1244 (2d Cir. 1972); Fortune Society v. McGinnis, 319

F. Supp. 901 (S.D.N.Y. 1970). But cf. Morales v. Schmidt, — F.2d —, 12 Crim. L. Rep. 2378 (7th Cir. Jan. 17, 1973).

5 E.g. Goodwin v. Oswald, note 4, supra.

6 Lamont v. Postmaster General, 381 U.S. 301 (1965).

"[T]he use of the mails is almost as much a part of free speech as the right to use our tongues." Milwaukee Social Democratic Publishing Co. v. Burleson, 255 U.S. 407, 437 (1921) (Holmes, J. Dissenting); see also opinion of Justice Brandeis, rejecting the view that use of the mails is merely a privilege and not a right. 255 U.S. at 427. At this point of constitutional development, the "privilege-right" distinction has been definitively rejected as an analyatical tool in cases involving important freedoms. E.g Morrissey v. Brewer, 408 U.S. 471, 481–482 (1972).

7 See Nolan v. Fitzpatrick, 451 F.2d 545 (1st Cir. 1971); Note, "Prison Mail Censorship and the First Amendment," 81 Yale L.J. 87 (1971); Stern, "Prison Mail Censorship: A Non-Constitutional Analysis," 23 Hastings L.J. 995 (1972); Note, "The Right of Expression in Prison," 40 S. Cal. L. Rev. 407 (1967); Singer, "Censorship of Prisoners' Mail and the Constitution," 56 A.B.A.J. 1051 (1970).

8 Wilkinson v. Skinner, 462 F.2d 670 (2d Cir. 1972); Goodwin v. Oswald, 462 F.2d 1237 (2d Cir. 1972); LeVier v. Woodson, 443 F.2d 360 (10th Cir. 1971); Carothers v. Follette, 314 F. Supp. 1014 (S.D.N.Y. 1970); State ex rel. Thomas v. State, 198 N.W.2d 675 (Wis. 1972).

9 E.g. United States ex rel. Gabor v. Myers, 237 F. Supp. 852 (E.D. Pa. 1965).

10 Martinez v. Procunier, — F. Supp. —, 12 Crim. L. Rep. 2420 (N.D. Cal. Feb. 2, 1973) (three-judge court).

11 This fundamental right of access to the courts also protects jailhouse lawyers, Johnson v. Avery, 393 U.S. 483 (1969), and requires adequate prison law libraries, Gilmore v. Lynch, 319 F. Supp. 105 (N.D. Cal. 1970), aff'd sub nom. Younger v. Gilmore, 404 U.S. 15 (1971). See also Novak v. Beto, 453 F.2d 661 (5th Cir. 1971). See Carothers v. Follette, 314 F. Supp. 1014 (S.D.N.Y. 1970) (sealed letters to judges); Palmigiano v. Travisono, 317 F. Supp. 776 (D.R.I. 1970); Smith v. Robbins, 454 F.2d 696 (1st Cir. 1972); Moore v. Ciccone, 459 F.2d 574 (8th Cir. 1972); Wilkinson v. Skinner, 462 F.2d 670 (2d Cir. 1972); Morales v. Turman, 326 F. Supp. 677 (E.D. Tex. 1971); and Peoples v. Wainwright, 325 F. Supp. 402 (M.D. Fla. 1971) (sealed letters to attorneys, courts and public officials).

12 See Guajardo v. McAdams, 349 F. Supp. 211 (S.D. Tex. 1972); Jones v. Wittenberg, 330 F. Supp. 707 (N.D. Ohio 1971); Jansson v. Grysen, 1 Prison L. Rep. 256 (W.D. Mich., June 1, 1972).

13 See Marsh v. Moore, 325 F. Supp. 392 (D. Mass. 1971); Merritt v. Johnson, — F. Supp — (No. 38401 E.D. Mich. Nov. 30, 1972); In re Jordan, 7 Cal. 3d 930, 500 P.2d 873 (1972).

14 See Smith v. Robbins, 454 F.2d 696 (1st Cir. 1972).

15 See Palmigiano v. Travisono, 317 F. Supp. 776 (D.R.I. 1970); In re Jordan, note 13, supra.

16 See Rhem v. McGrath, 326 F. Supp. 681 (S.D.N.Y. 1971); Haas v. United States, 344 F.2d 56, 67 (8th Cir. 1967).

17 Nolan v. Fitzpatrick, 451 F.2d 545 (1st Cir. 1971).

18 See Burnham v. Oswald, 342 F. Supp. 880 (W.D.N.Y. 1972); Washington Post v. Kleindienst, 1 Prison L. Rep. 141 (D.D.C. Apr. 5, 1972), stay granted pending appeal, 1 Prison L. Rep. 219 (U.S. May 12, 1972), remanded for further proceedings, 1 Prison L. Rep. 337 (D.C. Cir. Sept. 6, 1972), additional findings made, — F. Supp. — (D.D.C. Dec. 19, 1972). Despite the Burnham Court's apparent misreading of Sostre v. McGinnis, 442 F.2d 178 (2d Cir. 1971) as precluding *confidential* press interviews, the New York Department of Correction, in response to a subsequent suit, amended its regulations so as to permit them. See Barth v. Oswald, No. 72 Civ. 3775 (Stipulation dated Nov. 6, 1972 S.D.N.Y.).

19 Brown v. Peyton, 437 F.2d 1228, 1232 (4th Cir. 1971).

20 1424 16th Street, N.W., Room 404, Washington, D.C. 20036. Director: Al Bronstein.

21 1705 DeSales Street, N.W., Washington, D.C. 20036. Director: Richard Singer.

22 15th Floor Hoge Building, Seattle, Washington 98104.

23 See Doe v. Bell, 1 Prison L. Rep. 189 (N.D. Ohio Oct. 19, 1971) (attorneys permitted to visit potential civil rights clients); Ready v. Kreiger, — F. Supp. —, No. C72-1192 (N.D. Ohio Nov. 7, 1972) (same for solitary confinees); Seale v. Manson, 326 F. Supp. 1375 (D. Conn. 1971) (officials agree to allow potential defense witnesses to visit pretrial detainee); Jones v. Wittenberg, 330 F. Supp. 707 (N.D. Ohio 1971) (same); National Prisoners' Rights Association v. Sharkey, 347 F. Supp. 1234 (D.R.I. 1970) (meeting at the prison between inmates and ex-convicts was permitted, absent a showing of any real danger); Duren v. Procunier, 1 Prison L. Rep. 279 (N.D. Cal. July 28, 1972) (restraining order granted permitting woman to visit her imprisoned male friend); Jones v. Sharkey, — F. Supp. —, No. 4948 (D.R.I. June 12, 1972) (visits by children).

24 See Choice v. Johnson, — F. Supp. —, 12 Crim. L. Rep. 2298 (E.D. Pa. Dec. 28, 1972). But cf. Payne v. District of Columbia, 253 F.2d 867 (D.C. Cir. 1958); In re Flowers, 292 F. Supp. 390 (E.D. Wis. 1968).

25 Stanley v. Georgia, 394 U.S. 557 (1969).

26 Fortune Society v. McGinnis, 319 F. Supp. 901 (S.D.N.Y. 1970); Wilkinson v. Skinner, 462 F.2d 670 (2d Cir. 1972); Long v. Parker, 390 F.2d 816 (3d Cir. 1968); Rowland v. Jones, 452 F.2d 1005 (8th Cir. 1971); Brown v. Peyton, 437 F.2d 1228 (4th Cir. 1971); Hoggro v. Pontesso, 456 F.2d 917 (10th Cir. 1972).

27 See Sostre v. Otis, 330 F. Supp. 941 (S.D.N.Y. 1971); Guajardo v. McAdams, note 12, supra; Martinez v. Procunier, note 10, supra.

28 See generally Van Erman v. Schmidt, 343 F. Supp. 377 (W.D. Wis. 1972); Seale v. Manson, 326 F. Supp. 1375 (D. Conn. 1971); Cruz v. Beto, 405 U.S. 319, 323 (1972) (Burger, C.J., concurring) ("materials cannot be denied to prisoners if someone offers to supply them").

29 Freeley v. Henderson, 1 Prison L. Rep. 270 (N.D. Ga. June 29, 1972); United States ex rel. Katzoff v. McGinnis, No. 70 Civ. 272 (N.D.N.Y. 1970), aff'd sub nom. Rodriguez v. McGinnis, 456 F.2d 79 (2d Cir. 1972) (en banc).

30 In Sostre v. McGinnis, 442 F.2d 178 (2d Cir. 1971), the court held that the inmate could not be punished for possessing objectionable, but uncirculated, personal political writings. In Baker v. Henderson, No. 16, 746 (N.D. Ga. Oct. 5,

1972), the court ruled that a federal prisoner could not be punished for circulating a grievance petition, which was to be submitted to the Director of the Federal Bureau of Prisons. See also, Grene v. Britton, 455 F.2d 473 (5th Cir. 1972).

[31] Gray v. Creamer, 465 F.2d 179 (3d Cir. 1972).

[32] Trujillo v. Love, 322 F. Supp. 1266 (D. Colo. 1971). See also Kirkland v. Hardy, 1 Prison L. Rep. 312 (D.D.C. June 22, 1972) (consent order permitting publication of prison newsletter, "Alerts," under prescribed conditions).

[33] Scerbaty v. Oswald, 341 F. Supp. 571 (S.D.N.Y. 1972).

[34] E.g. Cooper v. Pate, 378 U.S. 549 (1964). However, some old and new religious groups have fared well, too. See Cruz v. Beto, 405 U.S. 319 (1972) (Buddhist); Theriault v. Carlson, 339 F. Supp. 375 (N.D. Ga. 1972) (Church of The New Song).

[35] See Walker v. Blackwell, 411 F.2d 23 (5th Cir. 1969); Long v. Parker, 390 F.2d 816 (3d Cir. 1968); Cooper v. Pate, 382 F.2d 518 (7th Cir. 1967); Fulwood v. Clemmer, 206 F. Supp. 370 (D.D.C. 1962); Barnett v. Rodgers, 410 F.2d 995 (D.C. Cir. 1969); Brown v. Peyton, 437 F.2d 1228 (4th Cir. 1971).

[36] Otsuka v. Hite, 64 Cal. 2d 596, 414 P.2d 412 (1966).

[37] But see Green v. Board of Elections, 380 F.2d 445 (2d Cir. 1967). See generally Note, "Collateral Consequences of a Criminal Conviction," 23 Vand. L. Rev. 939 (1970). The First Amendment rights of parolees and probationers are receiving increasing judicial protection. See Sobell v. Reed, 327 F. Supp. 1294 (S.D.N.Y. 1971); Hyland v. Procunier, 311 F. Supp. 749 (N.D. Cal. 1970); Porth v. Templar, 453 F.2d 330 (10th Cir. 1971).

[38] McDonald v. Board of Election Commissioners, 394 U.S. 802 (1969).

[39] Goosby v. Osser, 409 U.S. 512 (1973).

[40] In Love v. Hughes, — F. Supp. —, No. C-72-1081 (N.D. Ohio Oct. 27, 1972), a three-judge District Court, by a 2–1 vote, directed election officials to furnish paper ballots to the untried prisoner-plaintiffs.

[41] See Comment, "Labor Unions for Prison Inmates: An Analysis of a Recent Proposal for the Organization of Inmate Labor," 21 Buff. L. Rev. 963 (Spring 1972); Halverson, "Prisoners in Unions? Yes: in New England," Christian Science Monitor, Sept. 14, 1972, at 1; Rodriguez, "The Prison Union—They Aren't Kidding," New York Sunday News, Feb. 20, 1972; Taylor "R.I. Union is a Closed Shop Custom-Made for Prisoners," Boston Globe, Nov. 5, 1972.

[42] Goodwin v. Oswald, 462 F.2d 1237 (2d Cir. 1972).

[43] Prisoners Labor Union at Jackson v. State of Michigan, 346 F. Supp. 697 (E.D. Mich. 1972).

[44] See generally Reetz v. Bozanich, 397 U.S. 82 (1970); Askew v. Hargrave, 401 U.S. 476 (1971).

CHAPTER 5
DISCIPLINE AND DUE PROCESS

EDITORS' INTRODUCTION

The lack of due process in prison disciplinary proceedings is a subject of bitter concern to inmates. A prisoner may have his term of imprisonment increased by years or spend months in solitary confinement, virtually at the whim of prison officials.

Perhaps the most important element of due process protection in disciplinary proceedings is the involvement of persons outside the correctional system, either as members of the disciplinary tribunal or as inmate representatives. This presence of outsiders is the best way of assuring that procedural reforms are enforced in the prison disciplinary process.

DUE PROCESS BEHIND THE WALLS

MICHAEL MILLEMANN *

Despite its proliferation during the last several years, affirmative civil rights litigation on behalf of prisoners has had mixed results. On one hand, system-wide abuses have been invalidated as unconstitutional.[1] At least one judge has questioned whether incarceration itself, because of its inherent inability to coexist with constitutional rights, is unconstitutional.[2] On the other hand, decisions have held that archaic and discredited prison practices and policies, such as solitary confinement in dark cells, are constitutional.[3] Indeed, one prestigious court has held that the Eighth Amendment's proscription of cruel and unusual punishment must depend for a definition upon historical usage, the practices in other jurisdictions, and popular opinion.[4] The consequence of this view is the legitimization of policies and practices which have always existed in some jurisdictions and are accepted by the public, thus depriving the Eighth Amendment of its capacity for reform and making it an apologist for the status quo. Suits aimed at reforming the process by which prisoners are punished after they are in prison have been among the most successful types of litigation. Ironically, the development of this successful case law predates the landmark opinion of the Supreme Court in *Morrissey v. Brewer*,[5] requiring full "administrative" due process before revocation of parole, and postdates the decision of the Second Circuit in *Sostre v. McGinnis*,[6] requiring only minimal guaranties of due process before substantial prison punishment is imposed.

The relatively strong body of lower federal court case law [7] and the *Morrissey* decision forecast a potentially bright future for litigation in this area. Indeed, the *Morrissey* decision expressly rejected many of the traditionally proffered justifications for summary decision-making in holding that the interests of the state, as

* Director, Litigation Division, Legal Aid Service, Portland, Oregon; originator and former Director, Baltimore Prisoner Assistance Project; A.B. Dartmouth College; J.D. Georgetown University.

well as the interests of the inmate, are served by the observance of due process guaranties.[8]

This article will discuss the question of what process is due before inmates may be substantially punished. Substantial punishment, unless otherwise defined, will include any revocation of good time,[9] the imposition of solitary [10] or maximum-security [11] confinement, and any prison punishment which jeopardizes an inmate's chance for parole.[12]

The Factual Setting

Prior to recent court decisions, the process by which prisoners were punished differed little from prison system to prison system across the nation. The inmate would be accused of misconduct, usually by a prison guard. The prison guard would write a report which would be referred to his supervising officer and, in most cases, be passed on to a body responsible for prison disciplinary decision-making. This body was either the warden of the institution, one of his deputies, or a panel of prison personnel which usually included the supervisor of the guard force, a deputy warden, and perhaps a person from the "treatment" [13] staff.

While this process was taking place, the inmate was almost always held in a maximum-security section of the prison awaiting the disposition of his case.[14] The actual disposition was made solely on the basis of the guard's report or, in some prison systems, after a hearing at which the inmate had the right to appear but not to be represented, present witnesses, or confront his accuser. In many instances the person who was responsible for initiating the charges of misconduct sat as a member of the prison tribunal which decided the inmate's guilt or innocence.[15] In essence, when hearings were held they were nothing more than a sham procedure by which prison punishment was legitimized.

The consequences of prison disciplinary decisions are, in many instances, quite serious. Punishment can include revocation of all earned good time,[16] confinement in isolation or maximum-security cells for extended periods of time,[17] and the revocation of other important prison rights and privileges.[18] Equally damaging to the inmate are the collateral consequences of this punishment. A record of substantial prison punishment can seriously jeopardize any chance for successful parole consideration.[19] Prison punishment can also result in the inmate's inability to gain access to minimum-security jobs, work-release programs, education-release programs, and other meaningful programs which are important not only in themselves but also in securing parole.

The Test of Procedural Due Process

In order to decide whether a hearing is constitutionally required before the government may act in a way injurious to a private interest, it must first be determined that "the interest is one within the contemplation of the 'liberty or property' language of the Fourteenth Amendment." [20] If the interest is found to be constitutionally protected, the scope and content of the procedures which are due before that interest may be compromised must then be determined. The requisites of procedural due process are not inflexible and invariable; rather they are defined in each case by an ad hoc examination and analysis of several factors.

"[C]onsideration of what procedures due process may require under any given set of circumstances must begin with a determination of the precise nature of the government function involved as well as the private interest that has been affected by governmental action." [21] Thus, in determining the content and timing of a required hearing, the following factors must be balanced: (1) the nature of the particular governmental action involved; (2) the interest of the private party which is jeopardized by that governmental action; and (3) the interest of the government in having a summary decision-making process.

While this balancing test ultimately determines the content of procedural due process, if the plaintiff goes forward to show that governmental action in the nature of "adjudication" [22] threatens grievous injury to a private interest, it is then presumed that certain basic procedural standards must be observed. These protections, developed to prevent arbitrary decision-making, include: prior notice of charges; a hearing before an impartial tribunal at which the accused is able to confront his accusers, cross-examine opposing witnesses, present evidence (including the testimony of witnesses) and enjoy representation by counsel; and a written decision based upon the evidence produced at the hearing and containing findings of fact and reasons for the decision.[23] The government may then rebut this presumption by showing that the balance of factors renders some or all of these rudimentary procedural protections inappropriate in the particular factual setting.

Support for this "presumptive test" of procedural due process is found in pronouncements by the Supreme Court that one's right to a hearing before suffering substantial injury is implicitly recognized in the Constitution [24] and that, to satisfy this constitutional requirement, the hearing must be "meaningful." [25] Professor David states, "The true principle is that a party who has a sufficient interest or right at stake in a determination of governmental action should be entitled to an opportunity to know and to meet, with the weapons of rebuttal evidence, cross-examination, and argument, unfavorable evidence of adjudicative facts, except in the rare circumstances when some other interest, such as national security, justifies an overriding of the interest in a fair hearing." [26]

Procedural Due Process Within the Prison

Until recently, the traditional judicial response to inmate allegations of unconstitutional treatment has been to deny relief in deference to the expertise of prison administrators.[27] Exemplifying this studied noninvolvement [28] is the response of the Tenth Circuit to an inmate assertion that he had been unfairly disciplined: "The discretion of the prison officials on matters purely of discipline, within their powers, is not open to review." [29]

This uncritical judicial deference to prison administration legitimized the plenary power of penal administrators to discipline as they saw fit. An attendant consequence of the denial of judicial review was the reinforcement of the prison community's isolation. The court's refusal to consider the validity of prisoner complaints prevented the public from acquiring knowledge of prison conditions and hindered possible reform efforts.

Erosion of the "hands-off" doctrine began with dicta contained in several decisions. In *Landman v. Peyton*,[30] for example, the Fourth Circuit Court of Appeals stated:

". . . Under our constitutional system, the payment which society exacts for transgression of the law does not include relegating the transgressor to arbitrary and capricious action. . . . [W]e cannot, without defaulting in our obligation, fail to emphasize the imperative duty resting upon higher officials to insure that lower echelon custodial personnel are not permitted to arrogate to themselves the functions of their superiors. Where the lack of effective supervisory procedures exposes men to the capricious imposition of added punishment, due process and Eighth Amendment questions inevitably arise." [31]

Subsequently, a decision holding racial segregation within prisons unconstitutional stated, "[I]t is well established that prisoners do not lose all their constitutional rights and that the Due Process and Equal Protection Clauses of the Fourteenth Amendment follow them into prison and protect them there from unconstitutional action on the part of prison authorities. . . ." [32]

Later, in holding unconstitutional a prison regulation which prohibited one inmate from giving legal assistance to another, the Supreme Court stated that, while "discipline and administration of state detention facilities are state functions . . . in instances where state regulations applicable to inmates of prison facilities conflict with [federal constitutional] rights, the regulations may be invalidated." [33]

These statements, although made in the context of cases not involving disciplinary questions, were irreconcilable with the earlier law that prison inmates were "slave(s) of the state" [34] and undermined the position that judicial review of disciplinary proceedings within a penal institution was "wholly unwarranted." [35] By recognizing that the Constitution's protections extend through prisons walls, the decisions set the stage for the application of due process principles to prison disciplinary proceedings.

Lower court decisions and *Morrissey v. Brewer* [36] have elevated the dicta of these cases to holdings and rejected many of the traditional arguments offered by the state in support of summary decision-making. These decisions have held that various aspects of life in prison are entitled to constitutional protection. They have analyzed the question of what process is due inmates before they are punished, by weighing the interest of the inmate in procedural fairness, the interest of the prison officials in summary decision-making and abbreviated procedures, and the nature of the prison disciplinary process. An analysis of these factors follows.

The Inmate's Interest

Although incarceration in a penal institution is viewed by many as an inflexible dichotomy—one is either in or out of prison—it is clear that gradations of institutional freedom exist after the denial, by incarceration, of liberty in its traditional sense. These gradations are both inter- and intra-institutional. Institutional freedom reaches its ebb at maximum-security prisons.[37] Its summit is attained at various camp centers, which are marked by an absence of walls and of maximum-security devices and practices.[38]

Moreover, the presence or absence of various privileges or rights hinges upon the nature of the confinement. Thus vocational and work-release programs are for the most part designed for those in minimum-security institutions.[39] Eligibility for parole increases radically as an inmate progresses through the chain of maximum-medium-minimum-security institutions.[40] Since the penitentiary is an institution concerned almost exclusively with security, its purpose and nature are functionally distinct from those of the minimum-security penal institutions, where emphasis is upon preparation for return to the outside world.[41]

Intra-institutional liberty also exists in gradations. For example, in most maximum-security institutions the degrees of incarceration range from solitary isolation,[42] the most restrictive form of imprisonment, through confinement in "maximum-security" quarters,[43] to confinement in the "general population."

In addition to forfeiting some or all of their institutional liberty, inmates adjudged guilty of misconduct may be denied "good time" credit, which is a statutory device that shortens the length of time to be served [44] and expedites a prisoner's eligibility for parole.[45] Insofar as the accumulation of "good time" advances a prisoner's release date, it can be said to represent traditional liberty—freedom from incarceration.

Thus, there is a significant quantum of institutional and traditional liberty to which every inmate is presumptively entitled while incarcerated.[46] Disciplinary decisions can directly affect institutional liberty and can result indirectly in a denial of traditional liberty insofar as they cause the denial of parole and the inability to earn "good time." [47] It is this quantum of liberty which deserves constitutional protection. The holding in *Morrissey* that conditional liberty, in that case the liberty of a parolee, is entitled to constitutional protection is persuasive authority for the proposition that the unconditional and conditional liberty at stake in prison disciplinary proceedings deserves similar safeguarding.

The Interest of the Prison Officials

Prison administrators raise several arguments in response to suggest that an adversarial administrative hearing is required prior to the imposition of punishment. They contend that summary ex parte action is necessary in many instances to deter conduct that, in the restricted atmosphere of a prison community, may explode into a large scale disturbance or violence. The ex parte nature of these proceedings is also defended on several grounds, the first being that there is no right to "good time" or to maximum institutional freedom. Officials also argue that the imposition of discipline is not truly adversarial in nature but merely a component part of the rehabilitative and therapeutic scheme of incarceration. Finally they state that the requirement of an adversarial hearing prior to punishment would greatly complicate administrative problems, result in an additional expenditure of public funds, and constitute a security risk. An analysis of these proffered justifications follows.

Withdrawal of Privileges

Prison administrators are on constitutionally unsound ground when they argue that, because "good time," parole, and other forms of institutional freedom are bestowed upon inmates not as a matter of right but as privileges accorded by the legislature or prison officials,[48] procedural due process need not be observed when they are forfeited or withdrawn. The Supreme Court has expressly "rejected the concept that constitutional rights turn upon whether a governmental benefit is characterized as a 'right' or as a 'privilege' "[49] and has stated that the initial question of whether any due process protections may be invoked depends upon a determination that the interest threatened by governmental action is "within the contemplation of the 'liberty or property' language of the Fourteenth Amendment'."[50]

The Second Circuit in *Sostre v. McGinnis* [50a] also recognized this principle by holding that prison officials "may not avoid the rigors of due process by labeling an action which has serious and onerous consequences as a withdrawal of a 'privilege' rather than a 'right'." The court went on to add that the "distinction between a 'right' and a 'privilege'—or between 'liberty' and a 'privilege' for that matter—is nowhere more meaningless than behind prison walls." [51]

Disciplinary Proceedings as Therapy

Another proffered justification for denying inmates an adversarial determination of guilt prior to the taking of disciplinary action is that the injection of the adversarial process into prison disciplinary proceedings would destroy the therapeutic and rehabilitative nature of those proceedings.[52] The premise of this theory is that the prison staff can best determine an inmate's needs when it functions free from the pressures of an adversarial proceeding.

A threshold criticism of this argument is that in most cases the person imposing prison discipline is neither a psychologist nor a psychiatrist nor one trained in related fields of knowledge. It is generally the case that the warden of the institution or a multiple-member panel of custodial personnel (those in charge of prison security) and classification personnel (counselors) determines what disciplinary action is appropriate.[53] Very rarely do classification personnel have extensive psychological training,[54] and the educational requirements for custodial personnel are minimal.[55] The therapeutic model of disciplinary proceedings is a fiction.

In addition, the punishments imposed in prisons cannot be described as therapy. Confinement under the conditions heretofore described,[56] or increase in the term of confinement in institutions which lack programs for rehabilitation,[57] can hardly be considered therapeutic. Indeed, the usual result of such "therapy" is frustration and despair. Penological experts recognize this: "[t]he routine use of severe disciplinary measures usually serves to embitter inmates rather than deter them. . . . It is good disciplinary practice to be cautious in the imposition of penalties which remove the possible incentive for future good behavior [e.g., revocation of 'good time']." [58]

Because the corrective measure imposed is incarceration under harsh conditions, the determination to take such a measure is punitive rather than therapeutic. Therefore, traditional adversarial procedural protections are particularly appropriate to the prison disciplinary process.[59]

A more fundamental infirmity in the therapeutic rationale for disregarding procedural safeguards at prison disciplinary proceedings is suggested by an examination of the legal principles governing juvenile commitments and the commitment of persons to hospitals for the mentally ill. In re Gault [60] established that invocation of the doctrine of parens patriae does not justify an arbitrary restraint on a child's liberty. The Court in Gault rejected the contention that the good will and compassion of juvenile authorities were adequate substitutes for procedural safeguards: "It is of no constitutional consequence—and of limited practical meaning—that the institution to which he is committed is called an Industrial School. The fact of the matter is that, however euphemistic the title, a 'receiving home' or an 'industrial school' for juveniles is an institution of confinement in which the child is incarcerated for a greater or lesser time." [61]

Similarly, the psychiatrist-patient relationship does not preclude judicial protection of personal liberty for mental patients. Hospitals for the mentally ill have no license to disregard the requirements of procedural due process,[62] nor may they deny or abridge the basic rights of their patients under the guise of therapy or treatment. This was the holding of *Covington v. Harris*,[63] where the District of Columbia Circuit Court of Appeals reversed the District Court's dismissal of a habeas corpus petition filed by a patient who challenged his continued confinement in maximum-security quarters within a hospital for the mentally ill.

The court there recognized the primary responsibility of the hospital in making decisions affecting a patient's liberty and the narrow scope of judicial review of such decisions. Nevertheless, it stated that this does not detract from the principle that "additional restrictions beyond those necessarily entailed by hospitalization are as much in need of justification as any other deprivations of liberty; nor does [such recognition] preclude all judicial review of internal decisions." [64] The court explained the need for the imposition of constitutional strictures upon even beneficent or paternalistic institutions: "[n]ot only the principle of judicial review, but the whole scheme of American government, reflects an institutionalized mistrust of any such unchecked and unbalanced power over essential liberties. That mistrust does not depend on an assumption of inveterate venality or incompetence on the part of men in power, be they Presidents, legislators, administrators, judges, or doctors." [65]

The *Morrissey* [65a] decision provides the final answer to the "therapeutic" rationale for summary punishment. Summary parole revocation, the Court concluded, is inconsistent with the rehabilitative purpose of parole, since "fair treatment in parole revocations will enhance the chance for rehabilitation by avoiding reactions to arbitrariness." [66] Summary punishment within a prison creates the same reactions to arbitrariness—hostility, bitterness and anger—which threaten an inmates rehabilitation and, thus, can scarcely be justified as "therapeutic."

The Balance—Efficiency versus Freedom

There can be no doubt that prison administrators have a deep interest in conserving their allotted funds while at the same time maintaining adequate security within their penal institutions. These two legitimate interests must be considered and together weighed against the inmate's interest in liberty before it is decided what form the hearing should take and at what point the hearing should be held.

It has, however, been repeatedly held by the Supreme Court that fundamental constitutional rights may not be sacrificed in the interest of administrative and fiscal efficiency.[67] *Goldberg v. Kelly* [68] is a reaffirmation of this principle. There, the Court recognized that the requirement that a hearing be held prior to any termination of public assistance "doubtless involves some greater expense" [69] but explained:

> "[T]he State is not without weapons to minimize these increased costs. Much of the drain on fiscal and administrative resources can be reduced by developing procedures for prompt pre-termination hearings and by skillful use of personnel and facilities. . . . Thus, the interest of the eligible recipient in uninterrupted receipt of public assistance, coupled with the State's interest that his payments not be erroneously terminated, clearly outweighs the State's competing concern to prevent any increase in its fiscal and administrative burdens." [70]

The right to personal liberty deserves no less weight when balanced against the need for conservation of state finances.[71] A decision of an Arkansas federal court granting sweeping relief to inmates of the Arkansas penal system contains an implicit recognition that the rights of inmates may not be sacrificed to conserve state funds and avoid administrative dislocation. *Holt v. Sarver* [72] declared unconstitutional virtually the entire range of institutional practices in Arkansas prisons because of their extraordinary contamination with brutal sanctions and arbitrary procedures and because of the system's total lack of rehabilitative programs. The court acknowledged that "[i]t is obvious that money will be required to meet the constitutional deficiencies of the institution," [73] but held that the cost of change did not justify the existence of prison conditions which offered "no legitimate rewards or incentives," but only "fear and apprehension" and "degrading surroundings." [74]

Allegations that a requirement of prior disciplinary hearings would threaten security measures within penal institutions are reminiscent of *Cafeteria & Restaurant Workers Union v. McElroy* [75] and related cases.[76] The argument is twofold. First, holding a hearing utilizes personnel and resources needed to maintain security. For example, if inmates are given the right to confront accusers, who are usually prison guards, then these guards must appear at hearings instead of performing security functions. This would necessitate a significant diversion of security resources. Second, allowing inmates adversarial rights will erode the traditional inmate-staff relationship by placing inmates and staff on the same level for a brief period of time.

Neither of these contentions withstands scrutiny. The first contention, that security will be immediately jeopardized, is essentially another form of the conservation of resources argument. If additional personnel are necessary to render prison discipline constitutional *and* to maintain security, then they must be provided for in the budget.[77] "A prior hearing always imposes some costs in time, effort and expense, and it is often more efficient to dispense with the opportunity for such a hearing. But these rather ordinary costs cannot outweigh the constitutional right." [78]

The second contention, that further intangible injury to prison security will result from making adversarial hearings mandatory, presumes a staff-inmate relationship that should become archaic. The President's Commission on Law Enforcement and the Administration of Justice casts severe doubt on the necessity of such a relationship when it states in its report that "the 'collaborative regime' advocated in this volume is one which seeks to maximize the participation of the offender in decisions which concern him, one which seeks to encourage self-respect and independence in preparing offenders for life in the community. It is inconsistent with these goals to treat offenders as if they have no rights and are subject to the absolute authority of correctional officials." [79]

The Nature of the Proceeding

The nature of the disciplinary proceeding is adjudicatory. The issue before the prison disciplinary board is whether the inmate did what he was alleged to have done and, if so, was it a violation of prison rules. In thus applying general prison policy and law to a given set of facts to determine guilt, the disciplinary panel is performing a quasi-judicial function. It is anomalous to regard this proceeding as "non-adversarial" while concluding that proceedings which revoke parole, terminate welfare payments, or evict tenants from public housing are adversarial and therefore demand the complete observance of due process principles.

The leading opinion which rejects a full procedural due process model for prison discipline, *Sostre v. McGinnis*,[80] is based in part upon the court's conclusion that the relationship between prison officials and inmates is "not adversarial" and that "the evidence as to whether the prisoner has violated a prison regulation is likely to be simpler, more precise, and more readily at hand, than, for example, the evidence bearing on the question whether welfare payments should be terminated." [81] The court concludes that there is less need for a full due process hearing. This holding is substantially eroded by *Morrissey,* which decided that full procedural safeguards are necessary in order to arrive at the truth and avoid arbitrary decision-making and expressly held that the relationship between the parole officer and parolee, while initially "non-adversarial," may evolve into an antagonistic one when the parolee's parole is revoked.[82]

If, as the Second Circuit concluded in *Sostre v. McGinnis,*[83] inmates are entitled to be free from punishment imposed through arbitrary decision-making, it is a virtually inescapable conclusion that traditional protections of procedural due process should be used to preserve this freedom. Hundreds of years of Anglo-Saxon jurisprudence have developed and tested these techniques for discovering truth and insuring objective decision-making, including cross-examination, confrontation, and presentation of witnesses.

When there is no requirement of due process at a prison disciplinary hearing, the proceeding simply follows this scenario: the inmate comes before a disciplinary panel; he is told that he has been accused of committing a certain act of misconduct; he is asked what his side of the story is; then, in the overwhelming number of cases, he is told that he is guilty.[84] Without vehicles for discovering truth and insuring objectivity, administrative proceedings become a sham and a means for legitimizing arbitrariness.

The Court in *Morrissey* found that the traditional procedural safeguards are necessary to insure that parole is not revoked "because of erroneous information or because of an erroneous evaluation of the need to revoke parole. . . ." [85] It is this necessity for avoiding arbitrary punishment that mandates procedural safeguards and not the conclusional observation that a proceeding is "adversarial" or "non-adversarial."

The Case Law

Several lower federal courts prior to the *Morrissey* decision held that the traditional rudiments of procedural due process must be observed before inmates are substantially punished.[86] The leading case, *Landman v. Royster,*[87] holds that the essentials of procedural due process [88] are necessary whenever good time is revoked or whenever inmates are confined in solitary confinement, maximum-security confinement cells, or padlocked within their cells for more than ten days.[89]

One recent case, decided in the context of pretrial confinement, applies full procedural guaranties [90] to denials of visits, denials of the right to participate in religious services, the imposition of solitary confinement, and the revocation of commissary, gymnasium, library, movie, dayroom and other privileges for more than seven days.[91] The court in this case concluded that pretrial detainees who have been convicted of no crime and are presumed to be innocent, may not be denied any significant institutional liberty without full procedural protections. The widespread, arbitrary denials of rights and privileges and the state of chaos within the Baltimore City Jail were other reasons for expanding due process.

Even the decision of the Second Circuit in *Sostre v. McGinnis,*[92] which guarantees only minimal due process protections against arbitrary decision-making, recognizes that an inmate may not be subjected to punishment for an infraction of prison rules unless that punishment is "premised on facts rationally determined," and, in most cases, only after a hearing in which the prisoner is "confronted with the accusation, informed of the evidence against him, and afforded a reasonable opportunity to explain his actions." [93]

Components and Timing of the Required Hearing

Once it is established that the balance of interests mandates a hearing, then the well-accepted components of procedural due process are required, unless elements of that due process are held to be outweighed by an overwhelming governmental interest.[94] Due process presumptively requires that:

1. rules defining inmate misconduct be prepared and distributed to inmates;

2. prior specific written notice of charges of misconduct be given to the accused;

3. the accused inmate be afforded a hearing before an impartial tribunal;

4. the accused be entitled to present evidence, including witnesses, in his behalf;

5. the rights of confrontation and cross-examination be extended to the accused;

6. the decision be based upon substantial evidence, be written, and include reference to the evidence relied upon and reasons for the decision; and

7. the accused have the choice of representation by counsel or substitute counsel at the hearing.

Right to Written Rules and Specific Notice of the Charges

Prison rules are, in many instances, extremely vague and uncertain. For example, inmates in most penal systems may be punished for having a "disrespectful" attitude [95] and for using "vulgar" or "improper" language.[96] Moreover, written regulations specifically describing infractions of prison rules were not, until recently,[97] required to be conspicuously posted or distributed to new inmates.[98]

As an initial matter, procedural due process and fundamental fairness require that the rules of a prison or jail be reduced to writing and given all inmates.[99] Vague and meaningless prohibitions of misconduct, such as rules forbidding "misbehavior," "misconduct," or "agitation," should be replaced by more precisely drafted regulations.[100] The right to specific notice of the charges takes on added significance when the exact nature of the conduct in question is either unknown or vaguely and generally described. In such a case specific notice not only informs the accused, perhaps for the first time, of the alleged conduct but also serves the accused with initial notice that such conduct is considered improper.[101]

Right to a Written Decision

The harm caused by the vagueness of prison regulations in describing prohibited conduct is compounded when there is no written decision after a hearing. The lack of a written decision undermines the inmate's right to appeal his decision to higher administrative authorities and to seek judicial review of adverse determinations. Without a written decision, the reviewing body is unable to appreciate, with particularity, the nature of the conduct prohibited, the acts which the accused is found to have committed, and the evidence supporting a determination of guilt. The result has been complete deference to the decision of the lower administrative body, reflecting the traditional "hands-off" approach of the judiciary.

Right to Confrontation and Cross-Examination

The right to confront and cross-examine opposing witnesses has been accepted as being appropriate and necessary "[i]n almost every setting where important decisions turn on questions of fact. . . ." [102] The availability of this right has not been confined to criminal cases (although it finds express constitutional recognition only in that context),[103] but has been guaranteed, by virtue of the Fourteenth Amendment's due process clause, to those who have substantial interests at stake in administrative decision-making.[104]

Considering the significant quantum of personal liberty which is threatened,[105] the quasi-criminal nature of the disciplinary proceeding, the constructive and rehabilitative effect of a fair disciplinary hearing,[106] and the rather unique pressures and relationships existing in prisons,[107] it would seem that the requirement that prison disciplinary proceedings guarantee inmates the rights of confrontation and cross-examination is well founded and logical. This is so even though the introduction of these practices into prison administration might erode traditional inmate-staff relationships [108] and cause some administrative dislocation.[109] Significant denial of liberty based upon the unchallenged testimony of faceless informers is simply not consistent with concepts of fundamental fairness and traditional notions of procedural due process. The *Morrissey* requirement that cross-examination and confrontation be allowed unless there are exceptional circumstances [110] amply supports a similar right at prison disciplinary hearings.

Right to Present Witnesses

Inmates should also be entitled to call witnesses in their own behalf at disciplinary proceedings.[111] Decisions requiring full procedural protection when new findings of fact are made to determine the appropriate sentencing of a convicted felon [112] and before a person may be transferred from a juvenile to an adult penal institution,[113] expelled from a state school,[114] evicted from public housing,[115] terminated as a welfare recipient,[116] or denied the right to pursue a profession [117] cast grave doubt on the constitutionality of current policies and procedures of many correctional systems. These neither give inmates the right to confront and cross-examine accusers or opposing witnesses [118] at disciplinary hearings, nor allow inmates the opportunity to present witnesses in their own behalf.[119] The ability to adduce supportive or exculpatory testimony is critical to raising the inmate's defense above the suspect level of self-serving declarations.

Right to an Impartial Tribunal

It is essential that an impartial tribunal preside at any constitutionally required hearing.[120] To be impartial a tribunal should be as nearly free as possible from interests which conflict with its obligation to fairly and objectively find facts and apply law. This principle is violated when the same prison official assumes the dual responsibility of initiating and pressing charges of misconduct and subsequently determining, as a member of an administrative body, whether misconduct has occurred and assessing appropriate punishment.[121]

To assure that that tribunal is completely impartial, it would be preferable if at least one member was not an officer or employee of the penal system. With the proliferation of prison reform groups [122] and the increased public interest in corrections, reputable citizens could probably be encouraged to assume this responsibility. One leading decision in this area [123] requires that the disciplinary panel for major violations of prison rules disqualify correctional officers and contain at least one person, a "hearing officer," who is employed by the Division of Correction and *not* responsible to the officials of the particular institution in which he sits. Another [124] requires that major jail discipline be imposed only after a hearing before a single hearing officer who is a member of the bar and not responsible to jail officials but to the Jail Board, the policy-making body for the jail. Requirements of impartiality contained in other decisions, however, have allowed prison officials and personnel to sit on disciplinary panels.[125]

Right to Retained Counsel or Counsel-Substitute

Johnson v. Avery [126] established the constitutional right of inmate "writ-writers" to render legal assistance to fellow prisoners. The decision was premised on the fact that many inmates are illiterate and unable to adequately represent themselves. It would seem that these same factors would require the extension of *Johnson* to include at least the right to counsel-substitute at prison disciplinary proceedings. In all cases charging serious misconduct carrying substantial penalties, however, inmates should be allowed representation by counsel, because the ability of inmate or staff counsel-substitute to provide effective representation is compromised by practical considerations. Neither inmate nor staff representative has had formal legal training. The inmate representative may well incur disrespect and hostility, while the employee counsel-substitute faces an inescapable conflict of interest between the duty to report inmate misconduct and maintain harmonious relations with correctional officials who press charges of misconduct and the duty to give representation to the inmate.

Inmates particularly need counsel in cases where the misconduct is also a violation of criminal law and potentially indictable. In *Clutchette v. Procunier* [127] the court held that inmates in this position are entitled to the representation of counsel. Without counsel they are unable to resolve the dilemma of defending themselves before the prison disciplinary panel, with the attendant risk of self-incrimination, or exercising the constitutional right to remain silent at the price of effectively conceding guilt before the prison panel.[128]

The final justification for allowing retained counsel at prison disciplinary hearings is perhaps the most simple and persuasive. The Fourteenth Amendment's guaranty of due process mandates such a result in cases threatening "grievous loss." The courts in several recent decisions, including *Landman v. Roy-*

ster,[129] *Krause v. Schimdt,*[130] and *Collins v. Schoonfield* [131] have extended this due process protection to prison inmates threatened with serious punishment, the *Landman* court commenting: "In other instances where proceedings may result in the loss of substantial rights, the right to representation by counsel has been considered an essential element of due process." [132]

Recognition of the right to counsel at prison disciplinary proceedings raises the problem of resources and availability. One solution would be to allow retention of counsel only at disciplinary hearings that concern charges of serious misconduct. Equal protection problems could be resolved by relying upon the legal community to provide free legal assistance to indigent inmates in this limited class of cases.[133] *Goldberg v. Kelly,*[134] and *Mempa v. Rhay* [135] support this solution.[136]

The Timing of the Hearing

While normally there is no question that any required administrative hearing must precede the governmental action to which it pertains,[137] in extraordinary situations summary governmental action may precede administrative decision-making.[138] In a case where an inmate's conduct poses a substantial and present threat to the safety of others, immediate restrictive confinement without the benefit of a prior hearing may be warranted.[139] A hearing to determine the necessity to continue restrictive confinement should be held as soon thereafter as possible. The revocation of "good time" or denial of parole should always be preceded by the required disciplinary hearing since its summary forfeiture serves no valid purpose.

Conclusion

The reform of prison administrative practices by guaranteeing prodecdural due process is but one step toward effecting urgently needed large-scale penal reforms. It is a step, however, which both insures fundamental fairness and is, for the inmates concerned, rehabilitative. The language of Mr. Justice Frankfurter is apt:

"The validity and moral authority of a conclusion largely depend on the mode by which it was reached. Secrecy is not congenial to truth-seeking and self-righteousness gives too slender an assurance of rightness. No better instrument has been devised for arriving at truth than to give a person in jeopardy of serious loss notice of the case against him and opportunity to meet it. Nor has a better way been found for generating the feeling, so important to a popular government, that justice has been done." [140]

Footnotes

[1] See e.g. Holt v. Sarver, 309 F. Supp. 362 (E.D. Ark. 1970), aff'd 442 F.2d 304 (8th Cir. 1971); Landman v. Royster, 333 F. Supp. 621 (E.D. Va. 1971); Gates v. Collier, 349 F. Supp. 881 (N.D. Miss. 1972).

[2] Morales v. Schmidt, 340 F. Supp. 544 (W.D. Wisc. 1972).

[3] Novak v. Beto, 453 F.2d 661 (5th Cir. 1971).

[4] Sostre v. McGinnis, 442 F.2d 178 (2d Cir. 1971).

[5] 408 U.S. 471 (1972).

[6] Sostre v. McGinnis, note 4, supra.

[7] See, e.g., Landman v. Royster, note 1, supra; Clutchette v. Procunier, 328 F. Supp. 767 (N.D. Cal. 1971); Bundy v. Cannon, 328 F. Supp. 165 (D. Md. 1971); Krause v. Schmidt, 341 F. Supp. 1001 W.D. Wisc. 1972); Collins v. Schoonfield, 344 F. Supp. 257 (D. Md. 1972) (see interim decree); McCray v. Maryland, 10 Crim. L. Rep. 2132 (Cir. Ct. Maryland, 1971); Meola v. Fitzpatrick, 322 F. Supp. 878 (D. Mass. 1971); Morris v. Travisono, 310 F. Supp. 857 (D.R.I. 1970); Urbano v. McCorkle, 334 F. Supp. 161 (D.N.J. 1971); United States ex rel. Neal v. Wolfe, 346 F. Supp. 569 (E.D. Pa. 1972).

[8] Morrissey v. Brewer, note 5, supra, held that parolees are entitled to a full administrative due process hearing prior to revocation of their parole. The hearing must be before an impartial tribunal, and the parolee's own parole officer is disqualified from acting as the hearing officer. At the hearing the parolee is entitled to written notice of the claimed violations of parole, disclosure of evidence against him, the opportunity to be heard in person and to present witnesses and documentary evidence, the right to confront and cross-examine adverse witnesses (unless the hearing officer specifically finds good cause for not allowing confrontation), and a written statement by the fact-finders as to the evidence relied on and reasons for revoking parole. In addition, soon after the initial arrest of the parolee for alleged violation of his parole, the parolee is entitled to a preliminary hearing to determine whether or not there is probable cause to continue to hold him. In reaching the decision that procedural due process requires these hearings, the Supreme Court dismissed several arguments which normally are made by prison officials in support of ex parte decision-making within a prison. In this regard the Court rejected the idea that due process was inapplicable to revocation of parole since parole is a privilege, held that a simple factual administrative hearing will not interfere with the necessary exercise of discretion by a parole board, and concluded that it is in the interest of the state as well as the individual parolee that full due process procedures are afforded the parolee, since arbitrary decision-making can only

cause hostility and undermine the rehabilitation of the parolee. Perhaps most important to the topic at hand was the holding of the Court that qualified liberty —in Morrissey the qualified liberty of a parolee—was entitled to full constitutional protection.

9 Most states by statute authorize the diminution of the period of one's incarceration as an inducement to encourage good behavior and adequate performance in one's job or in the prison classroom. The effect of these statutes is to decrease the amount of time an inmate must serve in order to gain release, and, in some cases, to expedite his consideration for parole. See e.g. Md. Ann. Code, art. 27, §700(b)-(d) (1971).

10 Confinement in isolation or solitary cells is still traditionally used by many prisons as a form of punishment. While so confined, an inmate is usually totally isolated from others in a small unfurnished room, not allowed to exercise outside the cubicle, and denied visitation and other privileges. Isolation of this nature can last for significant periods of time. See e.g. "The Unconstitutionality of Prison Life," 55 Va. L. Rev. 795 (1969).

11 Maximum-security confinement shares many of the qualities of isolated confinement with the exception that inmates confined in maximum- or punitive-security cells are usually able to communicate with other inmates so confined and are allowed somewhat more expanded visitation and exercise privileges. However, the length of such confinement can be quite excessive, in some cases years. See e.g. Landman v. Royster, note 1, supra; Bundy v. Cannon, note 7, supra; Sostre v. McGinnis, note 4, supra.

12 While parole boards in most states are ostensibly independent from the correctional systems, there is, as a practical matter, great deference given by the parole board to prison decision-making. Misbehavior within the prison system will in many instances seriously jeopardize an inmate's chance for parole and result in the inmate's inability to progress through the maximum-medium-minimum security system and, thus, indirectly limit parole opportunities. See e.g. United States ex rel. Campbell v. Pate, 401 F.2d 55 (7th Cir. 1968).

13 See e.g. Landman v. Royster, note 1, supra; Bundy v. Cannon, note 7, supra; "Prison Discliplinary Practices and Procedures: Is Due Process Provided?" 47 N.D. L. Rev. 1 (1970).

14 See e.g. Landman v. Royster, note 1, supra; Bundy v. Cannon, note 7, supra; Sostre v. McGinnis, note 4, supra.

15 See e.g. Bundy v. Cannon, note 7, supra.

16 Revocation of all earned good time can mean the extension of a prison sentence for years. See e.g. Landman v. Royster, note 1, supra; Bundy v. Cannon, note 7, supra.

17 Maximum-security confinement can last for years. See e.g. Landman v. Royster, note 1, supra.

18 A recent decision, United States ex rel. Neal v. Wolfe, 346 F. Supp. 569 (E.D. Pa. 1972), holds that the rudiments of procedural due process are applicable whenever a prisoner may lose privileges such as a preferred job status acquired through good behavior.

19 See note 12, supra. The relationship between prison discipline and parole is even more closely connected in the federal system. Federal inmates whose

good time is revoked are unable to even be considered for parole until that good time is restored. See Meyers v. Alldredge, 348 F. Supp. 807, 824 (M.D. Pa. 1972).

[20] Morrissey v. Brewer, note 5, supra, 408 U.S. at 481.

[21] Cafeteria & Restaurant Workers Union v. McElroy, 367 U.S. 886, 895 (1961). The Supreme Court has, on numerous occasions, stated this flexible standard for satisfying the requirements of procedural due process and listed relevant factors to be considered in determining whether this standard has been met. See e.g. Goldberg v. Kelly, 397 U.S. 254, 262–263 (1970): "The extent to which procedural due process must be afforded . . . is influenced by the extent to which [one] may be 'condemned to suffer grievous loss' [citation omitted] and depends upon whether the . . . interest in avoiding that loss outweighs the governmental interest in summary adjudication"; Hannah v. Larche, 363 U.S. 420, 442 (1960): "The nature of the alleged right involved, the nature of the proceeding, and the possible burden on that proceeding, are all considerations which must be taken into account"; Joint Anti-Fascist Refugee Comm. v. McGrath, 341 U.S. 123, 163 (1951) (Frankfurter, J., concurring): "The precise nature of the interest that has been adversely affected, the manner in which this was done, the reasons for doing it, the available alternatives to the procedure that was followed, the protection implicit in the office of the functionary whose conduct is challenged, the balance of hurt complained of and good accomplished—these are some of the considerations that must enter into the judicial judgment"; Stanley v. Illinois, 405 U.S. 645 (1972); Bell v. Burson, 402 U.S. 535 (1971); Fuentes v. Shevin, 407 U.S. 67 (1972).

[22] By "adjudicatory" action is meant the application of preexisting policies or rules to particular factual determinations. See K. Davis, Administrative Law Text, §§7.02–.04 (1959).

[23] The Supreme Court in Goldberg v. Kelly, 397 U.S. 254 (1970), indicated that these are the basic components of procedural due process when no countervailing governmental interest is presented requiring omission of one or more of these ingredients. Accord Willner v. Committee on Character and Fitness, 373 U.S. 96 (1963).

[24] See e.g. Goldberg v. Kelly, note 23, supra; Green v. McElroy, 360 U.S. 474, 496–497 (1959); Joint Anti-Fascist Refugee Comm. v. McGrath, 341 U.S. 123, 168 (1951) (Frankfurter, J., concurring): "[T]he right to be heard before being condemned to suffer grievous loss of any kind, even though it may not involve the stigma and hardships of a criminal conviction, is a principle basic to our society."

Placing upon the government the burden of showing why the "basic" right to full procedural due process is inappropriate finds support in traditional equal protection and due process arguments, which require the government to justify with "compelling reasons" the abridgment of basic rights. See e.g. Shapiro v. Thompson, 394 U.S. 618 (1969); Levy v. Louisiana, 391 U.S. 68 (1968); Loving v. Virginia, 388 U.S. 1 (1967); Griswold v. Connecticut, 381 U.S. 479 (1965); Skinner v. Oklahoma, 316 U.S. 535 (1942). Judge Merhige stated a related principle in Landman v. Royster, note 1, supra, at 654, stating, "Where substantial sanctions are possible and the assistance of counsel may be of benefit, retained counsel is necessary to protect the fact-finding and adjudication process unless there is shown some 'compelling governmental interest in summary adjudication' . . . the fulfillment of which is inconsistent with the right to retained counsel."

25 See Armstrong v. Manzo, 380 U.S. 545, 552 (1965); Wong Yang Sung v. McGrath, 339 U.S. 33, 50 (1950).

26 K. Davis, Administrative Law Text, note 22, supra, §7.02, at 115.

27 See e.g. McCloskey v. Maryland, 337 F.2d 72 (4th Cir. 1964); Siegal v. Ragen, 180 F.2d 785, 788 (7th Cir. 1950); Roberts v. Peperseck, 256 F. Supp. 415 (D. Md. 1966); Ruark v. Schooley, 211 F. Supp. 921 (D. Colo. 1962).

28 The "hands-off" doctrine is not founded upon a claim by the federal courts of a lack of jurisdiction, since 28 U.S.C. §1343 clearly authorizes federal courts to hear claims of denial of constitutional rights and since 42 U.S.C. §1983 provides a specific vehicle for obtaining redress for denials of constitutional rights which are made under color of state law. Nor is the "hands-off" doctrine based upon concepts of abstention or exhaustion of remedies, since in almost no prison cases does there exist a statute the interpretation of which might negate the necessity of reaching the constitutional question, and exhaustion of state remedies is not required in order for one to bring suit under 42 U.S.C. §1983. See Wilwording v. Swenson, 404 U.S. 249 (1971). The doctrine is best described as a self-imposed limit on jurisdiction based upon respect for federal-state comity and on deference to the expertise of prison administrators. But see Rodriguez v. Preiser, — U.S.L.W. — (1973).

29 Kostal v. Tinsley, 337 F.2d 845, 846 (10th Cir. 1964). See Douglas v. Siegler, 386 F.2d 684 (8th Cir. 1967); McCloskey v. Maryland, 337 F.2d 72, 74 (4th Cir. 1964): "In the great mass of instances, however, the necessity for effective disciplinary controls is so impelling that judicial review of them is highly impractical and wholly unwarranted."

30 370 F.2d 135 (4th Cir. 1966), cert. denied 388 U.S. 920 (1967).

31 370 F.2d at 141.

32 Washington v. Lee, 263 F. Supp. 327, 331 (M.D. Ala. 1966), aff'd 390 U.S. 333 (1968). Accord Talley v. Stephens, 247 F. Supp. 683, 689 (E.D. Ark 1965). Similar statements were contained in Jackson v. Godwin, 400 F.2d 529, 532–533 (5th Cir. 1968), which invalidated certain restrictive correspondence regulations:

"Acceptance of the fact that incarceration, because of inherent administrative problems, may necessitate the withdrawal of many rights and privileges does *not* preclude recognition by the courts of a duty to protect the prisoner from unlawful and onerous treatment of a nature that, of itself, adds punitive measures to those legally meted out by the court. . . . [C]onstitutional safeguards are intended to protect the rights of *all* citizens, including prisoners, especially against official conduct which is arbitrary. . . ." (Emphasis added.) See Jackson v. Bishop, 404 F.2d 571 (8th Cir. 1968); Fulwood v. Clemmer, 206 F. Supp. 370 (D.D.C. 1962).

33 Johnson v. Avery, 393 U.S. 483, 486 (1969).

The President's Commission on Law Enforcement and the Administration of Justice recognized the demise of the "hands-off" doctrine: "There are increasing signs that the courts are ready to abandon their traditional hands-off attitude. They have so far been particularly concerned with the procedures by which parole and probation are revoked. But recent cases suggest that the whole correctional area will be increasingly subject to judicial supervision."

United States President's Commission on Law Enforcement and the Administration of Justice: Corrections, at 83 (1967) [hereinafter "President's Comm'n on Corrections"].

34 See Ruffin v. Commonwealth, 62 Va. (21 Gratt.) 790, 796 (1871).

35 McCloskey v. Maryland, 337 F.2d 72, 74 (4th Cir. 1964).

36 Note 5, supra.

37 Most maximum-security prisons are acknowledged as "warehouses" and were constructed years ago. The following description of the Maryland Penitentiary is true of many of these old penitentiaries. "The Maryland Penitentiary . . . is little better than a place to do time with a few positive treatment opportunities. The institution program is essentially industries-and-security oriented. The buildings are old and in poor state of maintenance. Limited space seriously impedes planning and expansion of programs. Recreation and general living space is inadequate, particularly when penitentiary inmates may live for decades within this small and crowded enclosure. There is no formal vocational training program. The development of any sophisticated plan for treatment would be an academic exercise in view of the almost complete lack of treatment facilities." The Commission to Study the Correctional System of Maryland, Minority Report to Governor Spiro T. Agnew, at 20 (1967) [hereinafter "Md. Correctional Comm'n Rep."]. Interinstitutional transfers of inmates for disciplinary reasons are made to the Penitentiary, which serves as a prison within a penal system. Maryland Department of Correctional Services, Policy Memorandum No. 21-68 (Jan. 17, 1968).

38 In Maryland, the camp centers (five in all) are recently constructed, modern facilities which have ample recreation areas. The vocational programs, including work-release programs, are superior to those offered at either the Penitentiary or the House of Corrections (a medium-security institution). Inmates at the camps have substantial contact with the communities in which the camps are located, and there are opportunities for inmates to spend time outside the camp centers. The purpose of these camps is to prepare inmates for release rather than to maintain a high level of security. Md. Correctional Comm'n Rep., note 37, supra, at 62–66.

39 See Md. Correctional Comm'n Rep., note 37, supra, at 62–66.

40 See footnote 12, supra.

41 Most penal systems have no mandatory requirement of a hearing prior to or soon after a transfer from a medium- or minimum-security institution to a maximum-security institution. Recent decisions indicate that the absence of a hearing in this regard is unconstitutional. See e.g. Bundy v. Cannon, note 7, supra; United States ex rel. Neal v. Wolfe, note 7, supra.

42 See footnote 10, supra.

43 See footnote 11, supra. In Maryland, maximum-security quarters are used for the severe punishment of inmates who violate prison rules. Inmates so punished are locked in a single cell for twenty-four hours a day except for brief exercise periods (ten to fifteen minutes two or three times weekly) and weekly showers. Other denials of liberty include: (1) exclusion from standard recreational activities (movies, television viewing, etc.); (2) restriction of library privileges; (3) refusal of permission to participate in vocational and educational

programs; (4) refusal of permission to work; (5) limitation of visitation privileges; and (6) restriction of socialization opportunities. See Affidavit of inmate of Maryland Penitentiary, "sentenced" to maximum security for one year, on file at the office of the Maryland Law Review. There is a thirty-day time limit on the use of this form of punitive confinement for inmates whose misconduct presented no "serious danger and threat to the security of the institution and the inmates," but there is only a requirement that the punishment be reviewed every thirty days in cases of those guilty of serious infractions. Maryland Department of Correctional Services, Administrative Directive No. 12-70 (June 1, 1970).

44 See footnote 9, supra.

45 Id.

46 The extent of liberty which is forfeited when "good time" is revoked can be very substantial, resulting in years of additional confinement. See e.g. Bundy v. Cannon, note 7, supra (punitive transfer of inmates from minimum-security to maximum-security institution, accompanied by forfeiture of "good time" of from seventy-eight days to over one year and, in three cases, by denials of parole). See also Hirschkop and Millemann, "The Unconstitutionality of Prison Life," 55 Va. L. Rev. 795, 831 (1969). See footnote 16, supra.

47 As mentioned before, throughout this article the focus will be on disciplinary action denying the three most substantial quanta of institutional liberty: (1) "good time" credit; (2) freedom from maximum-security confinement within an institution; and (3) freedom from confinement in a maximum-security institution. General references to serious disciplinary actions or substantial denials of prison liberty should be understood to refer to deprivations of one or more of these quanta of liberty.

48 See e.g. Douglas v. Sigler, 386 F.2d 684, 687 (8th Cir. 1967): "The diminution of sentence rests on legislative grace and not constitutional right."

49 Graham v. Richardson, 403 U.S. 365, 374 (1971).

50 Morrissey v. Brewer, note 5, supra, at 481.

50a Note 4, supra.

51 Id. at 196.

52 See e.g. Menechino v. Oswald, 430 F.2d 403 (2d Cir. 1970), holding that the initial parole hearing need not be adversarial, since parole hearings are part of the rehabilitative process; Alvarez v. Turner, 422 F.2d 214, 217 (10th Cir. 1970), parole revocation hearing need not be adversarial since "the decision to revoke parole is prognostic."

53 This was the case in Maryland prior to Bundy v. Cannon, note 7, supra. This panel, comprised of the assistant superintendent of treatment, a classification counselor, and a senior correctional officer, determined whether the inmate committed the infraction and, if so, the appropriate punishment. Maryland Department of Correctional Services, Administrative Directive No. 12-70 (June 1, 1970).

54 In Maryland, as of 1967, psychiatric services in the correctional system were virtually nonexistent. Md. Correctional Comm'n Rep. 14, at 20–21. Very recently a staff of psychologists instituted a special ten-cell therapy unit in the Maryland Penitentiary which provides therapy and counselling for a small number of inmates. See The Evening Sun (Baltimore), Dec. 7, 1970, Sec. C, at 1.

55 In Maryland there is no educational requirement beyond that of having a high school diploma. (This information was obtained by the author as a result of a conversation with officials of the Maryland penal system.)

56 See footnotes 10, 11, 43, supra.

57 See footnote 37, supra.

58 American Correctional Association, Manual of Correctional Standards, at 411–412 (1966).

59 See Mempa v. Rhay, 389 U.S. 128 (1967); Specht v. Patterson, 386 U.S. 605, 607, 610 (1967). In Specht, petitioner was convicted, under a Colorado statute which provided for a maximum sentence of ten years, of the crime of taking indecent liberties. He was sentenced to an indeterminate sentence, however, under a separate "sex offender" statute which allowed the imposition of such a sentence if the defendant "constitutes a threat of bodily harm to members of the public, or is an habitual offender and mentally ill." This sentencing was done without a prior hearing to determine his status as a sex offender. The Supreme Court held that this procedure violated due process since "the invocation of the Sex Offenders Act means the making of a new charge leading to a criminal punishment" and involves the litigation of a new and "distinct issue," thus requiring the rudiments of procedural due process. It is the fact that new and distinct issues are involved in prison disciplinary proceedings which requires compliance with procedural due process.

In Mempa v. Rhay, supra, the Court held that due process required the presence of counsel at probation revocation hearings, since the time of deferred sentencing is a critical stage in a criminal case. The analysis of the Court, that a forfeiture of conditional liberty based upon factual determinations may not violate due process, is applicable to the revocation of "good time" and to the imposition of punishment, which results in a denial of parole. See Hewett v. North Carolina, 415 F.2d 1316 (4th Cir. 1969) (applying Mempa to revocation of probation where a new sentence was not imposed).

60 387 U.S. 1 (1967).

61 Id. at 27.

62 The recent opinion in Lessard v. Schmidt, — F. Supp. — No. 71-C-602 (E.D. Wisc. 1972), CCH Poverty Law Rep. ¶16,255, holds that prior to involuntary civil commitment persons are entitled to full procedural safeguards, safeguards approximating those afforded criminal defendants. Decisions prior to this case insured procedural due process prior to involuntary civil commitment to a lesser extent. See e.g. Barry v. Hall, 98 F.2d 222 (D.C. Cir. 1938); In re Lambert, 134 Cal. 626, 66 P. 851 (1901); Petition of Rohrer, 353 Mass. 282, 230 N.E.2d 915 (1967). The above cases hold unconstitutional, as not following procedural due process, ex parte involuntary commitment to mental institutions. See also Baxstrom v. Herold, 383 U.S. 107 (1966), requiring, on grounds of equal protection, that full procedural standards be observed before a state may confine a prisoner in an institution for the insane after the expiration of his sentence; United States ex rel. Schuster v. Herold, 410 F.2d 1071 (2d Cir. 1969), requiring, again on grounds of equal protection, that a full adversarial hearing be held before a penal inmate may be transferred to a state institution for insane criminals.

63 419 F.2d 617 (D.C. Cir. 1969). See also Jones v. Robinson, 440 F.2d 249 (D.C. Cir. 1971).

64 Covington v. Harris, note 63, supra, 419 F.2d at 624.

65 Covington v. Harris, note 63, supra, 419 F.2d at 621.

65a Morrissey v. Brewer, note 5, supra.

66 Morrissey v. Brewer, note 5, supra, at 484.

67 See e.g. Harman v. Forssennius, 380 U.S. 528, 542 (1965); Carrington v. Rash, 380 U.S. 89, 96 (1965); Oyama v. California, 332 U.S. 633, 646–647 (1948).

68 397 U.S. 254 (1970).

69 Id. at 266.

70 Id.

71 The pronouncement of the court in Hamilton v. Love, 328 F. Supp. 1182, 1194 (E.D. Ark. 1971), is instructive: "Inadequate resources can never be an adequate justification for the state's depriving any person of his constitutional rights. If the state cannot obtain the resources to detain persons awaiting trial in accordance with minimum constitutional standards, then the state simply will not be permitted to detain such persons." See Long v. Robinson, 316 F. Supp. 22 (D. Md. 1970), declaring unconstitutional the classification, for criminal law purposes, in Baltimore City of children of sixteen and seventeen years as adults when they were categorized as "juveniles" throughout the rest of the state— the court so held despite the facts that the cost to the State of Maryland would be measured in millions of dollars and that the decision would result in substantial administrative confusion.

72 309 F. Supp. 362 (E.D. Ark. 1970), aff'd 442 F.2d 304 (8th Cir. 1971).

73 Id. at 383.

74 Id. at 379.

75 367 U.S. 886, 896 (1961). The Court held that due process did not require that the Navy advise an employee working on a military installation of why she was excluded from that enclave or that it provide her with a hearing at which she could attempt to refute the grounds for her exclusion. The interest of the government in maintaining national security was held to outweigh the need to preserve the opportunity of one person "to work at one isolated and specific military installation." But see the dissenting opinion of Justice Brennan at 901–902 for a different evaluation of the employee's interest.

76 Knauff v. Shaughnessy, 338 U.S. 537 (1950); Bailey v. Richardson, 182 F.2d 46 (D.C. Cir. 1950), aff'd per curiam 341 U.S. 918 (1951).

77 It is questionable whether the making of significant additional expenditures would in fact be necessary to assure procedural fairness. Indeed, the contrary might be true. If prison disciplinary boards included as a participating member a public citizen who lacked official ties to the penal system, prison employees would be able to spend more time performing security and rehabilitative functions; at the same time, procedural fairness would be better assured. Similarly, if law students were allowed to represent inmates at disciplinary hearings, then the time and energy of prison employees, who in accordance with the policies of several prison systems now perform this function, could be conserved. In the long run the guaranty of procedural fairness could result in the conservation of state funds. It is the opinion of many penal experts (see note 106, infra) that the fair and impartial treatment of inmates serves a positive rehabilitative func-

tion which might well reduce recidivism and thus prevent future expenditures of state funds.

[78] Fuentes v. Shevin, 407 U.S. 67, 90, n. 22 (1972).

[79] President's Comm'n on Corrections, note 33, supra, at 83.

[80] 442 F.2d 178 (2d Cir. 1971).

[81] Id. at 196–197.

[82] Morrissey v. Brewer, note 5, supra.

[83] 442 F.2d 178 (2d Cir. 1971).

[84] See underlying facts found by courts in Landman v. Royster, note 1, supra; Bundy v. Cannon, note 7, supra.

[85] Morrissey v. Brewer, note 5, supra, 408 U.S. at 484.

[86] See footnote 7, supra.

[87] 333 F. Supp. 621 (E.D. Va. 1971).

[88] Written notice, a hearing before an impartial tribunal, the right to present witnesses and cross-examine adverse witnesses, the right to counsel, the right to written reasons.

[89] Several opinions requiring that prison officials observe due process guaranties before imposing serious punishment do require less in the way of due process when the severity of the puishment is decreased and, in essence, set up a dual system for imposing punishment. See e.g. Landman v. Royster, note 1, supra; Bundy v. Cannon, note 7, supra.

[90] Collins v. Schoonfield, note 7, supra (see interim decree).

[91] Id.

[92] 442 F.2d 178 (2d Cir. 1971).

[93] Id. at 198.

[94] If a hearing is required, it must be fair, Wong Yang Sung v. McGrath, 339 U.S. 33, 50 (1950); and it must be conducted in a "meaningful manner," Armstrong v. Manzo, 380 U.S. 545, 552 (1965). The function of a disciplinary hearing is to determine "who did what, where, when, how, why, with what motive or intent." K. Davis, Administrative Law Text §7.02, at 116 (1959). After this initial determination, existing policies are applied to decide if an infraction of prison rules has occurred and, if so, to impose appropriate punishment. Therefore, the nature of such a hearing clearly is adjudicatory, warranting imposition of full procedural protections. See Goldberg v. Kelly, 397 U.S. 254 (1970); Willner v. Committee on Character and Fitness, 373 U.S. 96 (1963). See also In re Gault, 387 U.S. 1 (1967); Kent v. United States, 383 U.S. 541 (1966); Simmons v. United States, 348 U.S. 397 (1959).

[95] Maryland Department of Corrections, Handbook for Inmates §13, at 17 (1964).

[96] Id., §20, at 21.

[97] Many prison systems are now, for the first time, reducing rules to writing and distributing rule books to inmates. See e.g. Bundy v. Cannon, note 7, supra.

[98] See e.g. Collins v. Schoonfield, note 7, supra (interim decree); Rhem v. McGrath, 326 F. Supp. 681 (S.D.N.Y. 1970).

99 Id.

100 Landman v. Royster, note 1, supra.

101 Substantive due process questions are raised when inmates are punished for conduct that has not prior to the inmate's act been prohibited in writing (see Sostre v. Rockefeller, 312 F. Supp. 863, 871–872 (S.D.N.Y. 1970); Rodriguez v. McGinnis, 307 F. Supp. 627, 632 (N.D.N.Y. 1969), or for conduct which is forbidden only in vague and uncertain terms. See Landman v. Royster, note 1, supra; Douglas v. Sigler, 386 F.2d 684, 686 (8th Cir., 1967).

102 Goldberg v. Kelly, 397 U.S. 254, 269 (1970). See K. Davis, Administrative Law Text §§7.02, 7.05 (1959).

103 The Sixth Amendment to the United States Constitution provides in pertinent part, "In all criminal prosecutions, the accused shall enjoy the right . . . to be confronted with the witnesses against him. . . ."

104 See Morrissey v. Brewer, note 5, supra; Goldberg v. Kelly, note 102, supra (1970); Willner v. Committee on Character and Fitness, 373 U.S. 96, 103–104 (1963); Greene v. McElroy, 360 U.S. 474, 496–497 (1959); I.C.C. v. Louisville & N.R.R., 227 U.S. 88, 93–94 (1913).

105 See footnotes 9, 10, 11, supra.

106 "Denying offenders any chance to challenge arbitrary assertions of power by correctional officials" is inconsistent with "the need to instill [in the inmate] respect for and willingness to cooperate with society and to help the offender assume the role of a normal citizen." President's Commission on Corrections, at 82.

107 James V. Bennett, former Director of the Federal Bureau of Prisons, explained that, while prison officials control the institutions, subtle manipulations of prison discipline can and do occur: "The prison society has its way of enforcing its rules. Gambling, for example, is illegal in federal prisons . . . welching on a bet, however, is a sin to be avenged by some subtle method, such as planting dope or a knife beneath the offender's bed and tipping off an officer." J. V. Bennett, I Choose Prison, at 28 (1970). Judicial recognition of the especially real possibility of misuse of authority by prison guards is contained in Landman v. Peyton, 370 F.2d 135, 140 (4th Cir. 1966):

> "Acton's classic proverb about the corrupting influence of absolute power is true of prison guards no less than of other men. In fact, prison guards may be more vulnerable to the corrupting influence of unchecked authority than most people. It is well known that prisons are operated on minimum budgets and that poor salaries and working conditions make it difficult to attract high calibre personnel. Moreover, the 'training' of the officers in methods of dealing with obstreperous prisoners is but a euphemism in most states."

It is in order to guard against reliance upon the testimony of individuals who, as in the examples above, "might be perjurers or persons motivated by malice, vindictiveness, intolerance, prejudice, or jealousy," that we require confrontation and cross-examination. Greene v. McElroy, 360 U.S. 474, 496–497 (1959). While it is apparent that inmates called as witnesses at disciplinary hearings will be subject to the same institutional pressures as those described by Bennett, supra, this should not constitute sufficient ground for denying inmates the right to produce witnesses, but should only be a factor for the tribunal to consider in determining credibility.

108 It is apparent that traditional practices and accepted relationships must yield to constitutional obligations. See e.g. Morrissey v. Brewer, note 5, supra; Brown v. Board of Education, 349 U.S. 294 (1950).

109 See footnotes 70–72, supra.

110 Morrissey v. Brewer, note 5, supra, 408 U.S. at 489.

111 See Morrissey v. Brewer, note 5, supra, and cases contained in footnote 7, supra.

112 Specht v. Patterson, 386 U.S. 605 (1967).

113 Shone v. Maine, 406 F.2d 844 (1st Cir. 1969).
  Cf. Gomes v. Travisono, 353 F. Supp. 457 (D.R.I. 1973), a recent and important decision stating that a due process hearing must be had before inmates are transferred without their consent to another prison within the state or to another state.

114 Dixon v. Alabama State Bd. of Education, 294 F.2d 150 (5th Cir. 1961).

115 Escalera v. New York City Housing Authority, 425 F.2d 853 (2d Cir. 1970).

116 Goldberg v. Kelly, 397 U.S. 254 (1970).

117 Willner v. Committee on Character and Fitness, 373 U.S. 96 (1963).

118 By "opposing witnesses" is meant not only individuals who might testify against an individual at a disciplinary hearing but also any other person who might have supplied evidence affecting the decision.

119 Many prison systems, in the wake of the successful litigation mentioned in this article, have voluntarily adopted rules and regulations which provide most or all of the essentials of procedural due process. The Kansas penal system is a good example.

120 See e.g. Morrissey v. Brewer, note 5, supra; Goldberg v. Kelly, note 116, supra; In re Murchison, 349 U.S. 133, 136 (1955); Tumey v. Ohio, 273 U.S. 510 (1927).
  A recent decision, Taylor v. New York City Transit Authority, 309 F. Supp. 785 (E.D.N.Y. 1970), held that a requisite component of "quasi-judicial administrative adjudications" is an impartial tribunal. The court stated, "Confusion between the roles of judge and advocate has been rightly distrusted in English law since the Middle Ages. With possible exceptions not here relevant, the right to an impartial judge—one who has no interest in the outcome of a case before him and whose contact with the litigation does not suggest any reason for partiality—is required to meet minimum standards of due process." Id. at 788 (citation omitted).

121 See Bundy v. Cannon, note 7, supra. Holding that an inmate of the New York penal system had been arbitrarily denied "good time," the court in Rodriguez v. McGinnis, 307 F. Supp. 627, 632 (N.D.N.Y. 1969), questioned the constitutionality of the imposition of discipline under procedures not insuring a separation of functions, stating: "I am not sure the disciplinary officer . . . can assume legally the investigative mantle and [then] become prosecutor, judge and jury, and . . . Appellate Court of review." Other penal systems are sensi-

tive to this problem. For example, the policies of Missouri and Rhode Island explicitly exclude from membership on the disciplinary board any officer who initiated disciplinary charges or investigated the charges. See Morris v. Travisono, note 7, supra; Missouri State Penitentiary, Personnel Information Pamplet 3 (1967).

122 In Maryland, the Prisoners' Aid Association and the St. Johns' Council are two of the more active groups.

123 Bundy v. Cannon, 328 F. Supp. 165 (D. Md. 1971).

124 Collins v. Schoonfield, 344 F. Supp. 257 (D. Md. 1972) (see interim decree).

125 See e.g. Landman v. Royster, note 1, supra.

126 393 U.S. 484 (1968).

127 328 F. Supp. 767 (N.D. Cal. 1971).

128 Id. at 779.

129 333 F. Supp. 621 (E.D. Va. 1971).

130 341 F. Supp. 1001 (W.D. Wisc. 1972).

131 344 F. Supp. 257 (D. Md. 1972) (see interim decree).

132 Landman v. Royster, note 1, supra, at 654.

133 Cf. Madera v. Board of Education, 267 F. Supp. 356 (S.D.N.Y. 1967), where Judge Motley held that procedural due process required that a public school student be allowed to be represented by retained counsel at a conference to determine whether he should be suspended from school. This decision was reversed by the Second Circuit. 386 F.2d 778 (1967), cert. denied 390 U.S. 1028 (1968). Accord Wasson v. Trowbridge, 382 F.2d 807 (2d Cir. 1967) (a student has no right to representation by retained counsel at an expulsion hearing). These cases are distinguishable from prison disciplinary hearings in that (1) the amount of personal liberty at stake in prison disciplinary proceedings (for example, months of additional incarceration) is entitled to greater protection than the privilege which is lost on suspension or expulsion from school; and (2) inmates, as a class, are less able to assert and protect their rights, lacking the sophistication of college students and the parental protection enjoyed by younger students. See French v. Bashful, 303 F. Supp. 1333 (E.D. La. 1969) (holding that a student is entitled to representation by retained counsel at an expulsion hearing where the balance of sophistication favored the school).

The recent opinion of the Supreme Court in Argersinger v. Hamlin, 407 U.S. 25 (1972), establishes that criminal defendants are entitled to the representation by counsel, court-appointed if necessary, when they face prosecutions which may result in any incarceration. The logic and thrust of this opinion supports the argument that prison inmates, when faced with disciplinary action which may result in revocation of good time or which may defer parole consideration, are entitled to assistance of counsel also. Certainly, the opinions of the Second and Fourth Circuits in United States ex rel. Bey v. Connecticut Board of Parole, 443 F.2d 1079 (2d Cir. 1971), and Beardon v. South Carolina, 443 F.2d 1090 (4th Cir. 1971), which require, in most circumstances, that parolees faced with revocation are entitled to court-appointed counsel, provide additional support for allowing the representation of counsel at prison disciplinary hearings which threaten inmates' conditional liberty.

134 397 U.S. 254 (1970).

135 389 U.S. 128 (1967).

136 See also Williams v. Zuckert, 371 U.S. 534 (1963) (Douglas, J., dissenting from denial of certiorari); Maltex v. Nagle, 27 F.2d 835 (9th Cir. 1928) (counsel may be retained at deportation hearing).

137 See Fuentes v. Shevin, 407 U.S. 67 (1972); Boddie v. Connecticut, 401 U.S. 371, 378–379 (1971); Bell v. Burson, 402 U.S. 535 (1971); Stanley v. Illinois, 405 U.S. 645 (1972); Goldberg v. Kelly, note 116, supra; Sniadach v. Family Finance Corp., 395 U.S. 337, 339 (1969); Opp Cotton Mills v. Administrator, 312 U.S. 126, 152–153 (1941); Morgan v. United States, 304 U.S. 1, 25 (1938).

138 See F.P.C. v. Tennessee Gas Transmission Co., 371 U.S. 145 (1962); Fahey v. Mallonee, 332 U.S. 245 (1947); Yakus v. United States, 321 U.S. 414 (1944).

139 Collins v. Schoonfield, note 7, supra (see interim decree), holds that inmates may not be punished prior to a hearing unless: (1) the inmate's conduct poses a serious, immediate and substantial threat to the safety of himself or others or security of the institution; (2) the circumstances are such as to demonstrate strong probability of guilt; and (3) there is an appropriate investigation or due inquiry to insure that the punishment is not arbitrary or irrational. At any rate this decision requires that a hearing be held within forty-eight hours of solitary confinement and within seven days of revocation of any substantial jail privilege. Id.

140 Joint Anti-Fascist Refugee Comm. v. McGrath, 341 U.S. 123, 171–172 (1951) (concurring opinion).

CHAPTER 6
PRISON CONDITIONS

EDITORS' INTRODUCTION

On first impression one would think that the "cruel and unusual punishment" provision of the Constitution has been the decisional basis for the successful prison condition cases, but in actuality the Due Process Clause and not the Eighth Amendment has been more frequently utilized by the courts. The expansive concept of due process has apparently been more appealing to judges who were willing to spur reform and change. In recent years, prisoners' rights lawyers have tried to revise this historic Eighth Amendment anomaly. This article impressively collects, collates and analyzes the important Eighth Amendment cases in the prisoners' rights area. These should be utilized in a two-pronged attack, using the Due Process Clause and the Eighth Amendment to challenge prison conditions.

CHALLENGING CONDITIONS IN PRISONS WHICH VIOLATE THE EIGHTH AMENDMENT

WILLIAM BENNETT TURNER *

The Supreme Court has never applied the Eighth Amendment to prison conditions or practices. Therefore, the extent to which the Eighth Amendment provides in-prison protection has not been definitely resolved. This article considers lower court decisions applying the cruel and unusual punishment clause to prisons and draws analogies to Eighth Amendment decisions by the Supreme Court in other areas of the law.

The most comprehensive decision on the Eighth Amendment is the Supreme Court's death penalty decision in *Furman v. Georgia*.[1] In nine separate opinions the Justices expressed their views on cruel and unusual punishment, tracing the history and considering the contemporary meaning of the Eighth Amendment. It remains largely true that "what constitutes a cruel and unusual punishment has not been exactly decided,"[2] and *Furman* sheds little light on the Court's probable approach to questions of in-prison punishment. However, two points of relevance to prisoners' rights under the Eighth Amendment do emerge from the various opinion: first, the history of the amendment indicates that the word "unusual" adds nothing of substance to the word "cruel,"[3] and second, the judiciary is less reluctant to strike down punishments devised without statutory authority as opposed to punishments specifically authorized by state legislatures.[4]

Viewing the word "unusual" as surplusage is helpful to prisoners' rights, because the deplorable conditions in jails and prisons are anything but unsual. Accordingly, arguments that certain conditions are prevalent in most jails and prisons present no defense to a suit brought under the Eighth Amendment.

* Assistant Counsel, NAACP Legal Defense and Educational Fund, Inc., San Francisco, California; B.S. Northwestern University; LL.B. Harvard University.

The Court's apparent willingness to scrutinize punishments imposed without statutory authorization more carefully than punishments under laws passed by legislatures is pertinent to prisoners' rights suits because the conditions challenged in such suits are virtually never required by statute. The conditions are either the creation of officials acting without legislative authority, on a grisly frolic of their own, or they are the result of apathy, indifference, and public neglect. No considerations of deference to legislative judgment are involved.

While the Supreme Court has never applied the Eighth Amendment to prison conditions, it has established certain principles that apply with particular force to prison cases. Thus the Court has declared that the Eighth Amendment protects "nothing less than the dignity of man" and that its meaning must be derived by applying "the evolving standards of decency that mark the progress of a maturing society." [5] The lower courts have understandably had difficulty in applying these broad principles to specific and varying fact situations. Nevertheless, the lower courts have invoked the Eighth Amendment to protect prisoners from certain kinds of conditions or punishments.

In general, the cases break down into four categories: (1) the overall conditions of the jail or prison sink to an intolerably barbaric level; (2) physical punishments are impermissible; (3) denial of needed medical care in some circumstances is cruel and unusual; and (4) various kinds of disciplinary confinement violate the Eighth Amendment.

Overall Conditions of the Jail or Prison

The Arkansas prison case is the most dramatic example of a decision where the overall conditions were found constitutionally intolerable. The court in *Holt v. Sarver* [6] found that the living conditions in Arkansas prisons constituted cruel and unusual punishment. The opinion emphasized certain factors which, in the totality of the circumstances, led to the conclusion that the Eighth Amendment was violated: the trusty system, which placed power in the hands of favored prisoners rather than paid and trained correctional officers; inadequate supervision in the dormitories, leaving the prisoners vulnerable to homosexual attacks, stabbings, etc.; squalid conditions in isolation cells to which any prisoner could be summarily relegated; the lack of any meaningful rehabilitation program; poor sanitary conditions generally; inadequate clothing for prisoners; and the failure to furnish adequate medical care. Explicitly threatening to enjoin any imprisonment in Arkansas, the court ordered the prison officials to file a plan to remedy the deficiencies and bring about minimal standards of decency.

Another federal court recently came to a similar conclusion about the Mississippi prison, and condemned its overall conditions under the Eighth Amendment.[7] Although few prison systems are as primitive as those of Arkansas and Mississippi, the conditions in many county jails are comparable, and thus vulnerable under the Eighth Amendment. Indeed, a growing number of courts have not hesitated in using the *Holt* approach to condemn disgraceful conditions in local jails.[8] The decisions have emphasized that the prisoners are pretrial detainees who are presumed innocent and that the only purpose of holding them is to assure their presence at trial. The courts therefore conclude that any punishment unrelated to this purpose is unconstitutional.

The general approach of the cases is to consider the totality of the circumstances—overcrowding, poor sanitation, lack of recreational opportunities, limitations on visits and correspondence, absence of medical care, inadequate nutrition, etc. Some of the courts have entered sweeping decrees requiring even reduction of population through bail reform, training programs for guards and radical changes in physical conditions.[9]

Physical Punishments

It has always been assumed that the purpose of the Eighth Amendment was to proscribe, at the very least, tortures and other medieval punishments.[10] A leading case on prisoners' rights outlawed corporal punishment by use of the strap.[11] Beatings by officers have been held to constitute cruel and unusual punishment.[12] Unreasonable tear gassings of helpless prisoners should undoubtedly be treated the same as other excessive uses of force.[13]

Further, imposition of a bread and water or starvation diet has been treated as a species of physical punishment, and held cruel and unusual.[14] Where officials inflict some punishment that is physically debilitating, the courts can be expected to exercise Eighth Amendment scrutiny.[15]

Denial Of Medical Care

The courts have had difficulty with the frequent complaints of prisoners about denial of medical care. As noted above, the absence of any adequate medical care program may be one element in a decision that the overall conditions of a jail or prison are unconstitutional.[16] However, where the question is whether an individual prisoner has received proper medical treatment, most courts have held that no Eighth Amendment issue is raised unless the prisoner is denied needed medical care for some improper reason,[17] is forced to work by prison officials who know he is ill,[18] or has a very severe and obvious injury or illness that is deliberately overlooked by the officials.[19] Most courts have held that instances of simple negligence or medical malpractice do not give rise to a constitutional claim.[20]

Disciplinary Confinement

A few lower courts have held that solitary confinement, segregation, meditation, the "hole," isolation, maximum security or whatever euphemism may be used for the punitive confinement of a prisoner deemed recalcitrant, are cruel and unusual. As in the general conditions cases, these courts have considered the totality of the dehumanizing circumstances in punitive confinement and have held them violative of the Eighth Amendment.[21] Most of the cases have involved unconscionably unsanitary conditions in the cells, but the courts have not rested their decisions solely on that ground.[22] Rather, they have reviewed the totality of the sordid conditions and have condemned that totality as unconstitutional.[23]

A number of courts have said that solitary confinement *per se* is not cruel and unusual punishment,[24] but the significance of this depends on what precisely is meant by "solitary confinement." The conditions of such confinement can range from simple separation from the general prison population, with loss of only those privileges that involve no unnecessary deprivations, to confinement in a dark cell on a bread and water diet, without clothes, bedding or any of the usual prison privileges. Accordingly, it does not promote analysis to argue that "solitary confinement" is or is not cruel and unusual. A careful consideration of the precise conditions and deprivations involved is essential.

One of the significant factors in disciplinary confinement is its duration. The Second Circuit's important but very conservative decision in *Sostre v. McGinnis* [25] held that confinement for a year in segregation did not violate the Eighth Amendment. The court said that the precise conditions of the confinement raised it "several notches above those truly barbarous and inhuman conditions" previously condemned as cruel and unusual.[26] While the court's failure to put a durational limit on segregated confinement appears to have been strongly influenced by its view that the prisoner could at any time effect his own release by agreeing to abide by prison rules, this view is at odds with the reality of prison life. In any event, the court failed to articulate any coherent Eighth Amendment analysis to deal with a practice so widely used and abused in American prisons.

There is a growing body of recognized standards available for use by the courts in evaluating the conditions of disciplinary confinement.[27] Certainly any conditions that fall below accepted minimum standards should be constitutionally suspect, and the officials should bear a very heavy burden in justifying them.[28]

In the absence of any guidelines from the Supreme Court as to applicable Eighth Amendment principles governing prison practices, the lower courts have used three separate theories for holding that disciplinary confinement is cruel and unusual. First, several courts have found that the conditions are "shocking to the conscience" and in themselves constitute cruel and unusual punishment.[29] Second, where the conditions are not themselves cruel and unusual, the punishment may be unconstitutional because it is unnecessarily cruel in view of its purpose. The Supreme Court long ago established the basic principle that:

> "A punishment may be considered cruel and unusual when, although applied in pursuit of a legitimate penal aim, it goes beyond what is necessary to achieve that aim; that is, when a punishment is unnecessarily cruel in view of the purposes for which it is used." [30]

Under this principle, it can be assumed that some form of isolation of disruptive prisoners is needed to maintain order in prison, but conditions of isolation must not exceed that which is required to meet the need. Any conditions or deprivations that are not *inherent* in the separation of the troublesome prisoner from the general population should be subject to close scrutiny, with the burden on the officials to show that such conditions and deprivations are not merely gratuitous punishment but are actually required in order to fulfill the purpose of isolation.[31]

The third theory for determining that disciplinary confinement is cruel and unusual argues from the particular facts of a case that such confinement is wholly disproportionate to the prisoner's disciplinary offense. Thus putting a prisoner in the "hole" for trivial offenses that do not actually endanger prison security cannot be justified. The courts have said in a number of instances that excessive punishment is unconstitutional.[32] Disciplinary confinement should be reserved for extreme cases of disruptive conduct; reference to the kind of conduct punished is required because "a punishment out of all proportion to the offense may bring it within the ban against 'cruel and unusual punishment.' " [33]

Conclusion

While some barbarous prison practices will not be tolerated by the courts, the lack of Eighth Amendment guidance from the Supreme Court results in divergent approaches and results in the lower courts in prisoner cases alleging cruel and unusual punishment.

Footnotes

[1] 408 U.S. 238 (1972).

[2] Weems v. United States, 217 U.S. 349, 368 (1910). As a distinguished federal judge recently noted in a prison case, "This statement is as true today as it was in 1910." Novak v. Beto, 456 F.2d 1303, 1305 (5th Cir. 1972) (Wisdom, J., dissenting from denial of rehearing en banc).

[3] Furman v. Georgia, note 1, supra, 408 U.S. at 379 (opinion of Chief Justice Burger), and 408 U.S. at 322 (opinion of Marshall, J.).

[4] Id. at 384 (dissenting opinion of Burger, C.J.); and id. at 407 (dissenting opinion of Blackmun, J.).

[5] Trop v. Dulles, 356 U.S. 86, 100–101 (1958); Weems v. United States, note 2, supra, 217 U.S. at 373.

[6] 309 F. Supp. 362 (E.D. Ark. 1970), aff'd 442 F.2d 304 (8th Cir. 1971).

[7] Gates v. Collier, 349 F. Supp. 881 (N.D. Miss. 1972).

[8] See e.g. Brenneman v. Madigan, 343 F. Supp. 128 (N.D. Cal. 1972); Hamilton v. Love, 328 F. Supp. 1182 (E.D. Ark. 1971); Jones v. Wittenberg, 323 F. Supp. 93 (N.D. Ohio 1971), aff'd sub nom. Jones v. Metzger, 456 F.2d 854 (6th Cir. 1972); Wayne County Jail Inmates v. Wayne County Bd. Comm'rs, 5 Clearinghouse Rev. 108 (Cir. Ct., Wayne County, Mich. 1971); Bryant v. Hendrick, 7 Crim. L. Rep. 2463 (Ct. C.P. Phila., Pa., Aug. 17, 1970), aff'd sub nom. Pennsyl-

vania v. Hendrick, 444 Pa. 83, 280 A.2d 110 (1971). See generally Note, "Constitutional Limitations on the Conditions of Pretrial Detention," 79 Yale L.J. 941 (1970); Comment, "Incarcerating the Innocent: Pretrial Detention in Our Nation's Jails," 21 Buff. L. Rev. 891 (1972); Note, "Recent Applications of the Ban on Cruel and Unusual Punishments: Judicially Enforced Reform of Nonfederal Penal Institutions," 23 Hastings L.J. 1111 (1972).

9 See e.g. Jones v. Wittenberg, note 8, supra.

10 See Furman v. Georgia, note 1, supra, 408 U.S. at 382–384; Robinson v. California, 370 U.S. 660, 675 (1962).

11 Jackson v. Bishop, 404 F.2d 571 (8th Cir. 1968); cf. Gates v. Collier, note 7, supra.

12 See e.g. Inmates of the Attica Correctional Facility v. Rockefeller, 453 F.2d 12, 23 (2d Cir. 1971); Tolbert v. Bragan, 451 F.2d 1020 (5th Cir. 1971). Cf. Bethea v. Crouse, 417 F.2d 504 (10th Cir. 1969).

13 See Landman v. Royster, 333 F. Supp. 621, 649 (E.D. Va. 1971). Whether excessive force is considered cruel and unusual or a summary punishment without due process seems to make little difference. Cf. Anderson v. Nosser, 456 F.2d 835 (5th Cir. 1972), with Roberts v. Williams, 456 F.2d 819 (5th Cir. 1972).

14 See Landman v. Royster, note 13, supra, at 647. The court in Landman found that the diet was a "prolonged sort of corporal punishment." See also Dearman v. Woodson, 429 F.2d 1288, 1290 (10th Cir. 1970). Contra Novak v. Beto, 453 F.2d 661 (5th Cir. 1971), rehearing en banc denied, 456 F.2d 1303 (5th Cir. 1972), cert. denied sub nom. Sellars v. Beto 409 U.S. 968 (1972).

15 In Landman v. Royster, note 13, supra, at 647, in striking down the bread and water diet, the court said "the purpose and effect of such a diet is to discipline a recalcitrant by debilitating him physically."

16 See e.g. Jones v. Wittenberg, note 8, supra; Holt v. Sarver, 309 F. Supp. 362 (E.D. Ark. 1970), aff'd 442 F.2d 304 (8th Cir. 1971). In Sawyer v. Sigler, 320 F. Supp. 690 (D. Neb. 1970), aff'd 445 F.2d 818 (8th Cir. 1971), the court said: "When a state undertakes to imprison a person, thereby depriving him largely of his ability to seek and find medical treatment, it is incumbent upon the state to furnish at least a minimal amount of medical care for whatever conditions plague the prisoner."

17 See generally Coppinger v. Townsend, 398 F.2d 392 (10th Cir. 1968); Ramsey v. Ciccone, 310 F. Supp. 600 (W.D. Mo. 1970).

18 See Campbell v. Beto, 460 F.2d 765 (5th Cir. 1972); Woolsey v. Beto, 450 F.2d 321 (5th Cir. 1971); Black v. Ciccone, 224 F. Supp. 129, 133 (W.D. Mo. 1970); Talley v. Stephens, 247 F. Supp. 683, 687 (E.D. Ark. 1965).

19 See Corby v. Conboy, 457 F.2d 251 (2d Cir. 1972); Martinez v. Mancusi, 443 F.2d 921 (2d Cir. 1971); Redding v. Pate, 220 F. Supp. 124 (N.D. Ill. 1963); cf. Church v. Hegstrom, 416 F.2d 449 (2d Cir. 1969).

20 See United States ex rel. Hyde v. McGinnis, 429 F.2d 864 (2d Cir. 1970); Gittlemacker v. Prasse, 428 F.2d 1, 6 (3d Cir. 1970); Church v. Hegstrom, 416 F.2d 449 (2d Cir. 1969). Cf. Puckett v. Cox, 456 F.2d 233 (6th Cir. 1972) (negligence can be basis for relief but must be more than isolated instance of failure to protect).

[21] See Wright v. McMann, 460 F.2d 126 (2d Cir. 1972); Hancock v. Avery, 301 F. Supp. 786 (M.D. Tenn. 1969); Holt v. Sarver, 300 F. Supp. 825 (E.D. Ark. 1969); Jordan v. Fitzharris, 257 F. Supp. 674 (N.D. Cal. 1966); cf. Brooks v. Florida, 389 U.S. 413, 415 (1967).

[22] But see Novak v. Beto, note 14, supra.

[23] See generally Turner, "Establishing the Rule of Law in Prisons," 23 Stan. L. Rev. 473, 492 (1971).

[24] See e.g. Sostre v. McGinnis, 442 F.2d 178, 192 (2d Cir. 1971); Courtney v. Bishop, 409 F.2d 1185 (8th Cir. 1969); Ford v. Board of Managers, 407 F.2d 937 (3d Cir. 1969).

[25] 442 F.2d 178 (2d Cir. 1971), cert. denied sub nom. Sostre v. Oswald, 404 U.S. 1049 (1971).

[26] Id., 442 F.2d at 193–194, n. 24.

[27] See e.g. American Correctional Association, Manual of Correctional Standards, at 415, 420 (1966); Federal Bureau of Prisons, Policy Statement No. 7400.5 (Nov. 28, 1966); United Nations, "Standard Minimum Rules for the Treatment of Prisoners," 2 N.Y.U. J. Int'l L. & Pol. 314–332 (1969); President's Commission on Law Enforcement and Administration of Justice, Task Force Report: Corrections, at 210 (1967); National Council on Crime and Delinquency, "Model Act for the Protection of Rights of Prisoners," 18 Crime & Delinquency 414 (January 1972). In addition, a number of states have specific regulations governing conditions of segregated confinement. See e.g. New York Department of Correctional Services Regulations, 7 N.Y.C.R.R. §§300.1–301.9; Rules of the California Director of Corrections, ch. 4, art. 5 (Mar. 7, 1972); Morris v. Travisono, 310 F. Supp. 857, 868–870 (D.R.I. 1970). See also Appendix A-13 of this book.

[28] See Turner, note 23, supra, at 511; see generally Singer, "Confining Solitary Confinement: Constitutional Arguments for a 'New Penology'," 56 Iowa L. Rev. 1251 (1971); Hirschkop and Millemann, "The Unconstitutionality of Prison Life," 55 Va. L. Rev. 795 (1969).

[29] See cases cited in note 21, supra.

[30] Weems v. United States, note 2, supra, at 370. This principle has been followed in prison disciplinary cases. See Dearman v. Woodson, note 14, supra, at 1290 (10th Cir. 1970); Landman v. Royster, 333 F. Supp. 621 (E.D. Va. 1971); Hancock v. Avery, 301 F. Supp. 786, 791 (M.D. Tenn. 1969); Jordan v. Fitzharris, 257 F. Supp. 674, 679 (N.D. Cal. 1966). Chief Justice Burger's dissenting opinion in Furman v. Georgia, note 1, supra, 408 U.S. at 385–391, indicated great reluctance to review a legislature's determination that a particular punishment is "necessary" to a state purpose, but presumably the absence of any statutory authorization for conditions of disciplinary confinement would permit closer judicial scrutiny.

[31] Regarding problems of proof in such cases, see Turner, note 23, supra, at 494–495, 510–511, 515.

[32] See Wright v. McMann, 460 F.2d 126, 132–134 (2d Cir. 1972); Jackson v. Bishop, 404 F.2d 571, 577–578 (8th Cir. 1968); Landman v. Royster, note 30, supra; Carothers v. Follette, 314 F. Supp. 1014 (S.D.N.Y. 1970); Jordan v. Fitzharris, note 30, supra; Fulwood v. Clemmer, 206 F. Supp. 370, 379 (D.D.C. 1962).

Contra Novak v. Beto, note 14, supra. The "disproportionality" theory of the Eighth Amendment seems to stem from the "precept of justice that punishment for crime should be graduated and proportioned to offense." Weems v. United States, 217 U.S. 349, 367 (1910).

[33] Cf. Robinson v. California, 370 U.S. 660, 676 (1962). Most of the opinions in Furman v. Georgia, note 1, supra, indicated reluctance to develop the "disproportionality" theory of the Eighth Amendment. While some punishments may be patently arbitrary and excessive, there are apparent difficulties in developing standards as to how far the state can go in dealing with concededly punishable conduct.

CHAPTER 7
PRETRIAL CONDITIONS

EDITORS' INTRODUCTION

This short but comprehensive article singles out the special legal issues attached to conditions in pretrial detention facilities. It reminds us that in the enthusiasm for reforming these overcrowded inhumane institutions one ought not lose sight of the "crucial goal of incarcerating fewer individuals."

It should be noted that this article does not deal with those serving short-term sentences in a sector of a local county jail, since their legal status is comparable to that of convicted persons incarcerated in penitentiaries.

IMPROVING CONDITIONS IN PRETRIAL DETENTION FACILITIES

STANLEY A. BASS *

Accused persons who are not released on bail are usually detained in local jails, which have aptly been described as "the lowest form of social institution on the American scene."[1] A recent report by the United States Department of Justice Law Enforcement Assistance Administration confirmed in detail the decrepit state of affairs in the nation's jails.[2] Ironically, conditions in jails are consistently rated as being worse or harsher than those in penitentiaries, which house convicted felons.[3] Some evidence tends to suggest that the inhumane conditions of local jails may actually prejudice the disposition of the case, in terms of both guilt and sentence.[4]

One of the most serious problems in pretrial detention is overcrowding. There are too many, as well as the wrong kinds of, people behind bars. Pretrial release procedures in the lower criminal courts around the country fail to keep out of jail a substantial number of arrested persons whose presence at trial could be assured through means less restrictive of personal liberty than pretrial confinement.[5] The monetary bail system, which discriminates against the poor and other minorities,[6] the lengthy delays in the administration of criminal justice, and the lack of adequate defender services, all combine to swell the population of pretrial detention facilities. This undermines, on a grand scale, the fundamental presumption of innocence, which was "secured only after centuries of struggle."[7]

Thus, it would be a mistake to concentrate reform efforts merely against the internal conditions of local jails. It is also essential that workable programs be devised in every jurisdiction

* Staff Attorney, NAACP Legal Defense Fund; former Community Legal Counsel, Chicago; former Director, Council of Civil Legal Aid Service, Cook County Jail, Illinois. A.B. College of the City of New York; J.D. University of Chicago Law School.

whereby most accused persons awaiting trial are permitted to remain at liberty until their cases are finally adjudicated. In addition, speedy trials and competent representation by counsel must be made a reality.[8]

For those persons who are required to be imprisoned before trial, either because their future presence in court could not otherwise be guaranteed, or because they present a proven substantial danger to the community if released, humane and decent treatment must be accorded.

The Eighth Amendment's ban against "cruel and unusual punishment" has only limited utility in improving the conditions in pretrial detention facilities.[9] A more promising theoretical basis is the developing due process right not to be *punished* at all without trial. A related and equally useful rationale is the increasingly recognized equal protection right not to be treated substantially worse than either convicted defendants or bailed accuseds. The state must show that the restraints imposed upon prisoners awaiting trial are either inherent in the nature of confinement or are necessarily related to the state's legitimate interest of insuring the accused's presence at trial.

The Supreme Court has not yet scrutinized the conditions of jails under the due process and equal protection theories mentioned above. However, the Court has held that punishment may not be imposed without trial,[10] and it has recognized that the "traditional right to freedom before conviction permits the unhampered preparation of a defense, and serves to prevent the infliction of punishment prior to conviction."[11]

The lower federal courts, in a growing body of decisions, have rendered relief in a number of jail cases, ranging from the issuance of injunctions against specific practices,[12] to requiring jail officials to present periodic progress reports to the court on improvements,[13] to ordering an institution closed down,[14] to directing the release of inmates from confinement.[15] These courts have relied not only upon specific constitutional guaranties, such as freedom of speech and press,[16] religion,[17] petition for redress of grievances,[18] access to courts and to counsel,[19] and the right not to be subjected to cruel and unusual punishment,[20] but also upon the "preferred status" of unconvicted pretrial detainees.[21]

Adopting a "totality of the circumstances" approach, which considers such factors as overcrowding, poor sanitation, lack of recreational opportunities, limitations on visits and correspondence, absence of medical care, inadequate nutrition, and insufficient protection against assaults and other physical and psychological dangers, federal as well as state courts have often granted relief on an institution-wide basis to members of a class composed of most, if not all, inmates of a particular jail.[22]

In taking on omnibus class actions of this type, the following advice may be helpful:

"The importance of careful evidentiary preparation in such cases cannot be overstressed. It is necessary to demonstrate graphically the actual living conditions (enhanced, perhaps by judicial on-site inspection), and to press jail officials to justify their policies with facts as opposed to general conclusions. While jail records and files are often poorly maintained, they do occasionally contain information helpful to the inmates' side of the case and should be examined through pretrial discovery. Past grand jury inspection reports calling for improvements and studies by such organizations as the National Council on Crime and Delinquency are also helpful. In addition, expert witnesses such as psychiatrists, penologists, dieticians, and sociologists can provide the evidentiary basis for favorable factual findings by an enlightened court that the total treatment of the detainees does constitute 'punishment' and perhaps even 'cruel and unusual' punishment. It is important to try to present the case as a move by concerned citizens to counter the inertia of a neglected system rather than as a grudge contest between good and evil.

"Appropriate relief in jail suits may range from requiring prison officials to present periodic progress reports to the court, to ordering outright release of inmates from custody. The courts are naturally reluctant to order local political entities, which are responsible for most jails, to raise the funds required to replace outmoded facilities and to hire needed additional personnel. However, the defense of poverty by the county is insufficient justification for maintaining an unconstitutional facility. Accordingly, some judges may be persuaded to use the threat of releasing prisoners, perhaps with a timetable, in order to get officials moving on a project of significant improvements." [23]

In conclusion, jail and court reform cannot succeed meaningfully without a combination of grass roots political and litigative effort. Since jails, unlike prisons, are generally close to metropolitan centers, the opportunity is available to mobilize visible community support for needed changes and improvements.[24] However, in seeking to make life a little less unbearable for those unfortunate enough to be detained while awaiting trial, one ought not to lose sight of the crucial goal of incarcerating fewer individuals.

Footnotes

[1] McGee, "The Administration of Justice: The Correctional Process," 5 N.P.P.A. J. 225 (1959). See also Mattick and Aikman, "The Cloacal Region of American Corrections," 381 Annals of Am. Acad. Pol. & Soc. Sci. 109 (1969).

[2] 1970 National Jail Census.

[3] President's Commission on Law Enforcement and Administration of Justice, Task Force Report: Corrections, at 24 (1967).

[4] Rankin, "The Effect of Pretrial Detention," 39 N.Y.U. L. Rev. 641 (1964); Foote, "The Coming Constitutional Crisis in Bail: II," 113 U. Pa. L. Rev. 1125 (1965). See also Brooks v. Florida, 389 U.S. 413 (1967) (invalidating confession to prison riot, which had been obtained after prisoner was confined in solitary under barbaric circumstances).

[5] See e.g. 18 U.S.C. §3146 (release on nonfinancial terms and conditions). Cf. Williams v. Illinois, 399 U.S. 235 (1970) (allowing indigents to pay fines other than by serving sentences in jail).

[6] See Foote, note 4, supra.

[7] Stack v. Boyle, 342 U.S. 1, 4 (1951).

[8] See e.g. Rule of the Second Circuit Judicial Council, 8 Crim. L. Rep. 2251; Rule of the Florida Supreme Court, 8 Crim. L. Rep. 2453.

[9] See Turner, "Challenging Conditions in Prisons Which Violate the Eighth Amendment," Chapter 6 in this book.

[10] Kennedy v. Mendoza-Martinez, 372 U.S. 144 (1963).

[11] Stack v. Boyle, note 7, supra.

[12] E.g. Jones v. Wittenberg, 330 F. Supp. 707 (N.D. Ohio 1971), aff'd sub nom. Jones v. Metzger, 456 F.2d 854 (6th Cir. 1972); Palmigiano v. Travisono, 317 F. Supp. 776 (D.R.I. 1970); Davis v. Lindsay, 321 F. Supp. 1134 (S.D.N.Y. 1970).

[13] Hamilton v. Love, 328 F. Supp. 1182 (E.D. Ark. 1971).

[14] Hodge v. Dodd, 1 Prison L. Rep. 263 (N.D. Ga. May 2, 1972).

[15] Curley v. Gonzales, Civ. Nos. 8372, 8373 (D. N.Mex. Feb. 13, 1970). In Jones v. Wittenberg, note 12, supra, the court ordered the adoption of a pretrial release program.

[16] Fortune Society v. McGinnis, 319 F. Supp. 901 (S.D.N.Y. 1970).

[17] Barrett v. Rodgers, 410 F.2d 995 (D.C. Cir. 1969).

[18] Nolan v. Fitzpatrick, 451 F.2d 545 (1st Cir. 1971).

[19] Smith v. Robbins, 454 F.2d 696 (1st Cir. 1972).

[20] Wright v. McMann, 387 F.2d 519 (2d Cir. 1967).

[21] Seale v. Manson, 326 F. Supp. 1375 (D. Conn. 1971); Anderson v. Nosser, 456 F.2d 835 (5th Cir. 1972) (en banc).

[22] See Collins v. Schoonfield, 344 F. Supp. 257 (D. Md. 1972); Brenneman v. Madigan, 343 F. Supp. 128 (N.D. Cal. 1972); Jones v. Wittenberg, note 12, supra; Wayne County Jail Inmates v. Wayne County Bd. Comm'rs, 5 Clearinghouse Rev. 108 (Cir. Ct. Wayne Cty., Mich. 1971); Jackson v. Hendrick, No. 71-2437 (Ct. C. P. Phila., Pa., April 7, 1972).

[23] Bass, "Correcting the Correctional System: A Responsibility of the Legal Profession," 5 Clearinghouse Rev. 125, 148 (July 1971), reprinted by American Bar Association Commission on Correctional Facilities and Services.

[24] The organized bar has begun to give its attention to this urgent subject. See 12 Crim. L. Rep. 2169 (reporting the commencement, by the ABA Commission on Correctional Facilities and Services, of a nationwide effort to improve conditions in jails and local juvenile detention facilities).

EDITORS' INTRODUCTION

No discussion of pretrial detention facilities should take place outside the larger context of the money-bail system. Men and women imprisoned before trial are accused persons presumed to be innocent of the charges against them. Nevertheless, they normally endure conditions of incarceration far worse than those imposed on persons who are convicted of crimes.

The suffering of pretrial detainees, however, goes far beyond the physical deprivations which are imposed. As the study described below demonstrates, persons who are imprisoned before trial are far more likely to be convicted and to receive harsher sentences than those who have been released, yet the factor which determines who will be "in" and who will be "out" while awaiting trial is financial status. The persons crowded into our nation's jails have in common, virtually without exception, their poverty. Because they are poor, these people are not only punished before they are convicted but also face a much greater likelihood of being convicted and of receiving a substantial prison sentence. The text below is excerpted from a memorandum of law filed in support of a challenge to the bail system in the City of New York. It advances the major constitutional arguments against pretrial detention of the poor and describes the results of an in-depth study of the impact of the bail system on the outcome of a criminal case.

MONEY BAIL AS A DENIAL OF EQUAL PROTECTION
(Bellamy Brief) *

New York Supreme Court
Appellate Division—First Department

John Bellamy, *et al.,* on behalf of themselves and all other persons similarly situated,

Plaintiffs,

against

The Judges and Justices Authorized to Sit in the New York City Criminal Court and the New York State Supreme Court in New York County, *et al.,*

Defendants.

PLAINTIFFS' MEMORANDUM

Introduction

Plaintiffs submit this Memorandum in order to apprise both the Court and the numerous defendants at the very outset of this action of the nature and scope of the lawsuit, the facts and the data which form its basis and the legal points and authorities upon which reliance will be placed.

Parties

Plaintiffs bring this action on their own behalf and on behalf of all other clients of The Legal Aid Society of the City of New York (hereinafter referred to as "the Society") incarcerated prior to final judgment in a criminal proceeding against them in either the Criminal Court of the City of New York, New York County or the Supreme Court of the State of New York, New York County

---

* Prepared by Special Litigation Unit, Legal Aid Society, New York City, Robert H. Hermann, Attorney-in-Charge.

pursuant to a securing order issued under Title P of the Criminal Procedure Law (Articles 500 through 540) and in accordance with the practices and procedures which defendants have instituted under that title. The defendants are the District Attorney for New York County and each and every Judge and Justice of the afore- mentioned courts.

Summary of Facts and Issues

The present lawsuit is in substantial part predicated on the results of a detailed statistical study of the effect of detention on the outcome of a criminal case. This study was undertaken by the Society in the hope of proving by hard data something which has been known by veteran criminal lawyers for a long time: that the court's decision at arraignment to detain or release the accused is a crucial factor affecting the outcome of a case. Because the Society was able to use the highly advanced data processing services of the Columbia University Computer Center, which were obtained through the auspices of the Society's consultant on this project, the Columbia University Bureau of Applied Social Re- search, it was possible to conduct a far more sophisticated and in-depth study of the question than any previously undertaken (*e.g.,* Rankin, *The Effects of Pre-Trial Detention,* 39 N.Y.U. L. Rev. 641 (1964)).

The study, explained at length in the text, shows in essence the following: Those people who must wait in jail for the disposi- tion of the criminal charges against them because they do not have enough money to purchase their freedom are far more often convicted, far more often given a prison term, and far more often given a long prison term than those people who obtain their re- lease during this time. This disparity in treatment between those detained and those released is not accounted for by any factor related to the merits of the cases, such as the seriousness and nature of the charges, the weight of the evidence and the presence or absence of aggravated circumstances, prior criminal record, family and community ties, or the amount of bail. For example, a first offender who is detained in lieu of bail is more than three times as likely to be convicted and almost twice as likely to get a prison sentence as a recidivist with more than ten prior arrests who is released (see Table 18, *post*). The differences in outcome between the two groups of people, the detained and the released, are accounted for only by the fact of pre-trial detention itself.

The present bail system thus causes to be treated differently two groups of accused persons alike in all material respects save that one group lacks the funds to raise bail. This differentiation in treatment among persons because of their wealth or lack of it is a violation of the Equal Protection Clauses of the federal and state constitutions.

The defendants, in their implementation of the present bail system, have in addition denied plaintiffs due process of law in the following respects. They have failed to accord to plaintiffs a presumption in favor of release on their own recognizance. They have failed to investigate or utilize non-financial conditions of release; in so doing, they have also perpetuated an iniquitous system of bail bondsmen. They have failed to request or to set money bail in the minimum amounts needed to assure plaintiffs' continued appearance. They have failed to grant plaintiffs full and fair hearings on the issue of bail or release. They have failed to state their reasons for the bail conditions they have urged or imposed. They have based their recommendations and decisions on inaccurate, misleading and incomplete information. They have failed to provide meaningful procedures for prompt judicial review of bail determinations.

Plaintiffs seek a judgment declaring the operation of the present New York bail system to be in violation of the constitutional guarantees of equal protection of the laws and due process of law, as well as the statutory mandates of the Criminal Procedure Law. In addition or in the alternative, plaintiffs seek permanent relief against the continuation of the aforementioned practices, which deny due process of law, and an order requiring the defendants to submit to the Court a written proposal for rules setting forth plaintiffs' rights at any judicial hearing where bail may be set or modified.

The Study

(A) Purpose of the Study

The study was undertaken by the Society to determine and hopefully explain the relationship between pre-trial detention and the final outcome of a criminal case in order to demonstrate how pre-trial detention affects plaintiffs in an immediate and causal way.

The study sampled closed case files of 857 individuals who,

like plaintiffs, were all represented by counsel associated with the Manhattan Criminal or Supreme Court Branches of the Society. Like plaintiffs, all those in the sample population had gone through the bail-setting process. Unlike plaintiffs, many of those in the sample population—38%, to be exact—were not held in jail pending the outcome of their case. The major purpose of the study was to determine whether there was a disparity in outcome and sentence between the "ins" and the "outs"; and, if so, whether there was any legally relevant explanation for such a discrepancy, or whether it was solely due to the fortuitous circumstance of whether an individual was able to raise enough funds to make bail.[1]

Briefly put, the study shows the following: Those who stay in jail for lack of bail money are much more often convicted and, when convicted, go to prison more often and get much longer prison sentences than those who make bail. More significantly, however, even when factors which are specified in the Criminal Procedure Law as relevant to bail and which might be thought to affect the outcome—such as the seriousness of the charge, prior criminal record, weight of the evidence, amount of bail, community ties and employment history—are held constant, there is still a large disparity in results between the detained and the released. The study shows that pre-trial detention itself causes the detained to be more often convicted and to be sentenced more severely than the released.

Certain consequences flow from this observation, especially when it is kept in mind that the only thing which determines whether an individual is detained or is released before the disposition of his case is, of course, the amount of money he has. The bail system as it operates in New York County denies to a person detained in lieu of bail the equal protection of the laws because it causes him to be treated less favorably than another who is identically situated in every respect except wealth, a constitutionally impermissible basis for differentiation (Point I, *post*). Further, in light of the critical importance of the bail decision to

---

[1] "Fortuitous" because, all other things being equal, wealth or the lack of it, which alone determines whether an accused makes bail, bears no theoretical or empirical relationship to either the likelihood of guilt or the need for a harsh sentence. Consequently, the neutral term "in" and "out" are used frequently hereafter to refer to those who, respectively, were unable or were able to post the amount of bail set by the court.

the outcome of a given case, the summary procedures now employed by defendants in reaching that decision amount to a denial of due process of law (Point II, *post*).

(B) Design and Method of the Study

The manner in which the study was performed is set out in extensive detail in the affidavit of Eric W. Single of the Columbia University Bureau of Applied Social Research, which is annexed to this Memorandum as Appendix A [not included here].

(C) Portrait of the Sample Population

As noted, 857 closed cases were included in the study. It was thought desirable to have such a large sample population in order to permit the planned multivariate analysis of bail. The vast majority of the cases were ultimately disposed of in Manhattan Criminal Court. One out of every fourteen cases, however, reached final disposition in the Supreme Court for that same borough. This 13:1 ratio is the same as the ratio between Criminal and Supreme Court cases for the Society's Manhattan offices in years past. The 857 cases sampled are numerically representative of the class of parties plaintiff in this lawsuit, *viz.,* adult males charged with a crime in Manhattan whose cases have involved some bail or release decision and who have been represented up to at least the disposition stage by one of the Society's attorneys.[2]

The people in the sample population had generally been charged with serious offenses: most (55%) were charged with felonies, some (7%) with categories of offenses which, depending upon the proof, might be felonies or misdemeanors, and the rest (38%) with misdemeanors. A more detailed breakdown of the sample population by the type of crime charged is the following:

---

[2] Because Criminal and Supreme Court cases have been merged for analytical purposes, it should be borne in mind throughout the following discussion that such items as length of sentence are composite figures which may cross the jurisdictional lines between the two courts. This in no way affects the accuracy or significance of the analysis. Nonetheless, it seems desirable to caution against regarding these data as either Criminal or Supreme Court statistics alone. They are an amalgam which, because of the strong preponderance numerically of Criminal over Supreme Court cases, is closest to what the Criminal Court cases would exhibit if considered alone.

Table 1: Type of Crime Charged

	N [3]	%
Robbery with a Dangerous Weapon	57	7
Robbery (all other)	41	5
Sale of Narcotics	54	6
Possession of Narcotics	183	21
Assault with a Dangerous Weapon	65	8
Assault (all other)	26	3
Burglary; Larceny; Criminal Possession of Stolen Property	294	34
Other (all categories)	137	16
	857	100%

Examining the demographic characteristics of those in the sample population, it becomes possible to draw a composite portrait of the typical criminal accused in the sample. He is young, unmarried, poor, is probably unemployed, and has a history of prior arrests, as the following table shows:

Table 2: Demographic Portrait of Sample Population

	N	%
(A) *Age*		
21–24	241	28%
25–29	241	28
30–39	233	27
40–49	97	11
50 and older	39	5
N.A.[4]	6	—
	857	99%
(B) *Family Situation*		
Single	539	66%
Married, with children	151	18
Married, no children	106	13
Divorced	20	2
Widowed	6	1
N.A.	35	—
	857	100%

[3] Refers to the number of cases in each category.

[4] "N.A." means Not Ascertained. In the subsequent analysis, all cases where the particular variable under scrutiny was not ascertained have been, of course, excluded from that question.

	N	%
(C) *Other Family Ties* (e.g., regular contact with parent or relative)		
Yes	459	60%
No	302	40
N.A. (by Probation Dept)	96	—
	857	100%
(D) *Length of Residence in New York City*		
More than 5 years	610	79%
3 to 5 years	65	8
2 years or less	68	9
Not a N.Y.C. resident	33	4
N.A.	81	—
	857	100%
(E) *Employment Status at Time of Arrest*		
Employed	361	47%
Unemployed	414	53
N.A.	82	—
	857	100%
(F) *Weekly Income When Most Recently Employed*		
$50 or less	26	8%
$51 to $75	46	14
$76 to $100	112	34
$101 to $150	113	35
Over $150	28	9
N.A. (includes unemployed)	532	—
	857	100%
(G) *Prior Criminal Record: Arrests (I)*		
Felony arrest within last 3 years	360	43%
Other prior arrest(s)	241	29
No prior arrest	241	29
N.A.	15	—
	857	101%
(H) *Prior Criminal Record: Arrests (II)*		
No prior arrests	241	28%
1 to 3 prior arrests	138	16
4 to 10 prior arrests	249	29
More than 10 prior arrests	229	27
	857	100%
(I) *Prior Criminal Record: Holds*		
Pending charges	64	8% (all cases)
Outstanding detainers	130	15% (all cases)

(D) Bail Determination and Pre-Trial Status

Of the 857 people whose cases were sampled, 30% were released on their own recognizance at the time of their arraignment in Criminal Court. A like percentage (31%) were given bail of $500 or less. For another 15% of the people, bail of $1000 was set. Bail of more than $1000 was set in 24% of the cases.

In all but 3% of the sampled cases, bail, when set, was fixed in even multiples of $500. (In the remaining 3% of the cases, bail was set at less than $500.) In fully three-quarters of all cases in which bail was set, it was set at either $500, $1000 or $2500. Furthermore, the data from a study of the amount of time spent in fixing bail in each case [5] show how little time is given to the determination of the proper amount of bail for each individual. In conjunction, these observations provide telling evidence that, contrary to constitutional and statutory imperatives, there is scarcely any individual consideration given to what amount of bail is appropriate in any case.

An analysis in greater depth of the bail-determination process is annexed to this Memorandum as Appendix B [contained in Appendix A-12 of this book]. It demonstrates that the defendants have failed to follow the mandate of CPL 510.30(2) that certain specified factors (e.g., family ties) be considered in the bail decision. It further shows that the defendants have taken it upon themselves to rewrite that statute by making an accused's prior criminal record and the nature of the charge virtually the only determinants of the amount of bail.

As might have been expected, there was a strong correlation found between the amount of bail set and the accused's pre-trial status (i.e., released or detained), as the following table shows.

Table 3: Pre-Trial Status By Amount of Bail

Amount of Bail	N	Percentage of People Released
Under $500	18	39%
$500	248	21
$1000	131	10
$1001–2000	69	7
$2001–5000	124	2
More than $5000	10	0

[5] See Appendix D [not included here].

Thus, when bail was set at less than $500, 39%, or two out of five persons, made bail; when bail was set at more than $2000, only two out of 124 persons made bail.

(E) Relationship Between Pre-Trial Status and Outcome

For most of the accused in the sample population, there were only two possible outcomes: a finding of guilty pursuant to a guilty plea (69%) or a dismissal of the charges after a not guilty plea (30%). In less than one percent of the cases was the adjudication of guilt made after a trial.[6] When these facts are related to pre-trial status, it is seen that those who are detained plead guilty more often and have their cases dismissed less often than those who are released, as the following table shows.

Table 4: Disposition By Pre-Trial Status

| Disposition | Pre-Trial Status [7] | |
	In	Out
Guilty Plea	79%	49%
Case Dismissed	20	50
Trial	1	1
	100%	100%
	(490)	(246)

Another way of putting this is to say that a man who is released has a better than even chance of having his case dismissed, whereas a man unable to make bail has only one chance in five of having his case dismissed.

A further and pragmatic way of looking at the outcome is in terms of result. Thus, for much of the subsequent analysis four possible outcomes are considered: (1) "D cleared"—*i.e.,* the ac-

---

[6] All seven such cases were Criminal Court cases.

[7] The terms "detained" ("in") and "released" ("out") refer to detention or release status at the time of final judgment. In 4% of the cases (35 in all), the accused was incarcerated for part of the time but eventually made bail or was released on his own recognizance before final judgment. These cases are counted in the "released" ("out") category. Also, the numerical figures given here, as in several subsequent tables, add up to less than the total sample population because of the "bench warrant" cases, i.e., those where people failed to return to court for sentencing or some scheduled court appearance prior to sentencing.

cused is acquitted at trial or, more frequently, obtains a dismissal of the charges against him; (2) "D loses, avoids prison"—*i.e.,* the accused is convicted but is given probation or a discharge, conditional or unconditional; (3) "D loses, short sentence"—*i.e.,* the accused is convicted and gets a sentence of ninety days or less; and (4), "D loses, long sentence"—*i.e.,* the accused is convicted and given a sentence of more than ninety days.[8]

Looking at outcome in terms of whether the accused was able or unable to secure his release prior to disposition, it is again evident that the detained lose more often and, when they do lose, get longer sentences than the released, as the following table shows.

Table 5: Outcome By Pre-Trial Status

| | Pre-Trial Status | | |
Outcome	In	Out	Total
D cleared	20%	51%	31%
D loses, avoids prison	18	32	23
D loses, short sentence	41	14	32
D loses, long sentence	20	2	14
	99% [9]	99%	100%
	(490)	(246)	(736)

Thus, those released have one chance in six of going to prison; by contrast, three out of five of those jailed receive prison sentences, and much longer ones at that. Furthermore, 33% of the released who were found guilty got a prison term, as contrasted with more than 75% of the detained.

(F) Explanation of Relation Between Pre-Trial Status and Outcome

Having demonstrated rather starkly the discrepancy in case outcome between those who are detained and those who are released, the next inquiry must be whether there is any legally

---

[8] A sentence of "time served" was counted in one of the last two categories as a sentence. For example, a man who was detained for fifteen days before being sentenced to "time served" was considered as having received a fifteen-day sentence.

[9] Here, as in subsequent tables, totals of 99% or 101% are due to rounding to the nearest whole number for purposes of readability.

relevant explanation for the discrepancy. Do the detained fare worse than the released because they are charged with more serious crimes? Because the cases against them are stronger? Because they have worse criminal records? Because there were other aggravating circumstances? Because they had higher bail? Because they have weaker family structures or poorer employment histories? The answer to each of these questions is no, as the following analysis will demonstrate.

(i) Seriousness of Charge

The following table demonstrates that felons and misdemeanants are about equally successful in avoiding prison sentences entirely; among all those receiving such sentences, however, the felons as a class get longer terms. As might have been expected, therefore, the seriousness of the charge is related to the length of the sentence.

Table 6: Outcome By Seriousness of Charge

Outcome	Felony	Misdemeanor
D cleared	34%	28%
D loses, avoids prison	23	22
D loses, short sentence	24	46
D loses, long sentence	19	4
	100%	100%
	(415)	(269)

A greater percentage of felons (69% of 474) than of misdemeanants (51% of 325) also are detained pending disposition of their cases. However, when the seriousness of the charge is held constant, it is still observed that there is a large discrepancy in treatment between the detained and the released, as the following table shows.

Table 7: Outcome By Pre-Trial Status By Seriousness of Charge

Outcome	Felonies		Misdemeanors	
	In	Out	In	Out
D cleared	24%	59%	16%	45%
D loses, avoids prison	21	27	12	35
D loses, short sentence	29	10	65	19
D loses, long sentence	26	4	7	0
	100%	100%	100%	99%
	(300)	(115)	(161)	(108)

Thus, even among those charged with comparably serious offenses, those who are paroled or make bail end up with much more favorable dispositions than those who stay in jail.

(ii) Type of Crime

Among those charged with the same offense, there is still a wide variation in outcome between the detained and the released groups, as the following table demonstrates.

Table 8: Pre-Trial Outcome By Status By Type of Crime
Type of Crime: Narcotics [10]

Outcome	Ins	Outs
D cleared	14%	43%
D loses, avoids prison	20	42
D loses, short sentence	47	13
D loses, long sentence	19	2
	100%	100%
	(133)	(67)

Type of Crime: Theft [11]

Outcome	Ins	Outs
D cleared	22%	49%
D loses, avoids prison	9	33
D loses, short sentence	53	16
D loses, long sentence	17	2
	101%	100%
	(175)	(63)

Type of Crime: Assault [12]

Outcome	Ins	Outs
D cleared	11%	78%
D loses, avoids prison	23	19
D loses, short sentence	46	3
D loses, long sentence	20	0
	100%	100%
	(44)	(37)

[10] Includes both possession and sale.

[11] Includes all forms of burglary, larceny, and criminal possession of stolen property.

[12] With or without a dangerous weapon.

Type of Crime: Robbery [12a]

Outcome	Ins	Outs
D cleared	33%	(57%) [13]
D loses, avoids prison	32	(36)
D loses, short sentence	7	(0)
D loses, long sentence	27	(7)
	99%	100%
	(81)	(14)

Table 8 makes it dramatically clear that the type of crime in no way begins to offer an explanation for the different treatment —greater conviction rate and longer sentences—obtained by those detained versus those released. A released person charged with a narcotics offense is, *e.g.,* more than three times as likely to have the case against him dismissed as a person facing the same charge who is detained, and the detained person is about four times as likely to get a prison sentence. Similar results appear for each of the other categories of crimes.

(iii) Weight of the Evidence

The Criminal Procedure Law requires that the court in determining bail must consider the weight of the evidence against the accused. CPL 510.30(2)(a)(vi). Although presumably a case where the accused has confessed is stronger than one where a confession is absent, a smaller proportion of those who confessed were detained (57% of 177) than of those who did not give confessions (62% of 672).

There was little apparent relationship between whether or not a person confessed and the outcome of his case, as indicated in the following table.

Table 9: Outcome By Confession

Outcome	Confessed	Did Not Confess
D cleared	30%	31%
D loses, avoids prison	27	22
D loses, short sentence	29	33
D loses, long sentence	14	14
	100%	100%
	(155)	(574)

[12a] With or without a dangerous weapon.

[13] Where the total number of cases in a given category (N) is below 25, the percentage figures have been placed in parentheses.

Consequently, the factor of whether or not a person confessed did nothing to explain the disparity of treatment between those detained and those released, as evidenced by the following table.

Table 10: Outcome By Pre-Trial Status By Confession

		Confessed		Did Not Confess	
	Outcome	Ins	Outs	Ins	Outs
D	cleared	20%	47%	20%	53%
D	loses, avoids prison	19	38	18	31
D	loses, short sentence	40	12	41	15
D	loses, long sentence	21	3	20	2
		100%	100%	99%	101%
		(95)	(60)	(392)	(182)

Similarly, it might be thought that because a case in which evidence of the offense is found on the accused at the time of arrest is presumably stronger than a case lacking such evidence, that factor might help explain the differing treatment of detained versus released persons. Whether or not evidence of the offense was found on the person of the accused was a matter which was observed to be related to the outcome of the case, as shown in the following table.

Table 11: Outcome By Found Evidence of Offense

	Outcome	Evidence Found	No Evidence Found
D	cleared	29%	35%
D	loses, avoids prison	20	30
D	loses, short sentence	34	26
D	loses, long sentence	16	9
		99%	100%
		(525)	(198)

However, as the following table demonstrates, this index of the weight of the evidence does no more to illuminate the observed disparity than did the factor of confession versus no confession.

Table 12: Outcome By Pre-Trial Status By Found Evidence of Offense

Outcome	Evidence Found		No Evidence Found	
	Ins	Outs	Ins	Outs
D cleared	19%	50%	23%	54%
D loses, avoids prison	15	32	28	34
D loses, short sentence	43	15	35	12
D loses, long sentence	22	3	14	0
	99%	100%	100%	100%
	(357)	(168)	(124)	(74)

(iv) Aggravated Circumstances

It might be expected that cases in which the accused was detained pending the disposition of his case presented more aggravated circumstances than cases in which the accused was released, thus accounting for the disparity in treatment between the two classes. Circumstances might be said to be aggravated when, for example, the victim of the crime was injured, or a dangerous weapon was used in the commission of the offense, or the accused resisted arrest.[14]

What might be thought to be aggravating circumstances bearing on the seriousness of the offense, however, in fact bear little relation to whether or not a person is detained. In 63% of the cases presenting aggravated facts the accused was detained, compared with 61% of the cases where such facts were absent. Likewise, the presence or absence of aggravating circumstances is not related to the outcome of the case, as shown in the following table.

Table 13: Outcome By Aggravated Circumstances

Outcome	Aggravated Circumstances	No Aggravated Circumstances
D cleared	33%	30%
D loses, avoids prison	25	22
D loses, short sentence	23	36
D loses, long sentence	19	13
	100%	101%
	(213)	(523)

[14] The category "aggravated circumstances" accordingly consists of cases where one or more of these three factors was noted.

Consequently, aggravation of circumstances does nothing to explain the outcome disparity between the detained and the released; holding that factor constant, the gap between the two categories remains as wide as ever, as the following table shows.

Table 14: Outcome By Pre-Trial Status By Aggravated Circumstances

Outcome	Aggravated Circumstances		No Aggravated Circumstances	
	Ins	Outs	Ins	Outs
D cleared	20%	59%	20%	48%
D loses, avoids prison	24	29	16	33
D loses, short sentence	30	9	46	16
D loses, long sentence	26	3	18	2
	100%	100%	100%	99%
	(144)	(69)	(346)	(177)

Thus, whether or not there are aggravating factors in the case, the detained are convicted about 80% of the time, whereas the released are convicted about 50% of the time. In addition, whether or not there are aggravating circumstances, detained persons get prison sentences more than three times as often as released persons.

(v) Prior Criminal Record

Whether or not an accused has a prior criminal record [15] is a factor which affects both his pre-trial status and the outcome of his case. Of those (360) with one or more felony arrests within the past three years, 80% were detained; of those (241) with some other criminal record, 68% were detained; and of those (241) with no "priors," 27% were detained. It is also true, as the following table shows, that the extent of an accused's prior record is related to the outcome of the case.

---

[15] Prior criminal record here refers to the arrests listed on the "yellow sheet"; whether or not a conviction was later obtained, the defendants routinely consider an arrest as the equivalent of a conviction.

Table 15: Outcome By Prior Criminal Record

Outcome		Recent Felony	Other Record	No Record
D	cleared	27%	25%	45%
D	loses, avoids prison	16	26	32
D	loses, short sentence	37	36	18
D	loses, long sentence	20	13	5
		100%	100%	100%
		(321)	(219)	(184)

Nonetheless, when one holds constant the factor of prior criminal record, the disparity of outcome according to pre-trial status is as strong as ever, as expressed in the following table.

Table 16: Outcome By Pre-Trial Status By Prior Criminal Record

Outcome		Recent Felony		Other Record		No Record	
		Ins	Outs	Ins	Outs	Ins	Outs
D	cleared	21%	55%	18%	39%	18%	55%
D	loses, avoids prison	16	17	18	44	32	32
D	loses, short sentence	40	21	46	15	37	11
D	loses, long sentence	23	6	18	2	13	2
		100%	99%	100%	100%	100%	100%
		(274)	(47)	(153)	(66)	(54)	(130)

Thus, the detained are exonerated less than half as often as the released, even if both have the same prior record or lack thereof. Likewise, regardless of comparable prior criminal activity, the detained are at least four times as likely to get a long prison term as the released.

This disparity, furthermore, obtains even among hardcore repeaters (here, those with more than ten prior arrests), as shown in the following table.

Table 17: Outcome By Prior Record, Among Recidivists
(More than 10 prior arrests)

Outcome		Ins	Outs
D	cleared	18%	52%
D	loses, avoids prison	10	21
D	loses, short sentence	46	21
D	loses, long sentence	26	7
		100%	101%
		(184)	(29)

What this table demonstrates is that notwithstanding equally extensive histories of recidivism, a factor theoretically important at the time of sentencing, those repeaters who can stay on the street until their cases are settled get a prison term 28% of the time, while those who are in jail continue to stay in 72% of the time. Comparing Tables 16 and 17, one also observes that a first offender who is detained gets a prison sentence 50% of the time, whereas a recidivist (here, one with more than ten prior arrests) who is released gets a prison sentence about half as often (28% of the time), as shown in the following table.

Table 18: Outcome Among Detained First Offenders
Compared to Released Recidivists

Outcome	First Offender: In	Recidivist: Out
D cleared	18%	52%
D loses, avoids prison	32	21
D loses, short sentence	37	21
D loses, long sentence	13	7
	100%	101%
	(54)	(29)

Even when both seriousness of the charge and prior record are simultaneously taken into account, the detained receive a much less favorable outcome than those who are released, as shown in the following table.

Table 19: Outcome By Pre-Trial Status By Seriousness of
Charges By Existence of Prior Record

| | Prior Record | | | | No Prior Record | | | |
| | Felony | | Misdemeanor | | Felony | | Misdemeanor | |
Outcome	In	Out	In	Out	In	Out	In	Out
D cleared	22%	54%	18%	43%	27%	62%	(11%)	49%
D loses, avoids prison	21	30	10	35	33	25	(33)	40
D loses, short sentence	31	9	65	22	23	12	(50)	11
D loses, long sentence	26	7	7	0	17	1	(6)	0
	100%	100%	100%	100%	100%	100%	100%	100%
	(249)	(46)	(136)	(58)	(30)	(68)	(18)	(45)

(vi) Personal History

It might be imagined that differences in background, employment history, family situation or other personal matters could account for the discrepancy in outcome between those who do and those who do not secure their release pending disposition of their cases.[16] This thesis is examined below by analyzing two such variables, strength of family ties and employment situation.

Strength of Family Ties.[17] As might have been suspected, there was found to be a relationship between the strength of a person's family ties and the likelihood of his being detained pending the outcome of his case. Of the 286 people with weak family ties, 72% were detained; of the 342 with some ties, 61% were detained; and for the 229 with strong family ties, the comparable figure drops to 49%. Furthermore, a relationship between the strength of a man's family ties and the outcome of his case also was found to exist: the stronger the ties, the greater the likelihood of his obtaining a dismissal of the charges or getting a short sentence, as the following table shows.

Table 20: Outcome By Family Ties

Outcome	Weak Ties	Some Ties	Strong Ties
D cleared	24%	32%	37%
D loses, avoids prison	21	22	26
D loses, short sentence	38	31	27
D loses, long sentence	17	15	10
	100%	100%	100%
	(239)	(299)	(198)

Because there is a clear relationship between strength of family ties and both the likelihood of detention and the outcome of the case, one might speculate that the outcome disparity be-

---

16 The importance of such factors in the initial bail-determination process is discussed in Appendix B hereto [see Appendix A-12 of this book].

17 The strength of a person's family ties was measured in the following manner. One "point" was assigned to an individual for each of the following characteristics indicative of family ties which appeared on his ROR sheet: being married; having children; having regular contact with parents or relatives. A person with none of these characteristics was said to have "weak" ties; a person with any one of the characteristics, "some" ties; anyone with two or three of the characteristics, "strong" ties.

tween those detained and those released could be explained on that basis. However, the following table demonstrates that this is not so, since people with equally strong or weak family ties experience very different outcomes of their cases depending, once again, on whether they were detained or released.

Table 21: Outcome By Pre-Trial Status By Family Ties

	Outcome	Weak Ties Ins	Weak Ties Outs	Some Ties Ins	Some Ties Outs	Strong Ties Ins	Strong Ties Outs
D	cleared	19%	43%	22%	50%	20%	56%
D	loses, avoids prison	16	39	17	31	22	30
D	loses, short sentence	45	12	39	17	39	13
D	loses, long sentence	20	6	22	2	18	1
		100%	100%	100%	100%	99%	100%
		(188)	(51)	(198)	(101)	(104)	(94)

Regardless of family ties, then, the disparate outcomes for detained and released persons still obtain. Thus, a person with weak family ties who was released avoided jail 82% of the time. By contrast, a person with strong family ties who was nonetheless detained avoided jail only half as often (42% of the time).

Employment Status. Those who did not have a job when they were arrested (414) were a good deal more likely to be detained in lieu of bail than those who did have a job when they were picked up (361)—69% as opposed to 49%. In addition, the unemployed were somewhat more likely than the employed to be convicted and, once convicted, to get a long prison term, as is shown in the following table.

Table 22: Outcome By Employment Status at Time of Arrest

	Outcome	Employed	Unemployed
D	cleared	34%	27%
D	loses, avoids prison	25	22
D	loses, short sentence	31	34
D	loses, long sentence	10	17
		100%	100%
		(302)	(363)

Whether employed or not, however, the detained are still far more likely to be treated harshly than their counterparts who secure their release, as is evidenced by the figures in the following table.

Table 23: Outcome By Pre-Trial Status By Employment
Status at Time of Arrest

		Employed		Unemployed	
	Outcome	Ins	Outs	Ins	Outs
D	cleared	17%	54%	21%	47%
D	loses, avoids prison	23	27	16	40
D	loses, short sentence	43	17	42	10
D	loses, long sentence	17	1	22	3
		100%	99%	101%	100%
		(163)	(139)	(269)	(94)

It is illuminating to observe that an employed person who is detained has a 60% chance of getting a prison sentence, whereas an unemployed person who secures his release has only a 13% chance of getting a prison sentence.

(vii) Amount of Bail

Table 3, *ante,* demonstrates what common sense would dictate: pre-trial status is related to the amount of bail; the higher the bail amount, the smaller the percentage of accused who are released. The amount of bail is also related to the outcome of the case. For example, 86% of those released on their own recognizance never ultimately get a prison sentence, a rate twice as high as that (43%) for all those for whom a bail amount is set. Similarly, those who are released on their own recognizance are far less likely to get long prison sentences than those for whom $1000 bail or more was set, as the following table shows.

Table 24: Outcome By Amount of Bail

			$500 or		More than
	Outcome	ROR	Less	$1000	$1000
D	cleared	57%	26%	25%	18%
D	loses, avoids prison	29	18	16	26
D	loses, short sentence	12	51	43	21
D	loses, long sentence	2	5	16	35
		100%	100%	100%	100%
		(175)	(241)	(122)	(198)

It might be theorized, then, that the amount of bail explains the disparity in outcome between the detained and the released populations. In other words, it has been argued that the court sets bail in a manner which it predicts will correspond to the final outcome of the case; the amount of bail, under this theory, is a rough initial guess as to the likelihood of conviction and/or the length of the sentence, if any. If that is so, those with like bail amounts should not experience grossly different outcomes—whether or not they can actually raise bail.[18] This turns out not to be the case, as the following table shows.

Table 25: Outcome By Pre-Trial Status By Amount of Bail

	$500 or Less [19]		$1000 or More	
Outcome	Ins	Outs	Ins	Outs
D cleared	23%	37%	19%	(33%)
D loses, avoids prison	11	43	22	(33)
D loses, short sentence	59	20	30	(19)
D loses, long sentence	7	0	29	(14)
	100%	100%	100%	99%
	(187)	(54)	(299)	(21)

Putting it a different way, the discrepancy in treatment between those detained and those released persists even among cases which, under the proposed hypothesis, were viewed as comparable by the court which fixed bail. For example, two-thirds of those who make bail of $1000 or more will, even if convicted, not serve a prison term; but two-thirds of those who cannot make bail of $500 or less will be convicted and receive a prison term.

What Table 25 also shows is the very high "error rate" in the present bail system. Of those detained in lieu of $500 bail or less, 34% were ultimately given no prison term, and of those detained in lieu of $1000 bail or more, 41% were ultimately given no prison term. These cases represent errors by the bail-setting court in gauging the likelihood of either conviction or a prison sentence, or both.

---

[18] Unless, of course, the defendants are deliberately fixing excessive bail in a large percentage of the cases. See *ante*, n. 1.

[19] Excludes cases of those released on their own recognizance. The figures would obviously show an even greater disparity if the "$500 or less" category included these cases.

(viii) Summary

Because none of the factors examined even begins to explain the disparity in outcome between detained and released persons, it is very unlikely—and, in fact, it turns out not to be the case—that in combination they explain it either. To cite an example: Even when four factors—seriousness of crime, prior criminal record, family ties and employment status—are the same, those people who were detained were 41% more likely to be convicted and sentenced to prison than those who were released. Furthermore, in determining whether the accused will ultimately be convicted and given a prison sentence, his pre-trial status is more than three times as important as either the seriousness of the crime with which he was charged or his prior criminal record; in fact, his pre-trial status is more important in that respect than all those other factors combined. Thus, those factors which, considered alone, do not account for the different treatment of detained versus released persons do not explain it even when they are combined.[20]

(G) Conclusions

The study has shown that one factor—whether the accused is released or detained pending trial—above all others determines both the outcome of his case and the likelihood of his receiving a prison sentence. By examining seriousness of charge, type of crime, weight of the evidence, aggravated circumstances, prior criminal record, strength of family ties, employment status and the amount of bail, the study demonstrates that neither independently nor in combination does any of these factors account for the disparity in outcome and in severity of sentence between those detained and those released. The inescapable conclusion is that the fact of detention itself causes those detained to be convicted far more often and sentenced much more severely than those who are released. Thus, the present bail system creates two classes of accused distinguished by their wealth or lack of it: those who are released and are relatively more likely to have a favorable outcome in their cases, and those who are detained in lieu of bail

---

[20] Appendix C ("Effect of Pre-Trial Status On Likelihood of Prison Sentence") explains at length the manner in which the statistics presented in subsection (viii) were derived [this appendix is not included here].

and are therefore much more likely to be convicted and get a prison sentence.

ARGUMENT

POINT I

The present New York bail system denies to plaintiffs the equal protection of the laws.

The results of the Society's study of the institution of bail, as well as the conclusions necessarily to be drawn from it, are frighteningly clear. The bail system, as it now operates under defendants' control, creates two distinct classes of persons accused of crime, those who have been detained and those who have obtained their release. What the study shows statistically is that given two groups of people accused of crime whose cases and backgrounds are substantially alike, those who are not able to make bail are extraordinarily more likely to be convicted and, once convicted, to get a longer sentence than those who obtain their release. This difference in outcome depends solely on whether the accused does or does not have enough money to purchase his freedom before trial. In this manner, the present bail system operates to deny to plaintiffs the equal protection of the laws, in violation of the Fourteenth Amendment to the United States Constitution and Article I, Section 5 of the New York Constitution.

The purpose of the Equal Protection Clause of the Fourteenth Amendment is "that all persons similarly circumstanced shall be treated alike." *F.S. Royster Guano Co.* v. *Virginia,* 253 U.S. 412, 415 (1920). A statutory scheme which, on its face, need not be considered discriminatory nonetheless violates the Equal Protection Clause where, as here, it has come to be applied in such a way that it is only the poor who suffer under that system. *Williams* v. *Illinois,* 399 U.S. 235, 242 (1970).

In analyzing observed disparities in the treatment of people to determine whether they constitute a violation of the Equal Protection Clause, said the Supreme Court in *Williams* v. *Illinois,* it is essential to remember that "[t]he Constitution permits *qualitative* differences" only. *Id.* at 243 (emphasis added). As has been clearly established by the study, there are differences in outcome between those detained and those released, and these differences are not caused by any "qualitative" differences between the two groups of cases. "Qualitative" differences such as type and seriousness of charge, weight of the evidence, aggravation of circumstances, nature of prior criminal record and personal background, were shown not to be the reason for differing treatment. Rather, only detention itself explained the disparity in treatment. Detention in lieu of bail turns on wealth alone, and the amount of money an accused has is not a "qualitative" basis for treating him differently from other persons similar to him in all other respects.

The Supreme Court in *Williams* v. *Illinois* called attention to "[t]he need to be open to reassessment of ancient practices other than those explicitly mandated by the Constitution * * *," 399 U.S. at 240, a need which is especially important in a situation such as the present one. It has now been demonstrated how those "ancient practices" have over the years led to a system which treats some people more harshly than others only because they are too poor to buy their liberty. "Notions of what constitutes equal treatment for purposes of the Equal Protection Clause *do* change," *Harper* v. *Virginia Board of Elections,* 383 U.S. 663, 669 (1966), and "[l]ines drawn on the basis of wealth or property, like those of race, are traditionally disfavored." *Id.* at 668 (citations omitted). In constitutional litigation, "the passage of time has heightened rather than weakened the attempts to mitigate the disparate treatment of indigents in the criminal process." *Williams* v. *Illinois, supra,* 399 U.S. at 241. Thus, in order to ameliorate the possibility of unfairness arising out of a person's impoverished financial status, the Supreme Court has expanded concepts of equal protection in the criminal justice area. *E.g., Griffin* v. *Illinois,* 351 U.S. 12 (1956) (right of free transcript on appeal from felony conviction); *Douglas* v. *California,* 372 U.S. 353 (1963) (right to counsel on first appeal as of right); *Mayer* v. *Chicago,* 404 U.S. 15 (1971) (right of free transcript on appeal from misdemeanor conviction); see also *Gilmore* v. *Lynch,* 319 F.Supp. 105 (N.D. Cal. 1970) *per curiam*), *aff'd sub nom. Younger* v. *Gilmore,* 404 U.S. 15 (1971) (right of state prisoners to access to law library).

As Judge Skelly Wright has observed in a landmark opinion, whenever a "critical personal right" is infringed by an existing legal classification, that classification must be subjected "to the gauntlet of a judicial review searching for adequate justification * * *." *Hobson* v. *Hansen,* 269 F.Supp. 401 (D.C. Cir. 1967), *appeal dismissed,* 393 U.S. 801 (1969).

The need for investigating justification is strengthened when the practice, though not explicitly singling out for special treatment any of the groups for which the Constitution has a special solicitude, operates in such a way that one such group is harshly and disproportionately disadvantaged. * * *

The explanation for this judicial scrutiny of practices which, although not directly discriminatory, nevertheless fall harshly on such groups relates to the judicial attitude toward legislative and administrative judgments. Judicial deference to these judgments is predicated in the confidence courts have that they are just resolutions of conflicting interests. This confidence is often misplaced when the vital interests of the poor and of racial minorities are involved. 269 F.Supp. at 507.

Two recent Supreme Court decisions which have clear ramifications for the present bail system are *Williams* v. *Illinois, supra,* and *Tate* v. *Short,* 401 U.S. 395 (1971). In *Williams,* the Court held that the frequently used manner of sentencing an accused either to pay a fine or to work it off in jail at the conclusion of his jail term denied to an indigent the equal protection of the laws. The fact that the mode of sentencing which was invalidated was both venerable and non-discriminatory on its face did not rescue it, in the Court's view. Whatever valid justifications there may be for imprisoning a convicted person, the inability to raise a certain amount of money is not among them. 399 U.S. at 243. Consequently, in *Tate* the Court later held that to imprison an indigent for non-payment of a fine which had been imposed in lieu of a jail sentence was likewise a violation of the Equal Protection Clause. There was found to be "unconstitutional discrimination" because "petitioner was subjected to imprisonment solely because of his indigency." 401 U.S. at 398.

"The Supreme Court's decisions in [*Tate* and *Williams*]," it has recently been observed, "indicate that a man should not be kept imprisoned solely because of his lack of wealth." *United States* v. *Gaines,* 449 F.2d 143, 144 (2d Cir. 1971) (*per curiam*). In *Gaines,* the Second Circuit applied to the area of bail the equal protection analysis of *Tate* and *Williams.* Gaines, after being convicted and sentenced by a federal court, was returned to New York State authorities to face the state charges for which he was being held when federal authorities first acquired him by a writ of habeas corpus *ad prosequendum.* Because he was unable to post the amount of bail set by the New York court, Gaines could not begin serving his federal sentence. Ultimately, the state case against Gaines was dismissed. The Second Circuit held that federal authorities must credit Gaines with the time he spent in the New York jail after bail had been set. Gaines, said the Court, served "dead" time "solely because he lacked sufficient funds to post bond in the state court which held him in custody * * * Gaines' lack of wealth has resulted in his having to serve a sentence that a richer man would not have had to serve, an impermissible discrimination according to *Tate* and *Williams.*" 449 F.2d at 144. Likewise in New York often the accused's lack of wealth prevents him from making bail, and this in turn results in his having to serve a sentence that a richer man would not have had to serve.[21]

The present New York bail system creates a dichotomy in the treatment of persons accused of crime as invidiously and irrationally discriminatory as any scheme yet invalidated by the courts of this country under the Equal Protection Clause. The study has shown that in the criminal justice system in New York County there is one issue which, above all others, determines the outcome of the case: Was the accused released or detained while awaiting disposition of the charges against him? What is more, however, the detained fare more poorly than the released not for any reason —any "qualitative" reason—having to do with the merits of their case. They fare worse only because they are too poor to make bail. A disparity founded on such an impermissible basis is a denial of equal protection of the laws.

POINT II

The bail determination process in the Criminal and Supreme Courts in New York County violates the Due Process Clauses of the State and Federal Constitutions.

The point of intake into the criminal justice system was, for the majority of the plaintiffs, Part AR-1 of the Criminal Court at 100 Centre Street in Manhattan. As was recently observed in the *Harvard Law Review,* it is hard to imagine

---

[21] See Tables 10, 12, 14, 16, 19, 21, 23 and 25.

> * * * a dingier courtroom in which the men and women with business to do were mostly past caring, and the men and women—litigants—upon whom this business was to be done were mostly past hoping. Tigar, *Foreword: Waiver of Constitutional Rights: Disquiet in the Citadel,* 84 Harv. L. Rev. 1, 5 (1970).

In that courtroom, a decision of tremendous importance—whether the State will deprive a man of his liberty before it has proved it has a right to do so—is reached in an instant.

> Arraignment proceedings are handled at breakneck speed with the arraigning judge arriving at his decision on bail within seconds * * * In the vast majority of cases, the judge simply announces a sum and proceeds to the next case. Fabricant, *Bail as a Preferred Freedom and the Failure of New York's Revision,* 18 Buff. L. Rev. 303, 307 (1969).

The observation study (Appendix D [not included here]) reveals that the average arraignment takes from 1½ to 3 minutes, and that only a small portion of this time is concerned with the setting of bail.

It has previously been shown that whether an accused is detained or is able to secure release pending disposition of his case is a matter that drastically affects the outcome of his case. Seasoned lawyers have always been aware of what the study demonstrates by statistics—*i.e.,* that "the decision to incarcerate an accused by the fixing of bail in an amount too high for him to meet is perhaps the most critical decision in the criminal process." *Id.* at 314. Nonetheless, even though what has been documented here mathematically, *i.e.,* that the bail-or-release question is outcome-determinative, is also generally accepted as true, the process by which this crucial decision is reached is shockingly barren of basic guarantees for the accused. This lack of fundamental procedural safeguards violates the Due Process Clauses of the Fourteenth Amendment to the Constitution of the United States and Article I, Section 6 of the Constitution of the State of New York.

"Due process of law," it has been observed, "is not a rigid or static expression. It is a concept of what is fundamentally just, fair and right * * *." *People* v. *Colozzo,* 54 Misc.2d 687, 691, 283

N.Y.S.2d 409, 415 (Sup. Ct. Kings Co. 1967), *aff'd mem.*, 32 A.D.2d 927, 303 N.Y.S.2d 348 (2nd Dept. 1969). The extent to which procedural due process must be afforded, the Supreme Court indicates, is determined by considering "the extent to which [plaintiffs] may be 'condemned to suffer grievous loss' " and weighing "whether [their] interest in avoiding that loss outweighs the governmental interest in summary adjudication." *Goldberg* v. *Kelly,* 397 U.S. 254, 263 (1970).

As to the first branch of that inquiry, the extent of plaintiffs' losses is clear. In New York County in 1969, according to Department of Correction statistics, 38,771 people were remanded in lieu of bail. New York City Department of Corrections, *Annual Report* (1969), Table 3. Such incarceration entails many obvious losses. A man imprisoned in lieu of bail loses his liberty. His family is disrupted. He is deprived of any meaningful contact with other human beings, especially his family. His income and possibly his job are lost, which in turn causes additional hardships to those dependent on him. He is forced to survive at the most minimal level of human existence, and is subjected to overcrowding, inadequate food, sexual assaults and frequent acts of violence. He is exposed to people with wide-ranging criminal experience, and is housed with people suffering from mental illness or addiction to narcotics.[22] The pressures of this type of existence have caused the number of suicides and suicide attempts in New York's jails to mount steadily in recent years.[23]

Incarcerated persons suffer further loss with respect to the outcome of the case. They are hampered in the preparation of their defenses. They are denied the chance to demonstrate rehabilitation. It has additionally been shown now that all other things being equal they are convicted more often, get prison terms more often, and more often receive harsh sentences.

---

[22] For a description of present conditions in pre-trial facilities for adult male prisoners in Manhattan, see Appendix E (Affidavit of William Vanden Heuvel, Chairman of New York City Board of Correction) [this appendix is not included here].

[23] See Report, Proposed Legislation and Recommendations of the Subcommittee on Penal and Judicial Reform to the Committee on Public Safety of the Council of the City of New York, Minutes of November 16, 1971 at 576. Furthermore, the time spent in detention awaiting disposition of the case has for some time been notorious. A sample of the Society's case files on January 20, 1972 revealed that among Supreme Court cases, 110 people had been detained for at least three months and 92 had been detained for four months or more.

With regard to the other branch of the test enunciated, *viz.,* "the governmental interest in summary adjudication," one word sums up that interest: money. There is no legitimate interest other than the allocation elsewhere of its resources for the State of New York to want the bail-setting process to continue to be a mockery of the presumption of innocence and of due process of law. What the present study has demonstrated by statistics is the extent to which the bail decision is an extremely critical stage of any criminal proceeding. Since it showed that in many cases it is the ultimate constitutional right to liberty which defendants are adjudicating when they issue securing orders, it is not a sufficient answer to say that there is not enough money available to grant procedural due process. See, *e.g., Millard* v. *Cameron,* 373 F.2d 468, 472 (D.C. Cir. 1966) (indefinite commitment of psychopath without treatment cannot be justified on ground of lack of resources). Furthermore, it is far from clear that the present system is an efficient use of even existing resources. The Tombs alone, for example, holds about 1,400 men each day at an average cost per man of approximately thirteen dollars a day, for a total of over $6½ million per year. Improvement in the bail procedures would certainly reduce this cost.

*   *   *   *

The constitutional requisites which plaintiffs in this suit argued must be met at any hearing at which bail may be set are reprinted in Appendix A-12 of this book. They include: a presumption in favor of releasing the defendant on his own recognizance, a presumption in favor of nonfinancial alternatives to bail, a full and fair hearing on bail, a statement, a prompt, automatic and de novo review of bail, and an expedited appeal from the setting of bail.

CHAPTER 8
MEDICAL TREATMENT

EDITORS' INTRODUCTION

Lack of adequate medical attention is the single most consistent complaint heard from prisoners. As this article points out, litigation alone will not remedy the ills of prison medical services in this country. Judges are particularly loath to challenge the professional judgment of doctors. Only the concerted efforts of the public, legislators, and above all the medical community, can help bring humane medical treatment to prisons.

THE RIGHT TO MEDICAL TREATMENT

EDWARD I. KOREN *

One need only compare Alexander Berkman's remarkable memoirs about his late-19th century confinement in Pennsylvania's Western Penitentiary [1] with the 1972 McKay Commission Report on Attica [2] to see how little prison medical care and prisons have changed in a hundred years.

It is now becoming increasingly clear that part of the prison medical care problem documented in literature stems not from sadistic or cruel men but from a system that breeds mistrust between doctor and prisoner.[3] This basic mistrust is a function of the prison doctor's accountability, not to his patient but to the institution and the prison system.[4]

The reports and cases that have come in a flurry recently, the McKay Commission Report in New York, a report of the Health Law Project of the University of Pennsylvania Law School,[5] and Chief Judge Frank Johnson's decision concerning Alabama medical care to prisoners [6] confirm and document the need for immediate and basic changes in the way we provide medical care and treatment to those we have confined to our prisons.

One point emerges from the body of literature and documentation in this area: the way we have sought to deliver health care to prisoners is a notable failure. Even Judge Johnson's important decision and decree in the *Newman* case, setting federal standards for medical care to state prisoners, leaves intact the present method of providing care and treatment to Alabama prisoners.[7]

This article will focus upon the present state of the laws and will assess its effectiveness in relating to the area of medical care for prisoners. The first section will examine the standards historically used by the courts in entertaining claims of inadequate medical care. It will then describe the constitutional and factual

* Associate Director, American Civil Liberties Union National Prison Project, Buffalo; Adjunct Lecturer (prisoners' rights), State University of New York at Buffalo; Associate Editor, Prison Law Reporter; A.B. Brooklyn College; J.D. State University of New York at Buffalo Law School.

grounds upon which inadequate medical care may be challenged with illustrative examples of case law. The next section describes what the present and developing statutory and common law is. The last section discusses legal remedies and litigation strategy and concludes with suggested alternative systems for the future.

The Background

Until fairly recently, medical problems, like other prisoner grievances, were summarily dismissed by the courts. Inmates were left to the tender mercies of administrators under the so-called "hands-off" doctrine, which presumed expertise on the part of prison officials in the handling and care of inmates. Judicial review of administrators' conduct and the demise of the "hands-off" doctrine can be attributed to both commentators' attacks [8] and the Civil Rights movement in the early sixties.[9]

With the rise of judicial intervention, prisoners began taking their medical problems to court at an accelerated pace. We can draw some definite conclusions from the substantial body of law specifically devoted to the medical care of inmates.

The Case Law

Much of the reported case law concerning medical care for prisoners comes out of the federal courts [10] and the invocation of the Federal Civil Rights Act of 1871.[11] A state prisoner claiming that he has been deprived of his constitutional rights "under color of State law" [12] can utilize a federal forum as well as a state forum.[13] The federal constitutional rights involved in prison medical care are those derived from the Eighth Amendment, which prohibits "cruel and unusual punishment." The following is a summary of that case law which interprets the Civil Rights Law and the pertinent constitutional provisions.[14]

The threshold constitutional considerations required by the United States Supreme Court in medical care cases is whether the medical treatment afforded or the deprivation of that care is so "outrageous," "shocking," [15] or "barbarous" [16] as to "violate the evolving standards of decency that mark the progress of a maturing society." [17] The court will only scrutinize and criticize prison medical care where "extraordinary or exceptional circumstances" amount to a constitutional violation. Beyond these two general criteria of "shocking to the conscience" and "extraordinary circumstances," the law in this area has little consistency and must be viewed on a court-to-court if not a case-by-case basis. Nevertheless there are some discernible common threads.

Total Denial or Refusal of Care

In the early case of *Coleman v. Johnson,*[18] a state prisoner alleged that he had been shot in the leg incident to his original arrest, and that the state prison authorities had refused to treat his leg wounds, which led to amputation. The Seventh Circuit held that those facts constituted a valid claim under §1983. Federal courts have held similarly in other cases where there was total denial of care.[19] For example, the courts have held prison officials liable where there has been total denial or refusal of care in the presence of intense daily headaches,[20] dislocated and fractured vertebrae after an automobile accident,[21] epilepsy,[22] and histoplasmosis (a form of tuberculosis).[23] Therefore, the most effective way to withstand a motion to dismiss in a medical care case is to allege that the prison refused to provide any medical attention.

On the other hand, where *some* treatment or care has been provided and where there has not been a total denial, the courts have refused to intervene. The refusal is usually based on the theory that the courts should not second-guess the experts in the field, that is, the prison doctor or medical personnel. This of course is a variation of the "hands-off" doctrine.

In a Ninth Circuit case,[24] a state prisoner claimed he received inadequate care for his chronic back condition. The court, in dismissing his claim, said that the prisoner was occasionally permitted to visit the prison hospital for both medication and physical therapy.

Similarly, in *Startz v. Cullen,*[25] a recent Second Circuit case, the plaintiff claimed he received insufficient care for his heart condition. The complaint alleged that he had been prescribed a strict fat-free diet and that the prison authorities had failed to carry out those medical orders. The court upheld the dismissal of the complaint, holding that as long as the "prison authorities have made . . . a sincere and reasonable effort to handle Startz' problems . . ."[26] enough had been done to satisfy constitutional standards. The prison authorities, the court explained, had placed him in an outside hospital for observation, starting him on five medicines, and were attempting (albeit ten days after the complaint was filed), to meet the requirements of his fat-free diet.

In *U.S. ex rel Hyde v. McGinnis,*[27] a state prisoner was treated for muscle spasms with a tranquilizer, which was given in pill form. Upon transfer to another prison, he was prescribed the same tranquilizer in liquid form, which he found to be less effective for his condition. He sued, and the dismissal of his action was affirmed in the Court of Appeals.

In *Coppinger v. Townsend,*[28] the court explicitly stated that when a "difference of opinion" between the "the lay wishes of a patient and the professional diagnosis of the doctor" existed, there was no claim rising to a constitutional violation. Thus, mere dissatisfaction with the treatment that is provided is insufficient to state a claim for relief.[29]

In general, therefore, it would seem that prisoners asserting claims pursuant to §1983 have been unsuccessful. Even if by some chance a prisoner surmounted the jurisdictional obstacles and made the proper allegations to withstand a motion to dismiss, he would still be faced with proving his claim in court. The state need only prove in rebuttal that some degree of medical care was provided in order to prevail.[30]

Denial of Doctor's Orders by Prison Personnel as Grounds for Action

It is also apparently well established and fully in line with the logic of the "hands-off" doctrine that where there is defiance of doctor's orders by prison personnel, a cause of action exists under §1983. In *Martinez v. Mancusi,*[31] an inmate suffering from infantile paralysis was transferred to an outside hospital so that corrective surgery could be performed on his leg. Had the operation been successful, the inmate would have been able to walk again. Subsequent to the operation, the surgeons ordered Martinez to remain on his back. Twelve days after surgery, without the surgeons' authorization, the prisoner was forced to walk and was taken back to the prison on orders of the warden. The Second Circuit held that it proved the warden's conduct reflected "a deliberate indifference to [Martinez's] condition and surgeons' orders." [32] Other courts are in accord.[33] Moreover, in *Martinez* the Second Circuit went a step further and held that a cause of action against *prison medical* personnel was alleged where the personnel defied or overruled the advice of the experts, in this case the surgeons. After Martinez was returned to the prison, he was confined to the prison hospital for one day, then discharged by the prison doctor and placed in a cell. He was again forced to move his leg, and the operation ultimately proved unsuccessful. Commenting on the prison doctor's conduct, the court said "[H]is actions were in deliberate disregard of orders and hospital requirements. Obviously, courts cannot go around second-guessing doctors. But neither can they ignore gross misconduct by a doctor, especially when it violates specific orders by the specialists in charge of the case." [34]

Unhealthy Prison Conditions

Prisons themselves generate illness, disease, and other medical problems.[35] The federal courts, through §1983, have dealt with three types of cases in this context:

(1) the "jail cases" which involve over-all conditions in pretrial detention facilities;

(2) the segregation cases which deal with conditions in disciplinary units;

(3) the forced-work situation. These cases are usually brought as class actions under Rule 23 of the Federal Rules of Civil Procedure.

When courts have found constitutional violations in the "jail cases," [36] they usually have issued broad mandates directing that certain minimum standards be met. These orders usually contain provisions involving medical care for inmates as well as provisions forcing the upgrading of living conditions that have a direct effect upon the health of inmates.

Certainly one reason for federal court intervention in the "segregation cases" [37] is the proven inadequacy of medical treatment.[38]

Injuries Sustained Through Forced Work as a Ground for Action

Courts have been uniformly more sympathetic to inmates where forced work has led to injuries or aggravation of injuries.

Upon a writ of habeas corpus, the Western District Court of Missouri ordered that an inmate be reassigned from the prison barber shop because it was proven that such work would aggravate the inmate's hip problem.[39]

The other side of forced work is punishment for being medically unable to work or requesting medical treatment. Inmates in Kansas were punished by the deprivation of good time if they were in the prison hospital, in an idle company, or in their cells due to non-work-related illness or injury. The court in *Sawyer v. Sigler*[40] held this practice violated the inmates' right to equal protection of the law:

> "The policy of denying statutory good time has the effect of requiring prisoners to choose between their statutory good time, on the one hand, and their constitutional right to receive necessary medical treatment, including relief from work, on the other. Requiring that choice by the disabled necessarily has a chilling effect upon procurement of the constitutional right to medical treatment."

Statutory and Regulatory Standards

A number of jurisdictions[41] have enacted legislation which guarantees adequate medical attention for prisoners.[42] In several of these jurisdictions, the language of the relevant statutes clearly places an affirmative obligation upon the appropriate correctional and medical personnel to provide an adequate standard of medical treatment.[43] In other jurisdictions, the courts have interpreted the statutory language as placing such an affirmative obligation upon the appropriate personnel:

> "Thus the general common law duty of the custodian of a prisoner to take proper care of the inmate is specifically imposed on the penitentiary superintendent in Mississippi by statute Mississippi Code Ann. §7930 (Supp. 1968)."[44]

Some states have enacted enabling legislation pursuant to which administrative regulations can be promulgated.[45] Regulations in New York are particularly unambiguous, but they apply only to local jails and penitentiaries.[46]

The jurisdictions with explicit legislation, however, are the exception rather than the rule. Most states have neither statutes nor administrative regulation in this area.[47]

At this point, it is appropriate to note several nonstatutory standards of care which may be raised as guidelines in litigation. These guidelines may be used as a standard of comparison by showing that the particular prison does not comply with the acceptable standards set forth, or they may be used by the court as a guide in fashioning a remedy. The *Manual of Correctional Standards,* issued by The American Correctional Association, has a rather meager section concerning medical care, merely proposing certain ratios, which they consider to be appropriate, of doctors and psychiatrists to inmates.[48] The *Manual* has, however, been cited by several courts.[49]

The Federal Bureau of Prisons, a system highly respected by the federal courts [50] and the professional corrections community, has issued a policy statement concerning the medical care of federal prisoners. The statement provides for detailed physical examinations of every prisoner within ten days of arrival at the prison,[51] an immunization program,[52] a "sick line" with emphasis on quality care and maintenance of professional decorum,[53] and the emergency treatment of patients.[54]

The federal policy statement is, relatively speaking, the best of its type. However, the enforcement of the statement as policy in the federal system may leave something to be desired. Howard Levy, a medical doctor and a former inmate at several federal prisons including Lewisburg, has described the medical care as merely "good enough to keep prisoners alive." [55]

The United Nations Standard Minimum Rules for the Treatment of Prisoners has a section devoted to medical treatment. Rule 22(1) requires that every institution have at least one "qualified" medical officer. This medical officer, according to Rule 24, "shall see and examine every prisoner as soon as possible after his admission and thereafter as necessary with a view particularly to the discovery of physical or mental illness, and the taking of all necessary measures." A pretrial detainee, according to Rule 91, "shall be allowed to be visited and treated by his own doctor or dentist if there is reasonable grounds for the pre-trial detainee's application and he is able to pay any expense incurred." [56]

Pennsylvania has already taken steps to implement the *United Nations Standard* into their law,[57] a bill has been introduced into the United States House of Representatives embodying its principles,[58] and commentators have urged its adoption into American law.[59]

Tort Law

The prisoner's custodian, whether a sheriff, jailor, warden, or superintendent, has a common law duty to protect the prisoner from all unnecessary injury and must exercise reasonable and ordinary care for the prisoner's life and health.[60] The point upon which most jurisdictions are split is the issue of whether or not an inmate can collect damages for the breach of that duty of care.[61] The majority of jurisdictions hold the custodian liable; [62] neglect, fire, filthy conditions, disease, injuries resulting from physical abuse at the hands of guards and at the hands of other prisoners, have been held actionable.[63]

In addition, some courts have construed statutes as imposing a duty of care upon prison officials, a breach of which has been held actionable.[64]

In cases where prisoners seek to sue the state itself for breach of its common law duty, they, like all other plaintiffs suing the state, must overcome the state's sovereign immunity. In 1946 the Federal Tort Claims Act was passed permitting persons to sue the United States.[65] No specific language in the Act prevented federal prisoners from suing the government; yet some courts so interpreted the statute.[66] The matter was not resolved until 1962. In *United States v. Muniz,*[67] Chief Justice Warren, writing for the majority, held that federal prisoners indeed had a right to sue in the Court of Claims. The Court rejected the argument that such lawsuits would lead to increased disciplinary problems, citing legislative history as evidence in court.[68] The decision, however, stepped back from actually holding the government liable for discretionary or intentional acts of its employees.[69] (This rule is applicable to all actions, including non-prison litigation.)

Federal prisoners and their dependents can further be compensated for "injuries suffered in any industry or in any work activity in connection with the maintenance or operation of the institution where confined." [70] However, inmates or their dependents must elect compensation under either the Tort Claims Act or the Federal Prisons Industries Fund.[71]

New York, among other states, has also permitted lawsuits against itself by citizens, generally,[72] but state prisoners who are serving felony sentences are precluded from pursuing their claims for damages while confined,[73] under the statute that treats felony offenders as being "civilly dead" while serving their sentences. Thus, New York prisoners serving felony sentences cannot sue and recover damages for even the most compelling claims.[74]

Remedies

The appropriate remedy must be sought once the prisoner or lawyer has chosen the applicable body of law. The possible legal remedies and the practical effectiveness of each of these remedies is discussed below.

Damage Actions

State prisoners may sue for monetary relief [75] incident to a §1983 action in the federal district courts. Federal prisoners may sue federal officials for violation of their constitutional rights and recover damages [76] under the Federal Tort Claims Act.

Relatively few damage awards have been obtained. In *Sostre v. McGinnis*,[77] Martin Sostre won a judgment of $25 a day compensatory damages for 372 days of unlawful segregation. Not suprisingly, additional punitive damages awarded by the District Court were removed. In any event, the award was assessed against the warden, who died subsequent to judgment, and no money has as yet been collected from the estate. Damages of $1,500 were recently awarded because of cruel and inhumane treatment in *Wright v. McMann* [78] pursuant to a §1983 action; and $85,000 in *Roberts v. Williams* [79] for negligence resulting in blindness and possible brain damage.

Statistics are not available indicating what recoveries inmates have made in tort actions or under tort claim statutes. It can be said, however, that in New York, as in other jurisdictions where "civil death" prevails, prisoners are barred from recovery due to the fact that they cannot bring proceedings until they are released from custody.

In theory, damages serve two important legal purposes: making the victim whole, and deterring similar conduct by the defendant and others in the future. Certainly deterrence is not effective in jurisdictions having tort claim acts where the state is the party defendant and the cost of any recovery is borne by the state. Moreover, as in New York, the Attorney General often represents the jurisdiction before the particular Court of Claims, and thus even legal fees, usually paid by the individual at fault, are borne by the state.

In §1983 actions in federal courts, even though individuals must be named as party defendants, the Attorney General will appear for the state if the allegations involve on-the-job conduct by the employee. Further, because of the growing power of correctional personnel unions and organizations, states are beginning to enact legislation protecting employees against damage awards levied against individual employees for on-the-job misconduct.[80] The state thus insures its employees against damage awards. Apparently the trend is toward the successful organization of potential defendants to deflect damage actions, thereby lessening the chances that damage rewards will deter misconduct or raise the level of care. Of course such legislation may have the effect of lessening the reluctance of judges and juries to award damages against correction personnel when it is known that the state and not the individual will be liable. It should be recognized that, even in cases where maltreatment is established, the prisoner is in a particularly poor position before a judge or jury that is assessing damages. The fact of our legal and social systems is that a prisoner is not viewed as an appealing or sympathetic plaintiff vis-à-vis correctional personnel, especially poorly-paid correctional personnel.

Equitable Remedies

State prisoners may obtain declaratory,[81] injunctive, or broad equitable relief [82] incident to §1983 actions. Federal prisoners may sue for an injunction to restrain unconstitutional conduct or treatment [83] and may obtain a writ of mandamus,[84] or they may appeal by a writ of habeas corpus. Further, federal prisoners may invoke the provisions of the Administrative Procedure Act, under which "a person suffering legal wrong because of agency action or adversely affected or aggrieved by agency action . . . is entitled to judicial review thereof." [85] A federal prisoner is not entitled to monetary relief under the Act, but a prisoner can couple the lawsuit with a request for declaratory or injunctive relief.[86]

For example, injunctive relief was achieved for state prisoners in the case of *Talley v. Stephens.*[87] Here prisoners in the Arkansas State Prison system [88] filed suit in equity to restrain the superintendent from violating the Fourteenth Amendment and

§1983 by the denial of adequate medical care, the regulation of the number of inmates allowed to report for sick calls, and compelled physical labor beyond prisoners' physical capacities. The District Court held that petitioners were entitled to adequate medical care and were permitted to attend sick call at all reasonable times, and to be free from forced labor.[89]

Broad equitable orders concerning medical care were obtained in several jail cases noted earlier, e.g., *Jones v. Wittenberg* and the *Wayne County Jail Inmates* cases.[89a] In other cases, similar results were obtained by negotiation and subsequent consent orders entered by the court.[90]

In one other such case, *Batchelder v. Geary,*[91] a stipulation and order was filed directing that "a committee of doctors be designated to report to the Court on the status of medical facilities at the Santa Clara County Jail and the Elmwood Rehabilitation Center at Milpitas."

Recently Federal District Judge Frank M. Johnson, Jr. held that medical treatment and care afforded to prisoners in the entire Alabama prison system violated their constitutional right to be free of cruel and unusual punishment. The court ordered Alabama prison authorities, among other things, to:

(1) "bring the general hospital at the Medical and Diagnostic Center up to the standards provided in the United States Dept. of Health and Welfare Proposed Revised Regulations for Participation of Hospitals in Medical Programs of January 17, 1972;

(2) "ensure that each medical facility shall have written sanitation procedures approved by the medical director

(3) "institute a systematic program evaluating and updating all medical equipment. . . ;

(4) "file a . . . minimum staffing [proposal] . . . ;

(5) "ensure that every inmate who is in need of medical attention for diagnostic or treatment purposes, is seen by a qualified medical attendant when required and by a physician when necessary"; and

(6) "maintain a record system throughout the Alabama Penal system which will ensure that a complete medical record is available for each prisoner at the facility to which the prisoner is currently assigned."[92]

The proof in this case was rather gruesome, including: unsupervised prisoners screening sick-call patients, dispensing medication, giving injections, suturing and performing minor surgery. Judge Johnson cited numerous cases of pervasive and gross neglect, including the development of maggots in unattended bedsores of a quadruplegic, the death of an epileptic who was handcuffed to his bed, and a patient who was ordered to be fed intravenously, but who had not received nourishment in three days prior to his death.[93]

Injunctive relief may remedy the individual extreme or gross cases, and may force change in those jurisdictions which still refuse to enforce adequate standards, or condone shockingly horrible medical care systems. But what of the care in places such as Attica, the run-of-the-mill prisons where medical care is described as involving "a reasonable level of competence," [94] or Lewisburg, where the care is sufficient to "keep the inmates alive?" [95]

The response of the judicial system would thus fail where there is no proof of unusual or barbarous conduct. The courts use the very same standard of behavior which "shocks the conscience," a standard that has apparently been discredited in the search and seizure area [96] as well as other areas of the criminal justice system.[97]

The Merits and Priorities of Litigation

In light of the present state of law, should prisoners and their lawyers continue to litigate in the medical area, and if so, how?

Litigation in behalf of individual inmates for the remedy of their individual medical problems has achieved only spotty results —a single victory here, another victory there, but mostly a rather dismal record. Nevertheless, it seems valuable to maintain the pressure of this mostly pro se litigation. With the demise of the "hands-off" doctrine, the courts are beginning to rule on the merits of claims after trial rather than dismiss on the allegations in the complaints or on procedural grounds.[98] Thus more lawsuits should be successful in the long run. As judicial standards emerge, lawsuits will be screened out, but judges will begin to see that there are meritorious prisoner cases that should be dealt with.

Gradually the courts are becoming less willing to absolutely defer to the expertise of prison and even medical personnel in the treatment or care of inmates.[99] In *Lopez Tijerina v. Ciccone,*[100] the court went so far as to appoint an independent medical examiner to substantiate or refute the accuracy or efficacy of the challenged treatment. Although the plaintiff in *Lopez Tijerina* lost, the case might have gone the other way had there been a conflict between the prison's medical assessment and that of the independent examiner.

Another possible approach is to press for treatment and care by private, outside doctors. It is a rather small step from the *Tolbert* [101] case where the court held that a prisoner was entitled to privately-prescribed medicine and to an initial evaluation by a private doctor. Furthermore, if an inmate has a right to reasonable medical treatment, then the state must show some compelling state interest in order to justify any conditions imposed upon that right. Restrictions on time and place may be appropriate, but access should not be denied.

The priority in litigation should be placed upon egregious cases where the limited time, energy, and resources of the movement to effect changes in prison conditions can be focused upon cases where overwhelming evidence can be adduced and a broad order applicable to as many people as possible obtained. Perhaps a few well-chosen malpractice lawsuits might be utilized to indicate to prison doctors that they are not immune to lawsuits. The key is choosing the right set of facts, the right jurisdiction, and the right judge to make the appropriate impact.

The results of a litigational strategy alone cannot really hope to produce desperately needed change, because of the problems of implementation and sustaining enthusiasm in a system after reform personnel have left. The hope for long-term change lies in both creating a climate in which the public itself calls for change through its elected representatives and in the creation of an in-prison organization of inmates with outside support, which has real political and economic power.

Some have called for grievance machinery or an ombudsman [102] to solve these problems. New York has established a Medical Review Board to investigate deaths in their prisons.[103] Although useful in the short run, the history of regulatory agencies is that they are captured by the groups they have been directed to regulate. Until prisoners have enough power to at least help determine who sits on the grievance boards, the danger of capture is all too plain.

A Non-Litigational Strategy

At the same time that concerted litigational attack is made, a new medical delivery system must be developed and implemented.

If this system is to be effective at all, it must take into account the failures of the old system, and thus it cannot be related in any way to the correctional system in terms of money, staff, and resources. Independence of medical personnel from the correctional system may be the key to destroying that basic mistrust that the McKay Commission noted.[104] "Unfortunately, it is clear that prisoner-initiated actions, however dramatic, sensational and extreme, cannot guarantee reform unless accompanied by support and initiative from outside the prison walls." [105]

Perhaps this independence could be assisted by medical schools' assuming full responsibility for the care and treatment of a particular prison.[106] There is a precedent for such a proposal. For many years the General Hospital in Columbus, Ohio, was attached to the Ohio State Prison. The medical staff of the hospital and the academic staff of the local medical school tended to the medical needs of the prison population. The hospital provided medical treatment and care and was operating as a healing hospital. Many former prisoners at Columbus and others have spoken highly of the care and treatment afforded to inmates at the prison. With the building of the Lucasville prison, the relationship of hospital-medical school-prison was severed.

In the wake of the Attica uprising, a proposal was made to seek alternative ways of providing medical services at Attica.[107] The proposal suggests that "Work in [several areas] can provide us with an ideal mechanism for conducting the necessary evaluations while actively supplementing existing health programs." [108]

Conclusion

While the law can be a force for change in the prison medical area, it can only be the cutting edge. New ways to serve the medical needs of prisoners must be developed and implemented.

Litigation can serve to point out the problems and correct the more egregious or outrageous cases, but the most serious problems of prison medicine will remain until some serious thinking concerning alternative methods of delivery is done. Inherent in the analysis will have to be the basic assumption by courts, lawyers, and the public generally that prisoners are people entitled to basic human rights, including, but not limited to, the right to adequate medical care.

Footnotes

[1] A. Berkman, Prison Memories of An Anarchist (1970), at 246.

> " 'A young man with parchment-like face, sere and yellow, walks painfully from the line.
> 'Doctor, I seem to be gettin' worser, and I'm afraid—'
> 'What's the trouble?'
> 'Pains in the stomach. Gettin' so turrible, I—'
> 'Give him a plaster. Next!'
> 'Plaster hell!' the prisoner breaks out in a fury, his face growing livid. 'Look at this, will you?' With a quick motion he pulls his shirt up to his head. His chest and back are entirely covered with porous plasters; not an inch of his skin is visible. 'Damn yer plasters,' he cries with sudden sobs, 'I ain't got no more room for plasters. I'm putty near dyin', an' you won't do nothin' fer me'."

[2] N.Y. State Special Commission Report on Attica (1972), at 66 (hereinafter "McKay Commission"):

> "Inmates did use sick call to escape a boring job and see friends as well as to get treatment for illness, but the number of such 'malingerers' is not known. Both doctors claimed that the majority of those on sick call were not ill and that it was possible in a few seconds by 'looking into their eyes' to distinguish these from inmates with valid complaints. They also expressed the opinion that inmates make more demands for medical treatment than they would outside of prison. Inmates, however, complained that the doctors often didn't believe that they were sick and routinely dispensed a few drugs, such as aspirin, for almost all complaints. A few inmates expressed the opinion that the medication they were getting was harmful to them."

[3] Id.

[4] Rundle, "Medical Un-Care for Prisoners," 1 Prisoners' Rights Newsletter 53, 54 (April 1972) (from a paper originally presented at the Conference of the National Committee for Prisoner Rights in Chicago in November, 1971).

[5] "Prisons Assailed in Pennsylvania," N.Y. Times, October 29, 1972, at 23. The Governor of Pennsylvania appointed a panel to seek ways to improve health care for Pennsylvania inmates. He made public a report prepared by the Health-Law Project of the University of Pennsylvania Law School, funded by the Federal Office of Economic Opportunity.

[6] Newman v. Alabama, 349 F. Supp. 278 (M.D. Ala. 1972); "Alabama Inmates Win Health Edict," N.Y. Times, October 5, 1972, at 25.

[7] See McKay Commission, note 2, supra, at 69: "In long range terms solution to such (medical care problems at Attica) will depend on the development of some alternate system for delivery of care."

H. Levy and D. Miller, Going to Jail at 95–99 (Grove Press, 1970); Rundle, note 4, supra.

8 Note, "Beyond the Ken of the Courts," 72 Yale L.J. 406 (1963);Note, "Constitutional Rights of Prisoners: The Developing Law," 110 U. Pa. L. Rev. 985 (1962). However, the discredited doctrine has remained somewhat more viable in the medical care area, perhaps because inmates are generally not only asking to review decisions of prison officials but those of doctors and medical personnel.

9 See Monroe v. Pape, 365 U.S. 167 (1961); Cooper v. Pate, 378 U.S. 546 (1964).

10 Jurisdiction in the U.S. District Courts is founded upon 28 U.S.C. §1341.

11 42 U.S.C. §1983.

12 State action by state officials must always be alleged and proved.

13 State prisoners can also bring their §1983 actions in state courts but have generally chosen the federal forum due to its more hospitable judges and procedure. Sullivan v. Little Hunting Park, Inc., 396 U.S. 229 (1969), and Kates, "Bringing Federal Civil Rights Actions in State Court," 6 Clearinghouse Rev. 318 (October 1972).

14 For a full list of the cases as well as other expositions of the present law, see S. Alexander, "The Captive Patient," 6 Clearinghouse Rev. 16 (May 1972); Zalman, "Prisoners' Right to Medical Care," 63 J. Crim. L.C. & P.S. 185 (1972); South Carolina Department of Corrections, The Emerging Rights of the Confined, ch. 13, 146–157 (1972); Sneidman, "Prisoners and Medical Treatment: Their Rights and Remedies," 4 Crim. L. Bull. 450 (1968).

15 Rochin v. California, 342 U.S. 165 (1952).

16 Robinson v. California, 370 U.S. 660, 676 (1962) (Douglas J., concurring).

17 Trop v. Dulles, 356 U.S. 86, 100–101 (1958).

18 247 F.2d 273 (7th Cir. 1957).

19 See also McCollum v. Mayfield, 130 F. Supp. 112 (N.D. Cal. 1955); Elsberg v. Haynes, 257 F. Supp. 739 (W.D. Okla. 1966); Haigh v. Sindow, 321 F. Supp. 324 (S.D. Cal. 1964).

20 Redding v. Pate, 220 F. Supp. 124 (N.D. Ill. 1963).

21 Hughes v. Noble, 295 F.2d 495 (5th Cir. 1961).

22 Blanks v. Cunningham, 409 F.2d 220 (4th Cir. 1969).

23 Riley v. Rhay, 407 F.2d 496 (9th Cir. 1969).

24 Stiltner v. Rhay, 371 F.2d 420 (9th Cir. 1969), cert. denied 386 U.S. 997 (1967).

25 468 F.2d 560 (2d Cir. 1972).

26 Id. at 561.

27 429 F.2d 867 (2d Cir. 1970).

28 398 F.2d 932 (10th Cir. 1968). In accord Domingues v. Moseley, 431 F.2d 1376 (10th Cir. 1970); Shaffer v. Jennings, 314 F. Supp. 588 (E.D. Pa. 1970); Willis v. White, 310 F. Supp. 205 (E.D. La. 1970).

29 In accord Thompson v. Blackwell, 374 F.2d 945 (5th Cir. 1967); Medlock v. Burke, 285 F. Supp. 67 (E.D. Wis. 1968); Goodchild v. Schmidt, 229 F. Supp. 149

(E.D. Wis. 1968); Henderson v. Pate, 409 F.2d 407 (7th Cir. 1969); U.S. ex rel. Lawrence v. Ragen, 323 F.2d 410 (7th Cir. 1963); Prewitt v. Arizona, 418 F.2d 572 (9th Cir. 1969); Haskew v. Wainwright, 429 F.2d 525 (5th Cir. 1969); Weaver v. Beto, 429 F.2d 505 (5th Cir. 1970); Isenberg v. Prasse, 433 F.2d 449 (3d Cir. 1970); Paniagua v. Moseley, 451 F.2d 228 (10th Cir. 1971).

30 See notes 27–29, supra.

31 443 F.2d 921 (2d Cir. 1970), cert. denied 401 U.S. 983 (1971).

32 Id. at 924.

The Second Circuit in Startz v. Cullen, note 25, supra, distinguished the Martinez case by stating that the prison-authorized conduct in Startz was "far removed from the reckless failure to inform themselves of a prisoner's medical needs which we held in Martinez . . . to be the equivalent of intentionally inflicted harm." 468 F.2d at 562 (2d Cir. 1972).

33 Hirons v. Director, Patuxent Institution, 351 F.2d 614 (4th Cir. 1965); Edwards v. Duncan, 355 F.2d 993 (4th Cir. 1966); Tolbert v. Eyman, 434 F.2d 625 (9th Cir. 1970); Sawyer v. Sigler, 320 F. Supp. 690 (D. Neb. 1970).

34 Martinez v. Mancusi, note 31, supra, 443 F.2d at 924.

35 "Prisons Assailed in Pennsylvania," note 5, supra; S. Alexander, note 14, supra, at 21.

36 See e.g. Inmates of Cook County Jail v. Tierney, 4 Clearinghouse Rev. 388 (N.D. Ill. 1968); Jones v. Wittenberg, 323 F. Supp. 93 (N.D. Ohio 1971). See also state court decision in Wayne County Jail Inmates v. Wayne County Bd. Comm'rs, 5 Clearinghouse Rev. 108 (Cir. Ct. Wayne County, Mich. 1971); Hearings before House Subcommittee #3 on Corrections 92d Cong. 2d Sess. Part VIII, at 119–230; Bryant v. Hendrick, 7 Crim. L. Rep. 2463 (Ct. C.P. Phila., Pa. 1970), aff'd sub nom. Pennsylvania v. Hendrick, 444 Pa. 83, 280 A.2d 110 (1971).

37 See e.g. Wright v. McMann, 387 F.2d 519 (2d Cir. 1967), on remand 321 F. Supp. 127 (N.D.N.Y. 1970), aff'd 460 F.2d 126 (2d Cir. 1971); Jordan v. Fitzharris, 257 F. Supp. 674 (N.D. Cal. 1966); Talley v. Stephens, 247 F. Supp. 683 (E.D. Ark. 1965). But see Holt v. Sarver, 300 F. Supp. 825, (E.D. Ark. 1969), 309 F. Supp. 362 (E.D. Ark. 1970), aff'd 442 F.2d 304 (8th Cir. 1971).

38 Apparently this is one reason why the Second Circuit in the important Sostre v. McGinnis case, 442 F.2d 178 (2d Cir. 1971), found that there was no Eighth Amendment violation in Sostre's segregated confinement (distinguishing the cases of Wright, Jordan, and Talley, note 37, supra) at 193, n. 24: "[A] prison physician visited Sostre's segregation unit daily, and at no time did the physician observe, or did Sostre call his attention to any [adverse effects of segregation on his physical or mental health]."

39 Black v. Ciccone, 324 F. Supp. 129 (W.D. Mo. 1970). See also McCollum v. Mayfield, 130 F. Supp. 112 (N.D. Cal. 1955); McCrossen v. State, 277 App. Div. 1160, 101 N.Y.S.2d 591, lv. to app. denied 302 N.Y. 950, 98 N.E.2d 117 (1950); Talley v. Stephens, note 37, supra.

40 320 F. Supp. 690, 699 (D. Neb. 1970).

41 Including federal legislation relating to federal prisons, see 28 U.S.C. §4042.

42 Interview with Herman Schwartz, Professor of Law, State University of New York at Buffalo.

43 See e.g. Mich. Comp. Laws 1948 §800, at 15–17; Cal. Pen. Code (West 1970) §4023; Ill. Rev. Stat. 108, §§32-33; W. Va. Code ch. 7, §7-8-2 (1969).

44 Anderson v. Nosser, 438 F.2d 183, 194 (5th Cir. 1971). Although the court held state officers liable under §1983, it ruled on the pendent state claims of the plaintiffs as well. See also McCrossen v. State, note 39, supra, interpreting N.Y. Corr. Law §46 (McKinn. 1968). But see Bush v. Babb, 23 Ill. App. 2d 285, 162 N.E.2d 594 (1959). A former inmate brought suit for negligence against his former jailor, claiming that the Illinois Jail and Jailor's Act, ch. 75 Ill. Rev. Stat. §2 (1959), was violated. This Act states that the jailor "shall furnish necessary medical aid for all prisoners under charge." The inmate contracted tuberculosis. The court held that the Act merely required that the jailor decide whether, under particular circumstances, medical care was required. The duty imposed would be quasi-judicial rather than ministerial, and thus the jailor was immune from liability. The Act, the court explained, was a duty not directed toward individual inmates but for the good of the public in general.

45 See e.g. N.Y. Corr. Law §§112, and 70.2(c) (McKinn. Supp. 1970); and Mass. Ann. Laws.

46 7 N.Y.C.R.R. §5100.1 contained in the Minimum Standards for local jails and penitentiaries promulgated pursuant to N.Y. Corr. Law §46(7-a) (McKinn. 1968). See also, with respect to city jails, village and town "lock-ups," 7 N.Y.C.R.R. §5200.4.

47 See e.g. Texas and the comments thereon in Zalman, note 14, supra, at 187, n. 12.

48 American Correctional Association, Manual of Correctional Standards, at 439 (rev. ed. undated).

49 Wright v. McMann and Jordan v. Fitzharris, note 37, supra, and Wayne County Jail Inmates, note 36, supra.

50 See e.g. Wright v. McMann and Jordan v. Fitzharris, note 37, supra. The author has been present on several occasions in and out of court when federal judges have asked questions concerning the Federal Bureau (FBP) standard or policy statement on the subject. Apparently the judges look upon the FBP standards as a model in their §1983 state cases.

51 Bureau of Prisons, United States Dept. of Justice Manual of Policy Statement §37601.

52 Id.

53 Id. at §37602.

54 Id.

55 Levy and Miller, note 7, supra, at 97.

56 For a discussion of the United Nations standards as they related to the Attica demands, see Besharov and Mueller, "The Demands of the Inmates of Attica Prison and the United Nations Standard Minimum Rules for the Treatment of Prisoners: A Comparison," 21 Buff. L. Rev. 839 (1972).

57 New York Times, October 5, 1972, at 45, Cols. 6–8.

58 HR 11605, 92d Cong. 1st Sess. (1971). The bill was introduced by Rep. Charles Rangel of New York.

59 Besharov and Mueller, note 56, supra, at 854.

60 In general see annotation of Smith v. Miller, 241 Iowa 625, 40 N.W.2d 597 (1956) at 14 A.L.R. 2d 353 and Sreidman, note 14, supra. See e.g. Indiana ex rel. Tyler v. Gobin, 94 F. 50 (C.C. D. Ind. 1899); Ex parte Jenkins, 25 Ind. App. 318, 58 N.E. 560 (1906); Kendrick v. Adamson, 51 Ga. App. 402, 180 S.E. 647 (1935).

61 14 A.L.R.2d 353, 354–358.

62 Id.

63 Id. at 360–368.

64 Id at 358. See e.g. McCrossen v. State, note 39, supra; Pisacano v. State, 8 A.D.2d 335, 188 N.Y.S.2d 35 (4th Dep't 1959); Anderson v. Nosser, note 44, supra.

65 28 U.S.C. §§1346(b), 2671–2680 (1964).

66 Lack v. United States, 262 F.2d 167 (8th Cir. 1958); Jones v. United States, 249 F.2d 864 (7th Cir. 1957).

67 305 F.2d 285 (2d Cir. 1962); Winston v. United States 305 F.2d 253 (2d Cir. 1962), aff'd 374 U.S. 150 (1963).

68 Winston v. United States, note 67, supra, 374 U.S. at 163.

69 Id.

70 18 U.S.C. §4126 (1964).

71 United States v. Demko, 385 U.S. 149 (1966).

72 N.Y. Ct. Cl. Act (McKinn. 1963).

73 N.Y. Civil Rights Law §§79, 79-a-c (McKinn. 1971). Thirteen other states followed the medieval notion of "civil death"; see Jay, "Rights of Prisoners While Incarcerated," 15 Buff. L. Rev. 397 (1965).

74 See e.g. Lynch v. Quinlan, 317 N.Y.S.2d 216 (Dutch. Co. Sup. Ct. 1970). The statute creating the bar is now under attack in Johnson v. Rockefeller, — F. Supp. — No. 1699 (S.D.N.Y. complaint filed 1972 before Lasker, D.J.). Plaintiffs have moved for the impanelling of a three-judge District Court. A new law has recently been enacted in New York allowing prisoners to sue. L. of 1973 ch. 687 amending N.Y. Civil Rights Law, §§79, 79-a.

75 See Monroe v. Pape, note 9, supra; Wright v. McMann, note 37, supra.

76 Bivens v. Six Unknown Fed. Narc. Agents, 403 U.S. 388 (1971).

77 442 F.2d 128, 205 (2d Cir. 1971). See Schwartz, "A Comment on Sostre v. McGinnis," 21 Buff. L. Rev. 775, 790 (1972).

78 321 F. Supp. 127 (N.D.N.Y. 1970), aff'd 460 F.2d 126 (2d Cir. 1972).

79 302 F. Supp. 972 (N.D. Miss. 1969).

80 N.Y. 1972 Sess. L., ch. 283 §15 (McKinn. 1972) adding new §24 to the N.Y. Corr. Law, subdivision 3 of which reads:

> "3. The state shall save harmless and indemnify any officer or employee of the department from financial loss resulting from a claim filed in a court of the United States for damages arising out of an act done or the failure to perform any act that was (a) within the scope of the employment and in the discharge of the duties of such officer or

employee, and (b) was not in violation of any rule or regulation of the department or of any statute or governing case law of the state or of the United States at the time the alleged damages were allegedly sustained; provided that the officer or employee shall comply with the provisions of subdivision four of this section."

81 28 U.S.C. §§2201–2202 (1964).

82 42 U.S.C. §1983 (1964); 28 U.S.C. §1651 (1964); Fed. R. Civ. P. 65.

83 42 U.S.C. §1983 speaks of a suit in equity. Equity lawsuits have traditionally meant a flexible approach in terms of the remedy.

84 28 U.S.C. §1361 (1964).

85 5 U.S.C. §702 (1964).

86 See Jacob and Sharma, "Justice After Trial: Prisoners' Need for Legal Services in the Criminal-Correctional Process," 18 Kan. L. Rev. 493, 533 (1970).

87 247 F. Supp. 683 (E.D. Ark. 1965).

88 For a description of the medical care and abuses in the Arkansas system, see Murton, "Prison Doctors," in The Humanist, at 24 (May/June 1971).

89 Talley v. Stephens, note 87, supra, 247 F. Supp. at 686–687.

89a Note 36, supra.

90 Inmates of Cook County Jail v. Tierney, note 36, supra.

91 1 Prisoners' Rights Newsletter 39 (April 1972), — F. Supp. —, Civ. C-71-2017 (N.D. Cal. stipulation and order filed November 12, 1971).

92 New York Times, note 6, supra (decree 1-4).

93 Newman v. Alabama, note 6, supra, at 285.

94 McKay Commission, note 2, supra, at 67.

95 Levy and Miller, note 7, supra, at 97.

96 Mapp v. Ohio, 367 U.S. 643 (1961).

97 See e.g. Escobedo v. Illinois, 378 U.S. 428 (1964); Miranda v. Arizona, 384 U.S. 436 (1966). See also Zalman, note 5, supra at 193.

98 See Haines v. Kerner, 404 U.S. 519 (1972); Wilwording v. Swenson, 404 U.S. 249 (1971).

99 See the lines of cases beginning with Martinez v. Mancusi, note 31, supra, and Talley v. Stephens, note 87, supra.

100 324 F. Supp. 1265 (W.D. Mo. 1970).

101 Tolbert v. Eymon, 434 F.2d 625 (9th Cir. 1970).

102 Zalman, note 14, supra, at 199.

103 N.Y. 1972 Sess. L. Ch. 906 (McKinn. 1972).

104 See in this regard "Prison Health Projects—Three Proposals" (February 1972), authored by the Health Policy Advisory Center, Inc. (Health-PAC), 17 Murray St., New York, New York 10007.

105 Id. at 1.

106 This suggestion was made by the Health-PAC proposal noted in note 104, supra. The McKay Commission, note 2, supra, at 69, spoke of such a proposal in these terms:

"In long-range terms, solutions to such problems will depend in the development of some alternative system for delivery of care in which these essential services are provided for inmates of Attica by a large well-staffed medical center, or inmates in need of care are transferred to some facility with large enough volume to support more comprehensive staff pattern."

107 It is entitled "Proposal for University Participation in the Health Care Program for Attica," and prepared by Drs. E. Marine and J. McDaniel of the SUNY/Buffalo Medical School. A copy is on file with the author of this article.

108 Id. at 3. The several areas referred to included: (1) a mental health evaluation for all inmates; (2) a common inmate disease survey and evaluation of the present treatment delivery system; (3) vocational programs in health; and (4) drug education or rehabilitation program. As of the date of this article, the Proposal's recommendations that a "University Task Force" be appointed to conduct a study of the present health care programs, explore available models, develop a proposal to meet the health of Attica prisoners, and seek necessary financial support, have not been implemented.

CHAPTER 9
REHABILITATION

EDITORS' INTRODUCTION

Although one of the primary justifications for incarceration is to rehabilitate convicted criminals, little in the way of services which might be termed rehabilitative is offered in our prisons. In a time when we are faced with a rising crime rate and a great deal of recidivism, positive opportunities for change must be offered to our nation's prisoners if this situation is to change. The possibility of securing these services through litigation and the dangers of enforced involuntary rehabilitative attempts are discussed in the following article.

THE COMING RIGHT TO REHABILITATION

RICHARD SINGER *

The Right to Rehabilitation

The right to rehabilitation must be constructed upon recent court decisions establishing the right of mental patients to have a program of treatment inside the institution. The first of these cases is *Rouse v. Cameron,*[1] in which Judge Bazelon of the District of Columbia Court of Appeals held that under a Washington, D.C. statute which specifically provided for such a right, an inmate in St. Elizabeth's Mental Hospital had stated a cause of action in alleging that he was not being given proper psychiatric care.

Although the *Rouse* case depended rather clearly on the presence of a statute, Judge Bazelon did indicate in dictum that failure to provide such care might also violate the inmate's constitutional rights. The premise upon which such a statement was based may be identified as substantive due process, the theory being that if the state deprives a person of liberty for a specific purpose, it must thereafter attempt to fulfill that purpose or cede its authority over the individual.

In a series of cases in the ensuing years,[2] various courts either directly followed *Rouse,* finding statutory authority for a right to treatment for mental patients, or without making specific findings broadly hinted that constitutional arguments might be accepted by the courts under certain circumstances. A series of law review notes [3] and symposia [4] following this line of cases is a fertile source for much of the thinking which went into those and later decisions.

The next and perhaps most important step in establishing the right to treatment for mental patients was *Wyatt v. Stickney,*[5] which adopted the broad implications of *Rouse* and held that even in the absence of a statutory right to treatment there was an

---

* Project Co-Director, Resource Center on Correctional Law and Legal Services, ABA, Washington, D.C.; former Associate Professor of Law, University of Cincinnati; A.B. Amherst College; J.D. University of Chicago; LL.M. Columbia University.

affirmative constitutional duty upon the state either to provide meaningful services and treatment for persons in mental hospitals or to release them. In further orders, Judge Johnson specified the precise personnel ratios that must be followed in such an institution, and then proceeded to announce a series of sweeping remedies to bring the institutions up to constitutional minima of treatment.[6]

The implications of *Rouse, Wyatt,* and other cases for corrections are somewhat unclear. An argument can be made that the purpose of prison, much like the purpose of a mental hospital, is to rehabilitate and reform the incarcerated individual. One can further assert that, whether the state recognizes it in statutory language or not, virtually all penologists now agree that the primary purpose of a correctional institute is correction of the individual, and that incarceration without an attempt to correct violates the Constitution. The prime obstacle to this argument is that prison serves other purposes besides reformation. In fact, the main purpose of prison may not be to reform the individual at all but either to incapacitate or punish him, or to deter him or others.

In refutation of this, it is enough to note that the Supreme Court has renounced the goal of retribution,[7] that incapacitation is achieved simply upon the incarceration of the individual without precluding reformation, and that figures and studies on deterrence certainly undercut, if they do not totally destroy, the argument that deterrence works.[8] It may not be quite so easy, however, to convince a local judge that these other purposes of correctional institutions have been discarded and denounced both by correctional administrators and by other persons in the criminal justice system. Other ways by which the constitutional argument may be buoyed must therefore be considered.

The first and most obvious method is to find a state statute which clearly enunciates a purpose of reform.[9] If such a statute is found, then the constitutional argument can be used as a fallback. A judge, hesitant to read a right to rehabilitation into a state statute, may be persuaded by the lurking constitutional question to construe the statute to indicate that the purpose of corrections is indeed to correct.

The second source, perhaps less direct but nevertheless helpful, is statutes that establish programs of rehabilitation in the correctional system without specifically stating that the entire correctional system is geared to the purpose of corrections. These might include statutes establishing probation and parole, work-release programs, and furlough programs. Since all states have at least some of this legislation on their books, there is every likelihood that the statutory argument can be framed. Finally, statements of leading penologists and criminologists should be used to support any attempt to establish a right to rehabilitation.

These suggested techniques have already been used to some advantage in cases dealing with juveniles or young offenders. One of the first of these was *White v. Reid,*[10] where the District Court precluded the transfer of a juvenile to a correctional facility where he would not receive beneficial treatment. The *Reid* case was unclear in both its rationale and its facts as to whether it established a statutory or a constitutional right to treatment, or whether it was simply one judge's unique way of protecting juveniles.

The intervening two decades since *Reid* have seen courts around the country split on the question of whether transfer of juveniles to adult institutions is constitutionally permissible.[11] There is little doubt that at least some courts have endorsed the idea that a juvenile cannot be transferred to an institution in which he does not receive treatment. Similar holdings can be found for sex offenders.[12]

Two recent decisions in the District of Columbia lend further credence to the right to treatment. In *United States v. Waters,*[13] the court held that the young offenders (aged eighteen to twenty-six) must be sentenced under the Youth Corrections Act of the United States, unless the judge could give written reasons for not so sentencing the offender. In *United States v. Alsbrook,*[14] the court held that juveniles who were eligible to be sentenced to Lorton Reformatory could not be denied the treatment facilities at the institution simply because the institution was overcrowded.

These cases, of course, can be distinguished from normal adult-offender incarceration on the grounds that there are special statutes involved dealing with juveniles and young offenders, and that the law has always treated young offenders in a somewhat beneficent mood not generally applied to adult offenders. Nevertheless, these cases do bring the right-to-treatment cases for mental patients closer to the entire criminal justice system.

One of the most helpful decisions in this area is *Holt v. Sarver,*[15] which declared that one factor in determining that the Arkansas prison system as then managed was hopelessly unconstitutional was the absence of any rehabilitative program. Although stating, in dictum, that the absence of those programs would not alone render a system unconstitutional, the court also noted that "a sociological theory or idea may ripen into constitutional law."

Finally, a number of recent cases dealing with jail conditions [16] begin to establish the right of all criminal offenders, both accused and convicted, to basic decent standards of living. Some of these cases have gone further and required that institutions begin to establish rehabilitation programs for all inmates, whether convicted or still awaiting trial. In *Jones v. Wittenberg*,[17] for example, Judge Young announced that any plan which did not include a work-release component would not be accepted by the court as meeting constitutional standards.

Again, these cases do not specifically recognize the right to rehabilitative programs in a penal institution. They deal with institutions holding either pretrial detainees or convicted misdemeanants who, arguably, are more likely to benefit from programs of rehabilitation since they are not far removed from being "normal" citizens. Nevertheless, these cases do begin to develop a concept of right to rehabilitation in programs and treatment.

A major issue in this area is the definition of rehabilitation. Some correctional authorities appear to consider an inmate rehabilitated only when he has accepted white, middle-class, Christian values. Thus, for example, manufacturing license plates in prison, which is not a marketable skill in the free world, would be justified as "instilling work habits and modes," even if the Puritan ethic is not universally viewed as helpful. To the extent that the inmate cannot play some part in his own definition of rehabilitation, the concept may not be very useful and may even be counterproductive.

For the most part, however, we can agree that rehabiltation involves: (1) some change in the inmate's viewpoint concerning the use of violence in the community; (2) counselling by a psychiatrist, social worker, or similar professional; and (3) educational and vocational advancement. If this is what we mean by "rehabilitation," it is clearly necessary in today's prisons. In 1967, the Task Force on Corrections found that less than 20 per cent of the inmate population in the nation had graduated from high school, and that well over half (54 per cent) had not completed the eighth grade. Similarly, only one third had any real working skill before entering prison, compared with nearly double that number in the free world population.[18]

The resources available in prison to deal with these needs are pitiful; the shortage of trained professionals, such as social workers, teachers, psychologists, chaplains, and psychiatrists, is astounding. In 1964, Schnur estimated that if all of the full-time psychiatrists were distributed evenly throughout the nation's prisons, "it would mean that there is not more than 82 seconds of psychiatric help available for each inmate during a whole month," [19] and that each chaplain could give no more than ten minutes per month.

The same sorry state of affairs exists in vocational training and teaching. In 1967, the President's Task Force found that of 46,000 personnel in the corrections field, 31,000 were custodial, 2.4 per cent were professional, and about 3 per cent were educational. It is hardly surprising, therefore, that inmates leave institutions with no more skills, either social or vocational, than when they arrived.

Even where they exist, however, few current programs in correctional institutions are helpful. For the attorney, this raises a host of difficult and nonlegal issues. Does the right to rehabilitation mean that the program must be professionally run? Must it achieve some results? If so, how do we judge the effectiveness of any program?[20] When suit is contemplated, these issues should be faced directly, penological treatises consulted, and expert witnesses lined up.

The Right to Refuse Treatment

If a right to some programs of rehabilitation and treatment within the institution is established, there is a desperate need for a concomitant right to refuse programs of treatment. As suggested above, an inmate may well complain that the "treatment" he is receiving is designed to instill in him values which he and members of a culture to which he belongs simply do not accept. A good example might be a Black Muslim who is afforded an opportunity, or required, to participate in programs dealing with Christian or white middle-class ethics. Both of these concepts would be anathema to many Black Muslims and, indeed, to most Blacks, whatever their religious persuasion.

Even more disturbing is the prospect that programs of rehabilitation will be forced upon unwilling inmates. This occurs today when parole boards take into account the participation of inmates in programs considered to be reformative in nature. For example, an inmate who does not attend religious services may find that his plea to the parole board falls on deaf ears. An inmate may be told either at the time of his parole release hearing or at any time before or after such a hearing that the board generally considers participation in X program desirable, if not mandatory, to obtain early release.

Further considerations of the right to refuse treatment revolve around some shocking programs already present in some institutions, and undoubtedly to be established in more unless immediate action is taken. Frightening specters of *1984* appear when descriptions of drug-therapy and aversion-therapy programs at the Vacaville, California institute are considered.[21] In some instances, drugs are used to induce a paralytic death-like state in which the inmate finds it difficult, if not impossible, to breathe. During this time, subtle suggestions are made to him that his past behavior was wrong. Programs such as these are already in progress; they must be stopped before they proliferate.

Similarly, programs of lobotomies, electric shock, and other physical invasions of the inmate's bodily integrity must be attacked now before they spread.[22]

Some cases have already begun to suggest a right to refuse treatment or to describe limits on the discretion of correctional officers to "treat" an inmate. Perhaps the most important of this line of cases is *McNeil v. Director,*[23] in which the Supreme Court held that an inmate, sentenced for a crime but sent to the Patuxent Institute for determination as to whether he was a defective delinquent, must be released after his maximum sentence unless there was a finding that he was, in fact, a defective delinquent.

In *McNeil,* the inmate simply refused to talk with any of the administrators at the institution for a period of five years, maintaining silence in the face of every attempt to elicit from him responses by which his status as a defective delinquent could be determined. Although the *McNeil* case itself arose because the inmate was being kept beyond the maximum sentence for the crime of which he was originally convicted, a recent case filed in a state court in Maryland held invalid the institution's practice of holding an inmate at Patuxent past a six-month statutory deadline.

A second case which might be used in an attempt to establish a right to refuse coercive treatment is *In re Owens,*[24] in which the court placed limitations upon the ability of a warden of a juvenile institution to treat his wards with a series of stultifying drugs, which were used primarily to keep inmates quiet rather than to help them reform. The *Owens* case was highly critical of the use of any kind of coercive drug upon juveniles. While the case might arguably be limited as applying only to juveniles, its implications go far beyond the fact situation established there.

A third case which could be used to establish the right to refuse coerced treatment is *Theriault v. Carlson*,[25] which dealt primarily with the right of a newly formed inmate religious society to hold meetings. The court specifically forbade prison chaplains from writing reports on the religious activities—or inactivities—of inmates within the institution. One of the court's primary concerns was the fact that such reports were sometimes used by parole boards to determine whether an inmate was actually ready for parole. The *Carlson* case strongly suggests that failure to participate in programs the institution deems reformative cannot be used to retaliate against an inmate or to punish him with lengthier incarceration.

If inmates have the right to refrain from participating in certain religious activities, it would seem they also have a right to refrain with impunity from participating in other "beneficial" programs. The *Carlson* case is a "freedom of religion" case which might affect the opinion's applicability, but the thrust of the case cannot be diminished in that way.

The literature to the effect that offenders should not be coerced into participating in treatment programs is almost overwhelming. Primary among the considerations is the theory that coercive treatment will not work. If it is to be beneficial at all, a program must be purely voluntary, affording the inmate the opportunity to participate in its scope and breadth, but not requiring participation. Surely, in addition to whatever constitutional arguments might be made in this regard, common sense argues that inmates forced to participate in programs are less likely to be receptive to them.[26]

Summary and Conclusion

In the past five years, courts have begun to hold that there is a constitutional right to treatment for those who are committed to mental institutions. It is but a short step from those decisions to a holding that persons committed to penal institutions on the basis of criminal acts are also entitled to have programs of rehabilitation and education available to them.

The danger of this litigation and of postulating such a right lies in the possibility that we may win too much: we may in fact impose a duty upon the institutions to treat all who come within their walls, regardless of whether they themselves want that treatment and rehabilitation. There is, moreover, the question of standards when we seek reformation and rehabilitation of a person. We must ask whether, in pursuing the goal of helping people, we may force conformity with average middle-class, middle-American ideals upon all those who come within the grasp of the law. In striving to achieve the right to rehabilitation, the attorney in correctional law must vehemently and totally deny the concept of a duty on the part of the inmate to be rehabilitated.

Footnotes

[1] Rouse v. Cameron, 373 F.2d 451 (D.C. Cir. 1966).

[2] Director of Patuxent Institution v. Daniels, 243 Md. 16, 221 A.2d 397 (1966); Nason v. Superintendent of Bridgewater State Hospital, 353 Mass. 604, 233 N.E.2d 908 (1968); People ex rel. Blunt v. Narcotic Addiction Control Comm., 58 Misc.2d 57, 295 N.Y.S.2d 276 (Spec. Term, Part J, 1968).

[3] Birnbaum, "Some Remarks on 'The Right to Treatment'," 23 Ala. L. Rev. 623 (1971); Penegar, "The Emerging 'Right to Treatment'—Elaborating the Processes of Decision in Sanctioning Systems of the Criminal Law," 44 Denver L. J., 163 (1967); Note, 77 Yale L. J. 87 (1967); Note, 53 Va. L. Rev. 1134 (1967); Note, 1969 Duke L. J. 677; Morris, "The Confusion of Confinement Syndrome," 17 Buff. L. Rev. 651 (1968); Note, 60 Geo. L. J. 225 (1971); Mercer, "Right to Treatment or Release?," 5 Clearinghouse Rev. 290, 639 (1971, 1972).

[4] 36 U. Chi. L. Rev. 742ff (1969); 57 Geo. L. J. 673 (1967).

[5] 325 F. Supp. 781 (M.D. Ala. 1971); 334 F. Supp. 1341 (1971); 344 F. Supp. 373, 387 (M.D. Ala. 1972). The case is fully discussed in Drake, "Enforcing the Right to Treatment: Wyatt v. Stickney," 10 Amer. Crim. L. Rev. 587 (1972).

[6] 344 F. Supp. 373 (M.D. Ala. 1972).

[7] Williams v. New York, 337 U.S. 241 (1949).

[8] See G. Kassebaum, D. Ward, and D. Wilner, Prison Treatment and Parole Survival, at 27 and n. 4 (1971).

[9] A number of states declare such a purpose in their constitutions or statutes. Delaware, for example, states that, "A Department of Correction is established to provide for the treatment, rehabilitation and restoration of offenders as useful, law abiding citizens within the community." For a full discussion, see Note, 50 Neb. L. Rev. 543 (1971); see also Note, 38 U. Chi. L. Rev. 647, 659 (1971).

[10] 126 F. Supp. 867 (D.D.C. 1954).

[11] See generally Pirsig, "The Constitutional Validity of Confining Disruptive Delinquents in Penal Institutions," 54 Minn. L. Rev. 101 (1969). Note, 38 U. Chi. L. Rev. 647, 659 (1971), suggests that under Sostre v. McGinnis, one test of the Eighth Amendment is practices in other states: "[A]s progressively more states begin to experiment with programs for rehabilitation, the lack of such programs could come to constitute cruel and unusual punishment."

[12] In re Maddox, 351 Mich. 358, 88 N.W.2d 470 (1958).

13 437 F.2d 722 (D.C. Cir. 1970).

14 336 F. Supp. 973 (D.D.C. 1971), noted 41 U. Cin. L. Rev. 716 (1972).

15 309 F. Supp. 362 (E.D. Ark. 1970). Not all courts, however, have been receptive to the proposition set forth in Rouse and have either avoided the issue altogether or found some bar to judicial consideration. Thus in several cases where federal prisoners have complained either about initial placement or transfers which have, according to their complaints, deprived them of meaningful rehabilitation programs, courts have pointed to 18 U.S.C. §4082, which provides that the Attorney General may designate the institution where a prisoner shall be held in custody. Lawrence v. Willingham, 373 F.2d 731 (10th Cir. 1967); Jones v. Harris, 339 F.2d 585 (8th Cir. 1964); Frost v. Ciccone, 315 F. Supp. 899 (W.D. Mo. 1970); Thogmartin v. Moseley, 313 F. Supp. 158 (D. Kan. 1969); Mercer v. United States Medical Center, 312 F. Supp. 1077 (W.D. Mo. 1970); Foote v. United States, 306 F. Supp. 627 (D. Nev. 1969); Peek v. Ciccone, 288 F. Supp. 329 (W.D. Mo. 1968). See also Morris, " 'Criminality' and the Right to Treatment," 36 U. Chi. L. Rev. 784 (1969).

16 Wayne County Jail Inmates v. Wayne County Bd. Comm'rs, 5 Clearinghouse Rev. 108 (Cir. Ct. Wayne Cty. Mich. 1971) (opinions delivered May 18, 1971 and March 24, 1972; judgment entered March 24, 1972); Jackson v. Hendrick, No. 71-2437 (Ct. C.P. Phila., Pa., April 21, 1972); Hamilton v. Schiro, 338 F. Supp. 1916 (E.D. La. 1970); Hamilton v. Love, 328 F. Supp. 1182 (E.D. Ark. 1971); Jones v. Wittenberg, 323 F. Supp. 93, 330 F. Supp. 707 (N.D. Ohio 1971).

17 Jones v. Wittenberg, 323 F. Supp. 93 (N.D. Ohio 1970).

18 President's Commission on Law Enforcement and the Administration of Justice, Task Force Report: Corrections, at 1–4 (1967).

19 Schnur, "The New Penology: Fact or Fiction?" in Vedder and Kay, Penology, at 1, 3–4 (1964). In Newman v. Alabama, 349 F. Supp. 278 (M.D. Ala. 1972), Judge Johnson held that one part-time psychiatrist for 2,400 inmates violated the Eighth Amendment. The case is undoubtedly a landmark in the entire area.

20 In the cases dealing with review of programs of treatment in mental hospitals, the courts have generally said that there must simply be a bona fide effort to provide treatment, not that the treatment must be effective either for the individual concerned or even for the group of individuals to whom the treatment is afforded. The question of evaluating programs of this type will undoubtedly raise a great deal of litigation in the immediate future and will require the expert testimony of many witnesses who either have worked in those programs and can assess their validity, or at least penologists who have some idea of what might be effective.

21 See N. Kittrie, The Right to Be Different (Johns Hopkins, 1971); Schwitzgebel, "Limitations on Coercive Treatment of Offenders," 8 Crim. L. Bull. 267 (1972); Note, "Conditioning and Other Technologies Used to 'Treat?' 'Rehabilitate?' 'Demolish?' Prisoners and Mental Patients," 45 S. Cal. L. Rev. 616 (1972).

22 See the materials cited in note 21, supra, for arguments against these programs.

23 407 U.S. 245 (1972).

24 CCH Pov. L. Rep. 5663, ¶4355.83 (III. Circuit Court, Cook County, July 9, 1971).

[25] 339 F. Supp. 375 (N.D. Ga. 1972).

[26] The intrusions which civil commitment and treatment have made upon criminal law have raised serious questions of whether the two can really be differentiated in the future. Two recent cases indirectly pose the issue. In Humphrey v. Cady, 405 U.S. 504 (1972), the Court, in strong dictum, indicated that there appeared to be little difference between different kinds of civil commitment—in that instance, commitment under a sexual-psychopath statute and normal commitment of the mentally ill—and further suggested that prior criminal activity could not possibly justify differential treatment. In Jackson v. Indiana, 406 U.S. 715 (1972), the Court held that a state could not indefinitely confine an individual found to be incompetent to stand trial simply because of an alleged (and some readings of the case might even say admitted) criminal act, and that civil procedures must be inaugurated to justify further retention of the individual. The Court's language would also lend itself to an argument that incarceration, at least in a civil sense, could only be justified if the committee were "dangerous." A similar argument in the penal area would urge that check forgers, etc., are not dangerous, and must be "treated" in less drastic ways than full incarceration.

CHAPTER 10
PAROLE

EDITORS' INTRODUCTION

Penological developments over the last several decades have led to indeterminate sentences which theoretically allow an inmate's release date to be set when he is ready to reenter society. Parole is the major means by which inmates can earn their freedom before their sentences expire. Rather than serving as a stimulus to rehabilitation, it has become perhaps the single most shocking example of unbridled and arbitrary decision-making in the whole correctional field.

PROBLEMS IN PAROLE

HERMAN SCHWARTZ *

Few areas of criminal justice have been as free from legal restraints as the parole system. Parole has been the sacred cow of the correctional system. Everyone has agreed that prisons are terrible, that local jails are unspeakable, and that sentencing is a mess, but parole has been thought to be different. Protected by an image of benevolent expertise and shrouded by low visibility, parole boards have been seen by judges, legislators and the general public as experts in human behavior whose primary goal is to help the prisoner.[1]

To close students of the prison system, however, it has been clear that, rather than being apart from it, parole is central to the operation of corrections for many reasons. First, in many states parole is the primary road to freedom, and freedom is the prisoner's primary concern. Second, most parole personnel are close to the correctional and law enforcement bureaucracies and are quite willing to allow parole to be used for the control and management purposes of both. Finally, the goals of the parole system are so broad, the operating criteria so vague, and the standards for success so hard to pin down that there is no clear and independent function that the system can be made to serve.

The revolution in correctional law which has begun to make the correctional system more accountable to the demands of fairness and decency has also touched the parole system. Social scientists, lawyers, legislators, and others have begun to look more closely at the parole system and have reached a remarkably high degree of consensus.[2] As the New York State Special Commission on Attica put it, parole "was an innovation intended as a beneficial reform to promote rehabilitation. Instead, it became an operating evil."[3]

The Commission summarized its conclusions as follows:

"Based on interviews with inmates, correction officers, and parole officers, and analysis of over 60 parole cases,

---

* Professor of Law, State University of New York at Buffalo; Temporary Chairman, Steering Committee of the National Committee for Prisoners' Rights; former Director, American Civil Liberties Union Project on Prisoners' Rights. A.B., LL.B. Harvard University.

the Commission believes that many of the criticisms of the parole system are justified. The decisions of the Parole Board are fraught with the appearance of arbitrariness. Even when parole is granted, inmates must often wait in prison for months while searching for jobs and places to live. This is done through the mail, and they are given little assistance in this regard. Once on the street, parolees are subject to numerous petty and meaningless restrictions, and are at the mercy of a parole officer who can act arbitrarily in revoking parole."[4]

Courts also have begun to move, although gingerly, toward putting restraints on what has heretofore been uncontrolled and arbitrary discretion. The various parole boards have reacted with resistance, evasion, and at times with open defiance: a reaction that promises to breed a great deal of litigation before the parole system can be made accountable to a rule of law.

For the purposes of this survey of current law and problems, parole law can be divided into three areas: parole grant and denial of parole, the conditions imposed on the parolee, and the revocation of parole.[5]

The Grant or Denial of Parole

Few decisions are so important to a convicted person as whether he will gain parole, yet few decisions are so arbitrarily made. Operating in closed hearings, with the vaguest and most general of standards, with virtually no judicial or other review, parole boards have granted and denied parole in a manner that cannot be accounted for by any rational criteria.

To date, few courts have ventured into the area except in rather limited procedural considerations. Some judges, however, have shown an impatience with the process, indicating that more intervention is likely.[6]

Among the relevant issues are:

(1) How much of a hearing, if any, is the prisoner entitled to? Can he have counsel?

(2) Can the prisoner see his file?

(3) If he is denied parole, can he insist that he be given a statement of the reasons why? If so, how specific a statement?

(4) Are there any constitutional or other limitations on the reasons for parole denial?

Procedural Due Process

Most lawyers develop a particular concern for procedural due process and feel uncomfortable when it is absent. In parole release hearings it is virtually nonexistent. The leading case is *Menechino v. Oswald,*[7] in which the Second Circuit Court of Appeals rejected a claim for counsel at parole grant hearings, over a lengthy dissent by Judge Feinberg. Although the case focused on counsel, initially Menechino had asked for other due process protections such as cross-examination and presentation of witnesses. Although he abandoned these on oral argument, the court's wide-ranging opinion seemed to reject all forms of procedural due process.

For those seeking to expand prisoners' rights, the decision is most unfortunate and was premised on empty shibboleths. The first of these was that the parole board does not have an adversarial relationship to the inmate. In response, it must be noted that neither do judges, but counsel is required when a defendant's length of confinement is determined by a judge.[8] Next the court stated that there was no existing right involved, such as liberty already obtained or welfare benefits. However, the loss of a future or hoped-for benefit would seem as important as the loss of one already obtained. It does not seem reasonable to require procedural due process for the loss of property of possibly low value [9] but not for the denial of many years of liberty. Finally the court feared that the administrative burden would be too great. The burden could not have been any less, however, in cases granting the right to counsel in felonies [10] and misdemeanors,[11] or affording full due process protections to juveniles.[12]

The thrust of the opinion is that no procedural due process at all is required for the release hearings. Does this mean that the parolee should not be allowed to see some or all of his file, even though he believes there is demonstrably false information in it? This issue is currently being litigated in several cases in the federal system.

If the opinion denied all procedural due process, the result would be that the prisoner would never be allowed to present written or oral testimony on his behalf, and that the parole board need not give him or anyone else the reasons for a denial of parole.

It is unlikely that the court intended so far-reaching a ruling. Indeed, the case may have been ill-timed strategically, since there will indeed be a heavy financial burden on the system if appointed counsel is required—and if retained counsel is allowed, it is hard to see how appointed counsel for indigents can be avoided. Introducing due process into the parole system might better have started with a different issue than counsel. On the federal level, several courts have ruled that the Administrative Procedure Act [13] applies to parole boards, and this could have a great impact upon due process in parole-grant proceedings. [14]

Reasons

One of the most embittering and irrational aspects of the parole release process is its apparent arbitrariness. The criteria for parole usually will involve some variant of whether the offender will lead a law-abiding life and whether his release will be compatible with the welfare of society, generalities so broad and unpredictable as to be meaningless. [15] It is not clear how much more specific the criteria can be, but the reasons for denial can and indeed should be most specific.

Parole boards almost never give any reasons for their decisions. [16] Prisoners may wait hours, days, or months, and then simply be told "denied" or "continued" and informed when they will see the board again, perhaps twelve or eighteen months later. The inmate, who sees others getting paroled and who sometimes has a clean disciplinary record and a job or family waiting for him, is bewildered and infuriated. Since he rarely is given any help in preparing for the parole board, he knows no more about what the board considers adequate signs of rehabilitation than before.

It is the refusal to give reasons that demonstrates how far from any meaningful rehabilitational function the parole grant process is (assuming that the board or other correctional agencies have a meaningful conception of what it is to be rehabilitated and how to recognize it in the individual case). If the parole process is supposed to help a prisoner, surely the board should be required to tell the prisoner why he didn't make parole and how he can do so. The refusal to give reasons often gives rise to prisoner cynicism about the parole system and the belief that it is controlled by graft, corrupt political deals, and sheer whimsicality.

Only one court has required that reasons be given. In *Monks v. New Jersey State Parole Board,* [17] the court held:

> "[F]airness and rightness clearly dictate the granting
> of the prisoner's request for a statement of reasons. That

course as a general matter would serve the acknowledged interests of procedural fairness and would also
serve as a suitable and significant discipline on the
Board's exercise of its wide powers. It would in nowise
curb the Board's discretion on the grant or denial of
parole nor would it impair the scope and effect of its
expertise. It is evident to us that such incidental administrative burdens as result would not be undue; the reported experiences in the jurisdictions which have
long furnished reasons have given us no grounds for
pause." [18]

Giving reasons will be of little use, however, if all the
inmate gets is a check list with one item checked off, or merely
a recitation of the statutory criteria and a note that he does not
meet them.[19] The inmate must be told what in his own background
and performance currently disqualifies him for parole under the
specific criteria relied upon by the board.

One problem, of course, is that at least some of the reasons
are the result of broad policy judgments, such as: no offender
suspected of involvement in organized crime gets parole; a war
resistor must serve certain minimums, often despite the judge's
intention that he be paroled as soon as possible; or inmates who
do not go to church should not be paroled. At present there has
been no litigation of these issues, but such policies should be
smoked out and tested.

Substantive Due Process

There has been virtually no successful litigation alleging
that parole was wrongly denied on substantive grounds. However,
in *Novak v. McCune,*[20] pressure from a lawsuit presenting a particularly appealing fact situation induced the parole board to grant
an immediate parole. This may be a useful device in many cases.
Moreover, discovery may be available in suits alleging that the
board failed to comply with statutorily mandated procedures, such
as obtaining a psychiatric report. A decision in the Fifth Circuit
has held that arbitrary action by the parole board in refusing to
consider certain pertinent data is reviewable,[21] but the case has
been set down for rehearing *en banc.*

Discovery is also useful in that it can disclose material in
the files so embarrassing to the board that it will release the

offender rather than disclose the files. A class action may be able to produce both release in individual cases and discovery of grossly irregular policies and practices.

Another basis for possible challenge would be a contention that the board has acted discriminatorily, on grounds of racial, religious, or other forms of discrimination. Obviously, the problem here is one of proof. The boards have so much discretion, their actions are so immune to meaningful review, that they very likely will be able to come up with some statutorily adequate justification.

The Conditions of Parole

When a prisoner is granted parole, his release is subjected to a wide range of vague and intrusive conditions. (The State of New York has a standard list of conditions applicable to *all* parolees in that state.[22]) Curfew provisions may be added, and additional conditions may be imposed in individual cases.[23]

The stated purpose of the conditions is to insure that the parolee does not drift into illegitimate activity. In practice they are used by the parole officer and the police to maintain control over the parolee's activities. Parole officers freely admit that no one can possibly meet all the conditions and lead a normal life. When they suspect the parolee has engaged in illegitimate activity that they cannot prove, or when they want something else from him they charge him with a violation of the conditions.

There have been a few successful challenges to arbitrary conditions, some in the closely related area of probation. For example, the Virginia Supreme Court set aside a probation condition that a juvenile attend church. Two federal courts set aside restrictions on parolees' speech-making and politically-oriented travel.[24] Most efforts to challenge the nearly universal restrictions on travel have foundered.[25]

One of the most troubling parole conditions is the forced waiver of Fourth Amendment rights against arbitrary searches and seizures, and arbitrary home visitations. Some cases, particularly in California, have said flatly that a parolee has diluted Fourth Amendment rights, on the theory that he is still in the state's custody.[26] In other situations, parolees have been forced to sign consents,[27] or consent to a surprise visit has been implied from the permission "to visit me at my residence." [28] On the whole, the exclusionary rule has been held inapplicable to parole revocation proceedings; [29] however, a few courts have indicated a willingness to allow parolees the same Fourth Amendment rights as other citizens.[30]

Revocation

Parole revocation has been the area in which courts have found it easiest to justify intervention. The most significant development is, of course, the Supreme Court's landmark decision in *Morrissey v. Brewer*,[31] which required substantial due process protections for a parolee before parole could be revoked. Even before *Morrissey,* however, the parole boards were being somewhat limited in the manner in which they could revoke parole. While the *Morrissey* majority reserved the question of whether a parolee could have counsel at parole revocation, both the New York Court of Appeals and the Second Circuit Court of Appeals had held earlier that such counsel was necessary.[32] To date only one case has required appointed counsel on an equal protection theory.[33] Although some jurisdictions have held that even a hearing could be dispensed with,[34] most jurisdictions have required a hearing.

Revocation is, of course, easier for the courts to treat than other aspects of parole. Here there is deprivation of liberty and, often, factual questions are presented as opposed to those calling for expert judgment. Interestingly, virtually no decisions have dealt with the validity of the substantive basis for a revocation except for one cryptic but potentially far-reaching per curiam decision by the Supreme Court. In *Arciniega v. Freeman,*[35] the Court interpreted a federal parole condition of not consorting with ex-offenders as excluding a situation where the two ex-offenders simply happened to work at the same place. Although the decision can be viewed as merely interpretive of a federal regulation, the Court clearly adopted this narrow interpretation because it found the broader one objectionable.

Morrissey is, of course, of enormous significance. The due process protections that it requires go far beyond those afforded by any parole system in the United States. Compliance with *Morrissey* will require a major revision of parole procedures, and will turn what were formerly pro forma interviews, lasting no more than a few minutes, into full-blown adversary confrontations. One result may be to reduce the number of revocations because there simply will not be enough time or manpower to process many revocations if *Morrissey* is to be fully complied with.

The decision sets out a two-stage revocation procedure, which, except for counsel, will contain almost all of the due process protections normally involved in administrative proceedings. Seven members of the Court expressly reserved judgment on the issue of counsel for another day. Justices Brennan and Douglas would have required counsel as part of the *Morrissey* decision.[36]

In the first stage, which is similar to a preliminary hearing in a felony prosecution, the parolee is entitled to a tribunal excluding the parole officer who charged him with a violation, although it can include another parole officer. The parolee is also entitled to a finding of probable cause and prompt determination of the matter. The parolee should receive notice that the hearing will take place, that probable cause to determine whether a violation has been committed will be at issue, and a description of the particular violation alleged.

> ". . . At the hearing the parolee may appear and speak in his own behalf; he may bring letters, documents, or individuals who can give relevant information to the hearing officer. On request of the parolee, persons who have given adverse information on which parole revocation is to be based are to be made available for questioning in his presence. However, if the hearing officer determines that the informant would be subject to risk of harm if his identity were disclosed, he need not be subjected to confrontation and cross-examination. The hearing officer shall have the duty of making a summary, or digest of what transpires at the hearing in terms of the responses of the parolee and the substance of the documents or evidence given in support of parole revocation and of the parolee's position. Based on the information before him, the officer should determine whether there is probable cause to hold the parolee for the final decision of the parole board on revocation. Such a determination would be sufficient to warrant the parolee's continued detention and return to the state correctional institution pending the final decision. As in *Goldberg,* 'the decision-maker should state the reasons for his determination and indicate the evidence he relied on . . .' but it should be remembered that this is not a final de-

termination calling for 'formal findings of fact or conclusions of law.' " [37]

The proceeding must take place promptly and near the place of the alleged violation.

The revocation hearing itself must go beyond probable cause. It must be within a reasonable time after the parolee is taken into custody. "Two months . . . would not appear to be unreasonable." The Court listed the following minimum elements:

(a) written notice of the claimed violations of parole;
(b) disclosure to the parolee of evidence against him;
(c) opportunity to be heard in person and to present witnesses and documentary evidence;
(d) the right to confront and cross-examine adverse witnesses (unless the hearing officer specifically finds good cause for not allowing confrontation);
(e) a "neutral and detached" hearing body such as a traditional parole board, members of which need not be judicial officers or lawyers;
(f) a written statement by the fact-finders as to the evidence relied on and reasons for revoking parole.

Many questions remain open. The most obvious is the question of counsel, which has been answered in New York and other Second Circuit jurisdictions at least insofar as retained counsel is concerned.[38] That issue will soon come before the Supreme Court.

Other questions that have already occurred are:

1. Is a parolee entitled to bail pending the revocation? Justice Douglas thought a parolee should be entitled to bail, but the majority stated that a determination of probable cause "would be sufficient to warrant the parolee's continued detention and return to the state correctional institution pending the final outcome." Was this sentence meant to foreclose the bail issue?

2. How will the Board obtain the witnesses? Some, and perhaps most boards, may not have subpoena power or money for witness fees.

3. Who has the burden of proof at the hearing? Will hearsay be acceptable? The Court's language would seem to exclude it,

except in the specific instances mentioned by it. New York parole boards have relied heavily on hearsay, since, in many cases, the only evidence has been either the charge sheet or the parole officer's own testimony.

4. What are the implications for in-prison disciplinary proceedings? The Court relied heavily on *Goldberg v. Kelly,*[39] applying that decision to yet another administrative proceeding, but it also noted that summary treatment may be necessary "with respect to controlling a large group of potentially disruptive inmates in actual custody." [40] Was an exception intended here? Or did the Court only tentatively raise a possibility left for another day?

Remedies

There remains also the question of remedy: suppose the parole board does not comply with either the preliminary hearing or revocation proceedings. What relief is available?

Courts have given two answers to the failure to comply with the preliminary hearing requirements in jurisdictions where counsel is required, such as New York. Some courts have granted writs of habeas corpus and immediately released the parolee pending a new preliminary hearing.[41] Other courts have given the Board a few days in which to hold a hearing that meets *Morrissey* and *Menechino* standards. If the Board refuses to comply, then it would seem that no revocation could be imposed, since *Morrissey* implies that a valid preliminary hearing is a constitutional prerequisite to revocation. If the revocation hearing is faulty, it would seem that the same relief is appropriate.

Conclusion

The rule of law is gradually entering the parole area. Thus far parole boards have resisted fiercely, construing court decisions so narrowly as almost to ignore them. Persistent litigation and pressure will be necessary if the promise of *Morrissey* and other cases is not to be lost by the parole boards' massive resistance.

Footnotes

[1] For the historical development of parole, see Moran, "The Origins of Parole," N.P.P.A. J. at 71–98 (1954).

2 For a comprehensive collection of commentary and source materials on parole, see Corrections—Federal and State Parole Systems, Part VII-A,B, Hearings on H.R. 13118, Identical and Related Bills before Subcommittee No. 3 of the Committee on the Judiciary, 92d Cong., 2d Sess. (Feb.–May 1972).

3 Report of New York State Special Commission on Attica, at 93.

4 Id. at 95.

5 A recent comprehensive analysis of the legal aspects of parole is found in Comment, "The Parole System," 120 U. Pa. L. Rev. 284 (1971).

6 Cf. Menechino v. Oswald, 430 F.2d 403 (2d Cir. 1970), with Monks v. New Jersey State Parole Board, 58 N.J. 238, 277 A.2d 220 (1971).

7 Note 6, supra.

8 Mempa v. Rhay, 389 U.S. 128 (1967).

9 Fuentes v. Shevin, 407 U.S. 67 (1972).

10 Gideon v. Wainwright, 372 U.S. 335 (1963).

11 Argersinger v. Hamlin, 407 U.S. 25 (1972).

12 In re Gault, 387 U.S. 1 (1967).

13 5 U.S.C. §702ff.

14 See Sobell v. Reed, 327 F. Supp. 1294 (S.D.N.Y. 1971); Novak v. McCune, — F. Supp. — Civ. 421-72-R, E.D. Va. July 1972. See generally K. Davis, Discretionary Justice, at 103 (1970).

15 The federal criteria are:

> "§4203. Application and release; terms and conditions
> "(a) If it appears to the Board of Parole from a report by the proper institutional officers or upon application by a prisoner eligible for release on parole, that there is a reasonable probability that such prisoner will live and remain at liberty without violating the laws, and if in the opinion of the Board such release is not incompatible with the welfare of society, the Board may in its discretion authorize the release of such prisoner on parole." 18 U.S.C. §4203

The New York criteria are:

> "Discretionary release on parole shall not be granted merely as a reward for good conduct or efficient performance of duties assigned in prison, but only if the board of parole is of opinion that there is reasonable probability that, if such prisoner is released, he will live and remain at liberty without violating the law, and that his release is not incompatible with the welfare of society." N.Y. Corr. Law §213.

16 A recent survey found that only eleven out of fifty-one jurisdictions gave reasons. See O'Leary and Noffield, "Parole Decision-Making Characteristics: Report of a National Survey," 8 Or. L. Bull. 651, 663 (1972).

17 Note 6, supra.

18 Id., 277 A.2d at 199.

19 See the proposed federal practice in Hearings, note 2, supra, at 388.

20 Novak v. McCune, note 14, supra.

21 Scarpa v. U.S. Board of Parole, 453 F.2d 891 (5th Cir. 1971).

22 7 N.Y.C.R.R. §1.15 reads:

"Contents of parole and mandatory release agreement. [Additional statutory authority: Correction Law, §215] (a) Upon his release, a paroled person must proceed directly to the place to which he has been paroled and within a period of 24 hours must make his arrival report. At the time he reports to the proper area office or to the proper parole officer he must have in his possession the money he received at the time of his release, except the funds expended for necessary travel, food and shelter.

"(b) He must not leave the State of New York or the community to which he has been paroled without the written permission of his parole officer.

"(c) He must carry out the instructions of his parole officer, report as directed and permit the parole officer to visit him at his residence and place of employment. The parolee must not change his residence or employment without first securing the permission of his parole officer. The parolee understands that he is still in the custody of the superintendent or warden of the institution from which he is being paroled. He hereby consents to any search of his person, his residence, or of any property or premises under his control which the Board of Parole or any of its representatives may see fit to make at any time in their discretion.

"(d) He must make every effort to maintain gainful employment and, if for any reason he loses his position, he must immediately report this fact to his parole officer and he must cooperate with his parole officer in the officer's efforts to obtain employment for him. He must conduct himself as a good citizen, must not associate with evil companions or individuals having criminal records. He must abstain from wrong-doing, lead an honest, upright and industrious life, support his dependents, if any, and assume toward them all legal and moral obligations. His behavior must not be a menace to the safety of his family or to any individual or group of individuals. He must not use any drugs, the posesssion of which is illegal.

"(e) He must avoid the excessive use of intoxicating beverages and abstain completely if so directed by his parole officer.

"(f) He must not live as man and wife with anyone to whom he is not legally married, and will consult with his parole officer before he applies for a license to marry.

"(g) Immediately after his release on parole he must surrender any motor vehicle license which he had in his possession at the time of his conviction and sentence. While on parole he must not apply for a motor vehicle license, or own or operate a motor vehicle without permission of his parole officer. If, while on parole, a parolee purchases a motor vehicle without a valid license, it will be considered a violation of parole. A valid license will be deemed to be one issued subsequent to release on parole after permission has been obtained.

"(h) If a parolee carries firearms of any nature, it will be considered a violation of parole.

"(i) A paroled person must not carry from the institution from which he is released, or send to any penal institution, whether in the State of New York or elsewhere, any written or verbal message, or any object or property of any kind whatsoever, unless specific permission to do so has been obtained from the warden, superintendent, or other duly authorized officers of both the institution from which he is released and the institution to which the message, object, or property is to be delivered, and he must not correspond with inmates of correctional institutions without the written permission of his parole officer.

"(j) He must reply promptly to any communication from a member of the Board of Parole, a parole officer, or other authorized representative of the Board of Parole.

"(k) Any reports, either verbal or written, made or submitted by a parolee to a parole officer, which are subsequently found to be false, will be rejected by the Board of Parole, and will not be used in crediting parole time served and may be considered a violation of parole.

"(l) A parolee must report to his parole officer each and every time he is arrested or questioned by officers of any law enforcement agency and must state to the parole officer all the facts and circumstances which brought about the arrest or questioning.

"(m) As the right of franchise is revoked when a person is sentenced to a State prison, a person released on parole from an indeterminate or definite sentence to State prison, or from an indeterminate sentence with a commitment to the Elmira Reception Center, must not register as a voter and must not vote in any primary, special or general election.

"(n) No parolee can accept employment in any capacity where liquor is made or sold without the written approval of the State Liquor Authority permitting such employment.

"(o) Before being released on parole a parolee must agree in writing that if he is arrested in another State while on parole, he will waive extradition and will not resist being returned by the Board of Parole to the State of New York.

"(p) In addition to these general rules of parole which all prisoners released on parole must adhere to, the Board of Parole has the authority in any case to impose additional or special conditions of parole."

23 A current survey of parole conditions appears in Hearings, note 2, supra, at 1363–1365.

24 Sobell v. Reed, 327 F. Supp. 1294 (S.D.N.Y. 1971); Hyland v. Procunier, 311 F. Supp. 749 (N.D. Cal. 1970).

25 See Comment, "The Parole System," 120 U. Pa. L. Rev. 284, 313–320 (1971).

26 People v. Hernandes, 229 Cal. App.2d 143, 40 Cal. Rptr. 100 (1964), cert. denied 381 U.S. 953 (1965).

27 People v. Sickler, 61 Misc.2d 571, 573, 306 N.Y.S.2d 168, 170–171 (Dutchess Co. Ct. 1969).

28 United States ex rel. Randazzo v. Follette, 282 F. Supp. 10, 15 (S.D.N.Y. 1968), aff'd other grounds 418 F.2d 1319 (2d Cir. 1969), cert. denied 402 U.S. 984 (1971).

29 United States ex rel. Sperling v. Fitzpatrick, 426 F.2d 1161 (2d Cir. 1970).

30 Brown v. Kearney, 355 F.2d 199, 200 (5th Cir. 1966) (dictum); United States v. Lewis, 274 F. Supp. 184, 190 (S.D.N.Y. 1967). For a detailed analysis of the problem, see Comment, "The Parole System," 120 U. Pa. L. Rev. 284, 326–339 (1971).

31 408 U.S. 471 (1972).

32 See Menechino v. Warden, 27 N.Y.2d 376, 267 N.E.2d 238, 318 N.Y.S.2d 449 (1971); United States ex rel. Bey v. Board of Parole, 443 F.2d 1079 (2d Cir. 1971).

33 Ernest v. Willingham, 406 F.2d 685 (10th Cir. 1971).

34 Rose v. Haskins, 388 F.2d 91 (6th Cir. 1968), cert. denied 392 U.S. 946 (1968).

35 404 U.S. 4 (1971).

36 There is a curious feature to Justice Douglas' partial dissent. In style and structure it reads very much like a majority opinion and indeed concludes with the words "reversed and remanded." The last paragraph is written in the first person plural, as if it were being written for the Court, even though it is being written for only one Justice. The obvious inference is that Justice Douglas was originally supposed to write this opinion on behalf of the Court, but that he somehow lost his majority and decided not to rewrite his opinion. The ways in which he differs from his brethren will be discussed in the text.

37 Morrissey v. Brewer, note 31, supra, 408 U.S. at 487, citing Goldberg v. Kelly, note 39, infra, 397 U.S. at 271.

38 See Menechino v. Warden, note 32, supra; United States ex rel. Bey v. Board of Parole, note 32, supra.

39 397 U.S. 254 (1970).

40 408 U.S. 471, 483 (1972).

41 People ex rel. Angell v. Lynch, 71 Misc.2d 921, 337 N.Y.S.2d 556 (Sup. Ct. Westchester Co. 1972).

CHAPTER 11
CIVIL DISABILITIES

EDITORS' INTRODUCTION

The folly of prisons as breeding places of crime is surpassed only by the folly society perpetrates against itself when it imposes civil disabilities that make it almost impossible for ex-convicts to do anything but return to crime. The absurdity of these laws is described in this article, and the legal techniques for attempting to dismantle them are set forth in detail.

ATTACKING BARRIERS TO EMPLOYMENT: THE FORMER OFFENDER'S DILEMMA

JULIAN TEPPER *
HOWARD L. FEINSTEIN **

The Magnitude of the Problem

Of the many government-imposed deprivations suffered by the convicted criminal offender in the United States, the most far-reaching and personally damaging "civil disability"[1] is the continuing barrier to employment. While crime statistics are notoriously contradictory and elusive,[2] available studies estimate the number of persons with some criminal record to be from twenty million [3] to over fifty million.[4] The President's Task Force Report on Corrections points to the employment barriers faced by "untold millions" with criminal records.[5] The scope of the problem is even greater among particular groups—an estimated fifty to ninety per cent of males in poverty areas have criminal records.[6]

Employment barriers facing ex-offenders are particularly devastating because they are already likely to be in a class of relatively low employability.

> "They are frequently poor, uneducated, and members of a minority group. They may have personal disabilities—behavior disorders, mental retardation, poor physical health, overwhelming family problems. And they have in any case the stigma of a criminal record to overcome." [7]

* Director, National Law Office, National Legal Aid and Defender Association, Washington, D.C.; Lecturer (criminology), American University; A.B. University of Maryland; LL.B. Columbia University Law School; Dip. Crim. Cambridge University.

** Staff Attorney, National Law Office, National Legal Aid and Defender Association, Washington, D.C.; A.B. University of California; J.D. National Law Center, George Washington University.

The unemployment rate for ex-prisoners is three to four times higher than the national average.[8] As the President's Task Force on Corrections stated, a criminal record is a state-imposed disability that haunts the former offender for life.[9]

In surveying the increasing percentage of people employed in government jobs and the rapid growth in the number of occupations subject to state licensing, severe constitutional and social inequities become apparent. The need for change has been recognized by former Attorney General Mitchell:

"Finally, I propose for your consideration a more general problem—the need to elevate public attitudes toward the releasee. Studies have shown an appalling resistance to hiring ex-offenders, even by many governmental agencies at different levels, thus frustrating other efforts at correction. Some state laws prohibit the hiring of ex-offenders by government agencies, however well adjusted or corrected they may be. *When the releasee is thus denied the means of making an honest living, every sentence becomes a life sentence.*" (Emphasis supplied.) [10]

Nature and Scope of Disabilities

Because of the growing pervasiveness of government-imposed disabilities, it is generally agreed that "at present . . . an ex-convict probably stands a better chance of gaining entrance to private employment than to either public employment or licensed occupations." [11] The increase in both government employment and licensed occupations has spurred studies showing these barriers to be the greatest economic hurdle for the ex-offender.[12]

In 1970, state and local governments alone employed over 9.6 million persons, an increase of 3.6 million over the previous decade, and their projected employment for 1980 is approximately 13.5 million.[13] In over half the states, most government employment is not open to persons with criminal convictions; [14] the other states, with one exception,[15] use information regarding an applicant's criminal record in hiring decisions. "Many use this data to rule out any further consideration of applicants." [16] Until 1966, New York City barred ex-offenders from most city jobs. The decision is now discretionary, but information on criminal records is still sought.[17] The Federal Civil Service no longer flatly prohibits employment of ex-offenders but asks for criminal record information on job applications [18] and generally requires a two-year postsentence waiting period for felons and one year for misdemeanants.[19]

The great majority of statutes and regulations governing public employment do not refer to the nature of the offense committed. An application may be denied for any felony, or a crime involving "moral turpitude" or "infamous conduct." [20] The vague, often unrelated standards used by government civil service agencies are usually in effect a final barrier; the courts have been reluctant to interfere.

The factor most responsible for the increased concern over employment disabilities has been the rapid growth of private occupations subject to government licensing. Most states still have laws prohibiting the practice of certain occupations unless licensed.[21] Occupations for which licenses may be denied for criminal convictions include architect,[22] barber,[23] engineer,[24] realtor,[25] cosmetologist,[26] and dry-cleaning and laundry proprietor.[27]

The rationale justifying licensing professions such as law and medicine, to the extent they are valid, hardly applies to the many new fields which now require licensing:

"The extension of occupational licensing, with its built-in guild-like propensities, undoubtedly has diminished the traditional freedom to enter one's chosen calling—an erosion, some argue, without offsetting compensation to the public welfare. . . . There is little disagreement with the proposition that legislative licensing sanctions are justified only if they relate directly to the promotion of the public health, safety, and morals." [28]

The inequities and lack of standards which characterize public employment opportunities for previous offenders are also found in licensed occupations. State and federal courts have generally deferred to the decisions of licensing boards:

"An applicant excluded from licensed status on the basis of his criminal record must depend upon the courts for relief. In many instances, judicial review of the agency determination may be of limited scope. In the absence of a showing of arbitrary or capricious action, it is unlikely that a licensing authority's exclusion of a convicted criminal will be disturbed by the reviewing court." [29]

Most licensing boards are under no requirement to record evidence presented at hearings, hold open sessions, or adhere even to basic rules of evidence; with a generally narrow scope of judicial review, a hasty, one-sided hearing for an applicant with a criminal record is often his only, and futile, chance for employment in a particular occupation.

Licensing boards are also given broad discretion through vague, all-encompassing statutory language. Licensing provisions generally do not limit the use of a prior criminal record to situations where the offense bears a relationship to the applicant's ability to perform the job sought:

"A few statutes bar persons convicted of enumerated crimes. These provisions may limit exclusion to crimes that indicate unfitness for a particular occupation. The offense of receiving stolen property, for example, may prevent licensing as a junk dealer. . . . As a general rule, however, specificity is lacking in licensing legislation." [30]

Moreover, it is extremely difficult to conceive of criminal offenses which at all relate to a person's ability or fitness to perform cosmetology,[31] structural pest control,[32] or landscape architecture.[33] Statutes which do restrict consideration of criminal records to directly related grounds [34] not only are fairer, but also can be claimed to at least address the criterion of fitness, the stated rationale behind otherwise neutral licensing strictures.

The rapid and indiscriminate expansion of the scope of licensing provisions has brought forth the caveat that job training, in many fields, may prove of no value to prisoners:

"Let us not train women for jobs that they are barred from holding because of a prison record. Granted, many restrictive laws need changing but, in the meantime, it is inexcusable to give a woman a course in cosmetology if a state law where she will be seeking a job prohibits a license being issued to her." [35]

This "solution," however, merges with and is supportive of the problem. To some extent it would dilute ongoing efforts to break down existing barriers.

Yet another obstacle is bonding: employers in businesses of substantial size, including government and licensed occupations, secure fidelity bonding for their employees. The policies in most cases exclude persons with criminal records and require the employee and employer to obtain special exceptions. Often, the employer will not make the extra effort; some employers use the general rule as an excuse not to hire.[36]

Fortunately, programs aimed at bonding convicted persons have proven highly successful. Bonabond, the Washington, D.C. program initiated by Aetna Life and Casualty, funded by H.E.W. and managed by former offenders, was 100 per cent successful in its first year; nearly 150 former prison inmates were hired, and all were claim-free.[37] A companion program in Denver was similarly successful. According to the President's Task Force on Corrections:

"Efforts of this type need extensive expansion and support, and individual employers and insurers must be encouraged to eliminate flat restrictions on bonding for offenders." [38]

Persons seeking employment in private, unlicensed jobs may also be affected by civil disability statutes and regulations. A federal statute prohibits persons convicted of offenses involving "dishonesty or breach of trust" from working for a bank insured by the Federal Deposit Insurance Corporation.[39] Defense Department regulations bar many former offenders from government contract work through security clearance restrictions,[40] and the Landrum-Griffin Act prohibits felons from serving as officers or directors of labor unions.[41]

The diverse and wide-ranging nature of state-imposed barriers to employment dictates the need for a wide-scale attack:

". . . today the federal and state governments directly or indirectly control a great proportion of the nation's employment; if one is unable to hold public employment, his chances of personal economic success are significantly limited. Not only is he excluded from a substantial portion of the available jobs, ranging from postman to nuclear scientist, but his bargaining power with other employers is proportionately decreased." [42]

Counterproductivity of Disabilities

The irrationality of widespread, state-imposed barriers to employment becomes most evident when viewed in the context of the entire criminal justice and corrections system. Current restrictive policies belie the basic assumptions and goals of the criminal justice system. Empirical studies have uniformly demonstrated that steady employment is directly related to a low recidivism rate.[43] In surveying juvenile delinquency, the President's Commission on Law Enforcement and the Administration of Justice stressed: "To become a fully functional adult male, one prerequisite is essential: a job." [44] Yet,

"A recent study of federal releasees shows that, during the first month after release, only about 1 out of every 4 releasees was employed at least 80 per cent of the time, and 3 out of 10 were unable to secure jobs. After 3 months, only about 4 out of 10 had worked at least 80 per cent of the time, and nearly 2 out of 10 still had not been able to find work of any kind." [45]

Failure to obtain employment has been a major contributing factor to the increase in crime, directly contradicting the stated goal of crime prevention and perpetuating a vicious cycle:

"The position is also self-sustaining: each refusal to hire an ex-criminal contributes to a massive barrier to employment and thus encourages recidivism, which in turn justifies the next refusal to hire." [46]

The reduction of recidivism and crime is the primary purpose of North Carolina's "Jobs for Ex-Offenders Program" funded by the Justice Department.[47] Programs such as these are generally aimed at encouraging private employers to hire persons with criminal records; yet there has been a scarcity of similar government efforts aimed at breaking down state-imposed barriers:

"It is anomalous that men employed by the federal and state governments who devote a major portion of their time to persuading private employers to hire ex-prisoners are themselves extremely reluctant to hire men who have been in prison. Although government agencies frequently have taken the leadership in the employment of other types of handicapped persons, they lag behind private industry in the employment of men who have a criminal record." [48]

Unless their own barriers are removed, government efforts aimed at private employers will continue to appear hypocritical.

Barriers are also economically anomalous. The per capita cost of imprisonment is the most expensive part of the criminal justice system, but recidivism among unemployed releasees promises continuation of high costs.

"This is especially surprising from the standpoint of the government's economic interest, since any rehabilitation of an ex-prisoner through employment saves the government the cost of apprehension, trial, and reimprisonment, in addition to contributing to the ex-prisoner's character and to the protection of the public." [49]

Perhaps the clearest contradiction lies in the area of "rehabilitation." While "corrections" has been rightly criticized for its inadequate job training, the potential value of prison programs is limited by the employment restrictions. This situation is well known to inmates and, to some extent, destroys whatever incentive can be mustered for program participation.[50] It has been stated that nothing would do more toward achieving the correctional ideal of rehabilitation than the assurance of a decent chance for employment:

". . . barring them [offenders] from legitimate opportunities such as employment are inconsistent with the correctional goal of rehabilitation, which emphasizes the need to instill respect for and willingness to cooperate with society and to help the offender assume the role of a normal citizen.[51]

. . . .

". . . A general overhaul of all state and local licensing and employment regulations to eliminate such irrational barriers . . . would do much to help in the reintegration of offenders as useful citizens." [52]

A decrease in the number of jobs barred to previous offenders might thus prove instrumental in expanding the current meager effectiveness of prison employment and training. One step in this direction is a 1967 California statute prohibiting licensing agencies, on civil disability grounds, from rejecting former prisoners who received training in the occupation in question while in prison. However, even here the agency must find that the applicant is "a fit person to be licensed." [53] More recently, commissions recommending sweeping reforms in the state correctional systems of Ohio,[54] Wisconsin,[55] and Michigan [56] have stressed the importance of abolishing employment barriers.

Employment disabilities also frustrate the parole system:

"A traditional condition of parole is that the prisoner must have a bona fide job arranged before he is released from the prison. . . . In practice, usually it is difficult for men still in prison to procure promises of satisfactory employment upon expectation of release. As we have seen, inmates generally have little sustained work experience in the free community and few skills. They are predominantly from poor families and from broken homes, so that they are limited in the extent to which relatives can help to arrange jobs for them. Consequently some men granted parole remain in prison long after their parole date, waiting to secure a job." [57]

The anomaly is further substantiated by the record of success in prerelease-work programs. Over one half of the states and the federal prison system now have work-release programs.[58] During 1967, of 1,835 federal releasees who had participated in work-release programs, only 7.6 per cent were "failures," and only 2 per cent committed new felonies.[59] Community-based programs, particularly halfway houses, have also had some measure of success.[60] However, success in these prerelease programs, although evidence of job performance ability, does not overcome the very real barriers to employment still confronting the individual.

The Constitutional Challenge

Disabilities, now acknowledged to be generally dysfunctional, are being challenged on constitutional grounds. Cumulative case law, commentary, and developments in closely related areas are revealing their vulnerability to attacks based on the Equal Protection and Due Process Clauses of the Fourteenth Amendment.

It is the government-sanctioned restriction that is vulnerable on constitutional grounds, because of the "state action" requirement of the Fourteenth Amendment.[61] Jurisdictional allegations have generally been held satisfied by citation of the federal statutes commonly employed in actions claiming denial of constitutionally guaranteed rights.[62] The major obstacle in such suits has been in showing that state-sanctioned employment civil disabilities constitute substantive Fourteenth Amendment violations.

Right-Privilege Distinction

Traditionally, the foremost substantive obstacle to equal protection and due process attacks has been the view that government-related employment is not a right but a privilege and therefore is not subject to the shifting of the Fourteenth Amendment burden to the state, which takes place when "fundamental rights" are at stake. This rationale can be directly challenged on the ground that the severe economic consequences of employment disabilities should be sufficient to place these cases in the "fundamental rights" class:

> "It is difficult to articulate a general formula to distinguish interests regarded as 'fundamental' from other interests for purposes of the equal protection clause. The Court seems to have treated the cases on an ad hoc basis, occasionally pointing out reasons for regarding particular interests as important, but not formulating a comprehensive theory. However, it may be that a common thread can be found in the severity of the detriment imposed on a complaining party in 'fundamental interest' cases." [63]

However, the judicial trend has been to go beyond the right-privilege dichotomy, focusing instead on the reasonableness of individual decisions in determining whether government barriers to employment are permissible. This approach, analyzed by

Professor Van Alstyne in *The Demise of the Right-Privilege Distinction in Constitutional Law,*[63a] is particularly applicable to a deprivation grounded in arbitrary procedures and vague standards:

> "Even a privilege, benefit, opportunity, or public advantage may not be granted to some but withheld from others where the basis of classification and difference in treatment is arbitrary. . . . It may well be that no one has a right to secure or to maintain public employment. In determining whom to admit or whom to continue in public employment, however, government may not classify individuals as eligible or ineligible where the basis of classification is 'arbitrary or discriminatory.' A regulation which restricts the continuing eligibility of employees to the class willing to conform to an unreasonable rule of conduct ipso facto establishes an arbitrary classification. Such a regulation denies equal protection and is therefore unconstitutional." [64]

This standard of reasonableness has replaced that of right-privilege as the generally utilized judicial determinant:

> "When the nature of government interference with the private liberty of the individual has not been susceptible of categorization as an infringement of a well-defined 'right'—such as freedom of speech, freedom of religion, or freedom of association—the courts have been reluctant to interfere with governmental action. . . . Nevertheless, the view that a 'right' must be infringed before a remedy can be fashioned has been steadily eroded; the focus of inquiry has shifted from identification of individual rights to an examination of the reasonableness of governmental action." [65]

This approach was taken as early as 1952 by the Supreme Court in *Wieman v. Updegraff,*[66] which held unconstitutional an Oklahoma statute requiring loyalty oaths for state college employees:

> "We need not pause to consider whether an abstract right to public employment exists. It is sufficient to say that constitutional protection does extend to the public servant whose exclusion pursuant to statute is patently arbitrary or discriminatory." [67]

The Supreme Court again attacked the right-privilege distinction in *Schware v. Board of Bar Examiners of New Mexico*,[68] in an opinion reversing, on due process and equal protection grounds, New Mexico's refusal to admit Schware to law practice due, inter alia, to his arrest record. Justice Black specifically rejected the right-privilege distinction:

"A state cannot exclude a person from the practice of law or from any other occupation in a manner or for reasons that contravene the Due Process or Equal Protection Clause of the Fourteenth Amendment.[69]

. . . .

"We need not enter into a discussion whether the practice of law is a 'right' or a 'privilege.' Regardless of how the state's grant of permission to engage in this occupation is characterized, it is sufficient to say that a person cannot be prevented from practicing except for valid reasons. Certainly the practice of law is not a matter of the state's grace." [70]

Reasonableness

Once beyond "privilege" and onto "reasonableness," [71] the focus turns to the vital question of determining what comprises an unreasonable, and therefore constitutionally impermissible, denial of employment. In cases in closely-related employment fields, a pattern emerges which continues into the area of civil disabilities. The basic criterion for reasonableness is held to be whether the grounds for denial of employment bear a direct relationship to the applicant's ability to perform the job. Even cases decided on a somewhat different rationale generally cite this direct relationship test as a constitutional yardstick for review.

In *Griggs v. Duke Power Company*,[72] a unanimous Supreme Court held that Title VII of the Civil Rights Act of 1964 [73] prohibits employers from using standardized intelligence tests and a high-school education as employment determinants when the result is a substantially higher rate of disqualification of Black applicants. Chief Justice Burger found that these requirements were not significantly related to successful job performance, and that in enacting Title VII, "Congress has placed on the employer the burden of showing that any given requirement must have a manifest relationship to the employment in question." [74]

In another Title VII case, *Gregory v. Litton Systems, Inc.,*[75] an employer was restrained from using arrest records in hiring decisions, on the ground that the effect would be to discriminate against Black applicants. Central to the decision (recently affirmed by the Ninth Circuit) was the finding that arrest records bore no relationship to job performance:

> "There is no evidence to support a claim that persons who have suffered no criminal convictions but have been arrested on a number of occasions can be expected, when employed, to perform less efficiently or less honestly than other employees. In fact, the evidence in the case was overwhelmingly to the contrary. Thus information concerning a prospective employee's record of arrests without convictions, is irrelevant to his suitability or qualification for employment." [76]

In distinguishing arrests from conviction, the court specifically stated that it meant to express no opinion regarding the latter.[77] However, the court's use of the direct relationship test, as well as its reliance on empirical evidence regarding job performance by the class of applicants, is directly applicable to the instant problem.[78]

Similarly, in *Otsuka v. Hite,*[79] the California Supreme Court held that Article 2, Section 1 of the California Constitution, prohibiting persons convicted of "any infamous crime" from voting, could not apply to conscientious objectors who had pleaded guilty twenty years earlier to selective service violations on the ground that ". . . no reasonable relation is apparent between this result and the purpose of protecting the integrity of the elective process." [80] In *Schware,*[80a] Justice Black attacked the state's "good moral character" requirement (a typically vague standard used to bypass a job performance fitness test), noting, "[A]ny qualifications must have a rational connection with the applicant's fitness or capacity to practice law. . . . There is no evidence in the record which rationally justifies a finding that Schware was morally unfit to practice law." [81]

This direct relationship test has been urged by the President's Task Force Report on Corrections:

> "It is relevant to the offense they have committed to revoke the license of a lawyer convicted of embezzling the

funds of clients or a teamster convicted of vehicular homicide. But it is hard to see why, on the other hand, a man convicted of larceny should not be permitted to cut hair or run a restaurant." [82]

The direct relationship test satisfies both the due process requirement that a state restriction bear a rational connection to a valid state purpose and the equal protection proscription against impermissible governmental classifications. Although upholding the denial of a position as a policeman to a convicted felon in *Upshaw v. McNamara*,[83] the First Circuit pointed to law enforcement as a particularly sensitive area involving public trust and stated that its ruling in this case used a strict standard due to the special nature of the employment.

The Supreme Court also looked to the "special nature" aspect in *DeVeau v. Braisted* [84] in upholding Section 8 of the New York Waterfront Commission Act of 1953, an interstate compact between New York and New Jersey. The section, which prohibits any person from collecting or receiving dues for any New York waterfront union which has as an officer a convicted felon, was drawn to combat organized crime and corruption on the docks:

"New York was not guessing or indulging in airy assumptions that convicted felons constituted a deleterious influence on the waterfront. It was acting in impressive if mortifying evidence that the presence on the waterfront of ex-convicts was an important contributing factor to the corrupt waterfront situation." [85]

While one may disagree with the decision for its general approach to "ex-convicts," the case is obviously helpful in arguing for a limitation on disabling statutes.

Other Supreme Court decisions which sustain specific disability provisions are not overwhelmingly harmful to advocates for former offenders. For the most part they deal with the licensing of doctors and lawyers, occupations which not only involve the highest degree of public trust but which have been historically subject to strict professional and state regulation. They are in no way comparable to the numerous jobs that involve little or no public trust and have been licensed for only a short period. *Hawker v. New York*,[86] an 1898 Supreme Court case often cited as supporting the general policy of employment disabilities, not only involved a doctor but also a prior conviction for abortion, then an offense which bore a direct (negative) relationship to the applicant's profession.[87]

In *Barsky v. Board of Regents*,[88] the Supreme Court upheld a doctor's suspension for the misdemeanor of failing to provide papers to the United States House Committee on Un-American Activities. Dissenting, Justice Frankfurter recognized the special position of the professions with respect to occupational regulation, but noted that even for a physician a direct relationship test should have governed:

> "It is one thing thus to recognize the freedom which the Constitution wisely leaves to the States in regulating the professions. It is quite another thing, however, to sanction a State's deprivation or partial destruction of a man's professional life on grounds having no possible relation to fitness, intellectual or moral, to pursue his profession."[89]

Direct Relationship Test

One of the most telling arguments in favor of a direct relationship test is that the current vague and overbroad restrictions are based on the premise that former offenders will generally prove unreliable as employees, a conclusion unsubstantiated by evidence. This presumption of unsuitability has thus far put the burden on applicant-plaintiffs to show that they, and previous offenders generally, would be trustworthy employees—a difficult burden to meet in advance of actual employment. In the absence of supporting evidence, plaintiffs often could only attempt to shift the burden to the employer, claiming that the latter lacked evidence to the contrary.

Data now available demonstrate that the presumption of unsuitability is invalid. The federally-funded bonding programs in the District of Columbia and Denver, Colorado have proved overwhelmingly successful;[90] both went claim-free in their initial year. The District Court decision in *Gregory* indicated that persons with arrest records proved even more reliable than most employees.[91] The myth has been dealt a further blow by the findings of the Georgetown University Law Center study for the Labor Department's Manpower Administration.[92] A later article analyzing the Georgetown study concluded as follows:

> "Public agencies that do hire persons with arrest or criminal records find them to be about as honest, punctual, cooperative, accurate, industrious, and otherwise endowed with work-oriented qualities as other employees. For example, all police and most of the corrections agencies responding to this part of the survey found that employees with records are as honest as other workers; this was also true of 89 per cent of the other city, county, and State agencies." [93]

A major step forward was taken in *Perrine v. Municipal Court*.[94] There the California Supreme Court invalidated a Los Angeles County ordinance which made convictions for certain crimes of violence and sex permissible grounds for denying a license to operate a bookstore.[95] Part of the court's holding was based on the First Amendment, the ordinance in effect being a prior restraint on bookstore operators' dissemination of reading matter. The court also held that "it is constitutionally impermissible to deny an applicant a license to operate a bookstore solely upon the ground that he has suffered a prior criminal conviction," [96] focusing on the many basic infirmities of licensing legislation, particularly with regard to prior offenders.

In noting that the ordinance permitted license denials even if all requirements were met (the references to criminal convictions in the ordinance were "guidelines" for the licensing board), Chief Justice Wright found this latitude to be unconstitutionally vague and arbitrary.[97] That the board could, even in the absence of a conviction, reject if it "found" that an applicant had committed one of the enumerated offenses was held to be an overbroad discretion.[98] The court focused on the denial of due process, stating, "[A]n ordinance regulating the right to engage in a lawful occupation or business must bear a rational relationship to a valid governmental purpose." [99] It also shifted the burden of proof of reliability of former offenders onto the employer, based on present evidence: "We cannot assume that because petitioner was once convicted of violating Penal Code section 311.2, he will violate it again . . . ." [100]

Eventually, the greatest precedential value of *Perrine* may be its ruling that the Constitution requires a direct relationship test:

"Accordingly, standards for excluding persons from engaging in such commercial activities must bear some reasonable relation to their qualifications to engage in those activities. In the present case we perceive no reasonable relation between the qualifications of an applicant to operate a bookstore and any past conviction of any of the vast number of crimes listed in section 329.4 he or any of his coparticipants may have suffered . . . . Participants in the business of selling books require no special expertise. They are not like doctors or lawyers or school teachers, whose past convictions are often directly related to their occupational qualifications and may therefore be reasonably invoked to bar them from practicing their professions." [101]

Similarly, in ordering the issuance of a street vendor's license to a former prison inmate, the District of Columbia Court of Appeals in *Miller* [101a] expressed "serious concern about the constitutionality" [102] of the broad leeway enjoyed by the licensing authority:

"Unless there are some standards relating the prior conduct of an applicant to the *particular* business activity for which he seeks a license, the power to deny a license inevitably becomes an arbitrary, and therefore unlawful, exercise of judgment . . . ." (Emphasis in original.) [103]

Legislative Reform: Legal Challenges

Recently, some promising state statutory and administrative steps have been taken to combat the problems of disabilities. In Florida [104] and Illinois, [105] blanket licensing and civil service restrictions on ex-offenders have been abolished. New York's Alcohol Control Law was amended to permit the employment of ex-offenders in establishments selling beverages for off-premises consumption, [106] while Montana's state constitution was amended to include provisions for the restoration of full employment rights upon termination of sentence or parole. [107]

The Model Penal Code contains a relatively comprehensive, workable provision, which calls for a direct relationship test:

"No person shall suffer any legal disqualification or disability because of his conviction of a crime or his sentence on which conviction, unless the disqualification or disability involves the deprivation of a right or privilege which is . . . provided by the judgment, order, or regulation of a court, agency or official exercising jurisdiction conferred by law, or by the statute defining such jurisdiction, when the commission of the crime or the conviction or the sentence is reasonably related to the competency of the individual to exercise the right or privilege of which he is deprived." [108]

California's new reform licensing act includes this test, as well as specific procedural requirements for hearings on license denials.[109]

The Governor of Maine, by Executive Order, has prohibited state agencies from denying employment on the basis of prior criminal records,[110] and a Maryland Attorney General's opinion finds this discrimination by licensing authorities unconstitutional unless a direct relationship to job fitness is shown.[111]

While legislation may be the ideal solution, the absence of widespread and comprehensive statutes thus far suggests that the courtroom will be the major forum for debate and change, at least for the near future. There is, of course, some difference of opinion over specific tactics and goals in disabilities suits. Some favor removing jurisdiction of administrative licensing boards over questions relating to applicants' criminal records and assigning these determinations outright to the courts;[112] others would ask that adverse decisions of licensing boards based on criminal records be subject to de novo judicial review, with the direct relationship test as the determinative standard.[113] Challenges against existing statutory and administrative provisions by the affected class, grounded in the claim that these provisions and their implementation deny basic civil rights, may yet prove the most effective.

Footnotes

[1] For an exhaustive study of the history and nature of civil disabilities, including restrictions on voting, legal, judicial, and property rights and other deprivations as well as denial of employment, see "The Collateral Consequences of a Criminal Conviction," 23 Vand. L. Rev. 929 (1970).

[2] See D. Glaser, The Effectiveness of a Prison and Parole System (abr. ed. 1969).

[3] Trebach, "No. 1 Domestic Priority: New Careers," CITY, at 17 (Oct./Nov. 1970).

[4] Note, "Employment of Former Criminals," 55 Cornell L. Q. 306 (1970).

5 President's Commission on Law Enforcement and Administration of Justice, Task Force Report: Corrections, at 82 (1967) (hereinafter "Task Force Report: Corrections").

6 President's Task Force on Law Enforcement and Administration of Justice, The Challenge of Crime in a Free Society, at 75 (1967) (hereinafter "Task Force Report: The Challenge of Crime").

7 Task Force Report: Corrections, note 5, supra, at 32.

8 Trebach, note 3, supra, at 18.

9 Task Force Report: Corrections, note 5, supra, at 171.

10 Address by Attorney General Mitchell, "New Doors, Not Old Walls," National Conference on Corrections, Williamsburg, Va., Dec. 6, 1971.

11 23 Vand. L. Rev. 929, 1002 (1970).

12 For the most recent and comprehensive survey, see "The Effect of a Criminal Record on Employment with State and Local Public Agencies," a study by the Institute of Criminal Law and Procedure at Georgetown University, Prof. Herbert Miller, Director, commissioned by the Manpower Administration, U.S. Department of Labor (1971).

13 Marshall, "Criminal Records and Public Jobs," MANPOWER (Publication of Manpower Administration, U.S. Department of Labor), at 3 (Dec. 1971).

14 55 Cornell L. Q. 306, 310 (1970).

15 Marshall, note 13, supra, at 4. (Only Nebraska does not require information concerning arrest records on application.)

16 Id. at 3.

17 Task Force Report: Corrections, note 5, supra, at 90.

18 U.S. Civil Service Commission, Standard Form 171 (1968).

19 D. Glaser, note 2, supra, at 277.

20 See 5 C.F.R. §731.201 (1971), allowing rejection for criminal, infamous, dishonest, immoral, or notoriously disgraceful conduct, or ". . . any legal or other disqualification which makes the individual unfit for the service."

21 See e.g. Calif. Bus. and Prof. Code, §§1-300047; N.Y. Educ. Law, §§6501–7713; Va. Code Ann. §§54-1-54-915; Pa. Stat. Ann. tit. 63, §§9.1–1015; Mass. Ann. Laws ch. 112, 1-107; Mo. Ann. Stat §§326.001–343.250; Fla. Stat. Ann. §§454.01–493.56; Ind. Ann. Stat. §§63-101–63-3617.

22 N.C. Gen. Stat. Ann. §83-9 (1965).

23 N.J. Stat. Ann. §45:4-40 (1963).

24 Ky. Rev. Stat. Ann. §322.050 (1963).

25 Okla. Stat. Ann. tit. 59, §847 (1963).

26 Ariz. Rev. Stat. Ann. §32-552 (1970).

27 Calif. Bus. and Prof. Code §9540.3(d).

28 Note, "Entrance and Disciplinary Requirements for Occupational Licensing in California," 14 Stan. L. Rev. 533, 533–534 (1962).

29 23 Vand. L. Rev. 929, 1013 (1970).

30 Id. at 1011–1012.

31 Ariz. Rev. Stat. Ann. §32-552 (Supp. 1970).

32 Calif. Bus. and Prof. Code §8568(d).

33 N.C. Gen. Stat. §89A-7 (Supp. 1969).

34 See e.g. Me. Rev. Stat. Ann. tit. 32, §575 (Supp. 1970) (convicted embezzlers may not be licensed as collection agents); N.Y. Gen. Bus. Law §74 (McKinn. 1968) (security guards may not have convictions for possession of illegal weapons); Calif. Bus. and Prof. Code §5577: "The conviction of a felony in connection with the practice of architecture by the holder constitutes a ground for disciplinary action."

35 Statement of Elizabeth Koontz, Director, Women's Bureau, U.S. Department of Labor, before District of Columbia Commission on the Status of Women—Public Hearings on Woman and Girl Offenders, at 12 (Nov. 4, 1971).

36 Task Force Report: Corrections, note 5, supra, at 33; see also Lykke, "Attitude of Bonding Companies Toward Probationers and Parolees," 21 Fed. Prob. 36 (Dec. 1957).

37 See "Bonding Ex-Cons Proves a Success," National Underwriter at 1 (August 11, 1967).

38 Task Force Report: Corrections, note 5, supra, at 33.

39 12 U.S.C. §1829 (1964).

40 32 C.F.R. §§155.5, 156 (1970).

41 29 U.S.C. §504(a) (1959).

42 W. Van Alstyne, "The Demise of the Right-Privilege Distinction in Constitutional Law," 81 Harv. L. Rev. 1439, 1461–1462 (1968).

43 Trebach, note 3, supra, at 18; see also Glaser, note 2, supra.

44 Task Force Report: The Challenge of Crime, note 6, supra, at 74.

45 Task Force Report: Corrections, note 5, supra, at 32.

46 55 Cornell L. Q. 306, 317 (1970).

47 See Interim Report of the North Carolina Penal System Study Committee, North Carolina Bar Association, at 8 (1971); see also Memorandum from Governor Robert W. Scott to North Carolina State Department and Agency Heads, "Jobs for Ex-Offenders Program," at 1, 2 (May 3, 1971).

48 Glaser, note 2, supra, at 276.

49 Id.; see also North Carolina Governor's Memorandum, note 47, supra, at 1.

50 The anomaly was well recognized by the District of Columbia Court of Appeals in Miller v. D.C. Board of Appeals and Review, 294 A.2d 365 (D.C. App. 1972): "The Department's apparent policy of denying vendors' licenses to ex-convicts appears at cross-purposes with what other District government agencies are seeking and may frustrate entirely the legislative goal of vocational rehabilitation in our penal institutions." Id. at 370.

51 Task Force Report: Corrections, note 5, supra, at 82.

52 Id. at 33; see also 14 Stan. L. Rev. 533, 547 (1962).

53 Calif. Bus. and Prof. Code §23.8 (1967).

54 Final Report, Ohio Citizen's Task Force on Corrections at 117–118 (1971).

[55] Final Report, Wisconsin Council on Criminal Justice, Citizen's Study Committee on Offender Rehabilitation, at 46 (1972).

[56] Michigan Dept. of Corrections, "10-Point Plan for Prison Reform," April 19, 1972.

[57] Glaser, note 2, supra, at 214.

[58] 23 Vand. L. Rev. 929, 1162 (1970).

[59] Glaser, note 2, supra, at 285.

[60] See O. Keller and B. Alper, Halfway Houses: Community-Centered Corrections and Treatment (1970).

[61] See Civil Rights Cases, 109 U.S. 3 (1883).

[62] 42 U.S.C. §§1981, 1983; 28 U.S.C. §1343(3).

[63] "Developments in the Law—Equal Protection," 82 Harv. L. Rev. 1065, 1130 (1969).

[63a] 81 Harv. L. Rev. 1439 (1968).

[64] Id. at 1454–1455.

[65] Note, "Dismissal of Federal Employees—The Emerging Judicial Role," 66 Colum. L. Rev. 719, 734 (1966).

[66] 344 U.S. 183 (1952).

[67] Id. at 192.

[68] 353 U.S. 232 (1957).

[69] Id. at 238.

[70] Id. at 238, n. 5; subsequent Supreme Court decisions, notably Goldberg v. Kelly, 397 U.S. 254 (1970), and Graham v. Richardson, 403 U.S. 365 (1971), appear to have laid this distinction to rest.

[71] Federal courts have also noted this development in the area of government restrictions on employment of homosexuals, declaring the reasonableness test to be determinative. See Olson v. Regents of the University of Minnesota, 301 F. Supp. 1356 (D. Minn. 1969).

[72] 401 U.S. 424 (1971).

[73] 42 U.S.C. §2000(e) (1964).

[74] Griggs v. Duke Power Company, 401 U.S. 424, 433 (1971). Note also: "What is required by Congress is the removal of artificial, arbitrary, and unnecessary barriers to employment when the barriers operate invidiously to discriminate on the basis of racial *or other impermissible classification.*" 401 U.S. at 432 (emphasis supplied).

[75] 316 F. Supp. 401 (C.D. Calif. 1970), aff'd — F.2d —(9th Cir. 1972).

[76] Id. 316 F. Supp. at 402–403.

[77] Id. at 404.

[78] See also Carter v. Gallagher, 452 F.2d 315 (8th Cir. 1971), limiting use of criminal records because of racial impact (Minneapolis Fire Department).

[79] 414 P.2d 412, 51 Cal. Rptr. 284, 64 Cal.2d. 596 (1966).

[80] Id., 414 P.2d at 418. See also Stephens v. Yeomans, 327 F. Supp. 1182 (D.N.J. 1970).

80a Note 68, supra.

81 353 U.S. 232, 239, 246–247 (1957).

82 Task Force Report: Corrections, note 5, supra, at 33.

83 435 F.2d 1188 (1st Cir. 1970).

84 363 U.S. 144 (1960).

85 Id. at 159–160 (1960); see also Bradley v. Waterfront Commission of New York Harbor, 12 N.Y.2d 276, 189 N.E.2d 601, 239 N.Y.S.2d 97 (1963).

86 170 U.S. 189 (1898).

87 Note that in Muhammad Ali v. Division of State Athletic Commission, 316 F. Supp. 1246 (S.D.N.Y. 1970), license was ordered, on equal protection grounds, to issue to ex-offender in the *prize-fighting* profession.

88 347 U.S. 442 (1954).

89 Id at 470; see also separate dissent of Douglas, J., at 474: "So far as I know, nothing in a man's political beliefs disables him from setting broken bones or removing ruptured appendixes, safely and efficiently. A practicing surgeon is unlikely to uncover many state secrets in the course of his professional activities."

90 See note 38, supra.

91 See note 75, supra.

92 See note 12, supra.

93 Marshall, note 13, supra, at 5.

94 488 P.2d 648, 97 Cal. Reptr. 320 (1971).

95 Los Angeles County Ordinance 5860, §321 (1969). The California state courts have followed a particularly enlightened path in area of employment civil disabilities: see Yakov v. Board of Bar Examiners, 435 P.2d 553 (Calif. 1968); Morrison v. State Board of Education, 461 P.2d 375 (Calif. 1969); Comings v. State Board of Education, 23 Cal. App.3d 94, 100 Cal. Rptr. 73 (1972); these cases all employed a job fitness test in reversing employment disqualifications.

96 Perrine v. Municipal Court, note 94, supra, 488 P.2d at 649.

97 Id. at 651.

98 Id. at 652.

99 Id.

100 Id. at 653.

101 Id. at 652.

101a Note 50, supra.

102 Id. at 370.

103 Id. at 369.

104 Repeal of §112-01, Fla. Stats. (1971).

105 Illinois Uniform Code of Corrections, §525-5 (1972).

106 N.Y. Alcoholic Beverage Control Laws, A-11983 (ch. 340) (1972).

107 Constitution of Montana, §28 (Rights of the Convicted), 1972 amendment.

108 American Law Institute, Model Penal Code, §306.1(1).

[109] Calif. Sen. Bill No. 1349 (enacted and effective Aug. 15, 1972), amending Calif. Bus. and Prof. Code.

[110] Maine, Office of the Governor, Executive Order No. 8, Apr. 24, 1972.

[111] Maryland, Offices of the Attorney General, Dept. of Licensing and Regulations: Opinion of July 20, 1972.

[112] See Task Force Report: Corrections, note 5, supra, at 92; Note, 15 Hastings L. J. 355 (1964).

[113] 23 Vand. L. Rev. 929, 1168 (1970).

SECTION IIII
PROCEDURAL ASPECTS OF PRISONERS' RIGHTS LITIGATION

CHAPTER 12
JURISDICTION

EDITORS' INTRODUCTION

Jurisdictional questions, the threshold of every lawsuit in the prisoners' rights area, pose a number of thorny issues and choices to be resolved. The following article discusses the problems and alternatives and contains helpful suggestions on how to proceed.

FEDERAL JURISDICTION AND PRACTICE IN PRISONER CASES

WILLIAM BENNETT TURNER *

This chapter considers the procedural vehicles for vindication of prisoners' claims in federal courts. State court procedures are not considered. State judicial remedies are of course on the books in all states. They may take the form of habeas corpus, mandamus, actions for injunctions, special statutory proceedings, damage actions, etc. Although state remedies are theoretically available, most of the cases granting relief to prisoners have come from the federal courts. Accordingly, and because of the considerable variety in practice in different states, this chapter discusses only the procedural means for bringing prisoners' cases in federal courts. As a practical matter, the likelihood of obtaining relief in a prisoner's case depends to a great extent on the particular judge who decides it, and the choice of federal or state forum will be governed accordingly.

The Hands-Off Doctrine

For most of our history there was no judicial review of prison conditions. Review was avoided under the "hands-off" doctrine.[1] The courts deferred to the presumed administrative expertise of prison officials. Prisons were thus unique among American administrative agencies in enjoying an immunity from judicial scrutiny. Courts invoking the hands-off doctrine often said they lacked "jurisdiction" to supervise prisons or must "abstain" from intervening in prison management. The doctrine never had any jurisdictional basis, and there never was a well-reasoned decision holding that a federal court lacked power to reach the merits of a constitutional claim.

While many courts continue to express great reluctance to

---

* Assistant Counsel, NAACP Legal Defense and Educational Fund, Inc., San Francisco, California; B.S. Northwestern University; LL.B. Harvard University.

adjudicate prisoners' claims against their keepers, most recognize that in a properly pleaded case there are no jurisdictional barriers to review. The only lingering effect of "hands-off" is on the merits —whether the courts will hold that the facts show deprivation of a constitutional right. Here, in balancing whether officials' evidence of prison security considerations outweighs a prisoner's interest in exercising an asserted right, many courts still defer to the "discretion" of the officials and hold that the substantive right does not exist. In short, "hands-off" has nothing to do with jurisdiction or justiciability; at most it reflects a conservative judicial approach to review of prison practices on the merits.

In approaching the question of judicial review many older decisions cited a dictum from an inapposite Supreme Court case for the proposition that "lawful incarceration brings about the necessary withdrawal or limitation of many privileges and rights, a restriction justified by the considerations underlying our penal system." [2] On the other hand, courts exhibiting greater sensitivity to the realities of prison life and to the judicial duty to protect constitutional rights presume that "a prisoner retains all the rights of an ordinary citizen except those expressly or by necessary implication, taken from him by law." [3] Under this approach, restrictions of prisoners' rights must be justified by showing that they adhere in the very fact of imprisonment. The burden of showing this justification may be greater or less, depending on the character of the right involved.[4]

Habeas Corpus or the Civil Rights Act?

The two principal means of seeking federal judicial review of state prison practices [5] are habeas corpus petitions [6] and civil suits under 42 U.S.C. §1983.[7] In many cases, other routes are open.

The courts have broadened the scope of habeas corpus to allow it to be used to challenge most in-prison practices.[8] Habeas may be used even where release from custody is not the remedy sought; a number of prisoners' rights decisions have resulted from habeas petitions.[9] Although the courts have recently minimized the distinctions between habeas corpus and §1983 actions,[10] where there is a choice a §1983 suit will ordinarily be preferable for the following reasons:

Exhaustion

Exhaustion of state remedies is probably not required,[11] whereas the federal habeas statute requires exhaustion of state remedies.[12]

Discovery

Any significant prisoners' rights action will require extensive use of the liberal discovery techniques provided by the Federal Rules of Civil Procedure. These may be used as a matter of course in a civil suit under §1983, while in habeas corpus limited discovery may be had in certain circumstances but only by court order.[13]

Class Action

Maintenance of a class action under Rule 23(b)(2) of the Federal Rules of Civil Procedure is possible in a §1983 suit, assuming that the usual class action requirements can be met.[14] In habeas corpus, however, it is more doubtful whether a class action may properly be maintained.[15] Class actions avoid mootness problems if a particular plaintiff is released or transferred [16] and also provide a basis for claiming broad injunctive relief going beyond a particular prisoner's situation.

Equitable Relief

Exercise of the wide equitable powers of the federal courts can be justified in a civil suit but is inappropriate and probably unavailable in a habeas corpus action. For example, prison officials in a civil action may be required, by way of remedy, to promulgate new rules and regulations, to report to the court, or to file and implement a plan to remedy constitutional deficiencies in the prison system.[17] It would be difficult, if not impossible, to obtain this relief in an application for a writ of habeas corpus.

Exhaustion of State Remedies

As the law stands now, no state judicial remedies need be exhausted in prisoners' rights cases under §1983.[18] However, the Supreme Court has granted certiorari in a case involving this issue, and a more definitive statement will undoubtedly be forth-coming.[19]

Exhaustion of state administrative remedies is not required, at least where there is no adequate administrative procedure set up to provide a speedy and fair hearing of the prisoner's grievance.[20]

Abstention

The doctrine of abstention is inapplicable in prisoner cases unless construction of a state statute by a state court would avoid or modify the federal constitutional question presented.[21] As stated above, however, this doctrine is sometimes relied on by judges who wish to avoid a decision on the merits.

Test for Stating a Federal Claim Under §1983

A prisoner's complaint should not be dismissed for failure to state a claim "unless it appears beyond doubt that the plaintiff can prove no set of facts in support of his claim which would entitle him to relief." [22]

In order to state a claim under §1983, it is necessary to allege that (1) the defendants act "under color of state law," and (2) they have deprived the plaintiff of a constitutional (or federal) statutory right. The first requirement is never a problem if the defendants are state or local officials—if they act in their official capacity at all, they act under color of state law. The second requirement actually goes to the merits; §1983 is properly invoked to the extent that the allegations show deprivation of a federal right. Accordingly, prisoners' actions should almost never be disposed of on motion to dismiss before the court has an opportunity to appraise the complete factual situation.[23]

Three-Judge Courts

Where the action seeks an injunction against the enforce-ment of a state statute or administrative order made under a state statute, and the basis of the action is the unconstitutionality of the statute, federal law requires that the case be heard by a three-judge district court.[24] Where administrative regulations of state-wide applicability are involved, a three-judge court must be convened.[25] General practices not embodied in formal regulations apparently may be considered by a single district judge.[26] Regulations which are not of statewide applicability (for example, regulations governing only one prison in a multiprison state) do not require a three-judge court even though the regulations are promulgated pursuant to statutory authority and are approved by a state agency.[27] Even where a three-judge court is required, a single judge may grant temporary relief pending the hearing before the full court, at least where preferred constitutional rights are involved.[28]

The constitutional challenge to the statute or regulation must present a "substantial federal question" to justify the convening of a three-judge court.[29] This requirement can be strictly applied to foreclose consideration on the merits of a suit.

Federal Prisoners

No decision has spelled out in any comprehensive manner the appropriate procedural vehicles to be used by federal prisoners to gain access to federal courts.[30] Clearly it should be easier for federal prisoners to have their claims against officials heard in federal court than for state prisoners, because considerations of federalism and comity do not apply. However, §1983 is not available to federal prisoners—federal prison officials do not act under color of *state* law. Accordingly, federal prisoners must look elsewhere for means of airing their complaints. The possible procedures are as follows:

Habeas Corpus

Habeas corpus is an available remedy for federal prisoners.[31] The scope of habeas is broad enough to cover situations where release is not the remedy sought.[32]

Mandamus

Federal prisoners may bring a mandamus action against federal officials.[33] Reasoning that state prisoners can sue under §1983 to correct constitutional wrongs perpetrated by state officials and that "it would be unthinkable that the same Constitution would impose a lesser duty on the Federal Government," the courts have accepted jurisdiction under the mandamus statute without attention to the traditionally strict standards for mandamus.[34]

Federal Question Jurisdiction

Federal prisoners may of course sue under the general federal question statute.[35] However, this statute requires an allegation that at least $10,000 is in controversy. In many if not most cases, the deprivation of prisoners' rights cannot easily be evaluated in monetary terms. But since state prisoners need not allege any amount in controversy to invoke §1983, and since the federal courts must protect the constitutional rights of federal prisoners at least as diligently as they do the rights of state prisoners, it is likely that federal prisoners' good faith allegations of amount in controversy will not be too carefully scrutinized.

Federal Tort Claims Act

Where the prisoner is injured by a federal official's negligence, he may sue the United States for damages under the Federal Tort Claims Act.[36] However, it has been held that federal prisoners held in local county jails, pursuant to contracts between the Federal Bureau of Prisons and the local jails, are not entitled to sue the federal government if the local official is the negligent party.[37]

Administrative Procedure Act

A federal prisoner may be able to challenge action taken by the Federal Bureau of Prisons under the Administrative Procedure Act.[38] The Bureau is not expressly exempted from the provisions governing federal agencies generally, and many actions taken by the Bureau, involving both rule-making and adjudicatory activities, should arguably be subject to judicial review under the APA. No case, however, has so held, and an older case held that federal good time forfeiture proceedings were not subject to the APA's provisions.[39] Given the demise of the hands-off doctrine, there is no reason why the Bureau should be treated differently from other administrative agencies, and some development of the law in this area may be expected.

Exhaustion Of Administrative Remedies

It has been held that federal prisoners must exhaust administrative remedies within the Bureau of Prisons before they can file suit in federal court.[40] Under Bureau procedure, the prisoner may take an appeal from action at the institutional level to the Bureau's Office of General Counsel and Review by writing a sealed letter and depositing it in the prisoners' mailbox.[41] While the effectiveness of this administrative remedy may be open to some doubt, it is not a burdensome procedure and, except in cases of emergency, can easily be pursued. The courts have not considered whether this remedy must be exhausted in *all* kinds of actions by federal prisoners (e.g., habeas corpus, mandamus, federal question, etc.), but it is probable that it would be required absent unusual circumstances.

Venue

Actions against federal officials may properly be brought in the District of Columbia, as well as in the district of confinement.[42] However, the District of Columbia Circuit has held that prisoner actions brought in the District should be transferred to the place of confinement unless the action clearly involves national policy or regulations.[43]

Conclusion

Jurisdictional problems today pose less of a bar to prisoners' rights litigation in the federal courts. Novel theories may continue to cause some difficulties, as may shaky factual underpinnings. But on the whole it can be hoped that the day when courts erect jurisdictional obstacles to avoid consideration of the merits of prisoners' lawsuits has passed.

Footnotes

[1] See generally Turner, "Establishing the Rule of Law in Prisons," 23 Stan. L. Rev. 473 (1971). For a collection of judicial formulations of the hands-off doctrine, see Note, "Beyond the Ken of the Courts: A Critique of Judicial Refusal to Review the Complaints of Convicts," 72 Yale L. J. 506, 508, n. 12 (1963). The doctrine is thoroughly criticized in the Note, supra, and in Note, "Constitutional Rights of Prisoners: The Developing Law," 110 U. Pa. L. Rev. 985 (1962). A more recent comprehensive treatment of the problem may be found in Goldfarb

and Singer, "Redressing Prisoners' Grievances," 39 Geo. Wash. L. Rev. 175 (1970).

[2] Price v. Johnston, 334 U.S. 266, 285 (1948). The Price case actually held that a Court of Appeals has power to order a prisoner brought before the court to argue his own appeal. *Id.* at 278, 284. The case cannot be read as establishing any presumption that prisoners have only those rights they can demonstrate as not having been withdrawn by the fact of incarceration.

[3] Coffin v. Reichard, 143 F.2d 443, 445 (6th Cir. 1944), cert. denied 355 U.S. 887 (1945). A recent District Court decision, building on this presumption, is the first thorough attempt by a federal judge to expound a coherent theory of judicial review in prison cases. Morales v. Schmidt, 340 F. Supp. 544 (W.D. Wis. 1792).

[4] See generally Turner, note 1, supra, at 508–511; Morales v. Schmidt, note 3, supra; Gilmore v. Lynch, 319 F. Supp. 105, 109 n. 6 (N.D. Cal. 1970), aff'd sub nom. Younger v. Gilmore, 404 U.S. 15 (1971).

[5] This includes practices of both state prisons and local jails but not federal prisons.

[6] 28 U.S.C. §2242.

[7] Federal court jurisdiction to hear claims of §1983 violations is based on 28 U.S.C. §1343(3).

[8] See e.g. Armstrong v. Cardwell, 457 F.2d 34 (6th Cir. 1972) and cases cited therein.

[9] See e.g. Landman v. Peyton, 370 F.2d 135 (4th Cir. 1966); Coffin v. Reichard, note 3, supra, 143 F.2d at 443.

[10] See e.g. Wilwording v. Swenson, 404 U.S. 249 (1971); McClain v. Manson, 343 F. Supp. 382 (D. Conn. 1972).

[11] See text accompanying notes 18–20, infra.

[12] 28 U.S.C. §2254(b). But see Wilwording v. Swenson, note 10, supra, treating a proceeding brought in habeas corpus as a §1983 civil action.

[13] See Harris v. Nelson, 394 U.S. 286 (1969). See generally Note, "Developments in the Law—Federal Habeas Corpus," 83 Harv. L. Rev. 1038, 1179–1187 (1970).

[14] Class actions have been maintained in a great number of prisoner cases. A few examples are Hamilton v. Love, 328 F. Supp. 1182 (E.D. Ark. 1971); Jones v. Wittenberg, 323 F. Supp. 93 (N.D. Ohio 1971); Morris v. Travisono, 310 F. Supp. 857 (D.R.I. 1970). Cf. Inmates of the Attica Correctional Facility v. Rockefeller, 453 F.2d 12 (2d Cir. 1971) (class action permitted as to one claim but not as to another where conflicts of interest existed between members of the asserted class).

[15] See generally Note, "Developments in the Law," note 13, supra, at 1170–1173. In Mead v. Parker, 464 F.2d 1108 (9th Cir. 1972), the court rejected the suggestion that a habeas corpus petition cannot be treated as a class action and remanded for a hearing on whether the Rule 23 requirements were met.

[16] See Washington v. Lee, 263 F. Supp. 327 (M.D. Ala. 1966), aff'd 390 U.S. 333 (1968).

17 See e.g. Jones v. Wittenberg, 330 F. Supp. 707, aff'd sub nom. Jones v. Metzger, 456 F.2d 854 (6th Cir. 1972); Gilmore v. Lynch, 319 F. Supp. 105, 112 (N.D. Cal. 1970), aff'd sub nom. Younger v. Gilmore, 404 U.S. 15 (1971); Holt v. Sarver, 309 F. Supp. 362 (E.D. Ark. 1970), aff'd 442 F.2d 304 (8th Cir. 1971).

18 Wilwording v. Swenson, 404 U.S. 249 (1971); cf. Humphrey v. Cady, 405 U.S. 504, 516 n. 18 (1972); see generally Turner, note 1, supra, at 506.

19 Oswald v. Rodriguez, No. 71-1369 (O.T. 1972). The decision of the Court of Appeals is reported sub nom. Rodriguez v. McGinnis, 456 F.2d 79 (2d Cir. 1972).

20 See Houghton v. Shafer, 392 U.S. 639 (1968); McClelland v. Sigler, 456 F.2d 1266 (8th Cir. 1972); Jones v. Metzger, 456 F.2d 854 (6th Cir. 1972); Sostre v. McGinnis, 442 F.2d 178 (2d Cir. 1971); Edwards v. Schmidt, 321 F. Supp. 68 (W.D. Wis. 1971); Carothers v. Follette, 314 F. Supp. 1014 (S.D.N.Y. 1970); cf. Carter v. Stanton, 405 U.S. 669 (1972).

21 See Jones v. Metzger, 456 F.2d 854 (6th Cir. 1972); Wright v. McMann, 387 F.2d 519, 524–525 (2d Cir. 1967); Clutchette v. Procunier, 328 F. Supp. 767 (N.D. Cal. 1971); cf. Lindsey v. Normet, 405 U.S. 56, 62, n. 5 (1972); Zwickler v. Koota, 389 U.S. 241 (1967). Younger v. Harris, 401 U.S. 37 (1971), does not apply where there is no pending (or at least threatened) state proceeding. See Lake Carriers Association v. MacMullen, 406 U.S. 498, 509 (1972).

22 Cruz v. Beto, 405 U.S. 319 (1972); Haines v. Kerner, 404 U.S. 519 (1972); cf. Conley v. Gibson, 355 U.S. 41, 45–46 (1965).

23 See Dreyer v. Jalet, 349 F. Supp. 452 (S.D. Tex. 1972); cf. Campbell v. Beto, 460 F.2d 765 (5th Cir. 1972); Jackson v. Bishop, 404 F.2d 571 (8th Cir. 1968); Pennsylvania v. Brown, 260 F. Supp. 323, 332 (E.D. Pa. 1966), modified on other grounds, 373 F.2d 771 (3d Cir. 1967).

24 28 U.S.C. §2281; see Moody v. Flowers, 387 U.S. 97 (1967); Wilson v. Kelley, 294 F. Supp. 1005 (N.D. Ga. 1968); Washington v. Lee, 263 F. Supp. 327 (M.D. Ala. 1966), aff'd 390 U.S. 333 (1968).

25 See Gilmore v. Lynch, 400 F.2d 228 (9th Cir. 1968), on remand, 319 F. Supp. 105 (N.D. Cal. 1970), aff'd sub nom. Younger v. Gilmore, 404 U.S. 15 (1971); cf. McCarty v. Woodson, 465 F.2d 822 (10th Cir. 1972); Seale v. Manson, 326 F. Supp. 1375, 1378–1379 (D. Conn. 1971).

26 Cf. Dorado v. Kerr, 454 F.2d 892 (9th Cir. 1972); Gilmore v. Lynch, 400 F.2d 228, 279 (9th Cir. 1968).

27 See Hatfield v. Bailleaux, 290 F.2d 632, 635 (9th Cir. 1961). See generally, as to state statutes or regulations of only "local impact" and the Supreme Court's strict construction of three-judge court jurisdiction, Board of Regents v. New Left Education Project, 404 U.S. 541 (1972).

28 See Palmigiano v. Travisono, 317 F. Supp. 776 (D.R.I. 1970) (censorship of mail, interference with assistance of counsel, and restriction of access to the courts).

29 See e.g. McCarty v. Woodson, note 25, supra.

30 Probably the most thorough treatment of the procedural possibilities for federal prisoners is in Mead v. Parker, 464 F.2d 1108 (9th Cir. 1972).

31 28 U.S.C. §2241.

[32] See e.g. Taylor v. Blackwell, 418 F.2d 199, 201 (5th Cir. 1969); Long v. Parker, 390 F.2d 816, 819 (3d Cir. 1967). Where injunctive relief is sought, the petition may be treated as a petition for mandamus, as in the cases cited, supra.

[33] 28 U.S.C. §1361.

[34] See Mead v. Parker, 464 F.2d 1108, 1111 (9th Cir. 1972), quoting from Bolling v. Sharpe, 347 U.S. 497, 500 (1954).

[35] 28 U.S.C. §1331.

[36] 28 U.S.C. §2674; see United States v. Muniz, 374 U.S. 150 (1963).

[37] See Logue v. United States, 459 F.2d 408 (5th Cir. 1972), rehearing en banc denied, 463 F.2d 1340 (5th Cir. 1972), petition for cert. pending, No. 72- —,O.T. 1972.

[38] 5 U.S.C. §702, et seq.

[39] Lesser v. Humphrey, 89 F. Supp. 474 (M.D. Pa. 1950).

[40] See Paden v. United States, 430 F.2d 882 (5th Cir. 1970); O'Brien v. Blackwell, 421 F.2d 844 (5th Cir. 1970).

[41] Federal Bureau of Prisons, Policy Statement No. 7300.2B (August 7, 1972).

[42] 28 U.S.C. §1391(e).

[43] See Young v. Director, 367 F.2d 331 (D.C. Cir. 1966).

CHAPTER 13
TECHNIQUES
OF LITIGATION

EDITORS' INTRODUCTION

This article, prepared by three of the foremost litigators in the prison area, fulfills almost singlehandedly the need for a litigation manual for non-crisis litigation. It shepherds the lawyer from initial stages of pretrial preparation right through to the enforcement of the favorable court orders in a most detailed and thorough manner.

LITIGATING AN AFFIRMATIVE PRISONERS' RIGHTS ACTION

PHILIP J. HIRSCHKOP *
NANCY CRISMAN **
MICHAEL A. MILLEMANN ***

Introduction

It is hoped that this article will provide an insight into the litigation of an affirmative prisoners' rights suit. Based on the experience of the authors in litigating various prison suits in a number of states, it is not intended to be a statement of law in the traditional law journal form. The article touches upon all phases of the suit, commencing with a consideration of possible goals and concluding with methods to ensure enforcement of the final court order.

Appellate review rests outside the scope of the article and is mentioned briefly only to alert trial counsel to the problems that arise at the appellate stage but stem from the trial phase. The article concentrates on the affirmative prisoner's rights action, particularly the use of the class action, and therefore does not deal extensively with litigation based on habeas corpus or 28 U.S.C. §2255 motions, or with litigation which is a response to a crisis situation, such as a prison riot or strike.

* Co-Director, American Civil Liberties Union National Prison Project; Founder, Law Students Civil Rights Research Council; Adjunct Professor of Law, Georgetown University Law Center; A.B., B.S. Columbia University; J.D. Georgetown University Law School.

** Staff Attorney, American Civil Liberties Union, National Prison Project; A.B. University of Pennsylvania; J.D. Georgetown University.

*** Director, Litigation Division, Legal Aid Service, Portland, Oregon; Originator and former Director, Baltimore Prisoner Assistance Project; former Staff Attorney, American Civil Liberties Union National Prison Project; A.B. Dartmouth University; J.D. Georgetown University.

Pretrial

Ultimate and Immediate Goals

Before commencing the actual litigation in a prisoners' rights case, the attorney should define its ultimate objectives, a determination based in part on the circumstances which precipitate the need for court action. The attorney who represents a prisoner or prisoners in the midst of a riot faces an immediate objective: to tackle the problems generating the riot. Long-term litigation, on the other hand, permits a careful, studied approach to solving the fundamental problems of prisons.

The consideration of ultimate objectives inevitably involves the question of priorities. Is relief for the individual prisoner-plaintiff less important than the reform of prison regulations which ultimately will benefit more than just the individual? Does the problem demand immediate resolution, or can resolution be postponed pending complete discovery and ensuing litigation?

Crisis situation litigation, such as court action in the midst of a prison riot, requires immediate decisions and limits the tools available to the attorney. Discovery is almost nonexistent because of the demands of time. In addition, crisis litigation encounters the strongest defense that prison officials advance: institutional emergencies demand that administrative powers be paramount.

Clearly, lawyers representing inmates must respond to crisis situations with every tool at their disposal, understanding that crisis litigation often encourages hasty, and hence poor, decisions.[1] While counsel must not shirk crisis litigation if that constitutes the only available means to end repressive and vindictive punishment of inmates who challenge prison conditions, counsel should first seek to resolve the problem through administrative channels,[2] resorting to litigation only after other efforts fail.

In addition to considering the ultimate objectives, the attorney must also define the immediate goals of the litigation.[3] The issues in prison litigation are innumerable. Medical attention,[4] physical conditions,[5] communications,[6] books,[7] access to legal materials,[8] race relations,[9] religious freedoms,[10] punitive segregation,[11] hearings prior to the imposition of punishment,[12] and parole [13] are only a few of the issues.

The prisoner-plaintiff should make the decision as to the immediate objective of the litigation. An individual who seeks resolution of a particular problem should be the major influencing factor. An attorney who contemplates a class action should seek out and consult with the prison leaders to ascertain their assessment of the situation.[14]

Methods of Achieving Reform

Two basic methods exist to reform oppressive prison conditions or regulations: administrative and legal. Administrative channels should be explored first as a possible means for instituting change. Often the problem boils down to the poor judgment of one administrative official. Perhaps the official can be persuaded to pursue a different course of action.[15] In addition, counsel should confer with the prison officials. The potential assistance of liberal prison administrators should not be underestimated. Often, administrators who seek in good faith to implement positive changes in the prison system are as frustrated by their inability to change the system as the lawyers who challenge it. This inability usually flows from a recalcitrant state legislature which will not appropriate the necessary funds for prison reform. In these situations, administrative officials may welcome the threat of a potential law suit as a vehicle for increasing their ability to institute the reforms they seek, and consent decrees or quasi-consent decrees may result from negotiations with such administrators.[16]

In most cases, however, an administrative remedy will not suffice. Unless a prison administrator has been faced with a number of prior suits that have produced victories for the inmates, counsel will usually encounter an attitude of extreme arrogance, rendering administrative redress unlikely, and counsel must consider legal action.

Individual and class actions represent the two primary legal methods available to reform existing prison regulations and conditions. Financial and staff resources often determine the nature of the suit that is brought. The majority of prison suits fall within the individual pro se habeas corpus group. These suits are inexpensive, since the inmate can file in forma pauperis.[17] Relatively little, if any, discovery is available in pro se actions, and therefore the staff resources are unnecessary.[18] However, the number of pro se cases decided adversely to inmates presents major precedential problems for the attorney filing an affirmative prisoners' rights action.[19] Class actions, on the other hand, are expensive and necessitate extensive manpower to accomplish successful discovery. The majority of these affirmative actions require taking numerous, costly depositions from prison officials. An adequately prepared case challenging the arbitrary enforcement of various rules may also involve interviews and correspondence with hundreds of prisoners. To meet the demands for finances and staff, the attorney should explore the possibility of tapping various resources. For instance, counsel may use volunteers from social action organizations concerned with prison reform [20] and law students [21] to satisfy labor needs. To help meet the financial requisites of a class action, the attorney should file in forma pauperis [22] and request costs and legal fees.[23]

Investigation

Subsequent to the determination of the ultimate as well as the immediate objectives of the suit and the assessment of available resources, a complete investigation of the problem should commence. In an effort to locate potential witnesses and accumulate evidence, it is important to contact and interview as many inmates as possible. If the suit is filed pursuant to Rule 23,[24] the court can order that all parties be notified,[25] and an important method to reach inmates who might be useful as witnesses or sources of evidence may thus be provided. Unless notification to prison authorities will disrupt the ability to investigate and litigate the problem, an effort should also be made to secure information relating to the issue from the officials.

Counsel should collect all of the prison administration's rules and regulations concerning the issue to be litigated, in addition to reading the relevant state and official administrative codes. Investigations by executive offices and those conducted through legislative hearings, if available, are credible as evidence. Official and quasi-official reports and studies represent another source of information. For instance, grand juries often visit prisons and angrily describe what they find.[26]

Contact with social action organizations within a state can also be helpful. These groups may have received information from prisoners or their families which is pertinent to the problem. The morgues of area newspapers should be checked for recent articles relating to prisons. In addition, the attorney should probe the reports of various health agencies which serve the prison population.

A sympathetic prison official is an unparalleled source of factual information. Particularly in the major cities the chances are good for finding a cooperative guard or employee who has become dissatisfied with deplorable prison or jail conditions. The facts provided by these persons are especially important because their testimony is not subject to the credibility problem that the testimony of inmates presents.[27] Some states employ jail or prison inspectors who should also be contacted and interviewed.[28] Finally, the attorney should study presently pending suits or settled cases which involve the factual questions at issue.

Parties

The choice of plaintiffs and defendants is crucial to procedural questions of jurisdiction and venue as well as to the substantive issues of the case and its ultimate success. Plaintiffs should be named, if possible, as a class.[29] Although they are expensive and cumbersome, class actions avoid problems of mootness if inmates are subsequently released from the system.[30] They also enlarge the scope of both discovery [31] and the evidence which may be presented at trial.[32] In addition, a class action provides a basis for more sweeping relief than does an individual action.[33] A class action also ensures at least partial retroactive application of the decree to persons within the class at the time of the filing of the complaint.[34] Finally, the technical advantages of Rule 23 benefit the plaintiff.[35]

Where counsel contemplates actual litigation,[36] the choice of individual plaintiffs to represent the class again presents a substantial problem. First, the credibility barrier must be faced. The attorney must select as plaintiffs those inmates who will be the most believable and persuasive witnesses. Second, since the defense in most prison cases is prison security, inmates with the best disciplinary records and the fewest infractions make the best class leaders. Finally, the attorney should not underestimate the tensions and potential attorney-client problems inherent in prison litigation. Many inmates, for example, justifiably have little confidence in attorneys, and the enforced separation between a lawyer and his client often produces devastating results in the attorney-client relationship.[37] Plaintiffs should be those inmates who have the best ability to deal with these tensions.

As for the selection of the defendants, the attorney should consider a large number, possibly a defendant class.[38] A defendant class obviates many of the costs involved in discovery. For instance, defendants in the class can be compelled to produce documents and submit to depositions by notice without sub-poenas.[39] All members of the defendant class are subject to in-terrogatories that are not available against ordinary witnesses.[40] Furthermore, the use of a large defendant class usually permits a choice of venue with respect to divisions in a district and districts within a state. Thus the attorney gains the advantage of proceeding in the forum most favorable to the litigation.[41]

Defendants must be selected with various criteria in mind. In a defendant class action, they must truly represent the class.[42] The chosen defendants must be able to give adequate discovery,[43] and where the suit seeks damages they must not fall within the purview of existing immunities. They must also be capable of sat-isfying any judgment rendered against them.[44] Finally, the attorney should not name as defendants those individuals who would be beneficial to plaintiff during litigation.[45]

Complaint

The attorney must elect a legal theory for the action. Cen-sorship raises First Amendment questions.[46] Access to legal ma-terials and counsel falls within the "access to court" doctrine.[47] Suits that challenge arbitrary punishments rely upon the Fifth and Fourteenth Amendments, and those suits which contest punitive transfers rely on the Eighth and Fourteenth Amendments.[48] Cruel treatment, beatings, torture, and killing, as well as denial of treat-ment for narcotics addiction and alcoholism, obviously fall within the scope of the Eighth Amendment.

Often an attorney will find he or she can challenge a prison regulation or practice under several legal theories. For instance, placement of inmates in solitary without a hearing poses such a problem. Is isolation a violation of the Eighth Amendment as cruel and unusual punishment, or is it unconstitutional under the Four-teenth Amendment as arbitrary action at the hands of the state? Should the attorney plead both actions in the alternative? While many prison suits challenging these forms of punishment rely upon the Eighth Amendment, the authors contend that the Fourteenth Amendment due process theory presents the better vehicle. Cer-tainly the wide spectrum of prison abuses produces such emo-tional and psychological impairments in a prisoner that an Eighth Amendment question is ever present. However, many actions directed against prisoners by officials can be unconstitutional or otherwise illegal but not cruel in the physical sense often associated with the Eighth Amendment.[49] Very little precedent exists where counsel has successfully used the Eighth Amendment to effect a beneficial change for prisoners.[50]

The attorney who challenges the conditions existing in pretrial detention facilities can also rely on either the Eighth Amendment or the Due Process Clause. It is again suggested that the due process theory presents the better argument, as it has been successfully relied upon in challenging the constitutionality of confinement in certain pretrial facilities.[51]

Cause of Action and Forum

With the legal theory firmly in mind, the attorney should next explore the specific cause of action. Such a consideration forces the attorney to make a preliminary decision relating to forum—whether to sue in the state or federal court. Advantages and disadvantages attend either choice. Several factors favor the state court system. Strongest of these is the fact that the state judge who sentences often does so in the belief that the prisoner will be treated in a fair and just manner, and that rehabilitation programs exist. Prison litigation before the state judge may enlighten him to the reality of the conditions and operations of state penal institutions and tend to inhibit him from sending future offenders to the institution. An additional advantage of proceeding in some state courts is the recent expansion of habeas corpus jurisdiction. While traditionally habeas corpus jurisdiction was limited to the constitutionality and legality of one's detention, courts have recently broadened habeas corpus to encompass a challenge to prison conditions.[52] In those states where the courts have expanded the jurisdiction to allow these challenges and where judges sympathetic to the plight of prisoners preside, the attorney should seriously consider habeas corpus litigation. A state judge will probably not be bothered by problems of federalism and comity, both of which usually reduce the willingness of federal judges to grant wide-sweeping relief.[53]

State judges can also remedy archaic prison conditions by exercising what may be termed a general "supervisory" power which vests in all state judges, due to their having convicted and sentenced defendants to state prisons.[54] Furthermore, state judges can always supervise and control prison conditions by exercising their authority to provide a remedy for constitutional violations.[55] In addition, the state court of appeals may provide incentive to the litigator to file in the state court system. Certain state supreme courts may be more progressive on questions involved in the suit than the equivalent federal appellate court.

The attorney who has decided to file the prisoners' rights suit in the state court system may rely on three basic actions: habeas corpus,[56] damage actions at law,[57] and injunctive suits in equity.[58] Most states have declaratory judgment acts, but attorneys have found these to be fruitless.[59]

Several factors support filing the suit in the federal court. Very often local state judges are professionally related in some way to the defendants in the suit. The Attorney General's offices and those defending the suit on behalf of the state have greater access to and familiarity with the state judges. The defendant-prison officials are usually represented by the state prosecutor who is unfamiliar with federal litigation and is thus at a disadvantage when plaintiffs bring the suit in the federal forum. Distinct advantages may also result from choosing the federal forum. Principally, pretrial is controlled by wider and more flexible rules of discovery.[60] Also, greater powers reside in the federal courts to create and enforce remedies by the exercise of their conjunctive law and equity jurisdiction.[61]

In the federal forum, the attorney must choose a basis of jurisdiction. There is a wide range of possibilities. When the suit involves the federal or military penal system, the courts can premise jurisdiction on the Federal Mandamus Act,[62] The Declaratory Judgment Act,[63] and the Federal Habeas Corpus Act.[64] When counsel sues state institutions in federal court, an even greater spectrum of jurisdiction emerges.[65] The attorney can also file a federal habeas corpus action or a federal declaratory judgment action.[66] Some federal courts assume jurisdiction of criminal cases under the All Writs Act.[67]

Within the federal forum, the attorney must also elect between a one-judge court and a three-judge panel.[68] If the prison suit challenges the constitutionality on its face of a state-wide statute or administrative policy, a three-judge panel will probably hear the suit.[69] In those jurisdictions where the circuit judge who sits on the panels appears sympathetic to prisoners' claims, counsel should consider a three-judge court. Although the choice between a three-judge and one-judge court may appear to be dictated by statute, as a practical matter there is a certain degree of flexibility with respect to the final determination. Litigants can choose to challenge the constitutionality of a statute on its face and appear before a three-judge panel, or they can allege that a state-wide statute or administrative regulation is being applied in an unconstitutional manner and thereby draw a one-judge court.[70] Furthermore, where counsel challenges the constitutionality of a statute on its face yet seeks to avoid a three-judge panel, a request for declaratory relief without a request for injunctive relief would force a one-judge court.[71]

A further factor affecting the choice of forum, and thereby, indirectly, the cause of action, is a conglomerate involving questions of convenience—the distance to the courthouse and the proximity of the inmate-witnesses. In addition, the attorney should also consider the past rulings by the state judges and their respective counterparts in the federal system on similar issues. The length of each judge's docket, the availability of interlocutory relief,[72] and the scope of discovery allowable in the respective courts are yet other factors to assess in choosing a forum.

Filing

Once the cause of action has been determined, the forum selected and the complaint written, the attorney will file the action. Filing the prison suit differs from filing an ordinary legal action because an enormous amount of beneficial publicity can surround the former. The attorney must be equipped with evidence so the media can publicize the prison conditions and hopefully catalyze a response from the legislature and executive as well as from the general public. Publicity also serves to reach those persons, including former inmates and sympathetic guards, who might have evidence relevant to the suit. However, caution is advised: publicity can backfire and embarrass prison officials to the point of forcing them to adopt a hard line position where they refuse to enter into appropriate compromises or consent decrees.

Litigation

Preliminary Motions

The distinction between long-term and crisis litigation [73] becomes most significant at the preliminary motions stage. Preliminary motions in the crisis situation are crucial, since the substantive issue of the suit may well be decided during a hearing on a motion for a preliminary injunction, a temporary restraining order, or an order to show cause. While in long-term litigation the discovery phase ranks higher in importance than does the motions stage, the attorney involved in *any* affirmative action should still consider the following motions.

Protective Orders

The attorney should seek to protect those inmates who have volunteered either as plaintiffs or as witnesses. Otherwise, officials may find spurious reasons to retaliate for the filing of the suit by placing the inmates involved in solitary confinement or transferring them to another institution.[74] In addition to ensuring against such events, the order should also guarantee the access of counsel and the press to the prisoners.[75] Finally, the order should include a provision that allows counsel and the inmates to communicate confidentially through the mail.[76] One of the major problems faced by attorneys representing inmates is the risk of a gradual erosion of client confidence as the litigation stretches on; for instance, correspondence cannot be frank and informative if the prison officials have full access to it. Also, gathering information can be extremely difficult if it entails a personal visit to the prison or jail each time the lawyer has a factual question to resolve.

Motion to Dismiss

The defendants will inevitably file a motion to dismiss. Counsel should anticipate this motion and prepare responses at the prelitigation stage. Failure to state a cause of action or to name proper parties, improper joinder of certain parties, and sovereign immunity represent common rationales for such a motion. When counsel is confident that the motion to dismiss will not be granted, attempts to secure a hearing should be accelerated in order to force the defendants to file an opposition response. However, if the attorney suspects the judge will grant the motion to dismiss, he should delay the hearing so that discovery both for the suit and any necessary appeal can proceed prior to the dismissal.

Venue Motions

Where the plaintiff's attorney has forum-shopped,[77] a combination of a motion to dismiss certain parties and/or a motion for a change of venue may defeat the plaintiff's plans. Therefore, counsel should resist a hearing on such motions and, if possible, simultaneously bring several substantive motions before the judge. For instance, the attorney might file a motion for a temporary restraining order, a protective order, or a motion for summary judgment. Once the judge has heard a substantive part of a case, the chances of venue transfer diminish, since there is a stronger basis for arguing that the court should retain the case.

Discovery

Successful affirmative litigation requires complete and thorough discovery. In the authors' experience, prison suits are won neither on the testimony of the plaintiffs nor on modern theories of penology. Generally, the record and the defendants' testimony provide the basis for victory. Consequently, the attorney should be aware of the six basic discovery tools.

Requests for Production of Documents [78]

The attorney should always request prison documents, since they often lead not only to other documents but also to potential witnesses and possible candidates for depositions. Most prison officials maintain section logs,[79] daily work sheets,[80] inmate case files,[81] officer and employee files,[82] minutes of staff meetings, policy statements, internal memoranda dealing with specific problems,[83] and prison and jail manuals and rule books describing the prescribed policies and rules which govern the administration of the institution.[84]

Interrogatories [85]

Counsel should file interrogatories early in discovery. Although this method permits the defendants to discuss their answers with counsel, it also forces them to reveal cold statistics which are inevitably bad.[86]

Depositions [87]

In the opinion of the authors, the most dramatic discovery results from the production of documents, while the most important discovery stems from depositions. Depositions may be distilled into two basic questions: how and why. The lawyer must be persistent in his determination to secure the answers to these queries.[88] Officials must be pressed for responses. When challenged to justify and explain their rules, they usually fail. This alone represents a type of victory. Although depositions are expensive, the new federal rules provide for depositions by tape recording and then transcription by a typist.[89] Again, the attorney can rely on the volunteer to furnish the needed manpower.

Inspection of Facilities

It is imperative that the trier of fact as well as the lawyer inspect the prison, especially when the complaint attacks the facilities. It is useful to personalize the case rather than discuss the problem in the abstract. Counsel should also try to persuade the court to order an inspection tour for experts and the press.

Medical Examinations

Where the complaint alleges inadequate medical facilities, the attorney should request that the court order outside medical examinations of the inmates. Medical personnel in prisons prove to be far below the quality of average medical personnel and may become so integrated with correctional operations that their concern for the independent practice of quality medicine diminishes.

Prisoner Questionnaires and Interviews

Correspondence with prison inmates has proved invaluable in prison litigation. Each prisoner who corresponds with the attorney should be answered. When the letter is received it should be immediately catalogued. An alphabetical list of all prisoners should be kept. A second list should be maintained classifying prisoners by institution. Most important, a third topical list should record abuses.[90] An adequate system of volunteers to reply to the inmate's letters and the use of forms and questionnaires may be used to encourage prisoners to supply invaluable information about the actions of prison officials. If this mass of correspondence is not answered, the litigation may lose the vital support of the prison population, which is necessary for a successful outcome.

Settlement

The most advantageous time to negotiate a settlement arrives near the end of the discovery phase when the defendants are embarrassed and hard-pressed to justify rules and regulations. Psychologically, when discovery is productive, officials will be most vulnerable to a settlement. In contrast, settlement just prior to trial is often impossible or, if reached, perhaps not as favorable to the prisoner-plaintiffs, since the defendant officials have been prepared by their counsel, told how to flavor their testimony, and have begun to convince themselves that the rules and regulations are logical and necessary. Although it continues to be desirable to obtain complete vindication from the courts, major victories do sometimes result from compromise.[91] Counsel should have the litigational objectives in writing, and the offer can be made to drop the suit if the terms are met. Also, when the prison administrators seem reasonable and concerned about redressing the problems within their system, exploration of the possibility of a consent decree becomes appropriate.

Although consent decrees lose the tremendous advantages of a hearing and the attendant publicity given to the plight of the prisoners as well as that given to the irrationality of the prison administration, they are often the best solution for the client, particularly in view of the difficulties and expense of litigation. Moreover, consent decrees often enable the specifics of a given problem to be solved in a more satisfactory manner than is sometimes possible when a court order is entered. Finally, consent decrees are virtually unappealable.[92]

During pretrial negotiation, counsel may find it helpful to enlist prominent members of the legal community as amicus or co-counsel. Often, the support of such persons may aid in obtaining concessions from prison administrators.[93]

Trial

Trial strategy for the affirmative prison rights suit resembles the strategy for other constitutional litigation. The only novel factor in a prison suit is the use of model regulations. This, however, is but a variation of the standard trial memo and suggested findings of fact and conclusions of law submitted by attorneys in ordinary litigation.[94] The standard trial problems confronting the prison lawyer are analyzed below.

Selection and Preparation of Plaintiff's Witnesses

Counsel should divide the witnesses into three categories: inmates and favorable witnesses; defense witnesses; and experts.

Favorable Witnesses

The attorney must first select his witnesses. If an extensive prisoner file and index of complaints has been developed, the attorney should pull the file of each inmate who has complained about the problem at issue.[95] These inmates represent potential witnesses. Interviewers, preferably law students, should talk with all such prisoners. The interview questionnaire should be in a form that counsel can rely upon for examination of the prisoner at trial.

The attorney must be unusually cautious in selecting inmates as witnesses, to ensure that the prisoner will be a credible witness. Counsel may want to discard certain potential witnesses in light of their prison records or because of possible pressure from prison officials or other inmates. For instance, the attorney must consider a prisoner's history of escape, homosexuality, disciplinary infractions, and other problems that might be used to undermine the inmate's credibility.[96]

After the selection of plaintiff's favorable witnesses, requests should be made to the court in writing for writs of habeas corpus *ad testificandum* [97] or other appropriate orders to produce the prisoners to testify. Where prisoners are confined in divers institutions removed from the locale of the trial, the request should include provisions to ensure that the prisoners arrive in the vicinity several days prior to trial. This will afford the attorney the opportunity to consult with them on last minute details.

The named plaintiff must be in the court at all times.[98] This strengthens the rapport with the clients. Also, experience has demonstrated that a prisoner's presence during the testimony inhibits defense witnesses from distorting their testimony. In addition, because the inmates may be more familiar with the subject of the litigation as a result of their day-to-day exposure to prison life, they may notice and point out facts that an attorney may overlook.

Defense Witnesses [99]

Witnesses for the defense can be extremely helpful if properly used. For instance, counsel may wish to call defense witnesses and thus treat them as adverse or hostile. Where counsel has previously deposed these witnesses and believes they cannot justify or explain the application of particular prison rules, they should be questioned accordingly. Defense counsel may be lured into cross-examination of their own witnesses at that time and even forced to attempt to rehabilitate them during the plaintiff's case-in-chief. In addition, reliance on defense witnesses in plaintiff's cases-in-chief deprives the defense of part of its case. The defendants will thus appear to have a weak case, with only a few witnesses to call.

Experts

The defense will attempt to qualify prison officials as experts. The research done and the information about the official elicited during discovery prove invaluable in challenging the official's expert qualifications. The average penal official will have only a high school diploma with few courses in penology, criminology or sociology. He has perhaps attended a handful of seminars and possibly some conventions; he may be a member of the American Correctional Association. Plaintiff's counsel should explore in advance the administrator's familiarity with various published material relating to the prison field and should be prepared to examine on these materials. The majority of administrators or officials will be unable to answer specific questions about the President's Task Force Report on Corrections,[100] the American Correctional Association Standards,[101] or other standards which enjoy wide usage in the prison domain. Usually, they will be unfamiliar with the writings of Willard Gaylin [102] or Karl Menninger.[103] Counsel should also pose questions concerning major Supreme Court decisions relating to corrections and ask about written prison regulations or relevant state code provisions.

Nevertheless, despite prison officials' dubious expert qualifications, the court may still defer to their experience on a number of significant questions. Therefore, the expert witness for the plaintiff [104] must defeat the standard defense to prison suits: that change will jeopardize security and undermine the ability of prison officials to maintain discipline. For example, if the issue in the suit is whether or not inmates have the right to a fair hearing before punishment, expert testimony should destroy the argument that such a hearing would threaten prison security. Testimony in this regard should establish that the creation of a fair disciplinary process contributes to security by avoiding the hostility and anger which unfair punishment breeds and aids the inmate found guilty after such a hearing to confront his own misconduct. In addition, psychological testimony may be helpful to show that punishment imposed without an accompanying fair hearing is ineffective in deterring further misconduct.

Selection of Physical Evidence

Counsel should select exhibits with the objectives of the suit in mind. For instance, details and evidence of beatings should be avoided if the real issues involve communications. The press will concentrate on the brutalities.[105]

Trial Memorandum

Counsel should carefully prepare the trial memo to include model regulations covering the particular problems and conditions challenged in the suit. Submission of the finished product prior to trial is desirable. If the court reads a memorandum of law outlining relevant favorable cases already decided, the language of those decisions may be adapted to the case at trial. Accordingly, counsel should annotate the regulations with supporting case law, state and federal regulations, law journal notes and model codes. Thus, a detailed trial memo with specific proposed regulations as well as a summary of law becomes a valuable means of familiarizing the court with the issues at hand and places plaintiffs in the advantageous position of having their specific goals outlined.

Enforcement and Appeal

The aftermath of victory in the affirmative prison suit bears little resemblance to the finality which follows victory in other types of constitutional litigation. Prisons naturally resist change, and given the sweeping reforms which courts now order, enforcement presents a problem. When a judge rules favorably in a prison case, counsel should move for immediate implementation. Many courts have in fact attempted to ensure compliance with their orders, but this raises the question whether the prison decree is interlocutory or final. The attorney should request the court to indicate that the opinion is final and the time for appeal has commenced, and that the court will retain jurisdiction for implementation purposes. Some courts have indeed been persuaded to retain jurisdiction and have required the defendants to file implementation plans and reports with the court at regular intervals.[106]

Inevitably, those affected will be reluctant to implement substantial changes. Therefore it is useful to establish communications with the defendants or their counsel so that abuses can be monitored.[107] The attorney should insist that the court's ruling be published and circulated to each prisoner individually as well as being posted in a number of spots in the prison.[108] Guards should also receive instruction on the court's order from supervisors. Finally, to ascertain the degree of implementation, the attorney should supply questionnaires to as many prisoners as possible through the communications network already established.

Where counsel fears or knows that the abuses continue despite the court's decree, punitive damages [109] in addition to costs and legal fees [110] should be sought. Payment of personal damages will dampen the enthusiasm of prison officials for continuing abusive practices. If the prison officials are forced to realize that the continued abuse of inmates will result only in further court involvement, they may curtail objectionable actions. The court's power to hold the defendants in contempt perhaps constitutes the strongest weapon employable against continuing abuse. Counsel should not hesitate to ask the court for contempt process where the request can be supported by sworn testimony and affidavits. However, contempt action should not be brought prematurely or without sworn testimony. A premature contempt motion which might be supported by the court could open an avenue of appeal to the defendants to litigate the issue before the appellate courts. Counsel should not give this opportunity to the defendants.

Certainly the most drastic implementation measure is to request that the court place the entire prison system into what is tantamount to receivership. This can be accomplished by various means, ranging from orders to the officials to stop performing their duties to the actual placement of institutional management in the hands of others.[111] Little authority exists for such action, and again counsel should be cautious lest he lay the ground for an appeal by the defendants.

Affirmative prison actions generally conclude in a negotiated settlement or consent decree and rarely reach the appellate stage. Although review of an affirmative prisoners' rights suit lies beyond the scope of this article, passing mention will be made of certain problems inherent in the appellate stage but stemming from the trial phase. First, the merits of plaintiff's appeal will invariably rest on the strength of the factual record. Therefore, much of what counsel does during the course of litigation should be considered from the perspective of "making" the appellate record. Second, counsel for prison officials, whether they are appellants or appellees, will rely heavily upon case law that has been adversely decided to the prisoner. Thus, it is crucial that counsel for the prisoners indicate to the reviewing court that most of this case law stems from individual pro se suits filed by inmates who were without access to discovery, depositions, interrogatories, or legal advice. Thus, the average pro se suit and the law based thereon should arguably not be used as precedent by the reviewing court in deciding the legal merits of an affirmative prisoners' rights action.

Conclusion

The debate rages as to whether suits that improve prison conditions do not in fact precipitate more harm than good. The argument is that improvement of prison conditions renders penal institutions tolerable, a situation that only prolongs the use of prisons and penitentiaries in the criminal justice system. On the other hand, until prisons are abolished, litigation is often the only means of overseeing the institution and may create one of the few situations in which a prison official is forced to justify and explain his actions. This in itself represents a victory. Constitutional litigation alone cannot produce the demise of the prison system in America, but it can help. Therefore, the affirmative prison action must continue.

Footnotes

[1] See e.g. Banks v. Norton, 346 F. Supp. 917 (D. Conn. 1972) (petition for habeas corpus alleging poor prison conditions and punitive segregation without due process denied); Meyers v. Aldrich, Civil No. 72-132 (M.D. Pa. June 16, 1972), appeal docketed, No. 72-1819 (3d Cir. Sept. 5, 1972) (denial of preliminary and/or permanent injunction against further confinement in segregation without hearings which meet due process requirements).

[2] For a discussion of administrative solutions to prisoners' rights problems, see notes 15 and 16, infra, and accompanying text.

[3] Although it remains beyond the scope of this article to discuss litigation aimed at the release of individuals, such as habeas corpus and §2255 motions, these should, in the authors' opinion, assume at least the same priority as the improvement of prison conditions. See generally Turner, "Establishing the Rule of Law in Prisons," 23 Stan. L. Rev. 473 (1971). Litigation to enforce Supreme

Court decisions which invalidate incarceration for certain offenses (cf. Driver v. Hinnant, 356 F.2d 761 (4th Cir. 1966)) or certain sentences (e.g. Otsuka v. Hite, 64 Cal.2d 596, 51 Cal. Rptr. 284 (1966); Brawner v. Smith, 225 Ga. 296, 167 S.E.2d 753, cert. denied 396 U.S. 927 (1969)) must also continue, but again, is beyond the scope of this article. Finally, litigation which effects the release of large numbers of individuals must not cease. E.g. Tate v. Short, 401 U.S. 395 (1971); Long v. Robinson, 436 F.2d 1116 (4th Cir. 1971); Arthur v. Schoonfield, 315 F. Supp. 548 (D. Md. 1970).

4 See e.g. Sawyer v. Sigler, 320 F. Supp. 690 (D. Neb. 1970) (court ordered outside treatment recommended by physician for inmate possibly suffering from dangerous tumors); Talley v. Stephens, 247 F. Supp. 683 (E.D. Ark. 1965) (prison required to furnish reasonable medical attention for injuries and disabilities and to permit sick call at all reasonable times); Of Prisons and Justice, S. Doc. No. 70, 88th Cong., 2d Sess. 31–36 (1964); Barkin, "The Emergence of Correctional Law and the Awareness of the Rights of the Convicted," 45 Neb. L. Rev. 669, 673 (1966); Hollen, "Emerging Prisoners' Rights," 33 Ohio L. J. 1, 24 (1972).

5 See e.g. Hamilton v. Love, 328 F. Supp. 1182 (E.D. Ark. 1971) (prison conditions such as overcrowding, poor food, lighting and medical treatment, constituted cruel and unusual punishment); Holt v. Sarver, 309 F. Supp. 362 (E.D. Ark. 1970), aff'd 442 F.2d 304 (8th Cir. 1971) (conditions and practices including trusty system, open barracks and absence of meaningful rehabilitation programs were cruel and unusual punishment); Bryant v. Hendrick, 7 Crim. L. Rep. 2463 (Ct. C.P. Phila., Pa., Aug. 11, 1970) aff'd sub nom. Pennsylvania v. Hendrick, 444 Pa. 83, 280 A.2d 110 (1971) (overcrowding, filth, homosexual assaults and brutality by prison guards were found to be cruel and unusual punishment).

6 See e.g. Nolan v. Scafati, 430 F.2d 548 (1st Cir. 1970) (prisoner can write to the American Civil Liberties Union for the purpose of soliciting aid); Sigafus v. Brown, 416 F.2d 105 (7th Cir. 1969) (correspondence with courts cannot be confiscated); Carothers v. Follette, 314 F. Supp. 1014 (S.D.N.Y. 1970) (prison officials cannot read correspondence to courts).

7 See e.g. Sostre v. McGinnis, 442 F.2d 178 (2d Cir. 1971) (prisoner cannot be punished for mere possession of inflammatory or racist literature); Fortune Society v. McGinnis, 319 F. Supp. 901 (S.D.N.Y. 1970) (injunction against exclusion of newsletter published by former prisoners).

8 See e.g. Younger v. Gilmore, 404 U.S. 15 (1971) (affirmed injunction against enforcement of prison rule that established a list of legal materials permitted in the prison libraries and interpreted a second rule, prohibiting a jailhouse lawyer from retaining another inmate's papers, to apply only to storage of completed legal papers). But see Robinson v. Birzgales, 311 F. Supp. 908 (W.D. Mich. 1970) (state need not provide law library for inmates at a state mental institution).

9 Montgomery v. Oakley Training School, 426 F.2d 269 (5th Cir. 1970) (applies desegregation holding of Brown v. Board of Education, 347 U.S. 483 (1954), to prisons).

10 Walter v. Blackwell, 411 F.2d 23 (5th Cir. 1969) (right to gather for corporate religious services); Long v. Parker, 390 F.2d 816 (3d Cir. 1968) (right to consult minister of prisoner's choice); Fulwood v. Clemmer, 206 F. Supp. 370 (D.D.C. 1962) (right to wear unobtrusive religious medals).

[11] See e.g. Sostre v. Rockefeller, 312 F. Supp. 863 (S.D.N.Y. 1970) (punitive segregation for more than 15 days is cruel and unusual punishment); Jordan v. Fitzharris, 257 F. Supp. 674 (N.D. Cal. 1966) (confinement for 12 days in filthy 6′ x 8′ concrete strip cell that lacked light and heat constituted cruel and unusual punishment).

[12] See e.g. Landman v. Royster, 333 F. Supp. 621 (E.D. Va. 1971) (due process requirements such as written notice and presentation of evidence must be applied to disciplinary hearings that might result in solitary confinement transfer to maximum security, loss of good-time or 10-day padlock confinement); Clutchette v. Procunier, 328 F. Supp. 767 (N.D. Cal. 1971) (injunction against disciplinary hearings until due process rights such as notice of charges, calling of favorable witnesses, counsel and written findings of fact are required); Morris v. Travisono, 310 F. Supp. 857 (D.R.I. 1970) (requirement of hearing, investigation and review procedures before disciplinary punishment could be imposed).

[13] See e.g. United States ex rel. Campbell v. Pate, 401 F.2d 55 (7th Cir. 1968) (valid claim for relief presented when opportunity for parole hearing was lost due to unsubstantiated charge of prison guard).

[14] Writ writers provide other sources of information concerning prison troubles.

[15] Where the attorney cannot reason with the official, counsel should seek to convince higher executive officers to replace the official.

[16] For further discussion of consent decrees see notes 88–102, infra, and accompanying text. See e.g. Campbell v. Rodgers, Civil No. 1462-71 (D.D.C. Nov. 10, 1971), amended (D.D.C. Jan. 11, 1972); Taylor v. Sterrett, 344 F. Supp. 411 (N.D. Tex. 1972); Hamilton v. Love, 328 F. Supp. 1128 (E.D. Ark. 1971); Bundy v. Cannon, 328 F. Supp. 165 (D. Md. 1971).

[17] 28 U.S.C. §1915 (1970).

[18] Usually the inmate does not have the means to use interrogatories, requests for admissions, depositions, or motions for production of documents—discovery tools crucial to a successful prison suit. See notes 79–92, infra, and accompanying text.

[19] For discussion of how counsel can argue that these pro se cases are inapplicable to the case on appeal, see the paragraphs on appeal, infra, at 270.

[20] As examples, note the following: National Prison Project (Washington, D.C.); Prisoner Assistance Project (Baltimore, Md.); Fortune Society (most major cities); Offender Aid and Restoration Society (most major cities); Committee for Advancment of Criminal Justice (Boston, Mass.); Massachusetts Law Reform; and Massachusetts Council on Crime and Corrections.

[21] In Baltimore, Maryland, the Prison Assistance Project has provided legal service attorneys with volunteer law students who are supervised by staff attorneys. Where such projects exist, the attorney should employ their services; where they do not exist, they should be developed.

[22] 28 U.S.C. §1915 (1970). Permission to proceed in forma pauperis is at the discretion of the District Court judge. This discretion is involved in all cases and proceedings, criminal and civil, and without regard as to whether they are to initiate or commence action, defend or appeal. An affidavit must be made that states the inability of the affiant to afford the costs of the action, the nature of the case, and that it is the affiant's belief that he has good cause for redress.

23 Cf. Ojeda v. Hackney, 40 U.S.L.W. 2431 (U.S. Jan. 18, 1972) (district judge as federal chancellor possesses an equitable discretion to award fees in suit to recover state welfare benefits despite contrary provision of state law); Newman v. Piggie Park Enterprises, Inc., 390 U.S. 400 (1968) (fees awarded because petitioner is acting as private attorney general by bringing suit under Title II of Civil Rights Act of 1964, §204(a), 42 U.S.C. §2000a-3(a) (1970)); Knights v. Auciello, 453 F.2d 852 (1st Cir. 1972) (attorney's fees awarded in racial discrimination suit because plaintiffs were seeking to vindicate a public right at high cost in comparison with actual damages); Lee v. Southern Homes Sites Corp., 444 F.2d 143 (5th Cir 1970) (attorney's fees awarded in suit allowing racial discrimination to encourage private litigation enforcing statutory provision); Bradley v. School Board, 53 F.R.D. 28 (E.D. Va. 1971) (attorney's fees awarded because of unique character of school desegregation suits and in light of defendant's behavior before and during suit).

24 Fed. R. Civ. P. 23 (Class Actions) (hereinafter referred to as "Rule 23").

25 Fed. R. Civ. P. 23(c)(1). For a discussion of the effective use of the notice requirement, see note 35, infra.

26 E.g. Washington Post, Sept. 7, 1972, at B1, col. 7 (a report by the Anne Arundel County grand jury stated that the Maryland House of Correction, a 93-year-old medium-security prison at Jessup, had "long outlived its usefulness and ability to cope with the modern-day inmate").

27 For a discussion of the choice of plaintiffs see notes 29–37, infra, and accompanying text.

28 See e.g. Cal. Welf. & I. Code §18107 (West 1972); Mass. Ann. Laws ch. 124, §I(e) (1965); N.Y. Corr. Law §46 (McKinn. 1968).

29 Fed. R. Civ. P. 23 (a) & (b).

30 The issue of mootness arising from change in plaintiff's status subsequent to the filing of the complaint has been litigated in class action civil rights suits. E.g. Singleton v. Board of Comm., 356 F.2d 771, 773–774 (5th Cir. 1966) (holding that in challenge to desegregation of state reform school it was sufficient that class representatives show only past use of facility and possibility of future use).

31 Class actions enlarge the number of parties to the suit; Fed. R. Civ. P. 26–37 allow liberal discovery procedures to be used among parties without court order. A class action therefore enlarges the scope of discovery and permits it to be executed with greater ease.

32 The field of relevant evidence is enlarged because of the greater range of issues at trial in a class action. Evidence of the actions of defendants toward any of the members of the class rather than just toward a single plaintiff builds a more solid foundation for relief. See Fed. R. Civ. P. 43(a). Also, because of credibility problems which are likely to be associated with prisoners and a higher likelihood of impeachment, the solidarity of a class action will probably increase the weight of reliability given to inmate witnesses.

33 See e.g. Holt v. Sarver, 309 F. Supp. 362 (E.D. Ark. 1970) (holding that petitioners' individual claims did not present basis for individual relief, but the conditions at the prison as a whole constituted cruel and unusual punishment; the court ordered prison officials to present plans for correction of all unconstitutional conditions); McCray v. Maryland, 10 Crim. L. Rep. 2132 (Cir. Ct. Md. Nov.

30, 1971) (court ordered officials to submit proposed procedure for insuring due process in prison hearings, as well as to correct specific conditions found to be cruel and unusual); Wayne Co. Jail Inmates v. Wayne Co. Bd. Comm'rs, 5 Clearinghouse Rev. 108 (Cir. Ct. Wayne County Mich., 1971) (ordering widespread changes to be instituted within jail, including the transfer of prisoners to correct overcrowding, institution of procedures according due process to inmates, and the establishment of a system to identify and treat potentially suicidal inmates).

[34] In Long v. Robinson, 436 F.2d 1116 (4th Cir. 1971), the court ruled that a class action on behalf of plaintiffs and all those similarly situated was proper, where the class was narrowly defined as all those whose convictions were not yet final as of the date of institution of the suit, and affirmed the District Court in applying holding to all those properly in this class as of the date of institution of the action.

[35] Because of the nature of prisons, the class will be easily definable and so numerous as to render joinder of all parties impracticable. Fed. R. Civ. P. 23(a). A class action will promulgate a more effective and uniform relief, since all members of the class, hopefully all prisoners, will benefit from a positive decision. See Fed. R. Civ. P. 23(c)(3). There can be no dismissal or compromise without the approval of the court, Fed. R. Civ. P. 23(e). The court takes a much more active role in the conduct of the case in a class action. Fed. R. Civ. P. 23(d). But the greatest technical benefit may be the requirement of notice to members of the class. Notice provides an effective means to discover prisoners' complaints as well as to secure evidence suitable for trial. In 1970, a Rhode Island District Court required notice to be sent to all prisoners in a class action suit and provided for confidential replies from them regarding the case. The replies were only to be used if the prisoner signed a waiver. Thus, the class action notice requirement provided a safeguard discovery opportunity free from the possible harassment of prison officials. See Morris v. Travisono, 310 F. Supp. 857 (D.R.I. 1970).

[36] Where an attorney is formally retained on a private basis, he is limited to serving those who approach him. However, where a social action or prison reform group contemplates litigation and hires an attorney, a much more fluid situation exists. Accordingly, in N.A.A.C.P., Inc. v. Button, 371 U.S. 415 (1963), N.A.A.C.P.'s approach of potential plaintiffs was protected under the First and Fourteenth Amendments and was not prohibited under Virginia's power to regulate the legal profession, i.e., it was not considered improper solicitation in violation of Virginia statutes and the canons of professional ethics.

[37] For instance, the lack of private communication by mail between attorneys and their clients aggravates these problems.

[38] It is important to note, however, that Fed. R. Civ. P. 23(c)(2) grants members of a class in Rule 23 class actions the privilege of excluding themselves from the class. Counsel must recognize that the application of this provision to members of a defendant class in this type of action will render the suit unmaintainable. In Stinnie v. Gregory, Civ. No. 554-70-R (E.D. Va. filed Oct. 15, 1970), District Judge Merhige interpreted the provision in this manner.

[39] Fed. R. Civ. P. 30, 31, 34.

40 Fed. R. Civ. P. 33. See generally Harris v. Nelson, 394 U.S. 286, 289 (1969) (court may authorize discovery in habeas corpus proceedings, though generally the latitude of Fed. R. Civ. P. 33 is inappropriate to this proceeding).

41 For a discussion of choice of forum see notes 52–77, infra, and accompanying text.

42 Fed. R. Civ. P. 23(a).

43 Defendants with knowledge of prison conditions and with access to records should be chosen. Effective use may then be made of discovery rules.

44 Special consideration must be according to the possible defenses of immunity and hands-off doctrine. See generally Turner, note 3, supra, courts are reluctant to enter into areas that are considered discretionary or are properly executive rather than judicial functions due to considerations relating to the separation of powers. E.g. Upchurch v. Hawaii, 51 Hawaii 150, 153, 454 P.2d 112, 114 (1969) (dictum). This reluctance to deal with issues of prison administration is moderated by the propriety of judicial interference when constitutional violations are alleged. Coffin v. Reichard, 143 F.2d 443 (6th Cir. 1944) (per curiam) (holding that prisoners retained all constitutional privileges not expressly withdrawn and that the courts should be diligent in protecting such rights).

45 For instance, unnamed prison officials thus remain available for a negotiation without the presence of state attorneys.

46 E.g. Sostre v. McGinnis, 442 F.2d 178 (2d Cir. 1971), rev'g in part Sostre v. Rockefeller 312 F. Supp. 863 (S.D.N.Y. 1970), cert. denied Oswald v. Sostre, 405 U.S. 978 (1972) (prison officials cannot edit, censor or refuse to mail correspondence between inmate and court, attorney or public official); Jackson v. Godwin, 400 F.2d 529 (5th Cir. 1968) (arbitrary censorship of "Negro magazines" is an infringement of inmates' constitutional rights under First and Fourteenth Amendments); Nolan v. Fitzpatrick, 326 F. Supp. 209 (D. Mass.), rev'd 451 F.2d 545 (1st Cir. 1971) (held by trial court that inmate has constitutional right to uncensored use of mails to news media subject only to reasonable belief by prison officials that material contains risk to security or behavior within prison, reversed for mootness and control restricted to contraband and escape plans); Carothers v. Follette, 314 F. Supp. 1014 (S.D.N.Y. 1970) (with exception of escape plans and the like, inmates retain their constitutional rights to freedom from censored communication).

47 The "access to courts" doctrine was first enunciated in Ex parte Hull, 312 U.S. 546 (1941), where the court said that "the state and its officers may not abridge or impair petitioner's right to apply to a federal court for writ of habeas corpus." Id. at 549. U.S. Const. art. I §9.

See e.g. Johnson v. Avery, 393 U.S. 483 (1969) (regulation prohibiting inmate from assisting other inmates in postconviction relief is invalid); McDonough v. Director of Patuxent, 429 F.2d 1189 (4th Cir. 1970) (inmate has a right to free access to competent counsel); Rhem v. McGrath, 326 F. Supp. 681 (S.D.N.Y. 1971) (inmate has a right to private and uncensored access to attorney through the mails); Marsh v. Moore, 325 F. Supp. 392 (D. Mass. 1971) (inmate has right to free and uncensored access to attorney through the mails); Gilmore v. Lynch, 319 F. Supp. 105 (N.D. Cal. 1970) (access to federal legal materials is necessary in order that the inmate have reasonable access to the courts); In re Rider, 50 Cal. App. 797, 195 P. 965 (1920) (inmate has right to private consultation with counsel).

[48] For a discussion on arbitrary punishments, see note 12, supra; for a discussion on punitive transfers, see note 11, supra.

[49] The information explosion concerning prison conditions has forced prison officials to relinquish the use of more barbaric tortures such as strip cells, whips and electric shock punishments. Since the Supreme Court restriction of the death penalty, Furman v. Georgia, 408 U.S. 238 (1972), the vestiges of the death penalty remain as the only punishment involving the intentional infliction of physical harm. See Furman v. Georgia, supra, at 288. More subtle punishments, such as denial of good time, parole or work-release, and addition of time to prison sentences, are replacing the prior physical punishments. These penalties tend not to be cruel in the physical sense normally associated with the Eighth Amendment. Therefore, the more effective challenge concerns a denial of due process and equal protection of the Fourteenth Amendment.

[50] The Supreme Court has declared punishments to be in violation of the cruel and unusual provision of the Eighth Amendment in only four instances. Furman v. Georgia, 408 U.S. 238 (1972) (arbitrary imposition of the death penalty); Robinson v. California, 370 U.S. 660 (1962) (incarceration for narcotics addiction); Trop v. Dulles, 356 U.S. 86 (1956) (expatriation); Weems v. United States, 217 U.S. 349 (1910) (hard labor in chains). See generally Furman v. Georgia, supra, at 282, 322–328 (Brennan and Marshall, JJ., concurring, history of the Supreme Court decisions on the Eighth Amendment). For examples of lower court decisions declaring certain punishments to be cruel and unusual, see also Wright v. McMann, 387 F.2d 519 (2d Cir. 1967); Holt v. Sarver, 309 F. Supp. 362 (E.D. Ark. 1970), aff'd 442 F.2d 304 (8th Cir. 1971); Jordan v. Fitzharris, 257 F. Supp. 674 (N.D. Cal. 1966). But see Sostre v. McGinnis, 442 F.2d 178 (2d Cir. 1971), rev'g Sostre v. Rockefeller, 312 F. Supp. 863 (S.D.N.Y. 1970), cert. denied Oswald v. Sostre, 405 U.S. 978 (1972).

[51] Collins v. Schoonfield, 344 F. Supp. 257 (D. Md. 1972) (interim decree relief from inhumane prison conditions and discriminatory practices on the basis of the Fourteenth Amendment due process and equal protection of the law clauses).

[52] The cases which have recently expanded habeas corpus jurisdiction to encompass challenges to prison conditions include In re Riddle, 57 Cal.2d. 848, 372 P.2d 304, 22 Cal. Rptr. 472, cert. denied 371 U.S. 914 (1962) (denying petition of habeas corpus due to petitioner's failure to show guard's conduct constituted cruel and unusual punishment); Mahaffey v. State, 87 Idaho 228, 392 P.2d 279 (1964) (holding that hearing should be granted when petition makes a prima facie showing of cruel and unusual punishment); McCray v. Maryland, 40 U.S.L.W. 2307 (Cir. Ct. Md. Nov. 30, 1971) (finding that conditions of prison violated constitutional privileges of prisoners and ordering specific changes in practices); Commonwealth ex rel. Cole v. Tahash, 269 Minn. 1, 129 N.W.2d 903 (1964) (holding that conditions constituted threat to prisoner's health and safety and so were cruel and unusual punishment, justifying petitioner's transfer to another institution); People ex rel. Brown v. Johnson, 9 N.Y.2d 482, 174 N.E.2d 725, 215 N.Y.S.2d 44 (1961) (holding that transfer from state prison to hospital

for the insane without judicial proceeding could be protested through habeas corpus).

53 Federal courts have been reluctant to intervene in state prison matters where defendants are state officials vested with discretionary powers and acting pursuant to state statutes. E.g. United States ex rel. Lawrence v. Ragen, 323 F.2d 410, 412 (7th Cir. 1963) (citing the above rationale for refusal to grant relief to prisoner protesting inadequate medical care).

54 Wayne Co. Jail Inmates v. Wayne Co. Board of Comm., note 33, supra, discusses the inherent power of the court over the judicial process and its authority to make such orders as are necessary to assure efficient performance of its functions. This power justifies the court's interference in the handling of prisoners held in Wayne Co. Jail. Cf. Sheppard v. Maxwell, 384 U.S. 333 (1966) (holding that a trial court must take such steps as are necessary to protect processes from prejudicial outside influences); Noble Co. Council v. State, 234 Ind. 172, 125 N.E.2d 709 (1955) (deciding that power of court to appoint necessary personnel was inherent and that such power extended to related areas such as the Probation Dept); Zangerle v. Court of Common Pleas, 141 Ohio 70, 46 N.E.2d 865 (1943) (holding that the Domestic Relations Bureau was part of the judicial system and the court could make such arrangements as necessary to assure its efficiency). See also the Judicial Code, 28 U.S.C. §1651 (1970), which empowers federal courts to make such orders as are necessary for the exercise of their respective jurisdictions.

55 For cases involving state judicial authority based on the Eighth and Fourteenth Amendments of the U.S. Constitution, see e.g. In re Riddle, 57 Cal.2d 848, 372 P.2d 304, 22 Cal. Rptr. 472, cert. denied 371 U.S. 914 (1962) (excessive punishment is an invasion of fundamental constitutional rights); Wojnics v. Michigan Dep't of Corrections, 32 Mich. App. 121, 188 N.W.2d 251 (1971) (prisoner cannot be deprived of property without due process of law); Pennsylvania v. Hendrick, 444 Pa. 83, 280 A.2d 110 (1971) (unsanitary and unsafe prison conditions constitute cruel and unusual punishment). For federal authority, see e.g. Holt v. Sarver, 309 F. Supp. 362 (E.D. Ark. 1970), aff'd 442 F.2d 304 (8th Cir. 1971) (shocking prison conditions as cruel and unusual punishment).

56 28 U.S.C. §2241 (1970).

57 Basista v. Weir, 340 F.2d 74 (3d Cir. 1965) (a successful action for compensatory and punitive damages for violations of plaintiff's civil rights during arrest and detention); Roberts v. Williams, 302 F. Supp. 972 (N.D. Miss. 1969) (14-year old boy serving a sentence on the county farm was awarded $85,000 as compensation for injuries sustained as a result of cruel and unusual punishment—a gunshot wound received from a trusty of the prison). Where the attorney seeks damages at law he will often join his action with a claim for injunctive relief. The injunction would be to bar the continuance of the offending activities or to protect the prisoner from retaliatory acts. The damages would be to compensate for past injuries. See Sostre v. McGinnis, 442 F.2d 178 (2d Cir. 1971), rev'g in part Sostre v. Rockefeller, 312 F. Supp. 863 (S.D.N.Y. 1970), cert. denied Oswald v. Sostre, 405 U.S. 978 (1972).

58 See e.g. Hamilton v. Love, 328 F. Supp. 1182 (E.D. Ark. 1971); Jones v. Wittenberg, 323 F. Supp. 93 (N.D. Ohio 1971).

59 Goldfarb and Singer, "Redressing Prisoners' Grievances," 39 Geo. Wash. L. Rev. 175, 263 (1970). Goldfarb and Singer found declaratory judgments to be frequently denied, due to courts' reluctance to enter into areas of administrative expertise or to require changes where such change would necessitate expenditure of funds.

60 Cf. Fed. R. Civ. P. 26(b) (allows discovery of all unprivileged matter relevant to the action and reasonably calculated to lead to evidence admissible at trial) with Mass. Ann. Laws ch. 233 §36.

61 See generally Fed. R. Civ. P. 1 (distinction between equity and law abolished in federal court); 28 U.S.C. §1343 (1970) (jurisdiction for civil rights cases in equity and law); 42 U.S.C. §1983 (1970) (federal employee tort liability for infringement of civil rights under color of law). For examples of conjunctive law and equity jurisdiction see Wright v. McMann, 387 F.2d 519 (2d Cir. 1967) (while New York courts probably don't have jurisdiction over injunction and damages, federal court does have jurisdiction); Sostre v. Rockefeller, 312 F. Supp. 863 (S.D.N.Y. 1970), rev'd in part sub nom. Sostre v. McGinnis, 442 F.2d 178 (2d Cir. 1971), cert. denied Oswald v. Sostre, 405 U.S. 978 (1972) (injunction and money damages reversed on appeal); Jordan v. Fitzharris, 257 F. Supp. 674 (N.D. Cal. 1966) (injunction granted, damages refused). For the effect of Wright v. McMann, supra, see also Carothers v. Follette, 314 F. Supp. 1014 (S.D.N.Y. 1970).

62 28 U.S.C. §1361 (1970).

63 28 U.S.C. §2201 (1970).

64 28 U.S.C. §2241 (1970).

65 The majority of cases are brought under the 1871 Civil Rights Act, 42 U.S.C. §1981 et seq. and particularly §1983 of that title.

66 There is some question as to the usefulness of a federal declaratory judgment by itself.

67 28 U.S.C. §1651 (1970).

68 28 U.S.C. §§2281, 2282 (1970).

69 28 U.S.C. §2281 (1970) requires that a three-judge court be convened to hear cases asking injunctive relief from enforcement of a state statute or administrative order, where the challenge is based upon the unconstitutionality of the statute on its face. Gilmore v. Lynch, 400 F.2d 228 (9th Cir. 1968), on remand 319 F. Supp. 105 (N.D. Cal. 1970), aff'd 404 U.S. 15 (1971) (holding that prison regulations instituted by State Director of Corrections and applicable to all state prisons required three-judge court to consider injunctive relief); Hatfield v. Bailleaux, 290 F.2d 632 (9th Cir. 1961) (holding that challenge to regulations made pursuant to state statute but applicable only to one institution did not require three-judge court). 28 U.S.C. §2282 (1970) establishes similar requirements for challenges of federal statutes and orders. Under 28 U.S.C. §1253 (1970) appeals from orders of three-judge courts go directly to the Supreme Court.

70 See generally Faubus v. United States, 254 F.2d 797 (8th Cir. 1958) (three-judge court wasn't necessary where petition to enjoin governor from preventing implications of school desegregation plan did not challenge validity of any provisions of the Constitution or state laws conferring executive and military powers on governor but only claimed that the governor was using military force in violation of law and plaintiff's right under the U.S. Constitution); Sealy v. Dep't of

Public Instruction, 252 F.2d 898 (3d Cir. 1958) (where plaintiffs, seeking to enjoin building of proposed new high school in particular segment of township on ground that this would effectuate a segregated school system, did not attack state statutes but rather method in which statutes were applied by school authorities, single-judge court was proper); Murphy v. Benson, 151 F. Supp. 786 (E.D.N.Y. 1957) (in suit to enjoin spraying of trees on plaintiff's lands to eradicate gypsy moths, there was no necessity for a three-judge court, because complaint did not challenge the constitutionality of the Pest Control Act but merely charged at most an error in judgment by the secretary in carrying into effect the authority Congress had conferred on him).

[71] See e.g. Kennedy v. Mendoza-Martinez, 372 U.S. 144 (1963) (suit challenging the constitutionality of statutes which automatically deprived an American of citizenship for remaining outside U.S. jurisdiction in time of national emergency to avoid service was properly heard by a single judge because the issues "were not actually framed in contemplation of injunctive relief" even though requested in the amended complaint); United States v. Eramdjian, 155 F. Supp. 914 (S.D. Cal. 1957) (three-judge court was not required where only the interpretation and constitutionality of a statute requiring registration by narcotic addicts and violators crossing a U.S. border was involved and not an injunction against its enforcement). See also Bailey v. Patterson, 369 U.S. 31 (1962) (a three-judge court is not required when prior decisions concerning segregation in public schools make the complaint's constitutional issue frivolous).

[72] Federal interlocutory appeal is basically confined to refusal, modification, continuation or grant of injunctions as well as lower court orders where the trial judge is of the opinion that this order "involves a controlling question of law as to which there is substantial ground for difference of opinion and that an immediate appeal . . . may materially advance the ultimate termination of the litigation." 28 U.S.C. §1292(4)(b) (1970). Under the latter basis for interlocutory appeal, there must be a written statement by the trial judge as to his recommendation for appeal, and the appellate court must use its discretion as to whether to permit the appeal. Id. State laws regarding interlocutory appeals vary. See e.g. Cal. Civ. Pro. Code §904.1 (West 1972) (injunctions and various orders); N.Y. Const. art. 6, §3 (appeal allowed if the trial court certifies one or more questions of law have arisen which ought to be reviewed).

[73] For a discussion of crisis litigation, see note 1, supra, and accompanying text.

[74] Valvano v. McGrath, 325 F. Supp. 408 (E.D.N.Y. 1970) (injunction was granted to prevent violence by prison authorities acting in retaliation for statements made by prisoners concerning events following a prison uprising).

[75] Washington Post v. Kleindienst, 11 Crim. L. Rep. 2045 (D.D.C. April 4, 1972) (held that an absolute ban on press interviews violates First Amendment where inmate consents and the press exercises reasonable restraint as to time and place).

[76] Smith v. Robbins, 328 F. Supp. 162 (D. Me. 1971) (inmates must be allowed to be present when incoming mail from attorneys is opened by prison officials to inspect for contraband); Peoples v. Wainwright, 325 F. Supp. 402 (M.D. Fla. 1971) (on the court's inherent power granted under Rule 23(d) of the Federal Rules of Civil Procedure an injunction was given forbidding prison officials from

opening inmate-attorney correspondence); Marsh v. Moore, 325 F. Supp. 392 (D. Mass. 1971) (effective prison administration is not sufficiently jeopardized to deprive inmate of private communication with his lawyer); Palmigiano v. Travisono, 317 F. Supp. 776 (D.R.I. 1970) (prison officials forbidden to open or inspect incoming or outgoing correspondence between inmates and their attorneys).

77 For discussion of choice of forum, see notes 39–72, supra, and accompanying text.

78 Fed. R. Civ. P. 34, 45(b); Fed. R. Crim. P. 16, 17(c).

79 Documents reflecting the day-to-day events in a prison section.

80 Records that describe the more significant events which happen in a prison day.

81 A record of the individual's inmate's conduct while in prison.

82 Personnel files containing statements on the conduct and misconduct of prison guards and employees.

83 See e.g. Collins v. Schoonfield, 344 F. Supp. 257 (D. Md. 1972), in which documents produced in discovery not only substantiated inmate testimony and bolstered inmate credibility but provided tremendous weapons for impeachment of prison officials and insured that their testimony would be accurate. Furthermore, the documents, admissible as an exception to the hearsay rule, provided independent evidence of a significant nature. For example, the complaint alleged that inmates received contaminated food. Records obtained from the jail contained almost daily notations that the kitchen was overrun with rodents, that the food was infested with vermin, that the food trays were consistently dirty and contained roaches and other vermin.

Another issue in Collins centered around inadequate medical care. The records supplied during discovery indicated that only a quarter of the inmates who requested to see a doctor actually were able to see one; even then, the delay in obtaining medical attention was substantial.

84 Id.

85 Fed. R. Civ. P. 33.

86 Questions should range from the size of cells to the number and titles of books in the library. Prisoner classifications, work-release files and punishment criteria should also be discovered.

87 Fed. R. Civ. P. 27, 28, 30–32; Fed. R. Crim. P. 15, 17(f).

88 The authors in their experience have often received in response to questions "Why do you have this rule?" or "Why is the inmate treated thus?" or "How do you determine which prisoner is to go to solitary?" the answer, "We determine it in light of our experience . . ."

89 Fed. R. Civ. P. 30(b)(4); Fed. R. Crim. P. 15(d).

90 Therefore if a particular problem arises in the course of preparing for litigation, the index describing the problem or abuse can be pulled, and all prisoners who have complained can be contacted. The ability to select witnesses using this method is invaluable.

91 Morris v. Travisono, 310 F. Supp. 857 (D.R.I. 1970) (interim decree resulted from the good-faith bargaining between counsel for the prisoners and the prison authorities—prison conditions, discipline, and classification procedures were at issue).

92 Since a consent decree represents an agreement between the parties which settles the issues involved, neither party can claim to be prejudiced, and so there would be no grounds for an appeal. Therefore in the event of later dissatisfaction with the disposition of the case, the prison officials would be barred from further litigation of the issue.

93 In Bundy v. Cannon, 328 F. Supp. 165 (D. Md. 1971), the former United States Attorney for the District of Maryland and several prominent members of the bar assisted, as co-counsel and amicus respectively, in obtaining a good equitable consent decree that provided a fundamentally fair due process system for imposing punishment within the Maryland penal system.

94 See discussion of trial memo, infra, at 270.

95 In prison litigation, counsel must direct special attention to the rapid turnover in jail population. All efforts must be made to maintain files of forwarding addresses of inmates so they can be contacted.

96 Often procedural fights over the inmate's background divert attention from the essential issues at trial. This should be avoided. However, where prison officials have severely abused an inmate, he should not be discarded as a witness solely because of his background.

97 The writ of habeas corpus ad testificandum is directed to the custodian of any lawfully incarcerated witness and compels production of the witness to testify, either in his own behalf or for another. Petition for such a writ must show strict proof of the materiality of the testimony and the necessity of attendance. 97 C.J.S. Witnesses §30 (1955).

98 The prisoner client should be consulted on every material step of the litigation. Since the prisoner is removed from society, unable to choose an attorney and prevented from freely consulting where they do have counsel, there exists a justifiable paranoia about attorneys. The attorney must deal with this by frank and open discussion. Therefore, he should avoid bench and chamber conferences.

99 Counsel should ascertain prior to trial whom the defense plans to call as witnesses. All the exhibits (personal records, memos, letters) relating to that person should be assembled. Collect each incident involving that guard or administrator from the files and lists so that the witness may be asked why he placed a particular inmate in solitary or why he refused to mail another's letter.

100 The President's Commission on Law Enforcement and Administration of Justice, Task Force Report: Corrections (1967).

101 American Correctional Association, Manual of Correctional Standards (3d ed. 1966).

102 W. Gaylin, Meaning of Despair: Psychoanalytic Contributions to the Meaning of Depression (1968).

103 K. Menninger, The Crime of Punishment (1968).

104 Counsel can obtain the names of experts from the attorneys in prison suits from social action organizations active in the prison field, from major uni-

versities, and from congressional committees that have held hearings on prison matters and from authors of articles on prison.

105 See discussion of how counsel should effectively capitalize on the media's ability to disseminate information regarding horrendous prison conditions, regulations, etc., in the complaint section, supra, at 260.

106 See e.g. Wayne County Jail Inmates v. Wayne County Bd. Comm'rs, 5 Clearinghouse Rev. 108 (Cir. Ct. Wayne County Mich. 1972) (prior to a final order for general improvement of the prison facilities, the court gave an interim order requiring removal of dangerous mentally ill inmates, provision of drinking water and washing facilities to inmates confined to the "hole," and provision of bedding supplies to each inmate); Holt v. Sarver, 309 F. Supp. 362 (E.D. Ark. 1970), aff'd 442 F.2d 304 (8th Cir. 1971) (plans and reports from prison authorities showing intended as well as accomplished improvements in prison facilities required by court); Morris v. Travisono, 310 F. Supp. 857 (D.R.I. 1970) (jurisdiction retained for 18 months to allow time for prison authorities and inmates to establish a working scheme for enforcing negotiated regulations that resulted from court's interim decree); Bryant v. Hendrick, note 5, supra (30 days allowed for improvement of prison conditions). See generally Jones v. Wittenburg, 323 F. Supp. 93 (E.D. Ark. 1971) (injunction against continuation of such prison conditions as overcrowding, slow starvation and lack of recreational facilities and a date set for pretrial conference to consider the claims and a possible hearing date); but see Bundy v. Cannon, 320 F. Supp. 165 (D. Md. 1971) (injunction against prison disciplinary hearings was not granted, because state adopted adequate procedures and federal court did not want to supervise the continuous operation of state correctional system).

107 Counsel should bear in mind, however, that judicial officers do not want to become prison administrators and will be reluctant to have hearings on the same issue over and over. This fact, of course, must be balanced by the need to get back to the court while the matter is still fresh in the court's mind and the impact of plaintinffs' evidence still with the court.

108 Landman v. Royster, 333 F. Supp. 621 (E.D. Va. 1971) (court ordered preparation, distribution and posting of regulations to be formulated according to court guidelines); Morris v. Travisono, 310 F. Supp. 857 (D.R.I. 1970) (court ordered regulations prepared and distributed to prisoners under an order of notice permissible under Fed. R. Civ. P. 23(d)(2) and perhaps mandatory under Fed. R. Civ. P. 23(e)).

109 Sostre v. Rockefeller, 312 F. Supp. 863, 885–886 (S.D.N.Y.), rev'd in part 442 F.2d 178, 204–205 (2d Cir. 1970) (court awarded both compensatory and punitive damages, based upon a per diem rate, for unconstitutional confinement in solitary cell; on appeal the award of punitive damages was reversed, though the right to these damages exists in 42 U.S.C. §1983 suits).

110 Jordan v. Fitzharris, 257 F. Supp. 674, 684 (N.D. Cal. 1966) (awarding counsel fees). But see Turner, note 3, supra, at 519 (author found courts unwilling to grant these fees).

111 Receivership has never been granted by a court, but is the logical equitable remedy and so should be requested. Turner, note 3, supra, at 516.

EDITORS' INTRODUCTION

One of the most difficult situations that can confront the prisoners' rights lawyer is what to do when there is an emergency at the prison—a protest demonstration, strike, death, or violence. While the need for judicial relief may be urgent at such a time, the courts may be reluctant to act. What follows is a discussion of crisis litigation, with particular emphasis on its pitfalls and how they may be avoided.

CRISIS LITIGATION: PROBLEMS AND SUGGESTIONS

WILLIAM E. HELLERSTEIN *
BARBARA A. SHAPIRO **

Introduction

Rapidly growing concern about prisoners' rights and the outbreak of prison disturbances has created a need for the talents of what might be described as the "Prison-Crisis Lawyer." From what our own limited experience has taught us, this rapidly developing practice requires a combination of skills and resources that cut across various specializations. An individual attorney or legal organization confronted with a prison crisis will quickly discover that prompt and extensive action in many different spheres is called for and that personal and organizational resources will be, to say the least, heavily taxed.

A prison crisis may be defined as a situation in which prison officials respond with unnecessary force or excessive punitive and retaliatory measures to a prison disturbance or to some other activity which is viewed by them as a threat to prison security. Indeed, it has been the immediate aftermath of several major prison disturbances that has given rise to much of the complex litigation to be discussed herein.[1] This article will attempt to explore a number of problems that can occur in the course of dealing with a prison crisis and to offer some guidelines and suggestions.

Primary emphasis will here be given to litigation under the federal Civil Rights Act (42 U.S.C. §1983), since most prisoners' rights litigation has been undertaken pursuant to that statute.

Reprinted by permission of Buffalo Law Review (Spring 1972). Copyright © by Buffalo Law Review.

* Attorney-in-Charge, Criminal Appeals Bureau, and Director, Prisoners' Rights Project, Legal Aid Society, New York City; A.B. Brooklyn College; J.D. Harvard University.

** Associate Attorney-in-Charge, Prisoners' Rights Project, Legal Aid Society; A.B. Radcliffe College; LL.B. Columbia University.

However, state court remedies and administrative and political measures, either independently or in conjunction with federal litigation, should not be overlooked.[2]

Goals of Litigation

In a crisis situation, because of time pressures there is a great temptation to take legal action without advance thought as to the aims of the suit and techniques to be employed. However, as in any other kind of litigation, the goals of the lawsuits should be carefully thought out prior to filing. A suit commenced without a well-defined goal or theory in mind can become unwieldy and difficult to manage.

In a prison crisis suit, long-range goals may encompass some attempts at systemic alterations in prison life, but generally the litigation will be directed to securing permanent injunctive relief against various kinds of unlawful official conduct. Thus, in this type of suit, long range aims will frequently be secondary to the more immediate necessities—those of obtaining prompt protection of prisoners from acts of violence and other forms of brutality; securing adequate medical care; gaining relief from unduly harsh living conditions imposed in the context of an "emergency"; and thwarting attempts at summary punishment, such as administrative segregation. The paradox of this type of suit is that all too often the goal sought will be nothing more than restoration of the status quo as it existed prior to the disturbance.

In a suit brought primarily to challenge extreme punitive conditions in a prison rather than brutality, a good deal more attention will have to be paid to achievement of systemic changes within the prison. Therefore, such a suit may contain an attack on physical conditions, inadequate medical and psychiatric services, disciplinary procedures, censorship, visitation rights, and racial discrimination. Each of these abuses, however, could constitute a compact litigable unit by itself, with its own conceptual base. Thought should thus be given to whether an omnibus suit should be brought or whether it would be wiser to commence a series of actions challenging particular abuses separately. At times, omnibus suits can result in a hit-or-miss outcome where victory is secured on some points but not others because in the course of litigation some become obscured. Asking too much of a court at one time can be counterproductive. Goals that are achievable when the court's energies are not diverted by more serious issues may not be realized when made part of an omnibus suit. On the other hand in some cases the constitutional violations may result from the combination of many factors which, when viewed separately, might not seem to be of constitutional magnitude.[3] In such a case an omnibus suit might well be necessary.

A short-term purpose of crisis lawsuits not to be overlooked is the potential extra-legal consequence of the very commencement of the action. Involvement of a court in the crisis as quickly as possible brings needed exposure of official conduct by requiring state officials to account for their actions in answering papers or by testimony at a public hearing. Certain judges have proceeded immediately to the prison to hold such hearings and to inspect the conditions of the prison for themselves.[4]

Merely bringing the situation within the prison under public scrutiny may also have several important long range results. As the Second Circuit has recently observed:

> "The tragic events at Attica have deeply affected vital interests not only of those directly involved, including inmates and correctional personnel, but of the public at large. The public wants to know the facts, with a view to preventing the recurrence of conditions that led to the uprising." [5]

When the crisis results from an inmate disturbance, successful prosecution of a lawsuit can also legitimize some or all of the grievances of the inmates and can provide official recognition that the state has no qualms about engaging in its own brand of unlawfulness.

Some Threshold Problems

Resources

Prison crisis litigation requires the type of preparation that seldom can be accomplished by an individual attorney. Since an entire or substantial part of an institution is frequently involved, the task of gathering information alone can be overwhelming. Institutional defenders are usually best equipped to undertake this task as they possess the legal manpower and investigative staff that can be devoted to the project.[6] Much interviewing of inmates and others is required as is extensive legal research, either prior to the commencement of the suit or during its course. Coalitions of legal organizations can be effective in pooling their otherwise limited resources.[7] The use of law students and paraprofessionals should also be given serious consideration.

Access

In order to prepare effectively any lawsuit involving operations within prison walls, it is essential to gain firsthand knowledge of what is going on inside. It should be remembered that in every prison case the defendants have immediate access to witnesses and information often unavailable to plaintiffs' attorneys.

In a post-disturbance suit, the problems of access can be exceptionally severe.[8] Prison officials can be expected to make every effort to thwart attempts by outsiders to gain entry to the premises, including those by attorneys. When a request for entry has been turned down, there will be little alternative to seeking access by court order.[9]

In most other prison suits, however, the difficulties in gaining access are not nearly as severe. Relationships between inmates and attorneys (especially where institutional defender agencies are involved) have generally developed in advance of the suit either by the fact of prior or current representation of the inmate in his criminal case or through correspondence between the inmate and the attorney. Difficulties may occasionally arise only where, because of physical or personnel limitations, it has been impossible to obtain the express authorization of the inmates to commence legal action.[10]

Members of the state legislature and other public officials can also be of assistance in the attempt to gain information as to what is going on inside the prison. For example, in New York a legislator has a statutory right to enter a prison whenever he wishes,[11] and legislators have begun to utilize that right. Attorneys for inmates should therefore attempt to work closely with them in the hope they can provide a vital source of information. Not infrequently, legislators have furnished supporting affidavits and have testified as plaintiffs' witnesses as to their observations. In similar fashion, members of the press should not be overlooked as yet another source of vital information and possible eyewitness testimony.[12] Members of the clergy can also be helpful.

Preparation of the Complaint

In a prison crisis, attorneys may have to go into court on the basis of a very hastily prepared complaint.[13] Although it will not be possible under these circumstances to do the kind of factual and legal preparation that usually precedes the filing of a complaint in federal court, it must be remembered that the complaint will tend to determine the subsequent course of the litigation. Things added or omitted in haste may require extensive amendments to the pleadings and may delay or confuse the litigation. However, due to lack of time for preparation of the complaint, it will frequently be necessary to take advantage of the statutory right to amend the complaint at least once.[14]

The Plaintiffs

The first consideration in drafting pleadings is whether the suits should be brought as a class action. In most prison crisis litigation, such a large number of inmates will be involved that a class action under Rule 23 of the Federal Rules of Civil Procedure will be appropriate.

The courts have held that inmates may bring class actions against prison officials in a variety of situations. Class actions against widespread and unchecked brutality by prison officials [15] or by other inmates and inmate trustees [16] have been sustained. Class actions have also been deemed proper in prisoners' rights cases involving corporal punishment,[17] racial segregation [18] and general prison conditions.[19] Similarly, the use of class actions in cases involving widespread police misconduct has also been upheld.[20] However, class actions may be disallowed where the claims of each inmate rest on a distinct set of facts or where there exists a substantial conflict of interest among various members of the proposed class.[21]

A class action has many advantages in prison crisis litigation. The most obvious is that any relief obtained will protect all members of the class, not just a few selected clients. A class action will prevent the prison administration from rendering the case moot merely by transferring or giving special treatment to the individual plaintiffs.[22] If the case is brought on behalf of the entire class of inmates, the attorney will be given free access to all members of the class,[23] thereby avoiding difficulties that might otherwise arise in trying to interview potential parties or witnesses.[24] Additionally, when a suit is declared a class action, the members of the class must be notified of the suit and of the names and addresses of the plaintiffs' attorneys.[25] Once the inmates are thus notified of the class action, they will be able to correspond with the attorneys for the class.[26]

There may, on the other hand, be certain disadvantages to a class action which should be considered. Litigation of the case, including the class action question itself, may be more time-consuming than trying an action for individual plaintiffs only.[27] This will be a problem especially where personal injuries must be proved in a damage action. There may also be serious management problems in maintaining a class action in a large prison. The attorney for the class may receive voluminous correspondence from inmates on matters not pertinent to the class action. In sum, however, the advantages of a class action far outweigh the disadvantages except possibly where damages are sought. Therefore, suits for injunctive relief should be brought as class actions whenever possible.

In drafting a class action complaint, the statutory requirements of Rule 23 of the Federal Rules of Civil Procedure must be kept in mind.[28] However, particular attention should be given to those problems most likely to arise in a crisis situation. For example, an issue may be raised as to whether there are questions of law and fact common to the class,[29] whether the claims of the representative parties are typical of the claims of the class,[30] and whether the named parties will fairly and adequately represent the class.[31] The interpretations of the requirements of Rule 23 (a)(2), (3), and (4) vary from case to case, and tend to overlap to a large extent.[32] Attacks upon the propriety of the class under these sections generally resolve themselves into two basic questions. First, do the acts complained of affect, or are they likely to affect, all inmates? Second, to what extent will the relief sought by the named plaintiffs be beneficial to or desired by the other inmates? [33]

In cases involving brutality or other unconstitutional use of force, not all the inmates in the institution will have been subjected to such conduct. Nevertheless, if the brutality or force has been inflicted upon a large number of inmates and there is a continued threat or possibility of such action against the rest of the inmate population, a class action for injunctive relief can be maintained.[34]

Of course, if it had to be shown that the constitutional rights of all members of the class had already been violated, the value of the injunction as a preventive remedy would be destroyed.

A different situation might be presented if the plaintiffs, in addition to seeking injunctive relief against brutality, also seek damages for personal injury on the same facts.[35] Unless the damage claims arise from similar acts against a large number of inmates, a class damage action would not be advisable. Of course, an action may be maintained as a class action for injunctive relief, while damage claims are maintained only on behalf of the named plaintiffs.[36]

Although Rule 23(a) has been liberally construed to allow class actions, there may be cases in which the interests of the named plaintiffs are so antagonistic to those of other members of the class that a class action will not be allowed.[37] For example, in *Inmates of the Attica Correctional Facility v. Rockefeller* [38] it was held that the interests of inmates who expected to be indicted as a result of the riot, and of those who were not involved or who might cooperate with the prosecution, were sufficiently antagonistic to defeat a class action for an injunction against official interrogations.

If the interests of the named plaintiffs are not antagonistic to those of other members of the class, there is no need to establish that all, or even a majority, of the inmates actually support the action.[39] Class actions have been allowed even though a few members of the plaintiff class have testified for the defendants [40] or have objected to the action.[41]

In an action for injunctive relief, prison inmates as a class will generally satisfy the requirements of both 23(b)(2) [42] and 23(b)(3).[43] In such a situation it should be considered a suit under 23(b)(2),[44] so that the judgment will be binding on all members of the class.[45]

The Defendants

In determining who are to be the defendants, attention must be given to the question of who is directly or indirectly responsible for causing the acts complained of and who has the power to remedy any conduct or conditions which are the subject of the complaint. Any state or local official, such as the prison warden, the commissioner of correction, state judge or the governor, can be joined as a defendant if he or she has any power or duty to take corrective action. Thus, in *Rhem v. McGrath,*[46] the court, most significantly, held:

> "[W]hen conditions are permitted to exist which have the effect of violating a person's constitutional rights, the official charged with responsibility for those conditions has a *constitutional* obligation to alleviate those conditions, whether his statutory power to act be cast in terms of discretion or duty." [47]

In general, unless money damages are sought from individual prison guards, there is no reason to name them as defendants if the warden has been named. An injunction against the warden will be binding on all prison employees.[48] However, if enforcement against any of the warden's superiors or any other state officials is desired, these officials should be named in the complaint. It is possible that the state or a municipal or county government may also be added as a party defendant for injunctive relief.[49]

Even if damages are sought, it may be possible to add the state (or county or municipality) as a party defendant. Although 42 U.S.C. §1983 does not, by itself, authorize recovery of damages from governmental bodies,[50] it has been held that damages can be recovered under §1983 to the extent that there has been a waiver of immunity.[51] In addition, a pendent state law tort claim against the state or municipality and the responsible individuals may be added to the complaint.[52]

Damages

In drafting a complaint in a prison crisis, a determination will have to be made as to whether or not to sue for damages. Damages can be awarded for violations of constitutional rights by prison officials.[53] However, the amount of the recovery may be limited to compensatory damages,[54] which in most cases will not be great, particularly since inmates get free medical care and do not have any substantial income to lose as a result of injury or illness. Yet a small damage award may be very important to an inmate because of his indigency and should not be minimized by comparison of the inmate with a free citizen who has been slightly injured.

There are some strategic advantages to requesting damages. The damage claim will remain viable even if the claim for injunctive relief is rendered moot by the remedial actions of the defendants. If damages are finally recovered, either from individuals or from the state, the deterrent effect may be as significant as injunctive relief in the long run. Finally, the named plaintiffs may want damages, and failing to claim damages in the federal suit may bar them from recovering damages in any other manner.[55]

On the other hand, there may be serious disadvantages to adding damage claims. An attorney pursuing such a claim may find himself in the position of having to litigate separately the damage claims for each of the named plaintiffs. Litigation of a damage claim also may require considerable time and substantial expenditures for discovery, with only a small chance of a meaningful financial recovery.[56]

Scope of the Complaint

The Federal Rules of Civil Procedure allow a simplified form of pleading.[57] However, in pleading violations of prisoners' rights under the Eighth Amendment, relatively detailed pleadings may be required. To state a cause of action for injunctive relief under the Eighth Amendment it is necessary to allege both the original violation (such as beatings, unnecessary force, and violence) and facts that show that there is a real danger of continued or renewed violations (recurrent beatings, harassment, threats, verbal abuse, lack of affirmative action on the part of responsible officials).[58] If it is claimed that the conditions of confinement are so inhuman as to violate the Eighth Amendment, enough must be alleged to establish an overall picture of constitutional deprivation.[59]

In drafting a complaint for prisoners in this type of case, there may be a temptation to include a wide range of possibly unconstitutional acts or practices. Claims such as unwarranted confiscation of personal property, routine and harassing "strip searches," [60] mail censorship, lack of special diets or religious services for groups such as Black Muslims, arbitrary discipline, unsanitary conditions, and inadequate medical care may be made by the inmates. However, addition of a large number of these claims, some of which cannot easily be proved, may detract from the likelihood of success on the issues that are of a crisis nature.

Since it can be very difficult to check the information an

attorney receives from his clients, great care should be taken in making factual allegations in the complaint. Some of the information received may be rumor or hearsay; it may be difficult to find an eyewitness willing or able to testify to events that many inmates have described to the attorney.

Finally, in a post-disturbance situation, great care must be taken not to set forth information that might tend to incriminate any plaintiff. A suggested approach to this problem is to confine the allegations and claims of the complaint strictly to post-disturbance events. It should be remembered that plaintiffs are subject to pretrial discovery concerning all allegations in the complaint.

Trying the Issues

The nature of prison crisis litigation renders motion practice of crucial importance. Certainly where urgent relief is needed, as is most often the case in a post-disturbance suit, a trial on the merits may be too late to be very effective.[61]

In virtually every prison crisis situation, the first important motion will be an application for a temporary restraining order seeking immediate access to the institution and cessation of any brutality. Under Rule 65(b) of the Federal Rules of Civil Procedure, such an order may be granted without notice to one's adversary only if two conditions are met. It must clearly appear from facts set forth in an affidavit or *verified* complaint that immediate and irreparable injury will occur before the other side can be heard. The applicant's attorney must also certify to the court in writing the efforts that have been made, if any, to contact the other side, and why notice should be dispensed with. As a practical matter, most judges will insist or request that defendant's counsel be given informal notice. Since defendant's counsel will usually be the State Attorney General, City Corporation Counsel or County Attorney, this should not be difficult.

A problem that will arise in the preparation of initial papers is that much of the information that would bolster supporting affidavits may be obtainable only after access to the institution is granted. However, there is usually little time to worry about this dilemma, and supporting affidavits from attorneys reciting what they have learned from other sources have been sufficient in some cases.[62] When an attorney's affidavit is all that is submitted, it should be as specific as possible, setting forth the nature of the abuses complained of and the manner of their occurrence, including references to times and places. Whenever available, affidavits from inmates or other eyewitnesses should be obtained.

The application for a temporary restraining order must be accompanied by a complaint. However, in an extreme emergency it is possible that a court will act before a complaint has been filed.[63] Even if a temporary restraining order is granted, a motion for a preliminary injunction will have to be made. Counsel should press for an immediate evidentiary hearing on that motion. The court must grant a hearing whenever there is an actual dispute as to the facts.[64]

The hearing on the motion for a preliminary injunction should be approached with the greatest of seriousness. The plaintiffs must meet

> ". . . the burden of showing probable success on the merits and some irreparable injury or, where the showing of probable success is uncertain, that the balance of hardships tips decidedly in their favor." [65]

In establishing irreparable injury, the key factor is whether "there is some cognizable danger of recurrent violation." [66] The mere cessation of the practice or action complained of after the filing of the lawsuit will not itself justify the denial of relief.[67]

There are a number of important tactical determinations to be made concerning the actual conduct of the hearing. One is the location of the hearing. An effort should be made to persuade the judge to either visit the prison or to conduct some part of the hearing at the prison.[68] There may be competing factors as to the wisdom or desirability of having any part of the hearing at the institution. There exists the possibility that inmate witnesses may be intimidated by the immediate surroundings, especially if correction officers are permitted to remain in the hearing room. The warden will urge that security so requires. The court should be persuaded to exclude as many correction officers from inside the room as possible, particularly those who may be directly involved in the lawsuit. The use of federal marshals to maintain security should be urged as a reasonable alternative, with the correction officers maintaining their posts outside the hearing room. On the other hand, the judge's presence at the prison for part of the hearing may have a stabilizing effect. It may underscore the seriousness of the lawsuit and provide the inmates with additional assurance that their grievances are being given serious consideration.

Skill in the selection of witnesses and presentation of evidence is also of great importance. Prison crisis suits will always involve large numbers of potential witnesses—inmates, correction officials and others. First, efforts should be made to present whatever non-inmate witnesses are available if they have firsthand information, especially members of the press, clergy or legislature. Courts may be suspicious of prisoner testimony,[69] and corroboration by independent sources such as non-inmate testimony and prison disciplinary and medical records will be quite helpful.

An attempt should also be made to obtain as witnesses a wide cross section of the prison population. In addition to ethnic factors,[70] the inmate's criminal record, age, location in the institution, job status, prison disciplinary record, and articulateness or the lack of it should all be considered.[71]

Inmates called as plaintiffs' witnesses are in a delicate position, and every effort must be made to protect their personal interests. First, every prisoner must be warned that his testimony may lead to reprisals by prison officials, especially correction officers in whose immediate custody he is confined. Although courts are becoming increasingly sensitive to this danger,[72] the inmate should also be apprised that he cannot be fully protected against all future harassment in retaliation. A pretrial detainee must be advised that his being a witness could have an adverse effect on his criminal case, particularly in plea negotiations and at sentence.[73] A convicted prisoner should be forewarned of the risk of an adverse effect upon his prison assignment or parole status.[74]

The inmate's Fifth Amendment privilege against self-incrimination must also be protected zealously prior to his taking the stand and throughout the course of his testimony. The trial judge should be asked to restrict the scope of cross-examination to preclude inquiry into pending criminal charges or involvement in possible criminal conduct during a prison disturbance. In both *Valvano v. McGrath* and the *Attica* case, the District Court precluded cross-examination along these lines.

If parties or witnesses report that they are being harassed and intimidated, application should promptly be made to the court for their protection. A federal court has plenary power to take all steps necessary to safeguard its fact-finding processes, including the transfer of inmates confined in state or municipal facilities to federal custody during the course of the proceedings.[75] A court can even enjoin state criminal prosecutions if they are instituted in bad faith in order to intimidate parties or witnesses.[76]

In preparing a large number of witnesses in a short time, particular care should be taken to guard against conflicting testimony. Inmates will frequently describe events on the basis of hearsay or rumor rather than upon firsthand observation. It should be remembered that inmates' freedom of movement and thus opportunity for observation is limited by the very nature of their confinement. As a result, there may be serious variances in the descriptions of events, especially in the tense atmosphere of a crisis. Consequently, as much time and resources as possible should be devoted to the checking out of information before it is offered in court.

To prove an affirmative case at the preliminary injunction hearing, it will often be necessary to call prison officials. Absent time for extensive discovery, the examination of prison officials requires exceptional caution. Direct examination of prison officials should generally focus on what is being done to remedy the conduct or conditions which are the subject of complaint. However, prison officials may frequently disclaim any knowledge of unlawful conduct. Any conduct that is admitted will undoubtedly be defended on the grounds that it is necessary to the maintenance of prison "security." However, if the witness does not provide a more specific explanation of the conduct, it will subject his broader representations to doubt. Of course, he should be held to any specific representations he has ventured to make.

At the hearing, the defendants may seek to refute plaintiffs' case in several ways. They may rely solely on cross-examination of plaintiffs' witnesses or they may decide to call their own witnesses, including other inmates. Prison officials may attempt to exploit disunity among the inmate population. Possible bias of an inmate witness against the plaintiffs should be explored. Prison officials may offer inducements to inmates in exchange for favorable testimony. Such inducements might include preferred treatment within the institution, especially in job assignments; special consideration from the parole board; or offers to secure the district attorney's or the court's leniency in the inmate's criminal case.[77] Thus any inmate called by the defendants should be severely examined on the subject of inducements, and the records in his criminal case should be checked.

The defendants may also call prison officials and guards.

Much of the testimony will be based on their own "expertise" and the need for prison "security." The "expertise" of each witness should be closely scrutinized. He may lack familiarity with the rules, regulations, and operations manuals that govern the institution. Lower level correction officers can be especially vulnerable to this type of examination, since many have had limited training and may have spent little time reading the requirements of their own positions. Moreover, prison rules and regulations may be incomplete or contradictory. "Expertise" can also be challenged in the traditional manner by examination of the individual's background and credentials. Lastly, cross-examination may demonstrate that the issue in question has no relationship to the witness' proffered "expertise."

Particular attention should be paid to witnesses who have a special responsibility in connection with investigating the circumstances of a disturbance or charges of misconduct by prison guards. Examination of such officials should explore the possibility of conflicts of interest between their official responsibilities and their role as witnesses.

On occasion, it may also appear that the attorney for the defendants is vested with the responsibility of prosecuting prison personnel for misconduct. This type of conflict of interest has drawn comment from at least one federal court.[78]

Preliminary Relief

Various kinds of preliminary relief can be granted by the court in addition to an injunction against brutality or other flagrant constitutional violations. The court's order might include provisions for the enforcement of the injunction. For example, the court can provide for free access to all inmates by both attorneys and law students or paraprofessionals in their employ.[79] The court can appoint monitors,[80] or it might order the temporary suspension or reassignment of particular correction officers.[81] The court can also order that inmates be released from punitive segregation or solitary confinement unless they are given hearings on disciplinary charges.[82]

However, in dealing with a crisis it must be kept in mind that some concessions to post-crisis security may have to be made. For example, it has been held that a twenty-four hour lockup of prisoners for a period of several weeks following a riot is permissible as long as there are plans to return to normal at some time.[83] It has also been held that prison officials can temporarily isolate suspected "trouble makers" without any formal proceedings.[84] Prison officials may also be granted a reasonable period of time to restore exercise and other normal privileges following a riot or disturbance.[85] In general, where a strong argument is made that restoration of privileges will create a "security" risk, courts will hesitate before ordering an immediate return to pre-riot procedures.

Much of what we have discussed so far is also applicable to a trial on the merits. However, as in most federal litigation, the liberal provisions for pretrial discovery should be fully utilized. In prison crisis litigation, discovery will normally be directed to the following items: institutional disciplinary records of both inmates and guards; unpublished rules and regulations; medical records; criminal records of defendants' witnesses. Where actual conditions are in issue, a motion to inspect and photograph all parts of the prison should be made under Rule 34.[86] Detailed interrogatories, requests for admissions and extensive depositions into all aspects of prison management may also be called for.

Substantive Problems

Federal courts have repeatedly exercised their jurisdiction in the area of prisoners' rights,[87] and it is well established that they have the power, and even the duty, to step into a prison crisis to remedy flagrant violations of inmates' constitutional rights at the hands of prison officials. They have enjoined continuing physical brutality by prison officials [88] and by other inmates as well.[89] The use of corporal punishment has been enjoined,[90] as have barbaric forms of solitary confinement in "strip cells." [91] Federal courts have also acted in cases of alleged racial discrimination,[92] degrading and inhuman prison conditions,[93] disciplinary procedures which violated constitutional due process,[94] denials of access to the courts,[95] and interference with freedom of speech [96] or religion.[97]

However, there is a great difference between successfully invoking federal jurisdiction and establishing the right to relief. Although in cases involving first amendment rights courts have generally required prison officials to produce substantial justification for restricting the rights of inmates,[98] quite the contrary approach has been taken in cases arising under the Eighth Amendment where a heavier burden is placed on inmates. Since in a prison crisis reliance will generally be placed upon the Eighth Amendment's prohibition against cruel and unusual punishment, plaintiffs must be prepared to make a strong factual showing.

Although outright beatings and physical torture clearly violate the Eighth Amendment,[99] other forms of official conduct which can be labelled "punishment" may be insulated from constitutional attack:

> "For a federal court, however, to place a punishment beyond the power of a state to impose on an inmate is a drastic interference with the state's free political and administrative processes. It is not only that we, trained as judges, lack expertise in prison administration. Even a lifetime of study in prison administration and several advanced degrees in the field would not qualify us *as a federal court* to command state officials to shun a policy that they have decided is suitable because to us the choice may seem unsound or *personally* repugnant."[100]

Thus, courts have held that punishments violate the Eighth Amendment only in extreme cases.[101] The plaintiff in *Wright v. McMann,* for example, was placed unclothed in an unheated cell in freezing weather without soap or toilet paper. Such punishment was held to

> ". . . destroy completely the spirit and undermine the sanity of the prisoner. The Eighth Amendment forbids treatment so foul, so inhuman and so violative of the basic concepts of decency."[102]

Similarly, corporal punishment was held unconstitutional because it was degrading, counterproductive, subject to widespread abuse by sadistic guards, and also offensive to contemporary standards of decency, as evidenced by the fact that it had already been outlawed in all but two states.[103] However, punishments which the courts have found to be "counterproductive as a correctional measure," "personally abhorrent," and only "several notches above those truly barbarous and inhumane conditions heretofore condemned by ourselves and other courts as 'cruel and unusual' " have been held to be constitutional.[104]

Similar difficulties will be encountered when the state

asserts reasons of security, particularly in the wake of a prison rebellion, as justification for acts which might otherwise be held unconstitutional. For example, in the name of security, officials have been permitted to hold "suspected agitators" in administrative segregation without hearings.[105] Prison officials have been allowed to keep inmates locked in their cells twenty-four hours a day, without exercise, recreation, or family visits, and to otherwise restrict inmate privileges when the officials' actions were taken as temporary "security measures" following a prison rebellion.[106]

Even after a clear constitutional violation has been established, inmates may be required to show that there is a danger of repetition of such conduct before injunctive relief will be granted.[107] In determining the likelihood of repetition, a court will consider whether there has been a widespread pattern of conduct or whether initial unlawful conduct has been followed by harassment, and threats of repetition. The court will also consider whether officials have taken adequate steps to prevent a recurrence.[108] However, once a danger of repetition has been established, the court has a duty to act.[109]

Even without proof of likely repetition, it can be argued that in cases of particularly egregious violations of inmates' rights by prison officials, the courts should act if only to condemn the violations.[110]

> "It is of the highest importance to community morale
> that the courts shall give firm and effective reassurance,
> especially to those who feel that they have been harassed
> by reason of their color or their poverty."[111]

Such reassurance by federal courts is particularly important in cases involving prisoners, who have so few legitimate avenues for the presentation of their grievances.

Conclusion

Recent history has taught us that the manner in which state and prison officials respond to intolerable prison conditions and inmate disturbances protesting those conditions requires that lawyers be equipped to deal with the crises that ensue. The legal efforts made on behalf of prisoners caught up in a crisis may produce results ranging from changes in prison conditions to the saving of life and limb.

From the brief survey of case law presented above, it can be anticipated that inmates in a crisis situation may have unusual difficulty in establishing the right to relief in a federal court. Therefore, despite the pressures of time, lack of resources and the need for prompt action, able handling of a prison crisis lawsuit through planning, preparation, ingenuity and appreciation of the complexities of federal litigation is essential and should increase the chances for positive results.

Footnotes

1 The authors have been heavily involved in litigation arising out of three major prison disturbances: Queens House of Detention for Men at Kew Gardens in October, 1970 (Valvano v. McGrath, 325 F. Supp. 408 (E.D.N.Y. 1971)); Long Island City Jail (Branch Queens) in October, 1970 (Cender v. Lindsay, Civil No. 70-1225 (E.D.N.Y., Nov. 23, 1970)); Attica in September, 1971 (Inmates of the Attica Correctional Facility v. Rockefeller, 453 F.2d 12 (2d Cir. 1971)). In addition, the authors are involved in a challenge to conditions of confinement in the Manhattan House of Detention for Men (the Tombs) (Rhem v. McGrath, 326 F. Supp. 681 (S.D.N.Y. 1971)).

2 Several important suits challenging jail and prison conditions have been successfully prosecuted in state courts. Commonwealth ex rel. Bryant v. Hendrick, 444 Pa. 83, 280 A.2d 110 (1971); Inmates of Wayne County Jail v. Wayne County Bd. Comm'rs, 5 Clearinghouse Rev. 108 (Cir. Ct., Wayne County, Mich, 1971). As a general matter, however, many state courts have been exceptionally inhospitable to prisoners' rights suits. See Schwartz, "Prisoners' Rights and the Courts," N.Y. L. J., June 10–11, 1971, at 1, col. 4.

3 This has been particularly true in cases challenging generalized prison conditions of overcrowding, unsanitary facilities, etc. E.g. Holt v. Sarver, 309 F. Supp. 382 (E.D. Ark. 1970), aff'd 442 F.2d 304 (8th Cir. 1971); Jones v. Wittenberg, 323 F. Supp. 93 (N.D. Ohio 1971), aff'd sub nom. Jones v. Metzger, 456 F.2d 854 (6th Cir. 1972); Rhem v. McGrath, 326 F. Supp. 681 (S.D.N.Y. 1971). See also Note, "Constitutional Limitations on the Conditions of Pretrial Detention," 79 Yale L. J. 941 (1970).

4 See note 68, infra.

5 Inmates of the Attica Correctional Facility v. Rockefeller, 453 F.2d 12, 20 (2d Cir. 1971) (hereinafter "Inmates of Attica").

6 At present, there is still an absence of available resources in these agencies. Public Defender systems throughout the country have barely scratched the surface in the prisoners' rights area.

7 Coalitions can sometimes present more problems than they solve. Litigation by committee, especially among groups that may have divergent philosophies and goals, can be difficult to manage. When undertaken, it is suggested that all participants agree either formally or informally upon the designation of a chief counsel who will have primary responsibility for mapping litigation strategies in the absence of time for consultation. Frequently, the trial judge himself will urge such a designation to facilitate his communication with counsel.

8 After both the Attica disturbance and the death of George Jackson at San Quentin, attorneys' visits were suspended for several days.

9 Even with a court order, access may be difficult in extreme situations. In the Attica case, such an order was obtained. The prison was retaken by exceptional force on September 13, 1971. That evening, counsel for the inmates obtained, ex parte, a temporary restraining order from the United States District Court in Buffalo which ordered that 33 named attorneys, together with doctors and nurses accompanying them, be admitted forthwith to the prison. The order also enjoined any interrogation by state officials of inmates in the absence of counsel and provided that the state police were not to interfere with counsel as they were traveling from Buffalo to Attica. Such interference did not continue after the order was read to the state troopers. At the prison, however, admission was refused in the face of the order. The restraining order was vacated the following day, but two days later, after a national guardsman testified to having observed widespread brutality in the prison, correction officials in open court agreed to permit the attorneys to begin interviewing inmates. It ought not to be assumed that all prison officials will defy a court order as was done at Attica.

10 In the Attica case, the state strenuously contested the right of the legal groups seeking to represent the inmates on the ground that they had not been asked by the inmates to do so. Apart from the fact that time did not permit these amenities, only an extremely narrow view of the attorney-client relationship can support the position that an attorney or agency that has represented an inmate as his trial counsel or is representing him on appeal is not his attorney for purposes of helping him in the aftermath of a rebellion. The state's position was rejected by the Second Circuit. See Inmates of Attica, note 1, supra at 20–21.

11 N.Y. Corr. Law §500-j (McKinn. 1968) provides:

> "The following persons may visit at pleasure all county jails and workhouses: the governor and lieutenant-governor, secretary of state, comptroller and attorney-general, members of the legislature, judges of the court of appeals, justices of the supreme court and county judges, district attorneys and every minister of the gospel having charge of a congregation in the town in which such jail or workhouse is located. No other person not otherwise authorized by law shall be permitted to enter the rooms of a county jail or workhouse in which convicts are confined, unless under such regulations as the sheriff of the county, or in counties within the city of New York, the commissioner of correction of such city, or in the county of Westchester, the commissioner of correction of such county, shall prescribe."

12 In Cender v. Lindsay, note 1, supra, news photographers took photographs of beatings of inmates by correction officers which were used in the federal lawsuit and also figured prominently in subsequent official investigations into the conduct of the guards.

13 In fact, in Inmates of Attica, note 1, supra, Federal Judge John Curtin issued the order described in note 9, supra, before a complaint had been filed, on the basis of the emergency situation.

[14] Fed. R. Civ. P. 15(a). In an attempt to ameliorate the difficulties created by hasty drafting of pleadings, the Prisoner's Rights Newsletter has developed a "bank" containing briefs, memoranda, model complaints and other litigation aids for use by attorneys and inmates who plan to file such lawsuits.

[15] Inmates of Attica, note 1, supra; Valvano v. McGrath, Civil No. 70-1390 (E.D.N.Y., Feb. 1, 1971).

[16] Holt v. Sarver, 309 F. Supp. 362 (E.D. Ark. 1970), aff'd 442 F.2d 304 (8th Cir. 1971).

[17] Jackson v. Bishop, 404 F.2d 571 (8th Cir. 1968).

[18] Washington v. Lee, 263 F. Supp. 327 (M.D. Ala. 1966), aff'd 390 U.S. 333 (1968).

[19] Jones v. Wittenberg, 323 F. Supp. 93 (N.D. Ohio 1971), aff'd sub nom. Jones v. Metzger, 456 F.2d 854 (6th Cir., 1972); Rhem v. McGrath, Civil No. 70-3962 (S.D.N.Y., Oct. 26, 1970); Inmates of the Cook County Jail v. Tierney, 4 Clearinghouse Rev. 388 (N.D. Ill., Aug. 22, 1968) (oral opinion, transcript, at 7). See also Goodwin v. Oswald, 462 F.2d 1237 (2d Cir. 1972) (correspondence rules).

[20] BUILD of Buffalo v. Sedita, 441 F.2d 284 (2d Cir. 1971); Lankford v. Gelston, 364 F.2d 197 (4th Cir. 1966).

[21] In Inmates of Attica, note 1, supra, at 24, it was held that there could be no class action concerning interrogation by a special prosecutor investigating the riot when the proposed class included potential defendants, potential prosecution witnesses, and possibly uninvolved inmates.

[22] Transfer or release of the named plaintiffs in a class action does not make the case moot. E.g. Inmates of the Cook County Jail v. Tierney, note 19, supra; Washington v. Lee, 263 F. Supp. 327 (M.D. Ala. 1966), aff'd 390 U.S. 333 (1968); Ferguson v. Buchanan, Civil No. 64-107 (S.D. Fla., Mar. 12, 1965). In Jenkins v. United Gas Corp., 400 F.2d 28 (5th Cir. 1968), the named plaintiff in a class action to end employment discrimination on the basis of race was allowed to continue as the representative party even after he had been promoted out of the class.

[23] Inmates of Attica, note 1, supra; Valvano v. McGrath, Civil No. 70-1390 (E.D.N.Y., Dec. 8, 1970).

[24] For example, in prisons in New York State an inmate can normally be interviewed only by an attorney who already represents him or from whom he has requested legal assistance in writing.

[25] Fed. R. Civ. P. 23(c) requires notice to all members of a class under 23(b)(3). However, it has been held that due process requires notice in all class actions. Mullane v. Central Hanover Trust Co., 339 U.S. 306, 314 (1950); Eisen v. Carlisle & Jacquelin, 391 F.2d 555, 568 (2d Cir. 1968); Valvano v. McGrath, Civil. No. 70-1390 (E.D.N.Y., Feb. 1, 1971); Rhem v. McGrath, Civil No. 70-3962 (S.D.N.Y., Oct. 26, 1970).

[26] In Valvano v. McGrath, note 1, supra, the notice to the inmates informed them that they could write to the attorneys for either side. They were also allowed to address letters to the court, with instructions as to which attorneys should receive the letter, if they wanted to prevent anyone in the prison from learning the destination of the letter.

27 Of course, an evidentiary hearing on a motion for preliminary relief need not be postponed until after the determination of the class action issue. Evidentiary hearings were held prior to the class action determinations in both Inmates of Attica, and Valvano.

28 The complaints should allege that the proposed class meets all the requirements of Fed. R. Civ. P. 23(a) and the requirements of at least one subdivision of 23(b). Demarco v. Edens, 390 F.2d 836 (2d Cir. 1968); United States v. Preston, 352 F.2d 352, 354 n. 10 (9th Cir. 1965); Hickey v. Illinois Cent. R.R., 278 F.2d 529 (7th Cir. 1960), cert. denied 364 U.S. 918 (1960); Lunch v. Kenston School Dist. Bd. of Educ., 229 F. Supp. 740 (N.D. Ohio 1964).

29 Fed. R. Civ. P. 23(a)(2).

30 Fed. R. Civ. P. 23(a)(3).

31 Fed. R. Civ. P. 23(a)(4).

32 For example, it has been held that the requirement of Rule 23(a)(2) is virtually identical to that of 23(a)(3). American Airlines, Inc. v. Transport Workers Union, 44 F.R.D. 47 (N.D. Okla. 1968); Minnesota v. United States Steel Corp., 44 F.R.D. 559 (D. Minn. 1968). Rule 23(a)(4) has been held to require consideration of whether the interests of the named parties are coextensive with those of the class, whether they are antagonistic to the interests of other class members, the percentage of the class named as plaintiffs, and other factors. Advertising Speciality Nat'l Ass'n v. Federal Trade Comm'n, 238 F.2d 108, 119–120 (1st Cir. 1956). Other courts have held that less is required by 23(a)(4), looking mainly to whether or not the named parties will prosecute the case vigorously. Eisen v. Carlisle & Jacquelin, 391 F.2d 555, 562 (2d Cir. 1968); Mersay v. First Repub. Corp. of America, 43 F.R.D. 465, 469 (S.D.N.Y. 1968).

33 However, in one case, the opposition to the class action was on totally different grounds. It was argued that declaring the case a class action would require notice to the members of the class, and that the distribution of notice of the pending action concerning jail conditions would create a security risk. The case was declared a class action and notice ordered nevertheless. Rhem v. McGrath, Civil No. 70-3962 (S.D.N.Y., Oct. 26, 1970).

34 Inmates of Attica, note 1, supra, at 24 n. 11; Holt v. Sarver, 442 F.2d 304 (8th Cir. 1971); Jackson v. Bishop, 404 F.2d 571 (8th Cir. 1968). The individual situations of all members of the class need not be identical. The requirements of 23(a) generally have been liberally construed in this regard in favor of allowing individuals to bring class actions, particularly in civil rights cases. E.g. Johnson v. Georgia Highway Express, Inc., 417 F.2d 1122 (5th Cir. 1969); Schnell v. City of Chicago, 407 F.2d 1084 (7th Cir. 1969) (news photographer on behalf of all news media personnel); Norwalk Core v. Norwalk Redevelopment Agency, 395 F.2d 920, 937 (2d Cir. 1968); Eisen v. Carlisle & Jacquelin, 391 F.2d 555 (2d Cir. 1968); Lankford v. Gelston, 364 F.2d 197 (4th Cir. 1966); Potts v. Flax, 313 F.2d 284, 288–289 (5th Cir. 1963); Sullivan v. Houston Indep. School Dist., 307 F. Supp. 1328 (S.D. Tex. 1969); Broughton v. Brewer, 298 F. Supp. 260 (S.D. Ala. 1969); Wilson v. Kelley, 294 F. Supp. 1005 (N.D. Ga. 1968), aff'd 393 U.S. 266 (1968) (suit to desegregate correctional institutions).

35 Class damage suits have been allowed in other contexts under Rule 23(b)(3). E.g. Green v. Wolf Corp., 406 F.2d 291 (2d Cir. 1968); Foster v. City of Detroit, 405 F.2d 138 (6th Cir. 1968); Brennan v. Midwestern United Life Ins. Co., 286

F. Supp. 702 (N.D. Ind. 1968). Class damage suits have been preferred when individual suits would have been more time-consuming, Minnesota v. U.S. Steel, 44 F.R.D. 559 (D. Minn. 1968), although in other class actions the amount of damages had to be determined separately for each individual. American Trading & Prod. Corp. v. Fischbach & Moore, Inc., 47 F.R.D. 155, 157 (N.D. Ill. 1969). See Hobbs v. Northeast Airlines, Inc., 50 F.R.D. 76, 78 (E.D. Pa. 1970) (a class action may be proper in a personal injury case).

[36] The use of subclasses under Rule 23(c)(4) should also be considered in this context.

[37] Wilson v. Kelley, 294 F. Supp. 1005 (N.D. Ga. 1968) (inmates of work camps could not bring a class action to abolish work camps because some other inmates might prefer work camps to the penitentiary). See generally Hansberry v. Lee, 311 U.S. 32 (1940); McArthur v. Scott, 113 U.S. 340 (1884); Schy v. Susquehanna Corp., 419 F.2d 1112 (7th Cir.), cert. denied 400 U.S. 826 (1970); Weiss v. Tenney Corp., 47 F.R.D. 283, 290 (S.D.N.Y. 1969); Mersay v. First Repub. Corp. of America, 43 F.R.D. 465, 468–469 (S.D.N.Y. 1968).

[38] Inmates of Attica, note 1, supra, 453 F.2d at 24.

[39] Berman v. Narragansett Racing Ass'n Inc., 414 F.2d 311, 317 (1st Cir. 1969); Eisen v. Carlisle & Jacquelin, 391 F.2d 555, 563 n. 7 (2d Cir., 1968) ("[a] class action should not be denied merely because every member of the class might not be enthusiastic about enforcing his right").

[40] In Valvano v. McGrath, Civil No. 70-1390, at 15–18 (E.D.N.Y., Nov. 11, 1971) several inmates testified on behalf of the defendants at the first hearing on a motion for preliminary relief.

[41] Berman v. Narragansett Racing Ass'n, 414 F.2d 311, 315–316 (1st Cir. 1969), cert. denied 396 U.S. 1037 (1970) (share of recovery due each member of class subject to dispute); Dierks v. Thompson, 414 F.2d 453 (1st Cir. 1969); Coskery v. Roberts & Mander Corp., 97 F. Supp. 14 (E.D. Pa.), appeal dismissed, 189 F.2d 234 (3d Cir. 1951) (owners of 1,600 shares out of 330,000 opposed to the action). But see Fitzgerald v. Jandreau, 16 F.R.D. 578 (S.D.N.Y. 1954).

[42] Fed. R. Civ. P. 23(b)(2) provides for a class action when:

> "[T]he party opposing the class has acted or refused to act on grounds generally applicable to the class, thereby making appropriate final injunctive relief or corresponding declaratory relief with respect to the class as a whole. . . ."

[43] Fed. R. Civ. P. 23(b)(3) provides for a class action when:

> "[T]he court finds that the questions of law or fact common to the members of the class predominate over any questions affecting only individual members, and that a class action is superior to other available methods for the fair and efficient adjudication of the controversy. The matters pertinent to the findings include: (A) the interest of members of the class in individually controlling the prosecution or defense of separate actions; (B) the extent and nature of any litigation concerning the controversy already commenced by or against members of the class; (C) the desirability or undesirability of concentrating the litigation of the claims in the particular forum; (D) the difficulties likely to be encountered in the management of a class action."

44 Inmates of Attica, note 1, supra, at 24; Rhem v. McGrath, Civil No. 70-3962 (S.D.N.Y., Oct. 26, 1971); Van Gemert v. Boeing Co., 259 F. Supp. 125 (S.D.N.Y. 1966); cf. Technograph Printed Circuits, Ltd. v. Methode Electronics, Inc., 285 F. Supp. 714 (N.D. Ill. 1968).

45 In Valvano v. McGrath, Civil No. 70-1390 (E.D.N.Y., Oct. 21, 1971), the court allowed inmates to "opt out" of the class to bring individual damage suits even though it was a properly constituted class under Rule 23(b)(2).

46 Civil No. 70-3962 (S.D.N.Y., Dec. 16, 1971).

47 Id. at 3–4. See also BUILD of Buffalo v. Sedita, note 20, supra. A careful check of state statutes may reveal that a substantial number of state and local officials can be joined as defendants. E.g., N.Y. Corr. Law §504 (McKinn. 1968) (presiding justice of Appellate Division in cases involving New York City jails).

48 Fed. R. Civ. P. 65(d) provides:

> "Every order granting an injunction . . . is binding only upon the parties to the action, their officers, agents, servants, employees, and attorneys, and upon those persons in active concert or participation with them who receive actual notice of the order by personal service or otherwise."

Cf. Regal Knitwear Co. v. NLRB, 324 U.S. 9, 14 (1944).

49 A number of courts have held that injunctive relief cannot be granted against a municipality under 42 U.S.C. §1983. E.g. Patrum v. City of Greensburg, Ky., 419 F.2d 1300 (6th Cir. 1969), cert. denied 397 U.S. 990 (1970); United States ex rel. Gittlemacker v. County of Philadelphia, 413 F.2d 84 (3d Cir. 1969), cert. denied 396 U.S. 1046 (1970); Wallach v. City of Pagedale, 359 F.2d 57 (8th Cir. 1966); Spampinato v. City of New York, 311 F.2d 439 (2d Cir. 1962), cert. denied 372 U.S. 980 (1963). Other courts have allowed such injunctive suits under §1983. E.g. Garren v. City of Winston-Salem, N.C., 439 F.2d 140 (4th Cir. 1971); Harkless v. Sweeny Indep. School Dist., 427 F.2d 319, 321–323 (5th Cir. 1970), cert. denied 400 U.S. 991 (1971); Dailey v. City of Lawton, Okla., 425 F.2d 1037 (10th Cir. 1970); Adams v. City of Park Ridge, 293 F.2d 585 (7th Cir. 1961). See generally Comment, "Injunctive Relief Against Municipalities Under Section 1983," 119 U. Pa. L. Rev. 389 (1970).

50 Monroe v. Pape, 365 U.S. 167, 187–192 (1961).

51 Carter v. Carlson, 447 F.2d 358, 368–370 (D.C. Cir. 1971), cert. granted sub nom. District of Columbia v. Carter, 404 U.S. 1014 (1972); McArthur v. Pennington, 253 F. Supp. 420, 430 (E.D. Tenn. 1963). But see Sostre v. McGinnis, 442 F.2d 178, 205 (2d Cir. 1971), cert. denied sub nom. Oswald v. Sostre, 404 U.S. 1049 (1972).

52 E.g. United Mine Workers v. Gibbs, 383 U.S. 715, 725 (1966) (the pendent claim and the federal claim must "derive from a common nucleus of operative facts"); Price v. United Mine Workers, 336 F.2d 771 (6th Cir. 1964) (pendent state punitive damages claim in suit under federal labor-management laws); Rumbaugh v. Winifrede R.R. Co., 331 F.2d 530 (4th Cir. 1964) (state damage claim joined with federal claim under the Railway Labor Act). The pendent state claim need not be for the requisite jurisdictional amount under 28 U.S.C. §1331. Wilson v. American Chain & Cable Co., 364 F.2d 558 (3d Cir. 1966); Stewart v. Shanahan, 227 F.2d 233 (8th Cir. 1960); American Fidelity & Cas. Co. v. Owensboro Milling Co., 222 F.2d 109 (6th Cir. 1955). The defendant in the pendent claim need not be a defendant in the federal claim as long as the state claim can be joined under the rule of United Mine Workers v. Gibbs, supra. See Leather's Best, Inc. v. S.S. Mormaclynx, 451 F.2d 800 (2d Cir. 1971).

53 Sostre v. McGinnis, 442 F.2d 178, 204–205 (2d Cir. 1971); Wright v. McMann, 387 F.2d 519 (2d Cir. 1967); Roberts v. Williams, 302 F. Supp. 972 (N.D. Miss. 1969), aff'd 456 F.2d 819 (5th Cir. 1971), cert. denied — U.S. —, 10 Crim. L. Rep. 4011 (Oct. 13, 1971).

54 Sostre v. McGinnis, 442 F.2d 178, 205 (2d Cir. 1971); Wright v. McMann, 321 F. Supp. 127, 144 (N.D.N.Y. 1970), aff'd in part, rev'd in part 460 F.2d 126 (2d Cir. 1972).

55 Cf. Valvano v. McGrath, Civil No. 70-1390 at 6 (E.D.N.Y., Oct. 21, 1971).

56 There are still relatively few cases in which prisoners have been awarded damages. Sostre v. McGinnis, 442 F.2d 178, 205 (2d Cir. 1971) ($25 a day for 372 days of unlawful segregation); Anderson v. Nosser, 438 F.2d 183 (5th Cir. 1970), modified en banc No. 28971 (Mar. 3, 1972); Wright v. McMann, 321 F. Supp. 127 (N.D.N.Y. 1970) ($1500); Roberts v. Williams, 302 F. Supp. 972 (N.D. Miss. 1969) ($85,000 for negligence resulting in blindness and possible brain damage).

57 Rule 8(a)(2) of the Federal Rules of Civil Procedure provides that all that is required is "a short and plain statement of the claim showing that the pleader is entitled to relief. . . ." See also BUILD of Buffalo v. Sedita, note 20, supra.

58 Cf. Inmates of Attica, note 1, supra, at 22–23; Valvano v. McGrath, Civil No. 70-1390 at 26–29 (E.D.N.Y., Nov. 11, 1971); Cender v. Lindsay, note 1, supra.

59 In cases in which conditions have been held unconstitutional, the courts have relied on a combination of a large number of specific factors which individually might not violate the Eighth Amendment. Hamilton v. Love, 328 F. Supp. 1182 (E.D. Ark. 1971); Jones v. Wittenberg, 323 F. Supp. 93 (N.D. Ohio 1971), aff'd sub nom. Jones v. Metzger, 456 F.2d 854 (6th Cir. 1972).

60 "Strip searches" are thorough body searches (which often include a rectal examination) of inmates, often conducted before and after court appearances or visits, including attorney visits, and at other times as well.

61 Counsel should also be aware of Rule 65(a)(2) of the Federal Rules of Civil Procedure which states that "[b]efore or after the commencement of the hearing of an application for a preliminary injunction, the court may order the trial of the action on the merits to be advanced and consolidated with the hearing of the application."

62 See note 9, supra. In Cender v. Lindsay, Civil No. 70-1225 (E.D.N.Y., Nov. 23, 1970), the application for a temporary restraining order was based upon radio and newspaper reports of brutality.

63 In Inmates of Attica, note 1, supra, the temporary restraining order was issued before a complaint was filed. See note 9, supra.

64 SEC v Frank, 388 F.2d 486, 490, 492 (2d Cir. 1968); Hawkins v. Board of Control, 253 F.2d 752, 753 (5th Cir. 1958); City Line Center, Inc. v. Loews, Inc., 178 F.2d 267 (3d Cir. 1949); Sims v. Greene, 161 F.2d 87 (3d Cir. 1947).

65 Inmates of Attica, note 1, supra, at 20; Checker Motors Corp. v. Chrysler Corp., 405 F.2d 319, 323 (2d Cir. 1969); Clairol, Inc. v. Gillette Co., 389 F.2d

264 (2d Cir. 1968); Dino DeLaurentiis Cinematografica, S.p.A. v. D-150, Inc., 366 F.2d 373, 374–375 (2d Cir. 1966).

66 United States v. W. T. Grant Co., 345 U.S. 629, 633 (1953). See also NLRB v. Raytheon Co., 398 U.S. 25 (1970); Bailey v. Patterson, 323 F.2d 201 (5th Cir. 1963).

67 Inmates of Attica, note 1, supra; Matthews v. Hardy, 420 F.2d 607 (D.C. Cir. 1969); Lankford v. Gelston, 364 F.2d 197 (4th Cir. 1966); NAACP v. Thompson, 357 F.2d 831 (5th Cir. 1966); Strasser v. Doorley, 309 F. Supp. 716 (D.R.I. 1970); United States v. Richberg, 398 F.2d 523 (5th Cir. 1968). But see Belknap v. Leary, 427 F.2d 496 (2d Cir. 1970); Valvano v. McGrath, 325 F. Supp. 408, 410 (E.D.N.Y. 1971).

68 There is a growing body of precedent for this procedure: Arif v. McGrath, Civil No. 71-1388 (E.D.N.Y., Dec. 9, 1971); Valvano v. McGrath, 325 F. Supp. 408 (E.D.N.Y. 1971); Hamilton v. Love, 328 F. Supp. 1182 (E.D. Ark. 1971). Counsel should be alert to thwart efforts to give the judge only the "Red Cross tour"— where prison officials seek to show only those parts of the institution that will reflect favorably on their conduct.

69 An interesting contrast is presented in the court's decision in Valvano, vacating the findings of a magistrate whom the court had designated to take testimony and make factual findings on the issue of post-riot brutality. The only witnesses called by plaintiffs were inmates whose testimony was totally rejected by the magistrate. The court wrote:

"Where all the witnesses on one side have been considered untruthful and all the witnesses on the other side have been considered credible, it is almost inevitable that the conclusion is mistaken at least in part.

"The Special Master appears to have given considerable weight to the fact that plaintiffs' witnesses had prior felony convictions and many had records of addiction. A trial judge knows that the government frequently relies on convicts and addicts to prove its case and that juries frequently believe their testimony beyond a reasonable doubt, depending on the independent corroboration or impeachment that may be provided by documentary evidence and other oral testimony." Valvano v. McGrath, Civil No. 70-1390 at 24 (E.D.N.Y., Nov. 11, 1971).

70 Inmate differences may follow racial patterns or a prison disturbance may be blamed by the authorities on a particular ethnic or religious group. For example, where a major role in a prison disturbance is attributed to the black population, supportive testimony from white inmates can be persuasive.

71 An inmate's inability to express himself may add to, rather than detract from his credibility. Preparation of inmate testimony will be greatly facilitated if, from the outset, a separate file is maintained for each inmate interviewed.

72 Inmates of Attica, note 1, supra, at 23. "The situation here is unique in that plaintiffs, being prisoners, are at the mercy of their keepers."

73 A pretrial detainee's criminal lawyer should always be contacted prior to his participation in the suit.

74 In Valvano v. McGrath, 325 F. Supp. 408 (E.D.N.Y. 1971), the court sought to protect those who testified by enjoining the defendants "from forwarding any information to any other penal institution or employee thereof concerning any testimony given in court by any inmates, or any involvement in this lawsuit or the making of any charges against any Correction Officer." Id. at 411.

75 This was done in the Valvano case. Cf. Coffin v. Reichard, 143 F.2d 443 (6th Cir. 1944). In addition, the court in Valvano ordered:

"I. That the defendants take all reasonable steps to assure the safety of all inmates who have given statements to representatives of either side in this action, or have been interviewed by representatives of either side or have testified in court in this proceeding, or who may testify in any other action or proceeding arising out of the disturbance of October 2 to 4, 1970 or out of this action.

"II. That the defendants and all Correction Officers and other personnel in Queens House of Detention for Men are restrained until further order of the court from making any threats against any person who has been interviewed or has given a statement or testified as set forth above.

"III. That all inmates of Queens House of Detention for Men are restrained until further order of the court from making any threats against any person who has been interviewed or has given a statement or testified as set forth above." 325 F. Supp. at 411.

76 The Supreme Court's decisions in Younger v. Harris, 401 U.S. 37 (1971), Samuels v. Mackell, 401 U.S. 66 (1971), Boyle v. Landry, 401 U.S. 77 (1971), and Perez v. Ledesma, 401 U.S. 82 (1971), should not be considered obstacles to the court's issuing any injunction which is necessary to protect essential witnesses and parties, and thereby to "protect its jurisdiction" under 28 U.S.C. §2283. See the discussion of Dombrowski v. Pfister, 380 U.S. 479 (1965), in Younger v. Harris, supra at 47–54.

77 In Valvano, the court noted that an inmate who testified for the defendants was permitted to withdraw his plea of guilty to manslaughter in the second degree and to plead instead to criminally negligent homicide with a sentence to time served. See Valvano v. McGrath, Civil No. 70-1390, at 24a (E.D.N.Y., Nov 11, 1971).

78 Id. at 6.

79 Arif v. McGrath, Civil No. 71-1388 at 21–23 (E.D.N.Y., Dec. 1971).

80 Inmates of Attica, note 1, supra, at 25 (holding that the District Court should consider the use of federal monitors to enforce its injunction against brutality and harassment); Valvano v. McGrath, 325 F. Supp. 408, 411–412 (E.D.N.Y. 1971) (requesting the New York City Board of Correction to serve as monitors and report to the court).

81 Cf. Valvano v. McGrath, Civil No. 70-1390 at 29–30, 34–45 (E.D.N.Y., Nov. 11, 1971), where the defendants were ordered to begin independent departmental prosecutions of correction officers alleged to have been involved in acts of brutality against inmates. See also Biehunik v. Felicetta, 441 F.2d 228, 230–231 (2d Cir. 1971), cert. denied 403 U.S. 932 (1971).

82 Davis v. Lindsay, 321 F. Supp. 1134 (S.D.N.Y. 1970); Smoake v. Fritz, 320 F. Supp. 609 (S.D.N.Y. 1970). But see Inmates of Greenhaven v. Zelker, Civil No. 71-4676 (E.D.N.Y., Nov. 15, 1971). See also Nieves v. Oswald, Civil No.

1971-526 (W.D.N.Y., filed Nov. 16, 1971); Clutchette v. Procunier, 328 F. Supp. 767 (N.D. Cal. 1971).

[83] Rhem v. McGrath, 326 F. Supp. 681 (S.D.N.Y. 1971).

[84] Inmates of Greenhaven v. Zelker, note 82, supra; Arif v. McGrath, Civil No. 71-1388 at 16–20 (W.D.N.Y., Dec. 9, 1971).

[85] Rhem v. McGrath, 326 F. Supp. 681, 690 (S.D.N.Y. 1971).

[86] Rhem v. McGrath, Civil No. 70-3962 (S.D.N.Y., Apr. 21, 1971).

[87] It is well settled that inmate claims of denials of constitutional rights are within the jurisdiction of the federal courts under the Civil Rights Act, 42 U.S.C. §1983 (1971). 28 U.S.C. §1343 (1971); Haines v. Kerner, 404 U.S. 519 (1972); Johnson v. Avery, 393 U.S. 483 (1969); Lee v. Washington, 390 U.S. 333 (1968); Inmates of Attica, note 1, supra; Landman v. Peyton, 370 F.2d 135 (4th Cir. 1966), cert denied 388 U.S. 920 (1967). It is also clear that exhaustion of remedies is inappropriate in these cases. Wilwording v. Swenson, 404 U.S. 249 (1971); Houghton v. Shafer, 392 U.S. 639 (1968); Monroe v. Pape, 365 U.S. 167 (1961); Rodriguez v. McGinnis, No. 34567 (2d Cir., Jan. 25, 1972); Wright v. McMann, 387 F.2d 519 (2d Cir. 1967). And abstention is unwarranted because there is generally never any need for construction of a state statute so as to avoid a constitutional question. Wisconsin v. Constantineau, 400 U.S. 433 (1971); Rodriguez v. McGinnis, No. 34567 (2d Cir., Jan. 25, 1972); Wright v. McMann, 387 F.2d 519 (2d Cir. 1967). See generally "Prisoner's Rights Under Section 1983," 6 Crim. L. Bull. 237 (1970); Turner, "Establishing the Rule of Law in Prisons: A Manual for Prisoners' Rights Litigation," 23 Stan. L. Rev. 473 (1971).

[88] Inmates of Attica, note 1, supra.

[89] Holt v. Sarver, 442 F.2d 304 (8th Cir. 1971).

[90] Jackson v. Bishop, 404 F.2d 571 (8th Cir. 1968).

[91] Wright v. McMann, 387 F.2d 519 (2d Cir. 1967); Jordan v. Fitzharris, 257 F. Supp. 674 (N.D. Cal. 1966).

[92] Wilson v. Kelley, 294 F. Supp. 1005 (N.D. Ga. 1968); Washington v. Lee, 263 F. Supp. 327 (M.D. Ala. 1966), aff'd 390 U.S. 333 (1968).

[93] Holt v. Sarver, 442 F.2d 304 (8th Cir. 1971); Jones v. Wittenberg, 323 F. Supp. 93 (N.D. Ohio 1971).

[94] Sostre v. McGinnis, 442 F.2d 178 (2d Cir. 1971); Landman v. Royster, 333 F. Supp. 621 (E.D. Va. 1971); Clutchette v. Procunier, 328 F. Supp. 767 (N.D. Cal. 1971); Bundy v. Cannon, 328 F. Supp. 165 (D. Md. 1971), aff'd sub nom. Jones v. Metzger, 456 F.2d 854 (6th Cir. 1972).

[95] Johnson v. Avery, 393 U.S. 483 (1969); Ex parte Hull, 312 U.S. 546 (1941); Gilmore v. Lynch, 319 F. Supp. 105 (N.D. Cal. 1970), aff'd sub nom. Younger v. Gilmore, 404 U.S. 15 (1971).

[96] E.g. Nolan v. Fitzpatrick, 326 F. Supp. 209 (D. Mass. 1971); Fortune Society v. McGinnis, 319 F. Supp. 901 (S.D.N.Y. 1970).

[97] Cooper v. Pate, 378 U.S. 546 (1964); Sostre v. McGinnis, 442 F.2d 178, 189 (2d Cir. 1971). See also Cruz v. Beto, 405 U.S. 319 (1972).

[98] "Only a compelling state interest centering about prison security, or a clear and present danger of a breach of prison discipline, or some substantial inter-

ference with orderly institutional administration can justify curtailment of a prisoner's constitutional rights." Fortune Society v. McGinnis, 319 F. Supp. 901, 904 (S.D.N.Y. 1970).

[99] Inmates of Attica, note 1, supra, at 22–23.

[100] Sostre v. McGinnis, 442 F.2d 178, 191 (2d Cir. 1971).

[101] E.g. In re Birdsong, 39 F. 599 (S.D. Ga. 1889) (chaining inmate by neck; held unconstitutional); Hancock v. Avery, 301 F. Supp. 786 (M.D. Tenn. 1969) (no light or ventilation; no regular toilet; no soap, towel, toilet paper; restricted diet; held unconstitutional); Jordan v. Fitzharris, 257 F. Supp. 674 (N.D. Cal. 1966) (similar to Hancock; plaintiff naked, no bed; held unconstitutional).

[102] 387 F.2d at 526.

[103] Jackson v. Bishop, 404 F.2d 571, 579–580 (8th Cir. 1968).

[104] Sostre v. McGinnis, 442 F.2d 178, 193–194 (2d Cir. 1971). See also Ford v. Board of Managers, 407 F.2d 937 (3d Cir. 1969) (no running water or wash bowl; bread and water diet except one regular meal each third day; held constitutional); Landman v. Peyton, 370 F.2d 135 (4th Cir. 1966), cert. denied 388 U.S. 920 (1967) (diet of bread and water for two days, two meals on third day; no tooth brush or personal items; tear gas used; held constitutional); Knuckles v. Prasse, 302 F. Supp. 1036 (E.D. Pa. 1969), aff'd 435 F.2d 1255 (3d Cir. 1970), cert. denied 403 U.S. 936 (1971) (400 days segregation; held constitutional).

[105] Inmates of Greenhaven v. Zelker, Civil No. 71-6476 (E.D.N.Y., Nov. 15, 1971).

[106] Rhem v. McGrath, 326 F. Supp. 681, 684–685 (S.D.N.Y. 1971). See also Edwards v. Sard, 250 F. Supp. 977, 981 (D.D.C. 1966).

[107] United States v. W. T. Grant Co., 345 U.S. 629, 633 (1953); Inmates of Attica, note 1, supra, at 23–25; Belknap v. Leary, 427 F.2d 496 (2d Cir. 1970); Valvano v. McGrath, Civil No. 70-1390, at 27–28 (E.D.N.Y., Nov. 11, 1971); Cender v. Lindsay, Civil No. 70-1225 (E.D.N.Y., Nov. 23, 1970).

[108] Inmates of Attica, note 1, supra, at 23–25.

[109] Id. at 22; United States v. Richberg, 398 F.2d 523, 531 (5th Cir. 1968).

[110] Strasser v. Doorley, 309 F. Supp. 716, 725–726 (D.R.I. 1970) (declaratory relief on the basis of one incident of unconstitutional police conduct).

[111] Lankford v. Gelston, 364 F.2d 197, 204 (4th Cir. 1966).

CHAPTER 14

REMEDIES

EDITORS' INTRODUCTION

All too often, decisions in prisoners' rights cases utilize a great deal of sympathetic language, but decree little when it comes to actually ordering relief. This article discusses some of the more effective remedies which can be mandated by the courts, and points to the ways in which lawyers and the general community can aid in the enforcement of those orders.

ENFORCING PRISONERS' RIGHTS: REMEDYING THE REMEDIES

RICHARD C. HAND *
ROBERT PLOTKIN **

The true success of a lawsuit is not measured by the publicity it generates nor by flowery judicial language declaring principles of human rights. Rather, successful litigation is determined by the client's degree of satisfaction and the ultimate benefit he or she reaps from the protracted consumption of time and energy. Experience shows that prisoners have rarely reaped actual benefits from court decisions. Although the successful prison litigant can pursue the full range of declaratory, monetary and injunctive remedies, it is one thing to decree that an inmate is entitled to relief but quite another to *enforce* that decree and to assure that prison officials, hidden behind locked doors, will voluntarily comply with judicial orders.

It is not the law alone that must be faulted, although it does regularly fail to provide devices for implementing its decisions. The law historically has dealt with straightforward decrees —damages to be paid, trespasses removed—things which can readily be examined and measured. It is infinitely more difficult to determine if daily harassment or general brutality has been reduced in a closed institution. Lawyers as well as the courts are to blame, for they seek the finality of a judgment in order to close the file on another "victory" that has taken its toll in long hours of hard work. They relax or turn to new battles, assuming that the law will be complied with by correctional administrators. These administrators must also share responsibility for nonenforcement of judicial orders. They return to their closed societies, make

* Staff Attorney, Resource Center for Correctional Law and Legal Services, Washington, D.C.; A.B. Holy Cross College; J.D. Georgetown University Law Center.

** Staff Attorney, National Law Office, National Legal Aid and Defender Association, Washington, D.C.; A.B., J.D. University of Cincinnati; LL.M. New York University.

token gestures of compliance, and settle back into their familiar routines. The public demands no further accountability, expends few additional funds or energies, and prison life continues much the same as it did prior to the courtroom charades.

Thus, a discussion of remedies in prison litigation must go beyond the usual statutory and equitable avenues of relief and suggest methods for the continual enforcement of these decrees. Such suggestions reflect only a review of what is already possible and in the end they too may become as co-opted and as valueless as the remedies themselves.

Framing the Relief

As fundamental as the decision to file a lawsuit attacking prison conditions and practices is the determination of the lawsuit's precise objectives. Developing a sound lawsuit and theory for relief depends heavily upon tactical decisions made at the outset. Lawsuits born out of shortsightedness, haste, or an inability to perceive realistic objectives in terms of the underlying facts and the legal remedies available can end in failure. Not only might bad law result but, even worse, the prison inmate may again be the victim of a selective system of justice.

In deciding what relief to seek, the immediate needs of the client are paramount. Actions taken by litigators in prison crisis situations dramatize the importance of this rule. In the aftermath of prison riots and work stoppages, brutal and summary punishment meted out by prison guards is a documented reality.[1] The primary concerns of the lawyer are to gain immediate access to his client, to stop or attempt to minimize whatever brutalization is going on, and to secure needed medical relief.[2] Quite properly, all other considerations, including long-range goals and other implications of the lawsuit, become secondary. For these reasons, seasoned prison litigators are reluctant to file a comprehensive, affirmative action in response to crisis situations.[3] The optimum conditions for filing an affirmative action, particularly in an omnibus lawsuit encompassing a variety of issues, should permit careful definition of client objectives, both short and long range, assessment of available resources in light of those objectives, and selection of the procedural mechanism best fitted for achieving the relief desired.

When the conditions or practices which form the basis of the complaint are systemic and pervasive, affecting large and recognizable groups of inmates, a claim for class relief should be made, since widespread relief, rather than limited benefit to a few named plaintiffs, can result.[4] A decision must also be made whether to proceed in state or federal court.[5] All procedural and remedial advantages presented by the federal system will be of little use if the presiding judge is biased against prisoner cases, for whatever reason. Traditionally federal courts have been more sympathetic to prisoners' claims, but the state forum should never be subject to automatic exclusion.[6]

Federal courts have the power to issue equitable coercive relief in the form of preliminary and permanent injunctions.[7] They may define the rights and obligations of the parties involved under the Declaratory Judgment Act; [8] issue writs of mandamus [9] and habeas corpus; [10] and award damages.[11]

The inclusion of a plea for damages raises some questions for the lawyer. It may move edgy prison officials to seek settlement through negotiation, or, conversely, it may solidify official intransigence and increase the possibility of reprisals against the complaining prisoners. Even if the primary objective of the lawsuit is to change and improve prison conditions rather than to seek restitution for injuries that may be difficult to prove, damages should be sought both as a safeguard against mootness [12] and as a bargaining lever.

Where individual prisoners seek relief or monetary damages, the lawsuits are not unlike other habeas corpus or tort cases: they turn upon the particular facts involved. The problem of shaping the remedy occurs most often in those cases dealing with policies and conditions which exist on an institutional level and affect a substantial portion of the inmates.

Initially, administrative relief should be pursued in these instances through letters or informal negotiating sessions with the proper officials. While these officials are generally resistant to changes, they may be persuaded that prior case law and adverse publicity make settlement the wisest course. This saves the energy and resources of the litigators and can result in fast, meaningful changes for the inmates. Often administrators are more willing to cooperate *after* the complaint has been filed, so the option of negotiating should be left open.

Remedying Unlawful Procedures

In cases challenging prison procedures and policies, the common remedies are declaratory judgments and injunctions. Practices particularly susceptible to such relief are mail censorship,[13] limitations on reading materials,[14] religious restrictions,[15] punitive transfers,[16] and disciplinary rules,[17] but other administrative regulations that violate substantive constitutional rights should prove equally vulnerable. Litigators have had greater, more consistent success in these kinds of cases, probably because they involve the straightforward application of constitutional theories to administrative policies, a function familiar to both judges and lawyers.

Under the court's equitable powers, a judge can both prohibit prison officials from enforcing unconstitutional regulations and order implementation of new plans consistent with legal principles. The prisoners' lawyer should not only point out flaws in the existing system but he or she should also be prepared to offer workable alternative proposals, thus maintaining initiative and assuring substantial participation in the relief ordered. Requiring the prison to publish and distribute these new regulations [18] achieves an element of monitoring, for every inmate is then made aware of the new rules and is thereby in a position to report violations directly to the court or to the attorneys.

A remedy often overlooked, but of great importance to individual inmates, is the expunging of illegal administrative actions from prison records. Since all official determinations concerning a prisoner are made a part of his institutional file, and this record, in turn, forms the basis for future parole and classification decisions, care must be taken that no further disability results from past unlawful procedures. At a minimum, notations should be entered in an inmate's record reflecting that such decisions were reached absent adequate procedural safeguards,[19] but ideally total expungement offers the greatest protection.[20]

Landman v. Royster [21] is illustrative of both a well-litigated procedural case and the kinds of resistance one is likely to encounter from prison officials. In *Landman,* the court held the disciplinary practices of the Virginia penal system unconstitutional, enjoined their further use, and ordered that new procedures meeting minimum constitutional standards be developed.[22] The prison was required to distribute the resultant regulations to the inmates.[23] Within six months new complaints of failure to adhere to the order were filed,[24] and in less than a year it became obvious that the prison officials were not properly implementing the decree. The officials were subsequently held in contempt of court and faced with a $25,000 fine if further delays took place.[25]

Unfortunately, the difficult procedural victories such as

Landman are of limited value. Procedures alone are no more than a framework that gives an appearance of fairness. Their ultimate effectiveness is wholly dependent upon the attitudes of those charged with enforcement, since courts have refused to review the substance of the proceedings.

> "The struggle to expand and implement procedural due process in prison should be viewed as transitional and not be allowed to become terminal. Even with this important limitation much remains to be accomplished before the rights gained on paper are likely to result in changes in official behavior . . . [this] implies further that most prison authorities—like law enforcement officials reacting to the Warren Court—will seek minimal compliance and maximum avoidance when a ruling is viewed as impairing efficiency or creating the potential for disorder." [26]

Remedying Unlawful Conditions

The remedies to be pursued by the litigating attorney in cases challenging jail or prison conditions should be no less sweeping than the conditions themselves. Conditions in an Arkansas facility are typical of those found in many prisons and most jails.

> "The building and equipment have deteriorated greatly over the years. Much of the original equipment is no longer operative. Apparently this is true with respect to the original ventilation system. The very elaborate cell locking mechanisms . . . are presently inoperative. Most of the toilets are of the old niche, recessed type. The plumbing is bad and requires constant attention. The washing and showering facilities are completely inadequate. There are no safety vestibules and some windows have detention screens and some solid metal covers.
> "When the Court first inspected the jail . . . it came away with the impression that the cell areas were dark, dirty, very unsanitary, poorly ventilated, overcrowded, smelly and, overall, unhealthy and depressing places.
> "At the time this action was commenced, the jail had

no recreational, exercise, vocational or educational programs of any kind. No community resources were being utilized." [27]

Shaping an effective remedy in prison conditions suits depends upon a judicial willingness both to counter extraordinary illegality with extraordinary relief and to compel a state or county to enforce that relief. Since this often requires the expenditure or reallocation of state monies, an attorney must be prepared to convince a court that such action is not a usurpation of the legislative function but rather a constitutionally mandated responsibility to adjudicate, decide, and enforce the rights of citizens.

"Let there be no mistake in the matter; the obligation of the Respondents to eliminate existing unconstitutionalities does not depend upon what the legislature may do, or upon what the Governor may do, or, indeed, upon what Respondents may actually be able to accomplish. If Arkansas is going to operate a Penitentiary System, it is going to have to be a system countenanced by the Constitution of the United States." [28]

Moreover, increased appropriations may not actually be necessary. It may be possible to demonstrate that *reallocation* of monies already budgeted, rather than *additional* expenditures of funds, will absorb the cost of implementing changes required by the relief. This argument was successful in *Wyatt v. Stickney,*[29] where, after testimony firmly established a lack of adequate habilitation in a mental hospital, it became clear that budget revisions would not only help remedy critical staff shortages but would allow for sorely needed repairs and improvements in the existing structure.

Where the costs of bringing facilities to constitutionally acceptable levels are prohibitive, the state may be required to shut down the institutions. At least two courts have found conditions in local jails so intolerable that they have ordered the facilities closed. In Louisiana, the Orleans Parish Prison will cease operation by March, 1975, since "the present physical facilities are so deteriorated, so expensive and so difficult a structure in which to supervise and maintain security that, especially in light of the impending new prison, no reasonable expenditures could remedy all of the unconstitutional conditions which exist." [30]

Likewise, a federal court found a Georgia jail, used to house adult pretrial detainees, unfit for human habitation, declaring that "the cost of repairing the present structure would appear to be prohibitive. . . ."[31] It should be noted, however, that the inmates were *not* released; rather they were transferred to other institutions.

Short of closing an institution, courts may order reductions in population where prisoners are housed in overcrowded and punitive conditions. Although this remedy is most persuasive in instances where pretrial detainees are being held in lieu of bond,[32] several judges have found a basis for reducing prison populations under state or local housing codes.[33] Other courts have attempted to achieve constitutional compliance within existing facilities by ordering state officials to make personnel and programmatic changes. Thus courts have required that additional guards,[34] administrative staff,[35] and medical personnel[36] be hired. A few of these courts, sensitive to the less visible problem of staff attitudes, have required sensitivity training[37] or enrollment in specific courses for new and old employees.[38] Courts aware of the needs of the inmates have required psychiatric care[39] and group counselling, basic education courses, or work-release programs.[40]

Damages are a two-edged sword. Besides providing prisoners compensation for injuries personally suffered, recovery of damages is likely to have a deterrent effect on many of the more flagrant abuses documented in early prisoners' rights cases. Although judgments thus far have been limited to recoveries of nominal and compensatory damages,[41] it is clear that the federal Civil Rights Act authorizes, upon the appropriate showing of proof, recovery of punitive damages as well.[42]

Sostre v. McGinnis,[43] though unhelpful in many other respects, may lead to future recoveries of compensatory and punitive damages where conditions and practices are sufficiently onerous to support such a penalty. The Second Circuit, in affirming the lower court's compensatory award to a prisoner in the amount of $9,300, ruled that the offending warden would be required to pay this judgment out of his own pocket.[44] Moreover, the court held that punitive damages are available to prisoners in §1983 cases upon a showing that the defendant-official's acts reflect a pattern of knowing misconduct but reversed the lower court's award of punitive damages in that particular case.[45]

In addition to compensatory and punitive damages, courts also have equitable power to grant attorneys' fees[46] and expenses.[47] In *Newman v. Alabama,*[48] the court awarded the prisoners' lawyer $12,000 in fees, plus out-of-pocket expenses, to be paid by the state.

Finally, in *Landman v. Royster,* [49] three inmates recovered $21,000 in compensation against the warden of a state penitentiary for injuries sustained while incarcerated in punitive segregation.[50] Awards of this dimension, aside from setting a valuable precedent in terms of deterrence, could provide new incentives for involvement in prison litigation by lawyers heretofore unwilling to become involved without the promise of remuneration for their efforts.

Enforcement of Remedies

To be effective instrumentalities of meaningful change, court orders must be actively enforced. There are several ways this can be accomplished. One is to require the defendant prison officials to submit, within a certain time, a plan describing how and when unconstitutional conditions and practices will be eliminated.[51] By this action not only are the defendants committed to a court-endorsed timetable of their own making but also both the court and the plaintiffs are provided an opportunity to review and challenge any portions of the plan which evade or fall short of the original order. Moreover, requiring such plans renders more feasible the issuance of contempt citations for noncompliance with judicial orders. This seldom-used remedy recently made a dramatic and telling reappearance when a federal judge held three state prison officials in contempt of court, ordering immediate implementation of past decrees.[52]

One of the more significant developments in prison cases which calls for complex, and therefore long-range, relief and remedies has been the initiative taken by courts in appointing some kind of "overseeing" or "monitoring" body. In at least two jail conditions cases such monitors have been appointed to

> ". . . make frequent inspections of the jail . . . participate in meetings and conferences directed towards the reduction of the jail's population . . . consult with various governmental officials and agencies to assist in the implementation of directives relative to inmate medical and psychiatric care, jail sanitation and inmate recreational activity and . . . investigate inmate complaints of noncompliance with the Court's orders." [53]

In *Wyatt v. Stickney,* an Alabama judge designated a "Human Rights Committee" to monitor implementation of the minimum standards decreed by the court.[54] Another device to enforce judicial mandate is the appointment of a "special master" [55] to closely supervise an institution's activities.[56]

The presence of the monitors may serve a two-fold purpose. The monitors may not only report violations of the court's order in connection with contempt proceedings but also may report violations of the *criminal* law to the proper state officials. Although traditionally the use of criminal proceedings against prison officials has not been satisfactory,[57] perhaps the presence of a respected neutral body would increase the value of such a threat.

The ultimate enforcement of remedies may simply be outright release or release to parole supervision of prisoners who are held in unconstitutional circumstances. This may be the implied threat in many prison cases, such as *Holt v. Sarver,*[58] where the court concluded that if the state wants to run a penitentiary it must do so according to constitutional standards. The dramatic impact of such a drastic remedy would certainly galvanize legislative and public support to implement necessary changes. Outright release of prisoners has already occurred in at least one case, *Curley v. Gonzalez,*[59] where a federal court limited a crowded local jail to a maximum of sixty inmates. The defendants reduced the population by simply releasing all but sixty of their charges, although such action was not the clearly mandated method of enforcement.

Conclusion

Institutions such as prisons tend to perpetuate themselves; they develop a keen survival instinct that surfaces most adroitly, and least definably, when faced with outside threats to their continued existence. Court orders that seek to improve and make lawful the conditions under which men and women are imprisoned often become as insignificant and powerless as the prisoners themselves are made to feel.

To remedy the remedies, the vigilance and energy of judges and lawyers must overcome the durability and seeming immortality of prisons as institutions of despair.

Footnotes

1 See e.g. The Official Report of the New York State Commission on Attica, Final Report, at 426–449 (Bantam Books, Inc., New York, 1972).

2 Hellerstein and Shapiro, "Crisis Litigation: Problems and Suggestions," Chapter 13 of this book.

3 For example, adverse decisions were reached for the most part in cases filed responding to the Attica crisis: Inmates of the Attica Correctional Facility v. Rockefeller (hereinafter "Inmates of Attica"), 453 F.2d 12 (2d Cir. 1971); and a strike at the Lewisburg federal prison, Meyers v. Alldredge, 348 F. Supp. 807 (M.D. Pa. 1972).

4 Fed. R. Civ. P. 23. Class actions have been allowed in numerous prison cases, ranging from claims against widespread prison conditions, Holt v. Sarver, 309 F. Supp. 362 (E.D. Ark. 1970), aff'd 442 F.2d 304 (8th Cir. 1971); to racial segregation, Washington v. Lee, 263 F. Supp. 327 (M.D. Ala. 1966), aff'd 390 U.S. 333 (1968); to claims of brutality, Inmates of Atica, note 3, supra.

5 Obviously, federal prisoners do not have the choice. For the jurisdictional problems of federal prisoners, see Chapter 12 of this book.

6 In framing remedies, it should be kept in mind that the remedies in state codes are usually equivalent to the full range available in federal courts. See e.g. Jackson v. Hendrick, No. 71-2437 (Ct. C.P. Phila., Pa., April 7, 1972).

7 Fed. R. Civ. P. 65.

8 28 U.S.C. §§2201, 2202.

9 28 U.S.C. §1361.

10 28 U.S.C. §2241.

11 Since state laws relating to compensatory, nominal, and punitive damages differ widely, federal courts have attempted to bring a degree of uniformity to their decision-making by holding that §1983 should be read against the background of tort liability, which makes a man responsible for the natural consequences of his actions. Monroe v. Pape, 365 U.S. 167 (1961). For cases allowing recovery under 42 U.S.C. §1983, see also Jenkins v. Averett, 424 F.2d 1228 (4th Cir. 1970); Mansell v. Saunders, 372 F.2d 573 (5th Cir. 1967); Stringer v. Dilger, 313 F.2d 536 (10th Cir. 1963); Hague v. CIO, 101 F.2d 774 (3d Cir. 1939); Rhoads v. Horvat, 270 F. Supp. 307 (D. Colo. 1967); McArthur v. Pennington, 253 F. Supp. 420 (E.D. Tenn. 1963); Rue v. Snyder, 249 F. Supp. 740 (E.D. Tenn. 1966); Antelope v. George, 211 F. Supp. 657 (D. Idaho 1962).

12 It is recognized that a claim for damages based on equity issues is not rendered moot by cessation of a wrong once done. E.g. Hudson v. Hardy, 424 F.2d 854 (D.C.C. 1970).

13 See e.g. Palmigiano v. Travisono, 317 F. Supp. 776 (D.R.I. 1970).

14 E.g. Rowland v. Sigler, 327 F. Supp. 821 (D. Neb. 1971), aff'd 452 F.2d 1005 (8th Cir. 1971); Fortune Society v. McGinnis, 319 F. Supp. 901 (S.D.N.Y. 1970).

15 E.g. Walker v. Blackwell, 411 F.2d 23 (5th Cir. 1968); Long v. Parker, 390 F.2d 816 (3d Cir. 1968).

16 E.g. Gomes v. Travisono, 353 F. Supp. 457 (D.R.I. 1973).

17 E.g. Landman v. Royster, 333 F. Supp. 621 (E.D. Va. 1971); Clutchette v. Procunier, 328 F. Supp. 767 (N.D. Cal. 1971); Bundy v. Cannon, 328 F. Supp. 165 (D. Md. 1971).

18 Sinclair v. Henderson, 441 F. Supp. 1123, 1128 (E.D. La. 1971).

19 Daniels v. Brown, 349 F. Supp. 1288 (E.D. Va. 1972). The court required prisoners' records to be noted as "void" under subsequent court decisions so that the disciplinary actions would not affect later parole considerations. It is questionable how much impact such a caveat would have with a parole board.

20 E.g. Colligan v. United States, 349 F. Supp. 1233, 1238 (E.D. Mich. 1972).

21 333 F. Supp. 621 (E.D. Va. 1971).

22 Id. at 653–656.

23 Id. at 656.

24 See e.g. Holland v. Oliver, 350 F. Supp. 485 (E.D. Va. 1972), where the court found that prison officials had provided inmates appearing before disciplinary boards with prior notice of only one hour.

25 Washington Post, January 30, 1973, at Co. This contempt order appears herein as Appendix A-10.

26 Cohen, "The Discovery of Prison Reform," 21 Buff. L. Rev. 854, 878 (1972).

27 Hamilton v. Love, 328 F. Supp. 1182, 1188–1189 (E.D. Ark. 1971).

28 Holt v. Sarver, note 4, supra, 309 F. Supp. at 385; see e.g. Gates v. Collier, 349 F. Supp. 881 (N.D. Miss. 1972); Hamilton v. Love, 328 F. Supp. 1182, 1192–1194 (E.D. Ark. 1971); Wayne County Jail Inmates v. Wayne County Bd. Comm'rs, 5 Clearinghouse Rev. 108 (Cir. Ct. Wayne County, Mich. 1972) (opinions of May 18, 1971, March 24, 1972 and supplemental opinion of March 24, 1972, hereinafter "Wayne County"); Jackson v. Hendrick, note 6, supra. See also Note, 79 Yale L. J. 941, 955 (1970): "If the level of resources is always taken as given, it can justify anything . . . even depriving detainees to the point of starving them, with the lower level [of finances]." See generally Comment, "Enforcement of Judicial Financing Orders: Constitutional Rights in Search of a Remedy," 59 Geo. L. J. 393 (1970).

29 Wyatt v. Stickney, 344 F. Supp. 387 (M.D. Ala. 1972).

30 Hamilton v. Schiro, 338 F. Supp. 1016 (D. La. 1972) (Final Report of the Special Master, at 1).

31 Hodge v. Dodd, 1 Prison L. Rep. 263, Civ. A. No. 16171 (N.D. Ga. May 2, 1972).

32 Brenneman v. Madigan, 343 F. Supp. 128 (N.D. Cal. 1972).

33 E.g. Wayne County, note 28, supra.

34 See e.g. Holt v. Sarver, 309 F. Supp. 362 (E.D. Ark. 1970), aff'd 442 F.2d 304 (8th Cir. 1971); Jones v. Wittenberg, 330 F. Supp. 707 (N.D. Ohio 1971).

35 Jones v. Wittenberg, note 34, supra.

36 Newman v. Alabama, 349 F. Supp. 278 (M.D. Ala 1972); Wayne County, note 28, supra.

37 Taylor v. Perini, Civ. No. C-69-275 (N.D. Ohio 1972) slip opinion, at 8.

38 Jones v. Wittenberg, note 34, supra.

39 Newman v. Alabama, note 36, supra.

40 Jones v. Wittenberg, note 34, supra; Wyatt v. Stickney, note 29, supra.

41 Sostre v. McGinnis, 442 F.2d 178 (2d Cir. 1971), cert. denied Oswald v. Sostre, 405 U.S. 978 (1972); Wright v. McMann, 460 F.2d 126 (2d Cir. 1972); Sigafus v. Brown, 416 F.2d 105 (7th Cir. 1969); Whirl v. Kern, 407 F.2d 781 (5th Cir. 1969); Dewitt v. Wilkins, 335 F.2d 1 (2d Cir. 1964); United States ex rel. Motley v. Rundle, 340 F. Supp. 807 (1972). For cases authorizing recovery of damages by federal prisoners under the Federal Tort Claim Act, see United States v. Muniz, 374 U.S. 150 (1963); Close v. United States, 397 F.2d 686 (D.C. Cir. 1968).

42 Caperci v. Huntoon, 397 F.2d 799 (1st Cir. 1968), cert. denied 393 U.S. 940 (1968); Basista v. Weir, 340 F.2d 74 (3d Cir. 1965). The Basista court, in a helpful examination of the federal common law tort theory, also held that even where no allegations as to nominal or actual damages have been made, this is no bar to recovery of exemplary or punitive damages. Other cases acknowledging the availability of punitive damages under a §1983 action include: Washington v. Official Court Stenographer, 251 F. Supp. 945 (E.D. Pa. 1966); Brooks v. Moss, 242 F. Supp. 531 (W.D.S.C. 1965).

43 Sostre v. McGinnis, 442 F.2d 178 (2d Cir. 1971), cert. denied Oswald v. Sostre, 405 U.S. 978 (1972).

44 Id. at 205.

45 Id.

46 E.g. Newman v. Piggie Park Enterprises, 390 U.S. 400 (1968).

47 E.g. Jones v. Wittenberg, note 34, supra; Jordan v. Fitzharris, 257 F. Supp. 674 (N.D. Cal. 1966).

48 349 F. Supp. 278 (M.D. Ala. 1972).

49 333 F. Supp. 621 (E.D. Va. 1971).

50 Washington Post, Nov. 23, 1972, at B1.

51 Gates v. Collier, 349 F. Supp. 881 (N.D. Miss. 1972); Collins v. Schoonfield, 344 F. Supp. 257 (D. Md. 1972); Wayne County, note 28, supra.

52 Washington Post, Jan. 30, 1973, at C1. See also Goldfarb and Singer, "Redressing Prisoners Grievances," 39 Geo. Wash. L. Rev. 175, 278–281 (1970).

53 Wayne County, note 28, supra, opinion of March 3, 1972, slip opinion at 23. See also Jackson v. Hendrick, note 28, supra.

54 344 F. Supp.387, 392 (M.D. Ala. 1972). See also Gates v. Collier, 349 F. Supp. 881, 903 (N.D. Miss. 1972), where Law Enforcement Assistance Administration officials appointed a three-man committee of disinterested penologists to offer technical assistance.

55 See Fed. R. Civ. P. 53.

56 Hamilton v. Schiro, note 30, supra.

57 Goldfarb and Singer, note 52, supra, at 275–278. See also Biehunik v. Felicetta, 441 F.2d 228, 230–231 (2d Cir. 1971); cert. denied 403 U.S. 932 (1971).

58 Note 4, supra, 309 F. Supp. at 385. See also Note, 44 S. Cal. L. Rev. 1061 (1971).

59 Civ. No. 8372 (D.N.M. July 29, 1970).

CHAPTER 15
ALTERNATIVES
TO LITIGATION

EDITORS' INTRODUCTION

The prisoners' rights lawyer must not neglect the alternate avenues to litigation by which he can attempt to resolve his client's problems. These include both short-run attempts at negotiation and administrative resolution, and longer-range efforts to establish programs which will reduce the need for law suits. A number of interesting suggestions for programs that might be developed are discussed in the following article.

THE LIMITS OF LITIGATING – ALTERNATIVES TO A LAWSUIT

HILLEL HOFFMAN *

The recent upsurge of concern about conditions in the nation's prisons has inevitably drawn the legal profession into the movement for penal reform. Lawsuits involving disciplinary proceedings, parole hearings, solitary confinement, corporal punishment, political literature, mail censorship, medical treatment and legal assistance have already changed many aspects of prison life. In a few cases litigation has resulted in the restructuring of entire penal systems or entire institutions. During the past five years, as the number of lawsuits has proliferated, the amount of books, articles, reports and symposia dealing with prisoners' rights has increased enormously. At this juncture, with the first wave of major lawsuits open to retrospection, it is appropriate to examine the limits of litigation and to ascertain whether there are viable alternatives to lawsuits.

Without question, litigation has been and always will be the most important weapon in a lawyer's arsenal. Litigation brings issues into sharp focus and utilizes techniques that lawyers are well suited to perform. In instances where public apathy has been great or prison administrators have been recalcitrant, lawsuits have been the only available means of stimulating much-needed changes in prison conditions. Nevertheless, there are serious drawbacks to litigating which may not be reckoned with in the rush to publicity that accompanies many large-scale suits.

Litigation is enormously time-consuming from the point of view of the practitioner because of the need to interview prospective witnesses and to examine records and documents, and because of the time involved in trying cases, reading voluminous minutes, and writing extensive briefs. Litigation is extremely slow-moving, because trial calendars are crowded and parties are

---

* Assistant Attorney General, State of New York; LL.B. Columbia University; LL.M. New York University.

entitled to adjournments and delays in filing papers and making court appearances. Litigation is costly, because witnesses have to be transported long distances, experts have to be employed, depositions have to be taken, lengthy transcripts have to be prepared, and volunteer attorneys have to sacrifice time from their private practices. Litigation is sometimes ineffectual because of conservative decisions at the trial level, reversals on appeal, or the inability of judges to order legislators to appropriate more money for penal reforms.

In view of these difficulties and the risk of failure after many months of work, it is worthwhile to explore other approaches that may bring about the same results without the friction and animosity that often accompany lawsuits. One such approach would be for prisoners' rights lawyers and other interested members of the bar to work for the establishment of programs at the institutional level, which would deal with inmate problems expeditiously and fairly. For example, the establishment of an administrative grievance procedure that would operate within the prison on a weekly or monthly basis might be an important innovation.

In a model drafted by this writer and Ms. Michele Hermann for the Second Circuit Committee on Pro Se Litigation, volunteer lawyers would be asked to serve as hearings examiners along the lines of the Small Claims Courts in New York City. This would have the advantage of insuring an impartial tribunal, while acquainting private lawyers with the facts of prison life.

The hearing officer would have the power to issue subpoenas, administer oaths and assign some form of representation to the inmate in complex cases where the inmate needs assistance. Under this procedure the inmates-plaintiffs would be able to raise the issues normally raised in lawsuits when grievance procedures are unavailable. The hearing officer would be empowered to order corrective measures in the same way that a judge may order an inmate released from disciplinary confinement or order the restoration of an inmate's good time.

At the close of the hearing the parties would be entitled to a written determination and to judicial review on a standard of whether there was substantial evidence to support the findings. Decisions arrived at after full and fair hearings would be presumed to be correct in the same manner as in federal habeas corpus proceedings under 28 U.S.C. §2254(d).

Another program which would alleviate day-to-day prison problems would be the establishment of an ombudsman or inspector general to receive inmate complaints and bring them to the attention of the prison administration. This is currently being utilized by the New York State Division for Youth at its training schools for juveniles. Under this plan, four ombudsmen who were formerly Legal Aid attorneys specializing in Family Court matters travel to the state schools and receive complaints from the residents on matters involving their legal rights.

If the ombudsman believes the complaint falls within his jurisdiction, he will investigate it by interviewing staff members and other residents and by examining records. If he finds the complaint to be legitimate, the ombudsman will prepare a factual report which is forwarded to the superintendent of the school, the director of the Division for Youth, the director of the ombudsman project, and an independent review board. The review board is composed of two judges, a professor of law, a clergyman, an attorney, and an administrator. Its function is to offer expertise in solving problems raised by the reports and to act as an external check on the project's effectiveness.

Staff members are protected by being able to rebut unfavorable statements in the reports, and by requesting the ombudsman to investigate accusations made against them by the residents. Ombudsmen cannot initiate disciplinary proceedings against staff members, nor can they testify against staff members except as to incidents that occurred in their actual presence. Ombudsmen reports cannot be placed in a staff member's personnel file.

A third program that might ultimately reduce the need for litigation would be the establishment of a correctional information service to provide legal advice and representation to prison inmates in the same manner as the Mental Health Information Service provides assistance for mental patients in New York State. Under this program an autonomous state agency would be created, having no connection with the Department of Correction and providing legal services on the institutional level in the same manner as health care services are provided. The agency would hire its own attorneys, receive grants, and contract with recognized legal defender organizations to aid it in its work.

The attorneys of the correctional information service would be empowered to represent inmates in non-damage actions involving conditions of incarceration, legality of detention, and matters before the board of parole. The attorneys would also give the inmates advice on private legal problems. If the correctional information service should find that an inmate is presenting a claim that is frivolous or not made in good faith, the service could decline to represent the inmate, setting forth its reasons in a report to the court or the board of parole which assigned it to handle the case. However, this refusal of representation would not preclude the inmate from obtaining legal assistance from other sources or from proceeding pro se.

The presence of a correctional information service at penal institutions would be beneficial in at least two respects. First, the attorneys would be helpful in screening out worthless claims and in narrowing the issues in many cases. Secondly, the presence of attorneys at the institutions on a regular basis would act as a lubricant to prisoner-guard and prisoner-administration relationships. The attorneys would be able to resolve minor disputes informally and would present inmate grievances more articulately and less emotionally than the inmates.

The establishment of a correctional information service, an ombudsman program, or an administrative grievance procedure cannot be accomplished without extensive groundwork by members of the bar. This involves drafting new statutes and rules, lobbying in appropriate legislative committees, conferring with high level correctional officials, enlisting the support of bar associations, civic groups and religious organizations, seeing that new proposals receive favorable public attention, and, most of all, using the political acumen and skill that lawyers are noted for in protecting their own interests and the interests of more affluent clients. All of this activity may prove time-consuming and frustrating but no more so than spending months on a major lawsuit and then having a favorable decision reversed on appeal or having the court issue an order it is effectively powerless to enforce.

In addition to extensive lobbying efforts, another approach that needs fuller exploration is direct negotiation between inmates' lawyers and the administration and the correction officers. While the dramatis personae in most lawsuits are the inmate-plaintiffs on the one hand and the warden and the commissioner on the other, it is often forgotten that the line officers and their immediate supervisors play a very important role in prison life. Indeed, in some cases the administration is forced to take a position against liberal innovations because it is fearful of the opposition of the guards. This opposition is sometimes justified, because the guards have dangerous jobs to perform and they are understandably suspicious of new programs they think will weaken security and make their jobs more difficult.

Direct negotiations between prisoners' rights lawyers and the guards and the administration would go a long way to solve internal problems if all three sides were willing to talk seriously with each other. In many respects the interests of the officers and the interests of the inmates are not mutually adverse, because they spend so much time together in the same institution. An improvement in the inmates' living conditions helps the guards because it reduces tensions, and an improvement in the guards' salaries and working conditions helps the inmates because it brings better people into the system. Perhaps in the future we will see tripartite negotiations along the lines of present labor-management-government models, where inmate grievances and guard demands will be looked on as two sides of the same coin.

Finally, specialists in prison law must ask themselves whether the time and effort that is put into litigation has any effect on the ultimate rehabilitation of inmates. Although the establishment of fairer procedures and the elimination of physical abuses is unquestionably necessary and beneficial, litigation has a tendency to solve problems by legalistic means that do not touch upon the underlying causes of criminal behavior. While we know in a general way that there is a correlation between poverty, racism and crime, we do not know what motivates one individual to engage in criminal behavior while another person from the same environment or the same family remains law-abiding. At best, we can only look at an individual's background after he has been caught and try to determine retrospectively what went wrong.

Although it is not the function of attorneys to act as sociologists or psychologists, the question remains whether the establishment of legal procedures for almost every aspect of prison life will necessarily make much difference when an inmate is released from jail. The argument is often advanced that by forcing prison officials to obey the law, a good example is set for the inmates. This may be helpful to some of the men who sincerely wish to change, but it is not clear that it will be helpful to a professional criminal, a former drug addict, a compulsive gambler, an emotionally disturbed sex offender, or the other angry and sick people who were previously undeterred by the strictures of ethics, morals, religion, and penal law. As Claude Brown recently pointed out in an article in The New York Times (Sept. 24, 1972, §6 (magazine), at 95) most violent street crimes are committed by adult criminals with extremely low mentalities and by impoverished ghetto youths and drug addicts, all of whom are driven by a sense of ultimate desperation. Whether this sense of despair can be alleviated by what is accomplished in lawsuits is debatable.

Perhaps the primary value of litigation in the rehabilitative process is that it attempts to make an inmate's incarceration more decent and humane. This is a valuable goal and one that could not be accomplished without attorneys who sacrifice their time in numerous court battles. However, if we are concerned with what happens to people when they are released from prison, the legal profession must decide what the word "rehabilitation" really means and how to obtain the money and programs to bring it about. Filing lawsuits against a small group of prison officials who could not solve the problems even if they wanted to is not the ultimate answer.

SECTION IV
THE PROBLEMS
OF SPECIAL
GROUPS IN PRISON

CHAPTER 16
WOMEN AS PRISONERS

EDITORS' INTRODUCTION

Female prisoners in this country are often the victims of a number of unfair and discriminatory practices. This article discusses some of the major problems of women in prison and describes one program currently operating in this area.

WOMEN IN PRISON

MARILYN G. HAFT *

Increasing concerns have recently developed in our society for the problems of women and the problems of prisoners. Unfortunately, these concerns have rarely coalesced. As a group, women in prison suffer the mutually reinforcing problems of both women and prisoners. However, due perhaps to their relatively small number, their predominantly nonmilitant posture, and the apparent infrequency of overt brutality by their keepers, women prisoners have been neglected, even by the women's rights and the prisoners' rights movements.

This article will discuss many of the legal and social problems faced by women in the criminal justice system. The emphasis will be on the special problems of adult women incarcerated in institutions, although some attention will be paid to the uneven manner in which females are sentenced, including problems of juveniles.

The criminal justice system has shown little interest in the problems peculiar to female offenders. There are practically no statistics showing where women are incarcerated, what crimes they have committed and what sentences they have incurred. Even the comprehensive study of crime published in 1967 by the President's Commission on Law Enforcement and Administration of Justice had no statistics on women.[1,a]

Women derive one major benefit from being ignored by the system: proportionately fewer of them are arrested than men, and an even smaller proportion are convicted and incarcerated.[1]

While it could be argued that this merely reflects the rarity of criminal activities by females,[2] it seems more likely that the reason fewer women are actually subject to the system is due in large part to the fact that most law-enforcers, from the police to judges, are males and as such are more lenient towards adult females. They are merely reflecting the attitudes of men in the larger society who act out what is euphemistically known as the "chivalry factor."[3] They more often look the other way, excuse, forgive, and are thus unwilling to report and hold women.

---

* Ms. Haft is Co-Editor of this Sourcebook. Her biography appears at the front of the volume.

Although it is believed that women generally serve shorter sentences than men, there are a number of statutes which either explicitly or in effect sentence women to longer terms than men for the same crimes. In Connecticut, Maryland, Ohio, Massachusetts and Kansas, women may be sentenced for longer terms than men for the same crimes.[4] Primary among these crimes is prostitution, which labels only the conduct of the woman as criminal. In states where participation in prostitution is illegal for both males and females, unequal enforcement of the laws results in prosecution of the woman only. This phenomenon, although so very common, is a blatant violation of the equal protection clause and should be challenged by those accused of prostitution.[4.1]

Certain jurisdictions have statutes dictating indeterminate sentencing for women only; those sentenced under indeterminate sentences must receive the maximum punishment for that crime. For example, if burglary is punishable by statute by one-and-one-half to three years, the judge must sentence the prisoner coming under the indeterminate sentencing laws to three years. Therefore, in jurisdictions where indeterminate sentencing applies to women only, a woman's sentence may be potentially longer than the time a man can serve for the same violation.

It was originally believed that indeterminate sentencing was a progressive measure beneficial to women. This was based on the theory that women are more amenable to rehabilitation and therefore should be benefited with longer confinements and exposure to rehabilitative atmosphere. Needless to say, these measures have been and should be challenged in court on grounds of unequal protection of the laws.[5]

A careful study is needed to determine how many states have longer sentences for women than men. The laws in each state are not explicit in this area; some states have obscure provisions. For example, Maine has provisions for indeterminate sentencing for male and female alike. However, men can be sentenced under this law up to age twenty-six, while women are subject to it until age forty.

All unequal sentencing provisions may be, and should be, challenged on unequal protection grounds.

Female Juveniles

The chivalry factor can be a double-edged sword. For instance, the male role of protecting women has worked to the detriment of female juveniles. The double sexual standard in this society has caused the sexual and moral misbehavior of girls to be considered more serious than similar behavior by boys, and it is consequently more strictly repressed and punished. Girls are incarcerated for far less serious offenses than boys, and they are kept incarcerated for longer periods of time. According to the President's Commission on Law Enforcement and Administration of Justice, more than half of the girls before juvenile courts in 1965 were referred for conduct that would not be criminal if committed by adults, while only one fifth of the boys were referred for such conduct.[6] Incarcerated girls are often "criminals without crimes," having been committed for such offenses as running away from home, being incorrigible, ungovernable and beyond control of parents, being promiscuous, engaging in sexual relations and becoming pregnant.[7]

There is also some evidence that although girls are confined on less serious charges, they in fact spend longer periods of time in institutions.[8] Although there is no clear reason for this disparity, it may stem from fear that the young girls may become pregnant or morally depraved. Since they are seen to be weaker than males and less able to care for their moral beings, they are kept incarcerated for their own protection. Girls may also be kept on parole for longer periods of time than is required of boys.

One successful legal challenge to the practice of committing to institutions juveniles who have not been convicted of crimes was brought in New York State. In that case, the "wayward minor" statute permitted youths between ages sixteen and twenty-one to be confined in adult prisons if they were found to be "wilfully disobedient to the reasonable and lawful commands of parent, guardian or other custodian and . . . morally depraved or . . . in danger of becoming morally depraved." [9]

In *Gesicki v. Oswald,*[10] a three-judge federal court ruled that the statute was unconstitutionally vague and that it impermissibly punished a status or condition rather than a criminal act.

Another successful legal attack on the unequal treatment of female juveniles was mounted in the case of *Matter of Patricia A.*[11] There the New York statute which subjected females to the jurisdiction of juvenile courts for longer periods of time than males was declared unconstitutional.

The language in that opinion deals directly with the double sexual standard applied to young girls and boys.

"The argument that discrimination against females on the basis of age is justified because of the obvious danger of pregnancy in an immature girl and because of out-of-wedlock births which add to the welfare relief burdens of the State and city is without merit. It is enough to say that the contention completely ignores the fact that the statute covers far more than acts of sexual misconduct. But, beyond that, even if we were to assume that the legislation had been prompted by such considerations, there would have been no rational basis for exempting, from the PINS definition, the 16 and 17-year-old boy responsible for the girl's pregnancy or the out-of-wedlock birth. As it is, the conclusion seems inescapable that lurking behind the discrimination is the imputation that females who engage in misconduct, sexual or otherwise, ought more to be censured, and their conduct subject to greater control and regulation, than males." [12]

Statutes in other states which particularly victimize female juveniles should be equally vulnerable to litigation.

Women In Prison

Lack of Equal Facilities

Because so many women are screened out in the earlier stages of the criminal justice system, it is widely believed that only hard-core offenders are finally incarcerated.[13] Many of the women are poor and often black. "Chivalry" does not seem to extend to these minority women.[14] Mounting evidence supports the conclusion that the criminal justice system as a whole screens out the middle-class offender, while leaving the poor and often racial minorities to be imprisoned.

There are approximately 16,000 adult women incarcerated in the United States. About 800 are in the three federal reformatories for women. Six thousand are in state institutions, and about 8,000 are in more than 3,500 local jails scattered throughout the country. Only twenty-six states, plus Puerto Rico and the District of Columbia have separate institutions for women. Sixteen other states have women housed in facilities that are under control of wardens of male prisons,[15] or the women are transferred to sister states for incarceration.[16] This causes even greater separation between the women and their families than would normally be experienced in the isolation of prison.[17]

As women are always housed separately from men, they may often be held in prisons within male prisons.[17.1] In small county jails, women may be virtually confined to solitary as a result of rules that forbid mixing with the opposite sex. In jails where some facilities are available, women are frequently denied their use in order to prevent any contact with the more numerous male population. For example, use of the law library, when there is one in a county jail, may be denied to the female detainees. Similarly, recreation, education, and vocational programs may not be available to women in the county jails. There are many such instances of blatant violation of the equal protection clause of the Fourteenth Amendment suffered by women in jails.

Lack of Training

Despite all indications that women in prison are poor, undereducated, and lack the vocational training necessary to become self-supporting, there are very few institutions offering organized educational or vocational opportunities. The reasons usually given for the lack of programs for women are the relatively small number of women prisoners, the consequent high cost of training per prisoner, and the feeling that women criminals are less of a threat to society than male criminals and therefore do not necessitate the same financial expenditures.[18]

Sex-tracked Training

In those institutions where vocational training programs have been established for female offenders, they are almost always limited to training women as domestics or other "women's" occupations, such as hairdressing, typing, and sewing. Although all prison vocational training must be severely criticized for not being related to job possibilities after release, men may receive training in such higher paying occupations as auto repair, electronics, radio and television repair, printing, baking, and carpentry.[19]

Many women's institutions pride themselves in turning out good housekeepers; the emphasis is on behaving like a "lady," or looking attractive and keeping things clean and neat. It is little wonder that these women, poor, ill-trained and unskilled, may turn to prostitution upon their release and are prone to revolving-door recidivism. All released ex-offenders have enormous problems in finding jobs, but a female ex-offender has two strikes against her. Her sex and record put her at the bottom of the list of unemployed and unemployables in this country. There is no reason why women prisoners should not have the same vocational and educational opportunities as their male counterparts. If the legislatures and the departments of correction will not allocate the money to provide equal treatment, the courts should.

Children, Abortions, Contraceptives and Family Planning Education

A large number of women in prison have children or are pregnant. Most institutions make no provisions for pregnant women nor for women with children. Most jails do not permit children to visit, or where they are permitted to visit, glass or metal barriers often prevent any physical contact. In states where abortions are legal, pregnant prisoners are often not permitted to have them. When children are born in prison, the mothers are pressured to give them up for adoption.[20] Some prisons have nurseries where the babies can stay up to eighteen months after birth, but after that time the children must be sent away. There are no reports of child care facilities in prison nor provisions for contraceptive or family planning education.

Women who have children prior to imprisonment often see them placed in foster homes, thus breaking up the family during the time of incarceration, and upon release these women face great difficulty in regaining custody of their children. As most prisoners are released on parole, they are under the custody and supervision of their parole officers and are required to prove, in a series of informal steps, that they are willing and capable of caring for their children. This rule, which should consider the child's welfare, is subject to arbitrary enforcement if the parole officer or social agency caring for the child unjustifiably decides that the mother is unfit. In cases where custody is denied, the mother is entitled to a family court hearing on the issue of her fitness. Unfortunately, not enough women know about the right to a hearing. Although the emphasis here is on women prisoners, it is not in any way suggested that male prisoners should not be afforded the same rights in regard to their children as are women.

Children should be allowed to visit their fathers as well. Fathers should not be deprived of their custody rights either.

Parole

Another area where women prisoners may be subject to different treatment because of society's double standard towards the sexes is parole. Although there is still no established right to due process safeguards against arbitrary denial of parole, some attention should be given to different criteria which may be used in the decision to grant parole to men as opposed to women. Parole boards have been loath to divulge the reasons for their decisions to grant or deny parole, and to date most courts have not forced them to do so.[21] However, such information can be gathered by interviewing prisoners to ascertain what questions they were asked when they met the parole board.

The results may indicate a pattern whereby women are required to meet higher standards to show the board that they will not live "in sin" upon release. While it is a common condition of parole that all prisoners, male and female, may not live with any member of the opposite sex to whom they are not related or married, this rule may well be unequally enforced. Society's view that extramarital sex is normal for men but depraved for women is likely to cause parole to be refused or revoked more easily for women than for men. Unfortunately, proof of this assertion would involve enormous efforts to gather information in an area still too shrouded in secrecy. Perhaps a challenge that sexual conditions such as these violate all parolees' right to privacy will be more successful.

Legal Solutions

In the growing body of prisoners' rights law there has been a glaring absence of cases brought on behalf of women prisoners.[22] Because many of the class actions filed on behalf of male prisoners are brought on an institution-by-institution basis, their benefits are not extended to women. Therefore, the task of establishing the rights of women prisoners is formidable. Not only must those rights afforded prisoners generally be enforced for women, but also special attacks must be launched to solve those problems peculiar to women in prison.

Where women are excluded from training programs, work-release, halfway houses, furloughs and other advantages available to male prisoners, a challenge should be made under the equal protection clause of the Fourteenth Amendment. Under the Supreme Court ruling in *Reed v. Reed*,[23] different treatment of persons by the state on the basis of sex must bear a rational relationship to state objectives. In most instances of discriminatory treatment of female prisoners, that test cannot be met.

Attempts to force the state to admit women to educational and training programs may be met with the argument that since the right to treatment has not yet been generally established for prisoners, women cannot complain of exclusion from the few programs that do exist.[24] However, this argument may be countered by showing that the constitutional distinction between "rights" and "privileges" is disappearing. Even where the state or federal government is not required to provide programs, once it does it cannot exclude whole classes of prisoners from participation on the basis of sex.

Only one case is known where female prisoners successfully challenged their exclusion from a correctional program as a denial of equal protection. In *Dawson v. Carberry*,[25] inmates of San Francisco's female jail sued in federal District Court to gain participation in a work-furlough program from which they had been excluded. Jail officials claimed that it would be too expensive to provide this program for the few women prisoners. Although there was no final decision rendered by the judge in the case, he recessed for three months in order to give the correction officials an opportunity to formulate a program for the women.[26] The transcript of the hearing indicates that the judge considered the exclusion of the women from the program to be unconstitutional as a violation of the Equal Protection Clause.

The question of whether the state can be made to spend monies on separate facilities for women should be answered in the affirmative. In *Seidenberg v. McSorley's Old Ale House*,[27] a federal district court rejected the argument that a tavern could not accommodate women because it lacked the necessary restrooms, since only its past policy of discrimination had prevented it from making such an expenditure in the first place. In *Shapiro v. Thompson*,[28] the Supreme Court struck down a one-year residency requirement for the receipt of welfare payments, holding that although a state may limit its expenditures, it may not accomplish that limitation by invidious distinctions between classes of its citizens. Discrimination solely on the basis of sex is invidious. Both these cases point to the affirmative duty of the state to make equal expenditures on women's prison facilities. Legal actions need to be instituted to insure that the duty is fulfilled.

However, that duty can be a mixed blessing for women prisoners. As was pointed out, there are twenty-four states that do not even have separate women's penitentiaries. Theoretically the routes are open for courts and legislatures to force these states to expend untold sums of money to build "equal" prisons for women.[29] This would be a calamity, as this society does not need more fortress-like schools for crime and human degradation. Instead, this set of circumstances should be viewed as an unusual opportunity for those states that have unequal facilities and programs for women to spend monies on alternatives to prisons, such as community facilities, halfway houses where children can live with their mothers, vocational training programs, and extensive counselling services.

Model Legal Education and Counselling Programs

Women's prisons may not be as overtly brutal as male penitentiaries, but they are often institutions where covert oppression is wholesale. The women are treated like children, and even elderly prisoners are referred to as "girls." They are made to feel even more helpless and childlike than other prisoners. This psychological oppression has worked to such an extent that few women in prison have the sense of political consciousness possessed by many of their male counterparts, nor do they have confidence in their ability to help themselves legally or socially. Their ghastly self-image is consciously reinforced by the condescending boarding school atmosphere in the prisons.

There are, of course, female institutions, whether county jails or state penitentiaries, where barbaric conditions exist that are comparable to those in the worst male institutions. Due perhaps to women's self-image as helpless creatures, jailhouse lawyers are almost nonexistent in women's prisoners. As there is generally very little contact with the outside community, these conditions remain unchallenged.

Women inmates in all prisons are vitally concerned with the legality of their convictions and are distressed about their often complicated family law problems. Besides being so psychologically oppressed that they believe they cannot help themselves, they are handicapped by the lack of law libraries and training, which would help them solve their own legal problems.

One legal education and counselling clinic has been set up in response to this problem at Bedford Hills Correctional Facility. The prison is the only institution for women serving sentences above a year in New York State.

In the past, two approaches have been used to assist prisoners with legal problems. One, which is the legal services program, entails lawyers and law students making independent evaluations of legal problems and decisions about them, leaving the inmate passive and uninvolved, perplexed and often dissatisfied with the ultimate results. The other, which is the legal education program, aims at teaching inmates enough about the law to understand their own legal problems, but it leaves inmates frustrated and confused because it fails to provide enough legal assistance to actually remedy those problems.

After a study of these alternatives, a unique program was organized to offer a novel approach to the problems of women in prison. A clinical law program was established at New York University Law School utilizing law students and volunteer attorneys to provide *both* legal counselling and legal education to the inmates.

The project was made available to all the women in the prison, including those with reformatory sentences and those on work-release. Any inmate who is participating in the program is helped to fill out a comprehensive questionnaire to ascertain what her legal problems may be. The first six months of the program are devoted to instruction by the law students and lawyers on how to use the law library. These classes are conducted on an intensive, small group basis. Before each legal research class the students and lawyers provide counselling and legal services to remedy the women's most urgent legal problems, which are primarily in family law and criminal law areas. Periodically, general lectures are given on subjects of interest to all inmates, such as parole, court structure, jurisdiction and civil disabilities. During these months the law students study the law and procedure for postconviction remedies and family law at weekly seminars at the law school. The students must be well acquainted with both these areas in order to assist the inmates. They are also working on preparing a legal manual for inmates' use covering many substantive areas. After they have completed these legal studies and have considered the inmates' needs and desires, the students choose an area of expertise. The four major areas of specialization are criminal appeals, post-judgment motions, federal habeas corpus, and family law. All this work is done with close guidance from two supervising attorneys.

In the second six months of the year the inmates, lawyers and law students group into workshops where substantive law is discussed in the context of the inmates' individual cases. Each inmate may elect the class that deals with her most urgent legal problems. There are classes in criminal appeals, basic criminal law and procedure, habeas corpus, and family law. As the workshops progress, the inmates and lawyers work together on the preparation of individual cases.

The formation of the Women's Prison Project involved the complex process of bringing four separate groups together in mutual cooperation. First, the lawyers and law students had to meet to discuss and formulate the project. Next, the approval of the Department of Correction was needed, both from the administration at Bedford Hills and from the Commissioner of Correction in Albany. Thirdly, it was necessary to consult with the inmates. To this end, several informal meetings were held between the project directors and inmates at the prison (both on individual and group basis) to ascertain the desires, reactions, and suggestions of the women at the prison. Finally, it was arranged for the project to be offered as a clinical program at New York University Law School in order to facilitate the regular participation of law students in the program and to insure the continuity of the project.

The program has a number of goals. The common thread that runs throughout may be summarized in one word: change. Fundamentally, the program aims at changing the inmates' level of legal knowledge. The legal services component of the program hopes to change the life situations of the women by helping them to alleviate their own problems—family, medical, civil, criminal— in prison and out.

There are less tangible changes the program wishes to accomplish, the primary of these being to change the self-percep- tions of the inmates as prisoners and as women. More specifically, it is hoped that the prisoners can be aided to develop an in- creased sense of themselves and their rights and abilities, which will enable them to organize themselves and seek reforms within the prison. This is necessary because the militant mood which is so widespread in male institutions is totally lacking in women's prisons where submission and docility prevail.

Additionally, since one of the goals of the clinic is to reduce the isolation of the women, the clinic functions as an informal mobilizer of other community groups and professions. For example, doctors and social agencies have been encouraged to tend to the women's problems.

Since in recent years it has become increasingly clear that the entire prison system has become bankrupt and should be replaced, the best thing one can hope to do for women prisoners is to work for their release. The clinical program seeks to do this not only by aiding women in their individual criminal cases with the hope of winning their release but by teaching the women preventive law, so that in the future they will know how to avoid being sent back to prison.

Needless to say, legal education programs are not the whole answer to keeping women out of prisons and jails. Although litigation may help remedy the most egregious prison conditions, it cannot be seen as the solution to diverting women away from prisons. Legislative and administrative remedies as well as litigation will be necessary to form alternatives to prison.

Footnotes

[1a] The most recent comprehensive survey of correctional facilities for women is J. Lekkerkerker, Reformatories For Women In The United States (1931). This work has been updated only by an unpublished dissertation, K. Strickland, Correctional Institutions For Women In The United States, June 1967 (Ph.D. dissertation, Syracuse University, available through University Microfilms, Ann Arbor, Michigan).

[1] Uniform Crime Reports. These indicate that men and boys are arrested more often as compared to women on a 6-to-1 ratio and are convicted and admitted to federal and state institutions on a 20-to-1 ratio.

[2] The Uniform Crime Reports indicate that female crime has doubled in the last decade. Over all, arrests of women for violent crimes increased 69 per cent from 1960 to 1970, while the total crime rate for women rose 74.9 per cent during that decade. The percentage increase for men was 25 per cent. See Nagel and Weitzman, "Women as Litigants," 23 Hastings L.J. 171 (1971).

[3] See Reckless and Kay, The Female Offender (consultant report presented to the President's Commission on Enforcement and Administration of Justice (1967)).

[4] A Study in Neglect: A Report on Women Prisoners, at 5 (1972) (Survey of the Women's Prison Association in New York).

[4.1] See Portland v. Sherill, No. M-47623 (Circuit Ct. Multonah County, Oregon, January 9, 1967), defining prostitution as an offense that can be committed only by a woman as a violation of the equal protection clause. For a discussion of prostitution and the equal protection clause see generally, "The Equal Rights Amendment: A Constitutional Basis for Equal Rights for Women, 80 Yale L.J. 871, 962–965. L. Kanowitz, Women and The Law, at 16–17 (1969).

5 See Harvin v. United States, 445 F.2d 675 (D.C. 1971) (on rehearing en banc); United States ex rel. Sumrell v. York, 288 F. Supp. 955 (D. Conn. 1968); United States v. York, 281 F. Supp. 8 (D. Conn. 1968), where the court invalidated a statute requiring an indeterminate sentence for female offenders with a maximum of three years when male offenders convicted of the same offense would receive a maximum of twelve months—the state was required to but could not demonstrate that women required longer periods for incarceration; Liberti v. York, 28 Conn. Supp. 9, 246 A.2d 106 (1968), where the court invalidated a differential sentencing scheme because there was no basis factually and statistically for such differential treatment; State v. Costello, 59 N.J. 334, 282 A.2d 748 (1971), where the court required substantial empirically-grounded justification for the differential intermediate sentencing scheme, which the state could not provide on remand; Commonwealth v. Daniel, 430 Pa. 642, 243 A.2d 400 (Sup. Ct. Pa., 1968), where the court invalidated a statute which required the judge to fix an indeterminate sentence at the statutory maximum for female offenders only.

6 Report by the President's Commission on Law Enforcement and Administration of Justice: The Challenge of Crime in a Free Society, at 56 (1967).

7 See Singer, Women in the Criminal Justice System (1972) (an unpublished paper presented to the N.Y.U. School of Law Conference on Women and the Law, October 1972, on file with the author).

8 U.S. Department of Health, Education and Welfare, Children's Bureau, Statistics on Public Institutions for Delinquent Children—1964 (1965).

9 N.Y. Code Crim. Proc. §913-a(5)(b).

10 336 F. Supp. 371 (S.D.N.Y. 1971).

11 31 N.Y.2d 83, 286 N.E.2d 432, 335 N.Y.S.2d 33 (1972).

12 Id., 31 N.Y.2d at 88, 335 N.Y.S.2d at 37.

13 A national survey by the Women's Prison Association (A Study in Neglect: A Report on Women Prisoners, note 4, supra) indicates that women convicted in thirty-seven states and sent to prison are sent there for violent crimes.

14 The very few statistics that are available do support the conclusion. A survey of women prisoners at the three federal prisons (by the Labor Department) and Bedford Hills Correctional Facility, which is the only New York State women's institution for women serving more than a year sentence (by the Legal Education and Counseling Project) show that most of the women come from the city ghettos, from minority groups, and are very poor. Additionally, the very recent national survey by the Women's Prison Association in New York indicates that in the thirty-seven states studied, minority women are represented in disproportionately large numbers in prisons.

15 Figures provided by the U.S. Department of Labor, Women's Bureau, Washington, D.C. The American Correctional Association Directory lists all state institutions and populations.

16 Montana, North Dakota, and Wyoming all send their female offenders to Nebraska. New Hampshire, Rhode Island, and Vermont send theirs to Massa-

chusetts. Idaho sends theirs to Oregon, and Hawaii sends theirs to mainland federal prisons.

[17] See Park v. Thompson, Civ. No. 72-3605 (D. Hawaii, 1972), a case where a women inmate was transferred from Hawaii State Prison to the federal prison on Terminal Island in California because there was no facility to house her in Hawaii. The District Court has ordered the inmate back to Hawaii for a due process hearing on whether she was justifiably transferred. The state maintains that the inmate must be transferred back to a mainland institution because there are not sufficient vocational and educational programs and services for rehabilitation of women offenders in Hawaii. The inmate is challenging the lack of equal facilities and programs for women offenders as a denial of equal protection. On the issue of remoteness of women's institutions, see generally Note, "The Sexual Segregation of American Prisons," 82 Yale L.J. 1229 (1973). For a discussion of transfer of prisoners from one institution to another as a denial of due process, see Milleman, "Due Process Behind the Walls," Chapter 5 of this book.

[17.1] There are some sexually integrated state and federal prisons. The Federal Correctional Institution at Forth Worth, Texas is the only truly sexually integrated adult facility in the country. The Pennsylvania women's institution at Muncy, and the Massachusetts women's institution at Framingham have begun to take male inmates, but thus far few have been admitted, N.Y. Times, April 12, 1973, at 51 Col. 1. In the other states where women prisoners are technically housed in the same state institution as male prisoners, they are held in separate units of those institutions, with little or no mixing of the populations. This is the case, for example, in Florida, Mississippi, and New Mexico, ACA Directory supra, note 15, at 55–56. For a discussion of the present and future sexual integration of prisons, see Note, "The Sexual Segregation of American Prisons," note 17, supra.

[18] A Study in Neglect: A Report on Women Prisoners, note 4, supra.

[19] For descriptions of the difference in job training offered males and females in New York, Connecticut, and New Jersey, see Singer, Women in the Criminal Justice System, note 7, supra, at 39–40; The District of Columbia Commission on the Status of Women, Female Offenders in the District of Columbia, at 16 (1962); and Goldman, "Women's Crime," 22 Juvenile Court Judges J. 33–34 (1971); and Note, "The Sexual Segregation of Prisons," note 17, supra, at 1269–1273.

[20] Konopka, The Adolescent Girl in Conflict, at 22–23 (1966); Goldman, note 19, supra.

[21] Monks v. New Jersey, 58 N.J. 238, 277 A.2d 193 (1971).

[22] See Garnes v. Taylor, Civ. No. 159-72 D.D.C. filed January 25, 1972, an omnibus suit which raises many of the same issues as in class actions for men. This suit challenges the conditions in the District of Columbia Women's Detention Center. It also deals with problems peculiar to women, such as prostitution, and asks as part of relief that day care centers be set up for women with children. See also Park v. Thompson, note 17, supra; Dawson v. Carberry, No. C-71-1916 (N.D. Calif., filed Sept., 1971).

[23] 404 U.S. 71 (1971). In Frontiero v. Richardson, — U.S. —, 41 L.W. 4609 (May 14, 1973), four members of the Court held in that case that any classification based on sex was "inherently suspect" and subject to "strict judicial scrutiny."

[24] See articles in this book: Koren, "The Right to Medical Treatment" (Ch. 8), and Silbert and Sussman, "The Rights of Juveniles Confined in Training Schools" (Ch. 17); and Holt v. Sarver, 309 F. Supp. 362 (E.D. Ark. 1970).

[25] No. C-71-1916 (N.D. Cal., filed September, 1971).

[26] Another instance where women prisoners successfully asserted their right to participate in a correctional program offered men was in Mississippi, where female offenders won the right to conjugal visits, which had been given to male offenders for many years.

[27] 317 F. Supp. 593 (S.D.N.Y. 1970).

[28] 394 U.S. 618 (1969).

[29] See Note, "The Sexual Segregation of American Prisons," note 17, supra in which the probabilities of having courts mandate large amounts of money for building women's facilities is deemed unlikely. However, the Fourteenth Amendment is viewed as a likely vehicle to equalize programs and services in instances where comparatively little expense is required. The adoption of the Equal Rights Amendment is seen as a panacea for women's prisons. If the Amendment is adopted it can be used as a justification for the sexual integration of prisons whereby each prisoner will be placed within the system according to his or her individual requirements. Geographical location, programs and services to fit individual needs would be the sole legitimate basis for placement in an institution and in programs within the institutions. Sex would no longer be a basis for such placement. In passing the ERA, Congress clearly intended that benefits be extended whenever possible to those excluded previously, S. Rep. No. 92-689 92nd Cong. 1st Sess. 4–6 (1972). Therefore the advantages women presently have in prisons as compared with men, such as more privacy and lower security measures, may be extended to men where appropriate. Those benefits men presently have over women in prisons, including more programs, more services, homogeneity in security and offender classification because their larger numbers permit such classification, and more favorable geographical location, may be extended to women prisoners.

CHAPTER 17
JUVENILES AS PRISONERS

EDITORS' INTRODUCTION

The recidivism engendered by prison life is often less shocking than the criminal careers spawned in the training schools. Therefore, whatever need there is felt to be for a more humanitarian and socially useful treatment of adult offenders extends equally, or with even greater force, to the case of youthful offenders. This article describes the plight of juveniles in training schools and enumerates both their vested and emerging legal rights in a very comprehensive fashion.

THE RIGHTS OF JUVENILES CONFINED IN TRAINING SCHOOLS

JAMES D. SILBERT *
ALAN SUSSMAN **

Children in institutions are alone. Orphans, truants, runaways, and delinquents are deprived of their liberty in the name of treatment. Given neither the full constitutional protections of an adult nor the treatment, training, and rehabilitation promised, they suffer a cruel irony. They are often confined in penal-like institutions for noncriminal behavior, and if they do commit crimes, they are frequently confined for longer periods of time than adults are for committing similar crimes.

Unlike convicted adults, committed juveniles are not meant to suffer any civil disabilities while they are incarcerated. Children thus take with them to training schools not only all the rights that have been and are being granted to adult prisoners but all those possessed by free children as well. However, they are deprived of the right to leave the institutions at will and other rights absolutely necessary for and rationally related to "treatment," which is the purpose of confinement.

According to the National Center for Social Statistics in Washington, D.C., there are about 50,000 children in the United States living in public institutions for delinquent children. This article will focus on the rights of juveniles confined in training schools pursuant to juvenile court or family court placements. It will not cover older youths who are committed under "Youthful Offender" statutes nor those who are sent to reformatories pursuant to criminal court sentences.

* Ombudsman for juveniles, New York State Training Schools; Trial Attorney, Special Litigation-Law Reform Unit, Juvenile Rights Division, Legal Aid Society, New York City; J.D. Columbia Law School.

** Ombudsman for juveniles, New York State Training Schools; Special Litigation-Law Reform Unit, Juvenile Rights Division, Legal Aid Society, New York City; J.D. New York University.

Postadjudication Legal Rights Pertaining to Commitment

Right to Challenge the Legality of the Confinement

Once a child is placed in an institution by a court, he has the absolute right to challenge the legality of his or her confinement.[1] The confinement may be deemed improper because: (1) a legal irregularity occurred prior to confinement; or (2) he was placed in an inappropriate facility; or (3) the purpose for which he was sent to the institution is not being fulfilled. The confinement may be challenged by a direct appeal, by a writ of habeas corpus, or by a civil rights action under 42 U.S.C. §1983 in a federal court.

Grounds for Challenging the Confinement

Lack of Due Process in the Original Adjudication

Before a child may be committed to an institution he must be afforded the basic due process guaranties at the adjudicatory phase of the juvenile court proceeding. In 1967, the United States Supreme Court stated that "neither the Fourteenth Amendment nor the Bill of Rights is for adults alone."[2] The Court held that juveniles are entitled to adequate notice of the charges against them, the right to counsel, the privilege against self-incrimination, and the right of confrontation and cross-examination. Since 1967, this list of procedural guaranties has been expanded to include almost all those granted an adult except a grand jury indictment and a jury trial.[3] Consequently, children who have been deprived of any of these rights may challenge the legality of their confinement.

Statutory Vagueness and Unequal Protection

A juvenile may challenge the legality of confinement on the grounds that the statute under which he or she was adjudicated is unconstitutional because it is either too vague or discriminates unfairly against one sex. Some statutes which subject females to the jurisdiction of juvenile courts for longer periods of time than males have been declared unconstitutional.[4] Although statutes that permit commitment of juveniles for noncriminal behavior have been attacked successfully by older youths,[5] recent challenges of statutes permitting the confinement of younger juveniles for noncriminal behavior have been uniformly unsuccessful.[6]

Being Placed in an Inappropriate Facility

A child may challenge the legality of the confinement if he is placed in an inappropriate facility such as an adult correctional institution,[7] or in a facility where the conditions may be so unsuitable or unsafe as to violate the Eighth Amendment.[8] In many states all children are placed in the same institution without regard to the particular purpose for which they were brought before the court. Consequently a neglected child may be confined in the same institution with "hardened" delinquents. These neglected children may have the right to challenge the legality and appropriateness of their confinement on the grounds that they are being punished for their status and not for their behavior, in violation of the Eighth Amendment.[9]

Lack of Treatment

A child may challenge the legality of his or her confinement on the grounds that the purpose for which he was sent to the institution—treatment—is not being carried out.[10] Moreover, if in the name of "treatment" a child is abused, he has the right to challenge the appropriateness of the treatment.[11]

Right to an Attorney for Postadjudication Proceedings

If a child's right to challenge the legality of confinement is to have any significance, he must have the right to be represented by an attorney.[12] Most juveniles have neither financial resources to obtain independent counsel nor the educational sophistication to prepare pro se applications to a court. Therefore if they are to receive access to judicial relief, their right to confidential communications with a court or legal aid organization must be enforced.[13]

Right to Release Upon Expiration of Commitment Order or When It Is Determined That One Needs No Further Treatment, Whichever Is Sooner

In most states a juvenile is confined for an indeterminate term, often until he reaches majority. Since the purpose of confinement is treatment and not punishment, once it is determined that the child requires no further treatment he should be released, even if the legal time period has not expired.[14] To keep a child confined when there is no longer a need for treatment merely because he has no home is an unnecessary deprivation of liberty. In cases such as these the child should be considered "abandoned" or "homeless," to be cared for in an appropriate, nonpenal environment.[15]

Right to a Parole Revocation Hearing With Counsel

In New York a child has the right to a parole revocation hearing with the assistance of counsel before he or she can be sent back to an institution.[16] Strict rules and regulations governing these hearings have recently been promulgated.[17]

Right to Extension of Placement Hearing

Many states that authorize placements of juveniles for indeterminate terms provide that the need for continued confinement and/or parole supervision be reviewed periodically by the juvenile court.[18] Since such an extension is, in effect, a new sentence, a juvenile has the right to be present in court, the right to confront witnesses, and the right to an attorney.[19] Absent such a hearing, a juvenile's continued confinement and/or parole status is improper.

Right to Maintain a Civil Suit

Since there is no statutory loss of civil rights as a result of a juvenile court or family court adjudication, a child in an institution does not lose the right to sue civilly. Children maintain the right to sue for damages that may result from negligence or abuse incurred at the institution. These suits, however, may have to be brought by a parent, next friend, or law guardian. The claim for damages may be brought in a state or federal court as part of a civil rights action under 42 U.S.C. §1983.[20]

Right to Procedural Due Process Within the Institution

Right to Notice and Knowledge of Written Rules and Regulations

Just as certain states now mandate that meaningful written rules and regulations be distributed to adult inmates, the same right is developing for juveniles.[21]

Right to Be Free from Arbitrary Institutional Punishment

Juveniles must be afforded at least the basic elements of due process before being disciplined. It may not be necessary to hold a formal hearing, but as the Second Circuit stated in *Sostre v. McGinnis,*[22] the procedure must be "minimally fair and rational. . . ." This includes the right of the juveniles to be confronted with the accusations and the evidence against them and to have an opportunity to explain their actions. The criminal court in Chicago in *In re Owens* [23] specifically mandated that these basic guaranties be applied to juvenile institutional disciplinary proceedings.

Right to Be Free From Arbitrary Transfers

While many juveniles are initially placed in minimum-security training schools, they might be transferred administratively to maximum-security juvenile institutions, adult correctional institutions, or mental hospitals without first returning to court. These transfers are normally based on the juveniles' behavior in the former institution, not on the seriousness of the "offense" that brought them before the court in the first instance. Thus, a juvenile who was sent to a training school because of truancy may end up in a maximum-security institution because of poor "adjustment" at the open facility.

A juvenile has the right to the same basic procedural guaranties as an adult, namely, notice, the right to be heard, and the right to present evidence before being transferred.[24]

These transfers are generally not made for punitive reasons but rather to provide the juvenile with better care, treatment, and discipline. What in fact is delivered is more security. In view of the fact that the underlying philosophy of the juvenile court system is treatment, not punishment, the analogy of mental hospital transfer cases is applicable. In these cases the standard used by the courts is whether the transfer is the least onerous method of treating the patient.[25]

Right to Treatment

Juvenile court philosophy is firmly rooted in the concept that a child is not committed to an institution for punishment but rather for rehabilitation and treatment. Statutes under which juveniles (as well as mental patients and, in some jurisdictions, drug addicts and sex offenders) are civilly committed are constitutional *only* because treatment is to be provided.[26] Commitment of a juvenile without treatment, therefore, is a violation of the Eighth and Fourteenth Amendments.[27]

The first case to refer to a right to treatment for juvenile offenders was *White v. Reid.*[28] The court held that juveniles may not be detained in facilities (jails) that do not provide for their rehabilitation.[29] It was not until 1966, however, that the right to treatment received strong and clear judicial support. In the landmark decision of *Rouse v. Cameron,*[30] the D.C. Circuit Court held that involuntarily committed mental patients have a constitutional right to treatment, since the purpose of hospitalization is not to punish but to help the patient.

The strongest statement in support of the right to treatment is contained in *Wyatt v. Stickney,*[31] in which it was held that programs in a state hospital failed to provide treatment for the mentally ill. The court declared:

> ". . . The purpose of involuntary hospitalization
> . . . is *treatment* and not mere custodial care or punishment. This is the only justification from a constitutional standpoint . . . that allows civil commitments to mental institutions. . . .
>
> . . . .
>
> ". . . To deprive any citizen of his or her liberty upon the altruistic theory that the confinement is for humane therapeutic reasons and then fail to provide adequate treatment violates the very fundamentals of due process." [32]

Recent federal cases have specifically focused on this right as applied to juveniles in training schools.[33] They indicate that the term "treatment," while not specific, includes at the minimum adequate food, shelter and clothing; academic, vocational, and physical education; medical care; social services; psychiatric services; supervision by trained child care staff; recreation; and opportunity for visits and telephone calls.

Proof of insufficient staff [34] and inadequate psychiatric and medical care [35] has been held to evidence lack of treatment. Some courts have held that when the evidence supports the designation of an institution as "penal" it cannot be considered treatment-oriented,[36] and placement there of juveniles who had not committed any crime is considered to be harmful.

The right to treatment also has statutory support—with varying degrees of specificity—in some jurisdictions.[37] These statutes generally direct child care institutions to provide for the treatment or "reformation" of its inmates,[38] or for their treatment, rehabilitation, and "training." [39] Some specify vocational, physical, and academic requirements,[40] others the need for food and shelter,[41] and still others prescribe the maximum number of residents allowable in an institution or living unit.[42]

Right Not to Be Treated

Though it may seem contradictory, coupled with the right to treatment is the right *not* to be treated, that is, whenever institutional programs tend to degrade, dehumanize, punish, harm, or humiliate a child, they cannot be condoned merely because they fall within the category of "treatment." [43]

Not only must treatment not be allowed to become a justification for a denial of due process, but it may not serve to justify acts which, considered by themselves, constitute punishment, whether cruel and unusual or not.[44]

Individual Rights

Since the entire concept of juvenile commitment is treatment and not punishment, the issue is not what rights a child should possess while detained but rather which ones, if any, are forfeited.[45]

While legal literature on this matter is scarce, it is the opinion of the authors that the only rights lost by reason of commitment are the right to leave at will (liberty) and those others that are *absolutely necessary* to the furtherance of the rehabilitative program, and *not* those necessary to further the course of treatment of the individual child. Thus a juvenile may not be handcuffed to a chair in a classroom in order to derive the benefits of instruction, even though education may be deemed necessary under the treatment program as a whole.

Right to Be Free from Cruel and Unusual Punishment

Although certain constitutional amendments have not been extended to juveniles, such as the Seventh Amendment (right to a jury trial),[46] the Eighth Amendment prohibition against cruel and unusual punishment unquestionably applies.

Federal courts have held that extended periods of solitary confinement in juvenile institutions constitute cruel and unusual punishment,[47] and the conditions of a juvenile institution may be so unsuitable or unhealthy as to violate the Eighth Amendment.[48] Furthermore, the use of thorazine or other tranquilizers for the mere purpose of control has been prohibited by the Eighth Amendment.[49]

Abuse of children in any form, including corporal punishment, is prohibited in some states,[50] and disciplinary procedures that utilize the punishment of children by other children may violate the "unusual" aspect of the Eighth Amendment.[51] Additionally, confinement without treatment for a "status" rather than for criminal behavior, such as incorrigibility or truancy, may violate the Eighth Amendment.[52]

Right of Free Expression and Choice of Personal Appearance

Most training schools have on their premises public educational facilities which children must attend in order to comply with state compulsory education laws. Since the schools usually come under the jurisdiction of a state board or commission of education, rules applicable to student expression and dress in schools on the "outside" are equally applicable to training schools. At the very least, these rules are applicable while a child in training school is attending classes and perhaps—if the entire institution is considered a school—outside of classes as well. Furthermore, since juveniles in child care institutions lose none of their civil rights,[53] their right of free speech, both verbal and nonverbal, may not be abridged.

With regard to expression, the United States Supreme Court in *Tinker v. DesMoines School District* [54] established the fact that students do not forego their First Amendment rights by passing through the schoolhouse door. In *Tinker,* the Court declared unconstitutional the school district's ban on black armbands worn by students to protest the Vietnam war. This attire, the Court held, is protected when worn as a form of symbolic speech and when it does not substantially interfere with the operation of the school.[55]

With regard to the right of a student to determine the length of his hair, however, there exists a variety of precedents, in separate districts and circuits, holding both for and against freedom of choice.[56] The issue is further frustrated by the fact that the United States Supreme Court has refused to rule on the issue and that the holding in *Tinker* has been almost consistently distinguished as a First Amendment issue not applicable to the length of one's hair.

In New York, however, the Commissioner of Education has repeatedly ruled that the choice of one's hair style and the right, for girls, to wear pants to school is vested in the student and his or her parent. It has been held that no pupil may be excluded from instruction or extracurricular activities because of appearance unless the appearance poses a threat to the health, safety or welfare of the child or others or actually disrupts the educational process.[57]

The right to wear a beard has been upheld as belonging to adult prisoners awaiting trial so long as it presents no health hazard. A federal court recently held that a prison rule banning beards was not reasonably related to one's status as an unconvicted detainee.[58] Adjudicated children in detention centers and training schools are also unconvicted and should come under the scope of this decision.

Children in institutions are often compelled to wear ill-fitting uniforms with little or no variation in color or style. In some institutions a child suspected of planning to run away is forced to wear "breeze attire": extra-large pants with no belt, shoes without laces, or pajamas. While the justification for this type of clothing may be that it is necessary to maintain discipline and order or to identify a child in case of escape, the rationale is incompatible with the concept of treatment, for which the child was sent to a training school. These clothes, like prison stripes, serve not only to degrade and humiliate the child but to brand him in his own eyes as a prisoner.[59]

Certain states have regulations governing child care institutions which require each facility to furnish children with appropriate clothing, individually selected and properly fitted.[60] Properly fitted *state-owned* clothing, however, still dictates conformity. Needless uniformity reduces individuality. If the purpose of training schools is treatment and rehabilitation and instilling in the child a sense of dignity and pride, nothing is so essential to this goal or so directly related to an adolescent's self-image as his or her personal appearance. A child should have the right to wear varied, properly fitted, and, more important, personal clothing.

Right to Coeducational Activities

The early teenage years constitute a time of individual sexual awakening, experimentation, and identification. They also bring forth feelings of confusion and sexual frustration even among noninstitutionalized adolescents. Stringent sexual segregation during commitment, therefore, acts as an extra burden to be borne by juveniles in training schools and may be detrimental to the normal maturational and socialization process of youths supposedly confined for purposes of treatment and adjustment.[61]

In boys' institutions, the lack of privacy, the absence of females, the denial of appropriate stimuli, sheer sensual monotony, and the search for a meaningful relationship all contribute to the existence of homosexuality, either forced or consensual.[62]

Of female adolescent institutions it has been said, "The training school fosters homosexuality by putting girls of similar psychodynamic backgrounds together in a group living situation and depriving them of contact with the opposite sex." [63]

The frequent scheduling of mixed dances or other social events, if not the establishment of coeducational training schools, should be a part of a child's right to treatment. Moreover, the allowance or non-punishment of a modicum of autoeroticism should constitute part of a child's right to privacy.[64]

Right to Worship or Not to Worship As One Pleases

The right of a child to change his or her faith or abstain from religious activities altogether is not as well founded as other rights discussed herein. Most jurisdictions recognize the right of parents to control the religious upbringing of their children.[65] Training schools, therefore, must honor these wishes to the degree that they act in loco parentis.[66] Indeed, many statutes and regulations impose on training schools the burden of *fostering* as well as respecting the religious development of children,[67] which may be in violation of the Establishment Clause of the First Amendment. Thus, the judicial standards protecting the freedom of choice in matters of religious worship for adult prisoners may not apply in whole to juveniles committed to state institutions.[68] But the fact that most of the institutions are bound by the constitutional and statutory guaranties of an individual's freedom of religion and worship make them subject to constitutional attack.[69]

The question then arises as to when a child has the right to choose his or her own faith or no faith. Following the line of cases upholding the strict separation of church and state, it may be said that child care institutions are prohibited from imposing religion, either against the wishes of a child or his or her parents.[70] In pursuing the right of a child to make his or her own decisions independent of parental wishes, it might be argued that a child has the right to choose his or her own faith or no faith once he or she has reached "the age of discretion." [71]

At the minimum, it would appear as though the child has a right to follow the wishes of parents or guardians even when these wishes run counter to institutional policies. Therefore the training school is legally bound to respect the desires of the parent or guardian, regardless of whether the child is to be brought up according to the tenets of a particular religion, none at all, or according to the child's own decision.

Right to Receive and Send Uncensored Mail

Most juvenile institutions inspect, censor, and, at times, prohibit mail from coming in and going out of the facility. While courts have generally permitted prison officials to open and read all incoming and outgoing mail of *convicted* prisoners,[72] they have made a distinction between convicted inmates and those awaiting trial. In cases dealing with unconvicted inmates, it has been held that they may not be subjected to any greater hardship than necessary, and that they retain all rights of ordinary citizens except the right to come and go as they please. Thus, as the court stated in *Palmigiano v. Travisono*,[73] censorship of mail addressed to public officials, courts, and counsel cannot be permitted, and while incoming mail may be inspected for contraband and read in certain instances, outgoing mail cannot be inspected or read at all. Children in institutions have not been convicted of any crime, have not been denied any of their civil rights, and are not being held for punitive reasons; consequently their mail should be neither censored nor read.[74]

If the purpose of confidential communication is to have meaning for a child in an institution, it must be extended beyond that of judicial and legal personnel. Since most confined children do not have attorneys nor realize that they have access to them once they leave court, it is imperative that they have *someone* outside the institution in whom they may confide. For a training school to prohibit a child from writing a letter to his parents because it is "not in his best interest," contains "inaccurate information" or "profanity," or because it "may harm the parent-child relationship" is prior restraint on the freedom of expression in violation of the First Amendment and violates a child's right to privacy.

In addition to security as a justification for censorship, juvenile institutional authorities assert that their restrictive mail policy is related to the treatment program. However, isolating a child from potential bad news from the outside and preventing him from freely communicating his feelings about his treatment on the inside not only prevent a child from dealing realistically with these situations but stifle and frustrate his attempts to come to terms with his problems.

Right to Vote

Unlike incarcerated adults, juveniles in institutions do not lose any of their civil rights. In New York, the fact that a child has been adjudicated a juvenile delinquent *shall not* "operate as a forfeiture of any right or privilege or disqualify him from subsequently holding public office or receiving any license granted by public authority." [75] Certainly a child over eighteen who is committed to a juvenile institution does not lose the right to vote. The institution therefore should make ample arrangements to allow the juvenile to exercise the right to vote.

Right to Adequate Compensation for Work

The Thirteenth Amendment prohibition against involuntary servitude specifically excludes those convicted of a crime and imprisoned. Children in institutions, many of whom are committed for noncriminal behavior, have never been convicted of a crime. They are, however, forced to do tedious and boring work each day, such as mowing lawns, painting, and polishing floors. Often they are used as staff substitutes, which in some jurisdictions violates existing regulations.[76] For this work they receive little, if any, compensation. Work must be meaningful, constructive, and directly related to a proper vocational training program; tedious, menial labor without adequate compensation violates the Thirteenth Amendment.

Right to Confidentiality of Training School Records

Almost every jurisdiction considers its juvenile or family court proceedings confidential.[77] The privacy of these proceedings has been part of the philosophy and practice of the juvenile court system since its inception.[78] Even with the recent extension of certain procedural rights to juveniles, neither the protective nature of the court nor the confidentiality of its records has been altered.[79]

Similarly, a child's institutional records are private and are protected from disclosure, either through an extension of the statutes relating to court proceedings or by separate laws and regulations.[80]

Furthermore, a significant number of the reports contained in a child's training school records are generally filed by doctors, nurses, dentists, psychiatrists, psychologists, clergymen, and social workers. In every jurisdiction, communications with all or some of these professionals are deemed confidential and privileged, waivable only by the child or parent.[81]

Confinement Pursuant to Federal Adjudications

Jurisdiction

Under federal law, a juvenile delinquent is a person under the age of eighteen who has violated a law of the United States not punishable by death or life imprisonment.[82] Most young offenders, however, are turned over from federal to state authorities. Juveniles who come under the scope of the federal law may be proceeded against on the federal level as a delinquent only if both the child and the Attorney General consent. A child's election, therefore, is not in the nature of an absolute right, because the Attorney General has discretion to proceed against the juvenile by indictment just as in the case of an adult.[83]

Arrest, Detention, and Bail

Whenever a juvenile is arrested for violating a federal law, he must be taken "forthwith" before a committing magistrate.[84] If he is not so delivered, he may be detained in a juvenile home or "other suitable place" of detention designated by the Attorney General.[85] He may not be detained in a jail unless, in the opinion of the arresting officer, detention is necessary to secure the custody of the juvenile or to ensure the child's safety or that of others.[86]

The juvenile may not be detained either in an institution or jail for a period longer than is necessary to produce him or her before a committing magistrate.[87] This provision has been held to strict standards by the Second Circuit in *United States v. Glover*.[88]

Unlike pretrial proceedings in some states, juveniles brought before magistrates on federal charges may be released on bail, on their own recognizance or that of some responsible person.[89] In default of bail, the magistrate may commit the child to a juvenile home or some other suitable place of detention designated for that purpose by the Attorney General. The child may not be committed to a jail unless, in the opinion of the marshal, it appears this commitment is necessary to secure the custody of the child or to ensure the safety of the child or of others. If a juvenile is detained in a jail, he must be held in quarters apart from adults if segregated facilities are available.[90]

Hearing

Once delinquency proceedings have been initiated, the procedural rights that have been discussed earlier attach, including the rights to notice of charges, counsel, cross-examination, confrontation of witnesses, freedom from self-incrimination, and proof beyond a reasonable doubt.[91] While 18 U.S.C. §5033, which provides for an automatic waiver of the right to a trial by jury in federal delinquency hearings, has been declared unconstitutional as violative of the Sixth Amendment by one district court,[92] it is likely to remain in force in light of more recent circuit court and Supreme Court rulings on the same matter.[93]

When a child elects to be tried under the federal juvenile delinquency law, he must be advised of those procedural rights that normally accompany adult criminal proceedings but do not apply to delinquency proceedings.[94]

As with state delinquency hearings, federal adjudications are not to be considered convictions or sentences for crimes. The entire philosophy and purpose of the federal juvenile delinquency law is to avoid the prosecution of juveniles as criminals.[95]

Commitment

If a federal court finds a juvenile to be a delinquent, he may be placed on probation until his twenty-first birthday or committed to the custody of the Attorney General for like period.[96] The Attorney General in turn may commit the child to any public or private agency or foster home for the "custody, care, subsistence, education, and training of the juvenile." [97] While "care" and "training" are therefore required, no statute or provision dictates that an adjudicated juvenile must be sent to or remain in a national training school.[98] In fact, the Attorney General may place a child in a federal penitentiary or correctional institution if he so desires.[99] Some limits on the discretion of the Attorney General, however, have been judicially dictated. In *Stinnett v. Hegstrom,*[100] the court declared that the Attorney General could transfer a child from a national training school to more strict facilities only if they were in some degree comparable to those from which he was being taken, and that a transfer to a correctional institution would render the juvenile delinquency law a "hollow pretense" unless the latter institution maintained facilities for juveniles segregated from adult prisoners.

Under no circumstances, however, may the adjudicated juvenile remain committed for a period exceeding his or her twenty-first birthday or the term which might have been imposed had he been tried and convicted of the alleged violation for which he was determined delinquent, whichever occurs first.[101]

The crucial aspect of commitment, whether to a national training school or to any public or private agency, is that it must be for the care and training of the juvenile.[102] Courts have consistently stated that rehabilitation—rather than punishment—is the purpose of commitment under federal juvenile delinquency law.[103]

Judicial interpretations of the quality of treatment received by children committed pursuant to state juvenile court hearings would be equally applicable in determining the adequacy of treatment in federally operated institutions. Furthermore, constitutional prohibitions against cruel and unusual punishment, the creation of a "stigma" of criminality, and the treatment of residents as convicted criminals rather than as juveniles bearing a status, would be subject to legal attack if not upheld.[104]

Parole and Escape

Federal parole statutes pertaining to adult criminals and youthful offenders are not applicable to juvenile delinquents.[105] Instead, juveniles committed under federal law may be released on parole "at any time under such conditions and regulations as the Board of Parole deems proper" if the juvenile has given evidence of reformation and if there is a reasonable probability that the juvenile will remain at liberty without violating the law.[106] There is some conflict whether the federal escape statute, 18 U.S.C. §751, is applicable to juveniles.[107]

Particular Areas Vulnerable to Litigation

There are certain aspects of conditions and laws under which children are confined that are particularly vulnerable to litigation. The following list describes some of the areas that the authors consider especially open to attack.

Implementation of Gault

Although the Supreme Court ruled unanimously in 1967 that a juvenile must be afforded the basic fundamentals of due process before being confined in an institution, in many states children are still being denied the most basic element of due process—the right to counsel. Children and their parents are often not aware that a child is entitled to legal representation in a juvenile court proceeding. Moreover, certain juvenile courts deliberately disregard the *Gault* mandate, while others indirectly avoid its significance by accepting a child's unknowing waiver of counsel. Confinement of children so adjudicated can and should be challenged by writ of habeas corpus in the state courts or by a civil rights action under 42 U.S.C. §1983 in the federal courts.

Implementation of In re Winship

In 1970 the Supreme Court ruled that a juvenile court adjudication must be based on the same standard of evidence as a criminal court conviction—"beyond a reasonable doubt." [108] Furthermore, the Supreme Court considered this aspect of the juvenile court process so essential to the heart of the fact-finding process that it ruled in 1972 that *Winship* should be applied retroactively.[109] Many state juvenile court statutes only require that fact-finding hearings be based on the lesser standard of proof —preponderance of the evidence. Consequently, confinement pursuant to an adjudication based on a lesser standard of proof than "beyond a reasonable doubt" is invalid and should be challenged by writ of habeas corpus or by a civil rights action under 42 U.S.C. §1983.

"Status" Statutes

Practically all states have statutes that permit a juvenile to be confined for noncriminal behavior because he is "ungovernable," "stubborn," "incorrigible." In many jurisdictions these statutes are currently being attacked for vagueness as violative of the Fourteenth Amendment and as punishment of a status in violation of the Eighth Amendment.

Right to Treatment

The constitutional right to treatment which has been extended to the mentally ill is equally applicable to confined juveniles. Most successful right-to-treatment cases have been brought as civil rights actions under 42 U.S.C. §1983. Where state statutes provide that children in institutions be afforded "treatment and rehabilitation," recourse to state mandamus procedures may be a more direct and effective remedy. However, it should be noted that the earliest right-to-treatment cases [110] were brought as writs of habeas corpus.

Clearly the individual adjudications most vulnerable to attack are those where a child is placed in an institution for a *specific* problem, and the facility does not provide an adequate solution for that problem, for example, if a child is placed for truancy but the institution does not provide schooling, or if a child is placed for a drug problem but the institution has no drug treatment program, or if a child is placed because he is in need of psychiatric treatment but the institution provides little if any psychiatric care.

Discipline

Since children are confined in institutions for treatment—not punishment—severe disciplinary procedures are particularly subject to attack. Children are frequently forced to endure long periods of solitary confinement under conditions often as severe as those in adult institutions. Injunctions may be sought in the federal courts under 42 U.S.C. §1983 citing Eighth Amendment violations. This practice lends itself especially well to litigation, since it clearly points out the inherent contradictions within juvenile institutions and at the same time it is a narrow issue based on a strong constitutional foundation.

Conditions of Institutions

Many child care institutions are antiquated, hazardous facilities. Both pretrial detention facilities and posttrial placement facilities may be attacked for violating local health and fire regulations as well as certain state statutes that require that children be placed in a "home-like" setting. Moreover, if the conditions are so shocking, they may violate the Eighth Amendment, and a civil rights action in the federal court seeking an order closing the facility may be proper.

Parole Revocation Hearings

Most states do not provide for parole revocation hearings for children. In many states when children are placed in institutions, they are placed until they reach their majority. Therefore even if they are released from an institution, they may continue on parole for years, always subject to return for a parole violation.

Parole revocation hearings should be sought by writ of habeas corpus when a child is returned to a training school without a hearing for a parole violation. In New York where children are now entitled to a full parole revocation hearing with the assistance of counsel, the number of children returned to the training schools dropped from three hundred to fifty in one year. This probably was not attributable to the fact that children were successful in these hearings but rather to the fact that the existence of the hearing procedures dissuaded parole officers from initiating the return procedures.

Access to Courts and Censorship of Mail

None of the above-suggested areas of possible litigation can be effectuated unless children in institutions are able to reach the legal community. The normal difficulties of gaining access to the courts which adult inmates encounter are further compounded for children in training schools. Not only do they generally lack the financial resources and the educational sophistication often required for litigation but more importantly they are often unaware that they have any legal rights once they are confined, particularly the right of access to the courts.

In most training schools there are neither "jail-house" lawyers nor law libraries to apprise children of their legal rights. This is compounded by the fact that even if these resources did exist, due to age or educational disabilities many children would not know how to take advantage of them. Furthermore, if children are aware of their rights and are able to write, they frequently have no one to contact, since they are generally without counsel and often without sympathetic family. And even if a source exists, strict mail censorship often prevents meaningful communication. Suits based on the First and Sixth Amendments can and should be brought to establish the right to uncensored communication with courts and attorneys.

The lack of opportunity for private, meaningful contact with people outside the institution helps perpetuate a system of administration that is often based on secrecy and nonaccountability. Before broad litigation in the juvenile rights area can be effectuated, the shroud of secrecy that surrounds juvenile institutions must be lifted.

Footnotes

1 Morales v. Turman, 326 F. Supp. 677 (E.D. Tex. 1971); cf. adult parallel, Johnson v. Avery, 393 U.S. 483 (1969).

2 In re Gault, 387 U.S. 1, 13 (1967).

3 See McKeiver v. Pennsylvania, 403 U.S. 528 (1971).

[4] Matter of Patricia A., 31 N.Y.2d 83, 286 N.E.2d 432, 335 N.Y.S.2d 33 (1972).

[5] See Gesicki v. Oswald, 336 F. Supp. 371 (S.D.N.Y. 1971) "Wayward Minor Statutes."

[6] But see Gonzales v. Maillard, — F. Supp. — (N.D. Cal. 1971), CCH Poverty L. Rep. ¶¶866, 867, 4020.06, 4020.171, 4020.22, Weigel, J., No. 50424 SAW, where three-judge federal District Court struck down part of the California statute dealing with these children.

[7] White v. Reid, 125 F. Supp. 647 (D.D.C. 1954); Baker v. Hamilton, 345 F. Supp. 345 (W.D. Ky. 1972). But see Murray v. Owens, 465 F.2d 289 (2d Cir. 1972), which permitted incarceration of a 15-year old male in a correctional facility after a Family Court judge determined that he had committed a serious felony.

[8] Martarella v. Kelley, 349 F. Supp. 575 (S.D.N.Y. 1972).

[9] See Robinson v. California, 370 U.S. 660 (1962).

[10] See Robin R. v. Wyman, — F. Supp. —(S.D.N.Y. 1971), Motley, J., 70 Civ. 1402, May 26, 1971; United States ex rel. Wilson v. Coughlin, No. C 1793 (N.D. Ill., Nov. 22, 1971), CCH Poverty L. Rep. ¶4400.501; Martarella v. Kelley, note 8, supra.

[11] See Lollis and Pena v. Wyman, 322 F. Supp. 473 (S.D.N.Y. 1970) (extended periods of solitary confinement enjoined as violative of the Eighth Amendment).

[12] Morales v. Turman, note 1, supra.

[13] Id.; see also Ex parte Rider, 50 Cal. App. 797, 195 P. 965 (1920); cf. adult parallel, Palmigiano v. Travisono, 317 F. Supp. 776 (D.R.I. 1970).

[14] See e.g. N.Y. Exec. Law §511(3).

[15] N.Y. Exec. Law §523(1), (3).

[16] People ex rel. Silbert v. Cohen, 29 N.Y.2d 12, 271 N.E.2d 908, 323 N.Y.S.2d 422 (1971).

[17] See 9 N.Y.C.R.R. 169. See also adult parallel, Morrissey v. Brewer, 408 U.S. 471 (1972).

[18] N.Y. Family Court Act §756(b).

[19] People ex rel. Arthur F. v. Hill, 29 N.Y.2d 17, 271 N.E.2d 911, 323 N.Y.S.2d 426 (1971).

[20] See Lollis and Pena v. Wyman, note 11, supra, where $10,000 was sought by 14-year old girl who was in solitary confinement for fourteen days.

[21] In re Owens, 9 Crim. L. Rep. 2415 (Cir. Ct. Cook County, Ill., 1971), specifically spoke to this point in a case involving an Illinois maximum-security training school for boys. Cf. adult parallel, Rhem v. McGrath, 326 F. Supp. 681 (S.D.N.Y. 1971); Landman v. Royster, 333 F. Supp. 621 (E.D. Va. 1971). See also An Act to Provide Minimum Standards for the Protection of Rights of Prisoners, §4, Committee of the Model Act for the N.C.C.D., 18 Crime and Delinquency 10 (January 1972).

[22] 442 F.2d 178, 198 (2d Cir. 1971).

[23] Note 21, supra.

[24] Cf. adult parallel, Bundy v. Cannon, 328 F. Supp. 165 (D. Md. 1971).

25 See Baxstrom v. Herold, 383 U.S. 107 (1966). In Covington v. Harris, 419 F.2d 617 (D.C. Cir. 1969), the court questioned the transfer of a patient to the hospital's maximum-security wing and asked, "Is this the least drastic method of treating the patient?"

26 Robinson v. California, note 9, supra; Millard v. Cameron, 373 F.2d 468 (D.C. Cir. 1966); Miller v. Overholser, 206 F.2d 415 (D.C. Cir. 1953); Commonwealth v. Page, 159 N.E.2d 82 (Mass. 1959); see also symposia on the right to treatment, 57 Geo. L. J. 673 (1967) and 36 U. Chi. L. Rev. 742 (1969); "The Courts, the Constitution and Juvenile Institutional Reform," 52 Boston Univ. L. Rev. 33 (1972).

27 Martarella v. Kelley, note 8, supra, at 599; cf. Robinson v. California, note 9, supra; Rouse v. Cameron, 373 F.2d 451 (D.C. Cir. 1966); Nason v. Superintendent of Bridgewater State Hospital, 233 N.E.2d 908 (Mass. 1968).

28 125 F. Supp. 647 (D.D.C. 1954).

29 See also Kautter v. Reid, 183 F. Supp. 352 (D.D.C. 1960).

30 Note 27, supra.

31 325 F. Supp. 781 (M.D. Ala. 1971).

32 Id. at 784, 785. See also Wyatt v. Stickney (Amended) Civ. Action No. 3195-N (April 13, 1972).

33 Robin R. v. Wyman, note 10, supra.

34 Nason v. Superintendent of Bridgewater State Hospital, note 27, supra; Martarella v. Kelley, note 8, supra.

35 Matter of Ilone I., 64 Misc.2d 878, 316 N.Y.S.2d 356 (N.Y. 1970); Wyatt v. Stickney, note 31, supra.

36 Londerholm v. Owens, 197 Kan. 212, 416 P.2d 259 (1966). In Matter of Jeanette P., 34 A.D.2d 661, 310 N.Y.S.2d 125 (2d Dep't 1970), lv. to app. denied 34 A.D.2d 657, 311 N.Y.S.2d 965 (N.Y. 1970), it was determined that treatment did not exist—and placement would be "harmful"—when a girl who merely misbehaved was confined with those who had committed criminal acts. See also Matter of Lloyd, 33 A.D.2d 385, 308 N.Y.S.2d 419 (1st Dep't 1970).

37 See generally Standards and Guides for the Detention of Children and Youth (2d ed.), National Council on Crime and Delinquency (1961).

38 18 U.S.C. §5011; Ill. Ann. Stats., Charities & Pub. Welf. (23) §2518; Cal. Welf. & Inst's Code §§800, 1002.

39 N.Y. Exec. Law §511; Ill. Ann. Stats., Charities & Pub. Welf. (23) §§2502, 2627, 2656; Cal. Welf. & Inst's Code, §1251.

40 Ill. Ann. Stats., Charities & Pub. Welf. (23) §§2520, 2627, 2652; Cal. Welf. & Inst's Code §§1122, 1123; Rev. Stats. Mo. §219.020.

41 Ill. Ann. Stats., Courts (37) §701-12.

42 Ill. Ann. Stats., Charities and Pub. Welf. (23) §2628; Cal. Welf. & Inst's Code §886.

43 See Lollis and Pena v. Wyman, note 11, supra; Matter of Ilone I., note 35, supra; Rubin, "The Concept of Treatment in the Criminal Law," 21 S. Car. L. Rev. 3 (1968).

[44] See remarks of Richard Wasserstrom contained in N. Kittrie, The Right to Be Different, at 386–388 (Johns Hopkins, 1971). Contra see Cal. Welf. & Inst's Code §1768.

[45] Cf. adult parallels, Coffin v. Reichard, 143 F.2d 443, 445 (6th Cir. 1944), cert. denied 325 U.S. 887 (1945); Washington v. Lee, 263 F. Supp. 327, 331 (M.D. Ala. 1966), aff'd Lee v. Washington, 390 U.S. 333 (1968).

[46] McKeiver v. Pennsylvania, 403 U.S. 528 (1971).

[47] Lollis and Pena v. Wyman, note 11, supra; see also Inmates of Rhode Island Boys Training School v. Affleck, 346 F. Supp. 1354 (D.R.I. 1972).

[48] Martarella v. Kelley, note 8, supra.

[49] United States ex rel. Wilson v. Coughlin, note 10, supra.

[50] 9 N.Y.C.R.R. 168.1(a).

[51] Certain states prohibit this discipline by regulation. 9 N.Y.C.R.R. 168.1(d). See also Holt v. Sarver, 309 F. Supp. 362, 384 (E.D. Ark. 1970), aff'd 442 F.2d 304 (8th Cir. 1971) (inmate-trustee disciplinary system enjoined).

[52] Martarella v. Kelley, note 8, supra. Cf. Robinson v. California, note 9, supra.

[53] N.Y. Family Court Act §872.

[54] 393 U.S. 503 (1969).

[55] But see contra Gruzick v. Drebus, 431 F.2d 594 (6th Cir. 1970), cert. denied 401 U.S. 948, a lower court case distinguishing facts from Tinker, note 54, supra, in order to uphold a ban on the wearing of all symbols not related to school.

[56] See a list of these cases and their finding in Richards v. Thurston, 424 F.2d 1281, 1282 n. 3 (1st Cir. 1970), and in Note, 38 Brooklyn L. Rev. 802, 803 n. 5 (1972).

[57] Matter of Dalrymple, 5 Ed. Dep't Reps. 113 (1966); Matter of McQuade, 6 Ed. Dep't Reps. 36 (1966); Matter of Vartuli, 10 Ed. Dep't Reps. — No. 8297 June 21, 1971).

[58] Seale v. Manson, 326 F. Supp. 1375 (D. Conn. 1971).

[59] See H. Barnes and N. Teeters, New Horizons in Criminology, at 351 (3d ed. 1959).

[60] See 18 N.Y.C.R.R. 5.13.

[61] Catalino, "Boys and Girls in a Co-educational Training School Are Different— Aren't They?" 14 Can. J. Criminology & Corr's 120 (Ottowa, 1972).

[62] Gagnon and Simon, "The Social Meaning of Prison Homosexuality," 32 Fed. Prob. 23 (1968).

[63] Halleck and Hersko, "Homosexual Behavior in a Correctional School for Adolescent Girls," 32 Am. J. Orthopsychiatry 911, 915 (1962). See also Kosofsky and Ellis, "Illegal Communications Among Institutionalized Female Delinquents," 48 J. Soc. Psychology 155 (1958).

[64] See Griswold v. Connecticut, 381 U.S. 479 (1965), for its discussion of the First Amendment's "penumbra" of privacy; Olmstead v. United States, 227 U.S. 438, 478 (1928), for Justice Brandeis' dissent articulating the "right to be left alone."

65 Meyer v. Nebraska, 262 U.S. 390, 399 (1922); Pierce v. Society of Sisters, 268 U.S. 510 (1925); Portnoy v. Strasser, 303 N.Y. 539, 544, 104 N.E.2d 895, 898 (1952).

66 N.Y. Soc. Services Law §§373, 403; N.Y. Corr. Law, §610(3); Ill. Ann. Stats., Courts (37) §701-16. But see recent changes mentioned in S. Polier "Religion and the Child," N.Y. L. J., May 25, 1970.

67 18 N.Y.C.R.R. 5.17(a), (c); Ill. Ann. Stats., Courts (37) §705-7(2); Ill. Ann. Stats., Charities and Pub. Welf. (23) §§2627, 2656.

68 Sostre v. McGinnis, 442 F.2d 178 (2d Cir. 1971); Pierce v. LaVallee, 293 F.2d 233 (2d Cir. 1961).

69 U.S. Const. amend. I; N.Y. Const. art. 1, §3; N.Y. Exec. Law §526; Cal. Const. art. 1, §4; Ill. Ann. Stats., Const. art. 1, §3.

70 School District of Abington Township, Pa. v. Schempp, 374 U.S. 203 (1963). See also the important parallels of Anderson v. Laird, 466 F.2d 283 (D.C. Cir. June 30, 1972), cert. denied — U.S. — (1972) No. 72-653, December 18, 1972, wherein the Supreme Court let stand a decision prohibiting West Point and Annapolis from requiring students to attend religious services as part of their training.

71 See right of child to choose between the religions of either parent in Martin v. Martin, 308 N.Y. 136, 123 N.E.2d 812 (1954) (age 12); In re Vardinakis, 160 Misc. 13, 289 N.Y.S. 355 (Dom. Rel. Ct., N.Y. Co. 1936) (ages 13 and 15). See also Paolella v. Phillips, 27 Misc.2d 763, 209 N.Y.S.2d 165, 167 (Sup. Ct. Suffolk Co. 1960).

72 Sostre v. McGinnis, note 68, supra.

73 317 F. Supp. 776 (D.R.I. 1970).

74 See Note, "Prison Mail Censorship and the First Amendment," 81 Yale L. J. 87 (1971).

75 N.Y. Family Court Act §782.

76 18 N.Y.C.R.R. 5.15; see N.Y. Exec. Law §518.

77 N.Y. Family Court Act §§166, 783; Cal. Welf. & Inst's Code §827; Ill. Ann. Stats., Courts (37) §§702-8, 702-10.

78 Sussman, "The Confidentiality of Family Court Records," 45 Soc. Serv. Rev. 455 (Dec. 1971) and N.Y. L. J., Jan. 6–8, 1971.

79 In re Gault, note 2, supra, at 25.

80 N.Y. Soc. Services Law §372; Rev. Stats. Mo. §219.180; cf. adult parallels, Tarlton v. United States, 430 F.2d 1351 (5th Cir. 1970); Goble v. Bounds, 186 S.E.2d 638 (N.C. App. 1972).

81 N.Y. Civil Prac. Law & Rules, §§4504, 4505, 4508; Cal. Evidence Code, §§912, 992 et seq.; Ill. Ann. Stats., Evidence (51) §§5.2, 48.1, and Mental Health (91½) §406.

82 18 U.S.C. §5031.

83 18 U.S.C. §5032; Ramirez v. United States, 238 F. Supp. 763 (S.D.N.Y. 1965); United States v. Webb, 112 F. Supp. 950 (W.D. Okl. 1953).

84 18 U.S.C. §5035.

85 18 U.S.C. §5035.

86 18 U.S.C. §5035.

87 18 U.S.C. §5035.

88 372 F.2d 43 (2d Cir. 1967).

89 18 U.S.C. §5033. See also Trimble v. Stone, 187 F. Supp. 483 (D.D.C. 1960), as distinguished from Fulwood v. Stone, 394 F.2d 939 (D.C. Cir. 1967).

90 18 U.S.C. §5035.

91 In re Gault, note 2, supra; United States v. Costanzo, 395 F.2d 441 (4th Cir. 1968), cert. denied 393 U.S. 883; In re Winship, 397 U.S. 358 (1970).

92 Nieves v. United States, 280 F. Supp. 994 (S.D.N.Y. 1968).

93 Cotton v. United States, 446 F.2d 107 (8th Cir. 1971); McKeiver v. Pennsylvania, note 46, supra.

94 United States v. Morales, 233 F. Supp. 160 (D. Mont. 1964).

95 Cotton v. United States, 355 F.2d 480 (10th Cir. 1966); United States v. Fotto, 103 F. Supp. 430 (S.D.N.Y. 1952); Fagerstrom v. United States, 311 F.2d 717 (8th Cir. 1963).

96 18 U.S.C. §5034; United States v. Flowers, 227 F. Supp. 1014 (W.D. Tenn. 1963), aff'd 331 F.2d 604 (6th Cir. 1964).

97 18 U.S.C. §5034.

98 A Note on a national training school:
     The Robert F. Kennedy Youth Center in Morgantown, West Virginia opened in 1969, replacing the National Training School in Washington, D.C. It is operated under the jurisdiction of the federal prison system and receives federal law violators from the eastern section of the United States. (Most violators from the West are sent to the Federal Youth Center in Englewood, Colorado.) In 1971 it became and is to this day a coeducational institution. Most of its residents are from the ages of sixteen to twenty-one, and approximately two-thirds of them are committed for violating the Dyer Act (driving a stolen automobile across state lines). Others are committed for forging government checks, stealing from the mails, "moonshining," and committing crimes on federal property.

99 Suarez v. Wilkinson, 133 F. Supp. 38 (M.D. Pa. 1955); Arkadiele v. Markley, 186 F. Supp. 586 (S.D. Ind. 1960); Sonnenberg v. Markley, 289 F.2d 126 (7th Cir. 1961).

100 178 F. Supp. 17 (D. Conn. 1959). See also White v. Reid, note 7, supra, and accompanying text; United States v. Alsbrook, 336 F. Supp. 973 (D.D.C. 1971).

101 18 U.S.C. §5034; United States v. Hall, 306 F. Supp. 735 (E.D. Tenn. 1969). See also Fish v. United States, 254 F. Supp. 906 (D. Md. 1966).

102 18 U.S.C. §5034.

103 Nieves v. United States, note 92, supra; United States v. Borders, 154 F. Supp. 214 (N.D. Ala. 1957), aff'd 256 F.2d 458 (5th Cir. 1958).

104 United States v. Fotto, note 95, supra; United States v. Webb, note 83,

supra; United States v. Hoston, 353 F.2d 723 (7th Cir. 1965); United States v. Borders, note 103, supra.

[105] 18 U.S.C. §§4201; 4202 n.; 5026.

[106] 18 U.S.C. §5037. See also United States v. Hall, 306 F. Supp. 735 (E.D. Tenn. 1969); Fish v. United States, 254 F. Supp. 906 (D. Md. 1966).

[107] United States v. Becker, 444 F.2d 510 (4th Cir. 1971); United States v. Kinsman, 195 F. Supp. 271 (S.D. Cal. 1961).

[108] In re Winship, note 91, supra.

[109] Ivan v. City of New York, 407 U.S. 203 (1972).

[110] E.g. Rouse v. Cameron, note 27, supra; White v. Reid, note 7, supra.

CHAPTER 18
SPANISH-SPEAKING PRISONERS

EDITORS' INTRODUCTION

There are many Spanish-speaking inmates in this nation's prisons, particularly on the East and West coasts and along the Southern borders. During their incarceration, many suffer additional deprivations caused by a failure to provide an adequate means of communication and services for this large group. The following article describes some of the major problems of Spanish-speaking inmates; it contains a complaint prepared by a group of these prisoners detailing the conditions at one of New York's maximum-security institutions.

THE PROBLEMS OF SPANISH-SPEAKING PRISONERS

MARILYN G. HAFT *

The first time I was allowed to enter a prison and mix freely with the general population, a Spanish-speaking inmate approached me with another inmate standing at his arm. He pleaded with me in very broken English to do something for him which I could not understand. The inmate standing with him broke in when he saw my bewilderment and in a barely more understandable English explained to me that his friend had heard that his children were being sent to foster homes, and that one was sick. He had been trying to communicate with people on the outside for a month without success, trying to find out where the children were going and the state of his child's health. The social worker at the prison did not understand Spanish and had been slow in processing his request. His mail took weeks to get out because there was only one Spanish-speaking censor for a population of approximately three hundred Spanish-speaking inmates. Could I call his friend and find out where his children were? All this was communicated to me in twenty minutes of faulty simultaneous interpretation. Similar incidents occurred repeatedly there that day and in other prisons on subsequent visits.

The complaints and needs of the numerous Spanish-speaking prisoners in this country go unheeded. The prisons in New York, California, and a number of the Southwestern states contain a large population of Spanish-speaking inmates. Many of these inmates cannot read, write or understand anything but Spanish. They are therefore isolated in a system where adjustment, and indeed survival, are largely dependent upon communication.

Most prisons are not equipped in staff or attitude to change this set of circumstances. A Spanish-speaking prisoner entering

---

* Ms. Haft is Co-Editor of this Sourcebook. Her biography appears at the front of the volume.

the prison system is ushered through orientation sessions that are meant to explain the programs available, the institution rules, and what is generally expected during the length of imprisonment. All this is done in English, and as a result many of these inmates do not fully understand what is available or what is expected of them. The ramifications of the language barrier are pervasive and often amount to violations of the First and Fourteenth Amendments.

Denial of Due Process

If prison rules and regulations are printed at all, they are rarely printed in Spanish. This has serious consequences for those inmates who can only read Spanish. They often violate a regulation they are unaware of and are disciplined by a committee on which no Spanish-speaking person sits. In a clear violation of the Due Process Clause, the inmates are left unaware of the rules and the proceedings, and are unable to defend against the filed charges. Not only may this result in unjust punishment but the results of the proceedings are recorded on the inmate's record, and chances for parole and early release are unduly prejudiced.

One of the oft-cited malaises of prison systems is the isolation of prisoners from the outside world. If prisoners generally are locked in a communications tomb, the Spanish-speaking inmate is trapped in a tomb within a tomb where both the inside and outside worlds are cut off. Announcements, both written and spoken, are not understood, recreation programs are in English only, and world news is cut off, as only English television and radio programs are played.

More serious consequences arise from the inability of these prisoners to receive proper medical care, as most prison doctors cannot speak Spanish, and from their inability to participate in all-English vocational and academic programs and job-release programs. These prisoners are thereby being denied their emerging right to receive rehabilitation and treatment.

Service units within the prisons, which are supposed to alleviate personal problems within the facility, are unavailable to Spanish-speaking inmates. (Although the unwritten rule within prisons is that no complaints are made to the administration against another inmate, sometimes the inability to communicate with the administration can cost an inmate's life.) Additionally, in some prisons inmates are doomed to almost complete silence: there is an outrageous rule that prisoners are not allowed to speak among themselves in Spanish because the guards cannot understand and monitor the conversations. Also, parole officers inside and outside prisons often do not understand Spanish. Needless to say, the resulting lack of communication can lead to dire consequences for inmates seeking parole and for those on the street who are trying to abide by parole officers' demands.

The most frequent complaints from Spanish prisoners relate to correspondence. As the mail may be and indeed still is read and censored in most prisons, the Spanish-speaking inmate endures long delays in sending and receiving mail because there is usually only one censor who can read Spanish, and sometimes none. The personal problems caused by this situation are many, but the legal problems can be even more serious. The unreasonable delays frequently interfere with the inmates' rights to have access to the courts, as legal mail also must often wait censorship.

In the decision of *Younger v. Gilmore* (404 U.S. 15 (1971)), the Supreme Court held that as part of prisoners' right to have access to the courts, legal libraries must be installed in prisons. As a result, legal libraries have been installed in more and more institutions across the country, and one legal publishing company has been training prisoners in techniques of research. In New York those inmates who show legal talent are hired, as a prison job assignment, to work as legal librarians and aid others in their legal research and work. Again Spanish-speaking inmates suffer, as the law books are available in English only. In the legal education program at Bedford Hills Women's Prison in New York, we have alleviated the problem by having a bilingual inmate trained and hired as an inmate librarian.

These and many other problems emanating from the language barrier could be ameliorated by awareness, creative thinking, and the desire to help. Where the administration refuses to recognize and rehabilitate a large number of the prisoners under its custody, it thereby violates its legal obligation. When the recognized constitutional rights afforded other prisoners are denied to the Spanish-speaking prisoners, court action claiming unequal protection of the laws becomes necessary.

In one New York prison such action was required. What follows is the complaint filed in a §1983 class action suit by the Spanish-speaking inmates of Comstock prison.

"CRUZ" COMPLAINT

UNITED STATES DISTRICT COURT:
NORTHERN DISTRICT OF NEW YORK:

CIVIL ACTION NO.: ——————

EDUARDO CRUZ;
LOUIS MARTINEZ;
FRANK PERALES, Jr.;
JOSE ROSA;
GEORGE RIEVES;
JUAN FRANCISCO SOTO, Jr.; and
GLIDDEN SANTIAGO,

Prisoners at the Great Meadow Correctional Facility, at Comstock, New York, on behalf of themselves and all those similarly concerned and interested,

Plaintiffs,

–Against–

RUSSELL G. OSWALD,Commissioner of the Department of Correctional Services,at Albany,New York;

J.LELAND CASSCLES,Superintendent,of the GREAT MEADOW CORRECTIONAL FACILITY,at Comstock,New York; (et. al.)

NELSON A. ROCKEFELLER,Governor,of the State of New York, and as Executive Director of the New York State Department of Correctional Services,at Albany,New York.

Defendants.

STATE OF NEW YORK: SS.:
WASHINGTON COUNTY:

PETITION-COMPLAINT FOR DECLARATORY JUDGMENT, RELIEF AND DAMAGES.

ALL PLAINTIFFS AS ABOVE NAMED,being duly sworn according to law,do depose and state as follows:

That they institute this proceeding in their own behalf,and on behalf of all others similarly concerned and interested,and are proceeding pro se,being without the aid and/or the assistance and guidance of counsel due to their status of indigency,and that said plaintiffs hereto show the Court as follows:

JURISDICTION:

The jurisdiction of this court is invoked pursuant to and in accordance with the provisions of Title 28 United States Code, Sections 1331,1343,2201 and 2202; Title 42 United States Code Sections 1983 and 1985; and the Constitution of the United States, specifically but not limited to the Fifth,Eighth and Fourteenth Amendments thereto.

PLAINTIFFS:

1: Eduardo Cruz,Louis Martinez,Frank Perales,Jr., Jose Rosa, George Nieves,Juan Francisco Soto,Jr., and Glidden Santiago are all Puerto Ricans,and as such are United States citizens.

2: Eduardo Cruz is a prisoner at the Great Meadow Correctional Facility,at Comstock,New York; upon conviction of the alleged crime of "possession of a bomb",he was sentenced to a term of seven (7) years imprisonment on the 14th Day of December,1971, in the New York County Supreme Court by the Hon. Harold Bions,Justice

3: Louis Martinez is a prisoner at the Great Meadow Correctional Facility,at Comstock,New York; upon conviction for the crime of Manslaughter First Degree,he was sentenced to a term of imprisonment of not less than Ten (10) nor more than Twenty (20) years on the 3rd day of October,1967,in the New York County Supreme Court by the Hon.Davidson,Jr.,Justice.

4: Frank Perales Jr.,is a prisoner at the Great Meadow Correctional Facility, at Comstock,New York,upon conviction of the crime of Robbery in the Third Degree,he was sentenced to a term

of seven (7) years on the _____ day of _____ 19____,
in the Bronx County Supreme Court by the Hon.Edward J.Green-
field, Justice.

5:      Jose Rosa is a prisoner at the Great Meadow Correctional
Facility at Comstock,New York,upon conviction of the crime of
Grand Larcney in the third degree,Burglary and Criminal Trespass
in the First Degree,he was sentenced to a term of four (4) years
in the Bronx County Supreme Court,by the Hon.David Ross,
Justice on the 11th day of January,1970.

6:      George Nieves is a prisoner at the Great Meadow Correctional Facility at Comstock,New York, upon conviction for the
crime of Manslaughter First Degree,in the Kings County Supreme
Court,he was sentenced to a term of not less than seven and one
half (7½) nor more than fifteen (15) years by the Hon.Malbin,
Justice,on the 28th day of May,1964.

7:      Juan Francisco Soto,Jr., is a prisoner at the Great Meadow
Correctional Facility at Comstock,New York,upon conviction for
the alleged crime of "Murder in the First Degree," he was sentenced to a term of imprisonment of natural life,on the 17th day
of June,1966,by the Hon.John R.Starkey,Justice of the Kings
County Supreme Court

8:      Glidden Santiago is a prisoner at the Great Meadow Correctional Facility at Comstock,New York,upon conviction for the
crime of Criminal Posession of a dangerous drug in the fourth
Degree,in the New York County Supreme Court,he was sentenced
to a term of imprisonment of not more than seven (7) years,on the
22nd day of June,1972,by the Hon.Lawrence J.Tonetti,Justice.

DEFENDANTS:

9:      Nelson A.Rockefeller is the Governor of the State of New
York,and the Executive Director of the Department of Correctional
Services,at Albany,New York,as such,the Governor is responsible
for the appointment of the Commisisoner of the said Department
of Correctional Services,and is responsible for the management
and control,of all his appointees, and subordinates.He is the
ultimate authority in the State's Correctional System,and the
Commissioner and all subordinates are under his control and
jurisdiction.

10:      Russell G.Oswald is the Commissioner of the Department
of Correctional Services,appointed by the Governor as the Executive Director thereto,he is responsible for the control and management of all Correctional Facilities within the State of New York,

and is responsible for the appointment of all Superintendents, (et al.) to the State Correctional Facilities.He is also responsible for the conduct of all subordinates,and for the promulgation of Rules, Regulations,and the issuing of mandates and orders to his subordinates, and responsible for the mandates and orders being carried out and implemented.

11: J.Leland Casscles is the Superintendent of the Great Meadow Correctional Facility,being appointed to his position by the Commissioner of the Department of Correctional Services, and is responsible for the carrying out and implementation of mandates,directives,and orders as emanating from the Commissioner's Office,and he is also responsible for the actions,and all acts of subordinates under his control and supervision, and also for the general supervision and administration of the Great Meadow Correctional Facility,including all activities therein.

CLASS ACTIONS:

12: The plaintiffs are all members of a class of prisoners, consisting of the following:

They are all presently confined at the Great Meadow Correctional Facility at Comstock,New York, and those who will in the future be confined at Great Meadow Correctional Facility,and those who are presently confined at the Great Meadow Correctional Facility,all of the Puerto Rican culture,society and language, who have in the past,present and in the future will have requested the prison authorities and the named Defendants, to respect their ethnic backgrounds,culture and society,although they are of a minority within the facility, (grounds,contentions and allegations set forth in the Statement of Facts which follows).

All the heretofore named plaintiffs bring this proceeding and action pursuant to Rule 23 of the Federal Rules of Civil Procedure on behalf of themselves,all others similarly incarcerated at the present time who are likewise concerned and interested Puerto Ricans,and all those who will in the future be confined and incarcerated at the Great Meadow Correctional Facility which constitutes the above described class. The persons in this class are so numerous that joinder of all members is impractical. There are questions of law/and or fact common to the class; and the claims,contentions,allegations of the within named plaintiffs (representatives) are typical of the claims,contentions and allegations of the class,and the plaintiffs-representatives will fairly and adequately protect the interest of the class.

13:     All defendants are sued individually and in their capacity as State Officials.

STATEMENT OF FACTS:

14:     Due to the gravity of the situations,and the deplorable conditions which exist at the Great Meadow Correctional Facility, we the heretofore named plaintiffs in this proceeding are compelled to seek redress in this Court,in order to alleviate and to correct the discrimination which is and has been shown towards the Puerto Rican inmates incarcerated at this facility.We have petitioned the facility,and the Administration in Albany to correct the matters complained of, and in turn we were either ignored completely,or else the matter complained of was handled in a perfunctory and apathetic manner,with orders being issued,and thereafter not complied with or enforced. We are faced with a serious dilemma as created by the named defendants and their subordinates,and due to this dilemma we are forced to institute this proceeding and show unto the court as follows:

15:     The Puerto Rican population is approximately in the neighborhood of two hundred and sixty men,incarcerated and under sentence of imprisonment. The custodial staff of this facility consists,in addition to the Superintendent, of three (3) Deputy Superintendents,a Captain,nine Lieutenents,fifteen Sergents,and 342 Correction Officers. In addition thereto,there is a civilian staff of approximately one hundred fifty-five persons, of this complete total of *well over* five hundred prison personnel, approximately two (2) personnel speak and/or understand the Spanish language.

16:     Of the Puerto Rican population who are incarcerated at this facility,a great many cannot read,write,nor understand the English language;many cannot even read or write in their native tongue,and those who wish to learn the English let alone their Spanish language are not permitted to do so,and there are no qualified personnel within this facility to do so.

17:     There are no Spanish speaking personnel within the Hospital staff,and as a result,many of the Puerto Rican inmates who complain of sickness and ailments are not able to properly state their medical complaints to the doctors,and as a result, they are neglected and do not receive any medical treatment.

18:     There are no interpreters within the facility,other than for a Spanish speaking correctional officer,who is employed in the Correspondence Department to read and censor all incoming and outgoing mail and literature, his capacity to perform this function is limited,as he is also required to censor and read,plus handle, all incoming and outcoming legal mail,inter alia,and as a result, incoming and outgoing mail of the Puerto Ricans which are written in the Spanish language is often delayed for weeks before being received by the inmate or his family.

19:    There are no "rehabilitation" programs set up for the Spanish speaking inmates,especially for those who do not speak, write or understand the English language, contrary to the programs which are in force and effect for those inmates who do speak,read,write,and understand the English language.

20:    There are no cultural classes available to the Spanish speaking class of inmates,although there are available classes, for the studies of American and Black histories,their culture and backgrounds.

21:    There is a very critical area in which the Spanish speaking inmates are denied due process of law,and this is in the field where pre-parole interviews are necessary within the facility preparatory to meeting and seeing the parole board in order to be considered for release,without proper understanding,the Spanish speaking inmate is often neglected,and they cannot fully or in fact completely relate important matters to their interviewers, and/or in fact to their assigned parole officers,who cannot speak or communicate in the Spanish language,as a result, he is given a perfunctory and general routine pre-parole investigation,which usually results in his being denied a parole by the board of parole, and he is required to complete his full sentence.

22:    The Spanish speaking inmate is not allowed to receive foods native to his culture,while other inmates are allowed to receive foods from their families,which are native to their individual cultures;and further,the foods which any inmate may receive from their families,are contained on a list of foods which are published within the facility,which are not known or native to such Puerto Rican Spanish speaking peoples. Upon receipt of foods native to the Puerto Rican cultures here at this facility, it would be denied to the inmate,and it must thereafter be returned to the sender or else'destroyed',if returned to the sender, this embraces extra cost and postage which many inmates cannot afford.

23:    There is not available within this facility,any form of recreation native to the Spanish speaking inmates' culture, such as movies,stage shows,inter alia; the only "recreation" available to them,are certain records and tapes which are played repeatedy day after day for one hour at a time.The radio and television programs are geared to show and broadcast English speaking programs only,including News,worldwide and national. As aforestated,a great many of the Puerto Rican inmates are not able to understand the English language,and as a result of this discrimination,they remain in total ignorance of what is happening the world over,and within the Nation,and this is the same society which they are expected to be returned to,after they are finally granted a parole or release from prison,after serving a number of years. This is tantamount to an English speaking inmate being returned to a foreign land and expected to live a normal and respectful life,not being aware of what is expected of him,from such Society.

The English speaking inmates are allowed to have movies, and stage shows,(inter alia) which the Spanish speaking inmates cannot relate to nor understand.An example of this discrimination and dichotomy will be hereafter shown in toto.

24:     There are no Rules or Regulations published,or given to the Spanish speaking inmates in their native tongue. Such Rules and Regulations are published only in the English language,and distributed to the full inmate population, however, such Rules and Regulations are meaningless to an inmate,who cannot read (let alone speak or write) the English language,but yet,he is expected to abide by such Rules and Regulations,and a failure to do so will result in the inmate being "keep-locked" (that is,being confined to his cell as punishment,for periods of weeks,or longer if confined to a special housing Unit,or total segregation.) On many occasions,a Spanish speaking inmate has been unjustly "keep-locked" for a failure to abide by the Rules and Regulations of the facility,for allegedly doing something he was not allowed or permitted to do,not knowing that,such action was in fact not permitted according to facility Rules and Regulations, and when appearing before the facilities "Adjustment Committee" which dispenses punishments,he is not able to relate to,nor understand the charges filed against him,nor to understand the proceedings that are taking place.

25:     There is a Service Unit available within the facility,which is designed to alleviate problems within the facility upon request of the inmate,however,there are no Spanish speaking counsellors available,and as a result,only those able to relate problems with a counsellor receive any consideration,this creates a discrimination towards the Spanish speaking inmates who are not able to relate their problems in English.

26: That all requests for information to the facility personnel and to the Department of Correctional Services must be made in English,as to state such in the Spanish language would either not be answered,returned,ignored, or periods of weeks would ensue before an answer would be given. At times,an inmate does not wish to have another inmate write a request for him due to its personal nature, and he thus goes ignored.

27: That the announcements that are broadcast on the public address system connected with the radio,are spoken only in the English language,and as a result,those who do not understand the English language remain in ignorance of what is stated.

28: That there are no Spanish speaking Priest or Chaplains available within the facility,to conduct Services for those inmates who desire to have services available. They cannot relate to nor understand the Masses that are said, nor the Sermons that are spoken,as such are spoken only in the English language.

29: That there are no Spanish speaking personnel within the job release program that are and is available to the general inmate population. Due to a lack of Spanish speaking personnel within the facility, many Puerto Ricans are not able and/or not allowed to apply for such.

30: That upon arrival at this facility,there is an "Orientation Program" available,which is compulsory for the inmate to attend, however,this orientation program which is designed to explain the programs available, the conduct which is to be expected,and institutional life in general, is all spoken in English, and as aforestated,a great many of the Puerto Rican inmates are only capable of understanding the Spanish language. What is spoken and written in English is meaningless to them,and as a result, many inmates serve their whole sentence without ever knowing what has and is transpiring,and without any worthwhile or meaningful programs being utilized while so incarcerated.

31: That as heretofore mentioned, (23; sec.parag. [supra] . . .) the plaintiffs show unto the court the discrimination they are subjected to,which the inmates of other ethnic groups do not ordinarily suffer.

The plaintiffs Eduardo Cruz,Louis Martinez,and Frank Perales Jr., early in the month of October of 1972,requested an audience with the Superintendent J.L. Casscles,regarding the recognition of a Puerto Rican Holiday, "DISCOVERY DAY" which is celebrated throughout the Island of Puerto Rico on November 19th,1972. The request for an audience went ignored,and further requests were submitted . . . to the Superintendent and to Commissioner Oswalds' office.

While awaiting responses to these communications, the plaintiffs solicitated the support of various Legislatures, such as Hon.Herman Badillo,U.S.Congressman . . .; Hon. Arthur O.Eve, N.Y.S.Assemblyman . . .; Robert Garcia,U.S. Senator; Barbara Handschu, Esq. . . . The Puerto Rican Legal Defense Fund, Caesar A. Perales . . .; among others,and including The Governor of the State of New York.

As a result,it was decided by the hierarchy of the New York State Correctional System, to allow the inmates to celebrate their National Holiday,on the 19th of November,1972,and appropriate communications were sent to all Correctional facilities,and in fact,were announced in the Spanish-speaking newspapers,and the plaintiffs received confirmation of this fact from various sources. . . . However,although the Governor's Office, and the Commissioner ORDERED the holiday to be celebrated on November 19th,1972,the Superintendent of this Facility, J.L.Cassales, et al.,had no intention of following such directives.

First,the plaintiffs had an interview with the Protestant Chaplain,who informed them that the holiday would NOT be celebrated on the 19th of November,but instead on the 20th, and after repeated demands that such must and should be celebrated on the 19th,it was thus scheduled. The Protestant Chaplain had acted as a spokesman for the Superintendent,J.L.Casscles,and in turn, the plaintiffs requested the Chaplain to personally give to Superintendent Casscles a copy of the scheduled program. . . .

As can be seen by the scheduled program for the 19th of November . . . there was also an inmate show to be had, in conjunction with the entertainers that were to arrive here from outside sources.The holiday therefore was set to be had on the 19th of November,a Sunday,and a regular scheduled movie that was due to be shown to the general population was rescheduled for Monday,the 20th of November,and a stage show which had been scheduled for the 20th,was rescheduled for the 27th of November,1972.

Secondly,early on Sunday,November 19,1972,plaintiffs were informed by the facility,that,due to a "break-down" of the

bus[es] that were in the process of transporting the outside entertainers here to the Great Meadow Correctional Facility,the show
as scheduled would be cancelled.Request for direct telephone
communications to verify this were at first denied,then it was
decided to allow Eduardo Cruz to make telephone communication, and upon contacting one NOBERT LOPEZ,on the 19th of
November, he personally informed Eduardo Cruz, that the bus
indeed had broken down,but, that they would be arriving a little
later than originally scheduled,and after informing the officials
of this,they cancelled the entire show.Noberto Lopez also informed the plaintiff Cruz,THAT PREVIOUS TO THE BUS BREAK-
ING DOWN,THAT THE SUPERINTENDENT J.L. CASSCLES HAD
SENT TELEGRAMS TO PRACTICALLY ALL THE ENTERTAINERS
WHO WERE COMING HERE,AND INFORMED THEM THAT IF
THEY DID COME TO THIS FACILITY,THAT THEY WOULD BE
DENIED ADMISSION INTO THE FACILITY.

    This was the first indication that plaintiffs had that the
Superintendent J.L.Casscles et al.,did not intend to allow the
show to be had,and these telegrams that were mailed and sent
by the Superintendent to the entertainers were never known or
revealed to the plaintiffs until Noberto Lopez informed them of
such.

    Thirdly,and in sum, the facility personnel then scheduled
a movie for the entire prison population after cancelling the celeb-
rities for the Puerto Rican "Discovery Day" Holiday. No consideration whatsoever was given to the fact,that,even if there were
no deceit in the cancelling of the celebration, and the scheduled
entertainers would not be able to make it here in time to help the
Spanish speaking inmates in the celebration of their National
Holiday, *there was still available the inmate program that could
have been utilized,without the outside entertainers presence.*But,
this was scheduled to be cancelled also, in a cruel, callous and
vindictive manner.No further explanation was ever given to any
of the plaintiffs. This is discrimination in its cruelest form,as
while other ethnic groups are allowed and permitted to celebrate
their National Holidays without deceit and hypocrisy involved,the
Spanish speaking inmates are denied to celebrate theirs.

    The series of communications . . . show the attitudes of
the Superintendent and his subordinates here at this facility,and
the conspiracy they have invoked,to circumvent the orders and
mandates as did emanate from the Offices of the Governor,and

the Commissioner,and the lack of response and the disconcern displayed by the Offices of the Governor and Commissioner is the failure to implement their mandates and orders as issued to the Superintendent here.

32:   That as a result of all the foregone mentioned matters as set forth,each and all of the named plaintiffs,and the class of prisoners which they represent,have been denied fundamental constitutional rights,in that they have,and are still being denied, and subjected to,discrimination,due process and equality with other ethnic groups,cruel and unusual punishments,and the equal protection of the laws, pursuant to the United States Constitutions Fifth,Eighth and Fourteenth Amendments.

33:   That due to the nature of the complaints herein, plaintiffs request the court to grant them preference in the deciding of the within matters,as it is being contended they are suffering irreparable and immediate injury,due to the arbitrary acts of the defendants.

CAUSES OF ACTION:

34:   Defendants under color and guise of State laws, Rules and/or Regulations within the State of New York,have individually and collectively subjected the plaintiffs and the Classes they represent to be deprived of certain rights,privileges and immunities secured to them by the Constitution and Laws of the United States as follows:

Defendants have deprived the plaintiffs Eduardo Cruz, Louis Martinez, Frank Perales,Jr.,Jose Rosa,George Nieves,Juan Francisco Soto,Jr., and Glidden Santiago of the guarantees as enumerated in the Fifth Amendment,to wit:

"No person shall be . . . deprived of life, liberty, . . . without due process of law. . . .".

Plaintiffs contend,that the acts and actions of the named defendants,as heretofore set forth, amount to a denial of due process of law,and regardless of the fact that they are incarcerated wtihin a prison,their right to live a life and to be at liberty to do and receive what is their due,and which is native to the Spanish speaking peoples,cannot be denied to them.

35:   Defendants have deprived the plaintiffs as heretofore named, of the guarantees of the Eighth Amendment,to wit:

". . . nor (shall) cruel and unusual punishments be inflicted."

Plaintiffs contend,that the acts and actions of the named defendants,as heretofore set forth,amount to cruel and unusual punishment,and solely due to the fact of the plaintiffs backgrounds being of a Puerto Rican culture,which is foreign to the defendants' way of life.

36:    Defendants have deprived the plaintiffs as heretofore named,of the guarantees of the Fourteenth Amendment,to wit:

". . . No State shall make or enforce any law, which shall abridge the privileges or immunities of Citizens of the United States;nor shall any State deprive any person of life,liberty,or property, without due process of law; nor deny to any person within its jurisdiction the equal protection of the laws."

Plaintiffs contend,that the acts and actions of the named defendants,as heretofore set forth,amount to a denial of due process of law;equality with other ethnic groups within the prison system; equal protection of the law;the right to observe their national holidays as do other ethnic groups;the right to receive proper medical attention and the safeguarding of their lives, health,well being,which is denied to them due to their inability to speak or to understand the English language; the right to be free from punishments,due to a lack of understanding of Rules and Regulations which are written and spoken in English,and which cannot be understood due to a lack of interpreters within the facility ; the right to be allowed to participate in the "rehabilitation" programs, simply due to the fact they are unable to speak or to understand the English language; inter alia,and as set forth in the foregone Statement Of Facts.

37:    That the acts and actions of the defendants as named herein,are likewise contrary to the Statutes made and in force,to guarantee the United States Constitution,to wit:

Title 42 of the United States Code, Section's: 1981;1983 and 1985.
Title 28 of the United States Code,Section 1343.

38:    Accordingly,unless this court restrains the unconstitutional actions of Defendants,the individual plaintiffs, and the classes of people they represent will continue to suffer the most serious immediate and irreparable injury in that they will continue to be discriminated against,due to their Puerto Rican background and culture,and due to their inability to understand the English language,and no attempt being made to assist them to become familiar with the English language,and with no interpretators being available,they will be prevented from exerting their rights and from exercising elementary and fundamental federal Constitutional rights.

WHEREFORE, Plaintiffs respectfully pray that this court,on behalf of themselves and the classes they represent:

A: ENTER AN ORDER

Granting a temporary restraining order,restraining and enjoining defendants,their successors in office,and all their agents, and subordinates,from denying the Plaintiffs any further rights, and prohibiting them from interfering with, and to immediately create a program,wherein interpretors are made available to all Spanish speaking people within the facility,in order to alleviate and abolish the discrimination which has been created due to the language barrier which exist between Puerto Rican inmates and the facility personnel,in *all* the matters relative to and as set forth herein.

B: Granting a preliminary and permanent injunction restraining the defendants and enjoining them,their successors in office,and all their agents and subordinates,from denying them the Puerto Rican prisoners,the equal rights,which are accorded to other ethnic groups within the Great Meadow Correctional Facility,in the observing of holidays; in the observing of equal treatment in the area of recreation,medical attention,rehabilitation programs, pre-parole routines to enable them to also have an opportunity for release upon parole,orientation within the facility in the Spanish language,Rules and Regulations to be published in the Spanish language to alleviate and abolish the arbitrary and capricious punishments which are inflicted upon the Puerto Rican-Spanish speaking prisoners,who are not aware of,nor understand the English language,and do not understand what is expected of them;

That the granting and issuing of this preliminary and permanent injunction,should embrace all the matters as set forth more fully in paragraphs fourteen (14) through thirty-two (32),and although not repeated singly,it is only due to avoid being repititious.

C: Enter a declaratory judgment pursuant to Title 28 United States Code Section 2201,declaring that the following acts and actions of the Defendants and their agents and subordinates deprived plaintiffs and the classes they represent of rights guaranteed to them by the Fifth,Eighth and Fourteenth Amendments to the United States Constitution.

(1) Equality,and due process of Law, and the displaying of discrimination towards them due to their inability to understand the English language;

(2) The denial and refusal to recognize the Puerto Rican-Spanish speaking prisoners cultural and racial backgrounds,and their ethnic culture,and the denial of the plaintiffs to celebrate their National feast and holidays by the defendants,by way of deceit and hypocrisy,and in the allowing of other ethnic groups of prisoners to celebrate and observe their National feast and holidays.

(3) In the discrimination that is displayed openly by the defendants towards the Plaintiffs and the classes they represent,due to their inability to speak the/or to understand the English language, and the failure of the defendants to implement proper programs, wherein said Plaintiffs and the classes of prisoners which they represent could learn to speak and to understand the English language, and to be put and placed on a par with other inmates of different ethnic cultures and backgrounds.

D: The Plaintiffs are seeking judgments against the defendants singly and jointly, in an amount to be determined by a jury for the humiliation, public scorn and derision suffered by them; and granting all Plaintiffs herein and the classes of prisoners they represent judgment against the defendants and each of them, jointly and severally in an amount to be determined by a jury for the deprivations of Constitutional rights; and granting all Plaintiffs and the classes of prisoners that they represent judgment against the defendants and each of them, jointly and severally in an amount to be determined by a jury as punitive damages for the aforesaid conduct;

E: Granting a jury trial for damages as a matter of right, as well as for other issues triable by a jury, or in the alternative granting the empaneling of an advisory jury for the determination of issues for which such a request is made.

F: And for the granting of any and all other relief as the Court deems to be just and proper in the premise.

JURY TRIAL IS DEMANDED.

All of which is respectfully submitted by

/s/ Eduardo Cruz,#29358

/s/ Louis Martinez,#30188

/s/ Frank Perales, Jr.,#28144

/s/ Jose Rosa,#27581

/s/ George Nieves,#29702

/s/ Juan Francisco Soto, Jr., #30446

/s/ Glidden Santiago,#30053

ADDRESS FOR ALL PLAINTIFFS:
P. O. Box 51, Comstock,
New York 13821

Sworn and subscribed to before me
a Notary Public on this 29 day of
Nov. 1972.

Notary Public   /s/ James W. Phair

(Seal)

CHAPTER 19
THE CRIMINALLY INSANE

EDITORS' INTRODUCTION

Perhaps the most abandoned and despised of any group of prisoners today are those locked away in institutions for the criminally insane. They have been ignored because the public fears these criminals most of all, and because lawyers have been reluctant to become involved in the difficult task of disputing the professional judgments of psychiatrists. This article focuses on the legal problems peculiar to the criminally insane and helps to point to the urgently needed solution of those problems.

THE RIGHTS OF
THE CRIMINALLY INSANE

MONROE E. PRICE *

One of the most cruel aspects of the criminal justice system is the absence of treatment and general lack of adequate procedural protections for persons classified as "criminally insane." Three groups are often lumped together under this label: persons held incompetent to stand trial; persons held not guilty of a crime by reason of insanity; and persons transferred to a mental institution during the pendency of their prison term.

States have additional categories, such as "defective delinquent" and "sex offender," designed to cover people considered to be both "mad" and "bad." In *Baxstrom v. Herold* [1] and *Specht v. Patterson,* [2] the process by which these twice-cursed individuals were institutionalized was put in grave question. In *Baxstrom* the Court held that, before being civilly committed as a dangerously mentally ill person, a prisoner whose criminal sentence expires is entitled to the same jury review as is afforded anyone civilly committed under the New York Mental Hygiene Law. In *Specht,* the Court held that a person convicted under a Colorado statute bearing a ten-year maximum sentence, but sentenced to an indeterminate life term under the Sex Offenders Act, was entitled to a hearing before sentence, wtih full due process protections, on the ground that invocation of the Act entailed a separate criminal proceeding. In *Jackson v. Indiana,* [3] the Court took the additional step of inviting courts to investigate the "nature and duration" of commitments of the mentally ill.

A few states have already begun the substantial changes in legislation and administration which are the logical extension of these cases, but in most states there has not even been a beginning. Litigation and judicial intervention will still have to play a major role.

Litigation is hindered by the fundamental ambiguity in the classification of persons who are called "criminally insane."

* Professor of Law, University of California, Los Angeles; member, States Citizens Advisory Council on Mental Hygiene; board member, Center for Law and Social Policy, Washington, D.C.; B.A., LL.B. Yale University.

Those held because they are incompetent to stand trial have, of course, only been accused. They are frozen in an institutional limbo, although they have not been convicted of any crime. Persons "not guilty by reason of insanity" and then involuntarily committed are also, by definition, not convicted.[4]

Public suspicion and legislative ambivalence exacerbate the difficulties. The subject of release from a state institution for the criminally insane raises enormous fears and is clouded with public stigma. Administrators are often unwilling to experiment or to bring meaningful review procedure into the institution. On the other hand, statutes that commit persons for indeterminate periods on the basis of their danger to others—without providing any meaningful treatment—represent an unjustified and intolerable extension of preventive detention. Therapy should be a *sine qua non* for continued custody, but with stringent budgets and the overlay of fear, an adequate therapy program is often sacrificed to meet the prevailing demand for security. At times there is true conflict between the right to treatment and the need for security. But institutions, too often without judicial review, prefer security over rehabilitation.

The end of this article deals with the emerging right to treatment, but as a prelude there is a need to discuss the various closely related procedural rights. A fundamental right is the right not to be specially institutionalized at all unless treatment in a segregated context is essential. The right to treatment implies a right to be respected as a person, and the recognition of procedural rights is an emblem of individual respect in our legal system.

Historically, development of the procedural due process doctrine has anteceded the articulation of a right to treatment. Courts, concerned with the constitutional and budgetary implications, avoided broad right-to-treatment holdings by relying on procedural deficiencies to invalidate the manner in which particular individuals were held in a suspect mental health system. Even this was an advance. Here as elsewhere in the relationship between court and institution, the pernicious "hands-off" doctrine denied persons in custody any meaningful right to review. The application of equal protection doctrine to invalidate state procedures reflected deep distrust of the substance of what states were doing.

A time comes, as it has in the mental health context, where a judge breaks through from process to substance. Equal protection decisions and concern with procedural due process may be only way stations. Ultimately, the courts must deal with the reality of the care or punishment itself. In the interim, the equal protection cases must be implemented.

A few procedural issues have been and will continue to be of great importance in defining the obligations of state prison and mental health officials.

Procedural Rights

Present Mental Illness

By some remarkable fiction, in most jurisdictions a defendant's continuing mental illness is presumed from the fact that a jury found him not guilty by reason of insanity at the time of the offense.[5] All mandatory commitment statutes share a little in this fiction, though some are more rational than others. Some states require commitment unless the judge determines that the person has "fully recovered." Other states, such as Alabama, mandate commitment if the mental illness continues "to any degree." Clearly a jury finding that a defendant is not guilty by reason of insanity does not speak to the issue of present mental illness. Even a mandatory commitment statute should provide for a prompt determination of the person's current status.

Evaluations of persons who are found not guilty by reason of insanity often differ greatly from evaluations in a civil context, both in their timing and content. In California, for example, the state has no more than five days to evaluate a person subject to civil commitment because he is "dangerous to others." For persons undergoing evaluation after a jury determination that they are not guilty by reason of insanity, the permissible time of evaluation is ninety days.[6] In practice, as has been seen from recent Supreme Court cases, the evaluative period can stretch on for years.[7] This degree of differentiation between "civil" and "criminal" procedure is intolerable and unjustified. We know, from *Baxstrom,* that however flexible the state can be in distinguishing between categories of persons thought mentally ill, on the question of whether a person is "mentally ill *at all*" the room for differentiation is not so great.[8]

Persons who are "administratively transferred" from a purely correctional setting to a treatment center or treatment ward should have the same right to evaluation as civilly committed patients. Prior to *Baxstrom* many states applied less stringent tests than those applied to the civil population to hold prisoners beyond their term. But as *Baxstrom* makes clear, inmates should have the same right to be evaluated for mental illness as persons not in prison. And the evaluation should not be more taxing or drawn out.

Periodic Review

A state's scheme for the incarceration of the criminally insane must also be examined to determine the validity of review provisions. Since the implication of *Robinson v. California* [9] is that the state cannot hold involuntarily as "criminally insane" a person who no longer is mentally ill, the state must assure regular review of an inmate-patient's status. The Supreme Court has not articulated absolute limits on the period of time a person can be detained without a meaningful review of his status, but such limits are on the horizon. A limit which has some legitimacy would deprive the state of the power to hold a person in any of the categories of so-called criminal insanity for a period longer than the maximum sentence for the underlying offense. [10]

Assuring meaningful periodic review is a reform of the utmost importance. Grant Morris, in his study of incarceration of the criminally insane in New York, demonstrated that the median length of stay for the criminally insane was nine years, as compared to a median four-month stay for patients in state civil mental health hospitals. [11] The discrepancies between the periods of stay are largely a function of the lack of review in the institutions for the criminally insane (as well as some discrimination in the provision of treatment). The Supreme Court in *Jackson v. Indiana* [12] has already emphasized that the cruelty of indeterminate stays without meaningful review will no longer be tolerated when the justification for detention is evaluation and preparation for trial.

Elements of Meaningful Review

Reliance on habeas corpus petitions is hardly an adequate solution. Initiating a claim and fashioning a right is too heavy a burden for persons who have been institutionalized as criminally insane for a considerable length of time and have felt the enormous dehumanizing impact of the system. Although the review need not be by a judge, the internal administrative review procedures are perfunctory and meaningless. And courts, unlike hospital administrators, are equipped to understand the emanations of due process and equal protection.

Whether there is a patient-initiated filing or not, there should be a meaningful review each three or six months by a court, with the state bearing the burden of demonstrating why the patient should continue to be classified as criminally insane. Ideally, there should be counsel or an equivalent independent third party. Ideally, too, the reviewing medical authorities should not be the same as the treating authorities. An independent evaluation is desirable because, even where there is no real treatment, there may be a psychological need on the part of hospital personnel to indulge in the illusion that treatment is being provided.

Standard for Release

In many states, persons termed criminally insane must meet more stringent standards for release than "dangerous" persons civilly committed. Thus even when there is periodic review by the institution, "mental inmates" are discriminated against by the application of overstringent standards.[13]

Proof that the harsher standard is unnecessary is seen in the results of "Operation Baxstrom," the systematic release of persons from Dannemora and Matteawan in New York as a result of the Supreme Court's decision in *Baxstrom v. Herold*.[14] About one thousand persons who had been previously held in maximum-security institutions for the criminally insane, many for decades, were suddenly released to state civil institutions or released outright. Contrary to the fearful expectations of many, only a handful needed to be returned to a more secure institution.

The discrimination in release standards comes both from the legislature and from the administrators. The statutes themselves have a kind of "throw-away-the-key" tenor. A civil commitment statute may carefully provide for the automatic release of persons (originally found dangerous to others) unless there is clear proof, presented to a judge and jury, that a person continues to be dangerous and has manifested that danger. A statute for the release of the criminally insane in the same state may require that the person has "fully recovered."

The legislative standard aside, administrators of institutions for the criminally insane undoubtedly have a policy of reluctant release. In every jurisdiction where there is an effort to reduce incarceration without treatment for the criminally insane, it is essential to study release patterns to determine what the review standard is in fact and how it relates to standards used for similar classes of persons in the civilly committed population. The enormous popular prejudice against mental illness and the tremendous fear of persons classified as criminally insane contributes to this administrative discrimination.

Here as elsewhere in the mental health system there needs to be developed a greater flexibility, a richer sense of alternatives. Like other mentally ill persons, the criminally insane can often be better, and more inexpensively, treated in more normal, less restrictive settings. Those incompetent to stand trial and those not guilty by reason of insanity would also appear to have a clear constitutional right to be treated in the least restrictive setting necessary to accomplish legitimate governmental treatment goals. Too often for the criminally insane, the choice is continued incarceration or outright release. Often there is insufficient cooperation between the institutions for the criminally insane and the state civil mental health hospitals and community mental health programs. Other alternatives, such as a kind of parole or involuntary outpatient status, are now only in their infancy.

Due Process, Procedural Protections

Segregation or commitment to a specially designated institution is not merely an administrative matter for the criminally insane already within the jurisdiction of the state. It is a special kind of punishment, an oppressive, stigmatizing, debilitating kind of punishment. While we argue for a right to treatment, until the treatment needs of persons so incarcerated are fulfilled their removal to these special institutions is punishment and punishment alone. Persons categorized as criminally insane, i.e., those who are administratively transferred, not guilty by reason of insanity, incompetent to stand trial, may have a reduced opportunity for parole, may lose valuable procedural rights (such as the right to petition for the vacation of the underlying judgment against them) and may have special restrictions placed on their access to courts.[15] As has been well documented,[16] a lengthy stay in a mental prison, far from providing a therapeutic environment, contributes to the individual's disintegration. Finally, there is a special, odious stigma attached to having been branded "criminally insane" that is far worse than the stigma attached to conviction alone.

Thus to be classified as "criminally insane" is a punishment over and beyond the classification as a "criminal" and must be accompanied with adequate procedural safeguards. Right to counsel, right to confrontation, right of cross-examination, the placing of the burden of proof on the state, the right to a unanimous jury verdict, the privilege of the Fifth Amendment—all must be explored and defined in determining whether a person is criminally insane. Moreover, these procedural protections should be available not only at the initial determination but also at the time of periodic reviews. To be confined as a person who is criminally insane, at least under circumstances where treatment is not provided, is to be subjected to continuously renewed punishments.

The Right to Treatment [17]

The right to treatment is a constitutional embodiment of common sense: the state, it is asserted, should be permitted to do more to an individual than is necessary to carry out a valid legislated objective.[18]

Such an appeal, enforced by litigation, has already had an impact on the administration of mental health institutions. To some administrators it has come as a great shock that their role is to provide treatment, and not mere custodial care, to persons in their charge.

The need for judicial intervention was confirmed as administrators were asked to justify an entire range of restraints, including censorship of mail, and restrictions relating to dress, freedom of discussion, and religion. The sole reason given for most deprivations, including the fundamental deprivation of medical attention, was either lack of resources or administrative convenience.

The reply of the courts was, simply, that if the hospital was not acting like a hospital and was really a prison in disguise, non-convicted persons (and this label would include those incompetent to stand trial and those not guilty by reason of insanity) cannot be sent there.

In a very important case in the related area of civil commitment, a federal District Court in Alabama recently held that all those mentally ill and mentally retarded persons involuntarily confined to the state's mental institutions had a *constitutional* right to treatment. In its initial decision [19] the court found that defendants had failed to promulgate and effectuate minimum standards for adequate treatment and called for a hearing to set objectively measurable and enforceable standards for minimum adequate treatment and adequate habilitation.

In preparation for this hearing, plaintiffs and amici toured the Partlow institution in Tuscaloosa with a team of experts, presented testimony on conditions presently existing at Partlow, formulated standards for constitutionally adequate habilitation, and made proposals concerning implementation. Prior to the ordered hearing, plaintiffs, defendants, and amici met to discuss a number of proposed standards and entered into a series of stipulations which were presented to the court for approval.

A final order and opinion setting standards for minimum constitutionally and medically adequate treatment, and establishing a detailed procedure for implementation, was handed down on April 13, 1972. These standards include, inter alia, a provision against institutional peonage; a number of protections to insure a humane psychological environment; minimum staffing standards; detailed physical standards; minimum nutritional requirements; a provision for individualized evaluations of residents, rehabilitation plans and programs; a provision to ensure that residents released from Partlow will be provided with appropriate transitional care; and a requirement that every mentally retarded person has a right to the least restrictive setting necessary for habilitation.

The Judge also appointed a seven-member "human rights committee" for Partlow and included a patient on this committee. The human rights committee "will have review of all research proposals and all rehabilitation programs, to insure that the dignity and human rights of patients are preserved." It will also advise and assist patients who allege that their legal rights have been infringed or that the mental health board has failed to comply with judicially ordered guidelines. The case is currently on appeal before the Fifth Circuit Court of Appeals.

Since the right to treatment must be gained as a matter of law rather than common sense, it is necessary to distinguish among the categories of the criminally insane to articulate the separate justifications for each classification. The easiest case is the person who is committed because he is incompetent to stand trial. As Justice Blackmun has pointed out,[20] the sole reason for confinement in that situation is to prepare the person to understand and participate in the criminal trial. The state is authorized to institutionalize a person who is incompetent to stand trial so as to enhance his Sixth Amendment rights. Any institutionalization which does not serve that objective is unconstitutional.

After *Jackson,* the state must promptly indicate to the judge what steps are being taken to provide the kind of treatment that will increase the prompt likelihood that a trial can be resumed. If the state concludes that the person will never be able to assist at his trial, or that recovery of competency is remote, other procedures must be initiated.[21] The extraordinary luxury of holding a person indefinitely, with neither treatment nor prospect of release on the pleasant fiction that he is awaiting trial, is no longer legal.

The right to treatment of persons who are found not guilty by reason of insanity has several bases. First, literally, the person who is being committed has not been convicted of a crime. He is not being held criminally responsible. Yet he is being deprived of his liberty, and usually without the panoply of safeguards that surround a criminal trial. If treatment is withheld, then the institution becomes a penitentiary and the person is being criminally incarcerated without due process of law.[22] Second, even if due process procedures were strengthened, the criminally insane would still have a constitutional right to treatment. Commitments for criminal insanity are made on the basis of continuing mental illness as well as danger to the community. The person who is institutionalized as criminally insane is treated differently from other persons who are merely dangerous. He is deprived of valuable rights—the right to a determinate term, for example. What justifies the separate classification and institutionalization of the person called not guilty by reason of insanity can only be the state's commitment to provide treatment to him. Third, for all the categories of the criminally insane, we know quite well that it is cruel and unusual punishment to confine persons to prison for the condition of mental illness.[23] Yet, an institution which does not provide treatment is a prison. "Mandatory confinement in a mental hospital . . . rests upon a supposition, namely the necessity for treatment of the mental condition which led to the acquittal by reason of insanity and this necessity for treatment presupposes in turn that treatment will be accorded." [24]

For the person who is a member of the prison population and is administratively transferred to an institution for the criminally insane, the right to psychiatric treatment is much like the right to medical treatment. There is this essential difference. As discussed earlier, assignment to an institution for the criminally insane is potentially a special and additional kind of punishment, subject to its own stigma. The need for restraint alone cannot justify imposition of this additional stigma on a person merely because (s)he is an inmate in need of psychiatric assistance. The additional burdens, the additional deprivations imposed, can only be justified if the state is fulfilling the legitimate objective of providing treatment.

The decision of the D.C. Court of Appeals in *Rouse v. Cameron* [25] was the seminal case in the right-to-treatment field. After noting that "[t]he purpose of involuntary hospitalization is treatment, not punishment," Judge Bazelon described confinement without treatment as "shocking."

The Court of Appeals for the Fourth Circuit has also had occasion to consider the constitutional rights of persons confined for involuntary psychiatric treatment. This consideration has involved the Patuxent Institution, a psychiatric facility in Maryland in which mentally impaired habitual criminals are civilly confined for an indeterminate period for purposes of treatment. Lengthy hearings on the adequacy of treatment in Patuxent were held in state courts,[26] and then in the federal District Court.[27]

The courts found that staffing was adequate in number and professional competence; that group therapy was available to all inmates; that follow-up work with the inmates was better than in most private hospitals; that the institution had established a halfway house for parole consultations and an outpatient clinic; that vocational rehabilitation facilities were excellent; that speech therapy programs had been instituted; and that the unit system was effectively functioning with adequate staff, including, for each ninety-patient unit, two psychiatrists, two psychologists, and two social workers.[28]

The Patuxent litigation was considered by the Court of Appeals for the Fourth Circuit under the name *Tippett v. Maryland.*[29] The Court of Appeals reviewed the District Court's findings concerning adequate treatment and, stressing the high ratio of psychiatrists, psychologists and social workers to patients in the institution, sustained the District Court's findings. Nonetheless, the court emphasized that it was not resolving for all time the question of whether the administration of Patuxent was adequate to meet constitutional standards.[30] In his opinion concurring in this part of the court's decision, Judge Sobeloff, citing *Rouse v. Cameron,*[31] emphasized that adequacy of treatment was one matter which would have to be reviewed in the future:

> "One of the issues we should consider open for future evaluation is the adequacy of treatment at Patuxent. Our approval of the Maryland Defective Delinquent Act is grounded partly on the assumption that the state will continue to furnish Patuxent with sufficient funds, personnel and facilities to justify realistic hopes of rehabilitating its inmates."

Enforcing the Right to Treatment

In Maryland the state courts and the federal courts together have undertaken a sweeping review of the care and treatment available at Patuxent Institution. The Court of Appeals for the District of Columbia has been in the forefront in articulating and implementing rights for persons categorized as not guilty by reason of insanity. The states of Massachusetts and New York have initiated basic changes in their systems as a result of litigation that had an understanding of the right to treatment at its heart.

It is important, however, to recognize the complexity of right-to-treatment litigation. Successful cases have involved immense discovery and preparation for trial. What constitutes adequate treatment has been a matter of great debate, although it is not difficult to ascertain when virtually no treatment at all is being provided. Considerable expertise in the interplay of psychiatric issues and legal issues is needed. Factual investigations must be extensive; courts are interested in conditions as they are in addition to the statutory mandate and statements of administrators. The running of a right-to-treatment case approximates the running of an antitrust case. Any group considering such a case should consult either the Mental Health Law Project or other similar organizations that have accumulated expertise.

The cases illustrate several important aspects of litigation strategy. At least initially, it has been important to demonstrate that the institution is virtually bereft of treatment. The courts are understandably loath to substitute one notion of adequate treatment for another. But there are certain indices of lack of treatment that have been persuasive. These include lack of hygiene, physical sickness and deaths, shocking staff-patient ratios, and length of stays that are out of proportion to current trends. Second, it has been important to develop a distinguished body of experts willing to provide support in deposition for the lack of treatment at the institution under scrutiny. Third, it is important to think creatively about potential remedies and for the establishment of standards that will demonstrate to the court that the question is within judicial competence. By focusing on the necessary *preconditions* for any valid form of treatment—and leaving decisions as to the actual treatment modality to professional discretion—the courts can avoid difficult problems of justiciability.

The litigation theory should depend on the statute involved as well as on the Constitution. Most involuntary commitment statutes have treatment as a goal, though in some cases the therapeutic motivation may be more subtle and hidden than in others. The legislative history and the statements and writings of the institution administrators must be closely searched for articulation of therapeutic goals of the institution. Such a search is particularly necessary when dealing with the rights of the criminally insane, since there will be constant attempts to establish that the sole legislative aim was protective and constitutionally justified. The right to treatment has recently begun to prevail because it is a human concept, an important example of bringing the rule of law to the previously unreviewed acts of administrators.

Footnotes

[1] 383 U.S. 107 (1966).

[2] 386 U.S. 605 (1967).

[3] 406 U.S. 715 (1972).

[4] But see Goldstein and Katz, "Abolish the Insanity Defense. Why Not?" 72 Yale L. J. 85 (1963).

[5] See N. Dain, Concepts of Insanity in the United States (1964).

[6] Calif. Penal Code §1026.

[7] E.g. Jackson v. Indiana, note 3, supra.

[8] Baxstrom v. Herold, note 1, supra, 383 U.S. at 111.

[9] 370 U.S. 660 (1972).

[10] As part of the review process the burden could be placed on the institution to demonstrate why less onerous alternatives are not sufficient. The state should be forced to justify continuous holding of a person in a mental institution. See generally Chambers, "Alternatives to Civil Commitment of the Mentally Ill, Practical Guides and Constitutional Imperatives," 70 Mich. L. Rev. 1107 (1972). As the Operation Baxstrom follow-up indicated, the release of supposedly dangerous criminally insane to more "normal" and therapeutic settings can be

THE CRIMINALLY INSANE / 417

accomplished without a sacrifice in security. The less onerous alternative may, of course, include return to the regular prison population or release pending trial (in the case of a person held as not competent to stand trial). For the criminally insane, various civil commitment alternatives must demonstrably be explored. Counsel and court must however be careful to determine whether alternatives are being meaningfully explored or whether the new rules merely force the medical facility to adopt new boilerplate.

11 Robinson v. California, note 9, supra.

12 Note 7, supra.

13 Baxstrom v. Herold, note 1, supra.

14 Id.; Morris, "Habeas Corpus and Confinement of Mentally Disordered in New York," 6 Harv. J. Leg. 27 (1968).

15 Baxstrom v. Herold, note 1, supra.

16 "Family Therapy as an Alternative to Psychiatric Hospitalization," Psychiatric Report No. 20, American Psychiatric Association (February, 1966) at 188; Langsley, et al., "Follow-up Evaluation of Family Crisis Therapy," 39 Am. J. Orthopsychiatry.

17 The constitutional rights of the mentally impaired in mental institutions are not limited to the right to receive adequate treatment. In dealing with other issues, federal courts have found that other aspects of confinement must pass constitutional scrutiny. Covington v. Harris, 419 F.2d 617 (D.C. Cir. 1969) (right to least restrictive alternative wihtin mental institution); Jones v. Robinson, 440 F.2d 249 (D.C. Cir. 1971) and Williams v. Robinson, 432 F.2d 637 (D.C. Cir. 1970) (procedural due process applies to decision to confine inmate in maximum security within mental institutions); United States ex rel. Schuster v. Herold, 440 F.2d 1334 (2d Cir. 1971) (serious constitutional question raised by inadequate access to legal research materials in mental institution); Winters v. Miller, 446 F.2d 65 (2d Cir. 1971) (forcing medication on Christian Science practitioner in mental institution violated First Amendment).

In recent cases, the courts have held that the failure to provide adequate medical care to prisoners constitutes cruel and unusual punishment. Newman v. Alabama, 349 F. Supp. 278 (M.D. Ala. 1972); Ramsey v. Ciccone, 310 F. Supp. 600 (W.D. Mo. 1970); Campbell v. Beto, 460 F.2d 765 (5th Cir. 1972); Schack v. State of Florida, 391 F.2d 593 (5th Cir. 1968). The district court in Newman explicitly held that constitutionally required treatment includes psychiatric care for mentally disturbed prisoners.

18 Every state restraint should be measured by the likelihood that it contributes to the goal set forth by the law-making body. There can be quibbles about the stiffness of the principle. Some may argue that no state action should be permitted unless it is necessary or indispensable. Others argue that the state interest should be "compelling" and that no restraint should be tolerated unless the state meets a heavy burden of showing that the restraint was productive. For others, it would be sufficient if the state showed some reasonable relationship between a restraint and a legislative purpose.

19 Wyatt v. Stickney, 334 F. Supp. 1341 (M.D. Ala. 1971).

20 Jackson v. Indiana, note 3, supra, 406 U.S. at 738.

21 Ragsdale v. Overholsen, 281 F.2d 943, 950 (D.C. Cir. 1960) (concurring opinion, Fahy, J.); Martarella v. Kelly, 349 F. Supp. 575 (S.D.N.Y. 1972); Nason v. Bridgewater, 233 N.E.2d 908 (Mass. 1968); maybe Rouse v. Cameron, 373 F.2d 451 (D.C. Cir. 1966).

22 Cf. Robinson v. Calif., 370 U.S. 660 (1962).

23 Director of Patuxent Institution v. Daniels, 243 Md. 16, 221 A.2d 397 (1966); Murel v. Director, 240 Md. 258, 213 A.2d 576 (1965); Sas v. Maryland, 295 F. Supp. 389 (D.C. Md. 1969).

24 Ragsdale v. Overholser, 280 F.2d 943, 950 (D.C. Cir. 1960) (Fahy, J.).

25 Note 21, supra.

26 Director of Patuxent Institution v. Daniels, note 23, supra; Murel v. Director, note 23, supra.

27 Sas v. Maryland, note 23, supra.

28 Id.; see also Director of Patuxent Institution v. Daniels, note 23, supra.

29 436 F.2d 1153 (4th Cir. 1971), cert. denied sub nom. Murel v. Baltimore City Criminal Court, 407 U.S. 355 (1972).

30 Id., 436 F.2d at 1158, n. 21.

31 Note 21, supra.

SECTION V
FUTURE TRENDS

CHAPTER 20
ADMINISTRATORS AND REFORM

EDITORS' INTRODUCTION

Logically, it would seem that the simplest and speediest method of effectuating major prison reforms would be by appointing new, concerned prison administrators. What follows are discussions about the ways in which an administrator can make these changes and the problems he may face. One view is advanced by the former head of the Minnesota Department of Corrections, who instituted a remarkable number of innovations in that state. Another is expressed by a penologist who sees a bleak future for penal reform.

CORRECTIONS
IN THE YEAR 2000
– SOME DIRECTIONS

As a college teacher I would, on occasion, ask a criminology class to imagine that all incarcerative institutions burned down on the same day. There was no loss of life, and the prisoners and staff were willing to wait near their respective heaps of ashes for instructions from the budding criminologists. The question was, Armed with unlimited resources, what would you do?

Lively discussions would then ensue. Responses ranged from immediate remedial programs of tent cities, to relocation on a safe island, to community-based facilities. The deeper we investigated the problem, the more uniform became the ultimate response. Invariably, classes recommended the separation of "hardened" from the less "hardened," property offenders from the violent, old from the young, and finally they reached the conclusion that maximum-security facilities are needed for the "few" and should be built first. Who, I usually asked, will inhabit the maximum-security facility—the violent, the failures in community-based facilities, the ones with track records of incorrigibility, the habitual criminals, the really dangerous ones? The more time we spent in discussion, the more the new system began to resemble the old. There seems to be some abiding or residual value which incarceration serves. It may not be rational or effective, but it is significant and tenacious and hangs about our necks like the proverbial albatross. This forces us to ask what purpose incarceration serves and why incarceration produces a feeling of security.

Although as the year 2000 approaches decriminalization efforts may continue to gain ground, there will remain some forms of deviant behavior that shock the sensibilities of the public. These can be classed under the rubrics of (1) acts of force (mur-

* Director, Department of Corrections, State of Illinois; former Director, Minnesota Department of Corrections.

der, kidnapping, rape, assault); (2) acts that endanger life (bombing, arson, robbery); and (3) acts of deviance (sexual molestation of children), all of which arouse deep personal fears. Even as decriminalization seeks to widen degrees of behavioral freedom for victimless acts, these three categoies of conduct are not likely to develop constituencies supporting general nonincarcerative treatment.

For this serious victim-producing behavior, incarceration does accomplish the major goal of calming public outrage through incapacitation of the perpetrator. On another level, incarceration may, as Durkheim noted, produce solidarity in the social organism (through universally demonstrated outrage), and it may give an appearance of control by affording both the offender and society the opportunity for treatment. An admixture of other motives, such as vengeance, retribution, and deterrence, may also support incarceration. Although not necessarily utile, they seem to be present in varying degrees when incarceration is under discussion.

Adherents of incarceration are often called upon to produce results which available evidence suggests are unrealistic. Yet even nonadherents believe that incarceration will continue to be required in some form because certain behavior will always so outrage public sensibilities that, regardless of the evidence concerning the nonutility of incarceration, the need to calm public fear and anger will prevail. Indeed, the credibility of other methods of dealing with offenders is linked in the public mind with the system's ability to keep the more highly visible and serious actors off the streets. The question becomes, therefore, not whether to give up incarceration as a tool in corrections but rather how to make it a more rational process.[1]

Our social and political organization has done much to shape the present correctional system. Naturally, the structure of corrections in the future will dictate much of its ability to function as well. Currently we have state-by-state fragmentation as the price of federalism. There is no great mystery about correctional growth—the richer states have simply been able to develop more facilities. They do not necessarily demonstrate greater total progress in effectiveness or humaneness, they simply have more. It is not surprising in such a system to find jungle-like facilities coexisting with paradise-like programs within a single state. Conditions between states can be as different as those in foreign cultures.

There are many reasons for the sad state of the field of corrections as we enter the final quarter of the century. Among these are financial problems, regional attitudes, uneven staff training, development, commitments and philosophies, public neglect, lack of a correctional constituency, the absence of a correctional morality, and above all the low visibility of the correctional system. When these problems are placed in the context of lethargic state government bureaucracies with the usual two-year political perspectives, the extent of the structural and functional deficiencies begins to emerge.

The "two year perspective" is one of the key barriers to correctional change. This phrase refers to the political timidity that usually accompanies correctional innovation each time either a legislature or a governor stands for election. Since most major program changes require at least a two-year lead time, it takes an extraordinary coalition of political forces to accomplish it. Bright, creative people enter this milieu anxious to bring about change but find themselves with one foot mired in the quicksand of state government inertia while the other gropes for a toehold on the few resources available. Practically speaking, we may have to accept the "two year perspective" as political reality and build a sufficiently powerful correctional constituency to overcome it.

An effective correctional system cannot depend upon benign political leadership. Since correction is almost by definition a political process, one cannot naively assume that "de-politicizing" is an answer, although it may present a partial solution. Removing corrections from its present location in state government might improve its ability to focus on its primary task. If corrections were not considered to be a governmental function beyond the point of sentencing, administrators could be freed from devoting their time and energy in organizational boundary maintenance functions. This goal could be accomplished in the short run by contracting correctional work to nongovernmental agencies.[2]

Quite aside from the proposition that private sector operation may be more efficient, this approach begins to address itself to the larger political problem. The more contracts, the more involvement. The wider the involvement, the greater the probability of the development of a political constituency with clout.

The current thrust toward community-based correctional programs provides a good testing ground. Taking a halfway house or other localized program and contracting it out to an indigenous group could open channels of communication long lacking between neighborhoods that produce correctional clients and departments of corrections which hold them. If a correction department moves into the neighborhood as the operator, the program may be rejected as being a community-based San Quentin or Stillwater. When an indigenous group contracts to run a program, however, and to inform the community about it, the probability of public acceptance is greatly increased. This can lead to the development of another constituency for correctional change in these involved neighborhood groups.

Still another area of constituency-building can come from alliances with private business interests. This sector of the community has shown its flexibility in responding to social problems in recent years, although not always with outstanding success, in low-cost housing, education, job corps, the war on poverty and the war on crime.[3]

Many state governments have initiated "loaned executives" programs. Legislators respond well to such success models. Some corporations, RCA, Honeywell, Westinghouse, Thiakol, Ford, and others, have already established track records for operating with correctional clients in both probational and institutional programs. Currently, Bethlehem Steel and the United Steel Workers are working on a community-based program along with the National Council of Crime and Delinquency in Pennsylvania. This sort of involvement of business in corrections can create a powerful and sophisticated correctional constituency.

Assuming, however, that efforts such as those described above cannot entirely dispel the governmental environment, we must seek a modus operandi for state correctional services which insulates them from the perils of the "two year perspective." One solution might be to emulate the structure of the board of regents used by university systems. These regents should serve fairly long terms with staggered incumbencies and be limited to serving two such terms. The board of regents would then select the administrator of corrections.

Correctional reforms must also be viewed on a broader and more theoretical level. The ability to make corrections a more viable service may lie in understanding impacts from other criminal justice subsystems and other human services. We seem to be at the threshold of discovery and response in this area, which might be called macro-criminology. For example, early retirement might effect correctional change more rapidly than building institutions closer to urban areas or increasing pay for correctional officers. Similarly, one case decision could save ten years of staff training, since corrections is still a paramilitary operation where court orders are followed better than academic dicta. It may make better economic and human sense to pay the family of an incarcerated man a monthly allowance—the Puritan ethic notwithstanding—in order to keep the family from fragmenting and distributing itself into other subsystems of corrections and welfare.

The macro approach may eventually lead to the development of Departments of Human Services. Some jurisdictions are already well on their way to this, while others are beginning to form human services councils at state levels to deal with problems of manpower, education, corrections, human rights, veterans, welfare, medical, youth, and mental health services. From a political perspective, welfare and corrections will need to amalgamate with noncontroversial services having traditional constituencies, such as veterans and public health. We are still technologically very weak in the human services area. The structural outlines are visible, but manpower needs are critical, and administrators need special training. With the severe fragmentation federalism brings, this appears to be a field ripe for private foundation input and development.

The Dickens adage that the times were never better, they were never worse, applies to today's correctional scene. While Attica was not a watershed in American correctional history, it did occur at a significant time. Public knowledge, understanding, and support of correctional reform has never been higher, particularly in the current milieu of a human rights explosion and a favorable judicial climate. There has been more correctional case law produced in the last few years than in the previous century. The federal government, under a conservative administration, is providing leadership in the way of financial support and progressive standards.[4] Yet we remain saddled with a fortress prison system, and corrections administrations have no agenda for decisive change. The public seems to be more interested in incapacitation than in rehabilitation as an end in corrections. Legislatures still respond only to crisis instead of engaging in long-range planning for prevention. There is a vacuum, with some few exceptions, in political, moral and professional leadership in the field.

Nor does it appear that state legislatures will provide sufficient support in the foreseeable future to dramatically change correctional services, even if a plan for such change were available. Strategically, new services will probably be dependent upon conversion of traditional resources into new programs. Since institutional services usually consume the overwhelming proportion of corrections budgets, they represent a fruitful area for conversion.

While many complex problems confront correction officials in their quest for improvement, the most significant is to formulate a comprehensive statement of what the public can expect from corrections in its present context and what might be expected if corrections can successfully emerge from the fortress prison era as this century draws to a close.

In order to do this we must accept the research findings of the last two decades and respond not by redoubling our continuing efforts but by developing a new approach. The research findings have been summarized in two studies and clearly suggest that we need to give up some highly vaunted sacred cows.[5] Both reviewed a variety of punishments and treatments including warning, probation, fines, short imprisonment, long imprisonment, counselling, training, psychotherapy, halfway houses, and work-release. Both concluded that no treatment or punishment can be shown to be particularly effective.

The Hood and Sparks survey in relation to effectiveness of punishment and treatment concludes:

1. ". . . Research shows that probation is likely to be at least as effective in preventing recidivism as an institutional sentence. . . . However, [this] cannot be interpreted as showing that probation is especially effective as a method of treatment." [6]

. . . .

2. ". . . fines and discharges are much more effective than either probation or imprisonment for first offenders and recidivists of all age groups (. . . fines are especially effective for those convicted of theft) . . . It must be emphasized that this finding does *not necessarily* support the view that any offenders now sent

to penal institutions should as a matter of policy, be dealt with by non-institutional methods instead. Such a course could itself affect the recidivism rates of these and other offenders, as well as reducing the general-preventive effect of the penal system. *More-over, even if recidivism rates did not rise, a shift to non-institutional sentences would lead to an increased crime rate, since it would mean that some offenders now sent to institutions (and so not 'at risk') for a time would instead be at liberty in the community during that time.* [Emphasis added.] The social cost of these extra offenses would have to be balanced, in any policy calculation, against the excess cost of keeping the offenders in institutions rather than leaving them in the community." [7]

. . . .

3. "Longer institutional sentences are no more effective in preventing recidivism than shorter ones. Without exception [studies] . . . show that in general, longer sentences—even of an avowedly reformative kind— do not produce lower reconviction rates." [8]

. . . .

4. "Medium risk offenders are most likely to be affected by new penal methods. The persistent and low risk offenders are least likely to be affected. All groups are identifiable by prediction methods now in use." [9]

The authors conclude, "It must be admitted that a very large number of studies of the effectiveness of punishments and treatments have negative results: that is, they reveal no significant differences between the types of treatment investigated . . . even a marginal improvement in the overall 'success rate' from 60 to 70 percent, for example, would . . . reduce recidivism by one-quarter; and this would be no mean achievement." [10]

In a nutshell, under present conditions nothing much works effectively. Hood and Sparks believe that future effectiveness may lie in the direction of . . . "new forms of treatment, for particular types of offenders," while Greenberg believes that there is ". . . a gap between theory and experiment. Most rehabilitation programs have had little or no link with any plausible theory of why convicted persons were previously involved in crime or why they might return to it. Random experimentation is not a very efficient way of generating new knowledge, as [the] studies reported . . . prove so well." [11]

If both studies are right—Hood and Sparks in suggesting that we should concentrate on the middle-risk offenders with new forms of treatment, and Greenberg in seeking a link between a "plausible theory of why convicted persons were previously involved in crime and why they might return to it"—a working hypothesis can be formulated for correctional reform. This theory postulates that the greatest number of crimes are committed by treatable offenders who have not learned to respond lawfully to an environment that does not provide them with a feeling of "stake" in their society and/or enough opportunities to change their life's circumstances in a satisfactory manner. This theory assumes the career felon to be the least treatable.and excludes the dangerously violent as presenting psychiatric problems not responsive to present methods of treatment.

After separating individuals, the psychiatric and high-risk career felons would receive separate living and care programs: for the former, a concentration of psychiatric services and indeterminate sentences; for the latter, flat time sentences in a milieu of austere but humane and reasonable constitutional care. The largest remaining group, the middle-risk group, would be engaged in a "justice model" of treatment. [12]

The basic premise of the justice model is that non-law-abiders can be taught to be law-abiding by treating them in a lawful manner. This system attempts to bring the entire effort of the correctional agency to bear in teaching lawful behavior by program and example. The justice model seeks to place inmate population and staff within a lawful and rational arena. In a prison, elements of this model would include:

1. some form of self-governance;
2. a system-wide ombudsman independent of the department of corrections;
3. a law library;
4. civil legal assistance for inmates;
5. fair wages for prison industries;
6. opportunity to provide community service as a form of moral restitution;
7. programming for different ethnic groups;
8. due process safeguards built into internal behavior-management systems;

9. no mail censorship;
10. an extensive furlough program;
11. a contract system for parole with objective criteria for progression through the incarceration experience;
12. introduction of adversary and appeal procedures into the parole revocation process;
13. open press access to the correctional system;
14. a method of victim compensation and offender restitution.

Programs would include educational, recreational and vocational training, and industrial work opportunities. For those who wish to receive social, psychological, or psychiatric services, a voucher system would be provided. A separate internal police force would be employed to enforce, when necessary, the explicated norms of this new prison society. Only a small part of the staff would have police functions, while the major effort would be carried out by a nonuniformed counselling staff. This model aims at a prison experience that would allow men to learn to be agents in their own lives, to use legal processes to change their condition, and to wield lawful power. Men who can negotiate their fates do not have to turn to violence as a method of achieving change.

This plan might provide the keeper and the kept with a rationale and morality for their shared fates in a correctional agency.

Part of the goal would be the end of the fortress prison, to be replaced by rehabilitation centers in or near urban complexes. These new rehabilitation centers would house up to three hundred residents and would have the following characteristics:

1. They would be programmatically divisible into units of thirty to fifty residents.
2. They would provide a core of central services with from eight to ten different rehabilitations: intake—diagnosis-classification; psychiatric; high-risk career felons; education, both vocational and academic; chemical abuse; work and study release; preparole release; family treatment; conjugal visiting; crisis short-term return.
3. They would be urban-oriented to serve a region because (a) the professionals who will work at these

centers are urban-oriented; (b) except for the psychiatric unit, professionals should not be full-time state employees; [13] if residents want social, psychological or psychiatric services, they can contract for them; and (c) most offenders will continue coming from the urban areas and will return to them.
4. They would accomplish security through sophisticated electronic and sensory devices maintained by a small perimeter staff. Internally, the type of security housing would depend upon risk classification.
5. They would permit the assignment of staff to manageable groups of residents by subunits. Staff skills could be matched to the needs of each rehabilitation option unit.

It can probably be assumed that corrections will continue to receive individuals from all levels of risks in the foreseeable future. Even if we bend our efforts to diagnose, classify, and place lower risk categories into separate sets of community-based rehabilitation options, we will always have a stable population in secure custody. The justice model can be used for both the higher risk groups and for the community-based residential programs.

The key to the justice model is to continue fairness and due process atfer a defendant is convicted. It is sadly ironic that in our present system of criminal justice we insist on the full majesty of due process for the accused until he is sentenced to an institution, and then say that justice has been served. Our penal codes mandate that before a criminal sanction can be imposed there must be a finding beyond reasonable doubt that the accused's behavior was a union of *act* and *intent:* it was volitional. We are strict in standards of arrest, and we protect the defendant with a mantle of innocence. The defendant can stand mute in court and is protected from conviction by his own mouth, but he can challenge anything brought before the court to support a prosecution. We believe that this system is civilized; that under it the lowliest stands protected from the capriciousness of constituted authority.

While this system may not function perfectly, the great irony occurs after the conviction when the judge commits the defendant to prison. There we find the attitude that the person convicted of a crime does not need or even deserve justice but rather, having proved himself "unworthy," does not merit such treatment.[14] How else has the judicial dictum defining the prisoner as a "slave of the state" endured so long, accompanied by a judicial "hands-off" policy in relation to prison administration? This view is also found in legislatures and in prison treatment services, which view the prisoner as sick, leaving him little room for responsible behavior.

The justice model seeks to engage both the keeper and the kept in a joint venture, which insists that the agencies of justice shall operate in lawful and just manner. It is founded on the belief that because the prisoner did not use lawful means outside the prison, he should be provided with greater opportunities to learn lawful behavior within the institution. The effort must be turned to teaching a prisoner how to use lawful processes to achieve his ends and to have responsibility for the consequences of his behavior. In the absence of a continuum of justice in the prison, most ends are reached unlawfully, and unlawful behavior is punished without those standards of due process so revered outside the prison. This teaches the convict that lawful behavior does not pay; he is dealt with arbitrarily and usually responds by treating others in the same manner. The justice model would allow the prisoner to experience lawful ways of dealing with problems and would try to assure that the prisoner will be exposed to and participate in the life-style society expects him to pursue when he is released.

With the justice model, we are at the threshold of moving from perceiving offenders as clients to seeing them as constituents. This stems from the understanding that the state cannot, as historical experience makes clear, hire anyone to rehabilitate anyone else. The person who is troubled or in trouble must be an equal partner, must want something to happen. The best way to engage him is to treat him with dignity. The billions spent in criminal justice are wasted if the offender does not buy the program. It is up to corrections to sell that program through fair and honest involvement with its constituency.[15]

Footnotes

[1] The first task of those with administrative responsibility for incarceration should be to insure that it does not have an iatrogenic effect, that is, giving the incarcerated a disease they didn't have before entering the institution. Incarceration should be humane, safe, and afford constitutionally reasonable care.

2 A vehicle for such process was introduced in the Minnesota Legislature in 1971. It failed in committee. It was too new, too scary. However, Minnesota continues to contract services out, as do most jurisdictions. The 1972–1975 Mission Statement for Minnesota Department of Corrections reads in its preamble:

"The primary role of the Department of Corrections is to develop correctional policy, orchestrate a wide variety of correctional alternatives involving the private sector and the community and to *solely operate only those segments of the corrections system where* major professional corrections resources are required." (Emphasis supplied.) Id. at 1.

3 A more cynical colleague, an engineer, once reminded me that "all you have to do is dangle a buck and Yankee ingenuity will be there!"

4 National Advisory Commission on Correctional Standards.

5 D. F. Greenberg, "The Special Effects of Penal Measures: A Descriptive Summary of Existing Studies," Staff Memorandum #2 for the Committee on Incarceration (March 29, 1972); R. Hood and R. Sparks, Key Issues in Criminology (World University Library, 1970).

6 Hood and Sparks, note 5, supra, at 187–188.

7 Id. at 188–190.

8 Id. at 190.

9 Id. at 191.

10 Id. at 192.

11 Id. at 68.

12 Concentrating "treatment" on this group is reminiscent of a bit of folklore recently told me by Johnny Maher of the Delancey Street Foundation in San Francisco. He compared the German battlefield medical strategy with that of the British in W.W. I. Maher contends that the British treated the more severely wounded first, thereby allowing the less seriously wounded to deteriorate. The Germans assumed that they could salvage more manpower by treating the less severely wounded first. According to Maher, the German strategy returned more men to the field faster, while the British strategy, ostensibly a more humanitarian one, worked adversely both in humane and military terms.

13 Although professionals claim that their presence in authoritative settings has humanized treatment regimens, there is little evidence to support this. Rather it appears that their entry has cost them their identities in a process not unlike the one which has seen those who have invaded China over the years become Chinese.

14 How deeply our culture divides the offender from the accused may be seen in typical behavior of actors in the system. For example, a defendant on bail for up to a year, upon being pronounced guilty is immediately put into handcuffs. This same process occurs when a person surrenders himself.

15 The roots for the justice model theory are deep. They seem to be a congruence from several disciplines. Edmund Cahn, the legal scholar, coined the phrases, "the imperial perspective" and "the consumer prespective." Philip Selznick, the sociologist, developed the notion of "private government" and influenced the work of Eliot Studt and Sheldon Messinger's work on the idea of

justice as treatment. Edgar and Jean Cahn (son and daughter-in-law of Edmund Cahn), in relation to the "War on Poverty," wrote of "the military perspective" and "the civilian perspective."

Richard Korn's and Donald Cressey's ideas of "justice as negotiation" with the demonstration of existing dual systems of justice also contributed to the trend just now taking the shape of a model of justice. Disillusionment with the "medical model" by many behavioral scientists and the emergence of group and milieu therapy, guided group interaction, self-governance, student revolts, deepening commitments to ideas of personal, informal democracy and "local control" in the 1960's, all helped to create an atmosphere for an idea whose time is ripe.

Philip Selznick has conceptualized the major themes involved in the justice model:

"(1) *The postulate of normality, competence, and worth.* If offenders are to be dealt with as human beings, it must be assumed that they are basically like everyone else; only their circumstances are special. Every administrative device that negates this principle, and any therapy that ignores it, must be questioned and, if possible, set aside.

"(2) *Salience of the micro-world.* Men live out their lives in specific settings, and it is there, in the crucible of interaction, that potentialities are sealed off or released. The micro-world is the world of here-and-now; if an inmate's future is to be affected, that future should have a dynamic, existential connection with the experienced present.

"(3) *The poverty of power.* An administration that relies solely on its own coercive resources can make little contribution to the reconstruction of prison life or to the creation of environments that encourage autonomy and self-respect.

"(4) *Order as tension and achievement.* Quiescent conformity imposed from above is a parody of social order, not its fulfillment. A system that validates the humanity of its participants, and engages their full resources, accepts the risk of disorder and even, from time to time, of searing confrontations.

"(5) *Justice as therapy.* A concern for fairness and civic validation should permeate the entire administration of criminal law, including the daily life of the prisoner. That treatment will be most effective which does the most for the inmate's sense of self-worth and responsibility. Nothing contributes more to these feelings than a social environment whose constitutive principle is justice, with its corollaries of participation, giving reasons, and protecting personal dignity. . . .

"Without questioning the worth of these objectives, it may be asked: Is it the public policy to punish offenders, especially young offenders, beyond the fact of imprisonment itself? If not, does humane and respectful treatment, not as therapy but as civilized conduct, require a special justification?

"In seeking to make criminal justice more redemptive and less punitive, we may have asked too much of institutions that can barely hold their own, let alone develop the competence to be curers of souls. A retreat from rosy hopes may well be inevitable, if only because rehabilitation entails supervision, and ineffective rehabilitation coupled with open-ended control has little to commend it. As the dialogue proceeds and experience is assessed, we may well conclude that the real worth of the "treatment perspective," in its various forms, has been to serve as a civilizing influence on correctional systems. If that should be so, then a theory of corrections that envisions the creation of viable, working communities, based on a postulate of normality, will have most to offer." P. Selznick in the Forword to E. Studt and S. Messinger, C-Unit: the Search for a Community in Prison, at vii-ix (Russell Sage Foundation, 1968).

THE PRISONERS OF AFFIRMATION : CORRECTIONAL ADMINISTRATORS AS PENAL REFORMERS

RICHARD R. KORN *

The Destruction of People by Means of the Debasement of Their Language

Some months ago I visited a large church-supported correctional institution for children in Minnesota. In the course of my tour I passed a stout, solid door. Its thickness suggested a soundproof solitary confinement chamber. When I asked my guide, a young staff member, to open the door, he informed me that it was "occupied." I gently pressed—but when my guide told me that it would be "antitherapeutic to intrude at this time," I recognized the code words for a checkmate. I had to settle for a verbal description of a windowless, soundproof chamber called the "Time-Out Room." Children were placed in this room "when their acting out prevented them from participating in the program."

The dialogue in front of the locked door was associated with an unpleasant tension in my facial muscles, for as we talked, my guide and I occasionally exchanged smiles. We had made an unspoken agreement to do three things: to lie about what was actually taking place; to acknowledge that we were lying, thereby silently assuring each other of our intact inner integrity; and to refrain from an act that any ordinary man would have committed had he known the truth we silently shared: to batter down the door and rescue a child being tortured for the sake of a lie. Fortu-

---

* Director, Berkeley Institute for Training in Group Therapy and Psychodrama, Berkeley, California; author, Criminology and Penology (1959), Juvenile Delinquency (A Reader) (1967); Ph.D. New York University.

nately for us, the truths we shared with the child behind the door had been kept from the ordinary people of the world. These truths remain the private burden of a small group of professional altruists, typically liberal in thinking and gentle in speech, to whom have been entrusted the children of the poor.

The scene in front of the locked door could have taken place a thousand years ago. The visitor might have been a prelate from an outlying parish taking a tour of the Vatican dungeon. Passing the same room he might have made the same request. He would have been told that the "penitent" within could not be disturbed for the sake of his soul. The cell would be called "in pace," a place where he could be "at peace," and despite the differences in language, the smiles would have been the same.

Again both the visitor and his guide shared a certain secret. They were ministers of a religion in which neither any longer believed, and despite their inner doubts they had agreed to maintain appearances. A recent observer of the modern Church has described their situation:

> "[T]hough it was a world of faith, it was a world of deceptions too, and deliberate blindnesses; of things one should not see, and of consequent pretending not to see them. The attitudes, no matter how carefully inculcated, were strained—like the rapt composure one strove for on that mystic journey back from the communion rail. . . . One had been trained to put a different face on . . . for the sake of others. And in time the whole of one's own faith could be held for other people. Doubts were hidden for the sake of the children; or a priest's, for the sake of his flock; or the flock's doubts were minimized 'in front of Father'." [1]

The differences between the encounter in the papal dungeon and the visit to the modern "child-caring" institution a thousand years later are essentially liturgical, involving new verbal formulae for the mystical transubstantiation of reality by means of ritual. The objective remains constant: men must still find ways to resolve contradictions between their scruples and the testimony of their naked eyes. The instrumentality is a special language by means of which the distinction between the real and the ideal is itself obliterated.

Thus, the behavior of a child resisting mistreatment is

called "acting out." Since it is not acceptable to believe that staff will in fact mistreat children, the child's response must be otherwise explained. It is posited that the acting out stems from a hypothetical agent in the child's mind: a "character disorder." This malevolent agent operating independently of the child's volition—there are no malevolent children—makes it impossible for the child to defer gratification. It also lowers his frustration tolerance and makes him emit a self-destructive behavioral substance called uncontrollable aggression. (This behavioral emission is very different from the behavior of the staff person who packs the child off into a solitary confinement cell. The staff member is not expressing aggression: he is setting limits.)

Setting limits is one of several procedures by which the staff responds to the imaginary entities controlling the child. The totality of these procedures comprises a mystical rite known as the treatment program, which is designed to emit the appropriate correctives to the self-destructive behavior emitted by the child.

It is never the child as a person who is the target of these procedures, nor is it ever the staff member as a person who imposes them. The struggle taking place is between the child's character disorder and the treatment program. So, when one locks a minor in a six-by-eight foot cell, one is not locking up a child at all. One is locking up the malevolent force which lives in the child's brain and makes him do the things he does against his will. And when he screams so loud that he can be heard through six inches of soundproofing, it is not the child who is screaming but that demon within him, upon whom limits have finally been set.

It is by these means that the age-old problem of transforming the world in the direction of human ideals is solved with a magical economy of effort. One need no longer work and agonize to bring the millennium about. One need only assert that it has already been achieved, that it is happening now, before our very eyes. The costs of this procedure are minimal. What is sacrificed is only the integrity of the language, which must be debased, and the persons of those who have already been doomed by the unspoken, unspeakable judgment of those willing to sacrifice them for the sake of appearances.

Thus is fulfilled Orwell's prediction that, in our time, the killing of men will be made possible by the murder of their language. It is the special mission of the academic establishment to keep this language in repair, to replace concepts worn threadbare by use, and to train adepts in its vocabulary and syntax. At present this function is performed by the professional schools, which have largely displaced the theological seminaries in the work of training the moral henchmen of power. Nevertheless, from time to time, occasions arise when the process of repair cannot keep pace, when the strain between pretense and experience stretches even pretended belief to the breaking point. At this point the Old Dispensation—and perhaps even some of the Old Dispensers—may require replacement. This period is typically accompanied by a revival of the sense of outrage which had been put to sleep by the opiate of the old consensus.

The Flowering of the New Reform Movement From a Rhetoric in Decay

Penology has been witnessing a variety of movements around the nation in the last decade, all seeking to reform our prisons.

The flowering of this movement has been signalled by a general shift in mood on the part of correctional administrators from the self-congratulatory to the penitential. There is a general movement toward the confessional box, that is, toward its modern equivalent—the witness chair at a legislative hearing. Once seated there, the correctional administrator tends to strike an occasional note of critical self-examination to counterbalance his blame of others. Thus, Mr. Raymond Procunier, Director of the California Department of Corrections, testifying before the House Committee on the Judiciary in October of 1971—following a two-year period in which thirty-three men (personnel and prisoners) had violently died—observed:

> "Before I open for questions, I would like to suggest . . . there is no one in this field of any consequence at all that believes prison is the place to send a person for rehabilitation. None of us would suggest that a friend go to San Quentin for help." [2]

When it came to fixing responsibility for the wave of violence which had swept his constituency, however, Mr. Procunier confined his criticisms to the derelictions of others—a coalition of "violent, revolutionary inmates" and "radical reformers."

> ". . . The prison and parole system is being attacked by a group of radical reformers who will use apparently any

method—including attempts to provoke prison violence and publishing unconfirmed reports of physical brutality —to 'reform the system.' " [3]

But Mr. Procunier assured the Committee that:

"Prison is one place in which activist tactics, confrontation politics and revolutionary rhetoric cannot be tolerated." [4]

The Frustration of the Administrators of Reform

Part of the reform movement has been the appearance of new administrators on the correctional scene. These men are often drawn from outside the local system and sometimes from outside the correctional milieu. For such men, unencumbered as they are by any personal, professional or ideological commitments to the old system, the access to official authority comes as a dazzling opportunity to mobilize great power on behalf of basic innovations. As trenchant critics of the old system, they are aware of its capacity to do harm; to them it seems a reasonable assumption that the forces for promotion of reforms are at least roughly equivalent in potency to those that maintained pernicious conditions.

To the critical outside observer, the grim state of affairs in criminal justice and corrections may well give the appearance of an almost conspiratorial organization for the promotion of misery. Having finally gained entrance, the former observer, now a participant, discovers a shocking fact. Except for the universal penchant of bureaucrats to cover their own trails with as much dissimulation as possible, there is no conspiracy, nor need there be. Indeed, there is hardly any "organization" at all. What appeared at a distance to be a "system" turns out to be not a system but rather a concatenation of several systems and interest groups frequently operating at cross-purposes or, worse, without any reference to each other. In this administrative chaos, accident, apathy, and sheer inertia are fully capable of producing fortuitously what the most calculated and concerted effort might have failed to achieve by design—the near total frustration of any effort at change.

If a state administration is analyzed, the following power-and-interest groups can be identified and their purposes and interactions defined.

The Executive

For the Chief Executive the entire correctional apparatus (prisons, reformatories, etc.) is a necessary evil—a headache that ranges from the nagging to the severe. There is little political mileage in well-run prisons but great political vulnerability in their mismanagement. (Convicts don't vote, but their victims do.) The governor looks to his correctional administrators to run his prisons; they are the experts who must take the heat off him if things go wrong. Typically the governor wants a correctional administration that will keep costs down, maintain peace and quiet, and permit him to concentrate on more important matters.

The Legislature

The legislature divides itself into the different interests of the two political parties. The "ins" share the worries and concerns of the governor; like him, they bend a wary eye toward the taxpayer, the newspapers, and the opposition party. The "outs" are always on the alert for a politically pregnant scandal; their twin banners, "soft on crime" and "prison mismanagement," are rarely furled. As the temporarily unappreciated guardians of public morality, they are watchdogs hungry for any exposed shinbone. With astute cultivation and inspired leadership they can rise to higher (nonpartisan) things, but only when the millennium is at hand.

The Judiciary

Judges tend to protect themselves from uncomfortable knowledge about penal conditions in their jurisdictions. A vague, pervasive feeling that "the prison does not work, even though it is necessary," a nagging sense of guilt about the men they are sending away, a barrage of letters and writs from inmates claiming mistreatment, confront the judge. All of these things tend to make him willing to let the experts run the prisons, provided that individual rights of inmates are not clearly breached. By and large, the judiciary is willing to be inert in this area, responding only to the initiatives of others and then only in a narrowly legalistic context.

The Probation and Parole Authorities

In addition to carrying out their own onerous duties, the probation and parole authorities keep a wary eye on the press, on public opinion, on the opposition party, and on the state of institutional overcrowding. Particularly vulnerable to the accusation, "soft on crime," their longer-range efforts are subject to temporary or permanent revision under the pressure of critical incidents. Even thoroughly independent nonpartisan boards occupied by prestigious community figures have an Achilles heel: their budgets. Boards vary in their dependency on the advice of their professional staffs, which also may vary in response to the board members' attitudes and other influences. An imaginative and determined board, acting in cooperation with the judiciary, can serve as the source and sustainer of important innovations in correction.

The Correctional Establishment

Departments of corrections are well aware that their principal mandate is to protect the executive and his party from political embarrassment by keeping things under control and out of the public arena. But an old saw has it that the only way to keep out of politics is to play politics. Whether he wishes to or not, the commissioner must play the political game, if only to remain above it. The correctional administrator looks to his governor not for direction (which he will not get) but for protection and support. Quiet, economical housekeeping is his safest role. He can be the captain of his ship, so long as no one rocks it and he is content to keep it moored to the dock. If he resists the temptation to take it anywhere, he can have a quiet, ceremonious voyage (in port)— entertaining visitors at the captain's table and conducting tours of the staterooms.

The Citizenry

The best interests of the public is the most frequently invoked reason for any correctional action or inaction, and the least involved. Public Opinion is the sacred cow that is always deferred to and never consulted. Used as a shield or weapon in the hands of others in the correctional arena, it is inert in itself until stirred. Those who seek to use it try to manufacture it; those who fear it are half-aware that it is manufactured and despise it: both may dangerously underestimate it.

Two contradictory attitudes characterize the usual state of public opinion about crime and corrections. Citizens are "tough on criminals" but "soft on prisoners." The exploitation of one or the other of these available attitudes accounts for many of the pendulum swings in specific correctional systems. Typically, the shift occurs along the continuum of "hardness" versus "softness." An exposé of harsh prison conditions may inaugurate the brief reign of a humanitarian and reformist administration, but before long gradual disillusionment or disaster terminates the unlucky reign of reform and brings back the rule of repression.

The Media

The media are well aware that crime and correction are lively sources of news and potential public issues. Many journalists realize that the crucial determinants of correctional policies are political rather than scientific. Intuitively suspicious of any claim to superior morality or expertise, they have an inquiring nose for bodies buried under rhetorical flowers. Informed journalists have made distinguished contributions to public education about corrections. Molders as well as reflectors of public opinion, they are not only the eyes and ears of the slumbering giant but they have the power to amplify the voice of his uneasy conscience as well. They have often roused him to furious reaction, but they have not informed him adequately about what action to take.

The Social Scientist

The social scientist has long enjoyed the privilege of criticizing corrections from a comfortably safe distance. It is only in recent times that he has entered the field as a researcher, a participant-observer, a consultant, and an innovator. His performance is too recent and too variable to permit summary characterization, but the omens of promise are increasingly clouded with omens of foreboding. As the high priest of the victorious new religion of science, he may be treading confidently into a place that has been the graveyard of too many hopes before him. The fate of the professional clinician in correction may serve to warn him. The putrefaction is still fresh enough to reach even his high-held nose.

The Treatment Professionals

Once the glowing bride of corrections, Treatment has become its nagging wife. Treatment personnel are the little old ladies of any institution: vanity, as much as anything else, keeps them from behaving as viragos in the public company of their husbands, the correctional administrators. In any case, administrators, as with other neglectful husbands, are useful scapegoats who can be blamed for the failure of the marriage.

The professional, like other correctional employees, is largely preoccupied with saving his own image in the face of his failure. Since the image was more flattering to begin with, the task of face-saving is more preoccupying, and the professional must devote more time and effort to it. Within limits he can do this by laying the blame at the doors of the correctional administrator, the custodian, the politicians, and the public. But he has been careful to contain his complaining within decorous limits, and when anyone in authority looks askance, the professional tends to shift to his second role of martyr and long-suffering missionary. Unfortunately, the indifference and tolerant contempt in which most members of treatment staffs are held by most inmates testifies to inadequate ardor in this role as well.

The inmates have learned that the typical therapist will neither be his champion nor his antagonist. The activities of treatment staffs are rarely significant enough to be cited in lists of inmate grievances; lack of treatment is sometimes complained of, not its presence. When he is not seen as a little old lady, the prison therapist is often viewed as a professional snitch, a soft glove over the horny hands of custody, or as an ear and voice to exploit in hopes of recommendations for earlier release.

The Police

Prevalent police attitudes towards correction are direct and straightforward. They believe that prisons are good, especially when they are tough and punish the criminals caught by the police. Prisons become bad when they let criminals back into the streets where the police have to catch them all over again, which seems like a big waste of energy. Parole boards are especially bad because they let criminals out earlier than their maximum sentences ordain.

Through the highly articulate voices of their guilds, police-

men have given these attitudes an amplification that frequently
arouses legislators and other vote-conscious officials to action. As
one of the more effective lobbies for correctional retrogression,
the police establishment must be reckoned with. The aspiring
correctional innovator who refuses to engage it in dialogue does
so to the detriment of his own cause.

The Offenders

Prisoners are the ultimate consumers of corrections and
the ultimate determiners of its effectiveness. They are also the
least consulted of all the actors in the drama. These facts certainly contribute to the general correctional dilemma. To para-
phrase a noted phrase-maker: Rarely in the history of human
endeavor has so little been asked of so many who might have so
much to give.

> "It is not to be wondered at that prisoners reject a
> situation which has essentially rejected them. The spon-
> taneous human response to the denial of participation
> is subversion. Refusing to commit themselves to a pro-
> gram they had no part in making, and which they cannot
> trust because it will not trust them, the collectivity of
> exiles, thrown back on their own resources, create an
> underground program of their own. The overriding pur-
> pose of this program is to enable them to re-assert the
> autonomy which the official program has denied them.
> But the assertion of initiative in a situation which forbids
> it is explicitly illegal. It follows, in the nature of the case,
> that the representative institutional situation gives the
> offender no alternative to the loss of his autonomy except
> that of continuing his career of law-violation within the
> walls. The convicts have their own name for the program
> they create for themselves: they call it a School of
> Crime." [5]

The following conclusions can readily be drawn from this
model of the universe within which a state correctional system
operates:

1. Despite its authoritarian structure at internal local levels,
the system as a whole is essentially directionless and uncon-

trolled. It is not merely without any consistent, sustained external direction, it is equally incapable of directing itself.

2. None of the many individual forces that are singly capable of disturbing the system are singly capable of moving it in any sustained direction, nor of initiating and maintaining any fundamental change.

3. Vulnerable to a bewildering variety of disequilibrating influences, the system is preponderantly occupied with maintaining its own internal balance by means of constant minor adjustments. Unguided except on the level of rhetoric by any coherent plan, these adjustments are made on the level of many microscopically local arrangements, unknown and invisible to higher administrative authorities. At all levels, administrative opportunism and defensive readjustment are the rule.

4. In the face of a loss of actual control, correctional administrators have learned how to simulate the appearance of control by anticipating the thrust of many forces and predicting their probable resolution. By then "ordering" the system to move in the foreordained direction, they can create the appearance of steering while actually doing little more than holding on to the wheel.[6]

In operational terms, a combination of structural and socio-psychological processes join to frustrate attempts by any present combination of agents to direct the correctional endeavor. These include the coercive, noncontractual character of the system as it bears upon the offender and the restrictive character of administrative regulation, which limits the options, destroys the spontaneity, and degrades the status of personnel working with the offender. The hierarchical, bureaucratic structure, which seeks to coordinate control over personnel and inmates from a remote point, separated from both by many intervening levels of mediation each of which contributes uncontrolled variance, is another major factor that makes direction of the system impossible.

The paradoxical end result is that while severely limiting both creative and destructive initiatives, the system cannot eliminate them. Thus it fails to achieve its overall objective of coordinated control. Likewise, while they do not achieve the degree of self-direction and self-esteem necessary for a personal commitment to the program, the inmate and personnel participants can still rescue enough initiative to resist the stultifying effects of total standardization, thereby blunting and distorting the negative thrust of the overall program.

A roughly analogous stalemate exists on the ideological level. The humanitarian and reformative movements succeeded in undermining the monolithic powers of the custodial and security forces without succeeding in achieving the conditions required for effective treatment. The result is that the modern prisoner, though relatively freer within the walls, remains essentially without treatment. In the process, the real though brutal integrity of a frankly punitive ideology has been replaced by the casuistry of a hollow ritualistic pretense at treatment. This gives the prisoner irrefutable proof of the bad faith of his self-styled rehabilitators.

We must now face a consideration that makes much of the foregoing, however correct, virtually irrelevant. The fact that no "conspiracy" exists, the fact that correctional activities betray little functional coordination, is actually beside the point.

Men and women subject to extremities of power find it unendurable to believe their fates are being controlled by the whims of those who, in their own turn, are subject to the whims of even more remote figures and forces. Feeling like cogs, they are outraged by an indication that those immediately above them are also cogs and that the sources of real power are not only unapproachable but unfathomable. This combination of subjugation, uncertainty, and officials' inability to control official policy is an open invitation to paranoia. Indeed, from a mental health standpoint, paranoia might be preferable to an unresolvable situation of uncertainty. As the victim of planlessness, the prisoner is unrecognized and invisible. Hence prisoners insist as a matter of principle that anyone who can or does affect them be held personally accountable.

The deeply committed correctional administrator is cognizant of this resentment; indeed he might well share it, since he is subject to a similar situation. Like the inmate, he struggles to gain control of the forces that can affect his program. In so doing he will inevitably antagonize both those within his department who are apathetic, enjoying what is in effect an on-the-job retirement, and those who are engaged in defending their own private administrative empires.

In the course of this struggle to gain control, he may make a foolhardy promise to the inmates, committing himself to deliver more than he actually can. The danger in stimulating hope is that the frustration of hope leads to a feeling of deliberate betrayal. What happens next may be determined by who attacks him first and injures him the most—the militant inmates pressing him from the "Left" or the custodial and administrative old-liners blocking him and dragging him down from the "Right."

If the inmates, already skilled in the art of bypassing impotent authority, appeal over the administrator's head by means of an outburst, strike, or riot, the correctional reformer may have no alternative but to cast his lot with the old-liners who, having already inwardly repudiated him, will consent to save his face only if he abandons his program. Any move in this direction is likely to infuriate the prisoners, whose worst suspicions are now confirmed, and the reformer in turn is betrayed by those he sought only to help.

The sense of mutual betrayal may now trigger the tragedy foreordained by the correctional administrator's relative powerlessness. Aware of his humanity but distrustful of his intentions or his ability to fulfill them, the inmates may make a power play. Publicly humiliated by the defiance of his clients, outraged at being taken advantage of, and determined to refute the accusations from both sides that he is weak, the reformer may try to prove his strength by a harsh act of repression. The escalating consequences may complete the reformer's own disillusionment with penal reform, completing the destruction of the ideology of basic change by the sheer course of events.

A Grim Tomorrow

To this observer, the immediate and longer-range futures look exceptionally bleak. The prospects for a radical forward movement were much better a few years ago than they are today. The period spanned by 1960 to 1968 was one of quickening hopes for criminal justice and corrections in this country. Looking back at that period, one has the feeling of running out onto a long pier only to see the ship just pulling away from the dock. By now, four years later, the ship is far over the horizon.

These four years have been the most violent, most bloody in modern correctional history. Penal reform has failed in this country. There was too little of it; it was too slow; it fell too far behind the rate of social improvement taking place outside of the walls; it failed to take into account the revolution of rising expectations. What there was of it was inevitably dressed in a rhetoric so inflated that the actual achievement was always dwarfed by the pretense.

There may even be a more fundamental reason for the failure. None of the reforms, actual or proposed, has eliminated the element of coercion. When one asks why men resist coercion, one need only visualize the criminal's victim for a plausible answer. Offenders resist forcible correction for the identical reasons that the victims of crime resist crime: both reduce the victim to passivity, demanding that he renounce control of his own future and reducing him to an object.

An Alternative Prospect

In the face of this bleak picture, one might well wonder if there can be an effective program of correction. It would appear that most if not all of us repose great faith in reconciliation and restitution when it comes to dealing with our own transgressions. A system that might bring our treatment of strangers who offend us in line with the treatment we offer our friends, our kin, and our social equals would require the following changes.

Ideological: A transformation of the governing ethic from revenge-through-disablement and mutual alienation to mutual reconciliation based upon mutual restitution, including guaranteed compensation for the victims of crime. This ideological shift would be grounded upon the recognition that guilt and account-ability are social as well as individual, universal as well as isolable.

Theoretical: Recognition of the fact that crime is a social as well as an individual product, and that necessary changes in the individual can neither be substitutes for nor alternatives to necessary remedial social changes.

Organizational: Recognition of the fact that programs aimed at the promotion of self-sufficiency through exertion of individual initiative are incompatible with control by large-scale organizational structures whose sheer size and complexity sacrifice autonomy to system-needs of coordination.

Operational: Recognition that techniques of total control appropriate for the manipulation of materials and events in the physical world may be inappropriate in programs that seek facilitation of creativity and liberation from external forces and impersonal natural law. It follows that the reduction of the skills of human influence to a standardized technology that can be impersonally applied is inherently inimical to developing satisfying human relations.

In practical application, these changes would produce a program community-based and locally organized rather than institutional and bureaucratically controlled; informal and personal rather than formal and professional; evocative, enabling, and creative rather than repressive, inhibitory, corrective, or "therapeutic"; and mutually contractual rather than unilaterally obligatory.[7]

The prospects that such a system will ever be developed are slim, but they may well be our only hope.

Footnotes

[1] G. Wills, Bare Ruined Choirs: Doubt, Prophecy, and Radical Religion, at 8 (Doubleday & Co., New York, 1972).

[2] Testimony of Mr. Raymond Procunier, Director, California Department of Corrections. Prisons, Prison Reform and Prisoners' Rights: California, at 5 (U.S. Government Printing Office, Washington, D.C., October 25, 1971).

[3] Id. at 125.

[4] Id.

[5] Korn, "Correctional Innovation and the Dilemma of Change-from-Within," Can. J. Corrections 449–457 (July 1968).

[6] Korn, "Issues and Strategies of Implementation in the Use of Offenders in Resocializing Other Offenders," Offenders as a Correctional Manpower Resource, at 456 (Joint Commission on Correctional Manpower and Training, Washington, D.C., June, 1968).

[7] Id. at 80.

21

LEGISLATORS AND REFORM

EDITORS' INTRODUCTION

Courts traditionally are reluctant to tread where legislatures should. In prisoners' rights cases many judges have been loath to grant relief that embodies what they believe amounts to legislation, e.g., writing of new regulations and allocation of money for reform. The legislators, however, have fallen short of their duty to enact reform, leaving the situation unchanged. As these articles suggest, legislators have a great responsibility in the area of corrections.

THE LEGISLATOR AND THE LEGISLATURE: THEIR ROLES IN PRISON REFORM

HONORABLE ROBERT W. KASTENMEIER *

Few problems demand legislators' attention so pressingly as corrections. Seldom has the time been so ripe for action. The failings of our prisons have been extensively documented by the press, by official studies, and by firsthand accounts. The call for change has been sounded loudly by Attica and by a dozen other lesser-known prison uprisings.

Nonetheless, some basic barriers to change do exist. It is important to perceive these difficulties even if they have no clear solution, because they necessarily shape the course that a legislator, and legislatures, will take.

It is a troublesome fact that much that has gone under the rubric of reform in American penology has in fact become repression.[1] Consequently, any legislator searching for improved laws must probe the implications of change. Too many constituents of reformers have already suffered unforeseen consequences.[2]

Also, it must be recognized that prisons are merely the end of a long series of inequities in our criminal justice system. Even humane prisons would still be populated by the poor and the minorities. Thus, as the depth of the study of prison reform increases, so does the realization of how massive the task of achieving justice thereby really is.

Another problem is inherent in the legislative process itself. Legislators are expected to be well informed in voting on a myriad of issues. They are also responsible for servicing their constituents, and, to be practical, they are concerned about getting reelected. Rarely do such men and women have the knowl-

---

* U.S. House of Representatives (Wisconsin); Chairman, House Subcommittee No. 3 ("Subcommittee on Corrections"); LL.B. University of Wisconsin.

edge or time to develop a total grasp of the many matters before them. Consequently, legislators prefer laws set in a broad framework, leaving the interior design to administrators. It is easy in abstract terms to vote for a bill authorizing millions of dollars to fight disease, pollution, or hunger; the task of defining the details of that fight is one seldom welcomed by a legislator.

More than in most areas, that type of detailed, specific legislation is needed in corrections: so much of the lack of due process and decent conditions in prisons is the result of legislatures' failure to prescribe standards for prison administrators; so many of the abuses in parole systems are the result of legislative grants of broad powers, unrestricted by effective and meaningful statutory directives.[3]

However, particularity may well become a bar to meaningful reform, as statutory directives may limit administrative flexibility. The issue of specificity versus generality is especially relevant to the federal effort in corrections reform. An example of this may be seen in the Omnibus Crime Control and Safe Streets Act of 1968,[4] which created the Law Enforcement Assistance Administration as the primary source of federal funds for corrections on the state and local levels.

When this Act was amended in 1970,[5] there were extensive debates over the question of block grants versus categorical grants, e.g., provision of money largely without guidelines versus distribution of funds for specific purposes. The proponents of the block grant approach won out, having argued that administrative discretion in the use of funds would encourage innovation and flexibility. Four years later, however, it appears that flexibility did not bring about innovation [6] but only strengthened the status quo.

Finally, every legislator must face the eternal dilemma of either reflecting the views of his constituency or following his own persuasions even though the people he represents may disagree. This presents particular problems in the criminal justice area, because where criminals are concerned, reformers have not carried the day. Prison reform may be a popular subject of discussion, but it is not a politically popular program.[7] In my tenure as Chairman of the Subcommittee on Corrections of the House Committee on the Judiciary, few organizations have lobbied for prison reform. This apparent lack of interest creates little external pressure for action, while there is a growing and vocal opposition to penal reform based on the widespread sentiment that high crime rates can only be reduced by long and harsh incarceration.

The Avenues of Reform

If, notwithstanding these problems, a legislator does make the commitment to seek reform of our corrections system, there are four avenues available to him: (1) legislative amendment; (2) legislative innovation; (3) exposure function; (4) ombudsman function. For each of these roles the legislator—and the legislature—have some special competence, or at least advantage.

Legislative Amendment

Various statutory provisions impose bars to reform. For example, numerous provisions of the federal law apply to prison-made goods,[8] limiting the interstate sale and transportation of such goods, and thereby maintaining state prison industries within the confines of their own jurisdictions. In part, these restrictions account for the inability of state prison industries to develop adequate markets and pay adequate wages (assuming that wages are to be paid only from the proceeds of the sale of these goods). A service could be performed by removing these restrictions.

Many state statutes limit possible reform. For example, virtually every state has some restrictions on the right of inmates and ex-offenders to hold certain jobs and to vote.[9] Affirmative action is necessary to remove these restrictions, and, unless legal challenges can prevail in the courts, only the legislature is capable of taking the necessary steps.

At the risk of being presumptuous, I would advise any legislator interested in corrections reform to examine closely the laws in his jurisdiction and assess the statutory impediments, many of which, like the numerous state provisions barring ex-offenders from certain jobs, are of enormous importance;[10] then a concerted plan of action to remove these restrictions must be devised. In addition, the detailed review of existing correctional law will help the legislator to gain some understanding of the innovations needed to bring about meaningful reform.

Legislative Innovation

In changing the field of corrections, it is interesting to note that innovative legislation may not be necessary. For example, to my knowledge little or no legislation was necessary for Dr.

Jerome Miller, Commissioner of the Massachusetts Department of Youth Services, to undertake his program of closing all youth detention facilities in the state.[11] He apparently had the ability and the support to pursue this brilliant effort without looking to new, enabling legislation. Similarly, on the federal level there is a tremendous amount of flexibility available to the Federal Bureau of Prisons.

Notwithstanding these inherent potentials for change, the corrections systems in this country do not appear zealous in pressing for reforms within the broad mandates afforded them. For example, most of them could administratively adopt due process disciplinary procedures. Very few have, however, and in large part, the due process that does exist is the product of judicial imposition, not administrative discretion. Similarly, work-release—praised by most experts as a good, viable corrections program—is minimally employed in many systems, despite existing authority to implement it.

Since discretion has, generally, not been employed to pursue reformist courses but rather to maintain anti-reform methods, legislators may well have to enact detailed physical prison requirements and detailed due process disciplinary systems; legislate detailed parole procedures; and mandate work-release, education-release, halfway houses, and the like.

Exposure Function

It takes no special insight to recognize that corrections, in all its aspects, is largely hidden from the public. Correctional administrators seek to prevent public access as well as press access.[12] They do not want public scrutiny, nor is the public eager to scrutinize. In the main, the old saw, "out of sight, out of mind," characterizes the public's attitude toward our prisons, jails, and other correctional programs.

The congruence of administration resistance and public apathy is a significant hurdle to change. One major function a legislator can serve is to focus attention on corrections. Legislative hearings, general hearings, and political statements can all serve to raise the public consciousness and to stir the public conscience.

Legislative exposure can serve a more substantive role. It can assure that corrections systems do not operate in darkness. Very simply, some modicum of checks and balances must be introduced into a system which thus far has been largely devoid of them.

Hearings provide an excellent forum in which to raise critical questions. Why are press representatives barred from the prisons? Why is money being spent on a new prison rather than on increased training programs? Why is due process not being implemented in the disciplinary process? Why are people being transferred continually from one institution to another?

Although legislative bodies are not particularly well equipped to be investigative agencies, when they do perform this role and expose issues that have been obscured, they can perform a tremendous service.

Ombudsman Function

On a lesser, more individualized level, the exposure function can be performed by the individual legislator in his role as an ombudsman.

Any legislator who enters the corrections field quickly becomes a prime recipient of inmate mail.[13] He may soon receive more letters from prisoners than from his thousands of voting constituents. The problems these letters recount, the bitterness, the frustration, the pleas for help, cannot be ignored. On the other hand, no legislator is adequately equipped in terms of time or staff to handle all the complaints. To the extent that he can, however, he can effect investigations and changes. Moreover, the same complaint is often made by numerous prisoners. By pressuring the corrections administration, the legislator may be able to bring about an administrative improvement for all.

There is more to the ombudsman function than just servicing the inmates. Their letters are an educational experience, giving firsthand insight into what is happening in a given institution and the problems confronting inmates. This knowledge has been, so far as I am concerned, most worthwhile.

Conclusion

While there is much that legislators can and should do, how much they will do is problematical. Certainly I cannot point to the United States Congress as responding with alacrity to the crisis in corrections—a crisis by no means of recent creation but only of recent prominence. Nor am I aware that many states have rushed to reform.[14] Indeed, I think it a severe criticism of our governmental process that it is the courts that continue to be the primary agencies of change. But for them, the picture would be even more dismal. Yet the courts have been the victims of legislative inaction and legislative impotence and have been forced to act by legislative default.

I am not going to make a rhetorical call for action. These calls have been made time and again, and now deeds must replace words. We know where the responsibility lies, and in most, though not all, instances, we know in which direction to go. The test is whether we will act, and we should be measured critically by that test.

Footnotes

[1] Cf. D. Rothman, The Discovery of the Asylum: Social Order and Disorder in the New Republic (Little, Brown & Co., Boston 1971).

[2] Struggle for Justice, A Report on Crime and Punishment in America, at v (Hill and Wang, New York 1971):

> "The horror that is the American prison system grew out of an eighteenth-century reform by Pennsylvania Quakers and others against the cruelty and futility of capital and corporal punishment. This two-hundred-year-old experiment has failed."

[3] See generally Hearings before Subcommittee No. 3, Committee on the Judiciary, House of Representatives, Serial No. 15, Corrections—Federal and State Parole Systems, February–May, 1972.

[4] Pub. L. No. 90-351.

[5] Pub. L. No. 91-644.

[6] Several critical reports have been made concerning the Law Enforcement Assistance Administration. One of the most recent is a 55-volume study prepared by the National Council on Crime and Delinquency.

[7] In the 92d Congress, only approximately 25% of the membership of the House —119 Congressmen—have sponsored prison reform legislation. Since in many instances they were cosponsoring legislation introduced by another member, the actual number of substantive bills totalled approximately 45.

[8] See e.g. 18 U.S.C. §1761, 49 U.S.C. §60, etc.

[9] See generally Du Fresne & Du Fresne, "The Case for Allowing 'Convicted Mafiosi to Vote for Judges': Beyond Green v. Board of Elections of New York City," 19 DePaul L. Rev. 112 (1969); "The Equal Protection Clause as a Limitation on the States' Power to Disfranchise Those Convicted of a Crime," 21 Rutgers L. Rev. 297 (1967).

[10] See generally "The Collateral Consequences of a Criminal Conviction," 23 Vand. L. Rev. 929 (1970).

11 See testimony of Dr. Jerome Miller, Hearings before Subcommittee No. 3, Committee on the Judiciary, House of Representatives, Serial No. 15, Corrections—Prisons, Prison Reform, and Prisoners' Rights: Massachusetts, December 18, 1971.

12 Maurice Sigler, former President of the American Correctional Association, former Director of the Nebraska Department of Corrections, and current Chairman of the United States Board of Parole, recently stated in a speech delivered at the 1972 annual meeting of the American Correctional Association:

"The main reason these restrictions [on media access] are imposed is because we're afraid of the exposure and the resulting criticism."

13 See, for example, testimony of Assemblyman Alan Sieroty, California State Legislature, Hearings before Subcommittee No. 3, Committee on the Judiciary, House of Representatives, Serial No. 15, Corrections—Prisons, Prison Reform, and Prisoners' Rights: California, October 25, 1971.

14 See the report on the activities of the New York State Legislature in the year following Attica: Final Report of the Project on Correctional Legislation, prepared by M. A. Feit, R. A. Jackson, and V. K. Looper, Jr.

AN INTRODUCTION TO PRISON REFORM LEGISLATION

W. ANTHONY FITCH *
JULIAN TEPPER **

Although prison reform is a relatively new and undeveloped field, the prisoners' rights lawyer already has a number of sources to draw on for ideas and assistance. Stanley A. Bass and William Bennett Turner have recently published articles that provide valuable and relatively detailed guidelines to the numerous issues and strategies in prisoners' rights litigation.[1] Bass has also compiled a handbook, distributed to Reginald Heber Smith Fellows in the summer of 1971, containing many pragmatic suggestions and a number of helpful pleading models.[2] Even more recently, two newsletters primarily emphasizing prison case law developments have commenced publication.[3]

However, at the time that legal problems of the incarcerated poor are beginning to attract the attention of Legal Services and public interest attorneys,[4] many lawyers, especially those who have borne the brunt of prisoners' rights litigation thus far, are beginning to recognize the inherent limitations of litigation in this field as in any other. For this reason Bass spoke of the "enormous job [which] lies ahead," [5] and devoted a substantial portion of this article to nonlitigation approaches and goals. Professor Herman Schwartz, Director of the ACLU's project on prison reform and a cofounder of the National Committee for Prisoners' Rights, has recently suggested that at least some of the national prisoners' rights organizations, all of which are now primarily or entirely concerned with litigation, should consider reallocating a

* Chief of Prisoners' Rights Project of National Law Office, National Legal Aid and Defender Association, Washington, D.C.

** Director, National Law Office, National Legal Aid and Defender Association, Washington, D.C.; Lecturer (criminology), American University; A.B. University of Maryland; LL.B. Columbia University Law School; Dip. Crim. Cambridge University.

substantial part of their resources to education, clearinghouse, back-up and other nonlitigation activities.[6]

Assuming that the alleviation if not the resolution of the "prison problem"[7] requires additional approaches besides litigation, several responses seem possible. Within the litigation approach itself, plaintiffs' attorneys should have an inviolate policy of proposing detailed regulations covering every aspect of institution life at issue in the suit—the disciplinary process (including rules, prehearing status, and dispositional alternatives), correspondence, classification, medical services, treatment program alternatives, etc. Such quasi-legislative prayers for relief are necessary because often the allegedly unconstitutional practices or conditions at issue will have been caused or facilitated by the absence, vagueness, or arbitrariness of the institution's current rules. The submission of proposed rules and regulations is tactically advisable too. They should be supported by detailed case law, administrative practices in other jurisdictions (together with reports on the results of those practices), and data from the behavioral and other social sciences.[8]

A second response by some groups has been the collection and digesting of the policies and operating procedures of most of the state prison systems in this country.[9] These regulations provide data for persuasive arguments in opposition to prison administrators' claims that various changes will cause unreasonable administrative burdens. It is also becoming apparent that the material contains a number of innovative ideas regarding prison programs, needs, operations, and organizational structure, despite the generally primitive state of American corrections.

A third important alternative has been an attempt at administrative reform through cooperation with the prison authorities, who seem to have been rejuvenated by the recent attention lawyers have paid to the prison problem and have been frightened by the prospect of being entangled in—and losing— numerous lawsuits.[10] Thus, one group, therefore, has undertaken to analyze most institution rules and the current disciplinary procedure in one correctional system, to formulate substantially revised procedures, and to participate in the implementation of this new program.[11] Another organization has subsequently undertaken a similar project involving the administrative structure of an entire state department of corrections.[12] Such an approach, in which a number of other institutions have expressed interest, has the distinct advantage of avoiding the expensive and time-consuming litigation or legislative process. However, an equally important disadvantage is the potentially temporary nature of any reforms effected through this approach. A change of administration could lead to rescission of the new procedures, although such a retrenchment would probably be even more difficult for a prison head than the introduction of adequate procedures.

Fourth, at least two prisoners' rights organizations [13] are developing a collection of recent state legislative proposals for use as models in drafting other bills and as support for them. The remainder of this article describes the work one of these groups has already accomplished.[14] Hopefully, other organizations will submit similar legislative reform packages to the Clearinghouse.

An increased public awareness of prison problems has clearly resulted from the incidents at Soledad, San Quentin, Attica, Raiford, Pontiac, Walpole, and Rahway. Lawyers, however, must realize that for all of the publicity and accompanying "reform" attempts, daily life in most of the nation's prisons and jails continues in its same monotonous and cruel manner, completely unaffected by any criteria established by state legislatures or even by the safeguards of the United States Constitution. Indeed, it is not inaccurate to say that, because of a general lack of concern by the public, the abdication of rule-making responsibility by legislators, and, until recently, the courts' rigid reluctance to grant judicial review,[15] a miniature legal system, alien even to the rough and prejudicial structure of American law, has emerged within the prisons.

Significant statutory regulation of state penal institutions is rare. A prisoner is to be adequately fed and suitably clothed.[16] Beyond this, statutes have delegated unbridled discretionary powers to the corrections departments and provided them only the vaguest of standards. As a result, not only have they acquired virtually unlimited authority over human lives but, to the extent that they are challenged, they cite their experience and expertise, supposedly acquired from the exercise of such power, in support of their practices and policies.[17]

Many other state laws stipulate merely that security shall be maintained.[18] Such inadequate statutory criteria have permitted an overemphasis on security, so that prison systems perpetuate single-purposed and often illegal and unconstitutional procedures without restriction as a matter of course. From entrance and classification through daily living activities to post-release civil disabilities, the prisoner is subject, in the name of security, to severe curtailment or loss of rights which are constitutionally guaranteed to every citizen.

These two factors—tradition of delegating sweeping authority to the prison administrators, and their accumulation and abuse of great power—directly raise the first of two basic issues facing anyone interested in the legislative approach to prison reform. The first issue, broadly stated, is to what extent a statute should specify the manner in which the prison staff must operate in order to accomplish the statutory purpose. Despite the predilection of most lawyers for explicit, unambiguous guidelines as a means of monitoring bureaucratic functions, legislation in this country has traditionally provided only the vaguest guidelines for the administrative agencies. Indeed, it seems that the amount of legislative guidance is actually inversely proportional to the effect of the agency on citizens' lives; policing, probably the most crucial of functions, is an example. In spite of these traditions, the experiences of the past and the current conditions and practices in our prisons should, by now, have taught us a lesson. Our prisons are in their present state largely because of their isolation and freedom from public scrutiny and other controls. The armed fortresses we euphemistically call "correctional facilities" have been successful, if not in correcting, in keeping the enemy—the public, the families of prisoners, the lawyers, the press—out. Therefore, in drafting legislation dealing with any prison operations (e.g., discipline, prisoner conduct rules, mail censorship, classification standards and procedures), the presumption must be for specificity. Such legislation should, in most instances, be at least as specific as the court orders in *Clutchette v. Procunier*,[19] *Morris v. Travisono*,[20] *Palmigiano v. Travisono*,[21] and *McCray v. State of Maryland*,[22] for unlike some court orders, there is no retention of supervisory jurisdiction or other formal means of monitoring.

The second and even more difficult issue facing the prison reform legislator or legislative adviser is the effect his work will have on the ultimate purpose of the postconviction process and the reduction of recidivism by methods that are humane, constitutional, efficient, and do not intrude unnecessarily into a person's privacy. Many of the changes that can be effected through legislation will

almost certainly strengthen and perpetuate the large penal institution—jail or prison—at the very time when penologists are
unanimously advocating the abandonment of such facilities. Often
the lawyer who has been asked for "technical assistance" in connection with a particular piece of prison reform legislation will
not be in a position, because of restrictions on "lobbying" as it
is now defined and for other reasons, to broach this broader issue.
Frequently, however—and more and more often as the frustration
with today's penology intensifies, as it must—the lawyer will be
sponsoring or assisting in the preparation of more general legislation. It will thus be part of his duty to advise the legislator,
legislative committee, or citizen group on the ultimate effects
of any given alternative. Because penology is not in an advanced
state, because there is no extended theory about alternatives to
our present unsuccessful and conceptually bankrupt system, and
because in fact there is really only *one* alternative, the lawyer
again can rely on a simple rule of thumb: he must work for legislation that will end the unconstitutional, inhumane, and dysfunctional conditions and practices in prisons. *But,* in any situation
where the legislation will affect the amount and allocation of
public funds, the presumption must always be for community-
based programs. The choice of professional staff, vocational, educational, counselling and similar services, and new facilities must
all be resolved in favor of increased utilization of small, urban,
specialized facilities. Such a policy will benefit not only the
offender, but also the state in terms of substantially lower operating costs, and even more significantly, substantially reduced
recidivism.[23] Statistical studies and other data substantiating
these positions are now becoming available.[24]

Within the prison, at least five broad categories are appropriate subjects for legislation: the prison discipline process,
classification standards and procedures; inmate correspondence
and other first amendment rights; general standards for prisons
and for jails regarding housing of various groups of inmates,
sanitation, health and food standards, physical facilities, and
other facilities and services; and general requirements for "rehabilitation" programs.

The category of prison discipline raises three basic issues.
Although all are interrelated, the first can be called the question
of the rules that govern inmate conduct. The precise content of
the rules is generally left to the prison administration [25] on the
ground that this is dictated by the needs of each institution. It

is preferable to formulate rules through some process of collaboration between the department or the institution and outside lawyers, since the tendency at most prisons is to promulgate innumerable rules that are confusing and vague.[26] To meet this problem, legislation should at the very least provide the following: all rules enforceable by disciplinary sanctions should be posted around the institution and given in writing to each inmate in the form of a handbook during his orientation period at the prison; [27] inmates can be punished only for violations of published rules; [28] and conduct rules shall be developed by the prison or at departmental headquarters by a committee composed of outside lawyers, departmental lawyers, treatment personnel, administrators, members of the security staff, and prisoners.[29]

The second issue of prison discipline is the hearing procedure itself. Here the legislation should be particularly specific, dealing with such matters as when a prisoner is entitled to a disciplinary hearing (usually based on the severity of the sanction that can be imposed); [30] the composition of the disciplinary panel; adequate notice of the alleged rule violation and the time, place, and procedure of the hearing; the extent of the prisoner's right to confrontation, cross-examination, presentation of his own witnesses, counsel or counsel-substitute and appeal; and the standard of proof at the hearing.[31] The statute should also establish standards for the prehearing status of the prisoner; in most systems he can spend a week or more in a maximum-security or isolation cell after being accused of only a minor rule violation.[32]

A third problem within the disciplinary process is the sanctions to which an inmate can be subjected after a rule violation. A statute should require that every disciplinary disposition be chosen for its rehabilitative effect on the prisoner. This should be stated in writing by the disciplinary panel.[33] The statute should also provide that sanctions shall be proportionate to the seriousness of the rule violation. A slightly more specific approach would be a requirement that a schedule of possible sanctions be published, based upon a distinction between major and minor violations, with loss of good time, assignment to isolation, transfer to another institution, and transfer to higher security or custody status to be reserved for major violations, with lesser sanctions available for all violations.[34] The statute should also specify the particular visiting, housing, commissary, and other deprivations that may accompany confinement in isolation (if it is not prohibited entirely), as well as the maximum allowable period of such confinement.[35]

Legislation should also provide that these standards and procedures apply to *all* facilities of the department. Discipline in women's facilities, for example, is often administered even more arbitrarily and summarily—and with greater severity—than in men's prisons.

Furthermore, a large percentage of halfway house residents are returned to the prison by department orders on the basis only of reports alleging rule infractions and without any hearing whatsoever. Yet such transfers, and similar transfers (often termed "administrative") from one institution to another constitute sanctions or deprivations of liberty at least as severe as, for example, transfers from the general population to the maximum-security section of the prison.

Closely related to the disciplinary issue is the process of classification (including so-called "administrative segregation" and "administrative transfers") which, ideally, involves "the development and administration of an integrated . . . program of treatment for the individual, with procedures for changing the program when indicated." [36] The relation between classification and discipline should be clear. The two processes share many of the same purposes, including the appropriate development of the individual and the institution's order and security. They are performed through similar decision-making processes and on the basis of similar types of information including the behavior of the inmate. Most important of all, they often have similar conseqences for the inmate; as a result of each process, his program in the institution can be revised, his housing assignment can be changed, and his custody level can be altered. Thus, a decision by the classification committee—or by the same or nearly the same personnel acting as a classification rather than a disciplinary body—can, unless carefully regulated, entirely undermine the protections built into the disciplinary process. To guard against this, legislation should provide, as specified in *Morris v. Travisono*,[37] that the inmate is entitled to be informed of the subject and purpose of any classification conference affecting him and to submit information through some means to the committee. If downgrading (in terms of security status, housing, programs, etc.) is a possibility, additional procedural safeguards should be required. In particular, the classification committee should be prohibited from considering misconduct as a basis for reclassification unless and until the disciplinary panel has determined that the inmate is guilty of the alleged misconduct; then, the two disposition decisions should be coordinated or merged. The statute should also establish standards for changes in classification and require a written statement of reasons.[38]

A third area of prison life with which legislation should deal is inmate correspondence and related matters. In recent months a number of correctional systems, through either legislation or new administrative regulations, have reduced or ended mail censorship.[39] The present climate is therefore favorable for significant legislation on this topic.

It is convenient to distinguish six separate yet related issues within the correspondence category. They are: inmate correspondence with the courts; inmate-attorney correspondence; inmate correspondence with public officials; incoming publications (books and periodicals) and outgoing manuscripts; access of the press to prisoners and to the institution; and personal and business correspondence.

Despite clear case law prohibiting such practices,[40] a number of institutions continue to read, copy, delay, discourage, and even censor or stop legal pleadings filed by inmates. Therefore, a relatively simple statutory provision would still be useful, and probably uncontroversial. A similar provision for sealed mail to specified public officials (e.g., governor, state and federal representatives, departmental executive personnel, parole board members, etc.) would also be helpful and probably not overly difficult to achieve.[41]

The remaining types of mail present more serious problems for the legislative reformer. Inmate-attorney correspondence continues to be read in many prisons despite the growing body of case law in several other jurisdictions recognizing the confidentiality and effective assistance issues which this raises. One possible statutory provision in this regard is the external inspection of sealed inmate-attorney mail, on the theory that this level of precaution is proportionate to the relatively small risk that members of the legal profession will be involved in transmitting contraband, escape plans, and the like.[42]

Incoming publications are regularly censored by every prison. Even the most recent regulations provide that "inflammatory" material is prohibited. Legislation can be particularly useful here in controlling, if not ending, this practice by establishing a specific standard for such judgments (e.g., a *Roth* test together with a written statement of the precise ways in which some written matter threatens institution order and security) [43] and a procedure, including the participation of non-prison officials, for making determinations.[44]

A particularly common practice is the censorship, and usually the prohibition, of prisoners' manuscripts, especially those concerning institution life.[45] It would appear impossible to justify these direct state intrusions on the freedom of the press. Only three recent decisions have really dealt with this issue,[46] although decisions or regulations providing that all outgoing mail may be sealed [46a] would seem necessarily to preclude such censorship. (Earlier cases relied largely on the "hands-off" doctrine to rule in favor of the censoring prison authorities.)

Closely related to the manuscript issue is the interviewing of prisoners (and prison officials) by the news media. At least fifteen systems have implemented regulations allowing unrestricted contact with the press [47] and, apparently, most have followed their rules in good faith. (On the other hand, at least one state has adopted a new regulation which leaves so much discretion to the prison authorities that the access of the press may actually have been restricted further.) [48] In advising on such legislation, the lawyer should point out that no data have been produced to substantiate the asserted need for restrictions on manuscripts and access of the press. Simple, positively-stated statutory provisions directing the department of corrections to make reasonable provisions for press contacts and ensuring the rights of the inmates to write and distribute are desirable, but language allowing prison officials broad discretion for the security of the institution, for the safety or benefit of the inmate, or for emergencies must obviously be resisted.

As noted already, several of the foregoing problems could be subsumed in a general provision assuring uncensored outgoing mail. Here again one will encounter the unsubstantiated scare stories about institutional security needs and even claims that censorship is part of the rehabilitation program, but careful investigation into the manner in which current censoring is conducted should help counter these arguments. A necessary legislative compromise may be the authorization of censorship upon demonstration by prison authorities of a specific treatment need in each case, but any such provision is subject to abuse.

Incoming personal mail will probably remain subject at

least to inspection, with the attendant dangers of censorship, for as long as we have large institutions; but legislation should, ideally, contain a provision that only inspection and not delay or censorship is permissible,[49] thus making it possible for an inmate to litigate abuses without having to rely solely on constitutional grounds.[50]

The fourth area—general standards regarding housing, sanitation, food, physical facilities, and medical and other services [51]—is usually of less interest to the prison reform-prisoners' rights lawyer, perhaps because these matters less directly and visibly affect the inmate's First, Fourth, Sixth, and Fourteenth Amendment rights. But some of them raise, in extreme situations, questions of cruel and unusual punishment (and, it has been argued, other constitutional issues as well). These same matters also have an effect on the day-to-day life of the inmate as great or greater than any of the other topics considered so far. Many lawyers feel that they are not sufficiently informed on these topics to be of ready assistance as legislative advisers. However, in addition to marshalling this type of data through his own research, the lawyer can also be useful in identifying problem areas for which his clients might want to consider remedies. A list of such topics would include a prohibition on the housing together of pretrial detainees and convicted offenders in jails, of older, multiple offenders and youth or first offenders in prisons, and dangerous and non-dangerous offenders in all institutions; [52] the use of nationally recognized standards as a control on food,[53] medical services,[54] and overcrowding; [55] a requirement of initial and periodic medical and dental examinations; [56] a prohibition of disciplinary restrictions on diet; [57] required periodic inspections of prison facilities by local or state housing, medical, and health agencies with authority to require changes; the appointment of boards of supervisors or trustees (similar to hospital boards) with periodic inspection and reporting duties; statutory limits on the population of each institution and of specified areas therein (e.g., cells); the requirement of certain types of training for correctional personnel, especially guards; [58] subjection of the department of corrections to the provisions of the state's administrative procedure act; [59] promulgation of minimum wage scales for inmates; establishment of inmate grievance procedures in each institution and in the department through an independent board and hearing examiners,[60] or establishment of an ombudsman program; provision for regular telephone service for prisoners; [61] a requirement that part of each day be set aside for recreation; [62] and so forth.

The most crucial area of all—effective rehabilitation programs—is truly the most difficult for the lawyer. Indeed, it may not be susceptible to legislative control at all,[63] since the primary need in corrections today is a move away from poorly conceived, crudely executed, and single-minded, undifferentiated programs. But without assuming the role of a super social worker, behavioral scientist, and program planner and developer, the lawyer can suggest some general structural provisions that will facilitate the development of new correctional approaches. In this regard, the presumption for community-based programs and against the continuation or expansion of current programs and techniques, nearly every one of which is a failure by any standard, is particularly important.

Thus, the attorney will want to present data on and drafts for: the provision of initial and periodic classification studies of the inmate, including requirements that specific goals be established and that the inmate's program be altered if necessary after each reclassification to accomplish those goals; [64] general requirements for rehabilitation programs, provision of a high school equivalency program for all inmates who desire it; [65] establishment of parole eligibility in all cases upon completion of the minimum sentence; [66] authorization of emergency educational and (extended) evaluation furloughs; [67] authorization or preferably establishment of work-releasees' wages at the prevailing rate within the community; maintenance of halfway houses for first offenders and prereleasees as well as for parolees; and narcotic addiction treatment programs located in the community rather than in penal institutions.

In addition to community-based alternatives to imprisonment, at least two other non-prison areas of corrections will increasingly be the subject of legislation. It is not too great a generalization to say that every stage of the parole process in every state of the nation is in need of revision.[68] Parole may be most coveniently analyzed in three parts: the granting of parole; the period of parole supervision and the conditions governing that period; and the termination of parole.[69] Under the granting of parole fall such needs as the deduction of good time from the minimum sentence in calculating the first parole eligibility date; [70] the frequency of review if parole is denied; [71] specification of standards or factors by which a parole board decides to grant

parole,[72] including a presumption for parole; [73] the types of reports or data the board should use in considering parole; [74] and
at least a degree of participation by the prisoner in the hearing
granting parole.[75]

Regarding the parole program, the statute must enumerate
the conditions to which the parolee may be required to adhere
while on parole and the conditions that may not be imposed.[76]
Current parole conditions are frequently vague, highly invasive
of privacy, and unconstitutional. Other important issues include
the authorization of the parole board to dispense with supervision
in appropriate cases,[77] provision of a standard parole term,[78] at
least for mandatory releasees, and provision for good time deduc-
tions from a parolee's parole term or maximum sentence.[79] At
least two important changes are needed at the termination stage.
One is authorization of the parole board to discharge a person
from parole at any appropriate time, as opposed to the usual
requirement that a person remain on parole until the expiration of
his maximum term.[80] The other is the formulation of detailed
provisions regarding the grounds, process, and effects of the
revocation of parole, including the hearing procedures (notice,
counsel, cross-examination, etc.) to which the parolee is entitled.[81]

The third major issue in prison reform legislation is the
problem of civil disabilities. A dozen states still have civil death
statutes under which some or all sentences result in the loss of all
civil rights although the actual scope of these statutes has never
been defined.[82] Every state has numerous statutes that specifically
deprive former offenders of such rights as voting, public office or
employment, and occupational licenses. The most complete survey
of the numerous types of disabilities and the pertinent statutes in
each state appears in a recent law review note of three hundred
pages.[83]

Even in the case of such basic disabilities as the disenfranchisement of former offenders, litigation on constitutional grounds
has, with one or two exceptions, been unsuccessful.[84] Moreover,
the disabilities are so numerous as to render sweeping change by
litigation virtually impossible; legislation may be the only feasible
remedy. There are two possible approaches. First, a general statute may provide that conviction of crime does not result in civil
disabilities or that an offender's civil rights are fully restored upon
completion of his incarceration (or parole).[85] Alternatively, particular statutes excluding former offenders from certain benefits
may be repealed. Under either approach, care must be taken to

delete or define terms like "poor moral character" to prevent administrative agencies from relying upon such standards to discriminate against former offenders.

No one will agree with all of the proposals in this article, the provisions in the suggested acts, or even the definition of the most urgent issues. Indeed, the authors themselves still differ on several points and debated others until the publication deadline. Hopefully, further discussion and analysis of the prison problem will be stimulated by the foregoing review and the accompanying material, with the result that the prison system, regardless of its precise final form, will be returned to the purview of the people and the law.

Footnotes

[1] Bass, "Correcting the Correctional System: A Responsibility of the Legal Profession," 5 Clearinghouse Rev. 125 (July 1971); Turner, "Establishing the Rule of Law in Prisons: A Manual for Prisoners' Rights Litigation," 23 Stan. L. Rev. 473 (1971).

[2] Bass, "Protecting the Rights of Prisoners," Howard U. Law School, Reginald Heber Smith Community Lawyer Fellowship Program (Summer 1971). Pleadings are also available from the National Committee for Prisoners' Rights, S.U.N.Y.-Buffalo School of Law, 77 West Eagle Street, Buffalo, N.Y. 14202, and the NLADA National Law Office, 1601 Connecticut Avenue, N.W., Washington, D.C. 20009.

[3] Prisoners' Rights Newsletter, a publication of the National Committee for Prisoners' Rights and the ACLU Foundation (available from National Committee for Prisoners' Rights, note 2, supra); The Prison Law Reporter, a project of the Administration of Criminal Justice and Prison Reform Committee of the Young Lawyers Section of the American Bar Association (available from 15th Floor, Hoge Building, Seattle, Washington 98104).

[4] Speaker, Director's Column, 5 Clearinghouse Rev. 289 (October 1971):

"Legal Services lawyers have a right—indeed a duty—to examine the need for change in our correctional system, plan a strategy for overcoming the inertia of injustice, and participate in reform. This is not to suggest that other important fields of legal services to the poor should be downgraded or ignored. This is to suggest that correctional reform should be counted as one legitimate objective, which can best be attacked by determined and coordinated strategy."

[5] Bass, "Protecting the Rights of Prionsers," note 2, supra, Preface.

[6] Remarks of Professor Herman Schwartz at ACLU Conference on Prisoners' Rights, Chicago, Illinois, November 5–7, 1971.

[7] Bass, "Correcting the Correctional System: A Responsibility of the Legal Profession," note 1, supra, at 126; Speaker, Director's Column, note 4, supra, at 290 (both recognizing the impossibility of complete or prompt success).

[8] Such a package is now on file with the Clearinghouse under the case name of Hall v. Boslow, McCray v. Maryland, Clearinghouse No. 6493. In addition,

counsel from several of the more comprehensive prison suits will soon complete a model set of proposed regulations which should be useful in most litigation and which will be filed with the Clearinghouse.

9 The NLADA National Law Office, note 2, supra, has a substantial collection of such regulations, although it is not yet fully indexed.

10 Sixteen states have indicated to the NLADA National Law Office that they are presently revising their corrections regulations, and at least two others are revising as a result of recent court decisions.

11 Information on this project can be obtained from the NLADA National Law Office or the Institute for Studies in Justice and Social Behavior of the American University Law School, Washington, D.C.

12 Boston University Law School, Center for Criminal Justice, Boston, Massachusetts.

13 NLADA National Law Office, Washington, D.C.; National Committee for Prisoners' Rights, Buffalo, New York.

14 This article deals only with substantive issues in prisoner rights-prison reform legislation. A number of useful practical guidelines were recently suggested in Williamson and Folberg, "Legislative Law Reform: A New Challenge," 5 Clearinghouse Rev. 380 (November 1971). It is not expected that the legislative proposals suggested herein will meet with unanimous approval; the purpose of this article is rather to point out the important legislative issues, most of which can be resolved through any of several approaches. Some statutes or sections are suggested to illustrate certain important considerations; at other points, examples are drawn from proposed legislation. It will also be noted that the suggested provisions contain no attempt at definitions and omit such issues as bail reform and sentencing structure; see e.g. ABA Project on Minimum Standards for Criminal Justice, Standards Relating to Sentencing Alternatives and Procedures (1968); Model Penal Code Sentencing Provisions, ALI Model Penal Code (P.O.D. 1962); Advisory Council of Judges of the National Council on Crime and Delinquency, Model Sentencing Act (1963); National Commission on Reform of Federal Criminal Laws, Study Draft of a New Federal Criminal Code (1970); also available in Hearings on Reform of the Federal Criminal Laws, Before the Subcommittee on Criminal Laws and Procedures, Senate Comm. on the Judiciary, 92d Cong., 1st Sess. (February 10, 1971), and in House Committee on the Judiciary, 92d Cong., 1st Sess. (August 2, 1971) (Comm. Print, 1971).

Set out below are: a Suggested Prison Discipline Act; a Suggested Prisoners' Right of Communication Act; and a Suggested Parole Act:

Suggested Prison Discipline Act

Title I. Prisoner Conduct Rules

Section 101. The legislature finds and declares that prisoners in the correctional institutions of this state are entitled under the Constitutions of this state and of the United States to be clearly informed of the rules and regulations which govern their activities during incarceration. The legislature further finds that the promulgation of these rules and regulations sets a positive example which contributes to the rehabilitation of prisoners. The legislature further finds that participation by prisoners in the formulation of institutional rules and regulations

is of positive rehabilitative effect and should be encouraged whenever possible.
Section 102. A copy of the rules and regulations prescribing the duties and obligations of prisoners, the classification and disciplinary hearing procedure and hearing committee composition, and the authorized sanctions for the violation of such rules and regulations, shall be furnished to each prisoner presently incarcerated in a prison or other facility under the jurisdiction of the Department of Corrections, and to each prisoner when he enters the facility.

Section 103. No prisoner shall be punished for any reason other than violation of a published prisoner conduct rule.

Section 104. (a) Prisoner conduct rules shall be formulated and adopted by the Director of the Department of Corrections after consultation with lawyers, psychiatrists, psychologists, case workers, prison administration, prison security officers, and prisoners, and pursuant to [the state's Administrative Procedure Act].

(b) Modifications of and additions to the statewide prison conduct rules may be recommended by the Superintendent of each institution. Such modifications may be approved by the Director, pursuant to [the state's Administrative Procedure Act].

Section 105. For the purposes of Title III of the Act, the prisoner conduct rules required by this Title shall distinguish between rules the violation of which will constitute Major Infractions (hereinafter termed Major Rules) and those the violation of which will constitute Minor Infractions (hereinafter termed Minor Rules). A rule shall be classified as a Major Rule only if an infraction of said rule is likely to constitute a direct danger to the health or safety of other prisoners, personnel, or the institution generally.

Title II. Prison Disciplinary Procedures

Section 201. The legislature finds and declares that, under the Constitutions of this state and of the United States, prisoners in the correctional institutions of this state are entitled, before being punished for infractions of institution rules, to a fair hearing which will ensure a thorough examination, accurate determination, and appropriate disposition of every alleged incident at issue. The legislature further finds and declares that a fair hearing in which the prisoner and various institution personnel fully explore and consider the factual and personal issues can have significant positive effects on the treatment and rehabilitation of the prisoner.

Section 202. A copy of the disciplinary hearing procedures required by and established by and pursuant to this Title shall be included in the rules and regulations required by Section 102 to be furnished to each prisoner.

Section 203. Each institution shall develop and promulgate regulations by which alleged rule infractions are to be reported and investigated. Such regulations shall require that each report include the specific rule allegedly violated; the time, date, and place of the alleged violation; and a detailed description by the reporting officer of the behavior or incident at issue. Such regulations shall further require that the commanding officer of the shift investigate the incident before forwarding the report to the disciplinary committee.

Section 204. A copy of the investigation report required by Section 203, together with written notice of the time of and procedures at the disciplinary hearing shall be furnished the prisoner within twenty-four hours of the alleged incident and not less than seventy-two hours before the hearing.

Section 205. The Shift Commander shall determine the status of each prisoner for whom a disciplinary hearing is pending.

(a) The prisoner shall continue in his current housing and program assignments until the hearing, except that:

(1) The prisoner may be confined to his own cell or dormitory pending the disciplinary hearing if there is substantial reason, specified in writing by the Shift Commander and concurred in, upon review, by the Superintendent, to believe that the prisoner is dangerous to himself or others or in serious danger from others; or,

(2) The prisoner may be confined to administrative segregation pending the disciplinary hearing if the Superintendent determines in writing that there is substantial reason to believe that the prisoner is uncontrollable, extremely dangerous to himself or others, or in extreme danger from others and that confinement pursuant to Section 205(a)(1) is an insufficient safeguard.

(b) Prior to the disciplinary hearing, the prisoner who is alleged to have committed a rule infraction shall remain in his current institution program and retain his current rights and privileges except where changes in his program or privileges are necessitated by action pursuant to subsection (a)(1) or (a)(2) of this Section.

Section 206. (a) A disciplinary hearing committee shall be appointed for each institution as follows:

(1) One member of the committee shall be a professional staff member—psychiatrist, psychologist, or social worker—at the institution, appointed by the Superintendent.

(2) One member of the committee shall be a member of the correctional force at the grade of Captain or above, appointed by the Superintendent.

(3) One member of the committee shall be a Hearing Officer from the office of the Director of the Department of Corrections. The Hearing Officer shall be the Chairman of the disciplinary committee.

(b) No person shall sit as a member of the disciplinary committee which is hearing a matter in which he was directly involved, which he witnessed, or which he investigated.

Section 207. Disciplinary hearings shall be conducted according to the following procedures:

(a) The hearing shall be held within _____ days of the alleged incident, unless the prisoner requests a continuance for further preparation or other good cause.

(b) The prisoner shall be represented by a staff member or other prisoner. The prisoner shall be represented by counsel if the alleged violation constitutes a crime for which he could be prosecuted.

(c) The prisoner shall be present at the hearing and shall be read the report and advised of the charge.

(d) The prisoner shall be afforded an opportunity to explain his version of the incident and/or offer an explanation of his behavior.

(e) The prisoner shall be permitted to cross-examine the officer who filed the disciplinary report and other witnesses and to call witnesses of his own.

(f) At the conclusion of testimony, the committee shall privately review the testimony. If there is substantial reason to believe that the prisoner has committed the alleged infraction, the committee shall enter a dispositional decision pursuant to Title III of this Act. After a finding that the prisoner has committed the alleged infraction, the committee may consult with other professional personnel who are familiar with the prisoner and who may offer advice to the committee on the proper treatment of the prisoner.

(g) The prisoner shall be recalled and shall be informed of the factual findings and the dispositional decision of the committee and the reason for that decision.

(h) Whenever the committee finds that an infraction has not been committed by the prisoner, he shall be reinstated to his current status and his record shall clearly show that he was found not guilty of committing the infraction.

(i) The prisoner shall be advised of his right to appeal the decision to the Director and of the applicable review procedures.

(j) A full record of the hearing shall be kept, and the decision shall be entered on the disciplinary report form, along with all pertinent statements made during the hearing. Each voting member must sign the form and indicate his concurrence with or dissent from the decision.

Section 208. Every disciplinary proceeding in which the prisoner is found to have violated an institution rule shall be reviewed and may be appealed.

(a) The Director shall automatically review the record of every disciplinary hearing and may:

(1) Remand the case for further investigation and hearing;

(2) Suspend decision pending investigation; or

(3) Approve or modify the action of the committee, after consulting with the committee and advising the prisoner of any change in the decision.

(b) If the prisoner wishes to appeal the decision of the disciplinary committee, the following procedures shall be followed:

(1) The prisoner shall immediately notify the Director, on a form provided by the disciplinary committee for that purpose, of his intention to appeal.

(2) Within seventy-two hours, the prisoner shall transmit to the Director a written statement of the reason for his appeal.

(3) In reviewing the case, the Director may interview the prisoner or staff and order any other investigation or consultation.

(4) The Director shall notify the prisoner in writing of the action he has taken.

(c) Upon review or appeal of any disciplinary proceeding, the Director shall not impose any additional restrictions on the prisoner.

Title III. Disciplinary Sanctions

Section 301. The legislature finds and declares that the imposition of disciplinary sanctions has a significant impact on the individual and on his prospects for rehabilitation. The legislature further finds and declares that prisoners must not be subjected to, and have a right to be free from, disproportionate or other cruel and unusual punishment. The legislature further finds and declares that the practice of confining prisoners in isolation cells is detrimental to treatment goals and prospects for rehabilitation, constitutes extremely serious punishment, and should be used only in rare situations and, when so used, only for a short and temporary period of time. The legislature further declares that it is the policy of this state that every dispositional decision by a prison disciplinary committee shall be based upon, and be an integral part of, the treatment goals of the individual prisoner.

Section 302. If, after a disciplinary hearing, a prisoner is found to have violated a Minor Rule as defined in Section 105 of this Act, he is subject to one or more of the following sanctions, in addition to assignment to any additional program, therapy, counseling service, determined to be necessary:

(a) Reprimand.

(b) Loss of commissary for one week.

(c) Loss for not more than one month of movies, television, radio, recreation or athletic privileges (provided that all prisoners must be provided opportunity for daily exercise, which, weather permitting, shall take place outside).

(d) Twenty-four hour confinement to own cell, except for meals or with meals in cell, with or without curtailment of job assignments.

(e) Restitution.

Section 303. If, after a disciplinary hearing, a prisoner is found to have violated a Major Rule, as defined in Section 105 of this Act, he is subject to one or more of the following sanctions, in addition to assignment to any additional program, therapy, counseling or other service which the disciplinary committee determines to be appropriate:

(a) Any of the sanctions authorized in Section 302 of this Act.

(b) Transfer to the maximum security section (but not to an isolation cell) of the institution for a period not to exceed thirty consecutive days or sixty days in any six-month period.

(c) Transfer from the prisoner's current institution to any other institution in the state.

(d) Confinement in an isolation cell for a period not to exceed seven consecutive days or fourteen days in any six-month period.

(e) Withholding or forfeiture of the reduction of sentence awarded for good behavior, provided that the Director shall promulgate standards by which such withheld or forfeited reduction may be earned back by the prisoner.

Section 304. (a) No sanctions other than those specified in Sections 302 and 303 of this Act may be imposed upon a prisoner except after recommendation by institution superintendents and approval by the Director pursuant to [the state's Administrative Procedure Act].

(b) No prisoner shall be subjected to the sanctions authorized by Sections 302 and 303 of this Act except for violation of the published prisoner conduct rules.

Section 305. Cruel, corporal or unusual punishment; any treatment or lack of care whatever which injures or impairs the health of any prisoner; any deprivation, as a punitive measure, of clothing, a bed, bedding, the regular diet except as prescribed by a physician for dietary purposes, or normal hygienic implements required for basic sanitation that are provided to the general population of persons confined in a jail or a state prison; and the use of special isolation or restricted diets, straitjackets, gags, thumbscrews, shower baths, or the trussing up of prisoners, are illegal and hereby prohibited. Any state employee who violates the provisions of this Section or who aids, abets, or attempts in any way to contribute to the violation of such provisions shall be guilty of a misdemeanor. (Cf. Assembly Bill. No. 2904, California Legislature, 1971 Regular Session.)

Section 306. (a) Each prisoner in maximum security or in an isolation cell shall be examined daily by a psychiatrist and by a physician.

(b) Each prisoner in maximum security or in an isolation cell shall retain his full correspondence, reading, legal work, and visiting rights, and shall also retain those rights specified in Section 305 of this Act.

(c) Each prisoner in maximum security or in an isolation cell shall be allowed one or more daily exercise periods totaling at least three hours each day.

Title IV. Administrative Transfers

Section 401. The legislature finds and declares that in rare situations it may be necessary to separate a prisoner from the general population of the prison. The legislature further finds and declares that extended segregation can have no positive rehabilitative effect and may have serious anti-rehabilitative effects and that therefore the use of administrative segregation must be limited. The legislature further declares the policy of the state to be that administrative segregation shall not be utilized to increase or extend punishment resulting from violations of prisoner conduct rules.

Section 402. Administrative segregation shall be utilized only to provide a non-punitive confinement facility for those prisoners who are considered physically dangerous to themselves or others so as to require close supervision apart from the general population of the institution. However, such segregation must occur in a suitable, non-punitive security setting and any prisoner so segregated must be provided with an effective treatment program which will facilitate his return to the general population.

Section 403. (a) A prisoner may be recommended for transfer to administrative segregation only by his caseworker or by a correctional officer of the rank of Captain or above. Such recommendation shall be made only after consultation with the prisoner and shall specify the ways in which administrative segregation will contribute to the prisoner's treatment program and the factors clearly showing the prisoner to be uncontrollable, extremely dangerous to himself or others, or in extreme danger from others. If such prisoner requires hospitalization for medical or psychiatric treatment, he may be placed in the administrative segregation section of the hospital. Except in an emergency, all such recommendations shall be approved by the Superintendent before transfer of the prisoner to administrative segregation. A copy of the recommendation, approved and signed by the Director, shall be given to the prisoner.

(b) In an emergency, the prisoner may be placed in administrative segregation, for a period not to exceed twelve hours, at the order of the Shift Commander until the approval of the Director is obtained. In such instances an expedited investigation shall be conducted pursuant to the requirements of subsection (a) of this Section.

(c) A prisoner may be admitted to administrative segregation at his own request only after approval of the Shift Commander. All such requests and admissions must be immediately reported to the Superintendent. The Superintendent shall arrange for appropriate further investigation and examinations.

Section 404. No prisoner shall be detained in administrative segregation for more than thirty days unless the professional staff, upon review of the prisoner's record and following an interview with the prisoner, certifies during the last three days of confinement in administrative segregation that the factors specified in Section 403 (a) of this Act continue to exist and recommends that the prisoner remain in administrative segregation for not more than an additional thirty days with whatever modification of his program is necessary. All such reviews and recommendations require prior written approval by the Superintendent before implementation. A copy of each review and recommendation approved by the Superintendent shall be given to the prisoner. Each such recommendation approved by the Superintendent shall be reviewed and approved or overruled by the Director of the Department of Corrections within five days of the date of the professional staff's recommendation. Such approval must be obtained each time that a recommendation is made for continued confinement beyond the period last authorized by the Director.

Section 405. Upon discharge from administrative segregation, the prisoner shall be returned to the housing assignment and institution program from which he was transferred.

Section 406. The institution physician shall personally visit each prisoner confined in administrative segregation for routine sick call.

Section 407. Within forty-eight hours of a prisoner's transfer to administrative segregation, the professional staff of the institution shall develop and implement a special program designed to fulfill the purpose or underlying causes of the assignment of the prisoner to administrative segregation. The prisoner shall be given a copy of this program.

Section 408. (a) Unless specifically excluded by his special program, a prisoner in administrative segregation shall be allowed to have in his cell all items permitted to him in his current housing assignment.

(b) Unless specifically excluded by the prisoner's special program, a prisoner in administrative segregation shall continue to participate in his current institution program and shall retain all of his current rights and privileges.

[Title IV.—Alternative]

[This alternative is adopted from Assembly Bill. No. 2904, California Legislature, 1971 Regular Session.]

Section 401. The legislature finds and declares that in rare situations it may be necessary to separate a prisoner from the general population of the prison. The legislature further finds and declares that extended segregation can have no positive rehabilitative effect and may have serious anti-rehabilitative effects and that therefore the use of administrative segregation must be limited. The legislature further declares the policy of this state to be that administrative segregation shall not be utilized to increase or extend punishment resulting from violations of prisoner conduct rules.

Section 402. (a) If a warden or superintendent has reasonable cause to believe that a prisoner's presence in the general population of any prison will endanger the lives of others with whom he might come in contact, the warden or superintendent may, with the consent of the Director, file a petition to confine the prisoner in segregation with the court of the county in which the prisoner is held in custody.

(b) The petition shall state the facts upon which the warden or superintendent bases his belief.

Section 403. If the prisoner poses an immediate danger to others, he may be placed in segregation pending the outcome of the hearing. If for any reason the hearing is not concluded and a decision rendered within thirty days after the filing of the petition, the prisoner shall be released to the general population of a state prison.

Section 404. In any proceeding under this article the prisoner shall have the right to counsel. If he is indigent, the court shall appoint an attorney to represent him unless he [intelligently] waives the right to counsel.

Section 405. (a) The prisoner shall be brought before the court within two judicial days after the petition has been filed. The court shall inform the prisoner of the allegations in the petition and of his right to counsel. If the prisoner appears without counsel, he shall be informed by the court that he has the right to have counsel before proceeding further, and shall be asked if he desires counsel. If he desires and is unable to employ counsel, the court shall appoint counsel to represent him.

(b) The court shall ask the prisoner whether he admits or denies the allegations in the petition. If the prisoner denies the allegations, the court shall set the matter for hearing. The hearing shall be within ten days.

Section 406. At the hearing, the department shall have the burden of proving the allegations in the petition by a preponderance of evidence. The prisoner may present evidence, may cross-examine witnesses, and shall have the right to process for the purpose of presenting evidence.

Section 407. (a) If the court finds that the prisoner's presence in the general population of any prison will not endanger the lives of others with whom he might come in contact, it shall dismiss the petition.

(b) If the court finds that the prisoner's presence in the general population of any prison will endanger the lives of others with whom he might come in contact, or if the prisoner has admitted the allegation, the court may order the prisoner confined in segregation for not more than ninety days.

Section 408. At the end of the period of confinement ordered by the court the prisoner shall be released from segregation unless the warden or superintendent has filed a new petition pursuant to this article.

Suggested Prisoners' Right of Communication Act

Section 101. The legislature finds and declares that present restrictions on prisoners' correspondence and other communications are anti-rehabiliative, administratively inefficient, and, in many instances, unconstitutional. The legislature further finds and declares that it is in the best interest of the state and of prisoners incarcerated under the laws of this state to terminate such restrictions immediately. The legislature further declares that it is the intent of the legislature and the policy of this state that the provisions of this Act are minimum standards and that the Director of the Department of Corrections and the Superintendents of each institution under the jurisdiction of the Department shall strive to remove all restrictions on and otherwise facilitate prisoners' communications with family, friends, public officials, legal and business associates, past or potential employers, public and private service agencies, and others.

Section 102. No restrictions shall be placed on the identity of correspondents, on the number of correspondents, on the number of letters a prisoner may send or receive, or on the length of incoming or outgoing letters.

Section 103. Incoming and outgoing letters may be in any language.

Section 104. Each institution shall provide indigent prisoners with sufficient stationery, envelopes and postage for all legal and official correspondence and for at least three letters of personal correspondence each week.

Section 105. The institution shall provide free notary service to all prisoners.

Section 106. All outgoing mail may be sealed by the prisoner and shall not be inspected, censored, delayed, or otherwise interfered with in any manner. Outgoing packages may be inspected for contraband or stolen property.

Section 107. Incoming mail from any attorney; any court or official thereof, the Governor or Lieutenant Governor of the state; a member of the legislature of the state; a member of the United States Congress; a member of the Executive Branch of the United States Government; or an official of the Department of Corrections of this state shall remain sealed and be delivered directly and immediately to the prisoner.

Section 108. Incoming mail, other than that enumerated in Section 107 of this Act, may be opened by institution personnel only in the presence of the prisoner or his elected or designated representative, and may be inspected only for contraband as defined in the prisoner conduct rules and then immediately shall be delivered directly to the addressee.

Section 109. (a) Subscriptions to and receipt of newspapers, magazines, and other printed matter and the purchase and receipt of individual copies or issues of books, newspapers, magazines, and other printed matter, in any language, from any person, business, organization or other source, shall be permitted without restriction, with the exception of individual issues which are either obscene under applicable constitutional standards or constitute a direct and immediate threat to the security, safety, or order of the institution.

(b) Whenever it appears that a book, individual issue of a periodical, or other printed matter should be prohibited under the provisions of subsection (a) of this Section, the institution shall conduct an investigation pursuant to the following provisions:

(1) Prompt notice of the following shall be given to the addressee:

(A) Identification of the material;

(B) The interim prohibition of the material and the reason for such prohibition, including identification of the objectionable portions of such material;

(C) The addressee's right to a hearing, to be held within three days of such notice.

(2) At such hearing, the addressee may submit his arguments orally or in writing, or both.

(3) The hearing shall be conducted by a panel composed of one treatment or professional staff member, one administrative staff member and one non-institutional representative from the office of the Director of Corrections.

(4) Unless there is substantial evidence that an exception as stated in Section 109 (a) exists, the hearing panel shall order the immediate delivery of such material to the addressee. The panel shall announce its finding and the reasons for that finding immediately after the hearing.

(5) If the hearing panel finds the existence of an exception as stated

in Section 109 (a), such finding shall be reviewed by the Director of the Department of Corrections who shall affirm or revise such finding within five days of the decision of the hearing panel.

(6) Records of hearings provided for hereinabove shall be maintained at the institution for at least one year following the decision of the hearing panel. However, no such records, or reference to them, shall be placed in any prisoner's file or utilized in any other proceeding affecting the prisoner.

Section 110. (a) Manuscripts prepared and mailed by prisoners shall not be inspected, censored, delayed, or in any way interfered with. The institution shall not be responsible for the content of any manuscript; all such responsibility shall be that of the author.

(b) Each institution shall provide full access for the press and news media to inspect all areas of the institution and interview personnel and all prisoners.

Section 111. The Director and the Superintendent of each institution shall make reasonable provision for the use of telephones by prisoners.

Section 112. No additional restrictions on communications shall be permitted, for disciplinary, punishment or other reasons.

Suggested Parole Act

[The provisions suggested in the Act are based to some extent on Legislative Bill 1307, 80th Sess., Nebraska Legislature (1969); ch. 34, National Commission on Reform of Federal Criminal Laws (August 1970), Study Draft of a New Federal Criminal Code, also available in Hearings on Reform of the Federal Criminal Law, Subcommittee on Criminal Laws and Procedures, Committee on the Judiciary, U.S. Senate, 92d Cong., 1st Sess. (February 10, 1971), and in H.R. _____, Committee Print, Committee on Judiciary, U.S. House of Representatives, 92d Cong., 1st Sess. (August 2, 1971); and Tentative Final Draft of Illinois Uniform Code of Corrections (January 1971) (failed of passage). However, a number of important changes have been made. Although by no means constituting a complete "parole act," the various sections should suggest the issues of greatest concern at the present time to prisoners and parolees. Some of the provisions (e.g. Sections 101 and 112(b)) will probably necessitate changes in other state statutes (e.g. sentencing structure and appointment of counsel).]

Section 101. (a) Subject to the provisions of Sections 102 and 103 of this Act, every prisoner confined in a facility of the Department of Corrections shall be eligible for parole at any time during his sentence.

(b) Every prisoner shall be considered for assignment to parole status, pursuant to the provisions of this Act, at least once every twelve months.

Section 102. (a) If a prisoner is not otherwise paroled pursuant to the provisions of this Act, he shall be released upon the expiration of his maximum sentence reduced by the amount of earned good time and shall be considered a parolee subject to the provisions of this Act.

(b) Whenever the Board of Parole considers the assignment of a prisoner to parole, it shall order such assignment unless:

(1) There is a substantial reason to believe that he will engage in further specified criminal activity; or,

(2) There is substantial reason to believe that he will not conform to proper and appropriate specified conditions of parole.

Section 103. In making its determination, the Board of Parole shall take into account each of the following factors:

(a) The prisoner's personality, including his maturity, stability, sense of responsibility and any apparent development in his personality which may promote or hinder his conformity to law.

(b) The prisoner's mental or physical makeup, as evidenced by professional testing or examination, including any disability or handicap which may affect his conformity to law.

(c) The prisoner's ability and readiness to assume obligations and undertake responsibilities.

(d) The prisoner's family status, including whether his relatives display an interest in him or whether he has other close and constructive associations in the community.

(e) The type of residence, neighborhood or community in which the prisoner plans to live.

(f) The prisoner's employment history and his occupational skills.

(g) The prisoner's vocational, educational, and other training.

(h) The adequacy of the prisoner's parole plan, including his plans or prospects upon release.

(i) The prisoner's past use of addictive narcotics, or past habitual and excessive use of alcohol.

(j) The minimum sentence, if any, imposed by the Court, together with any reasons given for such sentence.

(k) The prisoner's attitude toward law and authority.

(l) The prisoner's conduct in the facility, including particularly whether he has taken advantage of opportunities for self-improvement.

(m) The prisoner's behavior and attitude during any previous experience of probation or parole and the recency of such experience.

(n) Any other factor which the Board determines to be relevant, provided that prior to the hearing, the Board informs the prisoner of such factors.

Section 104. In analyzing the factors specified in Section 103 of this act, the Board of Parole shall consider the following information:

(a) Reports prepared by the institutional caseworkers relating to the prisoner's personality, social history and adjustment to authority, and including any recommendations which the staff of the facility may make.

(b) Official reports of the prisoner's prior criminal record, including reports and records of earlier probation and parole experiences.

(c) The presentence investigation report.

(d) Recommendations regarding the prisoner's parole made at the time of sentencing by the sentencing judge.

(e) Reports of any physical, mental and psychiatric examinations of the offender.

(f) Any relevant information which may be submitted by the prisoner, his attorney, or any other person.

(g) Testimony by the prisoner at the parole hearing.

(h) Such other relevant information concerning the prisoner as may be reasonably available.

Section 105. (a) The Board of Parole shall make no final decision regarding assignment to parole before the prisoner appears at the parole hearing pursuant to this Section.

(b) The hearing shall be conducted in an informal manner. A complete record of the proceedings shall be made and preserved.

(c) The prisoner shall be permitted to consult with any person whose assistance he requires prior to the hearing. The prisoner may be represented at the hearing by an attorney, an employee of the Department of Corrections, or any other person granted leave by the Board.

Section 106. If the Board denies parole to the prisoner, it shall within two days following the hearing:

(a) Inform the prisoner in writing of the reasons for such denial, including the specific findings required by Section 102 (a) or (b), and the information or summary thereof upon which such reasons were based.

(b) Provide the prisoner with a reasonable opportunity to respond in writing to such reasons.

(c) Specify in writing the steps which the prisoner must take to facilitate his parole in the future.

(d) Schedule a re-hearing to occur within one year of such denial.

Section 107. (a) When a prisoner is assigned to parole status, the Board of Parole shall require as a condition of his parole that he refrain from engaging in criminal conduct.

(b) The Board may also require that the parolee:

(1) Work or pursue a course of study or vocational training.

(2) Undergo medical or psychiatric treatment, or treatment for drug addiction or alcoholism.

(3) Attend or reside in a facility established for the instruction or residence of persons on probation or parole.

(4) Support his dependents.

(5) Refrain from possessing a firearm or other dangerous weapon.

(6) Report to a parole officer as directed.

(7) Remain within the State of _____ unless granted permission by his parole officer to leave the State.

(8) Notify his parole officer of any change of address or employment.

(9) Satisfy any other conditions specifically related to the cause of his conviction and not unduly restrictive of his rights or liberty.

(c) Prior to being placed on parole, the parolee shall be provided with a written copy of the conditions under which the parole is to be served.

(d) After a hearing pursuant to Section 105, the Board of Parole may modify or enlarge the conditions of parole, in accordance with the provisions of this Section.

Section 108. (a) The parolee shall remain on parole for a period of _____ years, subject to the provisions of subsection (b) of this Section, regardless of the amount of time remaining unserved on his sentence, unless at the time of his release or thereafter the Board determines:

(1) That a shorter period of supervision is appropriate, or

(2) In cases where other than _____ years of the original sentence remains unserved, that a longer period of supervision, which in no event shall exceed the remainder of the parolee's maximum sentence, reduced by the parolee's earned prison good time, is appropriate.

(b) The Board of Parole shall reduce for good conduct in conformity with the conditions of his parole, a parolee's parole term by _____ days for each month of such term. The total of such reductions shall be deducted from his parole term to determine the date when discharge from parole becomes mandatory.

(c) Reductions of the parole term for good behavior may be forfeited, withheld and restored by the Board of Parole. The forfeiture and withholding of such reductions shall be made only if the Board finds a violation of parole conditions pursuant to a hearing as provided in Section 111 of this Act.

Section 109. (a) The Board of Parole may discharge a parolee from parole at any time if such discharge is compatible with the protection of the public and is in the best interest of the parolee.

(b) The Board of Parole shall discharge a parolee from parole when he has completed his parole term as reduced by his earned parole good time.

Section 110. (a) At any point during the period of parole, the Board may issue a certificate restoring all civil rights of the parolee.

(b) Whenever any committed offender or parolee is discharged from parole, the Board of Parole shall issue a certificate of discharge to such offender or parolee, and such certificate shall restore all civil rights of such committed offender or parolee.

Section 111. (a) Whenever a parole officer has reasonable cause to believe that a parolee has violated a condition of his parole other than by the commission of a criminal act, he may submit a written report to the Board of Parole which shall, on the basis of such report and such further investigation as it may deem appropriate, dismiss the charge of violation or order the parolee to appear at a parole redetermination hearing which shall be conducted within _____ days after notification of the charge is furnished to the parolee, unless the parolee requests a continuance.

(b) Prior to the hearing, the parolee shall continue in his current parole program, subject to such interim modifications as may be recommended by the parole officer and approved by one or more members of the Board.

(c) Whenever it orders the parolee to appear at a hearing pursuant to subsection (a) of this Section, the Board shall give the parolee written notice of:

(1) The conditions he is alleged to have violated.

(2) The time, date, place and circumstances of the alleged violation.

(3) The time, date, and place of the scheduled hearing.

(4) His rights under this Act.

(d) The hearing shall be conducted in an informal manner, provided that witnesses shall testify under oath and the Board shall consider no evidence which has been obtained by an unconstitutional search and seizure or otherwise in violation of the parolee's constitutional rights.

(e) If the Board of Parole finds substantial reason to believe that the parolee violated a condition of his parole, the Board may order that:

(1) The parolee receive a reprimand and warning.

(2) Parolee supervision and reporting be intensified.

(3) The parolee be required to conform to one or more additional conditions of parole imposed in accordance with the provisions of this Act; and/or

(4) Reductions for good conduct while on parole, awarded pursuant to Section 108 of this Act, be forfeited or withheld.

(f) Nothing in this Act or in the laws of this state shall be construed to authorize the Board of Parole to transfer a parolee to prison on the basis of a suspected violation or a violation of the parole conditions authorized by Section 107 (b) of this Act.

Section 112. (a) Whenever it is determined that a parolee has been arrested and charged with a criminal offense, the parole officer shall immediately investigate the circumstances of the arrest and submit a written report concerning the reason for such arrest to the Board of Parole.

(b) If the arrested parolee is released on bail by the Court pending trial and if there is reasonable cause to believe that the parolee has violated a condition of his parole, the conditions of the parolee's parole may be reviewed and modified pursuant to Section 111 of this Act.

(c) If the parolee is convicted of a criminal offense, the Board may promptly consider, at a hearing conducted within _____ days after the conviction unless the parolee requests a continuance, whether or not, as indicated by the circumstances of the criminal offense and other pertinent information, the public safety necessitates the reinstitution of the remainder of the original criminal sentence, pursuant to Section 113 of this Act.

(1) Whenever it orders a parolee to appear at a hearing pursuant to this subsection, the Board shall give the parolee written notice of:

(A) The purpose of the hearing.
(B) The time, date, and place of the scheduled hearing.
(C) His rights under this Act.

(2) At the hearing the parolee shall be represented by counsel unless he intelligently waives this right. If the parolee is indigent, the Board, within a reasonable time prior to the hearing, shall request the Court in which the parolee was originally tried and convicted to appoint counsel at state expense to represent the parolee in the parole proceedings.

(3) At the hearing the parolee or his counsel may subpoena witnesses and present evidence in his own behalf, confront and cross-examine witnesses against him, examine other evidence or information, and propose alternative dispositions to the Board.

(4) The Board shall not revoke the parolee's parole unless it has substantial reason to believe based upon the evidence at the hearing that the parolee may continue to pose a substantial danger to society at the expiration of his current maximum sentence.

Section 113. (a) A parolee whose parole is revoked shall be recommitted for the remainder of his maximum prison term, reduced by the amount of good time previously earned in prison and the amount of time served on parole.

(b) A parolee whose parole has been revoked shall be eligible for parole pursuant to Sections 101, 102, and 103 of this Act.

[15] See Note, "Beyond the Ken of the Courts: A Critique of Judicial Refusal to Review the Complaints of Convicts," 72 Yale L. J. 506 (1963).

[16] E.g. 51 Cal. Code Ann. §2084 (West):

"The wardens shall provide each prisoner with a bed of straw or other suitable material, and sufficient covering of blankets, and with garments of coarse, substantial material and of distinctive manufacture, and with sufficient plain and wholesome food of such variety as may be most conducive to good health."

See also, Miss. Code Ann. §§7930, 7945, recompiled vol. 6 (Supp. 1971).

17 E.g. Sobell v. Reed, 327 F. Supp. 1294 (S.D.N.Y. 1971); Landman v. Royster, 333 F. Supp. 621 (E.D. Va. 1971); Jones v. Wittenberg, 323 F. Supp. 93, 330 F. Supp. 707 (N.D. Ohio 1971), aff'd sub nom. Jones v. Metzger 456 F.2d 854 (6th Cir. 1972); Clutchette v. Procunier, 328 F. Supp. 767 (N.D. Cal. 1971); Kadish, "Legal Norms and Discretion in the Police and Sentencing Process," 75 Harv. L. Rev. 916:

> "[T]he new penology has resulted in vesting in judges and parole and probation agencies the greatest degree of uncontrolled power over the liberty of human beings that one can find in the legal system."

Cf. Rubin, "Needed—New Legislation in Correction," 17 Crime & Delinquency 392, 394 (1971), who, quoting Kadish, supra, states: "There is the central issue—uncontrolled discretion"; Hirschkop and Millemann, "The Unconstitutionality of Prison Life," 55 Va. L. Rev. 795, 811–812 (1969): "The central issue is the unreviewed administrative discretion granted to the poorly trained personnel who deal directly with prisoners."

18 E.g. Laws of Wisconsin Relating to Health and Social Service, Wis. Stat. §53.07 (1967); 24 Fla. Stat. Ann. §944.34 (1971–1972 Cumulative Annual Pocket Part).

19 328 F. Supp. 767 (N.D. Cal. 1971).

20 310 F. Supp. 857 (D.R.I. 1970).

21 317 F. Supp. 776 (D.R.I. 1970).

22 Misc. Pet. 4363 et seq. (Cir. Ct. for Montgomery County, Maryland, Nov. 18, 1971), 10 Crim. L. Rep. 2132.

23 President's Commission on Law Enforcement and Administration of Justice, Task Force Report: Corrections, at 38, 40, 42, 43 (1967); Keller and Alper, Halfway Houses: Community-Centered Correction and Treatment, at 136, 138, 140, 142 (1970); Mattick and Arkman, "The Cloacal Region of American Corrections," 381 Annals 116 (1969); Skoler, "There's More to Crime Control Than the 'Get Tough' Approach," 397 Annals 28, 32 (1971).

24 One of the best preliminary sources is Federal Probation, a quarterly that can be obtained free of charge from the Administrative Office of the United States Courts, Washington, D.C. 20544. Federal Probation is particularly useful as a guide to other, more technical journals and studies.

25 E.g. D.C. Code Ann. §24-442 (1967 ed.).

26 E.g. Maryland Division of Correction, A General Information and Guidance Handbook for Inmates (1971):

"Adjustment Violations:

* * * *

"(b) Disrespect to any officer or employee of the institution, or to any person visiting the institution.

* * * *

"(d) Swearing, cursing, or use of any other vulgar, abusive, insolent, threatening or any other improper language toward any other inmate or officer, or indecency in language, action or gesture at any time."

Mississippi State Penitentiary, Rules and Regulations for Inmates and Employees:

"Prisoners shall at all times be respectful to officers, guards and employees and be brief in their communications."

Idaho State Penitentiary, Rules and Information for Inmates (June 1, 1970):

"Agitation
"You are to conduct yourself in a constructive manner at all times by
"(a) not embarrassing visitors or annoying other inmates
"(b) not causing other inmates to violate rules by malicious mischief or
"(c) conduct of a destructive nature: [Examples include acts of fighting, violence, lying, use of profanity, loud or boisterous behavior, loitering, gambling or stealing.]"

Cf. Landman v. Royster, 333 F. Supp. 621, 654, 656 (E.D. Va. 1971):

"Few of the opinions to date on prison discipline treat in depth the real problem of vagueness in institutional regulations. . . . Particularly in a situation where the safeguard of a public trial is absent . . . and necessarily so, other procedural safeguards against arbitrariness should not be slighted.

* * * *

. . . The Court concludes, therefore, that the existence of some reasonably definite rule is a prerequisite to prison discipline of any substantial sort."

27 Suggested Prison Discipline Act, §102 (see note 14, supra, for the full text of this suggested Act).

28 Id. §103.

29 Id. §104 (a)

30 Id. §201 (requiring a full hearing in all cases. It may become necessary to compromise, providing for full hearings in situations of major, but not minor, alleged rule infractions).

31 Id. §§204, 206, 207, 208.

32 Id. §§204, 205.

33 Id. §301.

34 Id. §§105, 301, 302, 303.

35 Id. §§303, 305, 306.

36 Morris v. Travisono, 310 F. Supp. 857, 865 (D.R.I. 1970).

37 Id.

38 Id. at 870–871:

". . . Classification Procedures
* * * *

"B. Notice

"An inmate shall receive timely written notice of the subject and purpose of a classification meeting at which he is to appear. In cases where downgrading of classification grade is to be considered, said notice shall also inform the inmate of his right to be assisted by a classification counselor at the classification meeting. If an inmate requests assistance of a classification counselor, such assistance will be rendered a reasonable time in advance of the hearing.

"C. The Classification Meeting

* * * *

"2. The chairman of the Board shall explain the purpose of the meeting and the particular aspects of the inmate's record which may result in a classification change.

"3. No misconduct shall be considered by the Classification Board unless the Disciplinary Board has made a finding unfavorable to the inmate.

* * * *

"6. The inmate shall present pertinent information in relation to the classification procedure.

* * * *

10. A decision of the Classification Board must be based upon substantial evidence and reflect consideration of an inmate's entire record."

[39] Washington, Office of Adult Corrections, Memorandum No. 70-5 (1970); Pennsylvania, Bureau of Corrections, Administrative Directive No. 3, Inmate Mail Privileges (1970); Middlesex (Mass.) County Jail, Memorandum from Sheriff to Inmates of House of Correction, March 30, 1971; City of New York, Department of Corrections, General Order No. 17 (July 1, 1970); cf. (Proposed) Illinois Unified Code of Corrections, Tentative Final Draft (January 1971), §335-13 (failed of passage). See also, "Fogel Tells Congress of 'Modest' State Penal Reforms," Minneapolis Tribune (December 5, 1971); "Prison Mail Censorship Lifted Temporarily," Appleton, Wisconsin Post Crescent (December 1, 1971).

[40] Ex parte Hull, 312 U.S. 546 (1941).

[41] Suggested Prisoners' Right of Communication Act, §107 (see note 14, supra, for the full text of this suggested act); cf. Assembly Bill 6256, New York Reg. Sess., 1971–1972, "An Act to amend the correction law, in relation to the rights of inmates to mail certain uncensored communications" (March 2, 1971):

"Section 1. The correction law is hereby amended by adding thereto a new section, to be section one hundred thirty-nine, to read as follows:

"§139. Rights of inmate to mail certain sealed uncensored communications. An inmate may address a sealed communication to the Governor of the state of New York, the commissioner of correctional services, the deputy commissioner of correctional services, an elected member of the state legislature, the administrative head of the state or federal agency or board responsible for his custody or release, to a member of a state bar, or to a judge or to any federal, state, county or city official or agency or to any court which has jurisdiction of criminal matters. Such communications will not be censored.

"§2. This act shall take effect immediately."

42 Palmigiano v. Travisono, 317 F. Supp. 776 (D.R.I. 1970).

43 Cal. Penal Code §2600 (4), as interpreted in In re Van Geldern, 14 Cal. App. 3d 838, 92 Cal. Rptr. 592 (Cal. Ct. App. 3d Dist. 1971); cf. In re Harrell, 470 P.2d 640, 87 Cal. Rptr. 504 (Cal. 1970); Sostre v. Otis, 330 F. Supp. 941 (S.D.N.Y. 1971); McCray v. Maryland, note 22, supra; see, Suggested Prisoners' Right of Communication Act §109, note 14, supra.

44 Suggested Prisoners' Right of Communication Act, §109 (b), note 14, supra; Sostre v. Otis, 330 F. Supp. 941 (S.D.N.Y. 1971); McCray v. Maryland, note 22, supra.

45 E.g. California Department of Corrections, Administrative Bulletin No. 70/36, D 2502 (1970), and Hawaii Department of Social Services, Corrections Division, Regulations, Art. 6, D2.700, D2.701 (1965).

46 McCray v. Maryland, note 22, supra; Nolan v. Fitzpatrick, 451 F.2d 545 (1st Cir. 1971); Jones v. Wittenberg, note 17, supra.

46a See note 41, supra.

47 E.g. Georgia Rules of the State Board of Corrections, 125-1-2-.05, News Media Policy, amended (May 4, 1971) (revised); Pennsylvania, Bureau of Correction, Administrative Directive No. 9, Public Relations (Dec. 15, 1970); see Burnham v. Oswald, 342 F. Supp. 880 (W.D.N.Y. 1972), rev'd 10 Crim. L. Rep. 2187 (2d Cir. 1971).

48 Massachusetts, Department of Correction, Commissioner's Bulletin 71-6 (Aug. 3, 1971).

49 Suggested Prisoners' Right of Communication Act, §108, note 14, supra.

50 Id. §109(b).

51 See generally H.R. 11882, §4 (1)-(50), 92d Cong., 1st Sess. (Nov. 18, 1971).

52 E.g.: (a) The Director shall be responsible for the development and implementation of a prisoner housing program (including specialized institutions where possible) which embodies generally recognized penological standards for the grouping of prisoners and which includes consideration of the following factors: age of the offender; the crime for which he has been convicted; his prior criminal record; and his potential for rehabilitation. In no case shall persons waiting trial be integrated with convicted offenders.

(b) The Director shall establish limitations on each institution's population which shall be based on the standards of the American Correctional Association.

53 E.g.: (a) Dietary planning in the Department of Corrections shall be the responsibility of a qualified dietician, shall meet or exceed generally accepted minimum standards regarding quantity and nutritional value, and shall be reviewed semi-annually by the [State Department of Public Health or State Board of Medical Supervisors]. A uniform diet shall be maintained throughout each institution; no dietary restrictions shall be imposed for disciplinary or other reasons.

(b) No prisoner shall be required to violate any legitimate religious dietary restriction. To assure the effective implementation of this subsection, the Departmental Dietician shall promulgate a written list of nutritional substitutes for food items prohibited by religious dietary restrictions.

54 E.g.: (a) There shall be at each institution in this state at least one full-time doctor, with an adequate supporting staff, and one full-time or part-time dentist as may be required. A doctor or registered nurse shall be present at each institution at all times.

(b) The doctor and dentist at each institution shall be responsible for providing initial and, thereafter, annual medical and dental examinations for every inmate and other medical and dental services as needed.

(c) The Superintendent of each institution shall allow and make adequate provision for the examination of prisoners by their personal physician upon request.

55 Note 52, supra.

56 Note 54, supra.

57 Note 53, supra.

58 Note 51, supra.

59 Cf. Sobell v. Reed, 327 F. Supp. 1294 (S.D.N.Y. 1971); Monks v. New Jersey State Parole Board, 277 A.2d 193, 58 N.J. 238 (1971).

60 E.g. 4A Md. Ann. Code, art. 41, §204F (Replacement Vol., Cumulative Supp. 1971) (approved April 29, 1971), available from the Clearinghouse, Clearinghouse No. 7204 (4 pp.). See also Cal. Assembly Bill No. 1181, a bill to create the Office of Ombudsman for Corrections, Clearinghouse No. 7423, vetoed by the Governor on December 22, 1971, reintroduced as Assembly Bill No. 5, in the 1972 session of the legislature.

61 Suggested Prisoners' Right of Communication Act, §111, note 14, supra.

62 E.g.: (a) The Superintendent of each institution shall be responsible for establishing a daily recreational program for prisoners. Each such program must be approved by the Director and by the Board of Medical Supervisors.

(b) Prisoners in administrative segregation and punitive segregation or isolation shall be permitted a minimum of three hours of recreation each day.

(c) Adequate facilities shall be provided for indoor recreation during inclement weather.

63 But cf. Rubin, note 17, supra, at 403:

"[I]f we think [rehabilitative] programs are needed in prison, then we must add provisions that define these things as *rights* of prisoners, access to or denial of which should be subject to court review." (Emphasis in original.)

64 E.g. Legislative Bill 1307, 80th Sess., Legislature of Nebraska (1969):

"Section 10. Upon his initial admission to facility, each person committed to the division shall be given a physical examination and a thorough evaluation. He shall be kept apart from other persons committed to the division until he is known to be free from any communicable disease. [Preferable is "until the evaluation is completed."] The evaluation shall include such person's psychological, social, educational and vocational condition and history, and the motivation of his offense. A report shall be submitted on each such person to the chief executive officer of the facility containing the findings of the physical examination and evaluation. The report shall include recommendations regarding the facility to which such person should be assigned, the degree and kind of custodial control, and the program of treatment for his rehabilitation, including medical and psychological treatment and educational and vocational training.

"Section 9 (3). The program of each person committed to the division shall be reviewed at regular intervals and recommendations shall be made to the chief executive officer concerning changes in such person's program of treatment, training, employment, care and custody as are considered necessary or desirable."

65 E.g. "An Act concerning a special school district within the Department of Correction," Connecticut Public Act No. 636:

"Section 1. The commissioner of correction may establish a special school district within the state department of correction for the education or assistance of any person sentenced or transferred to any instiution of the department until released from its control, including but not limited to any person on parole.

"Sec. 2. The commissioner of correction, in consultation with the council of correction, shall administer, coordinate and control the operations of said special school district and shall be responsible for the overall supervision and direction of all courses and activities of said special school district and shall establish such vocational and academic education, research and statistics, training and development services and programs as he considers necessary or advisable in the best interests of the persons benefitting therefrom.

"Sec. 3. Said special school district acting by the commissioner of correction in consultation with the council of correction shall have the power to (1) establish and maintain within the department of corrections such schools of different grades as the commissioner may from time to time require and deem necessary in the best interests of those persons sentenced or transferred to any institution of the department, including but not limited to any person on parole, (2) establish and maintain within the department such school libraries as may from time to time be required in connection with the educational courses, services and programs authorized by this act, (3) purchase, receive, hold and convey personal property for school purposes and equip and supply such schools with necessary furniture and other appendages, (4) make agreements and regulations for the establishing and conducting of such schools as are authorized under this act and employ and dismiss, in accordance with the applicable provisions of section 10-151 of the general statutes, such teachers as are necessary to carry out the intent of this act, and to pay their salaries, (5) receive any federal funds or aid made available to the state for rehabilitative or other programs and shall be eligible for and may receive any other funds or aid whether private, state or otherwise, to be used for the purposes of this act.

"Sec. 4. Said special school district acting by the commissioner of correction in consultation with the council of correction may pursuant to agreements, cooperate with the federal government in carrying out the purposes of any federal acts pertaining to vocational rehabilitation, and may adopt such methods of administration as are found by the federal government to be necessary for the proper and efficient operation of such agreements or plans for vocational or other rehabilitation in correctional institutions, and may comply with such conditions as may be necessary to secure the full benefit of all such federal funds available.

"Sec. 5. This act shall take effect from its passage."

66 Cf. Suggested Parole Act, §101 (see note 14, supra, for the full text of this suggested act) which provides parole eligibility at any point in the sentence, thus assuming a sentencing structure without statutory minimums.

67 E.g. "An Act to amend the correction law in relation to the extension of limits of place of confinement," Assembly Bill 6358, New York Reg. Sess., 1971–1972 (March 2, 1971):

"Section 1. The correction law is hereby amended by inserting therein a new section, to be section twenty-three-a, to read as follows:

"§23-a. Extention [sic] of limits of place of confinement. The commissioner may extend the limits of the place of confinement of a prisoner as to whom there is reasonable cause to believe he will honor his trust by authorizing him to visit temporarily a specifically designated place or places for a period not to exceed thirty days. The commissioner may extend such limits for any reason consistent with the public interest.

"§2. This act shall take effect immediately."

See also, "An act concerning furlough for correctional institution inmates," Modified House Bill 6447, Public Act 272, Connecticut General Assembly (1969):

"The commissioner of correction at his discretion may extend the limits of the place of confinement of a prisoner as to whom there is reasonable belief that he will honor his trust, by authorizing him under prescribed conditions to visit a specifically designated place or places for periods not exceeding fifteen days and return to the same or another institution or facility. Such periods may be renewed at the discretion of the commissioner. Such furlough may be granted only to permit a visit to a dying relative, attendance at the funeral of a relative, the obtaining of medical services not otherwise available, the contacting of prospective employers, or for any compelling reason consistent with rehabilitation."

68 Cf. Rubin, note 17, supra, at 393:

"Probation and parole were innovations of the previous century. I think it must be said that they have not had the hoped-for impact on imprisonment and the prison system. The ratio of prisoners to the total population is higher than it was a hundred years ago. The length of prison terms has increased, not decreased. Prison conditions cause frequent riots. Parole has served to increase prison time rather than, as most people think, decreasing it; and in almost every investigation of prison riots, the inadequacies of parole have been faulted." [Footnotes omitted.]

During the past year, several commentators have even more seriously questioned the "beneficial" and "rehabilitative" purposes which parole is assumed to embody, charging that it is merely a device for restricting the liberty of ex-offenders, for discriminatorily releasing those inmates with sufficient influence of one type or another, or for achieving other hidden purposes. Speech by John Irwin, at Harvard Law School, October 18–19, 1971, reported in 53 Harvard Law Record 1, 16 (Oct. 22, 1971); American Friends Service Committee, Struggle for Justice 144 (1971). Although not necessarily disagreeing with these views, this section will assume the continued and probably expanded use of parole.

[69] E.g. Legal Manual of the Oregon Corrections Division, ch. 144 (1969–1970); Proposed Tentative Draft of Illinois Unified Code of Corrections, art. 315 (January 1971) (failed of passage); Study Draft of a New Federal Criminal Code, note 14, supra.

[70] Cf. Suggested Parole Act, §101, note 14, supra, which assumes a sentencing structure without minimum sentences.

[71] Id. §§101, 106.

[72] Id. §103.

[73] Id. §102.

[74] Id. §104.

[75] Monks v. New Jersey State Parole Board, 277 A.2d 193, 58 N.J. 238 (1971). Suggested Parole Act, §105, note 14, supra; cf. S. Bill 4156, New York Reg. Sess., 1971–1972 (February 22, 1971), "An Act to amend the correction law, in relation to the right of a prisoner to be informed of the reason or reasons for denial of parole":

"Section 1. Section two hundred fourteen of the correction law is hereby amended by adding thereto a new subdivision, to be subdivision six, to read as follows:

"6. If, after appearance before the board pursuant to subdivision four of this section, the prisoner is denied release on parole, the board shall inform such prisoner, in writing and within two weeks of such appearance, of the reason or reasons for such denial.

§2. This act shall take effect on the sixtieth day after it shall have become a law."

[76] Suggested Parole Act, §107, note 14, supra.

[77] Id. §108.

[78] Id. §109 (a); cf. Study Draft of a New Federal Criminal Code, note 14, supra.

[79] Suggested Parole Act, §108 (b), note 14, supra.

[80] Id. §109 (a).

[81] Cf. id. §§111, 112.

[82] Note, "The Collateral Consequences of a Criminal Conviction," 23 Vanderbilt L. Rev. 939 (1970); cf. Study Draft of a New Federal Criminal Code, note 14, supra. The ABA Commission on Correctional Facilities and Services has recently undertaken a state-by-state survey of employment disabilities.

[83] Id.

[84] Otsuka v. Hite, 64 Cal. 2d 596, 414 P.2d 412, 51 Cal. Rptr. 284 (1966); Stephens v. Yeoman, 327 F. Supp. 1182 (D. N. J. 1970); Perrine v. Municipal Court, 488 P.2d 648 (Cal. 1971); in Schware v. Board of Bar Examiners of New Mexico, 353 U.S. 232 (1957), the Supreme Court held that an arrest record, inter alia, was insufficient grounds for disqualification from law practice and stated that even if an offense was committed, it must have a rational connection with applicant's fiitness to practice law: "In determining whether a person's character is good, the nature of the offense which he has committed must be taken into account." 353 U.S. at 243.

[85] Suggested Parole Act, §110 (b), note 14, supra; Georgia H.R. No. 22-38 (1971), available from the Clearinghouse, Clearinghouse No. 7205 (2 pp.).

CHAPTER 22
COURTS AND REFORM

EDITORS' INTRODUCTION

In the past several years, pro se prisoners' suits seeking either habeas corpus or Civil Rights Act relief have comprised almost twenty per cent of the business of the federal courts.

These pro se lawsuits pose incalculable administrative problems for the courts, since the prisoner-petitioners are un-tutored in the law, often having little formal education of any sort. They are almost always indigent, and naturally their incarceration cripples their ability to prosecute the suits.

The sheer volume of cases forcloses assigning counsel in each suit, and the resultant screening is a burdensome task. There are no provisions to reimburse assigned counsel in a Civil Rights Act suit, and in habeas corpus the maximum authorized fee is $250. Furthermore, there is no means for the court to reimburse assigned counsel for expenses in prisoners' rights lawsuits even when the plaintiff is proceeding in forma pauperis. Thus costs of travel, transporting witnesses, investigation, and depositions may have to be borne by the court-appointed lawyer.

Two distinguished federal district court judges propose a number of innovations in the handling of these cases in the articles which follow.

ADMINISTRATIVE REFORM AND THE COURTS

HONORABLE JACK B. WEINSTEIN *

It is a great honor to work with those in the field of prisoners' rights—a small band that defends the front line of civil liberties forward positions that must stand if the citadel of the Bill of Rights for all of us is to remain unbreached. It is important to emphasize that there is no inconsistency between enforcement of the Bill of Rights and protection of the public against crime. They are not only compatible, they cannot exist without each other in a democratic society.

The people of our cities are entitled to and must get full protection, particularly against vicious street crimes. Punishment must also protect the public.

Each time a judge looks into the eyes of a defendant he is about to sentence, it is brought home to him that here is a human being who will ultimately return to society. He must return rehabilitated, not a more hardened criminal. Unconstitutional treatment embitters and inhibits rehabilitation.

As a citizen, a state prisoner is protected by the Fourteenth Amendment, which provides that no person shall be deprived of "life, liberty, or property without due process of law;" nor shall any person be denied "the equal protection of the laws."

Although we have greatly expanded the constitutional protections of defendants on trial, our system of safeguards has in large measure failed to protect defendants after they have been found guilty. The Chief Justice of the United States has pointed out that public safety depends in large part on the success of efforts to turn out prisoners ready for lawful employment and not for renewed crimes:

> "In part, the terrible price we are paying in crime
> is because we have tended—once the drama of the trial
> is over—to regard all criminals as human rubbish. . . .
> We lawyers and judges sometimes tend to fall in love

---

* U.S. District Court Judge, Eastern District of New York; Adjunct Professor, Columbia University School of Law.

with procedures and techniques and formalism. . . . The imbalance in our system of criminal justice must be corrected so that we give at least as much attention to the defendant after he is found guilty as before.

"Whether we find it palatable or not, we must proceed, even in the face of bitter contrary experiences, in the belief that every human being has a spark some-where hidden in him that will make . . . possible . . . redemption and rehabilitation. If we accept the idea that each human, however bad, is a child of God, we must look for that spark." [1]

In recent years prisoners have looked in increasing num-bers to the federal district courts, both via collateral attacks on their state court convictions through the habeas corpus mecha-nism and for damages and injunctive relief stemming from a variety of illegal acts allegedly committed against them—e.g. hostility and perjury of witnesses, assault by policemen, improper searches and unfair treatment in prison.

Sitting as constitutional courts, the federal courts have a clear obligation to redress constitutional grievances. The number of prisoner cases has risen sharply in the post-World War II era, for several reasons. Partly, it is because of procedural changes making it easier to attack state criminal convictions in federal district courts on the ground that they have been obtained in violation of the federal Constitution. Partly, it is because of the expansion of federal constitutional doctrines protecting defen-dants in state criminal trials. Partly, it is because we can no longer ignore the fact that prison conditions are intolerable, and that unfortunately, imprisoned men and women can, in most cases, look nowhere else but to the federal judiciary for protection of their federal constitutional rights.

Federal judges want to get out of the business of interfering in the operation of state prisons as soon as possible. They will do so just as soon as the states meet their minimum constitutional responsibilities. The prisoner pro se applications received by the federal courts raise some of the most troublesome current prob-lems in judicial administration. If there is merit in a prisoner's claim, every judge wishes to see justice promptly done. This is true whether the litigation is cast as a habeas corpus petition seeking to set aside a conviction or as a civil rights complaint seeking monetary damages for past harm or an injunction for continuing violations. Yet many of the strengths of our adversary system, which courts rely upon in doing justice, are absent in these pro se cases. There is not even the minimum screening by an attorney—an officer of the court—certifying that "there is good ground to support" the pleading.[2]

This poses a serious problem: how can we make the most effective use of our limited legal resources to insure that full attention is given to those cases that may have merit, but at the same time allow for prompt disposition of meritless claims? In this kind of litigation some modification of our adversary system may well be warranted. Such an innovation can hardly be provided by district judges on a case-by-case basis. New institutions, new rules laid down by appellate courts, and perhaps even new legislation will need to be considered. The cooperation of judges at all levels of the system, of attorneys, of law schools, and of legislators is called for.

In reviewing the special problems posed for the federal courts by pro se prisoner litigation, it must first be understood that in terms of numbers, the largest body of cases today are the habeas corpus cases. Nevertheless, habeas cases now present less of a problem to the federal courts than in the past, and they will continue to be of decreasing relative importance for several reasons.

The number of these cases seems to be levelling off or even decreasing after a dizzy spiral upward in the last decade. In 1961, 1,020 petitions for a writ of habeas corpus were filed in federal district courts by state prisoners. During the decade the number rose steadily each year, reaching a high point of 9,063 in 1970. In 1971, however, 8,372 petitions were filed by state prisoners, a 7.6 per cent decrease from the previous year.[3]

Expansion of the substantive constitutional doctrines seems to have halted, if not retrogressed. Therefore, applications from prisoners raising rights not available at the time they were first tried and convicted have become more and more unusual. The law has settled down: the courts have developed a body of similar cases on which they can rely, and they have been able to standardize their procedure for handling these cases.

Furthermore, the federal habeas statutes have certain built-in limitations. The rule that an adequate state hearing removes the necessity for an independent federal hearing and the rule that state remedies must be exhausted before there is a federal postconviction application permit disposition of most habeas corpus cases without any substantial effort on the part of federal trial and appellate judges. This is aided by the fact that to a greater extent, most state courts seem to be doing an adequate job in providing postconviction relief. In New York, state judges have been doing a generally fine job in the postconviction area.

The increasing facility with which we handle the habeas petitions should not, however, lead us to underestimate the number of cases with substantial grounds for relief. Although the prevailing attitude is that most, if not all, collateral prisoner petitions are frivolous, one study of 356 legal problems of inmates of the maximum-security federal penitentiary in Atlanta revealed that 21 per cent of the prisoners seeking to vacate their sentences under 28 U.S.C. §2255 had strong grounds for relief.[4]

By contrast with habeas corpus petitions, state prisoner civil rights actions under 42 U.S.C. §1983 have only recently begun to rise. In 1966, 218 complaints were filed in federal district courts; by 1971, 2,915 were filed. This represents a 1,337 per cent increase over five years.

As a federal district judge, I find that these civil rights cases are more difficult to deal with than the average habeas corpus petition, since in the latter there must be a state court record, which tends to focus the factual issues.[5]

In Civil Rights Act cases, however, the facts are often completely unresolved. Prisoner civil rights actions run the gamut from complaints about treatment in prison to complaints about witnesses, policemen, district attorneys, and newspapermen who offended before, during, and after trial.[6] Brooding on the past and supported by the legal skills of fellow inmates, there is almost limitless scope to drafting a complaint bottomed on *Monroe v. Pape,*[7] charging violation of constitutional rights. Pro se pleadings, we are instructed, must be construed as favorably as possible towards the plaintiff in determining whether he has stated a valid claim for relief.[8]

While some of the §1983 suits deal with constitutional violations at the time of arrest and trial, the bulk of them complain of constitutional violations in conditions in the prisons. Underlying these cases is the basic fact that present-day prisons are intolerable, and the imprisoned men and women look to the federal judiciary for protection of their federal constitutional rights. The challenge of safeguarding and implementing these rights is one that must be faced by our courts.

These are civil cases, and under our practice in the Eastern District of New York they are assigned to an individual judge, their treatment varying with each judge. Part of the problem encountered by the judiciary stems from the unsuitability of the Federal Rules of Civil Procedure to guide the course of pro se litigation, especially when brought by an incarcerated man. Partially, this derives from the fact that most prisoners have never seen the rules and are thus ignorant of their requirements. Even with access to the rules, however, problems such as meeting time limitations while restricted in the materials and opportunities needed to work on a case, or utilizing discovery devices from a prison cell, remain virtually insurmountable.

Another not inconsiderable problem the courts find in handling prisoners' rights suits is that of bringing prisoners from outlying state institutions to spend time in the federal house of detention preparing for and awaiting a hearing or trial. Not only is it expensive but it is disruptive of prison rehabilitative routine. Some prisoners may even utilize the device to break up the tedium of prison and to be brought, even for a short time, nearer to those who might visit them.

My own practice in all pro se prisoner cases is to immediately order the clerk to file the papers without prepayment of fees and to order the marshal to serve the defendants, who are often individual policemen, witnesses to crimes, wardens, and district attorneys, as well as governmental agencies. As in all civil cases assigned to me, I automatically order a pretrial hearing, but since the plaintiff is in prison he does not appear. It is impossible to know what the merits are at this stage since the Corporation Counsel's or Attorney General's representation often lacks force, and the individual policeman or witness (who must retain private counsel) very much resents being made a defendant.

I am reluctant to take the passive attitude usually adopted in civil cases, where the plaintiff decides how to move his case forward. The net result of that kind of attitude, bearing in mind the plaintiff's unfamiliarity with procedural devices and inability to physically attend sessions in court—unless he is brought into court (frequently at considerable expense) by order—would mean that these cases would lie dormant.

Thus, many judges find themselves unable to rely on the

traditional adversary processes to develop and clarify the legal and factual issues. The prisoner simply cannot prepare and try the case effectively. On the other hand, no statutory authority is given to pay appointed attorneys in civil rights cases. As a result, if counsel is appointed the court must select an attorney to represent the plaintiff without recompense, presenting undesirable conflict-of-interest problems. If there were a pool of talented lawyers who could be selected by rotation, or if the federal laws could be amended to provide for payment of appointed counsel, the problem of counsel could be solved. We then, however, would be left with the question of whether there is an obligation to appoint counsel for the policemen and the witness defendants who presently must retain their own lawyers.

In any event, appointing counsel for the petitioner in every case is not an ideal solution. Were courts to appoint counsel in all cases knowing that most were meritless, the ethical responsibility of the appointed lawyer might create intolerable burdens for himself and others. Once appointed he might feel compelled to utilize the full panoply of civil discovery devices including depositions and interrogatories. Just because he was appearing pro bono he might press the case more strongly than he would if financial considerations of the client mandated a more practical approach. Discovery might be as broad as the plaintiff's lawyer could manage, bearing in mind the possibility—no matter how remote—that some new fact might turn up, the significance of which the client might not have understood.

The lawyer would not be limited to the precise theory of his client but would seek to develop any other legal grounds that had the slightest possibility of success. The harassment of witnesses, policemen, and prosecutors, which might result were the scores of pending prisoner civil rights cases in New York City to proceed in this way, must be a matter of concern in this period when state criminal law enforcement is strained to the breaking point. The attorney who litigated assiduously, using all forms of discovery, might seriously interfere with state criminal processes, further exacerbating the relationship of federal courts to state law enforcement authorities. Furthermore, diverting legal resources from work for the ghetto poor, who ultimately might be helped by lawyers, to prisoners who cannot, seems nonutilitarian by any rational calculus.

One solution I have tried is to assume a more active role than that traditionally reserved for the trial judge. Before assigning counsel, I may at times write to a member of the bar in whom I have confidence, requesting an investigation of the matter before I take further action. I ask him or her to make a factual and legal inquiry to determine whether there is sufficient merit in the case to warrant appointment of an attorney, i.e., "whether counsel might possibly be of assistance." To avoid some of the burdens of the attorney-client relationship while affording the protection of the attorney-client privilege, I instruct the attorney as follows:

> "It should be clearly understood that you are not being appointed as counsel and you have no obligation or responsibility to the plaintiff or this Court as counsel. Nevertheless, for purposes of the attorney-client privilege, any communication with the client should be treated by you as if made in the course of negotiations between lawyer and client to determine whether representation will be undertaken. Thus, the attorney-client privilege will apply."

Although this technique has proven quite useful to me, the limitations on the possibility of the judge's assuming the role of investigator in these cases are obvious.

The problems presented by prisoner pro se litigation are, it is clear, enormous, but clearly the federal courts must meet and surmount the problems. Civil Rights Act suits frequently express legitimate constitutional complaints, and the courts would be abdicating a central part of their duty if they did not see to it that constitutional rights are vindicated.

A generalized inability of our judicial system to handle valid complaints contributes to an increased lack of public confidence in judicial institutions—confidence which has already been considerably eroded by the failure of the judicial system to deal with the rising tide of violent crime. These problems are not discrete. If we do not manage to improve the shameful conditions in our prisons, we will continue to turn out prisoners who are not fit to return to society in any role but that of a criminal. Failure to deal with well-founded prisoner complaints might also lead to a dangerous overreaction by the public, the government, Congress, or the judiciary, curtailing still further the opportunities for prisoners to assert their civil rights.

In part, the problem presents perplexing questions of federalism. Considerations of separation of powers and state sovereignty loom ominously on the horizon. Notwithstanding these factors, some have argued cogently that since the prisons are instruments of the courts, the courts have every right to *prescribe* how prisons shall be conducted, rather than limit themselves to *prohibition* of unconstitutional conditions.[9] Without going that far, I submit that there are a number of avenues we might explore to both improve the quality of judicial treatment of prisoner pro se litigation and to ease the burden these cases place on the federal courts.

We must recognize that real improvements often require new appropriations. The power of the courts to order reallocation of governmental resources is a most sensitive problem. Elected officials can properly decide whether schools or police or armed forces or prisons should get more money, and how that money should be raised. Allocation of resources is not an appropriate function for appointed judges except in the most extreme cases.

Inmate Legal Aid Programs

The Omnibus Crime Control and Safe Streets Act of 1968 established a Law Enforcement Assistance Administration to channel federal funds into state law enforcement programs.[10] Section 3731 of 28 U.S.C., setting forth those state programs and projects eligible for 75 per cent federal funding, could and should be easily amended to include a subdivision dealing with legal assistance programs for inmates in penal institutions. Pilot projects could also be funded at 100 per cent by the federal government.[11]

Full time legal assistance in the prisons would be of tremendous help both to prisoners and the judicial system. First, many frivolous claims would presumably never be filed if the petitioner had had even a perfunctory legal interview at the outset. Often the matter could be quickly adjusted administratively by the lawyer's intervention. Also, petitions prepared with the advice or aid of counsel would be clearer and would help protect prisoners' rights by assuring that the relief sought falls within the framework of existing rights and remedies.

The law schools and volunteer private attorneys are doing some of this work now, but it is doubtful that they are either willing or able to take on the entire job. Typical is the experience of the Columbia Law School. For the last two years Columbia has run such a project at the Greenhaven Prison facility. Prisoners seeking relief filled out a long information form. The law school group screened the questionnaires and filed petitions for these prisoners it accepted. Prisoners not accepted for the Columbia program were free, of course, to proceed on their own. This raised interesting questions of whether a court could be justified in assuming that any pro se petition from Greenhaven not drawn by the Columbia group was rejected after a preliminary screening as not warranting further work. Broader programs have been developed by other schools, many with the generous help of Counsel for Legal Education and Professional Responsibility, under the leadership of William Pincus.

In any event, after two years a combination of financial pressures, personnel shifts, and lack of a sustained substantial student interest resulted in the termination of the Columbia project. Even when the program operated it took care of the needs of only a few of the prisoners, because the students gave only a small portion of their time to the work. The need still exists at Greenhaven as well as at all other prisons. It can only be met by adequate government funding and by a staff of full-time attorneys working along with laymen, law students, bar associations, and volunteer attorneys.

Possibility of Deference to State Courts

Unlike habeas corpus, there is no requirement that the plaintiff in a §1983 civil rights action exhaust state remedies before commencing proceedings in federal court. There have been some suggestions that a deferral provision be engrafted onto §1983 to provide for prior action by some state body.

The deferral would probably be for a specified period of time in order to give an appropriate state agency time to act on the complaint; the state proceeding could be either administrative or judicial. At the end of the deferral period or at the close of the state proceedings, the federal court would be empowered to grant any legal or equitable relief it deemed necessary under §1983. Review of factual determinations would be the same as in habeas corpus cases, where findings derived from full and fair hearings are assumed to be correct.

There are pitfalls to a deferral statute. First, to cut back the protection of the constitutional rights of one group of citizens, i.e., prisoners, presents serious equal protection problems. Second, there is always the danger that in a political climate of fear and misunderstanding, cutbacks and revisions to the proposal might take place which would result in a drastic curtailment of protection of the constitutional rights of prisoners.

Creation of Adequate State Remedies

If the states provide an adequate remedy for prisoners' problems, it seems likely that the prisoners would utilize this voluntarily, without statutory mandate. A recent amendment to New York law seems to open the door for the first time to the institution by prisoners of state judicial proceedings to challenge the legality of arrest or detention.[12]

If the states were to adopt an administrative appeals procedure to settle grievances, most petitions might not need to be filed in any court. If a transcript of the administrative proceeding were kept, reasons given for the tribunal's decisions, and an Article 78[13]-type review provided for in state courts, any prisoner claim going to federal court could at the very least be expected to present clearly defined issues.

Development of a clear-cut code of prisoners' rights and responsibilities could also serve to eliminate many grievances before they arise and to stop prison officials from violating what should be uncontested rights. Such a code could be prepared jointly by prison authorities, groups such as the American Civil Liberties Union, and convicts. An excellent start in this direction is the comprehensive pamphlet, *The Emerging Rights of the Confined,* by the South Carolina Department of Corrections.[14]

Better Representation in Civil Rights Actions

Only recently have the district courts been authorized to provide payment for appointed counsel in habeas corpus cases. In civil rights cases, appointed counsel serve without fee, often outstandingly well. Nevertheless, it is clear that the pro bono resources of the profession are severely limited.

The section of the United States Code [15] dealing with proceedings in forma pauperis should be amended to provide for the payment of attorneys' fees and all costs and expenses of litigation for all indigent civil rights plaintiffs. Failure to cover fees deprives indigent plaintiffs of representation, penalizes the young practitioner, and forces such pro bono cases into the larger firms only.

Specialized Rules of Procedure
for Civil Pro Se Litigation

The Federal Rules of Civil Procedure simply do not contemplate this type of litigation. They depend on the adversary system to move a case ahead. Pro se litigants lack the envisioned familiarity with procedural devices; their incarceration prevents adequate research and makes their presence at frequent court sessions terribly expensive for the state.

It would seem sensible to authorize special national or local rules governing civil pro se litigation to alleviate these problems. These rules could set more flexible time periods, regulate proceedings in forma pauperis and generally create a more relevant and informal framework for the litigation. The rules would have the additional benefit of standardizing the handling of these cases, thereby eliminating the tremendous variety of unwritten and individual requirements and exceptions created by various clerks throughout the circuits.

Better Use of Federal Court Personnel and Facilities

It is clear that there are resources available to the district courts which are not yet being fully exploited. In this district the suggestion has been made that our magistrates actually visit the prisons and interview the prisoners. There are obvious problems connected with such a procedure, including that of how to treat plaintiffs and petitioners who insist on pressing their claims despite an adverse report from the magistrate. It is not clear whether the magistrate should be acting as investigator, judge or in some other capacity.[16] It would seem essential to fix his role as precisely as possible.

The possibility of increased use of pro se clerks should be explored. They have proven valuable on the circuit level. However, because I consider the matter important, requiring the exercise of a delicate balance of judgment, I prefer to handle all pro se prisoner applications myself with the aid of my own law clerks.

Sentencing should be coordinated with available facilities. It does little good to build new facilities if they are designed to accommodate outmoded concepts of sentencing. Conversely, innovative sentencing can be frustrating and fruitless if it is not done with the available resources in mind.

Innovative Treatment of Pro Se Cases
by the Federal Judiciary

Without structural changes, substantive and procedural innovations can do much to streamline pro se prisoner litigation. The federal courts could fall back on the well-established doctrine of abstention and refuse to consider certain classes of cases. The Second Circuit has declared its unwillingness to concern itself with "trivial questions of internal prison discipline":

> "The federal courts should refuse to interfere with internal state prison administration except in the most extreme cases involving a shocking deprivation of fundamental rights." [17]

I find this doctrine most troublesome. What is "trivial" to a judge on the court of appeals may be of overriding significance to a prisoner.

Perhaps we should accord a preferred status to certain types of claims. We might consider giving such treatment to cases arising under the Eighth Amendment to insure that no person is physically mistreated as a result of incarceration. A federal court in Montgomery, Alabama has relied on the Eighth Amendment to order drastic reform of prison health care services it found "barbarous" and "shocking." [18] Among other aggravating factors that should alert a court not to abstain would be racial prejudice or an independent design to deprive the defendant of a constitutional right, such as free speech.

Summary judgment would potentially be a useful tool in these civil cases, but in this circuit at least, district courts may not rely to any substantial extent on summary judgment predicated upon testimonial proof to avoid a full trial, even though a recovery seems hopeless. It may, however, be possible to judicially create a circumscribed form of summary judgment or to dismiss a complaint as construed in the light of facts judicially noticed. [19]

Judges should be encouraged to construe pro se prisoners' pleadings more liberally and to facilitate amendment of complaints by enumerating their failings in a conditional order rather than enter a final order of dismissal at once, and by requiring answering papers from the state. When similar complaints are received from a large number of prisoners, consolidation of actions, or a prisoners' class action should be considered.

Appeals from district court dismissals of prisoners' pro se petitions can also be streamlined. A circuit practice rule should implement a uniform system of advising a plaintiff of the steps he must take to appeal the dismissal of his petition. Courts should consider motions of counsel, under the rule of *Anders v. California*,[20] to be relieved on appeal on the grounds that the record presents no non-frivolous issues for appeal.

Finally, it would be highly desirable for the bar to take the initiative in working closely with the bench, correctional authorities, experts in penology and other disciplines, as well as with the legislature and executive, to meet the problems of the administration of criminal justice. One of the critical problems is in providing correctional facilities that prepare people for socially useful lives in a democratic society rather than for further lives of crime. Enforcing prisoners' constitutional rights aids in that task.

Footnotes

[1] 16 Vill. L. Rev. 1029 (1971).

[2] Fed. R. Civ. P. 11.

[3] Administrative Office of the United States Courts, Annual Report of the Director (table 14) (1971).

[4] Jacob and Sharma, "Justice After Trial: Prisoners' Need for Legal Services in the Criminal Correctional Process," 18 Kan. L. Rev. 493, 504 (1970).

[5] See 28 U.S.C. §§2244, 2254(1).

[6] See e.g. United States ex rel. Sabella v. Newsday, 315 F. Supp. 333 (E.D.N.Y. 1970); Sostre v. Rockefeller, 312 F. Supp. 863 (S.D.N.Y. 1970).

[7] 365 U.S. 167 (1961).

[8] See e.g. Dioguardi v. Durning, 139 F.2d 774 (2d Cir. 1944).

[9] See Spaeth, "The Courts' Responsibility for Prison Reform," 16 Vill. L. Rev. 1031, 1038 (1971).

[10] See 28 U.S.C. §§3701–3781.

[11] See 28 U.S.C. §3742.

[12] N.Y. Civil Rights Law §79 (as amended 1973).

[13] N.Y. Civil Prac. Law & Rules 7801 et seq.

[14] The Emerging Rights of the Confined, South Carolina Department of Corrections (1972).

[15] 28 U.S.C. §1915.

[16] Cf. Pub. L. No. 90-578, §636(b)(3) (1968); Note, "Proposed Reformation of Federal Habeas Corpus Procedure: Use of Federal Magistrates," 54 Iowa L. Rev. 1147 (1969); ABA, Minimum Standards for Criminal Justice: Post-Conviction Remedies §4.1 (masters for preliminary inquiry).

[17] Rodriguez v. McGinnis, 451 F.2d 730, 732 (2d Cir. 1971).

[18] Newman v. Alabama, 349 F. Supp. 278, 281 (M.D. Ala. 1972), citing Novak v. Beto, 453 F.2d 661, 671 (5th Cir. 1971).

[19] See, e.g. United States ex rel. Chubbs v. City of New York, 324 F. Supp. 1183 (1971).

[20] 386 U.S. 738 (1967).

PRISONER'S LITIGATION IN THE FEDERAL COURTS

HONORABLE WILLIAM WAYNE JUSTICE *

Introduction

Several years ago my knowledge of the area of prisoners' litigation in the federal courts was limited to problems raised by traditional habeas corpus [1] and its federal counterpart, the motion to vacate sentence.[2] Recently, however, a new area of prisoners' litigation has developed—the so-called prisoners' rights actions attacking the conditions of prison life and the management of the prison. While the traditional habeas cases are still very much with us, the provocative developments in the law now seem to be occurring in the prisoners' rights cases.

Whether we are dealing with traditional habeas corpus or with prisoners' rights, however, prisoners' litigation generally is more often difficult than routine for the federal judiciary. Until very recently, these cases were rarely initiated through the assistance of counsel; yet the law of habeas corpus, and now prisoners' rights, ranks with the most complex in our jurisprudence. While the overwhelming number of these lawsuits are without merit, the occasional successful claim—like Gideon's famous writ creating the right to appointed counsel—may revolutionize an entire phase of the criminal process.

Applications for Writs of Habeas Corpus

In recent years, the bar journals and law reviews have published an astonishing amount of material attacking the present habeas corpus system. The arguments are familiar. It is said that the staggering number of petitions filed has created an intolerable burden on the courts. As if numbers alone were not enough to discourage even the most indefatigable federalist, nearly every petition is inartfully drawn, requiring the judge to expend more

---

* U.S. District Court Judge, Eastern District of Texas.

than an ordinary effort to understand the basis of the claim. Moreover, valid claims are few and far between. Adding to this burden are the applicants who file writ after writ, raising a single, separate, and additional constitutional claim in each subsequent petition.

The habeas corpus problems are compounded immeasurably when it is considered that a prisoner's collateral attack may be instituted years after his conviction. Because of the death, or lapse of memory, of material witnesses, serious difficulties may occur in conducting a factual hearing on a claim and in retrying the prisoner if the habeas petition should be granted. In addition to these essentially administrative problems, the critics further complain that the habeas system adversely affects the ultimate rehabilitation of the prisoner and undermines respect for the law and for the courts.

Criticism has not been limited to the scholarly journals. The popular press has been less concerned about the administrative burden of habeas corpus than with the potential for federal court interference in state affairs. Indeed, some journalists simplistically ascribe a major share of the responsibility for our increasingly serious crime problem to the federal judiciary. Such critics are indignant that a prisoner, after his case has been affirmed by the highest appellate court of his state, is entitled to institute an entirely new attack upon his judgment in the federal system. They apparently seek to inflame the populace by conjuring up visions of convicted rapists, child molesters, and murderers roaming the streets upon release by federal judges. These carpers insist that prisoners are freed upon "mere technicalities." In point of fact, of the thousands of prisoners who have petitioned for habeas relief, only a small proportion have been released. Those released for the most part have been retried and convicted; those gaining total freedom comprise a miniscule proportion of the total number of petitioners.[3] Furthermore, one could hardly characterize the protections afforded against illegal search and seizure and against self-incrimination, for example, as "mere technicalities."

I must say that I cannot agree with the gloomy appraisals of the critics of federal habeas corpus. Granting the truth in the allegations of administrative snarls resulting from habeas applications, I am of the opinion that it is beneficial to maintain the system to serve as a check on the power of the state, that is, for the purpose of ensuring that prisoners are treated with scrupulous fairness at all stages of the state criminal process. That a check of the kind I have mentioned is beneficial was an unspoken premise of the expansion of the rights of the accused affected during the Warren era. It remains a valid premise today, especially with the repressive mood of the majority in this country.

Even so formidable a critic of the present system as Judge Henry Friendly has recognized as much.[4] Judge Friendly has argued that convictions should be subject to attack only when the prisoner supplements his constitutional plea with a colorable claim of innocence. He would make four exceptions to this rule, however, and allow the petitioner to proceed without maintaining his innocence:

(1) when a breakdown of the criminal process occurs;

(2) when there occurs a denial of constitutional rights claimed on the basis of facts outside the record, the effect of which was not open to review and consideration on appeal;

(3) when the state has failed to provide a proper procedure for making a defense at trial or an appeal; and

(4) when new constitutional developments relating to the criminal process occur, such as right to counsel, that are applied retroactively.

The exceptions he mentions would afford a check on possible miscarriages of the state criminal process; but it is a check that, in my opinion, can hardly be distinguished from what we have now. Even if we were to totally adopt Judge Friendly's system, I feel that we would eventually be right back where we started. Prisoners would soon learn which allegations to make to avoid summary dismissals of their claims, and the courts would then find it necessary to devise some procedure to determine whether the allegations had basis in fact.

Without discounting the significance of the problems raised by the critics, I suggest that some of the administrative burden, and much of the potential for federal-state friction, would be eased considerably if state judges and prosecutors would reexamine some of their basic techniques of handling postconviction remedies within the state system. I must add, parenthetically, that the suggestions I am about to make are based on my experience as prosecutor and judge within the forty-one-county area comprising the Eastern District of Texas. Although I cannot speak from personal experience about any other area, I have no reason to assume that some of my observations in the Eastern District would not be applicable elsewhere as well.

A recurring problem in federal habeas corpus is the failure of the state courts to hold evidentiary hearings on these claims. The Supreme Court decision in *Townsend v. Sain*,[5] as codified in Title 28 U.S.C. §2254, requires the federal court to grant a habeas petitioner a hearing on his claims if he has not received "a full and fair evidentiary hearing in a state court." Nevertheless, despite this oblique command to the state courts, I receive a surprising number of petitions raising substantial questions of fact on which the state courts have not attempted, even colorably, to hold evidentiary hearings. Typically, the transcript provided in such a case will contain a finding by the state trial judge that he is personally acquainted with the petitioner's case, and that his own knowledge convinces him that petitioner's claims are without merit. Frequently the record contains only a bare denial of the application without any findings of fact. I respectfully submit that the law requires more of state trial judges.

I can tell you from experience that granting a habeas hearing to remedy the situation causes inconvenience to the state—inconvenience that is interpreted by many of the state officials involved as interference. Assistant attorneys general must be dispatched to the court; witnesses must be subpoenaed. The prisoner, accompanied by guards, must be brought from the place of incarceration, usually several days in advance, so that he can consult with his attorney. At the conclusion of the hearing, the prisoner, upon his return to state custody, must again go through the thirty-day initial processing conducted by the department of corrections. Merely by setting a hearing, a federal judge is placed in the acutely uncomfortable position of having to rule that a brother judge did not give a fair and full hearing, and substantial court time must be devoted to adequately develop the facts.

On the other hand, when the court is provided with a transcript of a full-state evidentiary hearing on petitioner's habeas claims, the law calls for a simple review of the evidence and findings of the state trial judge. The case should receive a summary disposition unless the state proceedings taken as a whole do not fairly support the factual determinations of the state judge.[6] This procedure causes little interference with the state process and at the same time effects only minor imposition, relatively speaking, on the time of the court.

Guilty Pleas

Furthermore, state trial judges may want to consider, when taking pleas of guilty, a comprehensive examination of the accused regarding his basic constitutional rights. I would estimate that the majority of habeas matters filed in my court allege some infirmity in connection with a guilty plea. A common fact situation involves a petitioner who gave a statement of guilt to the law enforcement officers upon arrest or shortly thereafter and then decided to plead guilty. *McMann v. Richardson* [7] notwithstanding, the habeas opportunity arises when the state trial judge, upon receipt of the plea, fails to inquire into the details surrounding the giving of the statement. It takes very little time to determine if there is a statement, and if so, whether the defendant was given the *Miranda* warnings, whether he contends in any way that the statement was coerced, and whether the presence of the statement has, in any way, a coercive effect upon the defendant to plead against his will. In this regard, the court should point out to the defendant that if he feels he gave a statement against his will, he has the right to attempt to prove it on a motion to suppress. The court may then further inquire whether the defendant, knowing that he has this right against self-incrimination, wishes to waive it. By use of the kind of extensive inquiry I have described, the court obviates a possible claim that the plea was involuntary or that appointed counsel was ineffective.

The court, in similar fashion, should examine the accused regarding all the basic procedural and substantive rights afforded criminal defendants by the Constitution. Additionally, competency of the defendant to plead should be fully explored. Careful plea acceptance will enable the state trial judge to create a record that will stand up under scrutiny, alleviating the possibility of intrusive and offensive corrective action by the federal court. At the same time, the federal district judge's task will be simplified, because exacting and complete records of guilty pleas will enable him to dispose of very many habeas cases from his desk rather than from the bench.

Another problem related to acceptance of the guilty plea arises from contentions of ineffective assistance of appointed counsel. Many of these petitions are based solely on the fact that counsel was appointed only a few minutes or a few hours before the plea was entered. At the very least, this fact situation gives me pause. Some type of further examination, either of the record made in the state habeas hearing or of the facts after hearing in the federal court, is necessary. Litigation based on these narrow facts can be avoided entirely by the simple expedient of appointing counsel well in advance of scheduled pleas.

Prisoners' Rights Suits

Although there are many other observations I could make about traditional habeas corpus, the prisoners' rights cases arising under the various civil rights statutes also demand our examination. While the fiscal year 1971 recorded a 7.6 per cent decrease in traditional habeas corpus cases over the previous year, the prisoners' rights cases increased by 43.6 per cent.[8]

Without attempting to prove too much by these figures, I cite them as corroboration of what we have suspected for some time: that prisoners seem to be turning more of their petitioning energy against prison administration and less of it against law enforcement and the judicial process.[9]

Before raising some of the difficulties that I have encountered, or that I foresee, in the area of prisoners' rights litigation, I would like briefly to discuss some of the concepts that are no longer significant hurdles for the prisoner litigating in the federal courts. Gone forever are the days when judges could take refuge in the so-called "hands-off" policy that courts applied in the area of prison administration. Once intoned as the solution in nearly every order of summary dismissal,[10] the policy is now mentioned only as an historical preface. The law from the "good old days," if not good law, was predictable—as this notorious passage from an 1871 Virginia court affirms:

> ". . . [The prisoner] has, as a consequence of his crime, not only forfeited his liberty, but all his personal rights except those which the law in its humanity accords to him." [11]

Today the prisoner clearly has the right to be heard. Leave to proceed in forma pauperis should be granted as a matter of course,[12] since a district court may not refuse to docket the case of an indigent.[13] A motion to dismiss the prisoner's cause for failure to state a claim upon which relief can be granted [14] should be judged by the same standard as any other complaint in federal court. The complaint may not be dismissed on the pleadings "unless it appears to a certainty that the plaintiff would not be entitled to recover under any state of facts which could be proved in support of his claim." [15] The Fifth Circuit is following this command faithfully. During one recent month, various panels overturned nine summary dismissals of prisoner's complaints by district courts. [16]

Granting the prisoner the right to be heard does not require that the proverbial floodgates of litigation be opened. First, some complaints require only minimal research and analysis to determine that they do not state a federal claim. For example, a prisoner alleging no more than the denial of a club charter to certain inmates from the Toastmasters International, Inc. (an organization seeking "to increase the speaking ability and self-confidence of its members by means of forensic competitions"), does not raise a federal question absent any allegation that the denial had a racial or otherwise constitutionally impermissible motivation. [17]

In other cases, denial of the motion to dismiss will not necessarily mean a full trial on the merits. If the prisoner is proceeding pro se, the court should ordinarily appoint counsel and require that the attorney arrange a prompt conference with his client. Both the state and the prisoner may then rely on the full range of liberal discovery available in the federal courts to explore in depth the facts underlying the petitioner's allegations. Often discovery may be completed through the submission of interrogatories and requests for admissions. After the completion of discovery, many cases can be resolved on motions for summary judgment or settled in pretrial conference.

At least two other potential obstacles, in addition to summary dismissal, have ceased to pose substantial difficulty for the prisoners' rights suit. Exhaustion of state judicial remedies, normally required before the federal court can entertain an application for habeas corpus, is not required in the §1983 suit. [18] Moreover, the Supreme Court has indicated that exhaustion of state administrative remedies will not be required. [19]

The second potential hurdle, the doctrine of abstention, may still occasionally prevent federal cognizance of the prisoners' claims. Although the complexity of abstention (Professor Charles Alan Wright discusses four separate strains [20]) and the variety of fact situations in these cases render general discussion inappropriate, the notion of prior state law interpretation will often pale in significance when civil rights of high national concern are at stake.[21] The conscientious advocate would nevertheless be well advised to be prepared to meet the abstention problem.

Judicial Limitations on Review and Relief

Far more troublesome for the district judge than these preliminary decisions on the procedural aspects of the prisoners' rights claims is the struggle with substantive standards determining judicial review. Judge Tuttle, former Chief Judge of the Fifth Circuit, has declared, "[I]f a prisoner is serving time to 'pay his debts to society,' any further restraints or deprivations in excess of that inherent in the sentence and in the normal structure of prison life should be subject to judicial scrutiny." [22] Implementation of this affirmative policy, however, is difficult.

Courts have been asked to venture into other areas of law, of course, without definitive precedent; yet rarely have judges been asked to make rulings on the entire array of constitutional rights that should be afforded a significant portion of our population on such an accelerated basis. Appellate court guidelines are infrequent, vague, and often inconsistent.

With the exception of the few widely celebrated cases in this area, the majority, I fear, will suffer two infirmities: inadequate discovery and lack of focus on the kind of *specific* relief that can be afforded consistent with sound legal theory and practical implementation. Adequate discovery should not be a problem for the resourceful lawyer; he will meet little impediment in the federal rules pertaining to discovery. Generally, the rules permit discovery of any matter that is relevant to the subject matter, relevancy not being restricted to evidence that is admissible at trial but including any matter "reasonably calculated to lead to the discovery of admissible evidence." [23] The only limitations on discovery are exclusion of matters that are privileged or part of the attorney's work product, restrictions on physical or mental examinations, and certain protective orders issued for good cause to prevent annoyance, embarrassment, oppression, or undue burden or expense. The wide discretion granted district judges in shaping the appropriate protective order should encourage counsel to develop imaginative approaches to their lawsuits.[24]

The second failure—the lack of focus on the kind of

specific relief that can be afforded consistent with sound legal theory and practical implementation—is the more serious. Developing a theory on the applicable standard of judicial review—whether First Amendment, Eighth Amendment, equal protection, or due process—is of little help unaccompanied by specific theories of relief. Indeed, it probably would be helpful if counsel would think first in terms of the specific request for relief, and second in terms of the constitutional theory on which to base the law suit.

My observations on the limitations of judicial relief are general and should not dampen a lawyer's inventiveness. First, courts are likely to be most receptive to narrow requests to prohibit specific prison administration practices that exceed a constitutional limitation, such as the Eighth Amendment ban on cruel and unusual punishment, or those that invade a constitutionally protected area, such as First Amendment freedoms or the fundamental personal interests entitled to protection under equal protection analysis. Secondly, courts are likely to be receptive but cautious when confronted with a request to impose certain Fourteenth Amendment due process requirements on the disciplinary actions of the prison administration. Finally, courts are likely to be least receptive to requests for relief that require continuing supervision or the promulgation of extensive regulations or programs.

My first observation—that courts are likely to be most receptive to narrow requests to prohibit certain prison administration practices that exceed a constitutional limitation should not be surprising. Courts can rely on existing law for a framework of analysis and narrow issue formulation. The most serious drawback is, of course, the disappointing development of the law of cruel and unusual punishment by the appellate courts.

Judicial restraint involving the Eighth Amendment is well documented. Prior to the recent Supreme Court's 5-to-4 vote on the death penalty,[25] only three kinds of punishment had been determined by the Court to be cruel and unusual: twelve years in chains at hard and painful labor; [26] expatriation; [27] and imprisonment for narcotics addiction.[28] Generally lower courts have also demonstrated reluctance to invoke the Eighth Amendment, using the same restraint in reviewing punishments imposed by prison officials as they would in considering punishments determined by courts and legislatures. For example, in *Sostre v. McGinnis,*[29] the Second Circuit overturned Judge Motley's determination that segregated confinement in excess of fifteen days constitutes cruel and unusual punishment. The majority apparently concluded that the punishment was "counterproductive as a correctional measure and personally abhorrent" but not sufficiently "barbarous" or "shocking to the conscience" to warrant Eighth Amendment invalidation.[30] As Professor Herman Schwartz has observed, the dissent by Judge Feinberg put the problem in perspective: "What is 'cruel and unusual' to one man may be acceptable to another." [31]

The Fifth Circuit has shown similar reluctance in the Eighth Amendment area. In *Novak v. Beto*,[32] a majority, "deeply troubled" over the lightless cell, limited bedding, and minimal food provided the prisoner in solitary confinement did not find the conditions cruel and unusual. In *Anderson v. Nosser*,[33] the court, sitting in an en banc rehearing, decided that the treatment afforded certain pretrial detainees who had been arrested and imprisoned under conditions that included being stripped naked and force-fed laxatives constituted a denial of due process but did not constitute cruel and unusual punishment. Leading the dissenters in both cases was Judge Tuttle. Urging his brethren to take a short step in the development of the law of cruel and unusual punishment, he stated, "I do not hesitate to assert the proposition that the only way the law has progressed from the days of the rack, the screw and the wheel is the development of moral concepts. . . ." [34] With all respect for the able and cautious analysis of the majority, I am persuaded that Judge Tuttle's call should be heeded.

To the extent that judicial forbearance is founded on the notion, often unarticulated, that courts should defer to legislative guidance in the determination of what punishment is consonant with prevailing public attitudes and what punishment is cruel and unusual, I submit that this forbearance is inappropriate in the area of punishment assessed by prison officials. Many kinds of prison punishments are not expressly authorized by the legislature but are assessed pursuant to the prison administration's general delegation of authority. To contend that the "standards of decency" [35] of prison officials' activity have the same chance of evolution inside the prison walls as they do in the halls of the legislature is unrealistic. Theoretically, at least, the legislature is sensitive to the prevailing mores of the people and is well suited to the task of deciding when punishment offends human dignity. This argument loses all potency, however, when applied to the prison administrator's discretion to design the intensity and duration of punishment, limited only by his imagination and innate sense of decency.

It is hard to believe that any state legislature today would draft a statute providing that punishment include the conditions that the prisoner be confined in a dimly lighted or totally dark cell, provided one blanket, no clothes, no mattresses, sheets, pillows, no hot water, and only bread and water to eat.[36] Unfortunately, deference to legislative guidance for this determination —or the euphemism "evolving standards of decency"—has authorized this kind of punishment even in the absence of actual legislative imprimatur.

Even in those situations where the prisoner is subjected to discipline pursuant to an express legislative authorization—for example, many states have statutes permitting solitary confinement—the statutory grant is usually so broad as to impose no limits on the duration or intensity of the punishment. Although I find it plausible that a modern legislature might enact a statute allowing the prison authorities to confine a prisoner in solitary status for a limited period of time for severe disciplinary infractions, I find it inconceivable that the state's lawmaking body would authorize such treatment indefinitely, possibly for the entire length of sentence if a prison official so chooses.

My thesis, then, is that when prisoners challenge under the Eighth Amendment either (1) punishment initiated by the prison administration that is not expressly authorized by the legislature, or (2) punishment expressly authorized by the legislature but vague as to duration and intensity, the complaint should trigger a closer judicial scrutiny of the punishment than would normally be justified.

I am not unaware of other grounds for judicial uneasiness with the open-ended cruel and unusual punishment clause. The recent Supreme Court decision of *Furman v. Georgia*,[37] however, should provide some guidelines on formulation of a standard for its application. Justice Brennan, for example, suggests four: (1) punishment must not be so severe as to be degrading to the dignity of human beings; (2) the state must not arbitrarily inflict a severe punishment; (3) a severe punishment must not be unacceptable to contemporary society; and (4) a severe punishment must not be excessive.

When challenges are grounded in the First Amendment or in the fundamental personal interest category of equal protection analysis, judges may rely on more finely-honed judicial standards. Courts have heard First Amendment challenges in the area of freedom from censorship of reading material and correspondence, freedom of religion, and right to political expression and organization. Overlapping these First Amendment contentions are the claims in the area of personal fundamental interests. Challenges in this area include attacks on racial segregation, requests for more liberal visitation rights and conjugal visitation, and complaints regarding restricted access to the courts and legal materials.[38]

When the state infringes on a personal fundamental right, the burden ordinarily rests on the state to show a compelling state interest for the restriction.[39] Although the list of fundamental personal interests of prisoners will vary from that of the population at large, and although the compelling state interest may include the legitimate goals of sentencing rather than others that are analyzed with some frequency in non-prisoner areas, I think that the frame of reference is a useful one for the courts.[40]

I remarked earlier that courts are likely to be receptive but cautious when confronted with a request to impose Fourteenth Amendment due process requirements on the disciplinary actions of the prison administration. The most prominent example of this reluctance is the Second Circuit's rejection of the district court's decision in *Sostre v. McGinnis*.[41] The lower court had held that the imposition of serious disciplinary action required written charges, counsel or counsel-substitute, confrontation and cross-examination, an impartial tribunal, and a reasoned opinion. The court of appeals, in reversing the decision, held that due process required only notice of the charges, a reasonable investigation, and the opportunity to respond.[42]

I share the view that ordinarily the personal stake of the plaintiff in his liberty or property must be substantial before he can state a federal question under the due process clause, and I would therefore limit the claims in the prisoners' rights area to those of a serious deprivation. Nevertheless, I think that the judicial reluctance to delineate the specific minimal elements of due process that the prison administration must provide is unfortunate.[43]

William Bennett Turner suggests two administrative decisions that constitute serious deprivations entitling the prisoner to due process: (1) decisions transferring the inmate from the general prison population to maximum security, punitive segregation, or solitary confinement; and (2) decisions resulting in forfeiture or withholding of "good time." [44] I would require specific due process protections before such punishments could be imposed.

My final observation is that courts are likely to be least receptive to requests for relief that require continuing supervision of the prison system or the promulgation of extensive regulations or programs. Judicial experience here is limited. The mixed verdict on the courts' handling of the desegregation of the public schools will make the judiciary hesitant to undertake extensive affirmative relief in other areas. Moreover, courts will not be eager to assume additional jurisdiction for the initial review of another branch of cases. Although my conclusions at this point are tentative, I think that there is some utility in placing the initial burden of review or the burden of proposing programs and regulations on the appropriate state agency. For example, in *United States v. Texas,*[45] a suit initiated by the government to eliminate a number of the vestiges of segregation in the public schools, I placed the initial enforcement burden on the Texas Education Agency. That agency, pursuant to definite procedures, is now obligated to withhold funds and accreditation from school districts that fail to meet the constitutional requirements announced by the Supreme Court.

These observations on the limitations of relief anticipate consideration by the federal judiciary in the common law tradition of case-by-case decision. This approach necessarily avoids the underlying fundamental issue, that is, whether prisons as we know them today should continue or whether they should be replaced with other alternatives more consistent with the legitimate goals of sentencing. These aims are most often defined as protection of the public, deterrence, and rehabilitation. They must, however, be expanded to include the ideals of a civilized society—that we treat our fellow citizens, even those who have deviated from the norm, with some dignity and compassion.

Much of the literature of other disciplines, including sociology, psychology, and psychiatry, indicates that prisons should give way to other alternatives. Ideally these other disciplines are better suited to tackling this fundamental issue than are the courts. Yet the federal judiciary convenes to decide the hard cases as well as the routine; we would do less than our constitutional duty were we to refrain from a task that—although measured case-by-case, in sometimes faltering steps—nevertheless demands our decision.

Footnotes

[1] 28 U.S.C. §2254 (1971).

[2] 28 U.S.C. §2255 (1971).

[3] C. Wright, Law of Federal Courts, at 217 (1970).

[4] Friendly, "Is Innocence Irrevelant? Collateral Attack on Criminal Judgments," 38 U. Chi. L. Rev. 142 (1971).

[5] 372 U.S. 293 (1963).

[6] 28 U.S.C. §2254(d) (1971).

[7] 397 U.S. 759 (1970) (defendant who pleads guilty with the advice of competent counsel cannot attack his conviction collaterally if he alleges no more than that he decided to plead guilty because of a prior coerced confession).

[8] Annual Report of the Director of the Administrative Office of the United States Courts 1971, at 135 (1972).

[9] The prisoners' rights applications filed with one district judge in New York rose from 21 in 1966 to 585 in 1971. Wall Street Journal, Oct. 10, 1972, at 1, col. 1.

[10] E.g. Banning v. Looney, 213 F.2d 771 (10th Cir. 1954).

[11] Ruffin v. Commonwealth, 62 Va. 790, 796 (1871).

[12] See Cruz v. Hauck, 404 U.S. 59, 64 (1971).

[13] Campbell v. Beto, 460 F.2d 765 (5th Cir. 1972).

[14] Fed. R. Civ. P. 12(b)(6).

[15] Conley v. Gibson, 355 U.S. 41, 78 (1957); see Campbell v. Beto, 460 F.2d 765 (5th Cir. 1972).

[16] Bowman v. Hale, 464 F.2d 1032 (5th Cir. 1972); Brown v. Wainwright, 464 F.2d 1034 (5th Cir. 1972); Burroughs v. Wainwright, 464 F.2d 1027 (5th Cir. 1972); Dennson v. Tomkins, 464 F.2d 1033 (5th Cir. 1972); Hugenot v. Wainwright, 464 F.2d 1077 (5th Cir. 1972); McCray v. Fondre, — F.2d —(5th Cir. 1972); Gardner v. Thompkins, 464 F.2d 1031 (5th Cir. 1972); Richards v. Smith, 464 F.2d 1029 (5th Cir. 1972); Simon v. Wainwright, 464 F.2d 1038 (5th Cir. 1972).

[17] Fallis v. Toastmasters International, Inc., 467 F.2d 1389 (5th Cir. 1972); see also Tarlton v. Henderson, 467 F.2d 200 (5th Cir. 1972).

[18] Houghton v. Shafer, 392 U.S. 639 (1968); Monroe v. Pape, 365 U.S. 167 (1961).

[19] Wilwording v. Swenson, 404 U.S. 249 (1971).

[20] See generally, Wright, note 3, supra, at 196–208.

[21] See Wright v. McMann, 387 F.2d 519, 524–525 (2d Cir. 1967).

[22] Jackson v. Godwin, 400 F.2d 529, 535 (5th Cir. 1968).

23 Fed. R. Civ. P. 26(b)(1).

24 See generally Fed. R. Civ. P. 16, 26–37. E.g. Morales v. Turman, 326 F. Supp. 677 (E.D. Tex. 1972) (discovery order in right-to-treatment phase of juvenile detention case permitting four experts, trained in sociology and psychology, to live in the institution for four weeks under conditions experienced by the inmates and to report to the court at conclusion of study).

25 Furman v. Georgia, 408 U.S. 238 (1972).

26 Weems v. United States, 217 U.S. 349 (1910).

27 Trop v. Dulles, 356 U.S. 86 (1958).

28 Robinson v. California, 370 U.S. 660 (1962).

29 442 F.2d 178 (2d Cir. 1971).

30 For another view from the Second Circuit, see LaReau v. MacDougall, — F.2d — (2d Cir. December 15, 1972).

31 Schwartz, "A Comment on Sostre v. McGinnis," 21 Buff. L. Rev. 775, 784 (1972).

32 453 F.2d 661 (5th Cir. 1971).

33 438 F.2d 183 (5th Cir. 1971), aff'd in part, rev'd in part, remanded for further proceedings 456 F.2d 835 (1972).

34 Novak v. Beto, note 32, supra, at 672 (5th Cir. 1971).

35 Trop v. Dulles, 356 U.S. 86 (1957).

36 Novak v. Beto, note 32, supra, at 673–674.

37 408 U.S. 238, 257–306 (1972) (Brennan, J., concurring).

38 See the collection of cases and discussion in Turner, "Establishing the Rule of Law in Prisons: A Manual for Prisoners' Rights Litigation," 23 Stan. L. Rev. 473 (1971).

39 For a recent Supreme Court explanation of fundamental personal rights and equal protection analysis see Weber v. Aetna Casualty & Surety Company, 406 U.S. 164 (1972).

40 But see Morales v. Schmidt, 12 Crim. L. Rep. 2378, — F.2d — (7th Cir. 1973), rev'g 340 F. Supp. 544 (W.D. Wis. 1972). In reversing Judge Doyle, the Seventh Circuit concluded, inter alia, that rational relationship rather than compelling state interest is the acceptable equal protection test. As Judge Doyle points out, however, rational relationship as a standard of protection in the prison environment would appear to be no protection at all.

41 442 F.2d 178 (2d Cir. 1971), rev'g 312 F. Supp. 863 (S.D.N.Y. 1970).

42 In an area unrelated to prison discipline but presenting similar policy considerations—the rights of an untenured state-employed school teacher to procedural due process prior to termination of his contract—the Supreme Court has indicated that the number of due process applicants gaining entry to the federal forum will be limited. Board of Regents v. Roth, 408 U.S. 564 (1972); Perry v. Sindermann, 408 U.S. 593 (1972).

43 Cf. Morrissey v. Brewer, 408 U.S. 471 (1972) (prescribing in detail the minimum procedural safeguards required by due process when a state seeks to revoke parole.)

[44] Turner, note 38, supra.

[45] 321 F. Supp. 1043 (E.D. Tex. 1970), 330 F. Supp. 235 (1971), aff'd with modifications 447 F.2d 441 (5th Cir. 1971), stay denied 404 U.S. 1206 (Black, J), cert. denied 404 U.S. 1016 (1972). See also United States v. Texas, 342 F. Supp. 24 (E.D. Tex. 1971) (comprehensive educational plan for children from bilingual culture), aff'd 466 F.2d 518 (5th Cir. 1972), discussed in "Project Report: DeJure Segregation of Chicanos in Texas Schools," 7 Harv. Civ. Rights-Civ. Lib. L. Rev. 307, 376–391 (1972).

CHAPTER 23
PRISONERS AND REFORM

EDITORS' INTRODUCTION

The Fortune Society is a well-known and well-respected group that many ex-convicts turn to upon release from prison. It is an organization made up of and staffed almost totally by ex-convicts. Its purpose is to help the released prisoner in all phases of readjustment to society. This article discusses ways of bringing the community and the prisoner together towards this and other ends.

ORGANIZING TO HELP THE EX-OFFENDERS

DAVID ROTHENBERG *

Society has abruptly become aware of the problems facing the released convict. The man or woman coming out of prison is no longer part of an invisible society. We have finally come to realize that if we are concerned about reducing crime in our cities, we must begin to notice the released prisoner. In this new recognition there is a great tendency to obscure the real nature of the problems facing released offenders. Many state, city, and private agencies, with much concern, are establishing programs and plans. Unfortunately, they often have more to do with the backgrounds of their organizers than with the man or woman coming out of prison.

Last year I sat in on a meeting with members of the Chamber of Commerce. These successful business leaders from the State of New Jersey had gathered at the terrible state prison in Trenton. They had a tour of the industry, were prepared a palatable dinner—served by plantation-attired slave-inmates—and then gathered in the warden's conference room to discuss the problems of men returning to the streets.

It was an outstanding exchange of irrelevancies. Warden U. Samuel Vukcovich and I sat in stunned silence. One gentleman talked about insurance and hospital plans for the family when a man was released. Certainly from his split-level suburban existence this makes good and reasonable sense, but it is not what the man in the jail cell needs for his immediate future.

The warden and I haven't found ourselves in agreement on many penological issues, but as we tuned in to the businessmen we shared one realization: the solutions offered by these community leaders had little to do with the problems of convicts. It was clear to me that these men, all of them successful in business, were applying their values and their world to another group of men, most of whom had never made it in our system.

It is probably incumbent upon me, after offering this criti-

---

* Founder and Executive Director of The Fortune Society, New York City.

cism, to list what released prisoners do need. However, if it were that simple, the list would have been made available long ago and posted on church doors everywhere. At Fortune Society we meet hundreds of newly released prisoners each week. They range from men released after serving a week in the city jail to the man who came to us after serving thirty-four years and eight months. Their ability to perform in our society also covers a broad spectrum. There are ex-cons who hit the city and fall back into place with uncanny ease. There are also men and women unable to make basic decisions about survival outside.

There are people who do not know how to ride the subways, get on a bus, order a meal from a menu, put on a television set, dial a phone. They must slowly learn how to function, and this with Parole pressuring them to find a job and with the necessities of economic survival dictating their pursuit of alien patterns. They are confronted by housing, welfare, educational, and vocational choices that stagger their senses and terrify them at every turn.

These problems of readjustment exist no matter what crime caused the prisoner to be incarcerated. Civilians who meet with or work with released prisoners are usually preoccupied with the crime of the individual, due to their simplistic belief that if they knew the crime that sent the person away, this would guide them in their relationship. It is obviously necessary to know if the released prisoner was addictive, either to drugs or alcohol or gambling, or had a sexual hang-up, and to learn if the habit was maintained during incarceration. However, all men released from prison must be aided in their de-institutionalization, no matter what they once did. Their crime has been obscured by the prison time machine.

The overwhelming effect of the prison experience—infantile regimentation, a manipulative atmosphere, daily dehumanization and reinforcement of self-negation—takes its toll of men and women. In prison the reason for a person's incarceration is rarely confronted. The need to survive in prison subculture nurtures habits and behavior which all prisoners must learn to overcome if they are to survive outside the walls.

To help ex-offenders accomplish this, there must be immediate short-range programs as well as long-range planning. Obviously the long-range goals must embrace the notion that our criminal justice system has to be restructured. Men and women who have committed illegal acts against society (and the sacrificial lambs selected by economics and race who are imprisoned) must not become more alien while in the state's custody. A society that imprisons as ours does must question its entire moral fibre. Only by providing alternatives to our failing criminal justice system can we indicate some reexamination of the larger structure.

The more urgent and visible issue, however, is what happens to the man or woman being released from prison today and tomorrow. In this self-defeating, dungeon-dynasty, crime-prison-crime cycle, the prisoner who comes to some sort of self-understanding, growth, or maturity does so in spite of, not because of, the prison system, often at great pain and with great bitterness.

The rigidity of prison officials and the acquiescence of politicians, media representatives and, in turn, the public must first be softened. All censorship of literature and mail must be ended. Thousands of prisoners are totally isolated from the world to which they will return. Our prisons are filled with men and women, graduates of orphanages, foster homes, and homes in which they were unloved or unwanted children. It was the fact that they had no one to speak for them as youths that caused incarceration rather than probation. There must be conscoius attempts, belated as they might be, to reach the isolated and the alienated.

Mail is one step. The second, of course, is the appearance of outside people in the prisons. Not the antiseptic, prison-official tour highlighted by "Don't talk to the prisoners," nor long, boring lectures by prison officials. What is needed is continual, daily interaction between community people and prisoners. At the Bucks County Jail in Doylestown, Pennsylvania, a hundred and fifty citizens visit the jail each week. They come for bridge tournaments, chess games, Great Books seminars, rap sessions, drama workshops, prison councils (consisting of two inmates, two correction officers, and two civilians), job counselling meetings, current affairs discussions, etc.

These meetings do not undo the negativity of prison, nor do they bring into focus the real issue—the failure of the system. In the interim, they slow down the alienation of members of society, usually perceived by the prisoner as all those people who don't care, who neglect, negate, and deny him or her.

The influx of concerned people (who must insist that they be permitted in) will bring about several changes. As stated, it will keep the prisoner in touch with the outside world. It will also create a dedicated and informed constituency for meaningful penological change, since no one can enter the prison system, if only for a day, without becoming acquainted with its antiquity and waste. It would also keep the spotlight on correction people, whose abuses have long gone unchallenged, and no longer allow them to be unaccountable. The same people going in to the prisons could serve as a bridge at the time of release of prisoners, because they are known and familiar to the released offender. Thus, the regular presence of outsiders could lessen numerous barriers in the prison.

Who are these civilians who will be going in? Obviously they should represent all aspects of life. Having observed many community groups starting to get involved in prisons, it is my opinion that they should meet with established ex-con groups before they enter, and that the ex-cons should go in with them. There are many pitfalls in these meetings, usually provoked by civilians who attempt to fulfill their own needs rather than serve the problem. Certainly, individual gratification is essential, but only as it serves the problem, not at its expense.

I go into a state prison each Saturday morning at Rahway, New Jersey as coordinator of a two-hour current affairs class. I gain great satisfaction from it, but often I become overwhelmingly depressed. The gratification comes from seeing men's potential tapped, their curiosity aroused by a discussion, their recognition of their own potential awakened, and the realization of their intelligence fostered. The depression comes from wondering what a man with a forty- or fifty-year sentence does as he comes to understand his own manhood and his own sense of worth. My temptation is not to come back, to say that all is for naught, because why should this man be encouraged to believe in himself only to be subjected to more daily torture at the hands of the state.

One of the prisoners, a lifer, told me that my sense of gratification and depression, while not to be ignored, cannot be the issue of that classroom. Rather, it must be how the concerted, united effort of an enlightened group of student prisoners and a provoked citizenry can enable structural change to come about.

A few years ago someone called prison reform "the last frontier of social change." Prison reform is no longer what is needed. The idea of reforming prisons has become an anachronism at the same time it became vogue. The system, quite simply, does not work and it never has. The area of reform must be utilized for temporary conditions but not implemented to cement and legitimize the system. We can work at the long and short of it, simultaneously, if we are actively conscious of the needs and goals. An army of participants must be solicited. There is work to be done.

EDITORS' INTRODUCTION

Inmate self-government is usually viewed as a means of improving communications between the administration and the prisoners, where the prisoners "advise" the superintendent of their complaints and needs and suggested solutions. Some inmate councils have more power and are more representative of the general population's needs than others. However, none is viewed as a vehicle for complete prison reform.

The authors of this article present a convincing case for inmate self-government as a vehicle for complete prison reform. They trace four experiments in history in which inmates shared successfully in the actual decision-making and management of the prison with favorable impact on the rehabilitation of the prisoners.

Mr. Murton ran one of the successful experiments himself. He fails to disclose in this article why he was terminated as superintendent of Arkansas' notorious Tucker Prison Farm. Mr. Murton had uncovered a number of bodies of murdered prisoners on the grounds, and when he led a forceful investigation of the murders, he was fired.

SHARED DECISION-MAKING IN PRISON MANAGEMENT : A SURVEY OF DEMONSTRATIONS INVOLVING THE INMATE IN PARTICIPATORY GOVERNMENT

TOM MURTON *
PHYLLIS JO BAUNACH **

The "reformers" have been busy at the task of attempting to correct criminal behavior in a series of quaint models almost since the inception of the American prison. The Quakers bequeathed to us the legacy of corrections through religion. Some may have been converted but many also went insane.

The work ethic replaced religion in New York prisons. It gave rise to the industrial prison but did little to change the convict.

The reformers then gave us the reformatory wherein change was to be accomplished by education and vocational training. The criminals *did* become more educated but no less criminal.

Since World War II there has been a profusion of different kinds of institutional settings. We have seen forestry camps, halfway houses, reception and diagnostic centers, prerelease centers and, more recently, the current fad: community correctional centers. While the physical settings differ among these institutions, the treatment model does not.

The current model envisions a staff of treaters who attempt in some mysterious way to treat the criminal. The theory presumes

* Professor, Criminal Justice Studies, University of Minnesota; President, Murton Foundation for Criminal Justice, Inc.; Ed. and Pub., The Freeworld Times; former Superintendent, Tucker Prison Farm, Arkansas; D. Crim.

** Research Assistant and Ph.D. candidate, Department of Criminal Justice Studies, University of Minnesota; A.B. University of Rochester.

that the inmate is sick and that a nebulous cure called "rehabilitation" can be injected into the criminal as a cure for crime.

The various reform efforts have several things in common: they seek more money to hire more people to do more things to more inmates; they are founded on notions which are not based upon empirical evidence but rather on articles of faith; and they have uniformly failed to achieve the stated objective of reduced criminality.

With rare exceptions, all reform efforts have taken place with the assumption that the basic prison model is supportive. The medical treatment model has been grafted onto the prison dictatorship with the expectation that it will blossom.

In the bleak field of penology, there have been a few glimmers of hope. An occasional heretic has emerged to light a candle, briefly illuminating a possible pathway out of the abyss of traditionalism. There are several classic examples of efforts to involve the inmate in the decision-making process and thereby in self-determination.

Excluded from consideration are those prisons where inmates exercise illegitimate power to exploit their fellow inmates. The inmate guard systems in Arkansas, Mississippi and Louisiana are such examples.

Also excluded from discussion is the omnipresent inmate advisory council, which is proudly displayed by the warden as an example of "involvement" of the inmate in his destiny. Since these councils do not perform any decision-making functions, they are impotent. Such councils hold meetings, write proposals for change and make recommendations, but they cannot implement the desired change.

A classic example of the foregoing is the Resident Governmental Council (RGC) of the Washington State Penitentiary at Walla Walla. It has been in existence since December of 1970, yet, two years later, neither the warden nor the inmates were able to cite a single decision that had been made by the RGC.

In contrast, four case studies have been selected which demonstrate historical efforts to involve the inmate in prison management.

Alexander Maconochie (1787–1860)

Norfolk Island was established as a penal colony in 1788. A long succession of commandants (including the notorious Captain

William Bligh) supervised the colony in varying degrees of harshness until its abandonment in 1814. Ten years later, the colony was reestablished for the worst offenders in the colonial penal system. "[T]he felon who is sent there is forever excluded from all hope of return." [1]

Captain Alexander Maconochie of the British Royal Navy departed London in 1836 to serve as private secretary to Sir John Franklin who had just been appointed Lieutenant Governor of Van Diemen's Land (Tasmania) off the southern coast of Australia. Prior to leaving, Maconochie had been commissioned by the London Society for the Improvement of Prison Discipline to investigate the convict system in those colonies.

His report to the society and his subsequent writings, speeches and commentaries reflect his then-radical departure from accepted principles of penology.

> "The essential and obvious error in this system, is its total neglect of *moral* reasoning and influence, and its exclusive reliance, in every relation of life, on mere *physical* coercion.
>
> "I am inclined to question the *right* which society has assumed to itself of framing its laws so as intentionally to punish its erring members in reference, not to themselves, or to the abstract quality of their own crimes, but to the impression that may be so made on others.
>
> "This appears to me a sacrifice of their rights and interests to ours, which would be very difficult to reconcile with any abstract Christian principle; *for we may not do evil even that good may come; and in truth, so little real good ever does come from our attempting to seek it through evil, that we may almost draw an inference from this against the fact of our deriving any material advantage from acting on a principle, manifestly unjust in its very basis.* [Emphasis added.]" [2]

The theories Maconochie espoused gained some acceptance in London, and in 1839 he was offered the superintendency of Norfolk Island. Although it was not suited to implementation of his plan for resocialization of the convict because of its remoteness, he accepted the position and landed on the island in March of 1840 to assume his duties. The principle which was to guide his innovations is probably best summarized in Maconochie's own words:

> ". . . The first object of prison discipline should be to reform prisoners and thus prepare them to separate [from prison] with advantage both to themselves and to society after their discharge." [3]

The essence of Maconochie's "social management" theory was the "mark system" whereby the convict could make restitution for his crime by paying off his "debt" to society by earning marks through daily work. When he had accumulated a sufficient number, the convict was released on parole.

Maconochie rejected the arbitrary, punitive, and debasing nature of the traditional prison. "Man is a social being; his duties are social; and only in society, as I think, can he be trained for it." [4]

> "It is very interesting also to see social impulses strictly reciprocal, action and reaction equal, and the oppressor injured, both in character and in circumstances, by the result of his oppression.

> "It shews enlightened benevolence to be true practical wisdom, and cruelty or indifference to be folly as well as crime. The justice administered may be called poetical; but its sphere is amid the most ordinary realities of social life." [5]

In retrospect it would appear that Maconochie had a specific strategy to bring into existence his reform system. His first efforts were addressed toward restoring some self-concept of dignity to the convicts.

He provided markers for the graves of deceased convicts whereas previously only the graves of freemen were entitled to headstones. He allowed inmates to keep their earnings in their possession.

> "Those among the men who by any means accumulated money I used to encourage to keep it themselves, for I wished to extend the presence of temptation, and the practice of resisting it, in the body, and it was extraordinary how few losses were thus ever sustained; but on

extraordinary occasions, when men were near the period of their final departure, I would receive their little hoards, and give them orders on Sydney for their amount, that they might be sure to retain and receive them when they would be most useful to them." [6]

Maconochie was taking into consideration both the impact of self-concept and the development of trust between the administration and the inmates. The significance of this act can easily be overlooked. The essence of developing responsibility is creating experiences wherein the exercise is made meaningful because the inmate has the opportunity to *fail*. Thus success is real and self-reinforcing.

Maconochie took other steps to develop trust between the inmates and himself. He made himself readily available to the inmates by walking and riding among them almost daily and encouraging all to approach him with their problems.

He opened the courts to inmate attendance, and, in cases of great import, actually held court in the prison yard. Although, because of legal restrictions, he was not able fully to implement his plan to utilize inmate jurors, he did seek and consider inmate testimony and advice in matters before his court. He appointed inmates as defense counsel for the less sophisticated inmates with orders to provide the best possible defense and prohibitions against revealing to Maconochie any confidence. Maconochie would then wait twenty-four hours to allow time for reflection upon his decision.

Maconochie used trust as a basis for leading to responsibility. He chose trusted inmates from the population and placed them outside the prison camp in the Bush where they lived, worked and played together under the supervision of an inmate overseer.

"This distribution of men necessitated a greater employment of prisoner overseers and sub-overseers, and I was otherwise most favorable to this. In conducting a coercive system it often leads to tyranny and abuse, but in a reforming one it is most beneficial. It encourages the best men, increases their influence with others, and makes these aspire to similar trusts. The very possession of such trust is also a reformatory agent. I saw many instances of originally very indifferent men, thus, and thus almost alone, rendered trustworthy." [7]

The self-fulfilling prophecy of negative labeling is a reality. It could be argued that positive labeling might also lead to self-fulfillment. That is, granting an inmate trust through responsibility may in fact encourage him to attempt to live up to that trust and demonstrate responsibility.

Maconochie had the inmates assign themselves to small groups of six men and held them mutually responsible for each other until they had earned a cumulative total of 12,000 marks for the group. As Maconochie stated, "Superiors may be partial or deceived, but not equals." [8] It was assumed that through common earnings and common forfeiture peer pressure would tend to reinforce desired behavior.

According to Maconochie, there was considerable resistance to the plan among the inmates because it provided for the punishment of the innocent along with the guilty. He later modified the plan to allow for changes in the group composition. Whatever were the shortcomings of this method, these minimum-custody camps served as one of the prerelease stages in his plan to ease the transition from the prison to the free community.

Maconochie even appointed an inmate police force, which worked under the supervision of two free officers. They patrolled the island day and night and provided general law enforcement functions. This unusual delegation of power to inmates apparently was successful.

"I was four years in charge of Norfolk Island, with from 1500 to 2000 prisoners on it . . . (but) . . . I never had more than 160 soldiers and I never once called on (them) for other than routine duty. I had only five inferior free officers . . . instead of from forty to fifty who have since been attached to it. And my Police (force) was composed of men selected by me from the general body of prisoners, furnished only with short staves—instead of a large free and probationer force armed with cutlasses, and in some cases pistols, that has since been maintained.

"If, then, with this inferior physical force I was able to preserve perfect order, submission, and tranquility, it seems to me to follow incontestably—either that my measures were most singularly adapted to attain their end—or, as a general proposition, that restraints founded on self-interest, persuasion, exhortation, and other sources of moral influence, are in every case more stringent than those of brute force, even in dealing with the worst of men." [9]

In addition to the personal relations he developed with the inmates, Maconochie attempted to implement other portions of his master plan of 1840. He built a Roman Catholic and a Protestant church, obtained funds to hire churchmen, and conducted services himself in the Bush camps.

Each congregation was encouraged to form a band and a choir. The ministry was even extended to the jail, consisting of twelve separate cells. In the roof of each was a sliding panel to provide the inmate with the option of leaving it open to hear religious readings from the room above, or of closing it.

To deal with training, Maconochie established schools to provide basic educational instruction for the inmates. Since each man was to be released to the agricultural community of New South Wales, the principal training was in agriculture. Each convict on the island was given a plot of ground to raise a garden. Those men in the Bush camps had larger plots of ground and were allowed to raise produce for sale to the staff.

"I thus sought to distribute property among them, and from its possession acquire a sense and value for its rights; and the success of this policy was even extraordinary, petty theft becoming among the most unpopular of all offenses." [10]

The result of mutual trust and a chance to demonstrate responsibility was that, in fact, the inmates as a group *did* act responsibly, in prison and subsequently upon release. One example is cited by Maconochie wherein several inmates secured the release from prison of another inmate convicted of assault upon a convict. They were so sure of his reformation that they posted a bond in marks to be forfeited should he commit further crimes after release. One of the inmates posting security for his release was the victim.

Probably the most dramatic proof of the validity of Maconochie's system of trust occurred only ninety days after his appointment. One of Maconochie's biographers describes a most extraordinary celebration of the Queen's birthday at Norfolk:

"Never was Norfolk Island so gay, or its inhabitants so joyful as on the 25 May 1840. A proclamation had been issued by Maconochie, describing the pleasures and festivities he contemplated. On this occasion he resolved to forget the distinction between good and bad (inmates), and to make no exception from the general indulgence; but he entreated the men to remember that on the success of this experiment this confidence would greatly depend; he warned them to suppress the first tokens of disorder, and by retiring to their quarters at the sound of the bugle, prove that they might be trusted with safety.

"On the morning of the day, the signal colours floated from the staff, crowned with the union jack; twenty one guns, collected from the vessels and from the government house, were mounted on the top of a hill, and fired a royal salute.

"The gates were thrown open, and eighteen hundred prisoners were set free, and joined in various amusements, of which Captain Maconochie was a frequent spectator. Eighteen hundred prisoners sat down to dinner and at its close, having received each a small quantity of spirits with water, they drank health to the Queen and Maconochie—three times three for Victoria and the captain rent the air.

"They then renewed their sports, or attended a theatrical performance. New scenery, dresses, music and songs contributed to the hilarity of the party. . . .

"At the termination, no accident had occurred; the goal was completely unoccupied; no theft or disorder had disgraced the day; and thus the notion of Maconochie seemed to be illustrated by the experiment." [11]

Of the 1,450 prisoners discharged under Maconochie's system, less than 3 per cent of them were ever reconvicted of a crime. Of 920 doubly convicted convicts, only 2 per cent are known to have been reconvicted.

During Maconochie's four-year tenure, there was only one killing, four escapes, and no uprisings. Even the Secretary of State for the Colonies attested to the value of Maconochie's system—in his letter ordering Maconochie's dismissal!

". . . I gladly acknowledge that his efforts appear to have been rewarded by the decline of crimes of violence and outrage, and by the growth of humane and kindly feelings in the minds of the persons under his charge." [12]

In reading the writings of Maconochie and his contemporaries, one is impressed with his philosophy, strategy and grasp of the dynamics which underscored his administration. It is clear that he understood the basic evil of the prison and set about with notions of humanity to rectify that evil.

The records attests to the fact that Maconochie's system was successful insofar as the inmate population and the reduction of crime were concerned. However, he "failed" to secure his continued tenure and was fired at the height of his experiment in February of 1844.

Maconochie's major impact on the penal colony is best summarized in his own words:

"I found the island a turbulent, brutal hell, and left it a peaceful, well-ordered community . . . the most complete security alike for person and property prevailed. Officers, women and children traversed the island everywhere without fear." [To which Judge Barry added, "All reliable evidence confirms his statement."] [13]

Thomas Mott Osborne (1859–1926)

On June 13, 1913, the Westchester County grand jury condemned Sing Sing Prison and recommended to the Governor of New York the construction of a new prison to replace it. Shortly thereafter, following a series of riots and fires, the warden of Sing Sing was forced to resign under charges of malfeasance. Governor Glynn offered the post to Thomas Mott Osborne, who initially declined.

Osborne, a prominent citizen of Auburn, New York, his lifelong home, was deeply concerned with the issues of prison reform. His career as Mayor of the City of Auburn and as Democratic leader of upstate New York acquainted him with the problems of crime and criminals. For fifteen years he had served as Chairman of the Board of Directors of the George Junior Republic, an institution for juvenile offenders in which the inmates participated in community organization to develop a sense of responsibility. Osborne's experience with the Junior Republic laid the groundwork for his later reforms.

In 1913, Governor William Sulzer appointed Osborne Chairman of the New York Prison Commission. He focused his investigations on the Auburn prison, interviewing staff and inmates and observing obvious shortcomings. Osborne subjected himself to one week of voluntary incarceration at the Auburn prison to ascertain for himself the nature of prison discipline. On Sunday, September 28, 1913, he informed 1,400 inmates assembled in the chapel of his plan. He realized that his perception of the prison would vary considerably from that of a regular inmate, but he sincerely believed the experience would be valuable in his understanding of the prison system:

> "I have the feeling that after I have really lived among you, marched in your lines, shared your food, gone to the same cells at night, and in the morning looked out at the piece of God's sunlight through the same iron bars—that then, and not until then, can I feel the knowledge which will break down the barriers between my soul and the soul of my brothers." [14]

Osborne's experience as a prisoner gained him the respect and trust of the inmates and later their cooperation in implementing his reforms.

Superintendent of Prisons John B. Riley would not accept Osborne's refusal and insisted that he come to Albany for an interview. In response, Osborne gathered a group of twenty-five of his best friends from among the inmates at Auburn prison and discussed the matter with them. After a day and a half of debate, the inmates voted 18 to 7 in favor of his accepting the position. At the same time, Osborne received word from a trusted inmate at Sing Sing that the inmates there had signed a petition endorsing Osborne's appointment.

Prior to his acceptance of the post, Osborne had an interview with the newly elected Governor Charles S. Whitman and was assured of his support. With the assurance of official support and confidence in the inmates' cooperation, Osborne finally accepted the position on November 19, 1914.

Osborne rejected contemporary theories of criminality, which postulated that crime was a disease or a function of physical or mental deficiencies. He accepted the disease theory only as a metaphor. Criminals were neither physically nor mentally ill, but spiritually ill:

". . . [i]ll of selfishness, of a peculiar form of civic egotism which causes [them] to be indifferent to the social rights of other men." [15]

He rejected the notion of a "criminal type" because he believed that environment and training as well as heredity influenced behavior. He argued, however, that there was a "prison type" commonly mistaken for the "criminal type." The lockstep, shaved heads and striped clothing were hideous signs of degradation used to break the prisoner's spirit and crush his individuality. The "prison type" was the final product of the prison system:

". . . [L]arge numbers of men, broken in health and spirit, white-faced with the 'prison pallor', husky in voice —hoarse from disuse, with restlessness, shifty eyes and the timidty of beaten dogs . . . are creatures whom we ourselves have fashioned." [16]

In an address before the National Prison Association in 1904, Osborne attacked the evils of the prison system and enunciated his principles for the true foundation of prison reform:

"First—The law must decree not punishment, but temporary exile from society until the offender has proven by his conduct that he is fit to return.

"Second—Society must brand no man a criminal, but aim solely to reform the mental conditions under which a criminal act has been committed.

"Third—The prison must be an institution where every inmate must have the largest practicable amount of freedom, because it is liberty alone that fits men for liberty!" [17]

Osborne's approach was "anti-institutional" [18] in that he freed the inmates from the inflexible, uniform discipline of the old prison system and stressed their active participation in their own reformation. He was firmly convinced that the inmates' permanent reformation would occur only if they were trusted to exercise meaningful decision-making powers in the institution. Thus his efforts as warden at Sing Sing were directed towards creating an atmosphere in which the inmates could develop a sense of responsibility through self-determination.

Osborne's first task as warden was the reorganization of the Brotherhood of the Golden Rule, an inmate council created by his predecessor.

Although the Brotherhood had an elaborate constitution and by-laws, it was a sham for two reasons. First, inmates had been granted privileges without earning them:

> "The rewards were given out before they had been earned; the privileges enjoyed without the responsibility which alone made the exercise of such privileges valuable . . . prisoners were not being exercised in the bearing of responsibility; they were being bribed to be good." [19]

The inmates played Sunday baseball and watched movies, but they had no power to make or enforce the rules. They passively followed the lead of the administration.

Secondly, the administration had imposed the council on the inmates. Since the inmates had not taken the initiative to form the council, they had no vested interest in it; the council belonged to the administration, not to the inmates:

> "If a plan of self-government was to work at all, it must be worked by them; and they would certainly work their plan better than they could some outside plan—no matter how perfect. . . . The only self-government that would be successful in prison was the self-government which the prisoners would bring about—their own self-government." [20]

Osborne reorganized the council around the principles of self-determination embodied in the Mutual Welfare League, which had evolved from his voluntary incarceration at Auburn. The League was simple. Every inmate was eligible for membership. Two delegates from each shop were elected by secret ballot every six months. The Board of Delegates selected an executive board, which in turn selected a clerk and Sergeant-At-Arms. League members received privileges in return for self-discipline and loyalty to the administration. Discipline was handled through a judiciary board; infractions of the rules resulted in suspension of League privileges.

On the evening of his first day in office, Osborne met with the executive committee of the Brotherhood and *asked them* to draft a plan for a judiciary board. The inmates' proposal suggested that the judiciary board examine all minor cases of discipline. Osborne responded by turning over *all* cases of discipline to the judiciary board with the right of appeal to the warden's court, consisting of the warden, principal keeper, and prison doctor.

In addition, Osborne granted fifteen specific requests to change the prison rules within a week after he had assumed office. In so doing, he extended meaningful decision-making powers to the inmates, assured of their continued support and encouraged by their initiative.

Inmates traditionally marched to and from work under the watchful eye of the armed guards. Three days after Christmas, Osborne announced to the workers of the knit shop, "the most turbulent shop in the prison," that henceforth they would march under their own elected delegates instead of armed guards.

> ". . . [T]he whole prison population watched the strange sight of the worst company in the prison coming in from work under the leadership of their two delegates, one marching in front, one in the rear of the company. And such marching was never seen in Sing Sing before." [21]

Pleased with their performance, the following day Osborne removed the guards from the shop and left only the civilian foreman and elected delegates in charge. Thereafter, the disciplinary problems in the knit shop were minimal:

> "There has never since that time been any serious trouble in handling the discipline of the knit shop; although under the old system they used to have as high as ten or twelve cases of punishment a day, and many serious and bloody assaults a day." [22]

Shortly thereafter, the inmates initiated the move to march the men from all the shops under elected delegates and to remove the guards from the mess hall:

> "As the noon whistle blew and the men came marching out of their shops there was not a prison guard in sight.

> The nearly 1600 men came swinging down the prison yard under their own elected delegates, all prisoners. And when they had turned into the mess hall . . . not a single guard was to be seen. The men were eating their noon day meal, all in one big room and not a single guard in sight, only the elected Sergeant-At-Arms and his assistants." [23]

Osborne eventually placed all the shops under the charge of the civilian workshops, "like any work shop outside." [24] The removal of the guards improved the morale of the inmates and extended the new responsibilities to the prison delegates.

In addition to developing a sense of responsibility, Osborne endeavored to develop a community spirit among the inmates. He encouraged the growth of a knitting class, a choral society, a band and an education unit.

The education unit, called the Mutual Welfare Institute, was initiated by an inmate who succeeded in securing an enrollment of 80 to 90 per cent of the inmates. Subject matter was limitless: if a prisoner could teach the desired subject to another who wished it, the class was authorized.

The students erected a special school building to house the overflow of classes. The school staff met regularly to discuss educational policy and methods. The staff enjoyed the privileges of serving the inmate community:

> "All employees of the Mutual Welfare Institute perform their duties in connection with work for the State in addition to the time we give to the school. We consider it an honor to be connected with the school, and welcome the privilege of being permitted to serve our fellow inmates in this way." [25]

Permanent standing committees supervised every aspect of life in the prison:

> ". . . sanitation, athletics, entertainment, dietary, kitchen, finances, ways and means, reception of visitors, religious services, reception of new prisoners, employment, fire company, prison grave yard, a bank, a parole board." [26]

Osborne laid the foundation for inmate compensation with a system of token coins, although he left the prison before it was firmly established. The plan was to convert the token money into real money donated by the public. Each inmate received nine dollars a week from which he was expected to pay for his cell, his food, and his clothing.

Before long the inmates petitioned for a bank:

> "The bank was chartered and soon in active operation. Money was drawn out and deposited when needed; the depositors supplied with pass books; men were taught the use of saving institutions and how to economize." [27]

By May 2, 1916, after seven months of operation, there were 1,030 depositors and total deposits of $31,424.41 or an average of $30.50 credited to each depositor.

The greatest impact of Osborne's reforms was on the inmates' attitudes towards themselves and the prison community:

> "Since the League started, these men find it easier to be law-abiding; they find their self-respect restored as their belief in their own essential manhood grows stronger; they feel responsible for the acts of the community as well as for their own individual acts." [28]

Some of the prisoners formed an outside branch of the Mutual Welfare League. They met once or twice a year to give Osborne a public dinner and relate their successes and failures. They even tried to involve New York City Police Chief Colonel Arthur Woods in helping ex-inmates readjust to the street.

During the three years prior to Osborne's administration in Sing Sing, the prison hospital treated an average of 373 wounds per 1,450 inmates. After Osborne took office, the prison population increased to 1,600, but the number of wounds treated dropped to 155.

An average of thirty-five inmates were committed to Dannemora State Hospital in each of the three years prior to Osborne's administration. Under Osborne's administration, only nineteen inmates were transferred to Dannemora.

Industrial production increased 21 per cent.

The record for escapes indicates that in the first thirteen months of his administration there were three escapes. In previous years there had been ten escapes in 1913; six in 1912; four in 1911; seventeen in 1910; and nineteen in 1909.[29] Some escapees returned voluntarily upon learning that their behavior had dishonored Osborne and the League.

Judge William H. Wadhams of the Court of General Sessions in New York City observed that he had not one recidivist from Sing Sing since the creation of the League.

Osborne's tenure was short-lived. On December 28, 1915 he was indicted by the Westchester County grand jury for perjury and neglect of duty. He took a leave of absence to prepare his case. The case never came to trial. Because of the questionable nature of the evidence upon which the case was based, the court dismissed the charges.

Osborne resumed his position as warden on July 16, 1916, but resigned three months later. His resignation stemmed from an order by the Superintendent of Prisons that long-term convicts were forbidden outside prison walls. Trusties working in the administration building would have to be dismissed. Osborne interpreted this as an effort to reduce the effectiveness of his programs, since Sing Sing was the only prison with administrative offices located outside the walls.

While Osborne correctly surmised that it would take many years to gain widespread acceptance for his true principles of inmate government, he nonetheless demonstrated for the world that if given the opportunity, inmates can govern themselves responsibly:

> "In Auburn Prison for more than two years, in Sing Sing Prison for more than a year the new system has been in operation and *the thing works.* The truth of that fact no reluctant and no stupid politician can argue out of existence. It is a rock which affords a solid foundation for the future of prison reform." [30]

Howard B. Gill (1889–   )

In 1923, a special legislative committee was appointed to study relocation of the Massachusetts prison at Charlestown. The selected site was a part of 1,170 acres set aside in 1912 for a dipsomaniac hospital located about twenty-five miles from Boston in the Norfolk Township. A group of buildings known as "The Oval" and about 1,000 acres of land were transferred to the Department of Corrections in 1927. Construction of a wall around

37 acres to enclose the proposed new institution began in August of 1927.

Howard B. Gill was graduated from the Harvard Business School and worked for ten years in industrial and commercial research. He became a private business consultant in 1924 and thereafter studied prison industries in federal and state systems. He later worked as purchasing agent for the U.S. Bureau of Prisons and was responsible for developing prison industries.

When offered the Norfolk superintendency by Commissioner Sanford Bates, Gill protested that he was not qualified because he had neither the training nor the experience to operate a prison. Bates informed Gill that that was the precise reason he had been chosen to develop the new institution.

On November 10th of 1927, Gill was appointed superintendent of the new facility and given a free hand in establishing a new prison community. Gill proposed the combination of a community-type physical plant with the maximum opportunity for the inmates to develop a sense of responsibility through inmate participation. In this endeavor, he was influenced by his personal contact with Thomas Mott Osborne in 1925.

Gill contrasted his philosophy of prison management with the prevalent one:

> "The attitude of most people toward prisons is that the warden should be a despot and that the inmates should be noted for their docility. Nothing could be farther from the philosophy of Norfolk or the philosophy of modern penology. . . . These men are here because they could not take this responsibility in a free community. We need to reverse the old principle of the bastille prisons, which was that every man should be treated like every other man. We are apt to confuse uniformity with equality."[31]

Gill's oft-quoted basic rules consisted solely of "no escapes; no contraband." He did not believe in the use of stool pigeons because he despised and distrusted them. He refused to adopt the traditional system of informers but listened to any prisoner who wanted sincerely to inform him about prison problems.

The essential difference between the two systems is that in the traditional one the inmate "snitches" on his fellow inmates to achieve some personal gain. This gain could be favors from the administration or revenge for a personal grievance. In the new prison community of which Gill spoke, the inmates and staff had common goals and, consequently, common responsibilities. Hence, information provided to the warden by inmates was not a manifestation of desires for direct personal gains but rather a demonstration of responsibility in support of common prison goals.

One observer commented:

"Suffice it to say that through the ramifications of the work and the spirit caught up in the granting of inmate responsibility, many an inmate had learned the rudiments of community living which opened his eyes to the duties of good citizenship in the community. What some of the men needed for their social adjustment was exactly this sense of responsibility, not from official pressure, but of their own volition." [32]

Gill's first reform was rejection of the traditional prison planned to be built at Norfolk. He was granted permission to design and build his "community prison."

Gill believed that the needs of the inmates must take precedence over institutional needs and that changes, to be effective, must involve the inmate body. When a flurry of escapes occurred or construction work faltered, Gill called on inmate leaders (as well as staff) to help him solve such problems.

His criteria for staff selection were that the candidates must be "close to the earth, humane and willing to learn." Ultimately, he set two criteria for prison personnel: (1) like a shaggy dog (care for others); and (2) make something out of nothing (be innovative and creative).

He established an open press policy as "public institutions publicly administered." Casework was vested in social workers who were hired to supplement the traditional guards. The staff was dichotomized deliberately; the police force performed strictly custodial functions. Correctional officers had charge of the living units and shops as treatment staff and dealt with inmates' personal problems.

Classic evaluation and classification systems were established. However, these were later abandoned in favor of "problem solving" and "acculturation." In keeping with the philosophy of community, the inmates were housed in small units not exceeding fifty men and two officers. The housing officer on duty was required to live and eat with the inmates while on duty. Meals were partially prepared and were eaten in each unit (as a family) rather than in a centralized dining room.

The "small group principle" was applied to exercise and to all other activities such as school, medical care and industries. Each group developed other units including both security and treatment.

An outstanding feature of the institution emerged in the form of an inmate council. Patterned after Osborne's Mutual Welfare League, the inmates met as a group to pose problems or to suggest solutions to the warden. The staff were not involved initially.

At no time, however, did Gill envision the council as a form of "self-government" but rather as "inmate participation." In contrast to Osborne's League, the council had only advisory powers and did not handle inmate discipline. The joint committees, if approved by staff and council, carried out the activities of the prison.

> "Like the early Christian church which was truest and noblest in the days of its adversity, the council system of Norfolk was at its best when it was diligently forging the new plan, and the men involved in its creation were called upon to make sacrifices." [33]

The principle of "joint participation and joint responsibility" was adopted. The work of the council and the staff was divided among twelve committees (and numerous house committees) made up of sixty inmates and thirty officers.

After some disrupters took over the council a couple of times, the candidates for office had to be approved in advance by the administration, although the number of candidates was not limited. Gill appealed to the population as a whole, and the council was recalled. Staff members were included thereafter in all sessions of the council and were also assigned to committees.

The inmate council, which continued to evolve from 1928, developed into a coalition between staff and inmates and the sharing of responsibilities and decisions. The seeds were planted in the spring of 1928 with the Joint Committee on Construction. Thus in the new facility behind the walls, the housing officers became an integral part of the council system.

". . . [T]he real and most crucial accomplishments of
the council system lay in the intangibles. It was a spirit of
armistice where the two factions of social warfare forgot
the gun and the instruments of vengeance to live together in amity to think out and put into practice a plan
that would reduce the need for these conflicts." [34]

Adding staff to the inmate council was neither by accident
nor coercion but was deliberate, conscious action by Gill to
modify Osborne's plan. The Mutual Welfare League was like a
pyramid set on its peak. The warden and the inmates got together
and then told the guards what to do. According to Gill, resistance
by the guards to this method proved to be a major factor in
lessening the effectiveness of the League.

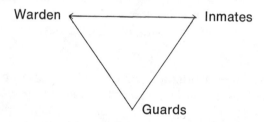

Gill reversed this arrangement and set the pyramid on its
base: the guards and the inmates got together and told the
warden what to do—with his consent. Gill recognized the defect
in Osborne's plans as the Norfolk council evolved and so modified
the structure to include both elements of the prison society
(guards and inmates) into a common effort at problem solving.
Thereafter, as Gill says, "it worked!"

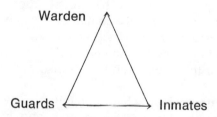

There are some direct measures of the effectiveness of
Gill's plan. Construction doubled after a joint committee of staff
and inmates was involved in supervision and planning projects
weekly.

During the five years of construction, 698 inmates were transferred to Norfolk. Of these, only 35 ran away although the minimum-custody section in the Oval had no security perimeter, nor did the Farm Colony outside the wall where 100 inmates were housed.

During the initial stages of construction, there had been a mutual sense of responsibility in the Oval. Staff members were an integral part of the system. Rapid expansion of the population and the staff, and the absorption following the opening of the wall, destroyed the homey atmosphere which had prevailed in the Oval and resulted in both inmate and staff problems.

The nostalgic attitude toward the "gold old days" in the Oval was characteristic of a few old-timers among the inmates who felt the loss of personal contact with the superintendent, who had to delegate such contacts to subordinates, many of whom were new to prison work and to the Gill philosophy.

Gill's greatest initial impact was no doubt upon the tractable, cooperative prisoner transferred from the state prison to Norfolk where, except for a few, they uniformly demonstrated the ability to act responsibly when offered the opportunity of self-determination. The discovery that only tractable cooperative prisoners could carry on at Norfolk was vital to the success of the Norfolk plan. Gill believed that some other plan would be needed in dealing with intractable and defective prisoners.

Gill's charisma enabled a highly qualified staff, imbued with the missionary zeal of the warden, to work together. Gill points with pride to the subsequent achievements of those who experienced the Norfolk experiment.

There is no statistical evidence regarding recidivism at Norfolk, but then that was never an objective of the plan. Gill's goal was merely to *change* prisoners. He rejected recidivism as a measure of the effectiveness of prison programs because of the other societal variables affecting failure after release from prison.

Nonetheless, Gill demonstrated rather forcefully that a community prison can work with increased production, less tension and a reduced number of institutional incidents. Unfortunately, the plan was cut short before further evaluation could resolve some of the questions which naturally developed with the experiment.

Gill's own words serve best to sum up his ideas about the effectiveness of inmate participation in prison management:

"Instead of letting it become the means whereby men can achieve anything they want, it is to be the means of teaching them what they should have. We have got to have certain standards of decency, order, quietness, industriousness, and patience which we must insist be the standards of the meanest, the most undesirable men in the place.

"On the other hand, with the proper plans, I think it has been demonstrated that the whole tone of an institution can be raised by this kind of participation, of exchange of ideas, of expression as contrasted with repression. We see men's faces light up and become normal, and that very atmosphere becomes a part of our therapy, because unless we meet that normal human feeling on the part of our men, we cannot do good case work with them. We cannot do the thing which we have set out to do—that is, to help them to help themselves." [35]

Gill was fired on April 5, 1934 following a political fight lasting five months. He was simultaneously removed as director of research to evaluate the effects of his experiment.

Thomas O. Murton (1928–)

Winthrop Rockefeller became a candidate for Governor of Arkansas in 1966. He expressed understandable indignation over a state police report, prepared in August of the year, which catalogued the cruelty practiced in the Arkansas prison system. He campaigned on a reform ticket and won election with a mandate from the electorate to end a century of decadence in Arkansas government.

Rockefeller took office in January of 1967 and was forced to deal with the prison issue promptly thereafter. To avoid a revolt at Tucker Prison Farm, Rockefeller fired three staff members and the superintendent who had been threatening the inmates with a submachine gun. This action left only two paid staff members and forty-eight guards under the nominal control of a state police detachment in charge of the institution, which consisted of three hundred inmates and 4,500 acres of land. The state police were not allowed by the inmate guards to carry their weapons.

Thus by February of 1967 there was a stalemate between the state administration and the inmates. The population agreed to nominal control by the police detachment but threatened to burn the prison to the ground and escape en masse if Governor Rockefeller did not keep his promise to reform the prison. More specifically, the inmates demanded appointment of a reform warden to run the prison.

Thomas O. Murton, then on the faculty of Southern Illinois University, was called to Arkansas as a consultant to evaluate the situation at Tucker. After his investigation, he reported to the Governor on the explosiveness of the situation and the total depravity of the system, and he made recommendations for reform of the prison.

Murton became intrigued with the challenge of the apparently impossible task to turn around an archaic prison and applied for the job as superintendent. Since there were no other applicants for the position and Rockefeller needed to fulfill his campaign promise to "hire a professional penologist," Murton was appointed to the position in mid-February of 1967.

Murton had been graduated from universities in Oklahoma, Alaska and California with degrees in Animal Husbandry, Education and Criminology, respectively. Ironically, it was the former degree and not the latter which assured his appointment in Arkansas because of the extensive agriculture operations for which the superintendent was responsible.

Murton was not interested in simply improving a decadent prison through traditional, evolutionary methods.

"Placing a man in prison to train him for a democratic society is as ridiculous as sending him to the moon to learn how to live on earth.

.   .   .   .

"The master can no more impose 'rehabilitation' upon the slave than a teacher can inflict 'education' upon the student.

.   .   .   .

"What is being suggested here is the substitution of legitimate power for the present illegitimate one. This new dimension in prison administration requires some courage and a great deal of perception by the reformer. To turn the prison around requires some skill and intuitive action which allows the formation of a new society.

A new prison community must be brought into existence which is unique in that it is a coalition between the staff and inmates as opposed to the traditional adversary relationship. This new community cannot emerge spontaneously; it must be developed and nurtured.

. . . .

"Truth is the cornerstone for mutual trust between staff and inmates which precedes change. The greater risk lies with the administrator because he must take the first step in establishing trust. In order to be meaningful, the opportunity to demonstrate responsibility must also include the possibility of demonstrating irresponsibility. Inherent in a true chance to succeed is the chance to fail." [36]

Murton rejected the basic concept of the prison as an autocracy and set about to revolutionize it. He immediately abolished corporal punishment, forbade torture, and removed the sadistic guards.

"My sole authority was that granted by the Governor. Nevertheless, we were able in a few months to feed and clothe the inmates, hire competent staff, upgrade the agricultural programs, establish educational and vocational training programs, provide rational religious counseling service (to replace forced church attendance under the gun) eliminate corruption, move the trusties into the barracks, and practically eliminate the rapes and other homosexual attacks." [37]

Death row inmates were integrated into all activities of the institution, including the new prison band. Dances were held at the prison which were attended by Tucker inmates, their wives or girl friends, and the freeworld staff. Thus, probably, the first interracial dances held in Arkansas occurred at the Tucker Prison Farm.

The band left the prison to play for patients at the state mental hospital. They were allowed to leave the prison escorted by an unarmed ex-inmate who had been hired as a freeworld guard. Two members of the band were men from death row.

"By Christmas of 1967, a woman supervisor was able to work at the prison laundry, female employees ate in the

> prison dining hall, female teachers conducted classes
> inside the institution with no guard present and the staff
> and their families attended programs, sitting with the
> general inmate population." [38]

These efforts were neither reckless abandon nor foolhardiness. They were all part of a plan to convey to the inmate some notion of self-worth.

Murton observed that "mutual degradation fosters mutual empathy" and proceeded to integrate the black inmates from death row into the all-white Tucker population without incident.

The dances, female supervisors, and female employees eating in the inmate dining room were all part of a plan to introduce a legitimate heterosexual element into the prison.

The purpose of requiring staff (and the prison board) to eat on the mainline was to demonstrate that there would be no caste distinction between freeworld people and prisoners. The same purpose was served in hiring ex-convicts to work at the prison.

All of these activities also included the element of trust. It was essential that the administration first trust the inmates before they could demonstrate responsibility. Allowing condemned inmates to accompany the band outside the prison was a classic example of this trust. The warden cannot say "I trust you" and then by his actions refusing a request, nonverbally indicate the opposite.

The operation of the prison was carried out in the context of an open press policy. This was done to inform and educate the public, eliminate suspicion of prison reform activities, persuade the free people that there was a need for reform and, hopefully, to enable the press to ensure that the atrocities of the past would not occur again.

After Murton gained nominal control of the prison in the first few weeks, he immediately sent out a request for assistance from staff with whom he had worked previously. His selection criteria were "simply" that (1) the individual must have integrity; (2) have empathy for other people; and (3) subordinate his personal welfare to that of the inmates.

To these factors, Murton added that "it helps to have been fired before." The reasoning behind this qualification was that the person would thus have demonstrated the quality of his commitment by having been tested "at the wall."

Former staff came from Missouri, California, Alaska, and Australia. They did not come to Arkansas for the climate or the meager pay. They did not come because Murton is particularly easy to work with. They came because they knew there was a challenge, a job needed to be done, and, perhaps, they needed to feel needed.

At the critical point in Murton's efforts to gain control of Tucker, several inmates with whom he had established confidence came forward to suggest the use of inmates to curtail the rash of escapes. The result was the immediate institution of the position of Inmate Sheriff as the chief law enforcement officer over the trusty guard force. More carefully, efforts were made to capitalize on inmate resources through representative government.

Without advance notice, the entire population was moved into the auditorium where the election process and purposes were explained.

> "[T]he 9th of March marked the first election for an Inmate Council at this institution. I had spent about two weeks in various contact with the inmates, telling them what the council could do, what the purpose of it is, what its functions would be, and the type of men who should get on it. That is, those who would stand up to me and not bow down to my desires; those who would truly represent the men. They should not be operators but those sincerely interested in trying to see what they could do to improve the lot of the prison.
>
> "This is in furtherance of my stated assumption that 'we,' meaning inmates as well as the staff, need to combine efforts in order to improve the situation here." [39]

While the creation of the farm council was the objective at the time, "the process," as Murton said, "was more important than the product." Extraordinary precautions were taken in the time-consuming process of democratic action. It would have been simpler to have appointed the first council members. But as Murton contended:

> "This process would have made all subsequent decisions suspect, and there was no assurance that the superintendent could select the proper inmates. Moreover, such a method would have negated an essential ingre-

dient of the council: the inmates had to become involved personally in the process if they were to have any commitment to the outcome. Finally, since the representatives were chosen by the inmates, they had credibility, were accountable to the inmate body and indirectly the general population was thus required to share the responsibility for managerial errors in the future." [40]

The creation of a farm council in Arkansas did not "just happen." As other reforms at Tucker, it was a planned ingredient of reform which was encouraged at the time the idea "originated" with the inmates. Murton had been superintendent of five other institutions prior to going to Arkansas, and his notions about inmate involvement in management of the institution evolved out of these experiences.

The Tucker Farm Council followed the usual pattern of dealing with housekeeping problems and then moved to weightier issues. When a rash of escapes occurred during Murton's third month as superintendent, the problem was taken to the council. While the escape of guards was a sign that the inmate power structure was being broken, the public became alarmed nonetheless.

The inmates on the council suggested many changes in security procedures including removal of some of the inmate guards from critical posts and a change in procedures which had become dysfunctional over the years.

With a desire to change the prison and a belief in the superintendent, the council members had a vested interest in perpetuation of the new administration. The inmates had information not available to the administration. Consequently they devised more appropriate rules for punishment in lieu of the then-abolished strap.

Within a month, it became apparent that most of the functions of the council centered around classification and discipline of inmates. To make the operation more efficient, the council was split in half. One inmate from each barracks and the superintendent constituted the Classification Committee and the other three inmates and the superintendent comprised the Disciplinary Committee. In each case, as on the larger farm council, the superintendent retained the right to veto—but it was never used.

The Classification Committee concerned itself primarily

with changing the inmate's custody grade or job assignment, which included deciding which inmates would become guards and carry rifles, shot guns and pistols.

> "We did make some good assignments today, I believe, and I'm well pleased with the contributions of the Classification Committee. These inmate members know the man, can make valid recommendations and I think that we are on the road to success in the area of control of the institution. If we can get adequate classification and adequate disciplinary measures taken, we can perhaps get control eventually. The fact that this is being done by inmates would send a chill down the back of any penologist but this is something that I want to experiment with here." [41]

One request for a job and custody change appeared to Murton to be a good choice but he was voted down unanimously by the inmate members of the committee. They explained that the inmate's mother had visited him the previous Sunday and had informed him that his neighbor was shacking with his wife. Hence, he wished to be reassigned to a position from which he could escape and solve his domestic problems. Such information is common knowledge among the inmates but is a secret from staff. By utilizing it through the council members, similar potential errors in classification were avoided thereafter.

The Disciplinary Committee met weekly to hear cases of infractions of the institutional rules. In many instances inmates were found not guilty by reason of insufficient evidence or lack of intent. No distinction was made between complaints filed by freeworld staff or inmate staff members.

Committee members took personal interest in many of the cases. A sixteen-year-old inmate continued to act irresponsibly and was in constant difficulty with the administration. One of the committee members suggested that the recalcitrant inmate be placed on "parole" to him. Murton was opposed to the plan, initially, but the committeeman argued that he had had the same attitude when he was the same age and thought he could change the boy's attitude.

The committee voted to parole the inmate from the "hole" to the committeeman after the latter agreed to forfeit his job as barracks orderly if the plan did not work. The committeeman thus had a vested interest in the success of the parole plan. As Murton contended, "the quality of commitment is directly related to the amount of personal jeopardy." That was the last time the young inmate came before the Disciplinary Committee. He subsequently became a model prisoner, attained promotions in the prison, eventually was paroled and has remained out of prison.

In spite of the fears expressed about the formation of the Tucker Farm Council, after it was fully operational there were no assaults, no fights and only one escape during the last five months of Murton's tenure at Tucker. (There had been thirty-eight escapes during the first five months.) The single escape was a runaway from a forced homosexual advance.

No inmate classified minimum custody by the inmates ever escaped.

No condemned prisoner ever attempted to escape even when outside the prison.

No woman was ever assaulted, attacked or insulted inside the prison.

The illegitimate power structure was destroyed.

No inmate in which trust was placed ever violated that trust—as long as Murton was superintendent.

Freeworld staff, women and children were free to mingle with the "convicts" without fear.

"The most significant change was in the attitude of the inmates. Fear had disappeared, a new community had been created and despair had been replaced by hope." [42]

The Tucker Farm Council could have been organized crime in lieu of the dictatorship previously in operation. Councilmen could have been elected through intimidation. They could have sold jobs and privileges to their fellow inmates. They could have manipulated the institution and the superintendent for their personal gain. All of these things could have happened but did not.

Murton's commentary on the council summarizes his assessment of the experiment:

"In review, it should be noted that the first requisite for change was that the superintendent did not consider himself omnipotent. Second, the idea for change had to

emerge from the inmates. Time was devoted to really involving the inmates in a legitimate self-help effort. Success fostered success and confidence. A by-product of
the farm council was the re-direction of traditional hostility from the superintendent to the inmate body. The
sharing of decision-making with the inmates carried with
it the implicit collective responsibility for the decision
made.

"Confidence was established through meticulous
procedures and credibility. Flexibility was the custom. I
did not last long enough to test the final phase wherein
the superintendent becomes an advisor and relinquishes
the veto power. The true success of inmate government
can only thus be validated. The correlation with recidivism would require additional experimentation beyond
the institution." [43]

Based upon the success of his plan at Tucker, Murton was
promoted on January 1st of 1968 to the superintendency of the
larger institution at Cummins and placed in charge of the entire
prison system. A statement by John Haley, Chairman of the Prison
Board, on March 2nd of that year assesses Murton's effectiveness:

"In my opinion, you have demonstrated near genius in
doing what you have been able to do at Tucker. You have
made drastic reforms, you have completely turned over
an inmate society in a period of a year, probably more
effectively than anyone else could. I don't know very
many penologists, but I do know that you are extremely
capable and have done a fantastic job. As concerns the
relationships with the inmates, as concerns dealing with
the inmate population, an inmate society, I cannot conceive of how anybody could find any substantial quarrel
with what you have done. . . . My personal opinion is
that, when it comes to dealing with the inmate population, you are superb . . ." [44]

Five days later Haley handed Murton his notice of dismissal and gave him twenty-four hours to vacate the farm.

"What success we had in gaining control of the Tucker
Prison Farm and revolutionizing it were the direct result

of the efforts of inmates who dared to believe and make a commitment to reform the prison. The whole key is that it was done 'with' and not 'to' them nor 'for' them." [45]

Conclusion

There are several common threads which characterize the reform efforts of these four reformers.

The men themselves possessed integrity, empathy and courage. Firmly committed to the welfare of the inmates, each jeopardized his personal tenure. They were fair yet firm in their dealings with the inmates. Their charisma and frankness captured the faith and trust of the inmates with whom they developed many lasting personal relationships.

They shared a common philosophy, strangely similar in many ways although some of them were unfamiliar with the work or writings of the others. They viewed the inmate as a human being with certain rights that should not be violated. They believed that reformation cannot be imposed from the top but must emanate from within. The individual must come to have self-respect, confidence, and belief in his net worth. To this end they rejected the iron-hand discipline of the prison dictatorship and replaced it with an environment conducive to the development of responsibility.

Each reformer ascribed to the thesis that man is more easily led than driven. They believed that fairness and honesty lead to mutual trust, which is the basis for developing responsibility. In this effort, the warden must take the first step. From trust come respect and credibility, and a vested interest in the continuation of the warden in power.

The prison was seen as a place to modify behavior, but only if it approximated the freeworld. That is, experience in meaningful decision-making must be available in the prison if the inmate is to become involved in self-determination. In this respect, the warden must risk the possibility that the inmate will act irresponsibly in learning to act responsibly.

Involving the inmates in the decision-making process forces them to share the responsibility for the decision made. Collective decision-making results in meaningful participation and a coalition of interests towards common goals.

Each reformer aggressively pursued an intuitive master plan to implement his "radical" innovations. The sequence, time lapse, and particulars of the plan were not rigid. Flexibility was a common characteristic which enabled the administrator to re-adjust to the changing situation as the need arose.

Each also demonstrated that "it works." At the very least, there was a reduction of tension, assaults, and escapes. At the best, there was a reduction in the recidivism rate.

Each reformer momentarily succeeded in alleviating the oppressiveness of a brutal system and therein unwittingly sowed the seed of his personal failure.

It should be fairly clear to even the modest scholar that historical penology has provided us with at least a clue to the valid techniques of modifying attitudes and behavior of the criminal offender. If so, why then have the appropriate programs not been put into effect?

Perhaps the answer to this question may be found in a consideration of the more fundamental issues involved in the dilemma of true prison reform: Is it not a peculiar logic which dictates that those institutional programs that have succeeded in achieving the stated objectives of the prison are doomed to fail, while those programs which fail in relation to the needs of the inmates tend to succeed in attaining longevity? But then, perhaps it is not a logic at all.

Footnotes

[1] J. V. Barry, Alexander Maconochie of Norfolk Island, at 90 (Oxford University Press, London, 1958).

[2] A. Maconochie, Australiana, Thoughts on Convict Management, at 7, 8, 114 (John W. Parker, London, 1839).

[3] Barry, note 1, supra.

[4] Id. at 68.

[5] Maconochie, note 2, supra, at 94, 95.

[6] Barry, note 1, supra, at 117.

[7] Id. at 113.

[8] Id. at 19.

[9] Id. at 166.

[10] Id. at 115.

[11] Id. at 104, 105.

[12] Id. at 147.

[13] Id. at 167.

[14] F. Tannenbaum, Osborne of Sing Sing, at 65 (University of North Carolina Press, Chapel Hill, 1933).

15 T. M. Osborne, Society and Prisons, at 32 (Yale University Press, New Haven, 1917).

16 Id. at 28.

17 Quoted in J. M. Holl, Juvenile Reform in the Progressive Era, at 277 (Cornell University Press, Ithaca, 1971).

18 Id. at 243.

19 Osborne, note 15, supra, at 204–205.

20 Id. at 159.

21 Tannenbaum, note 14, supra, at 119.

22 Osborne, note 15, supra, at 208.

23 Tannenbaum, note 14, supra, at 120.

24 Osborne, note 15, supra, at 207.

25 Quoted in Tannenbaum, note 14, supra, at 129.

26 Id. at 130.

27 Id. at 134.

28 Osborne, note 15, supra, at 230.

29 Tannenbaum, note 14, supra, at 146.

30 Osborne, note 15, supra, at 222–223.

31 C. R. Doering (Ed.), A Report on the Development of Penological Treatment at Norfolk Prison Colony in Massachusetts, at 77 (Bureau of Social Hygiene, New York, 1940).

32 Id. at 87.

33 Id. at 86.

34 Id.

35 Id. at 182.

36 Murton, "Inmate Self-Government," 6 U. San Francisco L. Rev. 87 (1971).

37 Murton, "One Year of Prison Reform," The Nation, Jan. 12, 1970, at 13.

38 Id. at 14.

39 Daily Log, Tucker Prison Farm, Arkansas, March 10, 1967, at 35, 36.

40 Murton, note 36, supra, at 94.

41 Daily Log, Tucker Prison Farm, Arkansas, April 13, 1967, at 76–77.

42 Murton, note 37, supra, at 14.

43 Murton, note 36, supra, at 101.

44 Extract from the transcript of an executive session of the Arkansas Board of Corrections at Cummins Prison Farm, Grady, Arkansas, March 2, 1968, at 73, 74.

45 Murton, note 36, supra, at 101.

CHAPTER 24
THE FUTURE

EDITORS' INTRODUCTION

Despite many deplorable prisons and practices, some innovative programs are currently being tried. While most are limited in scope and size, they may be of value in shaping the correctional systems of tomorrow. The following article describes the new trends in prison and parole and what should be done to implement them.

NEW TRENDS IN PRISON AND PAROLE

ROBERT PLOTKIN *

There is little certainty to the trend of corrections, and there is no guaranty that the future will be better than the past. Society's unsatisfied lust for retribution and punishment is simply not compatible with the system's mandate to "rehabilitate." Prisoners' lawyers are probably justified in their fears that lawsuits which make prisons more humane will also make prisons more acceptable to the public conscience.

Many thoughtful scholars of corrections contemplate a deep future commitment to the ideal of rehabilitation.[1] The problems of the past, according to this school of thought, have been caused by the penal systems' lack of funds, of trained personnel, and of scientific data, all of which are thought to be prerequisite to the success of the rehabilitation model. The solution, it is urged, is increased spending, training, and testing; placing less emphasis on security, greater stress on individualized treatment.[2] This is a respectable position, and pragmatically it probably represents the trend of the future.

However, certain rehabilitative proposals raise frightening prospects. It has been suggested, for example, that parole recidivists carry an electronic device to monitor their location and activities by sending signals to a "base station."[3] These devices would be constructed to assure that the wearer could not remove or obstruct the device, and the ultimate goal would be to develop "a therapeutic relationship" in which a parolee "could be rewarded, warned, or otherwise signaled in accordance with the plan for therapy."[4]

Other serious proposals for preventing crime by chronic offenders include techniques to induce vomiting at the mere thought of a criminal act,[5] and administering drugs to sex offenders, which would reduce sexual urges.[6] The Federal Bureau of Prisons has begun construction on a Behavioral Research Center

* Staff Attorney, National Law Office, National Legal Aid and Defender Association, Washington, D.C.; A.B., J.D. University of Cincinnati; LL.M. New York University.

at Butner, North Carolina, devoted to devising "more effective ways of programming the more difficult prisoners." [7] These prospects raise not only fundamental constitutional questions [8] but also address the broader "Clockwork Orange" issues of behavioral control in a free society.

Thus, the theory of rehabilitation does not face the future unchallenged. It presupposes that we know what rehabilitation means; it assumes that we possess techniques to implement our supposed knowledge; and it suggests that we have methods with which we can evaluate these techniques. In reality these underlying assumptions remain unproven,[9] and rehabilitation remains elusive. New thoughts suggest that treatment and punishment can never be compatible, and that society should not attempt to accommodate them both in its prisons. Perhaps the prison of the future should exist only to punish those for whom, out of an urgent need to protect society, no less drastic methods of punishment are available.

Simply confining people in a prison constitutes punishment; there is no reason to permit dehumanization, degradation, filth, and crowding; and there is no justification for forcibly attempting to program minds.[10] Ancillary services for the benefit of the inmates should be available on a voluntary basis only. The motivation to take advantage of them must come from the inmates and the quality of the services, or it should not come at all. It certainly must not come solely from the hope of pleasing the parole board.[11]

Regardless of the theory upon which we incarcerate people, however, it still appears that, at least for the foreseeable future, prisons will be a continuing fact of life until a maturing society is prepared to seriously consider alternatives to prisons.[12] While there may be legitimate disagreements as to the theory of confinement, there is little dispute as to the nature of the confinement. The degrading environment and treatment common in our prisons is universally deplored, and few would disagree that "the programs and policies associated with confinement should be directed at elevating and enhancing the dignity, worth, and self-confidence of the inmates, not at debasing and dehumanizing them." [13] Sadly, this is not a new trend. The corrections community has professed these values for nearly one hundred years; our institutions profess otherwise. This chapter explores, with little optimism, new efforts to confine people with dignity, all the while wondering if the "principle of enhancing human dignity can ever be implemented within the walls. . . ." [14]

Prison

The most visible change will probably occur in the physical appearance of prisons. Small, accessible prisons, similar to present halfway houses, will probably be built closer to urban areas. If the criminal justice system truly commits itself to the increased use of alternative forms of punishment and incarceration,[15] there should be a corresponding decrease in prison populations. As overcrowding eases, administrators should find their ability to deliver essential services improved, and decreasing security concerns should allow for stricter supervision of line personnel. Inmates may enjoy greater privacy and more time for eating, sleeping, and relaxing.

But appearances are deceptive. The heart of the problem still lies in attitudes, not architecture, and it is this that remains unpredictable. If the goal is to achieve fair and humane treatment for prisoners, to assure that they retain whatever dignity with which they enter the prison, the obstacle is the traditional emphasis placed upon security, which has led to dehumanizing practices by prison personnel intent upon breaking a man to make him accept his institutional status.[16] While correctional administrators are the first to reject these practices,[17] they have been unwilling or unable to prevent them.[18] Inroads on archaic attitudes have been made with some increased hiring of minority group members, former offenders, and persons sensitive to prisoners' needs. It is a slow process, one which depends upon the intuition and good will of employers and employees alike. The past has proven that such trust is not always well placed.

For these reasons there is a continuing need for an agent to mediate between the administration and the population. Continued expansion of prisoners' legal protections, codified to facilitate enforcement, offers the judiciary as one such mediator. Perhaps public scrutiny—by the news media, by lifting internal restrictions on communications, and by encouraging increased inmate-free world contact—is another possibility. Still other suggestions envision a formalized mediator in the guise of a prisoners' union [19] or an ombudsman.[20] Whichever method or combination of methods is finally adopted, it is clear that the most hopeful trend, from the prisoners' perspective, will be the increased availability of a system of checks and balances.

An important indicator of prison's future direction is the nature and quality of the institutional programs available to inmates. The past has seen fragmentary attempts by administrators to develop progressive programs which ameliorate the conditions of confinement, usually under the rubric of rehabilitation, and to the extent that these programs promote individual dignity and the community contact they should be encouraged. Certain of these programs, which are likely to figure prominently in the plans of correction administrators, merit further discussion.

Education

In theory, the value of prison education programs has long been recognized. The penal reformers of the 19th century insisted that rehabilitation could be achieved by improving inmates' self-perceptions as well as their opportunities upon release.[21] Courses offered in institutions have ranged from correspondence courses to educational television and college furlough programs. Some states provide teachers, texts, and similar materials, while others rely solely upon volunteers.

In fact, prison education has generally been poor, and except for a few instances the reformers' theory remains unproven,[22] for the programs have remained secondary to the interests of security and custody. Typical of this attitude is the case where a court upheld a warden's refusal to allow an inmate to enroll in a correspondence course because, upon release, the prisoner intended to apply his knowledge to writing a book about "brutal" prison officials.[23] Actual figures indicate that less than 10 per cent of all corrections personnel provide educational services to inmates.[24]

Existing programs suffer from the lip service and token support paid to correctional education by administrators and legislators. As a result, prison libraries are inadequate for independent research or reading, the classroom environment is not generally conducive to learning, and curriculum lacks diversity and stimulation, particularly for minority groups.[25] Inmates have complained that teachers, who often are not enthusiastic about teaching inside an institution, tend to moralize rather than to teach.[26]

Perhaps the heart of correctional education's failure lies

in its attitude: it has chiefly concerned itself with discovering what type of education is proper for an *inmate,* as if inmates are distinct and separate creatures. In the future it must be recognized that prisoners should receive the same education necessary for other groups in society; legislators and administrators should focus instead upon how this education can most effectively be delivered.[27]

Course attendance should not be required. Likewise, telling inmates "that their confinement may be shortened if their grade level increases" [28] should be discouraged, for it only increases enrollment in courses for the deceptive purpose of exhibiting rehabilitation to the parole board. The motivation for schooling comes, ideally, from the inmate himself and should be encouraged by the richness, quality, and variety of the curriculum rather than by extrinsic factors unrelated to education.

The quality of the teachers is as important as the quality of the curriculum. No longer can a person be hired to teach inmates simply because he or she has a diploma in a substantive area. The individual teacher must also be sensitive to a prisoner's needs, which may well result in the hiring of more minority group teachers as well as increasing the number of ex-inmate teachers. The use of current inmates as teachers is already widespread, although not always popular,[29] and perhaps the application of team teaching methods in prisons could blend the unique talents of inmates and civilian teachers. The limited use of programmed learning with computers has had some success [30] and can even reduce the number of teachers whose actual presence is required. Increased and genuinely interested faculties can also help to develop the kinds of courses necessary to motivate inmates to continue their studies. In Denmark, for example, courses in art, culture, and extemporanreous theater appear to have had limited success in motivating inmates,[31] and perhaps such broader horizons should be considered.

There is no reason why prison education must stop at the high school level. Southern Illinois University, for example, has had programs in Illinois prisons since 1952, and its experience shows that the courses are popular with inmates and cause no severe security problems.[32] An arrangement with a nearby university is especially useful in developing study furlough programs which allow inmates to get outside the walls and into the community to attend classes.

Likewise, education should not be limited exclusively to

inmates, since experience shows that the institutional personnel may also benefit from continued education.[33] Southern Illinois University offers numerous courses for prison staff, ranging from human relations to preparation of institutional food.[34] While this can hardly be called a trend, it does seem desirable to include staff in a broad-based educational program.

Work-Release

The idea of allowing prisoners to leave the institution to work at a job during the day and return to the prison at night is another not-so-new trend. Wisconsin's Huber Law,[35] the first day-parole program, was enacted in 1913,[36] and since that time at least twenty-eight jurisdictions have followed suit.[37]

The federal work furlough law [38] is fairly representative of work-release statutes. It allows inmate employment only after consultation with local labor unions, and only upon the conditions that there will be no displacement in the local labor supply and that the prevailing wage will be paid.[39] The Attorney General, who is authorized to collect "costs incident to the prisoner's confinement" from inmate earnings, may allow any prisoner who is deemed capable of "honoring his trust" to participate.[40]

Whether or not work-release actually engenders rehabilitation, there is little argument that it reduces isolation, encourages community contact, and potentially may be of value to certain offenders in maintaining their own sense of worth and dignity. But, as is too often the case with corrections, existing plans are marred by hesitancy, inconsistency, and half-hearted commitments.

As of 1969 only about half the states had such programs, despite widespread assertions that rehabilitation is a general correctional goal and that work-release is an important tool of rehabilitation.[41] Even states with legislative authorization have been slow in implementing work-release programs and in providing the necessary funds and manpower to run them properly.[42] Some states severely restrict eligibility for work-release, often excluding sex offenders [43] and perpetrators of violent crimes.[44] Broad administrative discretion, as found in the federal statute, often prevents many other classes of offenders from participating.

Moreover, work-release laws rarely take inmates into account. They usually contain detailed financial requirements that inmates must pay room and board and stipulate how other portions of their salary are to be spent. Few provisions are made, however, for easing the impact of the inmate's reentry into society. Although the prisoner has to make a continual readjustment between the institution and the free world and may find the stigma of "criminal" attached to him by fellow employees or others with whom he comes into contact,[45] there are few counselling programs available to help prepare him for this first real community contact. This minimizes the potential value of an outside job. Inmates are often employed in jobs for which they possess no skills, yet they receive little advance training or preparation; others perform only menial tasks with little future value. Generally there is a lack of coordination among the various state agencies involved in job placements.

The practical realities of life, over which correctional personnel have little control, also hamper work-release efforts. Periods of unemployment make jobs, particularly skilled ones, difficult for anyone to secure. Potential employers may be hesitant about hiring offenders, and powerful unions may frustrate other employment opportunities to protect their members. The rural locations of most prisons simply remove many major job markets from realistic consideration.

Authorizing and funding an entire program and the necessary supportive structure will not be sufficient to make extensive work-release programs viable in the future, for the plans cannot operate in a vacuum. As long as prisons remain in remote locations, removed from job markets, and as long as the public allows offenders to be barred from meaningful employment opportunities, the true potential of work-release will remain unknown. Furthermore, statutory requirements concerning matters such as wages and union approval need to be rethought. While job placement should be sensitive to economic realities, there may be justifiable situations in which an unskilled inmate should receive a lower salary than an experienced craftsman, or where local unions should not be able to thwart job placement.

Conjugal Visits

Restrictive visiting privileges have long been a major source of frustration and isolation for inmates. Marriages and families have disintegrated, sexual frustrations have intensified already serious prison homosexual problems, and general resentment toward prison officials is increased. In the future, prisons must move away from degrading and unnecessary visitation rules. There is already much precedent for such a movement. At present there are thirty-one foreign countries which either allow inmates to receive private visits from their wives (and in some countries even fiancées and prostitutes) or to leave the prison and visit their homes for short periods.[46]

Whether this country is ready for these hardly radical proposals is questionable. As recently as 1964 a poll indicated that roughly one half of America's penal administrators would be opposed to implementing conjugal visits in their prisons.[47] Interestingly, it should be noted that this concept is not a total stranger to these shores. Mississippi has successfully allowed conjugal visiting, progressing from blankets across cells to private guest houses, since 1918.[48] In-depth studies of the Mississippi program have indicated that inmates and guards alike regard it favorably and attribute it with preventing divorces and reducing homosexual behavior.[49]

California's Tehachapi Correctional Institution has experimented for the past few years with family visits.[50] Families, including children, are allowed to spend an unsupervised weekend in cottages at the prison. Inmates considered to be a minimum security risk with good conduct records are eligible for the visits. Preliminary results show reduced stress upon families and improved facilitation of inmates' ultimate return to the community.[51] Similar programs established at Soledad and San Quentin in California are believed to be the first of their kind at an American maximum-security prison.[52]

These cautious attempts represent the bulk of conjugal visiting programs in the United States. Prisoners have filed suits attemping to force wardens into granting extended visitation rights, on the ground that enforced celibacy is cruel and unusual punishment,[53] or that it is an impairment of the marital contract.[54] Thus far no court has granted relief. American morality, apparently shocked by the prospect of turning prisons into whorehouses, has been a significant factor in repressing conjugal visits,[55] just as the general attitude toward sex in Swedish society has encouraged its widespread use in that country.[56] However, as morals change and as the public becomes sensitized to inmates' isolation from their families, it is likely that conjugal visiting will be expanded.

Conjugal visiting is not the prisons' panacea. A visit can be most demeaning for wives entering a private room under the watchful eyes of guards and, possibly, other inmates. The facilities are often inadequate and unattractive, and not conducive to privacy.[57] Single and divorced inmates may resent being denied similar visits, and there are widespread assertions that these visits will have little effect upon homosexuality.[58]

Perhaps the real trend lies not in conjugal visits but in home furloughs allowing inmates to visit their families for short, specified periods. This plan would be available to all inmates regardless of marital status and would allow inmates to seek post-release employment. It also avoids the demeaning character of prison visits, although it may heighten the potential of administrative abuse. The California family visiting program at Tehachapi allows an inmate to visit home, during the last ninety days of incarceration, for two days and two nights to aid him in his readjustment problems.[59] Sweden has had a home furlough system since 1937, and 8,000 such visits are granted each year.[60]

The experiments and pilot projects of yesterday have become the hope for tomorrow. Conceivably they could be successful this time, particularly if there are checks and balances to control the traditionally vast discretion of prison wardens. But note the common thread in all of these new trends: they are not really new at all. Rather, they are the best remnants of today's crumbling system, and they will be difficult to salvage. If future prisons can promote individual dignity and allow inmates to leave the prisons while encouraging citizens to enter them, perhaps the changes will become that much easier.

Parole

Parole was originally established to ameliorate the punishment of offenders and to facilitate an offender's return to society,[61] a design that embodied all the ideals of individualized treatment and rehabilitation. In practice, parole has worked to increase the punishment inflicted upon prisoners and has made their return to the community more difficult. One should keep in mind, despite frequent assertions to the contrary, that no concrete evidence exists to show that parole reduces recidivism, or that parole reduces the median length of time an offender actually spends in prison.[62]

A significant factor in the development of parole has been the indeterminate sentencing structure, which carries the rehabilitation model one step further. As originally proposed, it envisioned committing an offender to prison until his keepers considered him cured,[63] but legislators were not willing to go quite that far. As a result, we now have a complex mixture of statutory provisions, which in general provide for maximum and minimum terms of confinement [64] and establish the point in time when an inmate *becomes eligible* for parole release (as opposed to being *released* on parole).[65]

When an inmate becomes eligible for parole, he then must await the board's decision to release him, if he is released at all, before his maximum term expires. This places the release decision solely in the hands of the parole board. Consequently inmates live in the uncertain limbo of never knowing when, or if, they shall be released, and the tensions caused by these uncertainties continually gnaw at them. The study of the causes of the Attica uprising concluded that "parole had become by far the greatest source of inmate anxiety and frustration." [66]

There are no standards governing decisions to release inmates on parole, and the process is often slow and "fraught with the appearance of arbitrariness." [67] Even more damaging to rehabilitation concepts, "there is no conceivably relevant knowledge in existence to support either the decision to grant parole or to deny it. . . ." [68] Data of this kind simply do not exist.

When an inmate is finally released on parole, he is then subject to numerous complex, technical conditions which in effect put him under constant surveillance.[69] The parole officers who are supposed to assist in his rehabilitation are underpaid, overworked, and undertrained.[70] Parolees are returned to prison for minor infractions of technical rules,[71] and are not entitled to earn good conduct reductions from their sentences while they are on parole. The time they spend on parole is not credited against their original sentences if their parole is subsequently revoked.[72]

If parole is to remain viable, change must occur in at least two major areas. A rational, equitable procedure for releasing inmates on parole at a specific time must be established, and nonsensical conditions and surveillance methods inherent in traditional parole programs must cease. Several alternatives for restructuring the parole-release decision are available. Legislation could provide that an inmate must be released when a certain portion of his sentence has expired, creating a statutory right to parole. The Model Penal Code has tentatively adopted this approach. It would create a presumption that the prisoner shall be released unless the parole board can demonstrate that there are compelling reasons not to release him.[73] Such a proposal begins to eliminate extensive discretion. Accompanying procedural safeguards could further protect against arbitrary decisions.[74]

An interesting proposal suggests the use of contracts in determining parole-release. Under this plan an inmate would negotiate an agreement with the parole board. The inmate would agree to enroll in certain prison programs and courses, and the board would agree to release him upon their successful completion. Hopefully, this would provide specific criteria upon which release could be determined, reducing the amount of discretion lodged in the board. It is also seen as a means of reducing an inmate's uncertainty while encouraging his participation in meaningful programs. One version of this plan has been in operation for over a year in Minnesota,[75] and another variation has been initiated in Arizona.[76] The Arizona plan, which places limits upon inmate eligibility for the contract, envisions a project coordinator assisting the inmate in preparing his proposals and in negotiating with the parole board and the corrections department.[77]

Because these projects are new, few data are available to measure their success, but it is evident that potential problems are present. For example, can an inmate truly negotiate with his keepers, and will his proposals be anything more than the usual efforts to please the parole board? Without corresponding legal rights to assure enforcement, the contracts may simply be shifting the board's exercise of discretion from the release decision to the negotiating table or to a completion of the contract determination. Nevertheless, these new decisions are of a more factual nature and are more amenable to review than past release decisions. Because caprice and uncrtainty are, to some extent, reduced, the parole contract is deserving of careful scrutiny.

It has also been proposed that custodial personnel, rather than the parole board, should make the parole release decision, on the theory that they have more firsthand knowledge of the person. The parole board's function would then be to act as an appellate body for inmates and as a final arbiter to settle close cases.[78] Despite this apparent procedural safeguard, institutional personnel have no more expertise or data than the parole board in deciding who to release, and their decision is more likely to be based upon how well an inmate has adjusted to the prison rather than upon all available extrinsic information.

Assuming that the future includes the continued use of parole, then the nature of parolee supervision must also be reexamined. There are no data indicating that numerous inflexible conditions facilitate reintegration into society, yet the present restrictive parole rules are routinely assigned to all parolees. There is no reason to require every parolee to conform to the same ten or fifteen conditions, but neither should special individual conditions be imposed unless clear and compelling reasons for doing so exist.[79] In Britain, parole conditions simply require a parolee to report to a parole officer upon release and thereafter to maintain contact with that officer; the parolee is required to report changes in residence and employment and must generally be of good behavior.[80] These conditions may be too vague to control arbitrariness, but a trend toward fewer, more specific rules related to the aim of parole appears to be desirable.

The ultimate solution to the parole problem may be to abolish the entire concept of supervised release.[81] By replacing indeterminate sentences with short, determinate terms, which would require all offenders to spend the full time in prison, the uncertainty and arbitrariness inherent in the sentencing and parole processes are effectively eliminated. Parole has not reduced the time spent incarcerated; it has not improved recidivist rates; and it has not significantly contributed to rehabilitating offenders. It has, on the other hand, increased anxiety, frustration, and unfairness. On balance it appears that inmates may be better off serving shorter sentences, with definite release dates already determined. But to eliminate parole would be to repudiate decades of self-styled progressive thinking, and such abolition is not likely in the immediate future.

Conclusion

In conclusion, we must hope that the future holds a general trend toward reduced incarceration. The system should reflect increased humane environments and public awareness. Most important, the theoretical basis of corrections must constantly be reexamined in the hope of answering the ultimate question—why do we have prisons at all.

Footnotes

[1] See e.g. American Correctional Association, Manual of Correctional Standards, at 3–10, (3d ed. 1966); V. Fox, Introduction to Corrections (1972); President's Commission on Law Enforcement and Administration of Justice, Task Force Report: Corrections, at 16 (1967) (hereafter "Task Force Report"); New

York State Special Commission on Attica, Official Report, XVI–XXI (Bantam Books, Inc., New York, 1972) (hereafter "Attica Report").

2 See e.g. authorities in note 1, supra.

3 Schwitzgebel, "Issues in Use of An Electronic Rehabilitation System With Chronic Recidivists," 3 Law & Soc'y Rev. 597 (1969).

4 Id. at 598.

5 Singer, "Psychological Studies of Punishment," 58 Calif. L. Rev. 405, 433 (1970).

6 Parade Magazine, July 25, 1971, at 15.

7 Washington Star and Daily News, November 5, 1972, at B-2.

8 See e.g. Note, "Conditioning and Other Technologies Used to 'Treat', 'Rehabilitate' and 'Demolish' Prisoners and Mental Patients," 45 S. Cal. L. Rev. 616 (1972). Note, "Anthropotelemetry: Dr. Schwitzgebel's Machine," 80 Harv. L. Rev. 403 (1966); Mitford, "Kind and Usual Punishment in California," The Atlantic, Vol. 227, p. 45 (March 1971).

9 See e.g. D. Glaser, The Effectiveness of a Prison and Parole System, at 204–210 (1969); Task Force Report, note 1, supra, at 13–14, 100–102.

10 American Friends Service Committee, Struggle for Justice: A Report on Crime and Punishment in America (1971); see also G. Jackson, Soledad Brother, at 29, 30 (1970).

11 Id.

12 See Chapter 25 of this book.

13 Attica Report, note 1, supra, at XVII.

14 Id.

15 See Chapter 25 of this book.

16 D. Clemmer, The Prison Community, at 100 (1940); E. Goffman, Asylums, at 14–28 (1961); H. Griswald, et al., An Eye for An Eye, at 8–22 (1970).

17 American Correctional Association, Manual of Correctional Standards, note 1, supra, at 354–355.

18 See e.g., Attica Report, note 1, supra, at 442–446.

19 See e.g. Note, "Labor Unions for Prison Inmates: An Analysis of a Recent Proposal for the Organization of Inmate Labor," 21 Buff. L. Rev. 963 (1972).

20 See Chapter 15 of this book.

21 Glaser, note 9, supra, at 173–177.

22 A. MacCormick, The Education of Adult Prisoners, A Survey and A Program (1931); Glecker, "Why Education in Prison," 17 J. Correctional Ed. 13 (1965).

23 Numer v. Miller, 165 F.2d 986 (9th Cir. 1940).

24 Task Force Report, note 1, supra, at 51.

25 Morris, "The University's Role in Prison Education," in H. Perlman and T. Allington, The Tasks of Penology, at 203–209 (1969).

26 Task Force Report, note 1, supra, at 54. The usual attitude exhibited in prisons is typified in the Attica Report, note 1, supra, at 41. "[T]he school was

used by the administration as a 'dumping ground', since the number of inmates in a class could be increased without an appreciable threat to security."

[27] Cassiday, "College in Prison," 14 Am. Benedictine Rev. 221 (1963); Glecker, note 22, supra.

[28] Glaser, note 9, supra, at 171.

[29] Id. at 180.

[30] Task Force Report, note 9, supra, at 53.

[31] G. Sturp, Treating the Untreatable, at 55–58 (1968).

[32] Task Force Report, note 9, supra, at 94.

[33] Morris, note 25, supra, at 202–203.

[34] Id. at 203.

[35] Wisconsin Stats. Ann. §56.08.

[36] S. Rubin, H. Weihofen, G. Edwards, and S. Rosenzweig, The Law of Criminal Correction, at 290–291 (1963).

[37] Johnson, Work Release: Factors in Selection and Release, at 24 (1969).

[38] 18 U.S.C. §4082.

[39] 18 U.S.C. §4082(c)(2).

[40] Id.

[41] American Correctional Association, Manual of Correctional Standards, note 1, supra, principle XXIII, at XXII.

[42] Carpenter, "Federal Work Release Program," in H. Perlman and T. Allington, The Tasks of Penology, at 185, 191 (1969).

[43] E.g. Rhode Island Stats. §13-2-35.

[44] E.g. Kentucky Stats. §197-140; South Dakota Stats. §24-8-1.

[45] Carpenter, note 42, supra, at 189–190.

[46] C. Hopper, Sex in Prison, at 5–6 (1969); H. Barnes and N. Teeters, New Horizons in Criminology, at 511 (3d ed. 1959).

[47] Balogh, "Conjugal Visits in Prisons: A Sociological Perspective," Fed. Prob. 53 (Sept. 1964).

[48] C. Hopper, note 46, supra, at 94–104, 117–136.

[49] Id.

[50] New York Times, August 4, 1968, at 57.

[51] Hayner, "Attitudes Toward Conjugal Visits for Prisoners," Fed. Prob. 44, 48–49 (March 1972).

[52] New York Times, April 23, 1972, at 62; New York Times, February 14, 1971, at 69.

[53] Tarlton v. Clarke, 441 F.2d 384 (5th Cir. 1971).

[54] In re Flowers, 292 F. Supp. 390 (E.D. Wis. 1968).

[55] Cavan and Zemans, "Marital Relationship of Prisoners in the United States," 49 J. Crim. L. C. & P.S. 50, 57 (1958); Cory, "Homosexuality in Prison," in C. Vedder and B. Kay, Penology, at 89 (1964).

56 Morris, "Lessons From the Adult Correctional System of Sweden," 30 Fed. Prob. 3, 11 (Dec. 1966).

57 Hayner, note 51, supra, at 44–45.

58 Some studies have indicated that homosexuality does not occur because of sexual deprivation; rather a major cause is the prisoner's need to assert an individual identity in a situation where both male and female prisoners are cut off from traditional sources of assertion and gratification. G. Sykes, The Society of Captives, at 95–99 (1958); Ward and Kassebaum, "Homosexuality: A Mode of Adaption in a Prison For Women," 12 Social Problems 159 (1964).

59 Hayner, note 51, supra, at 49.

60 Morris, note 56, supra, at 11. The Swedish experience also reflects a low escape rate among persons on home furlough. Id.

61 Rubin, et al., note 36, supra, at 543–548 (1963).

62 Task Force Report, note 1, supra, at 62.

63 Z. Brockway, Fifty Years of Prison Service, at 126 (1912).

64 Indeterminate sentences vary; there are those with maxima and minima lengths set by the legislature, Cal. Penal Code §1168 (West 1970); some have judicially set maxima and minima, New York Penal Law §70.00 (McKinn. 1967). The Model Penal Code §6.06 (Proposed Final Draft No. 1, 1961) would create legislative maxima and judicial minima. The totally indeterminate sentence does exist in some states, in the form of "psychopath" statutes, e.g. Md. Ann. Code art 31 B, §§6a, 9b (1971).

65 For example, in the federal system, 18 U.S.C. §4208 allows the sentencing judge to decide whether an offender must serve one-third of his sentence before becoming eligible for parole (§4208(a)) or whether the offender can immediately become eligible (§4208(b)). In either case, the inmate is not automatically released; that simply determines the time he first meets with the parole board.

66 Attica Report, note 1, supra, at 91.

67 Id. at 95.

68 Struggle for Justice, note 10, supra, at 71.

69 See e.g. Arluke, "A Summary of Parole Rules," 15 Crime & Delinquency, 267 (1969); see also Attica Report, note 1, supra, at 100.

70 Task Force Report, note 1, supra, at 94.

71 See e.g. Arciniega v. Freeman, 404 U.S. 4 (1971).

72 See e.g. Firkins v. Colorado, 434 F.2d 1232 (10th Cir. 1970); Canavari v. Richardson, 419 F.2d 1287 (9th Cir. 1969); Frierson v. Rogers, 289 F.2d 234 (5th Cir. 1961); Stevenson v. United States, 240 F. Supp. 859 (W.D. Mich.), cert. denied 389 U.S. 884 (1966).

73 Sec. 305.9 (Proposed Official Draft 1962).

74 See Chapter 10 of this book; Morrissey v. Brewer, 408 U.S. 471 (1972); K. Davis, Discretionary Justice, at 126–133 (1971).

75 New York Times, December 12, 1971, at 69.

76 Arizona Department of Corrections, Press Release, October 30, 1972.

77 Id.

78 V. Fox, Introduction to Penology, at 379 (1972); Task Force Report, note 1, supra, at 65.

79 See, on parole conditions generally, Comment, "The Parole System," 120 U. Pa. L. Rev. 284, 307–339 (1972).

80 Arluke, note 69, supra, at 274.

81 Struggle for Justice, note 10, supra, at 144.

CHAPTER 25
ALTERNATIVES TO PRISON

EDITORS' INTRODUCTION

All available information suggests that imprisonment serves neither to deter crime nor to rehabilitate criminals. The following critique of the current correctional system suggests some alternatives to imprisonment.

GUIDEPOSTS FOR PRISON REFORMERS LOST IN THE WOODS OF LITIGATION

DAVID F. GREENBERG *

The Crime Crisis and the Prison Crisis

Whether or not crime is actually increasing, fear of crime has become a prime topic of public concern and appears to have deeply affected the behavior patterns of many millions of Americans. Unflinching opposition to crime has replaced unyielding antagonism to Communism as the stock-in-trade of political speechmaking. That this development should coincide with growing doubts about the adequacy of imprisonment as a response to crime, and with a crisis within the prison walls of first magnitude, may provide unusual opportunities for, as well as serious obstacles to, fundamental progress with regard to crime *and* imprisonment.

The stage was set for a prison crisis by the political radicalization of the last decade. A high proportion of prison inmates are drawn from precisely those segments of the population—black and brown—whose world outlook and self-concept has been most drastically transformed by new radical insights concerning racial, class, and cultural oppression, and the role of the United States in world affairs. Prisoners coming to prison with this broadly radical conceptual framework are increasingly prone to interpret their situation not as the result of bad luck, personal deficiency, or evil but rather as the outcome of fundamental injustice in American society.

The rise of militant black, brown, red, and white organizations during the 1960's has provided highly visible models for translating these new insights and perspectives into active opposition to degrading and dehumanizing treatment in prison and has suggested strategies for dramatizing demands. Prisoners have begun to use the time-tested techniques of sit-ins, fasts, strikes,

---

* Founder, Chicago Connections (prisoner support group); Senior Fellow, Committee for the Study of Incarceration; B.S., Ph.D. University of Chicago.

and seizure of buildings in tense dramas whose audience extends far beyond the correctional establishment.

The prison system has curently lost much of its credibility with the public at large. Many people have come to believe that prisons contribute to crime rather than reduce it. Rising fiscal costs of imprisonment as well as fuller realization of its personal costs for the inmate have stimulated interest in alternatives to prison.

The Prison and the Treatment Model

Two hundred years ago confinement to an institution was almost always a pretrial measure. Persons convicted of crimes were embarrassed, whipped, mutilated, deported, or in the extreme executed, but rarely imprisoned. Incarceration was adopted as a punishment for crime in the early part of the 19th century for a number of reasons. Humanitarians wanted a method of deterring crime without annihilating or permanently incapacitating those punished.

New views of crime and insanity also encouraged an institutional response. Social deviation was increasingly interpreted not as the product of a conscious decision but rather as the predetermined outcome of a biological or social pathology, which could be cured by exposing deviants to an environment designed to foster the virtues of hard work, regular habits, abstention from vice, frugality, and submission to authority. The apparent decline of these virtues in the general population in the face of urbanization, industrialization, and class conflict was largely blamed for crime, insanity, and poverty.[1] The prison was introduced as something more than a therapy: it was the model of the reformers' ideal society.[2] As time went on it came to be seen as an ideal instrument for assimilating immigrant cultures [3] and providing obedient laborers for the farms and factories of a labor-short economy.[4]

For more than a century, the prison in one or more of its variants (jail, reformatory, training school, insane asylum) has been one of the dominant sanctions imposed on those found to have violated the law as well as on those regarded as insane or dangerous to themselves or others. The major justification for this response has been a constellation of ideas alternately known as "the rehabilitative ideal" [5] or "the individualized treatment model." [6] In this model, crime is to be prevented by curing individual criminals of the pathology that led to their violations of the law; they are to be released only when it has been determined that they will not break the law again. This view considers that prosecutors, judges, penal administrators, and parole boards should be able to exercise considerable discretion in order to select and administer the disposition best suited to the individual treatment needs of the criminal.

Critique of the Treatment Model

Although the treatment model claims to serve both societal needs for protection against crime and the interests of the prisoner in being rehabilitated and released as quickly as possible, the actual realization of this model has served neither interest very well. Treatment programs conducted in prison, or on probationers and parolees, when evaluated with controls seem not to succeed in reducing the rate of return to crime.[7] Thus the capability to rehabilitate on which the model is based does not exist, and it may now be questioned whether any rehabilitation program administered on a coercive basis will be able to succeed.

Instead of serving inmates' interests by helping them to avoid future imprisonment, the treatment model has harmed their interests in a number of ways. Indefiniteness in length of sentence, justified under the rehabilitative ideal, has increased the psychological hardship of imprisonment and lengthened actual time served. That it would do this should have been anticipated: there are many pressures on a parole board to be conservative and few, apart from overcrowding, to be lenient in release policy. From its perspective, a parole board can make two kinds of mistakes. It can release a prisoner who then goes out to commit a serious offense, or it can fail to release someone who, if released, would not commit an offense. The first mistake is highly visible, while the second is invisible, since the unreleased prisoner has no opportunity to prove the board wrong. This necessarily builds a conservative bias into the release system, a bias that confines a substantial number of persons who would not commit a serious crime if released in order to hold a limited number who would so act.[8]

The treatment model has had other harmful effects as well. When release is theoretically governed by treatment considerations, it is often used to control inmates by threatening parole denial as a sanction for misbehavior. This threat has inhibited many prisoners from protesting the conditions of their confinement. In addition, because the standards for decision-making in a rehabilitative system are typically either ill-defined or nonexistent, the existence of wide measures of discretion has made possible a pervasive discrimination against members of racial and cultural minorities, and against the poor and powerless.

The rehabilitative ideal has made it easier to invoke a harsh sanction by providing the rhetoric needed to clothe an essentially punitive response with a humane veneer. A recent example is provided by an article written by Mary Lindsay,[9] at one time Superintendent of the Women's House of Detention in New York, urging that the maximum sentence for prostitution be increased from two weeks to three months. She described the wonderful social services that could be provided for these unfortunate women in jail if only sentences were longer, justifying the coercion on the grounds that previous experience had shown prostitutes would not come to a voluntary program. Had Mrs. Lindsay written, "Prostitutes are evil, disgusting creatures. They should spend three months in jail because two weeks is insufficient punishment for their iniquity," the liberal community would have been up in arms. By attempting to justify a longer sentence on the basis of the women's "needs," that potential source of opposition was neutralized. To the women in jail, of course, three months is still three months; the experience of imprisonment is no less unpleasant despite expressions of good intent.

Finally, the treatment model has served as a politically conservative ideology. By attributing crime to personal pathology, it has diverted attention from broader questions of the distribution of wealth and political power which patterns of crime and law enforcement might otherwise have raised, both in the general population and among prisoners themselves.

For the public the price has also been high. It is expensive to imprison someone. The reforms associated with the treatment model have increased this expense by lengthening the period of confinement but have provided little or no additional long-term public protection. Less costly alternative ways of providing protection from crime have received scant attention, while resources and energy have been invested in rehabilitation programs that do not rehabilitate and preventive detention that detains but does not prevent.

The Purposes of Incarceration

No evaluation of imprisonment or alternatives can be conducted unless it is first established what purposes sanctions should legitimately serve. If there are no such purposes, our recommendation would be simple. We could advocate and work toward an abolition of prisons, insisting that no alternatives replace it.

The situation we face, however, is more complicated. Compliance with at least some rules appears to be necessary if diverse groups of people are to live together under tolerable conditions. The preservation of life, liberty, privacy, and the right to pursue happiness may require protection from the threat or actuality of interference by others. Although we may strive to create a society in which the protection of these basic values can be achieved without the use of any serious sanctions, to build a society whose members are morally sensitive yet tolerant of diversity, it is clear that neither the United States nor any other contemporary large-scale, heterogeneous society remotely approaches that libertarian's paradise. Now and in the foreseeable future the infliction of sanctions appears justified as an evil less to be feared than the damage that might ensue in the absence of any sanctions whatsoever.

To be sure, not all sanctions require the intervention of the state. Threats of disapproval, divorce, physical violence, loss of job or friendship, and fear of hellfire or a hangover, all do their bit to keep us in line. Informal sanctions have the advantage of flexibility; by contrast, law enforcement is a blunt instrument. But informal sanctions also have disadvantages and may be difficult to apply in many situations. Typically they make no provision for an established procedure to determine guilt, may allow the guilty to go unpunished when there is a strong interest in a penalty being exacted, and may result in unfairness or injustice. Thus for some offenses formal sanctions may be preferable to informal ones.

A sanction may reduce the incidence of specified behavior through various mechanisms. Among these are:

1. Incapacitation, which may physically prevent someone from violating the law for the duration of the incapacitation.

2. Rehabilitation, which changes attributes (e.g. attitudes, skills, values) of those who have violated the law in such a way as to prevent them from violating the law again.

3. Special deterrence, which inhibits punished law violators from returning to crime by instilling fear that they will be punished again if apprehended again.

4. General deterrence, which prevents lay violations by instilling in those who have not been punished a fear that they will be punished if they do break the law and are apprehended. At times the concept of general deterrence is stretched beyond compliance motivated by the conscious desire to avoid punishment to include "socialized deterrence," or compliance resulting from the long-range impact on attitudes toward violating the law which may be produced by consistent policies of enforcement or nonenforcement.

I have already alluded to evidence that the second of these functions, rehabilitation, has no present relevance to crime prevention because no one knows how to reform criminals. What of the other functions? As a large fraction of crimes are not reported, and law enforcement is highly inefficient, only a tiny fraction of the incidents classified as a serious crime result in imprisonment. Few of those convicted of a serious offense go on to commit another serious offense,[10] and it is not possible to predict in advance which ones these few will be. For this reason, incapacitation does not contribute substantially to crime reduction.

What of special deterrence? The evidence consistently suggests that lighter penalties (shorter sentences as compared to longer ones, flat release as compared to parole, probation as compared to imprisonment, more intense as compared to less intense street surveillance) are associated with rates of return to crime no greater than, and perhaps somewhat less than, those associated with more stringent penalties. For this reason, and because its numerical importance is limited by the same considerations applicable to incapacitation, special deterrence appears to have little relevance to crime prevention.

For most common offenses, general deterrence is, from a numerical point of view, probably the most significant way by which law enforcement reduces the incidence of prohibited behavior.

It must be noted, however, that some crimes seem to be more susceptible to prevention through deterrence than others. Some of the crimes now punished most severely may be among the least deterrable; however, retributive considerations preclude drastic lowering of penalties for these offenses.

It seems that a mild sanction will suffice to keep most people within the confines of the law most of the time. Within the existing range of sentence severity and certainty, crime rates for the seven F.B.I. index offenses do not vary.[11] Thus, sentences for these crimes appear to be much longer than could be justified on deterrence grounds and, in many instances, longer also than could be justified on retributive grounds.

The two areas in which an increase in the severity of the penalty could be expected to produce greater compliance are areas where enforcement is now minimal: business and governmental crime, and drunken driving. The former is usually unreported, unprosecuted, and, in the rare instances where prosecution does take place, is punished very lightly. The latter offense is one of the most dangerous in the United States, since drunken driving is considered responsible for more than 25,000 traffic deaths and a much larger number of injuries each year. Short jail sentences for driving while intoxicated have drastically cut traffic accidents and fatalities in several European countries and have created, as a by-product, a sizable middle-class constituency concerned about jail conditions. These offenses are, however, usually excluded from common definitions of "the crime problem" in the United States.

Alternatives to Prison?

Acceptance of the principle that sanctions should be imposed on those who break the law in order to reduce the incidence of law violation or to satisfy principles of retribution need not commit one to any particular sanction. Given the obviously unattractive features of the prison, it may be worthwhile to consider alternatives to it. The currently fashionable "alternative" is "community-based corrections."

Sometimes the term "community-based treatment" is used to describe small, residential facilities located in low-income neighborhoods and used as a supplement to, or in lieu of, conventional institutions located in rural areas. At other times, "community-based treatment" refers to programs in which convicted persons are conditionally released under supervision and required to participate in "out-patient" treatment programs located in their neighborhoods.

It is probably safe to say that no one really believes that merely locating an institution near an offender's neighborhood has in itself significant therapeutic value. The county jail, after all, was based *in* the community but hardly developed much of a reputation for rehabilitation. The difference is presumed to lie in the treatment, usually group counselling. Evidence indicates, however, that the rate of return to crime from these programs is no lower than it is for conventional penitentiary or reformatory commitments, or conventional probation. Such alternatives may still be defensible on grounds other than treatment, e.g., lower operating costs and less disruption of the lives of inmates. They do not, however, solve the problem of the prison, because they are usually intended as an adjunct to the prison or as a substitute for a small group of convicted persons.

Other alternatives may avoid the use of incarceration altogether. Though still at a primitive stage of development, it is possible that, in the future, behavior modification techniques will prove capable of preventing recidivist crime through forms of conditioning, psychosurgery, implantation of psychotropic drugs, or electronic monitoring of the brain.[12] Such measures appear sufficiently unpleasant to have considerable deterrent value. I find them highly objectionable because of their intrusiveness, disrespect for human dignity, and potential for political abuse, and I hope they will never be used on an involuntary basis.

Monetary fines are a more attractive alternative. In Sweden, more than 97 per cent of all sentences for criminal convictions are fines. Fines have a number of distinct advantages over imprisonment: they do not disrupt private lives or work careers, are psychologically less destructive than incarceration, and cost little to administer. If installment payments were permitted, fines of substantial magnitude could be levied and provisions made for victim restitution. Although little research has been done on fines, we know of no reason to believe they would be less effective as deterrents than other sanctions. The major impediment to the adoption of fines as the primary sanctioning technique would presumably be the inability of many persons to pay large fines. Denmark takes account of differential ability to pay by fining in proportion to income. This could be done in the United States also, but when a significant portion of the population has very little current income and limited prospects for the future, a small fine may be ineffective as a deterrent and therefore unacceptable to legislatures.

Prison Reforms

The large capital investment in prisons, the large number of employees they support, and the inevitably slow pace of change in a low-priority policy area make it unlikely that prisons will soon be abandoned. This being so, we must ask what reforms ought to be given priority consideration.

Prisoners would undoubtedly give first priority to shorter sentences rather than a modification of the conditions of confinement. It is remarkable that reformers in the past have paid so much attention to improvements in the physical plant and provision of treatment gimmicks but did so little to get prisoners out of prison. Evidence indicates that sentences could be lowered substantially without a perceptible rise in crime rates.

The goal of reducing sentences may under some circumstances conflict with another frequently proposed reform: greater use of probation or other diversionary schemes. At present one of the few pressures on a parole board to release prisoners is the necessity to make room for newcomers. A diversionary program relieving that pressure might well result in longer sentences for the smaller fraction of convicted persons sent to prison. If, simultaneous with the expansion of the diversionary program the number of prison beds were to be systematically reduced, this danger could be averted.

Continued expansion of probation and other street alternatives may eventually force us to confront another dilemma. To achieve a given level of compliance through deterrence, one may punish a few individuals harshly or a larger number more leniently. The latter alternative is clearly preferable, both for humanitarian reasons and for the pragmatic reason that certainty is probably more significant than severity of punishment for purposes of deterrence. Available evidence suggests that probation could be expanded considerably without loss of deterrent effectiveness, but there may be a limit to such expansion. Under some circumstances, then, it may be preferable to curtail the use of probation in favor of uniformly imposed short sentences rather than make wide use of probation, with stiff sentences for the few considered unworthy or unsuitable for probation.

Within the institution, the wide discretionary powers of prison authorities to discipline, transfer, disrupt and interfere with the lives of inmates, must be curtailed. Protection from involuntary lobotomies, shock treatments, and harmful drug programs must be provided. Rights, as distinguished from privileges, must be established, as the latter so readily become abusable control devices. Mechanisms must be established to prevent prison staff and administrators from infringing on rights established in court or in the legislature.[13]

The thrust to curtail discretion must be extended to the release process and ideally would culminate in the abolition of parole, with release automatic at the end of a legislatively prescribed sentence meted out equally to all convicted of the same offense and having the same prior record. A campaign to accomplish this goal would have to combat the ideology of individualization of justice, which has until recently dominated thinking about the criminal justice system.

In the drive to attain a nondiscretionary system of release, it may be tempting to aim at the establishment of due process at hearings on parole applications and revocations as a transitional measure. For tactical purposes this may be necessary, but there are dangers. In response to the U.S. Supreme Court decision granting limited but significant due process rights in parole revocation hearings,[14] the Adult Authority in California has already begun pressuring parolees to waive their newly granted rights by promising more lenient treatment in return. Moreover, *procedural* due process is of limited value in the absence of unambiguous *substantive* standards for determining eligibility for release or governing revocation.

At the pretrial stage an attempt should be made to abolish money-bail. The controversy over proposals for formalized pretrial detention has been allowed to obscure the fact that for the large proportion of defendants incapable of posting bond, preventive detention is an established fact. Recognizance programs fail to get to the heart of the issue: equal treatment before the law, regardless of wealth. Furthermore, because they affect too few, such programs have failed to reduce jail populations in large urban centers and have legitimized pretrial detention by placing the stamp of liberal approval on the principle that some people and not others should be confined before trial, on the basis of personal characteristics unrelated to the offense charged, prior criminal record, or history of appearance at previous trials. That the criteria generally used in recognizance programs, e.g., stability of job and residence, discriminate against the poor suggests the possibility of creating an alliance of groups disadvantaged by both bail and recognizance programs to eliminate these discriminatory elements in the administration of justice.

Preincarcerative Reforms

Thus far we have discussed only questions pertaining to jails and prisons. The input to these institutions is determined by the legislature, by police, prosecutors and judges, through processes systematically discriminating in favor of the politically powerful and affluent middle- and upper-income groups, and against the moneyless, the powerless, and cultural and political deviants. In the face of this pervasive discrimination and occasional outright repression, the expression "criminal justice system" is unjustified except as irony. Penal reform would be a cruel joke if it dealt only with the circumstances of confinement without touching the question of who should be confined and through what processes the decision to choose that disposition (or some other) should be made. Reformers should, therefore, broaden their sights and consider ways to expose and eliminate biases in the legislature and in the administration of justice. This will require tackling the question of discretion at all levels, not just the prison.

Civil commitments should be another focal point for reformers. To say that alcoholism and drug addiction are medical problems and should not be handled by imprisonment is of little benefit to addicts and alcoholics if as a result they are simply committed, under civil proceedings affording them less due process than is available in ordinary criminal trials, to an institution differing from the prison primarily in name.

Changing the System

As in many other social struggles, disinterested reformers cannot be counted on to fight or win the battle for a just and humane system of criminal justice alone. Those without a substantial stake in change are not likely to have the necessary persistence for a long struggle with slow and limited results. Much will depend, therefore, on those for whom the present system is profoundly dysfunctional—convicts, ex-convicts, the families of prisoners, and minority groups whose efforts to struggle against their own oppression or to transform the institutional arrangements of the larger society are met with repression at the hands of law enforcement officials. It is they who can put pressure on legislatures, educate and mobilize an ill-informed public, and force administrators to conform to court decisions.

In broad outline, the system for which they must strive will differ from the present one in several important ways. It will avoid excessive punishment. Rather than treating persons convicted of crime as if they were children or victims of a disease, it will regard them as fully competent adults. Coercion to achieve "treatment goals" will be prohibited, but uncoerced help, education, and training will be readily available to all who desire it.[15] Substantive rights not absolutely incompatible with the requirements of punishment—including the right to organize—will be guaranteed. In order to avoid arbitrariness and discrimination, fairness and equality of treatment will be guaranteed by measures reducing or eliminating the discretionary powers of law enforcement and prison officials.

The adoption of such a system would contribute to the elimination of some of the liabilities that many defendants now experience. Such a system would also reduce the harm suffered by those who are imprisoned. The complete elimination of those disabilities and the further reduction in harm to those punished, which might result from substituting fines for imprisonment on a large scale, awaits the realization of a society in which poverty and racial prejudice are not widespread.

The system described above would do little to ameliorate the crime problem, but there is no reason to believe that it would aggravate that problem. While the prison has something to do with crime prevention, the link between the prison and the reduction of crime is far more tenuous than has traditionally been believed. It is possible that changes at other levels of law enforcement could somewhat reduce crime rates, but this is speculation. It seems unlikely that any acceptable method of law enforcement could greatly reduce crime. Here, too, it is likely that we shall have to await more fundamental social change to solve our problem. Acceptance of the limited usefulness of law enforcement may facilitate the adoption of more equitable procedures of penal administration by relieving fear that increased crime will result from proposed reform. It may still be difficult, however, to overcome the traditional opposition to "coddling criminals," which perceived high crime rates may often exacerbate.

Footnotes

1 D. J. Rothman, The Discovery of the Asylum: Social Order and Disorder in the New Republic (Little, Brown & Co., Boston, 1971); R. B. Caplan, Psychiatry and the Community in Nineteenth-Century America (Basic Books, New York, 1969); S. J. Fox, Introduction, in B. K. Peirce, A Half-Century with Juvenile Delinquents (Patterson-Smith, Montclair, N.J., 1969) (originally published 1869).

2 Rothman, "History of Prisons, Asylums, and Other Decaying Institutions," Chapter 1 of this book.

3 A. M. Platt, The Child-Savers: The Invention of Delinquency (U. Chicago Press, Chicago, 1969).

4 E. C. Wines, The State of Prisons and of Child-Saving Institutions in the Civilized World, at 131–132 (Patterson-Smith, Montclair, N.J., 1968) (reprinted from the 1880 edition).

5 F. A. Allen, The Borderland of Criminal Justice: Essays in Criminology (U. Chicago Press, Chicago, 1964).

6 G. R. Bacon, et al., Struggle for Justice, Ch. 3 (Hill & Wang, New York, 1971).

7 This is the conclusion reached in D. S. Lipton, R. Martinson, and J. Wilkins, Effectiveness of Correctional Treatment: A Survey of Treatment Evaluations (New York State Office of Crime Control Planning, 1970, unpublished), based on a survey of more than 200 programs conducted between 1945 and 1967. My own survey, which brings their study up to date, confirms their conclusion. D. F. Greenberg, "The Special Effects of Penal Measures: A Descriptive Summary of Existing Studies," Staff Memorandum #2 for the Committee on Incarceration (March 29, 1972).

8 von Hirsch, "Prediction of Criminal Conduct and Preventive Confinement of Convicted Persons," 21 Buff. L. Rev. 717 (1972).

9 Lindsay, "Delinquency—Prostitution's Timebomb," 16 Crime & Delinquency 151 (1970).

10 This assertion may be reconciled with the widely circulated claim that recidivism is high by noting that most recidivists are returned to prison for technical violations of parole regulations or for minor property crimes.

11 F. E. Zimring, Perspectives on Deterrence, at 87 (U.S. Government Printing Office, Washington, D.C., 1971).

12 R. Schwitzgebel, Development of Legal Regulation of Coercive Behavior Modification Techniques with Offenders (U.S. Government Printing Office, Washington, D.C., 1971).

13 Greenberg and Stender, "The Prison as a Lawless Agency," 21 Buff. L. Rev. 799 (1972).

14 Morrissey v. Brewer, 408 U.S. 471 (1972).

15 Considerations of fairness suggest that such help should be made available equally to those who have not committed any crime but who simply find themselves in need of assistance.

APPENDIX A

A-1

SAMPLE COMPLAINT IN A §1983 CLASS ACTION CHALLENGING LACK OF DUE PROCESS IN PRISON DISCIPLINARY PROCEEDINGS

Clutchette v. Procunier

FLOYD SILLIMAN
SILLIMAN & HOUSE
130 West Gabilan
Salinas, California 93901
Telephone: (408) 424-0061

JOHN THORNE
510 North Third Street
San Jose, California
Telephone: (408) 286-1212

FAY STENDER
FRANCK, HILL, STENDER, HENDON, KELLEY & LARSON
2905 Telegraph Avenue
Berkeley, California 94705
Telephone: (415) 845-4123

WILLIAM BENNETT TURNER
1095 Market Street
San Francisco, California 94103
Telephone: (415) 861-8553

Attorneys for Plaintiffs

IN THE UNITED STATES DISTRICT COURT
FOR THE NORTHERN DISTRICT OF CALIFORNIA

JOHN WESLEY CLUTCHETTE and GEORGE L. JACKSON, individually and on behalf of all others similarly situated, Plaintiffs, vs. RAYMOND J. PROCUNIER, LOUIS NELSON and JAMES PARK, Defendants.	NO. C-70 2497 AJZ AMENDED COMPLAINT FOR DECLARATORY JUDGMENT, INJUNCTIVE RELIEF AND DAMAGES

Plaintiffs JOHN WESLEY CLUTCHETTE and GEORGE L. JACK-SON, as and for their amended complaint, allege as follows:

I. JURISDICTION

1. Jurisdiction of this Court is invoked pursuant to 28 U.S.C. Sections 1343(3), 1343(4) and 2201. This is a suit authorized by 42 U.S.C. Section 1983 to redress the deprivation under color of state law of rights, privileges and immunities secured by the due process and equal protection clauses of the Fourteenth Amendment to the Constitution of the United States. This is also a proceeding for a declaratory judgment as to plaintiffs' rights to be free from such deprivation by defendants acting under color of state law.

II. PARTIES

2. Plaintiff JOHN WESLEY CLUTCHETTE is a prisoner incarcerated at San Quentin State Prison, Tamal, California. He is a black citizen of the United States and a resident of the State of California.

3. Plaintiff GEORGE L. JACKSON is a prisoner incarcerated at San Quentin State Prison, Tamal, California. He is a black citizen of the United States and a resident of the State of California.

4. Defendant RAYMOND J. PROCUNIER is Director of the Department of Corrections of the State of California. He is sued individually and in his capacity as Director of Corrections. As such Director, defendant PROCUNIER has general supervision of California prisons including San Quentin State Prison.

5. Defendant LOUIS NELSON is Warden of San Quentin State Prison. He is sued individually and in his official capacity as Warden. He has general supervision and control of San Quentin State Prison.

6. Defendant JAMES PARK is Associate Warden of San Quentin State Prison. He is sued individually and in his official capacity.

III. CLASS ACTION

7. Plaintiffs bring this action on their own behalf, and, pursuant to Rule 23(b)(1) and Rule 23(b)(2) of the Federal Rules of Civil Procedure, on behalf of all other inmates of San Quentin State Prison subject to defendants' jurisdiction and affected by the policies, practices or acts of defendants complained of herein. The class is so numerous that joinder of all members is impracticable; there are questions of law and fact common to the class; the claims and defenses of plaintiffs are typical of the claims and defenses of the class; and plaintiffs will fairly and adequately protect the interests of the class.

IV. FACTS

A. Plaintiff CLUTCHETTE

8. On November 14, 1970, at approximately 1:15 p.m., plaintiff CLUTCHETTE was brought to the visiting room at San Quentin to receive a visit from a friend, Jacqueline Slaughter and a small child.

9. Upon entering the visiting room, CLUTCHETTE was told by a

correctional officer that he was required to sit next to an officer at the visiting room desk, instead of sitting at other empty places at the visiting room tables. CLUTCHETTE protested that he had never been required to sit in that place before and asked the officer on duty to speak with Lt. Wagner, who was in charge of the visiting room.

10. Plaintiff CLUTCHETTE and his visitors then sat down at one of the empty places at the visiting room tables. In the meantime, Lt. Wagner had stated that he did not want to speak with plaintiff and another correctional officer had informed plaintiff that it would be permissible for him to sit where he was sitting with his visitors.

11. Approximately 15 minutes later, two officers approached plaintiff and told him that his visiting time was over. Plaintiff responded that he would leave when his hour was up, since prisoners are customarily alloted one hour for visits.

12. Plaintiff then noticed that about 10 correctional officers had appeared in the hall to the visiting room and that they were armed with blackjacks and clubs. These officers began telling all persons in the visiting room to leave the room. Plaintiff, fearing for his safety, broke off part of a chair to arm himself.

13. One of the officers approached plaintiff and stated that he wanted to talk. Plaintiff put down the chair and walked toward him, completely unarmed, to discuss the matter, and was immediately assaulted without cause by the officer. The rest of the officers then attacked plaintiff, handcuffed him and commenced beating him with clubs. One officer beat plaintiff about the head several times while he was on the floor and handcuffed, opening a severe gash in plaintiff's forehead.

14. Another prisoner, Willie Thompson, attempted to defend plaintiff against this attack and was also beaten by the officers. Civilian witnesses in the visiting room who protested the beating, including Thompson's mother, were also pushed, shoved and abused by the guards.

15. The officers removed plaintiff CLUTCHETTE from the visiting room, photographed him and placed him in a strip cell. This is a concrete cell with a concrete slab and a one-inch mattress to sleep on, with no windows and no meaningful contact with the outside world. At this time, plaintiff's head was bleeding profusely, and he experienced dizziness, nausea and chills.

16. At approximately 11:30 p.m. the same day, plaintiff was taken to the prison hospital, where the gash in his forehead was sutured, he was given medication and placed in a hospital cell. At 8:00 a.m. the next morning he was taken from the hospital and confined again in the strip cell, despite a doctor's instructions that he should not be so confined. Although plaintiff was still in pain from his wound, he received no medication until approximately 4:00 p.m. that afternoon.

17. Plaintiff CLUTCHETTE was confined to an isolation cell for about a week, with no hearing or disciplinary proceeding whatever. On November 20, 1970, CLUTCHETTE was taken before a prison disciplinary committee at San Quentin and charged with misconduct regarding the visiting room incident set forth above. Specifically, CLUTCHETTE was

charged with "Refusing to obey a direct order by an officer, misconduct in the present of visitors, conduct that could lead to violence," and he was also charged with "assaulting an officer." Plaintiff was given no notice prior to the disciplinary proceeding, whether in writing or oral, of either the specific misconduct he was charged with or the prison rule he was charged with having violated. At the disciplinary hearing, the officials, because they thought a possible felony was involved, read CLUTCHETTE warnings regarding interrogations. They then asked plaintiff to plead guilty or not guilty to the charges. Plaintiff entered a plea of not guilty.

18. At the hearing on the charges, CLUTCHETTE was not permitted to be represented by counsel or counsel substitute. Defendant PARK had denied plaintiff's attorney's request to appear at the disciplinary hearing on plaintiff's behalf. No witnesses appeared at the hearing, and plaintiff was not permitted to confront or cross-examine any witnesses. Nor was plaintiff permitted to call any witnesses on his own behalf, even though civilian witnesses who were present in the visiting room at the time of the incident would have testified for plaintiff and established his innocence, and even though plaintiff asked to call a correctional officer and other inmates as witnesses. The request of plaintiff's attorney to supplement the evidence by affidavits of witnesses was denied. Plaintiff's request to see the disciplinary reports on which the charges were based was denied. No adequate record of the hearing was kept. There is no requirement that the decision of the disciplinary committee be based on substantial evidence adduced at the hearing or that the reasons for the disciplinary decision be either entered in the record or given to the inmate. There is no adequate appeal from the disciplinary decision.

19. As a result of the disciplinary "hearing" held on November 20, 1970, plaintiff was sentenced to (a) 60 days' loss of privileges enjoyed by prisoners at San Quentin, (b) 29 days in isolation in a strip cell, and (c) referral to the Marin County District Attorney for prosecution. Isolation is the most severe punishment which may be meted out by a disciplinary committee. Inmates in isolation are denied the normal prison privileges available to the general inmate population and are cut off from all meaningful human contact. They spend all or almost all of their time confined to their small cells in idleness. They are completely deprived of the right to participate in any rehabilitative program at San Quentin. Isolation is a form of solitary confinement which is calculated to undermine the sanity and destroy the spirit of any prisoner.

20. In addition to the above punishments imposed upon plaintiff CLUTCHETTE by the disciplinary committee, the action of the disciplinary committee will be referred by defendants to the California Adult Authority, which under California law is charged with the responsibility of setting plaintiff's sentence and term of imprisonment and determining whether plaintiff should be released on parole. Resolution No. 216 (6/5/64) of the Adult Authority requires that a report of all disciplinary actions involving an inmate be presented to the Adult Authority at the time when the Adult Authority considers the fixing of the sentence and parole date. On information and belief, the Adult Authority takes into

consideration and views unfavorably disciplinary records of the kind involved in plaintiff's case. Therefore, the action of the disciplinary committee in finding plaintiff guilty of misconduct and imposing serious punishment may seriously prolong plaintiff's actual term of imprisonment.

B. Plaintiff JACKSON

21. On November 18, 1970, at about 9:30 a.m., plaintiff JACKSON was brought to a visiting room at San Quentin to receive a visit from a friend, Joan Hammer.

22. JACKSON and his visitor seated themselves at a table. A correctional officer informed plaintiff that they should not sit on the same side of the table, and plaintiff's visitor moved to the opposite side of the table from JACKSON. An officer thereafter announced that visiting time was over, and plaintiff protested that the visit was being prematurely terminated. After JACKSON left the visiting room a scuffle ensued and plaintiff was set upon by a number of officers and handcuffed.

23. On November 25, 1970, plaintiff JACKSON was taken before a prison disciplinary committee at San Quentin and charged with misconduct regarding the visiting room incident set forth above. As in the case of plaintiff CLUTCHETTE, plaintiff JACKSON was not afforded any of the procedural safeguards set forth in paragraphs 17 and 18 above. His attorney's request to be present at the "hearing" was denied but, although he was not allowed to call witnesses in his behalf, he was allowed to submit the affidavit of Joan Hammer to defendant PARK.

24. As a result of the disciplinary "hearing" held on November 25, 1970, plaintiff JACKSON was sentenced to substantially the same punishments as plaintiff CLUTCHETTE set forth in paragraph 19 above, was confined in isolation in substantially the same conditions and was deprived of visits with Joan Hammer for a period of six months. In addition, the action of the disciplinary committee will be referred to the Adult Authority as set forth in paragraph 20 above, with the same consequences of such action.

C. General Policies and Practices

25. The disciplinary procedures described in paragraphs 17 and 18 above are followed in all disciplinary cases involving prisoners at San Quentin, and it is the general and uniform practice to deny San Quentin prisoners the minimum safeguards of procedural due process in disciplinary proceedings. However, a prisoner received in a state prison before January 1, 1948, is entitled to earn time credit reductions from his sentence and such credits may not be forfeited unless the prisoner is found guilty of a disciplinary charge in a hearing at which, under Penal Code Section 2924, he "may present evidence and witnesses in his behalf;" Adult Authority Resolution No. 86 requires that a record of the hearing be made. Thus, although the pre-1948 prisoners may have some procedural protections in certain disciplinary "hearings," the general policy and practice is to deny prisoners minimal procedural safeguards when charged with disciplinary infractions.

26. In addition, the conditions in isolation described in paragraph 19 above are uniform for all prisoners at San Quentin. Any prisoner at San Quentin may summarily be relegated to isolation in such conditions by the unfair disciplinary procedures described above. In addition, in accordance with the general policy and practice, the action taken by the disciplinary committee with regard to any inmate is reported to the Adult Authority as set forth in paragraph 20 above. Accordingly, the disciplinary action may directly affect any San Quentin prisoner's actual term of imprisonment. Indeed, as to prisoners whose sentence and release date have already been set, any finding of guilty by a disciplinary committee must be reported to the Adult Authority under its Resolution 216 and such finding in itself is sufficient ground for recission of the sentence and release date.

27. Plaintiffs and members of the plaintiff class on behalf of whom this suit is brought have no plain, adequate or complete remedy at law to redress the wrongs alleged herein, and this suit for declaratory judgment and an injunction is their only means of securing adequate relief. Plaintiffs and members of the plaintiff class are now suffering and will continue to suffer irreparable injury from defendants' policies and practices as set forth herein.

WHEREFORE, plaintiffs respectfully pray that this Court enter judgment granting plaintiffs:

(a) A declaratory judgment that defendants' acts, policies and practices complained of herein violate plaintiffs' rights and the rights of members of the plaintiff class secured by the due process and equal protection clauses of the Fourteenth Amendment;

(b) A preliminary and permanent injunction enjoining defendants from summarily punishing plaintiffs and members of the class and from inflicting serious punishments on them without providing them with minimal safeguards of due process of law;

(c) A preliminary and permanent injunction setting aside the disciplinary actions taken against plaintiff CLUTCHETTE on November 20, 1970, and against plaintiff JACKSON on November 25, 1970, expunging such actions from defendants' records, restraining defendants from reporting such actions to the Adult Authority and reinstating plaintiffs' normal prison privileges;

(d) Compensatory damages for plaintiff CLUTCHETTE in the amount of $15,000 and punitive damages for plaintiff CLUTCHETTE in the amount of $15,000;

(e) Plaintiffs' costs of this suit; and

(f) Such other and further relief as the Court may deem just and proper.

Dated: December 3, 1970.

/s/ Floyd Silliman

FLOYD SILLIMAN
SILLIMAN & HOUSE
130 West Gabilan
Salinas, California 93901

JOHN THORNE
  510 North Third Street
  San Jose, California

FAY STENDER
FRANCK, HILL, STENDER, HENDON,
KELLEY & LARSON
  2905 Telegraph Avenue
  Berkeley, California 94705

WILLIAM BENNETT TURNER
  1095 Market Street
  San Francisco, California 94103

Attorneys for Plaintiffs

SAMPLE COMPLAINT IN A §1983 ACTION

Oliver v. Schoonfield

IN THE
UNITED STATES DISTRICT COURT
FOR THE DISTRICT OF MARYLAND

ROSELLS OLIVER
Maryland Correctional Training Center
Route #3
Hagerstown, Maryland 21740

DORIAN WISE
1834 Druid Hill Avenue
Baltimore, Maryland

BENNIE WITHERSPOON, JR.
Patuxent Institution
Jessup, Maryland 20794

JAMES PALMER
Maryland Correctional Training Center
Route #3
Hagerstown, Maryland 21740
            and
JACKIE JACKSON
2829 West Garrison Avenue
Baltimore, Maryland

        PLAINTIFFS

        vs.   CIVIL ACTION NO.:

HIRAM L. SCHOONFIELD
Warden, Baltimore City Jail
401 East Eager Street
Baltimore, Maryland 21202

HOWARD PARKS
Deputy Warden, Baltimore City Jail
401 East Eager Street
Baltimore, Maryland 21202

EARNEST R. BARBOSA
3516 Langrehr Road
Baltimore, Maryland 21207

DONALD H. BROGDEN
2310 Winchester Street
Apartment H
Baltimore, Maryland 21216

B. O. McCUTCHEON
4024 Cranston Avenue
Baltimore, Maryland 21229

ANDREW STITCHALK
3927 Longley Road
Abingdon, Maryland 21009

ALBERT T. YOOR
746 South Curley Street
Baltimore, Maryland 21224
　　　and

UNKNOWN DEFENDANTS
　　Persons who have in the past,
　　or who are now, correctional
　　officers at the Baltimore City
　　Jail and whose names are now
　　unknown to Plaintiffs

DEFENDANTS

COMPLAINT FOR DAMAGES AND INJUNCTIVE RELIEF
JURISDICTION

1. Jurisdiction of this Court is invoked pursuant to and in accordance with the provisions of Title 28 U.S.C. Sections 1331 and 1343. This action arises under 42 U.S.C. Sections 1983, 1985, 1986 and 1988 and the Constitution of the United States, in particular but not limited to the First, Fifth, Eighth and Fourteenth Amendments thereto. In addition, pendant jurisdiction is invoked over state law claims.

PARTIES

2. All plaintiffs are citizens of the United States and Maryland. More specifically:

a. Rosells Oliver is a 20 year old black male presently confined at the Maryland Correctional Training Center;

b. Dorian Wise is a 19 year old black male currently residing at 1834 Druid Hill Avenue;

c. Bennie Witherspoon, Jr., is a 22 year old black male currently confined at the Patuxent Institution;

d. James Palmer is a 20 year old black male currently confined at the Maryland Correctional Training Center;

e. Jeffrey Johnson is a 19 year old black male currently confined at the Maryland Correctional Institution; and

f. Jackie Jackson is a 19 year old black male currently residing at 2829 West Garrison Avenue.

3. Defendant Hiram Schoonfield is Warden of the Baltimore City Jail. Article 1, Section 51 of the Baltimore City Charter authorizes and empowers Warden Schoonfield to "take charge of the prison and prisoners" committed to his responsibility. Defendant Schoonfield is generally responsible for the maintenance and supervision of the city jail and its employees and agents and the enforcement and implementation of policies, procedures and rules governing that institution. In addition, Defendant Schoonfield is responsible, in part, for the origination and promulgation of policies, procedures and rules governing the jail. Furthermore, Defendant Schoonfield is responsible, at least in part, for the hiring, training, disciplining and firing of correctional officers at the Baltimore City Jail.

4. Defendant Howard B. Parks is Deputy Warden of the Baltimore City Jail. He is responsible to Defendant Schoonfield for the enforcement and implementation of policies, procedures and rules governing the city jail and its employees and agents. In addition, he is responsible for the supervision of correctional officers at the jail and is particularly responsible for the administration of the jail in regard to security. He is also responsible, subject to and in conjunction with Warden Schoonfield, for the disciplining of correctional officers who violate jail rules.

5. Defendants Earnest Barbosa, Donald Brogden, B. O. McCutcheon, Andrew Stitchalk, and Albert Yoor are correctional officers presently employed at the Baltimore City Jail. They are either supervising or line officers whose obligation it is to guarantee jail security and provide for the health, safety and well-being of the inmates confined at the jail.

NATURE OF THE ACTION

6. This action is authorized by 42 U.S.C. Sections 1983, 1985, 1986 and 1988 and seeks to recover compensatory and punitive monetary damages for the deprivation under color of law of rights guaranteed to Plaintiffs by the United States Constitution and, further, seeks the recovery of compensatory and punitive damages for acts and conduct of certain defendants who intentionally, pursuant to a general plan, scheme and conspiracy and under color of law, denied Plaintiffs' rights to equal protection of the law and equal privileges and immunities guaranteed by law. In addition, Plaintiffs seek compensatory and punitive damages against certain Defendants for their reckless, negligent and intentional failure to prevent the continued commission of grossly improper, unlawful, illegal and unconstitutional acts by certain Defendants which denied Plaintiffs rights guaranteed by the United States Constitution and state and federal law. More specifically, Plaintiffs seek relief for acts and conduct which denied them, *inter alia:*

a. Their right, guaranteed by the Eighth Amendment, to be free from cruel and unusual punishment; and

b. Their right, guaranteed by the Fourteenth Amendment, to be free from arbitrary denials of liberty without due process of law.

This action is also authorized by provisions of Maryland law made applicable by the doctrine of pendant jurisdiction.

Finally, Plaintiffs also seek declaratory and injunctive relief to prevent the recurrence of the challenged acts and practices.

ALLEGATIONS OF FACT

7. All Plaintiffs have been, at one time, pre-trial detainees at the Baltimore City Jail awaiting trial in the Criminal Court of Baltimore City. While confined at the jail all Plaintiffs were physically brutalized either as a result of severe beatings by certain Defendants or as a result of the imposition, by certain Defendants, of even more vicious physical abuse which can only be termed torture. The facts supporting Plaintiffs' contentions are as follows:

a. On or about October 26, 1969, Rosells Oliver, Dorian Wise, and Bennie Witherspoon were pre-trial detainees confined in the Baltimore City Jail. All were confined on section K of the jail then used to house juveniles or youthful inmates. Either during the late evening of October 23rd or early morning of October 24th these three inmates were confined in their cells after the "lights-out" order had been given. There was some noise on the section at this time caused by inmate conversations and the section inmates were told to be quiet by, upon information and belief, correctional officer Andrew Stitchalk. Shortly thereafter, this officer, apparently irritated because the section was not quiet, told inmates Dorian Wise and Bennie Witherspoon to "pack their stuff" indicating that they were to be taken off the section. Within a short period of time a number of other officers, including, upon information and belief, Sergeant Earnest Barbosa, came upon the section and escorted Wise and Witherspoon from their cells. As they walked by plaintiff Rosells Oliver's cell, Oliver was told by the officers to come with the other two named plaintiffs. The guards walked the three inmates down the steps from the second tier of section K to the ground floor. From there the inmates were taken to a large hallway where they were ordered to remove their clothes. The inmates did so and then were confined in a small closet where supplies were kept.

Soon after their initial confinement in the closet, the door was opened and mace was sprayed upon the three inmates apparently in response to a comment made by one of the occupants of the closet. The result of this macing was that the inmates suffered painful and persistent burning of the eyes.

Sometime later, Bennie Witherspoon was taken from the closet into the hallway where some furniture (desks and chairs) had been arranged in pyramid fashion. Plaintiff Witherspoon was made to climb up onto a chair and ordered to turn so his back faced the iron grating which runs from the floor of the hallway to the ceiling and separates the hallway. While his back was to this grille a guard, Andrew Stitchalk, upon information and belief, handcuffed both his hands together from behind and attached them to the grille. The furniture was then removed leaving Witherspoon hanging with his hands above and behind his head and his feet off the ground. His feet were approximately three (3) feet from the ground floor. While he was hanging one of the officers present put a lighted cigarette near his feet causing him to jerk his body up and down and putting great strain on his wrists. During the time of his hanging Witherspoon began to cry and begged to be let down. He was in great pain and suffered great mental and physical stress. He was left hanging for approximately twenty (20) minutes to one-half hour and then let down. He was subsequently returned to K section.

During the time when Witherspoon was hanging from the grille other officers, unknown to plaintiff at this time, and a supervising officer, upon information and belief Lt. B. O. McCutcheon, observed this physical abuse and made no effort to prevent it or bring it to an end.

Soon after Witherspoon was let down, Rosells Oliver was taken out of the closet and the same treatment was repeated for him. The duration of his hanging was approximately five (5) to ten (10) minutes. While he was hanging a lighted match was placed close to his feet by, upon information and belief, Sergeant Earnest Barbosa. The flame touched and burned his right foot which was bare. While he was hung Oliver suffered great pain and mental and physical anguish.

Dorian Wise was the last to be taken out of the closet. He was hung in a manner similar to the other two inmates. While he was hung his wrists were cut by the handcuffs and he suffered great pain and both physical and mental agony. In addition, while he was hanging, a guard, unknown to plaintiffs at this time, climbed up behind Wise and with the use of his foot pushed Wise away from the metal grille to which he was attached by the handcuffs. This caused additional pain and suffering. After approximately twenty (20) minutes, inmate Wise was let down and returned to his cell.

All three inmates communicated both orally and in writing the fact of their treatment to Warden Schoonfield and Deputy Warden Parks. In addition, Witherspoon attempted to communicate this incident to his family by letters which they did not receive. This result of the hanging was to cause all three inmates great physical and mental anguish and to cause serious, substantial, and permanent physical and mental injury. Deputy Warden Parks and other supervising correctional officers, unknown to plaintiffs, subsequently met with the three inmates. No disciplinary action was taken, upon information and belief, against the guards who inflicted the injury upon the three inmates nor were any measures taken to insure that similar incidents did not occur in the future. Indeed, incidents of this nature were to recur again at least several more times.

b. On or about January 17, 1971, this same treatment, the hanging of juvenile inmates by handcuffs, occurred again. On that date inmates James Palmer and Leonard Cotton were confined as cellmates on K section. It was either late on the evening of January 17th, or early on the morning of January 18th, that they were taken from their cells because, upon information and belief, there was too much noise on the section. They were taken to the same place as the three above-named inmates by unknown officers and ordered to climb the same grille used in the hanging of the above-named inmates. Leonard Cotton was beaten and finally obeyed the order to climb the grille. When he did climb the grille he was handcuffed with his back to the grille, as in the above-mentioned cases, and allowed to hang freely for a period of time approximately fifteen (15) to twenty (20) minutes. While he was hanging from the grille, a large guard forcefully pulled down upon Cotton's legs inflicting great pain on his handcuffed wrists and then physically swung from his legs. During the course of the physical assault and the hanging Cotton was in great pain and suffered immense physical and emotional anguish.

Inmate Palmer was given a similar order, at approximately the same time as Cotton, to climb the grille. When he refused he was taken into a small room and severely beaten. This resulted in his face being swollen, bruised and seriously painful for several days after the beating. While this brutality was occurring other unknown correctional officers observed and made no effort to halt it.

Both inmates complained of their treatment to Deputy Warden Parks in person and communicated their outrage at their treatment in writing to Warden Schoonfield and Deputy Warden Parks. Other correctional officers, unknown to plaintiffs, were also informed of the treatment accorded Palmer and Cotton. No remedial steps were taken by defendants Parks and Schoonfield to insure that this physical brutality was not repeated.

c. In late October or early November of 1970, Jackie Jackson was confined on K section of the Baltimore City Jail. In the late evening or early hours of a morning during this period, Jackson was taken from his cell, upon information and belief, because of excessive noise on this section, and taken to the same area mentioned in the above incidents. As in the above cases, Jackson was forced to climb the grille and handcuffed with his back to the grille with his feet off the ground. Defendants Brogden, and Barbosa, as well as other unknown officers, participated in this brutalization. He hung in this position for approximately five (5) to ten (10) minutes. During this period of time he suffered great physical and mental pain and anguish. After he was let down he was then forced to strip naked and sit in a puddle of water from approximately 12 a.m. to 3 a.m. in the morning. After that he was returned to his cell.

Jackson attempted to report these abuses to jail officials but his attempts were ignored and disregarded.

d. In December of 1969, Jeffrey Johnson was a pre-trial detainee at the Baltimore City Jail. He was confined on section K of the jail. In the late evening or early morning hours of a day during that period Johnson was taken from his cell in K section, upon information and belief, because there was too much noise on the section, and taken to a solitary confinement cell in the jail. He spent approximately four (4) to five (5) hours in the solitary confinement cell until he was removed from the cell by Officer Yoor and another unknown officer and taken to the same area mentioned in the above incidents. Mr. Johnson was then forced by these officers to take his clothes off and was physically hung by his wrists from the same grille mentioned above. He was hung for approximately twenty (20) minutes with his feet off the ground. During this period of time Johnson suffered great pain and mental anguish.

e. The pattern and practice of imposing physical brutality and torture as described above has occurred on occasions other than the above-listed times. Other persons confined on J or K sections of the Baltimore City Jail have been similarly hung and brutalized. All named plaintiffs suffered, at the time of their brutalization, severe physical pain and mental anguish. All plaintiffs have also suffered permanent psychological injury and damage as a result of these vicious acts of brutality.

FIRST CLAIM

8. The above-described imposition of summary, harsh and brutal punishment and treatment upon plaintiffs by defendants Barbosa, Brogden, Stitchalk, Yoor and other unknown defendants has denied them the right to be free from cruel and unusual punishment and their right to life and liberty guaranteed by the Eighth and Fourteenth Amendments to the United States Constitution. These acts were executed and performed by defendants acting under color of law and their authority as correctional officers of the Baltimore City Jail. These unconstitutional, illegal and unprovoked acts include:

a. The physical assault and beating of plaintiff Palmer and the use of physical force by Defendants beyond that necessary for self-defense or to insure proper control and security of the institution.

b. The spraying of mace into a closed room containing plaintiffs Witherspoon, Wise and Oliver directly onto the body and faces of these plaintiffs when it was not necessary for the security and control of the jail or for the protection of any people or property within that institution.

c. The handcuffing and brutal hanging of plaintiffs Oliver, Wise, Witherspoon, Johnson and Jackson without any conceivable justification or excuse.

In addition to the direct brutalization of plaintiffs by the above defendants, the intentional failure of defendant McCutcheon and other unknown defendants to halt the brutalization they observed, the intentional, reckless and negligent failure of defendants Schoonfield and Parks to investigate the first incident of hanging and discipline those responsible and their refusal to take steps to prevent the recurrence of this brutality denied plaintiffs rights guaranteed by the Eighth and Fourteenth Amendments of the United States Constitution and make applicable to plaintiffs by Title 42 U.S.C., Sec. 1983.

SECOND CLAIM

9. Plaintiffs reallege paragraphs 1 through 7.

Plaintiffs allege that defendants Barbosa, Brogden, Stitchalk, Yoor and other unknown defendants did, in violation of 42 U.S.C., Section 1985(3), commit the above-described acts in furtherance of a conspiracy, scheme or plan designed and intended to personally injure plaintiffs and to, either directly or indirectly deny and deprive plaintiffs rights guaranteed by the United States Constitution and laws, particularly plaintiffs' right to equal protection of the laws and equal privileges and immunities under the laws.

THIRD CLAIM

10. Plaintiffs reallege paragraphs 1 through 7.

Plaintiffs allege that defendants Schoonfield, Parks, McCutcheon and other unknown defendants did, in violation of 42 U.S.C., Section 1986, have knowledge that the first illegal and unconstitutional acts set forth above had been committed and would be likely committed in the future and, having the power to prevent or aid in the prevention of the commission of these acts, neglected and refused to exercise reasonable diligence to prevent these acts of brutality.

FOURTH CLAIM

11. Plaintiffs reallege paragraphs 1 through 7 since claim IV arises out of the same facts supporting claims I, II, and III. For the purpose of this claim the defendants include all named defendants.

Plaintiffs have been denied rights guaranteed by Article 23 of the Maryland Declaration of Rights insofar as they were deprived of their liberty without adherence to the law of the land.

WHEREFORE, in consideration of all facts set forth in this complaint, plaintiffs petition this Court for the following relief:

1. That the defendants be ordered to reveal the names of the unknown defendants who were responsible in part for the acts complained of in this action. This is necessary due to the particular problems involved in this suit. Specifically, because the illegal action occurred late at night or in the early morning hours within the confines of the Baltimore City Jail, their identification by the named defendants is necessary to insure that proper relief against these Correctional Officers may be ordered by this Court.

2. That plaintiffs be awarded compensatory and punitive monetary damages against the defendants as specified below.

a. Plaintiff Rosells Oliver requests judgment against defendants' Earnest Barbosa, Andrew Stitchalk, B. O. McCutcheon, Hiram Schoonfield, Howard Parks, and unknown correctional officers, jointly and severally, in the amount of Ten Thousand Dollars ($10,000.00) and he further requests punitive damages in the amount of Fifty Thousand Dollars ($50,000.00) against each of the aforementioned defendants.

b. Plaintiff Dorian Wise requests judgment against defendants Earnest Barbosa, Andrew Stitchalk, B. O. McCutcheon, Hiram Schoonfield, Howard Parks, and unknown correctional officers, jointly and severally, in the amount of Ten Thousand Dollars ($10,000.00) and he further requests punitive damages in the amount of Fifty Thousand Dollars ($50,000.00) against each of the aforementioned defendants.

c. Plaintiff Bennie Witherspoon requests judgment against defendants Earnest Barbosa, Andrew Stitchalk, B. O. McCutcheon, Hiram

Schoonfield, Howard Parks, and unknown correctional officers, jointly and severally, in the amount of Ten Thousand Dollars ($10,000.00) and he further requests punitive damages in the amount of Fifty Thousand Dollars ($50,000.00) against each of the aforementioned defendants.

d. Plaintiff James Palmer requests judgment against defendants Schoonfield and Parks and unknown defendants, jointly and severally, in the amount of Ten Thousand Dollars ($10,000.00) and he further requests punitive damages in the amount of Fifty Thousand Dollars ($50,000.00) against each of the aforementioned defendants.

e. Plaintiff Jackie Jackson requests judgment against defendants Parks, Schoonfield, Barbosa, Brogden and other unknown defendants, jointly and severally, in the amount of Ten Thousand Dollars ($10,000.00) and he further requests punitive damages in the amount of Fifty Thousand Dollars ($50,000.00) against each of the aforementioned defendants.

f. Plaintiff Jeffrey Johnson requests judgment against defendants Yoor, Schoonfield, and Parks and other unknown defendants, jointly and severally, in the amount of Ten Thousand Dollars ($10,000.00) and he further requests punitive damages in the amount of Fifty Thousand Dollars ($50,000.00) against each of the aforementioned defendants.

3. That the Court enter a declaratory judgment pursuant to Title 28 U.S.C., Section 2201 declaring unconstitutional the acts and conduct described *supra,* and that a preliminary and permanent injunction be issued against named defendants, their agents and employees and those in active concert with them, enjoining them from continuing, allowing, participating in or countenancing the acts, practices and procedures described *supra.* Plaintiffs particularly request declaratory and injunctive relief:

a. Forbidding the handcuffing of inmates with their feet off the ground or any similar brutalization of jail inmates within the Baltimore City Jail;

b. Forbidding the promiscuous, unnecessary and unprovoked use of mace or tear gas when such is not necessary in order to safeguard the life or safety of jail personnel or inmates;

c. Forbidding the beating or physical assault of inmates in the Baltimore City Jail; and

d. Ordering defendants to devise a scheme or plan for the presentation, by inmates, of complaints and grievances including, at minimum the following features:

(i) A procedure whereby inmates are able to directly and privately communicate uncensored complaints to the membership of the Baltimore City Jail Board;

(ii) A procedure creating an independent body outside the jail administration, responsible for the review and evaluation of all inmate complaints and for recommendations to jail authorities and the Jail Board; and

(iii) A procedure providing for and requiring that all complaints made by jail inmates be made a matter of public record available to the public.

4. That plaintiffs be granted the costs of this action including

attorneys' fees and such other and further relief as this Court may deem
proper in this action.

/s/ Michael Millemann
_____

MICHAEL MILLEMANN
341 North Calvert Street
Baltimore, Maryland 21202
Legal Aid Bureau, Inc.

/s/ Joseph A. Matera
_____

JOSEPHIA MATERA
341 N. Calvert Street
Baltimore, Maryland 21202
Legal Aid Bureau, Inc.

/s/ Stephen Sachs
_____

STEPHEN SACHS
1605 Mercantile Bk. & Trust Building
2 Hopkins Plaza
Baltimore, Maryland 21202

/s/ Michael S. Elder
_____

MICHAEL S. ELDER
341 N. Calvert Street
Baltimore, Maryland 21202
Legal Aid Bureau, Inc.

/s/ Charles F. Morgan
_____

CHARLES F. MORGAN
1435 W. Baltimore Street
Baltimore, Maryland 21223
Legal Aid Bureau, Inc.

FORM: NOTICE TO MEMBERS OF CLASS OF COMMENCEMENT OF A §1983 CLASS ACTION

Collins v. Schoonfield

IN THE
UNITED STATES DISTRICT COURT
FOR THE DISTRICT OF MARYLAND

VERNON COLLINS, et al

    Plaintiffs

    vs.   CIVIL ACTION NO: 71-500K

HIRAM L. SCHOONFIELD, et al

    Defendants

APPROVED NOTICE TO ALL PERSONS CONFINED IN THE BALTIMORE CITY JAIL

This is a class action for declaratory judgment and equitable relief brought on behalf of all persons presently confined in the Baltimore City Jail and on behalf of those who will be confined in the future. This suit seeks to improve conditions in the Jail and challenges the legality and constitutionality of many policies and practices at the Jail.

The defendants are: Hiram L. Schoonfield, Warden, Baltimore City Jail; Howard Parks, Deputy Warden, Baltimore City Jail; Harry Harper, Deputy Warden, Baltimore City Jail; Paul J. Reid, President, Baltimore City Jail Board; Joseph F. George, Jr., Secretary, Baltimore City Jail Board; Dr. Bernard Harris, Jr., Member, Baltimore City Jail Board; Joseph L. Johnson, Member, Baltimore City Jail Board; Maurice A. Harmon, Ex-Officio Member, Baltimore City Jail Board.

The defendants are charged with having failed to maintain the City Jail in a manner consonant with the United States Constitution, in that, persons confined in the jail have suffered from: brutality, tear gassing, macing and beatings; improper interference with their communication and visitation rights; arbitrary punishment for innocent and/or constitutionally protected behavior; imposition of punishment without fair procedures; arbitrary and unconstitutional denials of religious freedom; discriminatory practices because of poverty; unconstitutional denial of books, magazines and other publications; inadequate food; inadequate light and heat; a lack of recreational facilities; a lack of adequate facilities for conferences with attorneys; a lack of adequate sanitation and hygiene facilities, a lack of adequate medical attention.

This case has been filed and is currently pending in the United

States District Court For the District of Maryland, before The Honorable Frank A. Kaufman, Judge of that Court.

Plaintiffs are represented by the following attorneys, who are serving as volunteers without fee:

Stephen Sachs
1605 Mercantile Bank
  and Trust Bldg.
2 Hopkins Plaza
Baltimore, Maryland 21202

Joseph A. Matera
341 North Calvert Street
Baltimore, Maryland 21202

Michael Millemann
412 North Bond Street
Baltimore, Maryland 21231

Luther C. West
Tower Building (7th Fl.)
222 East Baltimore Street
Baltimore, Maryland 21202

Stanley Bass
10 Columbus Circle
New York, New York 10019

Pursuant to Rule 23(c)(2), Federal Rules of Civil Procedure, each person confined in the Baltimore City Jail is hereby advised that:

A) The court will exclude him or her from the class of plaintiffs if he or she so requests in writing by   , 197 .

B) The final judgment, whether favorable or not, will apply to all persons confined in Baltimore City Jail who do not request exclusion; and

C) Any person confined in Baltimore City Jail who does not request exclusion may, if he or she desires, enter an appearance through his or her counsel.

Direct all replies to:

SAMPLE INTERROGATORIES PROPOUNDED BY PLAINTIFFS IN A §1983 CLASS ACTION CHALLENGING THE CONSTITUTIONALITY OF JAIL CONDITIONS

Collins v. Schoonfield

IN THE
UNITED STATES DISTRICT COURT
FOR THE DISTRICT OF MARYLAND

VERNON COLLINS, ET AL

    Plaintiffs

vs.   CIVIL ACTION NO. 71-500-K

HIRAM L. SCHOONFIELD, ET AL

    Defendants

INTERROGATORIES PROPOUNDED BY THE PLAINTIFFS

You are hereby requested to answer under oath the following interrogatories in accordance with Rule 33 of the Federal Rules of Civil Procedure. If any part of the following interrogatories cannot be answered in full, please answer to the extent possible. If you are unable to answer any of the interrogatories, or a part or parts thereof, please specify the reason for your inability to answer and state what other information or knowledge you have concerning the answered portion. For the purposes of these interrogatories, the term punishment is defined to include the withdrawal of any right or privilege, the denial of the opportunity to engage in any program or activity, the transfer of an inmate to isolation, mental seclusion, a lock-up section or any other section as a result of a breach of jail discipline or an infraction of jail rules and regulations by an inmate.

TO THE DEFENDANT SCHOONFIELD:

1. State your full name, address, age, title and nature and extent of your duties, educational background and work experience related to your present position, length of service in your present position and salary.

TO THE DEFENDANTS—THE BALTIMORE CITY JAIL BOARD:

2. State your full name, address, age, occupation and employer, title and nature and extent of your duties in regard to the Baltimore City Jail, educational background and work experience related to your position on the Board, tenure on the Board and salary, if any.

3. Describe in detail the function and responsibilities of the Board and state all sources of the Board's authority to act.

4. Describe in detail the procedures by which the Board promulgates rules and regulations for the government of the Baltimore City Jail and its inmates.

5. Describe in detail the means by which the Board is informed of the day to day events occurring in the jail.

6. State the frequency with which you have visited the Baltimore City Jail for the purpose of inspecting the facilities and conditions since you became a member of the Board.

7. State individually as best as you can the number of occasions and dates since you became a member of the Board on which you personally spoke with inmates in order to evaluate the operation of the jail and give, if you can, the names and/or location of the inmates to whom you spoke.

TO THE DEFENDANTS PARKS AND HARPER:

8. State your full name and address, age, title and nature and extent of your duties, educational background and related work experience, length of service and salary.

TO ALL OF THE DEFENDANTS:

9. Attach hereto a copy of the floor plan, if it differs from that contained in the City Jail Manual of the jail and produce the following information:

(a) When the jail was originally constructed.

(b) A description of any additions which have been made including the dates such additions were made.

(c) The number of cells presently fit for use exclusive of isolation or seclusion cells.

(d) The number of these cells which were originally designed to accommodate one person and which were subsequently modified to accommodate more than one person.

(e) The number of cells presently unfit for use and the reason therefor, exclusive of isolation or seclusion cells.

(f) The number of isolation and seclusion cells.

(g) The present capacity of the jail exclusive of isolation and seclusion cells.

10. State the inmate population on each of the following dates:

(a) January 1, 1970;

(b) February 25, 1971;

(c) May 4, 1971;

(d) Present date.

Also, state the population breakdown for these dates of:

(a) White inmates;

(b) Black inmates;

(c) Men;

(d) Women;

(e) Juveniles (those awaiting a juvenile court hearing, but not those waived to adult jurisdiction);

(f) Convicted inmates;

(g) Pre-trial inmates.

11. Has the Baltimore City Jail ever been declared obsolete, unsafe, unhealthful, unsanitary, in violation of any health or housing code, or otherwise deficient by any commission, grand jury, board, legislative body or commission, or any other federal, state or city agency?

(a) Attach hereto a copy of all Baltimore City Grand Jury reports concerning the jail for the last five years.

(b) Attach hereto a copy of any other report, memoranda or record prepared by any person, persons or agency in respect to any examination or inspection of the jail within the last five years.

12. Describe in detail all types of cells, including regular cells, medical seclusion cells, punitive isolation or seclusion cells, and all other types of cells presently existing in the jail.

(a) State the size of each such type of cell or area in height, width and length.

(b) Describe in detail the sanitary facilities in each such type of cell or area.

(c) Describe in detail provisions for heating, ventilation and lighting in each such type of cell or area.

(d) Describe in detail the furnishings provided in each such type of cell such as mattress, blanket, etc.

(e) Describe in detail the walls and doors of each such type of cell or area.

13. Describe the heating system at the jail, stating whether heating is controlled centrally or on each individual tier or row.

14. Describe the ventilation system at the jail, indicating:

(a) The means by which ventilation is provided.

(b) Who controls the ventilation system?

(c) Who can open or close windows?

15. Are you aware of, or do any reports, inspection records, etc. in your possession, indicate the existence of rats, mice, roaches, lice, or other insects or vermin in the jail?

(a) State what type of insects or vermin.

(b) State where they are infested.

(c) State what preventive or remedial measures are, or have been taken, in this regard.

16. Indicate what type of information is kept in regard to each inmate. Describe the content of the records which are kept in regard to each inmate.

(a) Enumerate each category of such information kept (e.g., medical, criminal record, etc.).

(b) Are letters of complaint or protest by an inmate ever retained or copied for or in an inmate's record?

(c) Are censored letters or other pieces of mail, either in-going or out-going, ever placed or copied in an inmate's file?

(d) Is an inmate's religious or political affiliation, such as being an adherent to the Islamic (Black Muslim) faith or a member of the Black Panther Party, ever notated in his records?

17. Indicate who is responsible for the formulation of the Baltimore City Jail budget.

(a) Describe the procedure by which the budget is formulated.

(b) Attach hereto a copy of any audit of the books or budget of the jail which may have been made during the last five years.

18. State with regard to the costs of maintaining each inmate during the last five years:

(a) The average total cost per year per inmate.

(b) The portion of such average total cost allocated to:

    (1) Medical care.

    (2) Food.

    (3) Clothing.

19. If there are differences in security provisions relating to individual sections of the jail, describe them.

(a) Which sections are lock-up sections?

(b) What are the criteria for assignment to a lock-up section?

(c) Which are the punishment sections?

(d) Who determines whether an incoming inmate is to be placed on a lock-up section? Using what criteria?

20. Describe in detail the difference, if any, with which inmates on lock-up sections are treated as compared to other inmates, especially in regard to:

(a) Feeding.

(b) Sick call.

(c) Recreation.

(d) Commissary.

(e) Showers.

21. What percentage of the inmate population of the jail was on lock-up sections, or on isolation, on each of the following dates:

(a) January 1, 1970.

(b) February 28, 1971.

(c) May 4, 1971.

(d) Date of signing interrogatories.

22. State in detail what provisions existed on each of the following dates for segregating the below listed sub-classes of inmates from the general population—January 1, 1969, May 4, 1971:

(a) Children under 18 awaiting trial in juvenile court.

(b) Children under 18 waived to criminal court.

(c) Escape risks.

(d) High or no bail inmates.

(e) Federal prisoners.

(f) Homosexuals.

(g) Suicidal inmates.

(h) Chronically ill or crippled inmates.

(i) Youths between 18 and 21.

(j) Convicted inmates.

(k) Emotionally disturbed inmates.

(l) Alcoholics.

(m) Drug addicts.

(n) Inmates who have exhibited aggressive tendencies.

23. State in detail in what respects juveniles were treated differently from other inmates on each of the following dates with special

regard to each of the following areas—January 1, 1969, May 4, 1971 and date of answers to interrogatories:

(a) Diet.

(b) Recreation.

(c) Showers.

(d) Medical treatment.

(e) Educational opportunities.

(f) Psychological or other counselling.

24. Please answer interrogatory No. 23 with respect to how sentenced inmates are treated differently from other inmates.

25. Provide a typical daily schedule including the time he gets up, the time he eats, amount of time locked in cell, amount of supervised activities, etc., for each of the following classes of persons prior to May 4, 1971:

(a) Juveniles.

(b) Sentenced inmates.

(c) Lock-up inmates.

(d) Other inmates.

26. Have day rooms, gymnasiums or other recreational facilities, after January 1, 1969, been used as dormitories or otherwise been used to house prisoners as a result of overcrowding? If so, state:

(a) How many day rooms there are.

(b) How many day rooms at one time have ever been used to house inmates.

(c) Whether the gymnasium has been used, since January 1, 1969, for this purpose.

27. How often do inmates receive clean sheets, towels, blankets and pillowcases.

(a) Do inmates ever receive torn half sheets for their mattresses?

(b) If an inmate's mattress is dirty or stained, can he request a clean one? If so, to whom is the request made? Will he receive a new mattress if his is dirty?

(c) Are inmates ever provided with hot water, mops, soap, disinfectant and other materials with which to clean their cells? How often?

(d) How often are the jail walls and floors scrubbed?

28. When, if ever, are inmates provided by the jail with fresh or clean clothing? What types of clothing are made available without charge to the inmates?

(a) What provisions exist for allowing inmates to launder their clothing?

(b) Are inmates provided with soap (other than hand soap) with which to wash their own clothing?

(c) Are there limitations on the amount and frequency with which an inmate may receive fresh or new clothing from the outside?

29. How often are inmates allowed to shower? How long?

(a) Are inmates required to take showers?

(b) What personal toilet articles does the jail provide to inmates?

(c) What provisions are made for shaving?

(d) How often is a fresh razor blade supplied each inmate?

(e) Do inmates have hot water in their cells?

30. Do inmates receive medical and psychological examinations upon entering City Jail? If so:

(a) State who gives such examinations.

(b) Describe the nature and extent of such examinations.

(c) State if records are kept of such examinations.

(d) Are inmate's prescription drug needs noted and cared for?

(e) Are such examinations administered at any time thereafter?

31. State the names and addresses of all doctors or dentists employed by the jail since January 1, 1969.

(a) State the ages of all such persons and the dates of their employment.

(b) State the salary of all such persons.

(c) State the educational and experience qualifications of all such persons.

(d) State the name of any such person who may have resigned or been discharged as a result of his protest of jail conditions.

32. Prior to May 4, 1971, how often each day was there a doctor in attendance at the jail:

(a) Who was in charge of meeting the medical needs of the inmates at other times?

(b) State the qualifications of such person or persons.

(c) State the number of such persons on duty each shift, each day.

(d) How often is there in attendance a dentist to treat inmates?

(e) Describe the nature and extent of dental work available to inmates.

(f) State whether or not there are other medical personnel, psychologists, or psychiatrists available for consultation.

(g) State the names and addresses of all such persons who have provided such services at the jail and the frequency with which they provided such services.

33. Describe in detail, the medical facilities available at the jail especially in regard to the following:

(a) State the available number of beds.

(b) State whether or not mentally disturbed inmates are ever placed in strip cells.

(c) Describe the medical seclusion cells.

(d) Describe the available medical equipment.

(e) Describe the type of medical treatment available there, e.g., emergency care, surgery, etc.

(f) State what provisions there existed prior to May 4, 1971 for the detoxification of narcotics addicts.

34. State the standard procedure employed by the jail prior to May 4, 1971 with regard to the treatment of inmates suffering narcotic withdrawal or from addiction to alcohol.

(a) State the substance of any court order entered against the jail within the last five years relating to the treatment of narcotics addicts.

35. How many incidents of suicide, attempted suicide, or self-inflicted injuries have occurred at the City Jail during the last five years?

(a) Describe in detail each such incident.

(b) Attach a copy of any report relating to any such incident.

(c) Is there any psychological, psychiatric or other counselling available to suspected or admitted suicidals?

(d) Describe in detail the "suicide-watch."

36. What procedure is followed by an inmate who complains of being sick or injured before he can see a doctor?

(a) How often is sick call held on each section?

(b) Who determines whether an inmate will get to see a doctor?

(c) What is the procedure in case of an emergency?

37. State the following with regard to inmates who are required to take regular medication or treatment:

(a) The procedure by which an inmate continues medication prescribed before his incarceration.

(b) Who is responsible for seeing that inmates receive their medication or treatment.

(c) State whether or not inmates working in the infirmary ever administer medication, dress wounds or perform any other function in relation to the treatment of other inmates.

38. With regard to the purchase, preparation and distribution of food to inmates:

(a) State who is responsible for the expenditure of funds in regard to the purchase of food.

(b) State who is responsible for the preparation and distribution of food to the inmates.

(c) State whether or not inmates are utilized to assist in the preparation and distribution of food. If so, which inmates?

(d) Which inmates are fed in the dining room?

(e) Which inmates are fed in their cells?

(f) Explain how cooking and eating utensils are cleaned.

(g) Explain how eating utensils used by inmates who are fed in their cells are cleaned.

(h) State whether there are occasions when inmates are not given regular diets as listed on menu, and if so, reason why?

(i) State whether inmates on lock-up or on isolation are ever fed differently from other inmates in respect to the type of food served and to the manner in which it is served (e.g., (1) inmates on isolation being fed two bologna sandwiches per meal, three meals per day; (2) inmates on L-Section being fed in paper cups).

(j) State what provisions there may exist to provide special diets for persons requiring such diets for medical purposes (e.g., diabetics).

39. State whether, prior to May 4, 1971, religious services were regularly conducted at the jail. If so, state:

(a) How often were services held?

(b) For what religious groups were services held?

(c) Which inmates were allowed to attend such services?

(d) Are inmates on isolation or on lock-up denied the right to attend religious services?

(e) Are inmates allowed to receive visits from their ministers or spiritual leaders other than during regular visiting hours?

(f) Were adherents to the Islamic faith allowed to conduct services? If not, why not?

(g) Are services ever conducted for Jewish inmates? Under what conditions?

(h) Do there exist special dietary provisions for adherents to the Islamic or Jewish religions?

(i) Are there any restrictions concerning which religious services an inmate may attend?

(j) Are there any restrictions concerning inmates receiving religious materials, books, newspapers, etc. through the mail or from family or friends?

(k) Whether any of the above practices were changed after May 4, 1971.

40. Describe in detail any recreational areas, programs or facilities which exist for the benefit of the inmates.

(a) Who is in charge of inmate recreational programs and resources and state his qualifications.

(b) State the frequency with which inmates have access to such programs and resources.

(c) Do inmates on isolation and lock-up have access to such programs and resources?

(d) State what provisions exist to insure that all inmates, including those on lock-up and isolation, are able to exercise.

(e) How often are inmates allowed the use of the day rooms?

(f) If any day rooms are used as dormitories, what provisions, if any, are made for inmates who would have used the day rooms for recreation, as well as the inmates housed there?

41. Describe in detail any vocational or educational programs, facilities or resources which were existing as of May 4, 1971.

42. State the vocational and educational programs which are in existence at the present time.

(a) State the date of inception or acquisition of such program or facility.

(b) State the name and qualifications of the person or persons who supervise such programs or facilities.

(c) Which inmates are eligible for such programs or allowed to use such facilities.

(d) State what provisions exist to allow juveniles to continue their education while incarcerated.

43. State in detail the procedure by which inmates can make their grievances concerning events or conditions in the jail known to responsible authorities.

(a) State the procedure by which inmates' complaints are dealt with within the jail.

(b) State the procedure by which inmates can make formal complaints to the Baltimore City Police Department.

(c) What restrictions, if any, are placed upon inmate access to the news media for the purpose of making their grievances known to the public?

(d) What restrictions, if any, are placed upon inmate access to the courts and public officials for the purpose of expressing grievances?

44. Who is responsible for hiring personnel to be employed at the City Jail?

(a) Are applicants given aptitude tests before they are hired? If so, attach hereto a copy of the test administered.

(b) Are jail employees ever examined or tested to determine their psychological suitability for correctional work? If not, why not?

(c) State the educational, training and experience requirements and job description for each of the following positions:

    (i) Warden.
    (ii) Deputy Warden.
    (iii) Captain.
    (iv) Lieutenant.
    (v) Sergeant.
    (vi) Correctional Officer.

(d) How are vacancies in regard to supervisory positions filled?

(e) State the full name, address, age, race, nature and extent of duties, educational background and related work experience, and salary of all supervisory personnel of the rank of sergeant or above presently employed at the City Jail.

(f) How is information concerning institutional policy disseminated to employees?

(g) State what provisions exist for the enforcement of regulations dealing with employee discipline.

(h) State the number of employees who have been discharged, suspended or otherwise punished since January 1, 1969, and in each case state the nature of the action taken against them and the reasons for this action.

45. State institutional policy concerning the use of force in regard to inmates.

(a) State institutional policy concerning the use of tear gas to subdue inmates.

(b) State institutional policy concerning the use of mace to subdue inmates.

(c) Are individual correctional officers authorized to use mace on inmates on their own discretion? Under what conditions?

(d) Have the ventilation system and ducts ever been used to disperse tear gas or any other chemical agent? If so, give all details including dates, locations, name of person authorizing such action, etc.

(e) State institutional policy concerning the use of high pressure water hoses to subdue inmates.

(f) State institutional policy concerning the use of riot sticks, blackjacks and similar weapons to subdue inmates.

(g) If tear gas, mace, high pressure water hoses, riot stick, blackjacks, etc. have been used since January 1, 1970 to subdue inmates, give the following information with regard to each occasion on which they have been used.

    (i) Date used.
    (ii) Location.

    (iii) Reason for use.
    (iv) What was used.
    (v) Amount used.
    (vi) How much was used.
    (vii) On whom used.
    (viii) Person authorizing use.
    (ix) Was anyone injured? Who?

46. State institutional policy concerning the use of isolation and lock-up as punishment as that term has been previously defined.

(a) Enumerate the offenses for which an inmate can be punished by placement on a lock-up section.

(b) Enumerate the offenses for which an inmate can be punished by placement on isolation.

(c) Enumerate other types of punishment which can be imposed on inmates.

(d) Are all punishable infractions reduced in writing in the handbook for inmates? Which are not so listed?

(e) Can an inmate be punished for conduct which has not been specifically prohibited by a written rule?

    (1) Who is responsible for determining that such conduct is punishable?

(f) Can an inmate be punished for conduct which is deemed to be merely disrespectful or vulgar?

(g) Is there a certain amount of punishment imposed for violation of each particular rule? If so, attach hereto a schedule indicating what punishment is imposed in regard to violation of each particular rule.

(h) State the procedure by which punishment is imposed on inmates.

(i) Are inmates given written or any other notice of charges against them and an opportunity to respond to an official other than their accusers?

(j) Are inmates ever given a hearing in regard to charges placed against them? If so, describe in detail how such hearings are conducted.

(k) Are inmates allowed to call witnesses to refute charges placed against them?

(l) Are inmates allowed to confront their accusers?

(m) Are inmates allowed to be represented by another person before jail officials in regard to charges placed against them?

(n) Are inmates informed of the conditions and length of their punishment?

(o) Are inmates ever punished for indefinite periods?

(p) Are there any restrictions on the length of time any inmate may:

    (i) Be placed on isolation;
    (ii) Be placed on lock-up; or
    (iii) Be otherwise punished?

If so, state such restrictions and who is responsible for enforcing them.

47. Do inmates who are being punished ever receive a review of their case for possible return to non-punishment sections? If so:

(a) Describe the procedure by which such punishment is reviewed.

(b) Under what circumstances does an inmate receive such a review?

(c) Is every inmate who is being punished entitled to a review?

(d) Who is responsible for any such review?

48. Are inmates who are on isolation or lock-up sections ever denied the following—if so, under what conditions:

(a) Showers.

(b) Regular meals (other than sandwiches).

(c) Running water.

(d) Toilet facilities (other than a hole in the floor).

(e) Visits from attorneys, friends or relatives.

(f) Toilet articles.

(g) Clothing.

(h) Mail.

49. Are inmates ever punished or placed on isolation or lock-up because of the length of their hair or the fact that they have a beard or other facial hair?

(a) Is an inmate ever punished by placement on isolation or lock-up for complaints concerning:

(i) The food;

(ii) Not receiving prescribed medication;

(iii) The condition of his mattress.

50. Indicate exactly what each of the following terms means in regard to their use on jail disciplinary slips and which of the Rules for Inmates is violated under each charge:

(a) Disrespect to an officer.

(b) Good of institution.

(c) Wise guy.

(d) Skating.

(e) For own protection.

(f) Insubordination.

(g) "Ball-busting".

51. Describe in detail the operation of the jail library.

(a) How many books are presently in the library?

(b) Where do the books in the library come from?

(c) Who selects these books?

(d) Which inmates have access to the library?

(e) Are books available to men on lock-up status?

(f) Does the jail accept contributions of books for use by inmates?

(g) Are certain types of books deemed unsuitable for the jail library? If so:

(i) What types of books are deemed unsuitable?

(ii) Does the jail accept contributions of such materials for inmate use?

52. Describe in detail the operation of the jail commissary.

(a) Describe in detail what is available to the inmates in the commissary.

(b) Who is responsible for the operation of the commissary?

(c) When and how often do inmates have access to the commissary?

(d) Are commissary rights ever withdrawn from inmates? If so, under what circumstances?

(e) Who receives the profits from the operation of the commissary?

(f) Attach hereto the commissary price list as of May 4, 1971 and a copy of the commissary financial statement for the year 1970.

(g) Does the commissary receive items donated for institutional use by manufacturers, governmental agencies, charitable groups, etc?

(i) Is it true that the commissary sells, at times, items which were donated and which are clearly marked not for sale? If so, why?

(h) Do any provisions exist to provide indigent inmates with toilet essentials? If so, explain in detail and list those articles which are provided.

(i) Do any provisions exist to provide inmates who are denied commissary privileges with essential toilet articles? If so, explain in detail and list those articles which are provided.

53. State exactly what provisions exist to allow a pre-trial detainee to participate in his defense of the pending charges against him.

(a) Are inmates allowed to have law books and legal materials in their possession?

(b) Are law books and legal materials ever confiscated from inmates? If so, under what circumstances?

(c) Are inmates allowed to interview witnesses in their case? If so, explain how.

(d) Are inmates allowed to telephone their attorneys or witnesses in their cases? If so, explain how and how often.

54. Describe in detail the procedure by which inmates are allowed to see visitors.

(a) Are there any restrictions on whom an inmate may receive as a visitor?

(b) May inmates touch and kiss their wives and families? If not, why not?

(c) Can the telephones through which inmates and their families communicate be monitored? If so:

(i) Are conversations ever monitored?

(ii) Under what circumstances are they monitored?

(d) Describe in detail the procedures by which inmates may receive money for their account and fresh clothing from visitors and any restrictions thereon.

(e) If there are any persons, or classes of persons who are presently not admitted to the jail to visit inmates, name them.

(f) Are visitation rights ever denied as a form of punishment? If so, under what circumstances are they denied?

55. Describe the procedure by which, if any, inmates are allowed access to telephones?

(a) Are incoming inmates allowed to make a telephone call upon arriving?

(b) Are inmates allowed to make telephone calls to witnesses and attorneys in relation to their case? If so, when and under what conditions?

(c) When inmates are allowed to make telephone calls, are their calls monitored in any fashion by jail employees? If so, explain how.

56. Describe in detail institutional policy in respect to censorship of in-coming and out-going mail and reading matter.

(a) What written or defined standards are applied in the censoring of mail?

(b) Is mail or reading matter sent to inmates ever refused or confiscated? If so, under what circumstances?

(c) Give the name and address of every jail employee who has censored mail since January 1, 1969.

(d) What becomes of mail sent by inmates which is censored and deemed objectionable?

(e) Are letters to or from inmates ever detained before delivery or mailing? If so, under what circumstances?

(f) Are letters or excerpts from letters ever photocopied or otherwise reproduced or noted by jail personnel?

(g) Are letters to or from courts, public officials and attorneys ever read? If so, under what circumstances?

(h) Are letters to or from courts, public officials and attorneys ever refused delivery or confiscated? If so, under what circumstances?

(i) Are there any restrictions on the types of reading material which an inmate may receive in the mail? If so, describe them in detail.

(j) May an inmate receive the Black Panther Party newspaper through the mail? If not, why not?

(k) May an inmate receive one of the local daily newspapers through the mail? If so, are certain articles ever excised or otherwise censored? Which articles?

(l) If there exists a list of objectionable reading material which cannot be received by an inmate, attach hereto a copy of such list.

(m) Who determines whether reading material sent to inmates is objectionable?

(n) Are there any written or defined standards applied to determine whether reading material is objectionable? If so, attach hereto a copy of such standards.

57. State the number of men on lock-up and isolation on each of the following dates:

(a) January 1, 1970.

(b) February 25, 1971.

(c) May 4, 1971.

(d) Date of Interrogatories.

58. What is considered a high bail for the purpose of placing an inmate on a high bail section?

59. What measures are taken to protect inmates who complain of violent or sexual assaults upon their person by guards or other inmates?

(a) Are all such complaints investigated? If not, why not?

(b) Who is responsible for investigating such complaints?

(c) Are written reports of such complaints and investigation, if any, made and retained?

(d) How many such complaints have been received since January 1, 1969 which concern guards? Other inmates?

(e) Attach hereto copies of all reports of such complaints since January 1, 1969 in your possession.

(f) How many complaints have you received of attacks on guards by inmates since January 1, 1969?

(g) Attach hereto a copy of all reports of such complaints in your possession.

(h) Give all details concerning any alleged attacks on officers by inmates since January 1, 1969, including the names of witnesses and all other relevant details.

/s/ Joseph Matera, Esq.
_____

JOSEPH MATERA, ESQ.
341 North Calvert Street
Baltimore, Maryland 21202
539-5340

/s/ Michael Millemann, Esq.
_____

MICHAEL MILLEMANN, ESQ.
412 North Bond Street
Baltimore, Maryland 21231
675-5218

/s/ Stephen H. Sachs, Esq.
_____

STEPHEN H. SACHS, ESQ.
Mercantile Bank & Trust Bldg.
Baltimore, Maryland 21202
539-5445

I HEREBY CERTIFY that a copy of the aforegoing Plaintiffs' Interrogatories were mailed postage pre-paid this   day of   , 1971, to George L. Russell, Jr., Esquire, Ambrose T. Hartman, Esquire, William Hughes, Esquire, and Carol S. Sugar, Esquire, Attorneys for Defendants, 508 Tower Building, Baltimore, Maryland 21202.

/s/ Michael Millemann
_____

MICHAEL MILLEMANN
412 North Bond Street
Baltimore, Md. 21231
675-5218

SAMPLE INTERROGATORIES PROPOUNDED BY PLAINTIFF IN A §1983 CLASS ACTION CHALLENGING THE CONSTITUTIONALITY OF PRISON CONDITIONS

Stinnie v. Gregory

UNITED STATES DISTRICT COURT
FOR THE
EASTERN DISTRICT OF VIRGINIA
Richmond Division

JOHN CHARLES STINNIE, et al,

      Plaintiffs,

  v.

E. W. GREGORY, JR., et al,

      Defendants.

CIVIL ACTION NO. 554-70-R

INTERROGATORIES

To: Each individual member of the
Defendant Class, comprising county
sheriffs, city sheriffs (city sergeants),
chiefs of police, in charge of lock-ups
and city jail farms, and other local county
and city jailers.

Plaintiffs propound the following interrogatories to each county sheriff, city sheriff (city sergeant) and chiefs of police, all individually as members of defendant class, pursuant to the Federal Rules of Civil Procedure, Rule 33. You are directed to answer the same fully, in writing, under oath.

1. State your name, official position, title and the Jurisdiction that you serve.

2. State the number of buildings that comprise your facility and the address and particular use of each building and wing (e.g., pretrial detention, juveniles, women, etc.).

3. Give the date that the original building was built as well as the dates of each wing and addition.

4. List the number of cells in each building and the number of bunks in each cell.

5. List the number of dormitories in your facility with the number of beds in each.

6. Give the *number, location* and *size* of each disciplinary cell in your facility.

7. Does each disciplinary cell have a window?

8. List the items of furniture in each disciplinary cell.

9. Does each cell have a commode capable of being flushed?

10. If the answer to question number 9 is no, what toilet facility is available and under what conditions?

11. List the total number of prisoners that have been held in your jail during the year 1971–72, stating also for that period the number of:

(a) alcoholics;
(b) narcotics addicts;
(c) women;
(d) men;
(e) pretrial detainees;
(f) those who could not meet bond prior to trial;
(g) sentenced prisoners;
(h) prisoners held for transfer to other institutions;
(i) prisoners serving time for fines;
(j) convicted felons;
(k) juveniles.

12. List the number of guards in your facility as well as the education and training of each.

13. Describe the work experience of each guard, prior to coming to your jail, in the area of corrections.

14. State verbatim (unless you attach a complete printed copy) each and every *written* rule, standard or regulation designed to control and regulate inmates *issued by the Division of Corrections or Department of Welfare and Institutions,* which is used or has been adopted for use at your jail or lock-up. Particularly any rules controlling: the use of mace, physical punishments, physical restraints, the imposition of punishments, correspondence privileges, diet, medical care, bedding, exercise, receipt of books and publications, library facilities, access to the courts, attorneys, press and social welfare institutions.

15. Give the date on which each of the rules listed in answer to question 14 were put into use at the jail or lock-up.

16. Name the person or persons who prepared the rules listed in answer to question 14 and who made the decision to adopt them for use at the jail or lock-up.

17. State verbatim (unless you attach a complete printed copy) each and every *written* rule and regulation designed to control or regulate inmates' conduct issued by *local authorities, public officials, administrators or jailers.* (Covering particularly those areas listed in question 14.)

18. State verbatim each and every *unwritten* legal standard, rule or regulation designed to control and regulate inmate conduct.

19. State verbatim (if not included in your answers to questions 14, 17, 18) each and every written or unwritten rule, standard or regulation which sets out the *punishments* or restrictions an inmate may receive, the *conduct* which merits each type of *punishment,* the procedure whereby an inmate is found guilty of a rule violation or other

improper or illegal conduct and the procedure whereby punishment is imposed on the inmate.

20. Give the date on which each of the rules listed in answer to questions 14, 17, 18, 19 were adopted for use and name the person or persons who prepared them and who made the decision to adopt them for use at the jail.

21. Do all of the above rules apply equally to persons confined in solitary or disciplinary segregation? If so, which rules do not apply?

22. State verbatim all rules that apply specifically to those inmates confined in solitary or disciplinary segregation.

23. Supply the following information for *all* of the above listed rules and regulations:

(a) Whether written copies of these rules are distributed to each inmate upon his arrival at the jail or lock-up. If not, whether each inmate receives such a copy at some time after the date of his arrival. If so, the length of time which passes after his arrival before he receives such a copy.

(b) Whether copies of these rules are posted conspicuously at any places within the jail or lock-up. If so, which ones, and where are they posted.

(c) Whether all jailers, guards, and other jail personnel who deal directly with the inmates are familiar with these rules. If so, the method by which they are familiarized with the rules.

(d) Whether these rules are intended to serve as an exclusive guide for what inmate conduct is considered improper and may result in the imposition of punishment, discipline or restriction.

(e) Whether inmates in the jail or lock-up have ever been punished, disciplined or subjected to restrictions for conduct considered to be improper but which is not a violation of the above *written* rules, standards, or regulations.

(f) The names and current addresses (where known) of all inmates disciplined or punished within the last year pursuant to the above written rules and regulations.

(g) The conduct deemed to be improper for each inmate listed in answer to question (f), the punishment given, and the date when the improper conduct occurred.

24. List separately for each question the following information for the institution under your control:

(a) The names and official position(s) of the person or persons who normally make the determination of *whether an inmate has violated* a rule of conduct or otherwise engaged in illegal or improper conduct.

(b) The names and positions held of the person or persons who normally make the determination of *what punishment,* discipline or restrictions an inmate is to receive after he is found guilty of having violated a rule of conduct or otherwise having engaged in illegal or improper conduct.

(c) Whether someone other than the person or persons listed above may determine whether an inmate has violated a rule of conduct or what punishment an inmate is to receive. List the names and positions of those persons who would make such a determination when the person or persons listed above in response to question 24 (a) and (b) do not.

(d) Whether the guard, jailer, or other person who has charged an inmate with a rule, violation or other illegal or improper conduct may ever make the determination, either on his own authority or jointly with others, of whether the inmate did, in fact, violate a rule or decide what punishment an inmate is to receive after he is found guilty of having violated a jail rule.

25. Answer in detail the following questions:

(a) If an inmate is accused of having violated a jail rule or otherwise to have engaged in improper conduct is he given written notice of the charges against him?

(b) Is an inmate so charged orally, presented with the specifics of the charge against him? Is he always presented with such specifics?

(c) Is an accused inmate given a hearing before those persons who will determine his guilt or innocence?

(d) Under what circumstances is a hearing not held.

(e) If such a hearing is held, is an inmate always given an opportunity to present evidence and witnesses in his behalf to rebut the charge against him at the hearing?

(f) Is an inmate so charged given an opportunity prior to such a hearing to gather evidence, talk to potential witnesses, and confer with a counselor, social worker or attorney?

(g) Is an inmate so charged allowed to be assisted or represented by a counselor, social worker, fellow inmate, or attorney at such a hearing? How often does this occur?

(h) During such a hearing, is the inmate so charged given an opportunity to orally question the person who brought the charges against him and any other witnesses against him?

(i) Is an inmate allowed to call his own witnesses to testify in his behalf?

(j) After a decision has been made as to whether or not an inmate so charged is guilty of the charges brought against him, is he given written notification of the decision, including reasons, findings of fact, and his punishment (if found guilty)?

26. Give specific data for your institution:

(a) Whether inmates in the jail or lock-up have ever been placed in handcuffs, shackles, or any other such form of physical restraints for other than transport. If so, list each and every such instance which has occurred within the last year, including the name and current address of the inmate involved, the type of restraint employed, the date when each instance occurred, the names and current addresses of any guards or jailers involved, the length of time such restraint was imposed upon each inmate, and the reason for the imposition of the punishment.

(b) Whether tear gas, Mace or any other chemical or gaseous agent has ever been used against any inmate in the jail or lock-up. If so, list each and every instance which has occurred in the last three years, including the name and current address of the inmate involved, the type of chemical agent used, the date when each instance occurred, the names and current addresses of any guards or jailers involved and the reasons for the use of the gas.

(c) Whether inmates in the jail or lock-up have ever been beaten, struck, manhandled, or in any other way subjected to physical violence. If so, list each and every instance which has occurred within the last year, including the name and current address of the inmate involved, the type of force used, the date when each instance occurred, the names and current addresses of any guards or jailers involved, and the reason for the use of physical force.

(d) Whether inmates in the jail or lock-up have ever been denied normal mail privileges such as the right to mail letters or the right to receive mail. Whether they have been denied free stamps, paper or envelopes. Whether they have been denied the right to buy such materials. If so, list each and every instance which has occurred within the last year, including the name and current address of the inmate involved, the specific privileges denied, the reasons for denial, the date when each instance occurred, the length of time the privilege was denied and the names and current addresses of any guards or jailers involved in each instance.

(e) Whether inmates in the jail or lock-up have ever been placed on a restricted diet or otherwise denied the normal meals, food or drink provided to other inmates. If so, list each and every instance which has occurred within the last year, including the name and current address of the inmate involved, the date when each instance occurred, the specific diet provided, the length of time the restricted diet was imposed, the names and current addresses of any guards or jailers involved, and the reason for the imposition of a restricted diet.

(f) Whether inmates in the jail or lock-up have ever been denied requested medical, dental or psychiatric care. If so, list each and every instance which has occurred within the last year including the name and current address of the inmate involved, the requested care which was denied, the date when each instance occurred, the names and current addresses of any guards or jailers involved, and the reason for the denial.

(g) Whether inmates in the jail or lock-up have been denied hygienic articles such as soap, razors, toothbrushes, etc. If so, list each and every instance which has occurred within the last year, including the name and current address of the inmate involved, the hygienic articles denied, the date when each instance occurred, the names and current addresses of any guards or jailers involved, and the reason for the denial.

(h) Whether inmates in the jail or lock-up have ever been stripped of their clothing or shoes or been denied clean clothes when needed. If so, list each and every instance which has occurred within the last year, including the name and current address of the inmate involved, the clothes denied or stripped from the inmate, the date when each instance occurred, the length of time the inmate was left without normal or clean clothing, and the reason for the denial.

(i) Whether inmates in the jail or lock-up have ever been denied normal bedding such as a mattress, pillow, blankets, sheets or clean sheets when needed. If so, list each and every instance which has occurred within the last year, including the name and current address of the inmate involved, the bedding denied, the date when each instance occurred, the length of time the inmate was denied normal bedding, the names and current addresses of any guards or jailers involved and the reason for the denial.

(j) Whether inmates in the jail or lock-up have ever been denied access to normal toilet facilities such as a toilet bowl capable of being flushed and a basin with working water spigots? If so, list each and every instance which has occurred within the last year, including the name and current address of the inmate involved, the toilet facilities denied, the length of time the facilities were denied, the date when the instance occurred, the names and current addresses of any guards or jailers involved, and the reason for the denial.

(k) Whether inmates in the jail or lock-up have ever been denied access to normal exercise or recreation areas or facilities. If so, list each and every instance which has occurred within the last year, including the name and current address of the inmate involved, the access denied, the length of time the access was denied, the date when the instance occurred, the names and current addresses of any guards or jailers involved, and the reason for the denial.

(l) Whether inmates in the jail or lock-up have ever been denied any normal visitation privileges, such as being able to meet relatives or friends once a week, etc. If so, list each and every instance which has occurred within the last year, including the name and current address of the inmate involved, the privileges denied, the length of time the privileges were denied, the date when the instance occurred, the names and current addresses of any guards or jailers involved, and the reason for the denial.

(m) Whether inmates in the jail or lock-up have ever been denied access to court officials or to attorneys by denial or restriction of mail or visitation privileges. If so, list each and every instance which has occurred within the last year, including the name and current address of the inmate involved, the access or privilege denied, the length of time the access or privilege was denied, the date when the instance occurred, the names and current addresses of any guards or jailers involved, and the reason for the denial.

(n) Whether inmates in the jail or lock-up have ever been denied access to ministers, religious services, or religious literature. If so, list each and every instance which has occurred within the last year, including the name and current address of the inmate involved, the access denied, the length of time this access was denied, the date when the instance occurred, the names and current addresses of any guards or jailers involved, and the reason for the denial.

(o) Whether inmates in the jail or lock-up have ever been denied access to the institution's library, books, periodicals, or newspapers or by having the inmate's own reading material removed from his possession. If so, list each and every instance which has occurred within the last year, including the name and current address of the inmate involved, the access or reading materials denied, the length of time this access or reading material was denied, the date when the instance occurred, the names and current addresses of any guards or jailers involved, and the reason for the denial.

(p) Whether inmates in the jail or lock-up have ever been punished, disciplined, or subjected to restrictions in any manner because they communicated with or received communications from any attorney or court official. If so, list each and every instance which has occurred within the last three years, including the name and current address of the inmate involved, the communication deemed punishable, a complete description of the punishment imposed, the duration and dates of the punishment and the names and current addresses of any guards or jailers involved. If punishment reports are available, please submit copies of the same.

(q) Whether inmates in the jail or lock-up have ever been punished, disciplined, or subjected to restrictions in any manner because they discussed, prepared or filed any writ, motion, complaint, or request to any court. If so, list each and every instance which has occurred within the last three years, including the name and current address of the inmate involved, the activities deemed punishable, a complete description of the punishment imposed, the duration and dates of the punishment, and the names and current addresses of any guards or jailers involved. If punishment reports are available, please submit copies of the same.

(r) Whether inmates in the jail or lock-up have ever been punished, disciplined, or subjected to restrictions in any manner because they complained or expressed displeasure about the treatment received or the conditions in the jail or lock-up. If so, list each and every instance which has occurred within the last three years, including the name and current address of the inmate involved, the activity deemed punishable, the person to whom the inmate complained and the substance of his complaint, a complete description of the punishment imposed, the duration and dates of the punishment, and the names and current addresses of any guards or jailers involved. If punishment reports are available, please submit copies of the same.

(s) Whether inmates in the jail or lock-up have ever been punished, disciplined, or subjected to restrictions because they requested medical, dental or psychiatric care. If so, list each and every instance which has occurred within the last three years, including the name and current address of the inmate involved, the activity deemed punishable, the nature of the request made by the inmate, a complete description of the punishment imposed, the duration and dates of the punishment, and the names and current addresses of any guards or jailers involved. If punishment reports are available, please submit copies of the same.

(t) Whether inmates in the jail or lock-up have ever been punished, disciplined or subjected to restrictions in any manner because they communicated with, attempted to communicate with or received communications from any public or governmental official or agency.

If so, list each and every instance which has occurred within the last three years, including the name and current address of the inmate involved, the activity deemed punishable, a complete description of the punishment imposed, the duration and dates of the punishment, and the names and current addresses of any guards or jailers involved. If punishment reports are available, please submit copies of the same.

(u) Whether inmates in the jail or lock-up have ever been punished, disciplined or subjected to restrictions in any manner because they communicated with, attempted to communicate with or received communications from a reporter, writer, editor, publisher, or other member of the press. If so, list each and every instance which has occurred within the last three years, including the name and current address of the inmate involved, the activity deemed punishable, a complete description of the punishment imposed, the duration and dates of the punishment, and the names and current addresses of any guards or jailers involved. If punishment reports are available, please submit copies of the same.

(v) Whether inmates in the jail or lock-up have ever been punished, disciplined or subjected to restrictions in any way because they communicated with, attempted to communicate with, or received communications from any social action agency, public service organization, or political group. If so, list each and every instance which has occurred within the last three years, including the name and current address of the inmate involved, the activity deemed punishable, the agency or organization involved, a complete description of the punishment imposed, the duration and dates of the punishment imposed, the names and current addresses of any guards or jailers involved. If punishment reports are available, please submit copies of the same.

27. List separately for each institution enumerated in your response to question 1, the following data:

(a) Each and every established standard, rule or regulation governing the visitors who may be received by an inmate.

(b) Whether the rules listed in response to question 27 (a) above are written or unwritten.

(c) Whether the above rules apply equally to those inmates among the general inmate population and those held in solitary confinement or any other form of segregation from the general inmate population. If they do not, specify in detail how the rules apply differently to those in solitary confinement or other types of segregation.

(d) Whether the rules governing visits by attorneys or court officials differ from those listed in response to question 27 (a). If so, specify the way in which they differ.

(e) For how many hours each week may an inmate receive visitors?

(f) On which days of the week may an inmate receive visitors?

(g) What is the basis used for determining whether an inmate will be allowed to receive a particular visitor? Who makes this decision?

(h) For what reasons will an inmate's privilege to receive visitors be revoked?

28. Give the following data for your institution:

(a) The name and address of each and every doctor, dentist or psychiatrist who is available to treat inmates in the jail or lock-up.

(b) The average number of hours per week spent in treating inmates at the jail or lock-up by each of the doctors, dentists or psychiatrists listed above. How many inmates, on the average are treated weekly by each?

(c) Whether there are established hours when an inmate can report for "sick call" and receive medical, dental or psychiatric treatment? If so, what are these hours?

(d) Whether there are any social workers, ministers, or counselors available to assist or counsel inmates in the jail or lock-up. If so, list their names, positions, qualifications, and addresses.

(e) The average number of hours per week spent by each of the social workers, ministers, or counselors at the jail or lock-up? How many inmates are treated weekly by each?

(f) Whether there are established hours when an inmate may receive the assistance of any of the above social workers, ministers or counselors? If so, what are these hours?

29. Supply in detail answers for the following questions about your jail or lock-up:

(a) Whether inmates being held pending their trials are segregated from or held in areas separate from those inmates who have already been tried or sentenced.

(b) Whether those inmates being held pending trial are treated in any way differently from inmates who have already been tried and sentenced. If so, list each and every way in which they are treated differently.

(c) Whether the jailer or keeper of the lock-up is considered to have authority to place any restrictions upon an inmate's dealings with bondsmen or any other persons performing the services of a bondsman. If so, specify the nature of such restrictions.

(d) The names of any inmates of the jail who have had such restrictions imposed upon them within the last year, the nature of the restriction, and the date on which it was imposed.

30. Supply the following data relative to the jail or lock-up under your supervision:

(a) Whether facilities have been made available for the purpose of inmate exercise and/or recreation. If so, list the amount of time each day each inmate is allowed to utilize these facilities for:

(1) Exercise;
(2) Recreation.

(b) Describe in detail the physical characteristics and dimensions of these facilities.

(c) Are inmates allowed to make and receive telephone calls?

(d) If so, what are the restrictions, if any, on inmate use of the telephone?

(e) Are these calls monitored or wire tapped in any way?

31. What educational or rehabilitative programs are available in

your institution? Are there treatment programs for alcoholics or inmates addicted to drugs available to inmates in your jail or lock-up?

> JOHN CHARLES STINNIE, et al.
> By Counsel

Counsel for Plaintiffs:

_____

PHILIP J. HIRSCHKOP
110 North Royal Street
P.O. Box 234
Alexandria, Virginia 22313
703-836-5555.

CERTIFICATE OF SERVICE

I hereby certify that a true copy of the foregoing Interrogatories was mailed, first class postage prepaid, on this the _____ day of _____, 1972, to:

> Van H. Lefcoe, Esquire
> Office of the Attorney General
> Supreme Court Building
> Richmond, Virginia 23219
>
> Jose R. Davila, Jr., Esquire
> Office of the Commonwealth Attorney
> 1012 Mutual Building
> Richmond, Virginia 23219
>
> Michael Jamgochian, Esquire
> Office of the Commonwealth Attorney
> City Hall
> Alexandria, Virginia 22314

SAMPLE INTERROGATORIES PROPOUNDED BY PLAINTIFFS IN A §1983 CLASS ACTION CHALLENGING VIOLATION OF FIRST AMENDMENT RIGHTS IN PRISON

Arey v. Oliver

IN THE UNITED STATES DISTRICT COURT
FOR THE EASTERN DISTRICT OF VIRGINIA
Richmond, District

CALVIN M. AREY
ROBERT J. LANDMAN
ROY E. HOOD
LEROY MASON and
THOMAS E. McLARN

    Plaintiffs

v.   CIVIL ACTION NO. 110-70-R

R. M. OLIVER
W. K. CUNNINGHAM
OTIS L. BROWN
D. P. EDWARDS
F. D. COX

    Defendants

INTERROGATORIES

To: W. K. Cunningham, Director
    Division of Corrections

Plaintiffs propounded the following interrogatories to the defendant, W. K. Cunningham, pursuant to the Federal Rules of Civil Procedure. You are directed to answer the same fully in writing under oath within the time provided by the Federal Rules.

1. List by name and address all penal institutions or institutions of correction and rehabilitation in Virginia such as: prisons, prison farms or ranches, juvenile or youth centers, halfway houses, county, city or town jails, or road camps, and other state and local penal or correctional institutions.

2. List separately for each institution enumerated in your answer to question 1, the following data:

    a. The total number of books in each library.

    b. List separately the number of books classed as fiction, non-fiction, reference.

    c. List the number of books about Negro culture (by or about Negroes).

    d. List by title the magazines, periodicals and newspapers received regularly.

    e. List the number and title of the *new* books received in the last year.

    f. List by title, series, volume, number and year the law books in each library.

    3. Answer for each institution listed in your answer to question 1 the following:

    a. State fully the rules governing inmate access to library facilities, (e.g., hours open for use, book loans, limits on materials that can be brought into the library, etc.).

    b. For what reasons are library privileges denied to prisoners? Who decides, and what is the process for taking away privileges?

    c. Do prisoners in isolation have access to legal materials?

    4. For each institution listed in your answer to question 1, supply the following information. If there are *limitations on any of the privileges,* state the policy reasons, the procedure for determining when a rule has been breached, and the possible punishment for such a breach. Answer each question for every type of mail, (e.g., personal, business, legal, package).

    a. How often are inmates allowed to write?

    b. To whom are they allowed to write?

    c. Is there a limit on the number of letters an inmate is allowed to send or receive?

    d. From whom are inmates allowed to receive mail?

    e. How much and how often are writing materials applied to inmates? What is the process for acquiring more than the normal supply?

    f. Is there a limit on the length of letters?

    g. Are prisoners freely allowed to write letters, legal memos, pleadings, etc., for other prisoners?

    h. Is an inmate's use of his personal typewriter limited in any way? Can other prisoners use the typewriter with the owner's permission? Can the owner of the typewriter type for other inmates?

    i. How much legal, regular, and carbon paper is a prisoner given each week?

    5. What is the criteria and procedure for making up each prisoner's "approved mailing list"? Is there a limit on the number of people on the list? Who makes up the list (e.g., what prison official)? Is the list the same for mail sent and mail received? What is done with letters sent or received not in accord with the list(s)? What are the procedures for putting a new name on the list? *Answer the above questions for each institution listed in question 1.*

    6. Quote in full the most recent regulations on prisoner correspondence for each institution enumerated in question 1. Include all types of correspondence (e.g., personal, business, legal, package).

    a. Who establishes these rules (e.g., state boards, officials of the immediate institution, etc.)?

    b. Is the application of the regulations supervised by state officials, or left to local discretion?

7. State *specifically* for each institution listed in question 1 how the regulations and procedures covered in questions 3 thru 6 differ according to place of confinement (e.g., the population at large, "C" cell house, "B" basement, maximum security, and any other divisions according to work or living quarters)?

8. Answer the following questions *separately* for each institution lisited in question 1:

a. Describe the procedures for censoring incoming and outgoing prison mail. That is:

(1) Is *all* incoming and outgoing mail censored? If not, what is excluded from censorship? How is that mail processed separately?

(2) Is all incoming and outgoing mail opened?

(3) What is the difference between "inspection" of legal mail and "censoring" of personal mail?

(4) If mail is "spot-checked" how is it determined which mail is checked (e.g., certain notorious inmates or notorious correspondents)?

(5) What are the grounds for censoring mail?

(6) Who inspects mail for censoring purposes? What persons other than the regular inspector (e.g., guards, prison personnel, supervisors) are allowed to read inmate mail? Under what conditions or restrictions?

(7) Are letters photocopied and sent on to prison authorities, the attorney general, etc.? For what reasons? How often? Has this been done in the last three years? If so, to whom was it sent and for what purposes?

(8) How long does the censoring process delay mail? Is mail delayed in order to be inspected by other prison officials?

(9) What is the procedure for forwarding mail to prisoners who have been moved (e.g., between prisons, between units, or cells within the prison) or have left the prison system? How long is the delay? Are there special policies for forwarding mail from the court or counsel?

(10) What is done with mail that is rejected by the censors? What is done with cash that is sent through the mail?

(11) Are there any restrictions on correspondence with: national, state and local service organizations; educational or scientific groups; public officials; lawyers and the courts? State specifically what they are. Are such letters ever confiscated? Why?

(12) What is the process for sending and receiving registered mail? Who signs for it? How is it payed for? Is it read by the censors?

(13) Do any of these procedures differ according to place of confinement (e.g. see Question 7)?

9. Describe the procedures for notarizing at each of the institutions listed in your answer to Question 1. Who performs the service (e.g. guards, supervisors, public notary)? How long must an inmate wait to have something notarized? Do prison officials who are notaries read the materials they are notarizing? Are special provisions made for men who have to meet court filing dates, etc.?

10. Quote specifically any written regulations on censorship which are in force in each of the institutions enumerated in Question 1.

Answer the following questions for each of the institutions named in your answer to Question One.

11. How often and for what reasons can a prisoner *initiate* and/or respond to urgent correspondence? Describe the procedure. Who gives the permission? How long does it take? Can a prisoner write to someone not on his "approved list"? Are these letters restricted in certain areas of the prison (e.g. can a man in solitary initiate correspondence with his lawyer or a petition for writ of habeas corpus)?

12. Answer for *each* of the institutions listed in your answer to Question One, the following:

a. State the regulations governing an inmate's receipt of publications (subscription or otherwise).

b. List by title the newspapers, magazines and periodicals that are approved for receipt by prisoners; that are disapproved for receipt by prisoners.

c. What is the policy and procedure for excluding certain publications? How are they chosen and screened?

d. Are there restrictions on subscriptions to Negro publications (e.g. *Muhammad Speaks, Ebony,* etc.)? If so, what are they (be explicit) and what is the policy?

e. List any religious periodicals or publications that are excluded because of the policies of the organization.

f. Are inmates in confinement such as C-Cell, B-Basement, maximum security and any other type of confinement, allowed to receive the same publications listed above? If not, what are the *specific* restrictions on each of the units?

13. Answer specifically and quote regulations if possible for each of the institutions in your answer to Question 1.

a. What are the regulations for letters to and from lawyers, the courts, etc.? What are the regulations in regard to the mailing of legal pleadings and the procedures for prisoners who have to meet filing dates?

b. Describe the methods used to examine legal mail. How long does it take?

c. What is the procedure necessary for a prisoner to get "special" permission to write to counsel, etc.? Do prison officials read the correspondence?

d. Are legal supplies, (brief paper, carbons, etc.) issued to prisoners? How much, how often, and what are the restrictions?

e. What are the rules relevant to writ writers?

f. Are law books, notes, etc., allowed to be received through the mail? Are they allowed to be kept in the cells? Are they allowed to be taken into restricted areas (e.g. Question 7)? Be specific as to the rules for each unit.

g. Is an inmate limited in the amount of funds he can spend on legal materials?

h. Which of the above rules are different for prisoners in restricted areas (e.g. see Question 7)? State specifically how they are different.

i. Are inmates allowed to *initiate* correspondence and pleadings with attorneys, the courts and to the Governor, from maximum security, B-Basement, C-Cell, and any other type of confinement. What are the procedures?

j. How is correspondence with an attorney determined to be "bona fide"? Is the correspondence read to make such a determination?

k. Is delivery to and from restricted areas (e.g. see Question 7) delayed longer than usual? How long?

l. May inmates receive books from attorneys? If not, why?

14. In regard to *"solitary," "meditation"* or similar confinement, answer separately for each of the institutions listed in your answer to Question One, the following:

a. What is the rationale for restricting mail from this type of confinement?

b. What is rational for denying reading material to men in this type of confinement?

c. Why are these men given a Bible as opposed to other literature?

d. Are Muslims allowed to have the Koran in solitary, meditation, etc.?

e. What is the text of the single letter men in solitary are allowed to send? Why are they required to sign it? To whom is it sent? In what other institutions is the letter used? What is the purpose of this letter?

15. Answer the following questions for each institution listed in your answer to Question One:

a. How much is each institution budgeted for paper? For postage? (answer per month, per institution).

b. How much paper is *used* per institution? How much postage is used? Answer per month, per institution.

c. How much paper and postage is allotted to each prisoner per week? Per month? If these amounts are restricted in confinement such as C-Cell, B-Basement, maximum security and any other type of confinement, list the different quantity allotted to an individual prisoner in each type of confinement. What is the rationale for restrictions?

Respectfully submitted

Calvin M. Arey, et al.
by Counsel

PHILIP J. HIRSCHKOP, Esquire
Counsel for Plaintiffs
110 North Royal Street
P. O. Box 234
Alexandria, Virginia 22313
703-836-5550

_____
/s/ Philip J. Hirschkop

PHILIP J. HIRSCHKOP

CERTIFICATE OF SERVICE

I hereby certify that a true copy of the foregoing was mailed this 28th day of August, 1970, to the following:

George R. Humrickhouse, Esquire
United Virginia Bank Building
Richmond, Virginia

C. Tabor Cronk, Esquire
Assistant Attorney General
Supreme Court Building
Richmond, Virginia 23219

FORM: REQUEST FOR PRODUCTION OF DOCUMENTS

Collins v. Schoonfield

IN THE
UNITED STATES DISTRICT COURT
FOR THE DISTRICT OF MARYLAND

VERNON COLLINS, et al.

        Plaintiffs

vs.

HIRAM SCHOONFIELD, et al.

        Defendants

CIVIL ACTION NO: 71-500-K

REQUEST FOR PRODUCTION OF DOCUMENTS
AND THINGS FOR INSPECTION,
COPYING AND PHOTOCOPYING

Plaintiffs, Vernon Collins, et al., hereby request, pursuant to Rule 34 of the Federal Rules of Civil Procedure, that defendants produce and permit plaintiffs, by counsel, to inspect and copy each of the following documents, writings, memoranda, reports, and records which have not already been made available to counsel for plaintiffs pursuant to earlier requests, particularly those *new* writings, memoranda, reports, records, and documents which have come into existence or been written since June, 1971 including:

(1) Written memoranda, regulations, policies and rules setting forth mandatory procedures which must be observed before inmates may be placed in maximum security quarters, isolation cells, or denied any right or privileges accorded other inmates.

(2) Written memoranda, policies and rules and regulations which describe and set forth what mandatory procedures govern the review, the re-evaluation, or reconsideration of decisions to discipline inmates.

(3) Written memoranda, policies, regulations and rules which regulate and set forth the maximum time an inmate may be held in maximum security or isolation cells.

(4) Written memoranda, policies, rules and regulations which govern the administration of the City Jail infirmary and the dispensation of medical and dental services to inmates of the City Jail including but not limited to records showing:

a. The schedule containing names of physicians, nurses and medical personnel, their responsibilities, position or title and the hours during which they are physically present at the jail and otherwise on duty.

b. The name of those inmates who have committed suicide at the jail during the past year and reports and records of these incidents.

c. The number of times and hours weekly that doctors at the jail conduct sick call.

(5) Written memoranda, policies, rules and regulations which set forth and describe the conduct of religious ceremonies at the jail and particularly the:

a. Denominations or religions which may hold group services at the jail.

b. Denominations and names of clergymen, ministers, religious leaders who conduct religious services at the jail or who meet with inmates on an individual basis.

c. Availability to inmates of special religious diets, religious materials, literature and books.

(6) Written memoranda, policies, rules and regulations which describe and set forth the type of food served inmates and the manner in which it is served.

(7) The daily worksheet for June, July, August, September, October, November and December, 1971. Logs for I, L, J, K, M, N, O, F and E sections, for October, November and December, 1970 and 1971.

(8) Memoranda, regulations or policies which govern the number of visits an inmate may have and the time, length and frequency of visits between inmates and:

a. Attorneys
b. Family members
c. Friends
d. Others

(9) Regulations, policies, memoranda, rules, and all other written documents setting forth the nature, extent and type of:

a. Educational programs offered to inmates while confined in the jail.

b. Vocational programs offered to an inmate while confined in the jail.

c. Rehabilitative programs offered to inmates while confined in the jail.

d. Other training programs offered to inmates while confined in the jail.

(10) All records of whatever type or kind including inmate profiles, medical records, disciplinary slips, incident reports, copies of correspondence, or any other written matter pertaining to the following former or present inmates of the Baltimore City Jail.

Vernon Collins
James R. Dailey
Frederick Freeman

Milton Gray
Sylvestor Morris
James E. Powell
Conrad Whitfield
Ronald Skillings

. . . .

Robert Lynch
Patrick Duba

(11) All records of whatever type or kind including employee profiles, medical records, record or memoranda of disciplinary action, incident reports, investigative findings, or any other written matter pertaining to the following former or present employees of the Baltimore City Jail.

Hiram Schoonfield
Harry Harper
Howard B. Parks
A. S. Tochterman
Kirkwood Wyatt
Joseph N. Cimino
Anthony R. Cimino
Charles T. Gales, Jr.
Homer D. Gerhart

. . . .

Barry L. Colbert
Edward Wegelein

(12) Copies of all minutes of Baltimore City Jail Board meetings since May, 1971, and copies of all press releases issued by the Jail Board, Warden or any other jail officials.

It is requested that the aforesaid documents be produced for inspection, copying and photocopying on January 3, 1972 at 12:00 noon, and each succeeding day until the copying of said documents can be completed. Productions and copying shall be made by counsel for the plaintiffs at 341 North Calvert Street.

/s/ Joseph A. Matera
_____
JOSEPH A. MATERA
341 North Calvert Street
Baltimore, Maryland 21202

/s/ Michael A. Millemann
_____
MICHAEL A. MILLEMANN
412 North Bond Street
Baltimore, Maryland 21231
675-5218

SAMPLE DEPOSITION OF A
FRIENDLY EXPERT WITNESS

Collins v. Schoonfield

IN THE UNITED STATES DISTRICT COURT
FOR THE DISTRICT OF ARIZONA

EDDIE WILLIE TAYLOR, suing on behalf of himself and all others similarly situated, 　　　　　　　　Plaintiffs, 　　vs. STATE OF ARIZONA; et al., 　　　　　　　　Defendants.	Civ. 72-21-Phx.
GEORGE YANICH, JR., suing on behalf of himself and all others similarly situated, 　　　　　　　　Plaintiffs, 　　vs. STATE OF ARIZONA; et al., 　　　　　　　　Defendants.	Civ. 72-58-Phx.

Phoenix, Arizona
November 9, 1972
9:30 a. m.

DEPOSITION OF JAMES V. BENNETT

PREPARED FOR:

MR. JOHN P. FRANK
Attorney at Law

. . . .

DIRECT EXAMINATION

BY MR. FRANK:

Q Mr. Bennet, would you please state your full name for the record?

A I am James V. Bennett, B-e-n-n-e-t-t. I am the former Director of the United States Bureau of Prisons, having been Director of the Prison Bureau for 27 years. I am now retired and serving as consultant to various groups connected with the operation of prisons and I am also a member of the Maryland Inmate Grievance Commission, which hears the complaints of inmates of any character, particularly those dealing with breaches of discipline.

Q   Mr. Bennett, have you been called upon from time to time to testify in various court cases on matters of prison administration?

A   Yes, sir, I have done so frequently since I have retired and on some occasions before I retired.

Q   In approximately how many courts have you been called upon to testify on these matters since—

A   In federal courts I have been called upon, in the last two years, four times.

Q   And of what organizations are you a member at the moment in the field of prison administration?

A   I'm a member of the Board of Directors of the American Correctional Association. I'm a member of the American Bar Association Commission on Correctional Facilities and Services, headed up by former Governor Richard Hughes, and a member of the American Law Institute, which has from time to time involved themselves in correctional matters. I am a consultant also from time to time to the Law Enforcement Administration.

Q   Mr. Bennett, is there some published place in which a biographical sketch of you appears in some concise form?

I will ask a stipulation that rather than spend further time on if here, we will attach as Exhibit No. 1 to the deposition a personal sketch of Mr. Bennett.

MR. DIXON: So stipulated.

THE WITNESS:

Q   (By Mr. Frank) Now I come to the subject at hand, which are the problems in connection with prison administration in this area, and I will ask you the following question: First of all, Mr. Bennett, there are in the United States, I take it, various forms of what is called segregation in prisons. Would you define, please, what the term "segregation" means?

A   Segregation in the terminology of most prison people consists of two kinds: One is so-called administrative segregation where inmates are placed who are in need of protection, who have some problem with regard to adjustment in the institution, which does not permit them to be released in general population. In addition to that, we have the so-called punitive segregation, where people are put for a predetermined period for some infraction of discipline.

Q   And in the course of this exchange, Mr. Bennett, I would like to have the record show that when we talk about segregation here, we are talking about punitive or disciplinary segregation, only, and not about the treatment of hospital cases, the mentally diseased or other types of problems.

A   Yes, sir, I understand.

Q   Now, in connection with punitive segregation, there are two types, one which is sometimes referred to by the term "isolation" and the other by the term "adjustment" or "adjustment center". What do those words mean as a prison man uses them?

A   Well, isolation is a section where they usually have, in addition to the ordinary barred door, they have another door which closes him in so that he is—he is isolated in there behind the bars and the closed door. Do I make myself clear?

Q   Yes. You are saying that in isolation, it's common to have a cell which can be blocked entirely by a solid front door, is that correct?

A   That's correct.

Q   And, now, what then is an adjustment center?

A   Well, that's a part of the same area, usually, but the door—he is not closed off from the corridor and not closed off, perhaps communicating with people in the corridor, if he cared to, or the inmate next door to him.

Q   Is the only difference between an adjustment center and isolation, as a physical matter, a difference in the doors?

A   Yes, yes, that's pretty largely the difference, although in some cases, the toilet fixtures are different because the inmates have a habit of breaking them up and they have what is known as a—it has a—the toilet in the floor, which is called an oriental toilet, usually, which can be flushed by the officer on the outside. That's put in there to prevent him from breaking it and prevent him from flooding his cell.

Q   And other than, then, these details, these two things are essentially identical, is that correct?

A   Yes.

Q   All right. Now, under what circumstances for disciplinary purposes is it customary in prison practice to put someone into an adjustment center?

A   Violation of the rules is the only valid reason for putting them in there.

Q   And how about into isolation?

A   That is likewise only for disciplinary—breach of discipline.

Q   In determining that there has been a breach of discipline and assessing a penalty, under what circumstances do you use the one and under what circumstances the other?

A   Well, it depends upon the character of the offense, whether the person is violent, whether he is noisy, whether he is shouting, whether he is threatening, and so on—that one you would put in the isolation. Now, if the person is, oh, amenable to regulations and will maintain good order, you put him in the adjustment section.

Q   Mr. Bennett, now I would like, please, to put that subject aside for just one minute and I will connect it up in a second, but I take you now to the matter of what is referred to here at least as good time. Is the phrase "good time" commonly used around the country?

A   Yes, it is.

Q   What does that mean?

A   It means a credit off the sentence for good behavior.

Q   And this is, then, a shorthand way of referring to the fact that if a person is in prison for, let us say, a five-year span, he can, by earning good time, reduce that five years to some shorter period and thus shorten the term of his imprisonment, is that correct?

A   That's correct.

Q   And if, on the other hand, he fails to be given allowance for that good time, he will lengthen the term of his imprisonment, is that correct?

A   That's correct.

Q   Now, Mr. Bennett, what is the relationship of the earning of good time to time spent in disciplinary confinement?

A   Well, ordinarily a person who is in disciplinary confinement receives no credit, no good time, while he is in disciplinary confinement.

Q   So that the practical result of being in disciplinary confinement is that one will have a longer prison sentence than he would have if he were out of disciplinary confinement, is that true?

A   That's correct, unless his good time he lost while in disciplinary segregation is restored to him, which is a common practice in most institutions.

Q   Now, Mr. Bennett, I direct your attention, please, to the currently developing law and practice in the United States as it relates to matters concerning loss of good time and will ask whether it is not now commonly regarded as proper that if a person's prison time is to be extended by loss of good time, that he is entitled to at least rudimentary constitutional procedures before there is such a loss of time and an extension of his sentence. Is that general?

A   Yes, I think it's generally accepted now that an inmate who suffers a lengthening of his sentence for any reason is entitled to at least fundamental due process.

Q   (By Mr. Frank) Mr. Bennett, you have just testified that the current understanding in prison administration is that the contemporary law requires that if a person is to have a lengthening of his sentencing, he is entitled to rudimentary constitutional protection. We then go to the question of what that rudimentary constitutional protection is, and I start first with the matter of notice. Is it commonly accepted that before a person can have a sentence extended, he is entitled to some clear form of notice of what it is that he is charged with?

A   That's correct, he is entitled to a notice and a statement of the charges.

Q   And how is that notice commonly given? What is the proper practice in that regard?

A   Well, ordinarily it's a charge sheet where whatever infraction the prisoner committed is written down by the reporting officer who saw or was witness to the infraction, and the circumstances of it.

Sometimes it is quite detailed and goes into considerable detail as to the character of the infraction. In other places at times it's rather short and cryptic and merely cites the violation of the rule.

Q   Mr. Bennett, when is that charge normally given to the inmate?

A   Well, it's usually given to him, oh, I should say within, oh—

oh, within 24 hours or, at most, I think most places, considering week-ends, we will say it would have to be given to him within 72 hours.

Q   But it's always given to him in writing, is that correct?

A   That's correct.

Q   And as nearly as possible, within 24 hours and to a maximum of 72 hours after the event, is that right?

A   That's right.

Q   Now, commonly, how long is the period of time between the time he gets that charge and the time of an actual hearing on the particular charge, itself?

A   Well, it depends when it occurred and sometimes depending upon the situation in the institution. If the institution is going through a critical period, it is delayed, but ordinarily, for the ordinary infraction, the prisoner would be given a hearing within, I should say, 24 hours, not counting holidays and Sundays.

Q   Mr. Bennett, during that period between the time of the episode, itself, the incident which gives rise to the proceeding, and the hearing, where is the prisoner normally kept?

A   Well, if it's a serious charge, if it's a serious charge of assault or homosexuality or something of the kind, he is isolated, he is put usually in the—what was just described as the adjustment center. If it's a minor charge like refusing to work or a minor charge relating to some altercation with another inmate over a sports event, he, in most institutions, in our institutions, would be kept in his regular cell.

Q   Mr. Bennett, how long is he normally kept in an adjustment center before the matter is heard, if he was, in fact, put into an adjustment center after the episode and before the hearing?

A   Well, certainly it ought not to extend more than 72 hours.

Q   Have you ever had the experience of having someone kept in an adjustment center for as much as 30 days between the time of the episode and the time of the hearing?

A   No, I couldn't say that that had ever happened in the federal system and it certainly doesn't happen now in Maryland and I don't think it happens in most states that way.

Q   And if a person were, in fact, held for 30 days—and I avow to you we have had one here of 90 or more days—is it fair to say that that is an absolutely deplorable system of prison administration?

A   Well, I don't like to characterize, Mr. Frank, but I would say that it certainly isn't in accord with modern practice and simply develops hostilities and problems and troubles that could well be avoided by an earlier hearing on the charge.

Q   Mr. Bennett, I will ask you to assume now that the individual has been charged in the manner you describe, and he does not, in fact, feel competent to handle the matter himself. I will ask you to assume that either he doesn't speak English comfortably or he is not very bright or for whatever reason, he just doesn't feel able to handle it. What is the federal practice in respect to furnishing anybody who can assist him in the presentation of his side of the matter?

A   He is permitted to select any officer or member of the personnel of the institution to come before the board and act as his, oh, interpreter or act as his counsel, using the word "counsel" not as, necessarily, legal counsel. He is permitted to have somebody come in and advise him, give any mitigating circumstances concerning the offense to the adjustment board, advise the prisoner on what he thinks would be the best plea for him to make, the best answer to the question.

Q   Mr. Bennett, is it accurate to say that at the present time, thinking amongst prison administrators is not settled as to whether the person should have private counsel or a law student or legal aides or a fellow prisoner or somebody from the treatment division, but that it is universally now regarded amongst prison administrators that within your liberal definition of counsel, he is entitled to have somebody?

A   That's right. The question as to whether or not he is entitled to legal counsel, a lawyer, qualified member of the bar, is now in litigation in several federal courts in the country.

Q   Mr. Bennett, I now come to the matter of the next of what I will label the rudimentary constitutional rights and take up the matter of confrontation. Is it now commonly regarded, first of all, that if the prisoner is going to have his sentence extended, he is entitled to actually hear evidence against him?

A   Yes, I think that is correct.

Q   And this would be, then, evidence from the person who saw or is reporting on the actual incident which is at the base of the problem?

A   That's correct, although on some occasions the adjustment committee may have reason to fear that such confrontation might result in violence and, therefore, will decline to have the reporting officer come before the committee, a situation of which I don't approve but it's sometimes done that way.

Q   In what general proportion of the cases now is it common to have the reporting officer actually there?

A   Oh, I would say 98 per cent.

Q   Mr. Bennett, I then reach the other phase of confrontation. What is the current practice in the United States as to the rights of the prisoner to ask questions of the person who is making the report?

A   I think it's assumed and I think he has the right to question the veracity of the report or the facts stated in the report.

Q   I will ask you now to assume hypothetically a prison administration system, Mr. Bennett, in which the practice is for members of the staff to go around and talk to people entirely outside the presence of the individual inmate and gather up statements from them and simply turn them in to the adjustment board without there being any opportunity for cross-examination by the prisoner or anybody, and then this uncross-examined material becomes the basis of a decision by the board.

I will ask you if that is regarded as acceptable practice in any system with which you are acquainted?

A   Well, it certainly isn't acceptable practice when the charge is a serious charge, when it's a question of—where there is some violence involved, where disciplinary action goes to whether or not the person was instigating a riot, whether or not the individual was a homosexual,

I should say that that, without giving the inmate an opportunity to have access to those materials, is, at minimum, undesirable.

Q And it is not the normal practice now in the United States?

A Let me say this: if the material is used or it comes before the adjustment committee.

Q Yes.

A But if that material goes only, perhaps, to the warden, that might be acceptable.

Q Yes. We want to exclude administrative investigation from discipline. I am talking in this exchange only about instances in which the individual's sentence is extended by virtue of disciplinary adjudication.

A Yes.

Q In that circumstance, I take it, it is virtually universally regarded now that there is a right to confrontation, is that correct?

A I should think so, yes, sir.

Q Now, Mr. Bennett, I come to the matter of the inmate's presentation of his own evidence. Let us suppose hypothetically that the charge is the usual business of a fight and the inmate is charged with having started the fight and he wishes to produce some bystander, whether another inmate or a guard, who observed the episode, to establish that he didn't start the fight.

What is the current practice concerning the right of the inmate to get either another inmate or a guard brought in to give his version of the episode?

A I should think that would be proper and feasible so long as it doesn't involve too many people. I mean he could call one or two or perhaps even three people, but to bring in 10, 15, 20, I should think that was unnecessary, cumulative evidence that shouldn't be permitted and unnecessary.

Q May we put it this way: That, certainly, I will note for the record that it is the position of the plaintiffs in this case that the adjustment board has all the rights of any court to avoid cumulative evidence and waste of time and so on.

A That's right.

Q But, on the other hand, there is clearly a constitutional right to call witnesses as well as to examine witnesses, is that not commonly accepted?

A I should think so, yes, that's right.

Q Now, I come to the matter of the impartiality of the tribunal, and the question arises: To what extent can persons, in current practice, who have been involved in the investigation of a matter be included in the board which passes upon the matter?

A The person should not be a member of the board. Any person who is witness to the event or makes the charges or, for any other reason, could be accused of partiality, should not be a member.

Q The system here is that we have what amounts to an adjustment committee or grievance committee which is the first one, and that then the decisions of that committee are reviewed by a second committee known as the classifications committee. At least some of the same personnel is on both of them, so that we have the situation in which, hypothetically, a Mr. B is reviewing the decisions of Mr. B.

If a prison has such a system, is that in accord with normal practice?

A   Well, it would not be in accord with normal practice so far as determining the penalty is concerned, or the fairness of hearing. The decision, for instance, of an adjustment board to transfer the man to some other work or some other section or some other kind of work is a matter that might properly go before the classification committee and the classification committee could be composed, perhaps, of a man who is on the adjustment committee is to review the determination of guilt or the determination of the penalty, I would think that it would be bad practice to have any member of the adjustment committee on that board.

Q   Mr. Bennett, let me go now to the matter of penalties. And I take it that one of the disciplinary penalties, of course, is the possibility of segregation, and with it the loss of good time. My question is: What are the views in your profession as to how long a person ought to be subject to disciplinary segregation?

A   Well, I think that the general impression now is that he should not be in disciplinary segregation for more than 15 days, and if for some reason he is not able to go back into the general population, he can be transferred to administrative segregation for another period of indeterminate length, that is to say he would have to be given an interview or a hearing by an officer of the institution from time to time to see whether or not he could be put into the general population.

Do I make myself clear?

Q   Yes, but I would like to pursue it from that preface, sir.

You have said that the current practice is that the outer limit of plain disciplinary segregation ought to be about 15 days?

A   That's right.

Q   That, then, if beyond that, he moves into administrative segregation, I would assume from your earlier answers that that would be so only if for some reason he was unfit to be in the general population because of violence or other things but that that would be nondisciplinary; is that correct?

A   That's correct, yes.

Q   And, therefore, the maximum disciplinary sentence would be a 15-day sentence, is that right?

A   I think that's the generally accepted practice now.

Q   And if something more serious is needed, the person would simply have to be referred to the courts for an actual conviction of a new offense, is that right?

A   Oh, yes. Well, that raises another question. A great many institutions who refer assault and what amounts to felonies to the courts do not bring them before the adjustment—or the disciplinary committee at all until after the court has acted, and then even after the court has acted they accept the decision of the court as to the penalty.

Q   Mr. Bennett, why is there the view that disciplinary segregation should be limited to 15 days?

A   I think it's a question of humanity, a question of, oh, fairness and of, well, just common decency, shall I say.

Q   Would you take up each of these? Would you explain, please, why it is inhumane and indecent to keep a person protractedly in disciplinary segregation? And for this purpose, I will ask you to assume hypothetically—and I avow this to be the case—that my client was kept in disciplinary segregation without a hearing for 90 days.

Now, why is the better view of prison administration that this is inhumane and indecent?

A   First of all, because of the conditions under which he lives in there—isolated, no contact with anyone else—he is apt to develop a situation psychosis, the doctors call it. He is deprived, usually, of reading materials, deprived of visiting privileges, deprived of exercise, and it just is not in accord with fair treatment.

Q   Well, Mr. Bennett, is it not true that in the common view of persons with whom you deal in your profession, all of this boils down to the fact that it is a plain denial of due process of law to treat a person that way?

A   Well, I don't know. Perhaps so, yes, yes, perhaps that—that's probably the way to phrase it.

Q   Let me come to the matter of exercise. I will ask you, please, what is the normal amount of exercise that a person ought to get who is in disciplinary segregation?

A   Well, ordinarily he doesn't get any. Ordinarily, in most institutions, he doesn't get any exercise. Some institutions will allow the fellow out in the corridor in front of the cells for an hour or so a day, but I should say the general practice is no exercise.

Q   What is the federal practice in this regard?

A   Our practice, likewise, is no exercise, although most of our —most of our commitments are for less than 15 days.

Q   But this is one of the key reasons why the commitment should be limited to 15 days, is that correct?

A   That's right.

Q   All right. Now, I come to the matter of the appellate phases of discipline.

We have proposed that there be a review, if one wishes it, without appearances or argument but simply on the record, by the state correctional authority to review any decision which had the effect of lengthening a sentence.

My question is: Is something of that sort common practice or uncommon practice in the United States at the present time?

A   Well, I should say that represents the better practice. I don't think that—I couldn't say that it prevails generally. I would say that is the better practice.

In many institutions the action of the adjustment committee is final.

Q   I now go to the matter of the bed, diet and so on. We have expressed the view that any sound rules for disciplinary segregation should provide that there be clean clothes, adequate light, heat and ventilation, healthful diet.

Are those commonly accepted as the norms for disciplinary segregation?

A Well, no, I'm not sure of that. You will have to take one at a time.

Q All right. How about clean clothing?

A Yes, he should be entitled to clean uniform frequently in the form of a coverall or something of that kind.

Q How about lighting?

A Well, that varies from time to time according to the inmate, but I should say that during the daylight hours the door would be left open and he would get barred light from the corridor, and because of the fact that those cells have to be proofed against destruction, there is frequently or usually a light outside the cell, which reflects into the cell, and which is turned on during the day, and sometimes for a period in the evening.

Q Mr. Bennett, what is the common practice in this regard? I will ask you to assume an isolation cell with a steel door with no light penetrating through it, so that the room is pitch dark when that door is closed unless the light is turned on.

What is the practice as to keeping prisoners in a completely black room for disciplinary purposes?

A Well, it formerly was quite common to keep them in a dark cell for two or three or four, sometimes as much as five days, but that practice is disappearing as being counter-productive, and there isn't any final categorical statement you can make with regard to it. It depends again on the character of the inmate, whether he is violent, assaultive, threatening.

Q I will ask you to assume that it is a routine case and that the prisoner is docile. For that purpose, how many hours of the day is the cell normally kept pitch black, if a person is in that situation?

A Well, I don't know. All I can say is that we wouldn't do it in the federal system except when, as I say, he is violent.

Q And you mean you wouldn't do it at all? What do you do, in short, between the hours of 11:00 at night, hypothetically, and 3:00 in the morning—

A Yes, that's right.

Q —in the federal system when—do you shut the door and leave it pitch black?

A Yes, although it's always open to observation. It depends on the inmate. Some of them are suicidal and some of them, as I say, are apt to develop a situation psychosis, and so we try to observe them regularly. The officer on duty is expected to observe them regularly.

Q Let me go now, please, to the matter of files and ask for the practice on this point.

We have all sorts of what I would call miscellaneous matters in the file of a prisoner, casual reports of a guard and so on. These may report claimed misconduct. They, in turn, if allowed to go to the parole board, may have an effect on whether the person is released and so affect the extension of his time. How much of the file material which reports alleged disciplinary infractions but which were never subject to any due process to determine whether the disciplinary infraction actually occurred, how much of that should go to the parole board?

A   Well, I don't know. I have doubt that any of that should go, in the event he was acquitted, so to speak, and if they do remain in the file, there should be a statement on the sheet that the matter had been investigated and the person found not guilty.

Q   Mr. Bennett, we are particularly concerned with reports which never come to that level at all, as, for example, a guard reports a minor infraction, nobody thinks it's worth having a hearing about and yet it looks bad on the parole record. Should that stuff go through to the parole board?

A   Well, I think I would be different from many people in this regard. I feel that the file must be comprehensive and that material of that kind should remain in the file, believing that the parole board is able to interpret that data and give it the right connotation. They have in the parole file the FBI flimsy which has a long number of charges on which he was arrested but no convictions and so on. Those remain in the file and the parole board presumably has the knowledge and the ability to give it the proper weight. I don't think you can keep away from the file statements about the prisoner that are made, although the person that makes the statement ought to be able to authenticate them and buttress them with facts.

Q   Mr. Bennett, I go to another topic, the matter of mail, and ask what is regarded as the normal practice as to the amount of mail a prisoner may receive or may send?

A   Well, formerly it used to be quite restricted but now I think almost all institutions have discontinued anything other than inspecting the incoming mail and inspecting the outgoing mail and put no limit on the amount of mail a prisoner may receive.

Q   For example, is there any reason why a person should not be allowed to correspond with a former inmate?

A   No reason.

Q   Now, you say that the mail should be inspected. What is the scope of that inspection?

A   It is the opening of the letter, to see that it doesn't contain any contraband of any kind.

Q   What is contraband?

A   Contraband could be anything from a hacksaw or a letter bomb or some drug, any of those—those things that might make possible escape or be used in some violence in the institution.

Q   I will ask you to assume that the local rule precludes any reference to any other inmate and also forbids derogatory remarks about the institution or its personnel.

Is that regarded as acceptable practice by those with whom you deal?

A   You mean is it acceptable practice to let it go out?

Q   To forbid it.

A   No. That, I think, is discarded notion. Let it go out, let it go out.

Q   All right. To what extent is the inmate allowed to have free access to letters from his counsel? How should those be opened and when and by whom?

A If the counsel has entered an appearance and has been recognized as his counsel over some time, the letter should go in without inspection of any kind. If the letter is from a person who alleges himself to be a lawyer and has not been recorded in the records of the institution as the counsel, that letter could be opened in the presence of the inmate and initials put on the letter to that effect and notation made that it comes from an individual who is not the inmate's counsel.

Q Mr. Bennett, how should the prison handle the possession of or the sending in of salacious, suggestive, obscene or any other kind of material of high sexual content?

A Personally, I am opposed to it, although there is a growing number of institutional people, psychiatrists and others, who say that is an acceptable outlet for sex urges.

Q In the federal practice, would a prisoner be allowed to have, hypothetically, the center girl from Playboy displayed upon his cell walls?

A Yes, he might, but someone might question his good taste in that regard and cause him to remove it.

Q And how about his incoming mail? Let us suppose that Miss Bunny Girl sends him a self-portrait and it comes in the mail. Will that piece of mail be confiscated?

A No—well, it is in some places now but I don't think that is necessary. I don't think it is proper.

Q Is there some reason by way of sound prison administration why you have to keep out of the prison salacious or suggestive material within your experience, or is it just a matter of good taste?

A It's a matter of good taste and also it must not be a means whereby a prisoner can pass it along to some other prisoner in return for some other favor. It must not be a form of exchange.

Q Mr. Bennett, I would like to get your comments on some of the internal regulations here. One of our rules provides that an inmate must be "orderly" and another says that it is a disciplinary offense if he agitates, unduly complains, magnifies grievances or behaves in any way that might lead to violence.

Now, the question is whether terms of this sort, as rules, are definite enough to be the basis of disciplinary sanctions.

What are your views on the problems of definiteness of the restrictions?

A Well, I think they ought to be, first, orderly and obey the instructions that the person must keep himself clean and in good order and sanitary and must not be boisterous or running around the institution and so on. I think that should properly be expected, and I think that is possible of definition.

Now, the question about whether or not he is creating dissension within the institution or possibilities of work strikes and so on, is that the question?

Q Well, it is just these words, Mr. Bennett. Let me give it concretely in terms of the federal regulation. Federal regulation Section

304 makes the offense of insolence toward a staff member a disciplinary offense.

Now, my question is: Have, within your knowledge, there, in fact, been people who have been given discipline for insolence?

A Oh, yes, for disrespect, yes, yes.

Q What does that mean? What is insolence or disrespect?

A Well, it means use of, oh, various terms that are common around an institution, use of terms concerning a man's sex and, oh, well, you know what they are.

Q Something we wondered about, Mr. Bennett, is that I suppose that very few people with the elegance of Lord Chesterfield are in prison and you are bound to get a certain amount of rough discourse.

How do you make allowances for that?

A Well, you have to make allowances on the extent to which it goes on and the tone in which it's done and the presence in which it's done. Prison officers now are coming to accept some of these terms as commonplace and don't take it too seriously. Now, if it's repeated and repeated in the course of—in the presence of others, why, that individual certainly ought to be charged with disrespect, in the minimum.

Q Another one is Section 306, which deals with conduct which disrupts or interferes with the security or orderly running of the institution.

And the question is: Is that sufficiently definite, so that people would know what it is that is legal and what is not legal? What is that kind of conduct?

A Well, those things are so difficult to define that we have to use general terms, and we have to leave it to the good sense of the disciplinary board as to whether it comes within the ambit of the definition.

Q Mr. Bennett, in the whole field of sexual relations, the rules have problems. Our rules use such terms as "immoral" or "debasement." Are the terms "immoral" or "debasement" sufficiently clear to prison people so they know what they are talking about? Do you know what debasement means?

A Well, no, no, I don't know how I would relate it to specific actions or specific words, but—

Q How about immorality? Is there a federal—

A No, I don't think so. You are reading—you were reading previously from this policy statement of the Federal Prison Bureau relating to inmate discipline.

Q That's right, and it does not have that kind of language. It does have the phrase in 554 that makes it an offense to use abusive or obscene language.

And if, in fact, prisoners use obscene language to each other, is there ever actually a disciplinary proceedings in the federal system?

A Yes, once in a while, once in a while when that obscene language is continued and of such character that it, shall I say, is inflammatory and calls or might bring on a fight.

They have a game, they used to call it a game, called "Playing the Dozen." That was a business of trying to think up terms which you called the other fellow that were more obscene, more—I don't know—more debasing, if you want, than others, and those, while it might have started out in a friendly way, lead frequently to fights and so on, violence, and so we have frowned upon that and disciplined people for engaging in interchange of that kind of term.

Q I will sum it up and put my last question this way, if Mr. Dixon will pardon it, as a deliberate summary. The common conception of what the constitution requires, where a person is likely to have his term extended because of his act, are the following: Number 1, there must be a clear, written charge.

A Right.

Q Number 2, there must be a right to counsel of some sort, whether professional or in the institution is still being debated.

A That's right.

Q Number 3, he is entitled to a right of confrontation which includes the right to hear the evidence against him and the right, within reasonable limits, to ask questions that bear on the matter.

A That's correct.

Q He has a right to present his own evidence, which includes a limited right, within reasonable administration, to bring in people who have something to say about it as witnesses.

A That's correct.

Q He is entitled to an impartial tribunal.

A That's right.

Q He is entitled to a speedy trial promptly after he has been put in a holding segregation.

A That's correct.

Q Protracted segregation is indecent, inhuman, as you have said. Disciplinary segregation therefore should be limited to two weeks, 15 days, something of the sort, and beyond that, if the person is psychotic or an impossible case, he should be handled as an administrative problem and not as a disciplinary problem?

A That's correct. I would like to add to that a prisoner in disciplinary segregation should be visited each day by some officer of the institution, and the fact that he did visit him should be logged in a log book.

There should be a log book in disciplinary segregation, noting who came in, any unusual events about the prisoner and noting anything else concerning him.

Q And finally, the prisoner should be entitled to one appeal to the correctional authorities of the state on the record, without the necessity of further oral appearances, but there should be review some place.

A That's right, that's correct.

. . . .

A-9

SAMPLE DEPOSITION OF A HOSTILE WITNESS (TOMBS CASE MANHATTAN HOUSE OF DETENTION FOR MEN)

Rhem v. McGrath

.   .   .   .

Q   What was the date of your appointment as Deputy Warden in Command?

A   I don't recall, I would have to get the teletype from my secretary.

THE WITNESS: May I?

MR. BERNIKOW: Yes.

Q   Do you become warden by a Civil Service examination?

A   At present the only way you can become a warden is to take the competitive examination for warden if you are eligible as a permanently assigned Deputy Warden who has been in that rank for at least one year.

Q   Are you eligible to take the test?

A   I am.

Q   Have you taken it?

A   I have not.

Q   Have you signed up to take it?

A   It has not been opened for filing.

Q   Do you know when it will be open?

A   I do not know.

Q   When did you take the examination for Deputy Warden, approximately how long ago?

A   I would say probably around December of 1965.

Q   What is your educational background?

A   I attended the Carlisle Institute through the Army, I attended Washington and Lee University, through the Army. I did not get a degree.

Q   How many years of college did you get?

A   I wouldn't know the total amount.

Teletype order 110-0 dated March 1971, designation of Deputy Warden.

Q   For approximately how many years did you take college courses?

A   I am still taking them. I am always taking a course. I have taken courses through the City of New York. I am going out in July and August of this year to the University of Colorado, hopefully, and take a course there. I don't know the subject yet.

Q   What date, or when did you join the Department of Correction of New York City, approximately?

A In May of 1949.

Q Did you have any prior work experience in correction?

A Prior to joining Correction?

Q Prior to joining here, in New York City, did you ever work for a Correction Department anywhere else?

A No.

Q Did you ever have any jobs prior to that related to the kind of work you do in Correction?

A Related to what?

Q Related to correctional work that you would consider?

A Would you please explain correctional work so we have a common understanding of that term?

Q Well, what jobs, what did you do right before you joined the New York Department of Correction?

MR. BERNIKOW: I will object to this, I don't think it is relevant.

MRS. SHAPIRO: Let's go on through his professional background and his job background.

MR. BERNIKOW: I am objecting to the question as being irrelevant, but I will permit the witness to answer the question.

Q What was your job, what did you do before you joined the Department of Correction?

A If I recall I came from the Department of Sanitation after just coming back from the Army.

. . . .

MR. BERGER: Let's go on with something else.

Q What do you do in a case with an inmate who repeatedly commits infractions? What would be the policy?

A What types of infraction does he repeat?

Q Being disrespectful or abusive to a correction officer.

A I have a review by the mental health staff to see what their recommendations are.

Q How many times have you had that occur since you have been at the Tombs?

A Innumerable.

Q Innumerable?

A Yes. Very often infractions will come before me where the disciplinary officer has recommended that the inmate not be punished and be seen by the mental health staff, and the mental health staff will concur that what he did was an episode of neurosis, psychosis, what have you, and would recommend no punishment. I go along with it.

Q What is the longest period of punitive segregation you would allow, that you have allowed?

MR. ROBERTS: Since when?

Q Since March 12.

A I don't think I have had any that extended beyond ten days.

Q What was the longest period of punitive segregation permissible?

A   Permissible?

Q   Yes. Is there any limit?

     MR. BERNIKOW: If you know.

A   I don't know if there is a limit.

Q   What constitutes disrespect to a correction officer? I have seen in the answer to interrogatories the infraction of being disrespectful to a correction officer. What is an example of that?

     MR. BERNIKOW: Objection.

     Off the record.

     (Discussion off the record.)

A   I wouldn't know what the gesture or what the incident was unless the investigating captain deemed it to be of such a nature as to require a hearing. Then after it was done, and the hearing was conducted, I would then review the entire thing.

Q   Some inmates have been disciplined for being disrespectful to correction officers?

A   What do you mean?

Q   Being placed in punitive segregation.

A   If it was of such a nature to be declared that serious by the captain.

Q   In your 22 years with the Department of Correction have you ever known a correction officer to have any action taken against him for being disrespectful to an inmate?

     MR. ROBERTS: Objection.

     MR. BERNIKOW: Objection.

A   How does this come to my attention?

Q   I am just asking you if you know.

     MR. ROBERTS: I will object to his responding to it.

     I will also object to the question as to form, as well as to relevance.

     MR. BERGER: It is perfectly good form.

     MR. ROBERTS: As to form as well as relevance.

     MR. BERGER: That is not grounds for not answering.

     MR. ROBERTS: As to form I think there is an objection. Reword your question.

     MR. BERGER: I don't have to reword it.

     MR. ROBERTS: Then he doesn't have to answer it. As to form he doesn't have to answer it.

     MR. BERGER: Unless it is to privilege he does have to answer it despite the objection.

     MR. BERNIKOW: Off the record.

     (Discussion off the record.)

Q   Defining disrespect as verbal abuse, or abuse by gesture, have you ever known a correction officer to be disciplined for that type of disrespect towards an inmate?

     MR. BERNIKOW: Objection.

     MR. ROBERTS: Objection. My objection is as to whether or not he has heard or not does not mean that it has not occurred.

Q   If you know, to the best of your knowledge.

     MR. BERNIKOW: Objection. You may answer.

A   Yes.

Q   Has it happened since you have been deputy warden in command?

A   Not since I have been in command, and not in this institution. I am going back maybe 10, 15 years.

Q   Ten, 15 years it has not happened?

MR. BERNIKOW: He said in this institution.

Q   In this institution?

A   Not in this institution. It is going back in my memory for 10, 15 years.

BY MRS. SHAPIRO:

Q   Are correction officers given any guidance or rules concerning what they are to consider is disrespect? Is a correction officer given any training or any rules as to what kind of language or gestures constitute an infraction, or is it up to each correction officer to determine whether something is or is not disrespectful?

A   They get a training at the correction academy. They get a break-in period here at the institution.

Q   What are they told constitutes disrespect?

M. BERNIKOW: Objection. I don't know if the warden can answer that question in view of the fact that he is not at the Rikers Island training facility.

MRS. SHAPIRO: He has been trained and he is in charge of the institution, and responsible for whatever in-service training the officers receive.

Q   When an officer comes to this institution is he given any guidance as to what kinds of remarks or abusive language he is to consider an infraction, and what he is not?

A   It depends on the circumstances. A remark is not the thing that causes the infraction. The circumstances causes it.

Q   Is there any general statement of policy that applies, that you give to people when they come to this institution?

A   They are taught in the academy how to handle people, how to recognize abnormal behavior in people. They are taught here in their break-in period how to handle people. They witness incidents taking place and how it is handled. It depends on the circumstance itself. Nothing is left to their judgment. Whatever they claim happened is reviewed by an investigating superior officer. He either concurs or dismisses it.

Q   Is any time that an inmate uses profanity to a correction officer, for example, is that considered an infraction of the rules, or is that often disregarded?

A   There may be extenuating circumstances where a prisoner uses profanity but we can allow it because we know what happened recently. Sometimes he had a bad court incident, possibly by sentence or otherwise, and when he comes back he is mad at the world and everyone, and he is asked to go along with the processes of receiving, or something that is normal, and he may utter an epithet, but it is forgiveable, we understand why.

Q   Is it the policy of this institution since you have been in charge to enforce strictly rules against use of profanity by inmates?

A   There is no strict enforcement of any rules and regulations by the head of this institution. There is always an allowance made for any physical or mental limitations. Never any strict enforcement.

I want to bring up something, please, in the questioning that was directed to me by counsel regarding what is or is not the type of training they get.

I am looking at a four-week schedule from academy training. I count maybe 20 to 30 sessions on human relations. So that the human relations is applicable to the type of on-the-job training that they are getting, or academic learning they are getting.

When they talk about, for instance, problems of adolescents in detention and mention human relations following it, they will talk about the various things adolescents do.

When they talk about searching and contraband, and it is followed by two sections in human relations, they will discuss what goes in the mind of the prisoner and how human relations is used in this search.

Q   When you were at the Academy years ago, were courses like that being given then?

A   They were given, but not under the name of human relations. I personally taught psychological reactions of prisoners in confinement. That is differing in sentence and detention institutions.

Q   As an assistant deputy warden for many years you reviewed many disciplinary proceedings, did you not? You are the disciplinary officer in many institutions, aren't you?

MR. BERNIKOW: Objection. What has this to do with the issues in the lawsuit?

MR. ROBERTS: He was a correction officer also many years before that.

Q   Since you have been deputy warden in command, how many requests have been made through the locked interview box by inmates to personally have an interview with yourself?

A   I have never received a request where they wanted to have an interview with me. I have received a request where they wanted something done.

Q   How many inmates have you actually interviewed since March 12, 1970?

MR. ROBERTS: Objection. If you can get that figure specifically, if that figure is available to you specifically.

MR. BERNIKOW: Give him your best recollection.

Q   The best you can remember.

A   Interviewed regarding complaints?

Q   Yes.

A   I haven't interviewed them personally, but I have sent deputy wardens to explain to hundreds of them at some time, or 50, 70, or 60, my feelings and what I was doing to alleviate their problem.

.   .   .   .

ENFORCEMENT OF A FAVORABLE DECISION BY A FINDING OF CONTEMPT: THE CONTEMPT OPINION IN LANDMAN v. ROYSTER

Landman v. Royster

IN THE UNITED STATES DISTRICT COURT
FOR THE EASTERN DIVISION OF VIRGINIA
RICHMOND DIVISION

ROBERT JEWELL LANDMAN, et al.

v.

M. L. ROYSTER, etc., et al.

CIVIL ACTION
NO. 170-69-R

MEMORANDUM

Under date of October 30, 1971, this Court issued a memorandum and order enjoining the defendants, who are responsible for the maintenance and running of the Virginia penal system, "from performing, causing to perform, or permitting the performance of any acts found in the memorandum of the Court to be violative of the prohibition against cruel and unusual punishment." The Court further directed that the defendants implement certain minimum due process procedures to be observed in administering discipline, to prepare and file with the Court a list of rules and regulations concerning standards of behavior, to take steps to make the inmate population aware of these rules, and to take all "necessary steps to inform all members of the custodial staff of all units of the Virginia State Penitentiary system of the injunctive terms of this order."

Subsequently, on July 18, 1972, the defendants filed a motion to vacate the injunction, alleging that the Court's injunction had contributed to a state of permissiveness and unrest which was endangering penal security. Thereafter, the plaintiffs, by written motion, petitioned for an order requiring the defendants to show cause why they should not be held in contempt of court for failure to obey the letter and spirit of the Court's order.

This matter came on for hearing on November 21, 1972. After the presentation of testimony by the defendants in support of their motion to vacate, the Court for the reasons stated from the bench granted plaintiffs' motion for a directed verdict. Not a scintilla of evidence was offered by defendants in support of their allegation concerning the existence of an emergency or of any link between any alleged unrest and the Court's injunction. A fair and reasonable conclusion is that the motion was precipitated by the plaintiffs' announced intention to seek an order of contempt against the defendants. Evidence was then heard on plaintiffs' contempt motion.

The evidence presented to the Court can be divided roughly into three contentions by the plaintiffs of allegedly contemptuous actions on the part of the defendants. First, there was evidence in support of a claim that the defendants arbitrarily placed certain maximum security prisoners on padlock, isolation and in the old death row cells without first providing them with the hearings required by the Court's order. Second, there was evidence concerning the alleged failure of the defendants to ensure that the Court's order was implemented throughout all levels of the penal system. Finally, evidence was presented in support of the plaintiff's contention that the defendants had failed to provide inmates at disciplinary hearings the procedural requirements made a part of the injunction. From all of the evidence adduced, the Court makes the following findings of fact and conclusions of law:

Throughout the Spring of 1972, it apears that tension was building in the maximum security section (C-Block) of the State Penitentiary.[1] By May, the tension had erupted into several disturbances, including the setting of small fires in the cells, floodings, and prolonged periods of yelling by the inmates. Prior to these disruptions, however, the custodial staff had begun to fear that a wholesale takeover of C-Block was being planned. In response, they ordered that all inmates in C-Block be placed on padlock. The effect of such padlock is the restriction of every inmate to his cell and the restriction of any congregation at all among those incarcerated in C-Block. The decision to padlock all of the prisoners seems to have been made jointly by the defendant Slayton, Superintendent of the penitentiary, and the C-Block custodial staff. No hearings were held prior to the step, and no charges were placed against any of the inmates.

Three of the inmates who seem to have contributed heavily to the existing tensions were Victor Cassara, Wiley Reynolds and James Peterson. Each appeared as a witness in this action. All have lengthy records of trouble with the prison authorities and other inmates. During the fall of 1971 and the spring of 1972, all were held, at one time or another, on C-Block padlock, isolation, and in the old death row cells, which are completely segregated from the rest of the inmate population. Peterson's case is of particular concern with reference to the pending motion.

In April of 1972, Peterson was transferred from the maximum security building at the State Farm to the general population of C-Block at the State Penitentiary. The guard in command of C-Block at the time was Lt. H. Catron, with whom Peterson had, slightly more than a year prior thereto, been involved in a serious altercation. Some three weeks after his transfer, Peterson was placed on padlock status at the order of Catron. The reasons assigned by Catron for his actions were that Peterson talked louder than other inmates in the mess hall, entered and

---

[1] The Court has visited the C-Block and unhesitatingly states that the physical arrangement and the procedures to which the inmates are subjected leave no doubt in the Court's mind that the cell block is in and of itself punitive in nature.

left his cell slower than the others, and evidenced anger over the failure to be given his typewriter and over the lack of ready access by the guards to fire extinguishers (this concern was precipitated by a fire in a cell near Peterson's). This transfer was effected summarily, without prior authorization by the Institutional Classification Committee (ICC). Subsequently, on May 30, Peterson was again summarily transferred by Catron, this time to isolation, for allegedly breaking the padlock on his cell. An Adjustment Committee hearing, which was not accorded Peterson until six days later, resulted in a decision to continue him in isolation for a certain number of days as punishment for his alleged misbehavior.

As the period for Peterson's incarceration in isolation ended, the C-Block officers expressed their concern over his return. Apparently, he was felt to be so disruptive and intimidating to other inmates that the security of C-Block was threatened by his return. Accordingly, the Institutional Classification Committee ordered that he be kept in isolation, which was done for a number of days. He was thereafter transferred to the old death row cells in East Basement (of A Building), then to what is described as the new ones in the basement of B Building, after Slayton decided that his incarceration in solitary might be violative of the Court's order. Peterson, as well as Cassara, Reynolds and several other inmates who were kept in these cells, remained confined on padlock, despite the fact that there was an exercise room available for just the new death row cells. Peterson had remained in such confinement from July, 1972, until after the hearing on this matter in November. The Court has learned, however, that he has now been transferred out of the penitentiary to a field correctional unit.

From the Peterson case, as well as from other testimony, the Court reaches several conclusions. First, there developed in C-Block, and the Court is satisfied in other areas throughout the penal system as well, an approach of ordering inmates into a higher security classification than they had previously been in prior to affording them a hearing. Such an approach violates both the letter and the spirit of the Court's order. By the precise and unequivocal terms of the order, the defendants are enjoined from the imposition of penalties prior to a hearing that conforms to the necessary due process requisites. Similarly, though not by express terms, the spirit of the Court's order mandates that an inmate who is transferred to a higher security classification for any appreciable period of time be afforded an opportunity for a hearing. This is theoretically accomplished by the Institutional Classification Committee. Common sense dictates, however, that there will be times when the exigencies of the situation require that an inmate be placed in confinement before a hearing can be convened. The Court recognizes this and has never suggested that such summary action prior to a hearing is prohibited.

The evidence before the Court, however, is that confinement prior to hearing became the rule in certain cases rather than the exception. The Peterson case cited previously is a prime example. The reasons presented to the Court, while they may have created suspicions which would justify greater confinement, do not show the sort of emergency conditions that would require immediate incarceration. More importantly, even if they did, an inmate such as Peterson was and is entitled to be afforded a hearing as soon as practicable after his confinement. The ICC normally held hearings according to a set schedule, as a consequence of which an inmate might have to wait several days or longer before being heard. Such a delay, in the absence as here of any reasonable justification therefor, cannot be tolerated.

The Court has for over three years endeavored to express its appreciation of the security problems which the defendants face, particularly in view of a crowded, antiquated facility, manned generally by an untrained, understaffed and in some instances potentially physically incapable guard force. It may well be that a sort of intuitive suspicion on the part of a guard is sufficient to confine a man to a greater security status in order to prevent difficulties. The Court is fully cognizant that we deal with a constant potential danger. But even in the face of this, the inmate must be afforded a hearing immediately thereafter in order that he may present his defense, if any, and in order that prison officials other than the acting officer might confirm that the latter's suspicions are justified. The defendants have knowingly failed to afford inmates such hearings as are required, not only by law but by simply fairness as well, and, in so doing, have failed to obey the Court's order.

The cases of Peterson, Reynolds and Cassara also present a rather disturbing use of the padlock system. All of these men were held on padlock or in the death row cells (under padlock conditions) for a number of months. Reynolds, for example, appears to have remained on padlock or in isolation continuously from October of 1971 until the present. Although the plaintiffs sought to characterize this detention as punitive in nature,[2] the Court concludes that there were genuine security reasons associated with the detention of these men.

Nevertheless, the Court is duty bound to be concerned over the apparent loss of privileges which these men suffered. Unless an inmate is intentionally deprived of his privileges by the Adjustment Committee as punishment, he should not be made to bear any of the incidents of same. To the contrary, he should receive at least those privileges as the exigencies of his special incarceration allow. Thus, there appears to be no reason why prisoners incarcerated in East Basement should not be allowed, as they have been deprived, to pursue educational opportunities or have access to the portable library. Unfortunately, it would seem from the evidence that, at least for a period, such amenities were not offered these prisoners.

Similar considerations apply to the matter of exercise, although the evidence before the Court was to the effect that there were security reasons for not allowing inmates on padlock or in the old death row cells to be freed for exercise purposes. If these problems can be overcome, however, as the Court is satisfied they can be, inmates so situated should be allowed exercise. Particularly in the new death row cells,

---

[2] Such detention was specifically declared unlawful in Ferrell v. Huffman, C.A. No. 490-72-R (E.D. Va. 1972).

where there is an exercise room that had formerly been utilized by death row inmates, there appears to be no valid reason for not allowing exercise. In any event, the defendants are duty bound to use their best resources to try to overcome any potential obstacles to allowing exercise.

The Court is further concerned over evidence which it heard concerning prolonged periods of isolation to which some inmates are subjected. Although the Court's order did not expressly address this issue, the defendants' own regulations place a maximum 15 days in isolation detention for each charge. However, by charging inmates with several different offenses growing out of one set of facts, prison officials have been able to greatly extend that limit. Both Reynolds and Peterson testified that since the Court's order they have been placed in isolation for a continuous period of over 40 days. Although part of this period in the case of these two men appears to have been imposed by mistake, the fact remains that they remained for a prolonged period in isolation.

The Court is convinced that this practice violates the terms of the injunction issued against the prison officials on August 13, 1968, in *Mason v. Peyton,* C.A. No. 5611-R (E.D. Va.). That order provided that "no inmate be placed in isolation or solitary confinement as punishment in such a manner or for such a period of time as would be detrimental to his physical and mental health, as determined by a qualified practicing physician." There is no evidence that the defendants ordered a doctor to visit on a regular basis the men kept in solitary for over fifteen days. Although this failure does not constitute contempt on the motion presently before the Court, it is a practice which the defendants must adopt in order to be in conformity with a prior order of this Court.

As to the plaintiffs' second claim, the evidence before the Court is virtually uncontradicted that there was considerable misunderstanding and confusion by lower level custodial staff throughout the penal system as to the meaning and effect of the Court's order of October 30. This confusion was revealed by the testimony of guards, higher prison officials, and even inmates. Indeed, the evidence presented by the defendants themselves in support of their motion to vacate suggests that any apprehensions felt by lower level security officers were less the result of the Court's order than of the failure to be informed as to the actual meaning and effect of that order.

The Court is convinced that any confusion that exists is directly attributable to the failure of the defendants to inform their lower level personnel as to the injunctive terms of the Court's order. The record is replete with explanatory memoranda issued by W. K. Cunningham, Director of the Department of Corrections, and his legal advisors to the various superintendents. There is a gaping absence, however, of such memoranda or other formal systematic communications by Cunningham or the superintendents to lower personnel. Further, there appear to have been few, if any, comprehensive oral explanations of the Court's decision.

On the other side of the coin, there was also a failure by the defendants to determine for themselves whether the Court's order was being implemented on the lower levels of the penal system. The testimony of Cunningham, in particular, reveals a serious lack of knowledge as to whether lower custodial personnel understood and were carrying out the terms of the injunction.

The failure to disperse information and to supervise the implementation of the Court's order constitutes a direct violation of the same, which specifically required the defendants to take the necessary steps to advise members of the custodial staff of the terms of the injunction. This requirement was not imposed lightly. As this Court's Appellate Court noted in *Landman v. Peyton,* 370 F.2d 135 (4th Cir. 1966), both the educational level and job training of prison guards leaves much to be desired. In order for them to perform their jobs in a proper manner, these guards must be carefully guided by their superiors. Particularly in a case such as this, when fundamental changes in the established order as instituted rapidly, there is an obvious need for clear and precise guidance. That guidance was here ordered, but not given.[3]

Defendants' failure to instruct their staffs on the Court's decision, in addition to violating the order on its face, has resulted in additional violations. The Court considers that the Peterson case, for example, can be attributed directly to the failure of the defendant Cunningham, through defendant Slayton, to inform his guards adequately as to the full purport of the Court's order.

In testimony before the Court, Lt. Catron stated that it was his understanding that under the Court's order he could place an inmate on padlock, or even in isolation, keeping him there until the ICC had had an opportunity to consider a status change. Catron's testimony, and the facts surrounding the Peterson case, made clear that he had no comprehension of the sort of emergency situation which must exist under this Court's order before such summary status shifts can be made. It was not until August of 1972, nearly ten months after the filing of the Court's order, that an express directive was made to Catron by A. E. Slayton, Superintendent of the Penitentiary, directing him to use padlocking prior to an ICC determination only "where absolutely needed." In sum, the Peterson incident presents a glaring example of the failure of a guard in a position of considerable authority to be apprised of an important aspect of the Court's order and of the deprivation to an inmate which resulted from this failure.

At least one official evidenced serious doubt that the guard force was intellectually capable of comprehending the Court's findings and order; a conclusion which, if accurate, placed upon the responsible officials an even greater duty and responsibility to explain in detail the requirements of law.

---

[3] Inherent in these proceedings is an undercurrent of disagreement by at least some of the penal officials of the propriety of the Court's injunctive relief. This attitude is even more disturbing in view of the Court's open encouragement, at and subsequent to the time of the injunctive order, directed to the State officials to appeal the Court's order. The Court recognized the full impact of its legal conclusions and their effect on the penal system and even more than usual encouraged an appeal to the end that there be no hesitancy on the part of the defendants to adhere to the law.

The evidence also is clear to the effect that the defendants failed to follow the Court's directive of taking "such steps as may reasonably be necessary to cause each member of the inmate population to be aware of the rules and regulations" required by the Court to be compiled. Although copies of these rules were posted at various places throughout the institutions, it appears they were, as the defendants by reason of their past experience ought to have known they would be, often torn down soon after posting by inmates who wanted personal copies. The result was that more often than not an inmate who desired to examine the list was unable to do so. Moreover, no provision was made to enlighten those inmates who were on padlock or otherwise unable to view the list at the selected posting areas.

It is perfectly obvious that the defendants did not take all steps practicable to ensure that inmates had access to the rules. Fortunately, this failure was resolved at trial by virtue of an agreement between counsel to prepare a booklet containing the rules for issuance to every inmate in the institutions. While this appears to resolve the problem of notice for the future, it does not excuse the neglect in the past.

The evidence that the Court has heard also compels the conclusion that the minimum due process procedures which the Court ordered have not been fully implemented. In particular, three shortcomings are evident. First, until September of 1972, attorneys who were retained by inmates to represent them at Adjustment Committee hearings were allowed only to observe such hearings and not to take an active part in them, a situation which borders on the ridiculous. Second, it was a practice of at least some of the Adjustment Committee officers to limit the number of witnesses which any inmate could call to two, regardless of circumstances. Thirdly, the right of cross-examination was in some instances denied *in toto* or severely restricted.

The first of these failures, concerning attorneys, gives rise to the unpleasant prospect that it was attributable either to an apparent failure on the part of the defendants and their legal counsel to comprehend the Court's order, or an intention to thwart same. The Court, quite frankly, cannot fully comprehend the motive of this failure. In recognizing that an inmate has the right to secure legal representation for certain hearings, the Court meant precisely that, legal *representation.* It is inconceivable that this should have been construed to mean that the attorney could play the role of only an observer. Nevertheless, the Court has concluded that the frustration which must be visited upon any humane prison administrator who has to work within the obviously limited resources available to the defendants, must in fairness be considered before reaching so drastic a conclusion as that the failure was designed to thwart the Court's order. The Court attributes the failure to a lack of appreciation of the recognition that a prison administration is not a fief unto itself. Coupled with this antiquated notion that a prison unit is not even peripherally a part of a community is the practice over the years, that has been shown the Court in this and in other prison cases, to envelope the system with a massive veil of secrecy. More concern seems to have been given to the image of the prison's administration than to the granting to its inmates not only such constitutional rights as they are entitled to in spite of their incarceration, or to the basic tenets of conduct which simple fairness, interpreted by even the most uneducated be accorded them as well. These cases are permeated by an apparent lack of understanding on the part of some of the defendants as well as on the part of at least some of their subordinates that the retribution required by law to be inflicted upon a convict had already, within the limits of the legislatively set boundaries, been pronounced by a trial court.

The other due process shortcomings appear, once more, to have resulted from the failure of the defendants adequately to instruct their staffs. Adjustment Committee officers were informed that they could place limits on the number of witnesses called. While reasonable limits for hearings in the prison context are necessary, an absolute limitation of two is arbitrary. Proper guidance by the defendants should have prevented this result from occurring. Similar limitations on the right to cross examination also seem to have been imposed, though the record does reveal that the defendants at least informed their subordinates that the inmates have such a right.

The Court heard considerable evidence on a wide variety of other matters which have occurred in the penal system since the issuance of the Court's order. Most of this evidence, though giving insight into the way in which the prison is operated, does not show acts constituting contempt of the Court's order. For example, the training of guards in riot tactics on the baseball field of the State Penitentiary, which clearly inflamed the inmates, may have been bad judgment, but it was not contemptuous. The case of James Boyd, a young inmate who was struck by guards during a struggle and subsequently placed in isolation without a hearing, may involve violations of the Court's order.[4] However, it is clear that any potential violations involve isolated acts by lower custodial personnel and do not amount to contempt by the defendants.

From all of the evidence presented to it, this Court can reach but one conclusion: the defendants have failed to implement and obey, both in letter and spirit, the directives of this Court's injunction. It follows from such a conclusion that the defendants have been in contempt of this Court's order.

The power of civil contempt, inherently vested in every court which exercises equity jurisdiction, makes the injunction an effective judicial remedy. Cf. United States ex rel Brown v. Fogel, 395 F.2d 291, 293 (4th Cir. 1968). Civil contempt, as distinguished from criminal, is designed to insure that the victorious party in an action secures the full relief which the Court granted to it. It does not seek, as does criminal contempt, to vindicate and protect the authority of the Court itself. See Gompers v. Bucks Stove & Range Co., 221 U.S. 418 (1911). Accordingly, the sanctions which are imposed for civil contempt are not

---

[4] The evidence here indicates that the use of force was occasioned by reason of the fact that the custodial personnel involved were men of such an age as to render them generally physically incapable of subduing a recalcitrant young man without the use of weapons.

punitive in nature, but rather seek "to enforce compliance with an order of the Court or to compensate for losses or damages sustained by reason of noncompliance." *McComb v. Jacksonville Paper Co.,* 336 U.S. 187, 191 (1949).

Viewing the evidence as a whole, and giving unto the defendants, as the Court deems it appropriate so to do, the benefit of every doubt, the Court cannot conclude that the defendants' violations of the injunctive order were wilful. For example, the Court is satisfied that the actions of the defendant Slayton were not done with a malicious intent to refuse to obey the directives of the Court. Nevertheless, the conclusion that he and other of the defendants did not maliciously refuse to obey the directives of the Court does not render the defendants immune from civil contempt, for wilfulness of behavior is not a necessary ingredient. As stated by Mr. Justice Douglas in *McComb v. Jacksonville Paper Co., supra,* at 191,

> "[t]he decree was not fashioned so as to grant or withhold its benefits dependent on the state of mind of respondents. It laid on them a duty to obey specified provisions . . . An act does not cease to be a violation of . . . a decree merely because it may have been done innocently."

Indeed, even the presence of good faith on the part of the defendants is no defense. This is because the purpose of civil contempt is not to punish, but to correct. If the plaintiffs have been deprived of that which the Court ordered, as has indeed occurred here, then the role of the Court is not to fix blame on the defendants, but rather to prevent a recurrence and to repair any damage that has been done. This duty devolves upon the Court regardless of whether the defendants tried in good faith to carry out the terms of the injunction. *Doe v. General Hospital,* 434 F.2d 427 (D.C. Cir. 1970).

During the proceedings on this matter, the Court heard much from the defendants about the complexity of the Court's order and the fundamental changes which it called for in the operation of the Virginia penal system. If these pleas were in support of an argument that the Court's order is too ambiguous to be followed, then they are not well taken. Although it is of course true that the failure to obey an injunction that is too vague or complex to be understood does not constitute contempt, *McComb v. Jacksonville Paper Co., supra,* at 195, (Frankfurter, J., concurring), the Court concludes after a careful reexamination of its order that it was not inexplicit. If the defendants had thought at any time that it was, they could have petitioned the Court for clarification or modification, or, more basically, could have appealed the Court's decision. They did not take either step, however, and that inaction coupled with the patently frivolous, baseless motion to vacate filed by the defendants, not only creates doubt in the Court's mind as to the sincerity of their pleas now made, but gives rise to a maxim not unfamiliar to football players to the effect that the best defense is a good offense. If that be the strategy of the defendants, their plan has been thwarted by the fact that the inmates at the penitentiary, for reasons perhaps best known to themselves, have apparently succumbed to the teaching that where there is a wrong there is a remedy, and the most effective place to effect such a remedy is through the judicial process. In any event, the Court rules as a matter of law that any alleged justification of their actions by the defendants on the ground that the Court's previous order was vague and hence unenforceable is devoid of merit.

It remains to be determined what steps the Court should now take in regard to these defendants. Imprisonment is clearly not in order. If the defendants had flatly and continually refused to obey the Court's order, then indefinite incarceration might well be needed. But the evidence before the Court does not suggest that the defendants wilfully disobeyed the Court's order or that they will do so in the future.

The violations most likely resulted from carelessness and perhaps from a failure to realize fully the gravity of the Court's order. Such an attitude stemmed no doubt from the long-held conception of prison administrators, noted previously, that their discretion over their charges is so great that they could not be held accountable for their actions to any outside body. Coupled with all of the foregoing is the Court's view that the limitations placed upon those directly in charge of the operation of the penitentiary are, by reason of an apparent lack of financial resources, so great as to make their task an almost impossible one. The Court cannot overlook the fact that there have been no serious disruptions on the part of the prison population. While this is a credit to the population, it is also indeed a credit to men such as Mr. Slayton, Mr. Oliver and certain of their subordinates. What each must be assured of, however, is that the Court has reached the end of the road insofar as searching for alternate punishments consistent with its duties.

What is needed to secure future compliance, therefore, is not imprisonment, but rather something which will impress upon the defendants the need to take all steps necessary to carry out all facets of the Court's order. A fine may be used for such purposes. *United States v. United Mine Workers,* 330 U.S. 258 (1947). Accordingly, the Court will impose a fine of $25,000, jointly and severally, on all of the named, living defendants in this action. The Court will, however, suspend the imposition of this fine on the condition that the defendants forthwith take such steps as are necessary to carry out the Court's order and, in particular, that they implement some means of insuring that the terms of the injunction are carried out on every level of the prison system.

The Court may also impose a fine, payable to the plaintiffs, to the extent of the actual loss incurred by the plaintiffs. *United States v. United Mine Workers, supra,* 330 U.S. at 304. In this case, however, there has been no evidence as to the extent of losses which the inmates have suffered and, indeed, the Court doubts that any injury that did occur could be quantified. Accordingly, compensatory damages will not be assessed against the defendants. Similarly, the granting of attorneys' fees does not appear to be an appropriate response to a finding of contempt. In order to secure such fees, plaintiffs must bring a separate motion before the Court.

In addition to the imposition of a fine, the Court will amend the original order to require the defendants to take further steps to ensure that the Court's order is fully implemented. Specifically, the defendants will be ordered to take steps to ensure that prisoners being held on higher level security classifications for security purposes be afforded as many of the privileges enjoyed by inmates in general population as the nature of their confinement allows. The defendants will further be ordered to ensure that custodial personnel are fully advised of the rules and regulations. The exuse offered by one official that he doubted the custodial staff would comprehend will, if accurate, simply require that the defendants either pierce any such suggested incomprehension by use of educational tools, or replace any such personnel with ones who are capable of understanding. Such steps may include memoranda, seminars and conferences. In addition, the defendants may be well advised to consider the establishment of some sort of formal grievance procedure by which inmates can make known any complaints which they may have over failure of the Court's order to be implemented or, for that matter, over any other issue. The Court will not, however, order such a procedure, since it has not heard evidence on its feasibility.

An order in accordance with this memorandum will issue within five days of this date, and the Court in the meantime will entertain a suggested form of order from any of the parties.

/s/ Robert R. Merhige, Jr.
United States District Judge

Date: Jan. 29, 1973

A-11

FORMS: PRO SE ACTIONS OF PRISONERS *

1. SUMMONS AND COMPLAINT
   a. SUMMONS—(This is based on the official form. You can get as many free copies as you need from the Clerk of the U.S. District Court for your district.)

IN THE UNITED STATES DISTRICT COURT
FOR THE _____ DISTRICT OF CALIFORNIA

NAMES OF ALL THE PRISONERS
WHO ARE BRINGING THE SUIT,

      Plaintiffs,

  v.   SUMMONS

NAMES AND TITLES OF ALL THE   Civil Action No.
PEOPLE YOUR SUIT IS AGAINST,
individually and in their official capacities,

      Defendants.

TO THE ABOVE-NAMED DEFENDANTS:
     You are hereby summoned and required to serve upon plaintiffs, whose address is
an answer to the complaint which is herewith served upon you, within 20 days after service of this summons upon you, exclusive of the day of service. If you fail to do so, judgment by default will be taken against you for the relief demanded in the complaint.

                            Clerk of the Court

DATE:

---

b. FORM FOR A COMPLAINT—(Number each paragraph in your complaint consecutively. The numbers here are only examples. An imaginary sample complaint based on this form begins right after this form.)

PRISONERS' NAMES
AND ADDRESS

IN PROPRIA PERSONAM

IN THE UNITED STATES DISTRICT COURT
FOR THE ――― DISTRICT OF CALIFORNIA

*NAMES OF ALL THE PRISONERS
WHO ARE BRINGING THE SUIT,*

        Plaintiffs,

v.

*NAMES AND TITLES OF ALL THE
PEOPLE YOUR SUIT IS AGAINST,*
individually and in their official capacities,

        Defendants.

COMPLAINT

Civil Action No.

(Civil Rights)

I. JURISDICTION

1. This is a civil action authorized by 42 U.S.C. sec. 1983 to redress the deprivation, under color of state law, of rights secured by the Constitution of the United States. The court has jurisdiction under 28 U.S.C. sec. 1343. Plaintiffs seek declaratory relief pursuant to 28 U.S.C. secs. 2201 and 2202.

II. PLAINTIFFS

2. Plaintiff *[PRISONER'S FULL NAME]* is and was at all times mentioned herein a prisoner of the State of California in the custody of the California Department of Corrections. He is currently confined in (name of prison), (name of town), California.

COMMENT: If any part of your lawsuit claims racial discrimination, state each prisoner's race. If you are concerned that something described in your complaint will harm any plaintiff's chances for parole, indicate that each prisoner is already eligible for parole or when he or she will become eligible.

If there are differences in the situation of the various plantiffs, use a separate, numbered paragraph for each. Otherwise you can use one paragraph for all the prisoners.

III. DEFENDANTS

3. Defendant *[FULL NAME OF HEAD OF CORRECTIONS DE-PARTMENT]* is the Director of the Department of Corrections of the State of California. He is legally responsible for the overall operation of the Department and each institution under its jurisdiction, including *[name of prison where Plaintiffs are confined]*.

4. Defendant *[WARDEN'S FULL NAME]* is the *[Superintendent or Warden]* of *[Name of Prison]*. He is legally responsible for the operation of *[Name of Prison]* and for the welfare of all the inmates of that prison.

5. Defendant *[GUARD'S FULL NAME]* is a correctional officer of the Department of Corrections who, at all times mentioned in this complaint, held the rank of *[Position of Guard]* and was assigned to *[Name of Prison]*.

6. Defendants *[FULL NAMES OF MEMBERS OF THE ADULT AUTHORITY]* are members of the California Adult Authority. As such they are responsible for fixing the terms of California State prisoners and for determining whether a prisoner will be released on parole before the end of his or her term.

7. Each defendant is sued individually and in his or her official capacity. At all times mentioned in this complaint each defendant acted under the color of California law.

COMMENT: Use only the paragraphs which fit your suit. Add numbered paragraphs for additional defendants. It is usually easiest to give each defendant a separate, numbered paragraph. Be sure to include paragraph 7 above, as the last paragraph in the section on Defendants.

IV. FACTS

State IN DETAIL all the facts that are the basis for your suit. What happened? Where? To whom? Who did it? When? Is it still happening?

Remember that judges may know very little about prisons. Be sure to explain how the prison works, so the judge can understand what happened. If you use words that are generally not used outside the prison system, or have a special meaning in prison—like "write-up," "segregation," "strip cell"—explain what those terms mean. Be sure to divide your descriptions into short paragraphs and to number each paragraph.

You may want to include some facts which you do not know personally. This may be general prison knowledge, or it may be information given to you by people who are not plaintiffs in your lawsuit. It is proper to include this kind of information. But you have to be sure— each time you give these kinds of facts—that you write that your statements are "based on information and belief."

Feel free to refer to documents, affidavits, and other materials which you have attached at the back as "Exhibits" in support of your complaint. Each document, or group of documents, should have its own letter—"Exhibit A", "Exhibit B", etc.

V. LEGAL CLAIMS

State which of your Federal constitutional rights you think were violated by which actions of which defendants. Show how their actions violated your rights. Use a separate paragraph for each violation of your rights, and number each paragraph.

Do not write long legal arguments in this section. Save your legal arguments for your Memorandum of Law. (The Memorandum is discussed in Chapter III, Part A.) It is best not to cite any legal cases in your complaint.

If you want an injunction, copy the following paragraph at the end of your Legal Claims section.

The plaintiffs have no plain, adequate or complete remedy at law to redress the wrongs described herein. Plaintiffs have been and will continue to be irreparably injured by the conduct of the defendants unless this court grants the declaratory and injunctive relief which plaintiffs seek.

Close the Complaint with the following sentence plus your requests for court action. Copy only the requests which fit your case. Rewrite the requests where necessary.

WHEREFORE, plaintiffs respectfully pray that this court enter judgment granting plaintiffs:

1. A declaratory judgment that the defendants' acts, policies and practices described herein violate plaintiffs' rights under the United States Constitution.

2. A preliminary and permanent injunction which:

a) Prohibits the defendants, their successors in office, agents and employees and all other persons in active concert and participation with them from harassing, threatening, punishing or retaliating in any way against any plaintiff because he or she filed this action or against any other prisoner because that prisoner submitted affidavits in this case on behalf of the plaintiffs;

b) Prohibits defendants *[LAST NAMES OF WARDEN AND DIRECTOR OF CORRECTIONS DEPARTMENT]* from transferring any plaintiff to any other institution, without that plaintiff's express consent, during the pendency of this action;

c) Requires defendant *[LAST NAME OF WARDEN]* to remove from each plaintiff's prison files and records any references to any events described herein or to the fact that plaintiffs filed this suit;

d) Requires defendant Adult Authority members to remove from plaintiffs' files any reference to the events described herein or to the fact that plaintiffs filed this suit, and prohibits defendant Adult Authority members from considering any such references in any way when they fix plaintiffs' terms or decide whether plaintiffs should be released on parole;

e) Requires defendants *[LAST NAME OF WARDEN AND DIRECTOR OF CORRECTIONS DEPARTMENT]* to allow plaintiffs and other prisoners: 1) to engage in any oral or written communication which is reasonably related to the conduct of this suit, including the preparation of affidavits on behalf of plaintiffs; and 2) to allow plaintiffs to confer with co-plaintiffs and prepare legal papers and do anything else, consistent with prison security, which is reasonably connected with the conduct of this suit.

COMMENT: Be sure to include only the sections that fit your suit. Then list everything else you want the court to order the prison officials to do or stop doing. Put each request in a separate paragraph that starts with a new letter. Indicate which defendants you want the particular order to apply to. You can put these paragraphs ahead of paragraphs (a)–(e), if you prefer.

3. Compensatory damages in the amount of $ from defendants *[NAMES OF DEFENDANTS WHO VIOLATED YOUR RIGHTS]*, and each of them, to plaintiffs, and each of them.

4. Punitive damages in the amount of $ from defendants *[NAMES OF DEFENDANTS WHO ACTED WILFULLY, ETC.]*, to plaintiffs *[NAMES OF VICTIMS OF WILFUL VIOLATIONS]*.

COMMENT: The words "and each of them" after "defendants" makes all the named defendants "jointly and severally liable" for compensating you, meaning you have a right to as much as you can get from each defendant up to the total award. You must request separate punitive damages from each defendant who acted willfully or in gross disregard for your rights.

The suggested language requests one lump sum of damages to be divided among the plaintiffs. If there is wide variation among the plaintiffs, or if you prefer separate amounts for each, do not put "and each of them" after "plaintiffs." Instead, indicate a specific amount requested for each plaintiff.

5. A jury trial on all issues triable by jury.

6. Plaintiffs' costs of this suit.

7. Such other and further relief as this court deems just, proper and equitable.

Respectfully submitted,

Date:

Prisoners' names and addresses

In Propria Personam

VERIFICATION

STATE OF CALIFORNIA ⎫
COUNTY OF _____ ⎬ ss.:

[FULL NAME OF PRISONERS] being duly sworn, depose and say, that they reside at   ; that they are the plaintiffs herein; and that they have read the foregoing complaint and know the contents thereof and that the same are true of their own knowledge except

as to the matters therein stated to be alleged on information and belief, and as to those matters they believe them to be true.

(signature)
Names of Plaintiffs

Subscribed and sworn to before me
this   day of   19

NOTARY PUBLIC

The note at the bottom of Form No. 2 "Affidavit" explains how to have this statement "notarized" and what to do if you have trouble getting it notarized. It is best if all the plaintiffs can sign in front of a Notary Public. If some can't, have as many sign as possible and try to have the others submit their own affidavits about the facts they know or believe.

c. SAMPLE COMPLAINT

This is an entirely imaginary document. It is here only to show how to use the form for a Complaint, in one imaginary kind of case. All the names and places are made up.

MICHAEL ACTIVIST
Box 21542
Repression, California

LAWRENCE LEADER
Box 72031
Repression, California

In propria personam

IN THE UNITED STATES DISTRICT COURT
FOR THE EASTERN DISTRICT OF CALIFORNIA

MICHAEL ACTIVIST
AND LAWRENCE LEADER,
        Plaintiffs,

      v.

BORIS BIGSHOT, individually and in his official capacity as Director of the California Department of Corrections; CHARLES CHIEF, individually and in his official capacity as Warden of Babylon Prison; Sergeant BULL, and Officer DOG, individually and in their capacities as correctional officers of the California Department of Corrections; ABNER ONE, BERTRAM TWO, CALVIN THREE, DAVID FOUR, EDGAR FIVE, FRANK SIX, GEORGE SEVEN, and HENRY EIGHT, individually and in their official capacities as members of the Adult Authority of the State of California,

        Defendants,

COMPLAINT

CIVIL ACTION NO.
(CIVIL RIGHTS)

I. JURISDICTION

1. This is a civil action authorized by 42 U.S.C. sec. 1983 to redress the deprivation, under color of State law, of rights secured by the Constitution of the United States. The court has jurisdiction under 28 U.S.C. sec. 1343. Plaintiffs seek declaratory relief pursuant to 28 U.S.C. secs. 2201 and 2202.

II. PLAINTIFFS

2. Plaintiffs MICHAEL ACTIVIST and LAWRENCE LEADER are, and were at all times mentioned herein, prisoners of the State of California, in the custody of the California Department of Corrections. They are currently confined in Babylon Prison, Repression, California. Both plaintiffs are eligible for release on parole under California law and are scheduled to appear before the Adult Authority of the State of California within the next year for a parole release hearing.

III. DEFENDANTS

3. Defendant BORIS BIGSHOT is the Director of the California Department of Corrections. He is legally responsible for the overall operation of the Department and each institution under its jurisdiction, including Babylon Prison.

4. Defendant CHARLES CHIEF is the Warden of Babylon Prison. He is legally responsible for the operation of Babylon Prison and for the welfare of all the inmates of that prison.

5. Defendant BULL, is a correctional officer of the California Department of Corrections, who at all times mentioned in this Complaint held the rank of Sergeant and was assigned to Babylon Prison.

6. Defendant DOG is a correctional officer of the California Department of Corrections who at all times mentioned in this complaint was assigned to Babylon Prison.

7. Defendants, ONE, TWO, THREE, FOUR, FIVE, SIX, SEVEN and EIGHT, are members of the Adult Authority of the State of California. They are responsible for deciding when California State Prisoners should be released on parole.

8. Each defendant is sued individually and in his or her official capacity. At all times mentioned in this complaint each defendant acted under the color of California law.

IV. FACTS

9. On May 1, 1970, at approximately 7 P.M., Defendant BULL approached the cell occupied by Plaintiff ACTIVIST, on Tier T of A Wing of the North Block of Babylon Prison. BULL demanded that ACTIVIST give BULL the several copies of the magazine "People's Struggles" which ACTIVIST had in his cell. ACTIVIST refused. He said the magazines were his and he had a right to them.

10. The magazine "People's Struggles" reports on the efforts of poor people around the world to achieve social, political and economic liberation. It does not advocate violence or incite to violence. A letter from the editors of the magazine, describing its content and purpose, is attached to this Complaint as Exhibit A.

11. About one-half hour later, at 7:30 P.M., Defendant BULL returned with Defendant DOG. BULL repeated his demand. ACTIVIST again refused. BULL ordered DOG to go into the cell, take the magazines, and "take care of ACTIVIST, too."

12. DOG and BULL entered the cell, hit ACTIVIST several times on the body with a wooden club. DOG and BULL walked out of the cell with the magazines, leaving ACTIVIST on the ground bleeding.

13. Plaintiff LEADER, who was confined in the adjoining cell yelled to DOG and BULL to leave ACTIVIST alone. He called to other prisoners on the tier who joined in. After DOG and BULL left ACTIVIST's cell, LEADER began to call for medical help.

14. Defendants BULL and DOG then entered LEADER's cell, beat him with a club and confiscated copies of "People's Struggle" that belonged to him.

15. Plaintiff ACTIVIST received no medical care until the following morning, May 2, 1970, at 8 A.M. As a result of the delay in providing medical care ACTIVIST now has scars on his legs and walks with a limp.

16. On May 3, 1970 and on several days after that, Defendants BULL and DOG warned plaintiffs that they would beat plaintiffs "worse" if they caught plaintiffs with "revolutionary" literature again or if Plaintiffs "cried to the courts" about what happened to them.

17. All the events described in paragraphs 10, 12–16 were witnessed by prisoners Carlos Cadre and Walter Warrior. Their affidavits are attached to this Complaint as Exhibits B and C. As indicated in these affidavits, BULL and DOG have also threatened prisoners Cadre and Warrior.

18. On information and belief, defendant BULL prepared "write-ups" against plaintiffs about the events of May 1, 1970. Write-ups are placed in a prisoner's file, which is reviewed by one or more of the Defendant members of the Adult Authority when they decide whether or not to grant parole to that prisoner. On information and belief, parole is frequently denied on the basis of write-ups.

19. On information and belief, BULL and DOG confiscated plaintiffs' literature on the basis of a policy directive issued by defendant CHIEF. Plaintiffs have not been able to obtain a copy of this directive. On information and belief, defendant CHIEF has encouraged his staff to "get tough" with "revolutionaries."

20. Defendant BIGSHOT either knew of defendant CHIEF's confiscation and "get tough" policies and practices or he should have known in the proper exercise of his official duties. Although defendant BIGSHOT has the power and the legal duty to end these practices, he has failed to do so.

21. On information and belief, the policy and practice of the California Department of Corrections is to forbid prisoners from corresponding with other prisoners or from talking with other prisoners who are in segregation or isolation, even when such communication is essential to the conduct of a lawsuit.

V. LEGAL CLAIMS

22. Plaintiffs have been deprived of their right to possess and read political literature, which is guaranteed by the First Amendment to the United States Constitution and the Due Process of the Fourteenth Amendment. The confiscation also deprived Plaintiffs of their property without the due process of law required by the Fourteenth Amendment.

23. The beatings which Plaintiffs suffered constituted cruel and unusual punishment in violation of the Eighth Amendment to the U.S. Constitution and the Due Process Clause of the Fourteenth Amendment.

The beatings also amounted to punishment without due process of law, in violation of the Fourteenth Amendment to the U.S. Constitution.

24. Defendants' failure to provide medical care needed by Plaintiff ACTIVIST constituted cruel and unusual punishment and punishment without due process of law.

25. Defendants' threats to punish plaintiffs for taking legal action, and their threats to punish prisoners who submitted affidavits on behalf of plaintiffs, violated plaintiffs' right of meaningful access to the courts, which is guaranteed by the Due Process Clause of the Fourteenth Amendment.

26. The Plaintiffs have no plain, adequate or complete remedy at law to redress the wrongs described herein. Plaintiffs have been and will continue to be irreparably injured by the conduct of the defendants unless this court grants the declaratory and injunctive relief which plaintiffs seek.

WHEREFORE, plaintiffs respectfully pray that this court enter judgment granting plaintiffs:

1. A declaratory judgment that the defendants' acts, policies and practices described herein violate plaintiffs' rights under the United States Constitution.

2. A preliminary and permanent injunction which:

a. Requires defendants CHIEF, BULL, and DOG to return the literature they took from plaintiffs.

b. Requires defendants CHIEF and BIGSHOT to rescind the policy directive concerning confiscation of "revolutionary" literature and to issue regulations which prohibit any such confiscation in the future;

c. Requires defendant CHIEF to remove from the plaintiffs' prison files any write-ups or other reports concerning the events described herein and any references to plaintiffs' possession of "revolutionary" literature, and prohibits defendant CHIEF from permitting any such reports to be placed in plaintiffs' files at any future time.

d. Requires defendant Adult Authority members to remove from plaintiffs' files any reference to plaintiffs' possession of "revolutionary" literature or to the events described herein and prohibits defendant Adult Authority members from considering any such references in any way when they fix plaintiffs terms and decide whether plaintiffs should be released on parole.

e. Prohibits defendants, their agents, employees, successors in interest and all other persons in active concert or participation with them, from harassing, threatening, punishing or retaliating in any way against the plaintiffs because they filed this action or against any other prisoners because they submitted affidavits in this case on behalf of plaintiffs, or from transferring plaintiffs to any other institution, without their express consent, during the pendency of this action.

f. Requires defendants CHIEF and BIGSHOT to allow plaintiffs and other prisoners to: 1) engage in any oral or written communication which is reasonably related to the conduct of this suit, including the preparation of affidavits on behalf of plaintiffs; and 2) to confer with co-plaintiffs and prepare legal papers, and to do anything else, consistent with prison security, which is reasonably connected with the conduct of this suit.

3. Compensatory damages in the amount of $10,000 to plaintiff ACTIVIST and $5000 to Plaintiff LEADER from all defendants and each of them, except defendant members of the Adult Authority.

4. Punitive damages of $10,000 to each plaintiff from Defendant BULL and from Defendant DOG.

5. Trial by jury on all issues triable by jury.

6. Plaintiffs' cost of this suit.

7. Such other end further relief as this court may deem just, proper and equitable.

DATED: May 30, 1970

Respectfully submitted,

LAWRENCE LEADER   MICHAEL ACTIVIST
Box 72031   Box 21542
Repression, California Repression, California

In Propria Personam

2. AFFIDAVIT

This form is for the plaintiffs, other prisoners, or anyone else who wants to make a sworn statement on behalf of the plaintiffs.

IN THE UNITED STATES DISTRICT COURT
FOR THE   DISTRICT OF CALIFORNIA

FULL NAME OF FIRST PRISONER LISTED IN THE SUMMONS AND COMPLAINT, et al.	
Plaintiffs,	
	CIVIL ACTION NO.
v.	
	AFFIDAVIT
FULL NAME OF FIRST DEFENDANT LISTED IN THE SUMMONS AND COMPLAINT, et. al.	
Defendants	

STATE OF CALIFORNIA

ss.:

COUNTY OF

FULL NAME OF PRISONER OR OTHER PERSON MAKING THE STATEMENT, being duly sworn, deposes and says:
WRITE STATEMENT HERE

(signature)

Name of person who made the statement

Subscribed and sworn to
before me this   day
of   19

NOTARY PUBLIC

Comment: The person who makes the statement should sign at the bottom and have his or her signature witnessed by a Notary Public. The Notary will sign at the bottom and stamp a seal on the affidavit. Every prison has some staff members who can do this. If a prisoner has trouble getting this done, he or she should have another prisoner witness the signature. Then the prisoner should add at the bottom of the affidavit:

I declare that I have not been able to have this Affidavit notarized according to law because *(explain here your efforts to get the affidavit notarized—who was asked, what they said, etc.).* I therefore declare under penalty of perjury that all of the statements made in this affidavit are true of my own knowledge, and I pray leave of the Court to allow this affidavit to be filed without notarization.

(signature)

Check Ch. III, Part A(2) for more information and citations to decisions which approve this procedure.

3. ORDER TO SHOW CAUSE AND TEMPORARY RESTRAINING ORDER

Be sure to submit, along with this paper, an affidavit (Form No. 2) stating how you will be hurt if you do not get temporary relief and how you tried to notify the defendants of your request for temporary relief. See Ch. III, Part E.)

IN THE UNITED STATES DISTRICT COURT
FOR THE DISTRICT OF CALIFORNIA

FULL NAME OF FIRST PRISONER LISTED IN SUMMONS AND COMPLAINT, et al.,
 	
     Plaintiffs,
 	
        v.
 	
FULL NAME OF FIRST DEFENDANT LISTED IN SUMMONS AND COMPLAINT, et al.,
     Defendants.
	ORDER TO SHOW CAUSE AND TEMPORARY RESTRAINING ORDER
	
	Civil Action No.

Upon the complaint, the supporting affidavits of plaintiffs, and the memorandum of law submitted herewith, it is

ORDERED that defendants *[NAMES OF DEFENDANTS AGAINST WHOM YOU NEED IMMEDIATE COURT ACTION]* show cause in room of the United States Courthouse, *[address]*, on the day of , 19 , at o'clock, why a preliminary injunction should not issue pursuant to Rule 65(a) of the Federal Rules of Civil Procedure enjoining the defendants, their successors in office, agents and employees and all other persons acting in concert and participation with them, from *[a precise statement of the actions you want the preliminary injunction to cover]*.

IT IS FURTHER ORDERED that effective immediately, and pending the hearing and determination of this order to show cause, the defendants *[NAMES OF DEFENDANTS AGAINST WHOM YOU WANT TEMPORARY RELIEF]* and each of their officers, agents, employees, and all persons acting in concert or participation with them, are restrained from *[a precise statement of the actions you want the temporary restraining order to cover]*.

IT IS FURTHER ORDERED that the order to show cause, and all other papers attached to this application, be served on the aforesaid Plaintiffs by *[date]*.

(signature)

Dated:

United States District Judge

4. IN FORMA PAUPERIS PAPERS

a. MOTION

Prisoners' Names and Addresses
IN PROPRIA PERSONAM

IN THE UNITED STATES DISTRICT COURT
FOR THE   DISTRICT OF CALIFORNIA

NAME OF FIRST PRISONER IN COMPLAINT, et al.,
     Plaintiffs
 	
     v.
 	
NAME OF FIRST DEFENDANT IN COMPLAINT, et al.,
     Defendants
	MOTION FOR LEAVE TO PROCEED IN FORMA PAUPERIS AND FOR APPOINTMENT OF COUNSEL
	
	Civil Action No.

     Plaintiffs move this court for an order permitting them to file this action in forma pauperis without prepayment of fees and costs or security therefor, and appointing *(Lawyer's name and address),* a member of the California Bar, to represent plaintiffs as provided in 28 U.S.C. sec. 1915(d) and 18 U.S.C. sec. 3006A(g), because, as their attached affidavits indicate, plaintiffs are unable to pay such costs or give security therefor, and they cannot afford to employ an attorney. This motion is based on the complaint, affidavits, and memorandum of law *[if any]* submitted herewith.

Dated:

(signatures)

Plaintiffs' names and addresses

In Propria Personam

b. PRISONER'S AFFIDAVIT

You need a separate affidavit for each plaintiff in the suit who wants to sue in forma pauperis or have counsel appointed.

IN THE UNITED STATES DISTRICT COURT
FOR THE   DISTRICT OF CALIFORNIA

NAME OF FIRST PRISONER, et al.,
        Plaintiffs,
 	
        v.
 	
NAME OF THE FIRST DEFENDANT, et al.,
        Defendants.
	AFFIDAVIT IN
	SUPPORT OF
	MOTION TO PROCEED
	IN FORMA PAUPERIS
	AND FOR
	APPOINTMENT OF
	COUNSEL
	
	Civil Action No.

STATE OF CALIFORNIA

ss.:

COUNTY OF

(NAME OF PRISONER) being duly sworn, deposes and says:

1. I am a plaintiff in the above-titled action.

2. I believe I am entitled and intend to bring this action in the United States District Court for the   District of California against the above-named defendants.

3. The action seeks to enjoin those defendants from *(The wrongful actions giving rise to this suit)* and seeks damages in the amount of $ for deprivation of Plaintiffs' civil rights.

4. I believe that I am entitled to the redress sought in this action.

5. I have read and know the contents of the complaint and believe them to be true.

6. I have assets of only $ in the form of   and no income other than   . *(Assets include cash in the canteen, bank accounts, a car, insurance, etc. If you have no assets, write "I am without assets and have no income other than   ." If you have no income, say that.)*

7. I need my income for my personal maintenance and that of my family. *(Use only if you have earnings. Mention family only if some of your money goes to them.)*

8. Because of my poverty I am unable to pay the costs of this action, to give security therefor, or to employ an attorney.

(signature)

(Prisoner's name)

Subscribed and sworn
to before me this   day
of   , 19   .

NOTARY PUBLIC

The note at the bottom of Form No. 2 "Affidavit," explains how to have an affidavit notarized and what to do if you have trouble getting it notarized.

c. PROPOSED ORDER

IN THE UNITED STATES DISTRICT COURT
FOR THE   DISTRICT OF CALIFORNIA

NAME OF FIRST PRISONER IN COMPLAINT, et al.,
 	
    Plaintiffs,
 	
     v.
 	
NAME OF THE FIRST DEFENDANT, et al.,
 	
    Defendants.
	ORDER
	
	Civil Action No.

THIS MATTER having come on regularly for hearing before the undersigned judge on the motion of the Plaintiffs for leave to proceed with this action in forma pauperis and for appointment of counsel, and it appearing to the Court that Plaintiffs are entitled to the relief they seek by this motion, it is hereby,

ORDERED that Plaintiffs are authorized to proceed with this action in forma pauperis, without being required to pay fees and costs or give security for them, and it is further

ORDERED that any recovery in this action shall be paid to the Clerk of the Court who may pay therefrom all unpaid fees and costs taxed against the Plaintiffs, and remit the balance to the Plaintiffs, and it is further

ORDERED that *(name of lawyer), (address),* a member of the California bar, is appointed to represent the Plaintiffs in this matter.

           United States District Judge

Dated:

5. MOTION FOR APPOINTMENT OF COUNSEL

Use this if counsel is not appointed at the start and you want to request counsel again after the court has denied the defendants' motion to dismiss or their motion for summary judgment.

PRISONER'S FULL NAMES
ADDRESSES
IN PROPRIA PERSONAM

IN THE UNITED STATES DISTRICT COURT
FOR THE   DISTRICT OF CALIFORNIA

NAME OF THE FIRST *PRISONER IN* *COMPLAINT,* et al., 　　　　Plaintiffs, 　　　v. *NAME OF THE FIRST* *DEFENDANT IN* *COMPLAINT,* et al., 　　　　Defendants.	MOTION FOR APPOINTMENT OF COUNSEL Civil Action No.

Plaintiffs move in this court for an order appointing *[Name and address of Attorney],* a member of the California Bar, to represent them because they cannot afford to employ an attorney. This motion is based on Plaintiffs' affidavits in support of their motion for leave to proceed in forma pauperis and for appointment of counsel. Legal authority for appointment and compensation of counsel is 28 U.S.C. sec. 1915(d) and 18 U.S.C. sec. 3006A(g), as interpreted in *McClain v. Manson,* 343 F. Supp. 382 (D. Conn. 1972).

(signature)

Dated:

Plaintiffs' Names and
Addresses
In Propria Personam

6. DISCOVERY PAPERS
a. REQUEST FOR INTERROGATORIES, WITH SAMPLE QUESTIONS

Prisoners' Names and Addresses
IN PROPRIA PERSONAM

IN THE UNITED STATES DISTRICT COURT
FOR THE   DISTRICT OF CALIFORNIA

NAME OF FIRST
PRISONER, et al.,
        Plaintiffs,
 	
        v.
 	
NAME OF FIRST
DEFENDANT, et al.,
        Defendants.
	PLAINTIFF'S
	FIRST SET OF
	INTERROGATORIES
	
	Civil Action No.

In accordance with Rule 33 of the Federal Rules of Civil Procedure, Plaintiff requests that Defendant *[NAME]* answer the following interrogatories separately and fully in writing under oath, and that the answers be signed by the person making them and be served on plaintiffs within 45 days of service hereof.

In responding to these interrogatories, furnish all information which is available to you, including information in the possession of your attorneys or investigators for your attorneys, and not merely information known of your own personal knowledge.

If you cannot answer the following interrogatories in full, after exercising due diligence to secure the information to do so, so state, and answer to the extent possible, specifying your inability to answer the remainder, and stating whatever information or knowledge you have concerning the unanswered portions.

These interrogatories shall be deemed continuing, so as to require supplemental answers if you obtain further information between the time answers are served and the time of trial.

Comment: The following are a few sample questions. Change them to fit your suit and add many new questions of your own.

1. What is your full name and address?
2. On *[DATE]*, were you employed by the California Department of Corrections as a correctional officer?
3. On *[DATE]*, were you on duty as a correction officer at *[NAME]* Prison?
4. If yes,
    (a) To what section or division of Prison were you assigned?
    (b) What is the full name, capacity and last known business

and residence address of the individual who was your immediate superior?

(c) At what time of the day did you go on duty?

(d) At what time of the day did you go off duty?

5. Did you have any encounter or contact with Plaintiff *[PRISONER'S NAME]* on *[DATE]*?

6. If yes, state specifically and in detail, as accurately as you can remember, the exact sequence of events that occurred subsequent to your initial encounter or contact with the Plaintiff on that date.

7. Did you at any time on *[DATE]* or on any other date, beat, strike, kick, spray with MACE, or with any other chemical, or otherwise abuse Plaintiff ?

8. If yes, were any other persons involved?

9. Was any written report made of the details of the conduct in interrogatory No. 7?

10. If yes, state:

(a) The name, badge or identification number, and present address of the person or persons who prepared each such report;

(b) The name, badge or identification number, and present address of the person or persons for whom each such report was prepared;

(c) The date, time, and place where each such report was prepared;

(d) The name, badge or identification number, and present address of the present custodian of each such report.

11. If the answer to question 9 is yes, was each such report written or reduced to writing?

12. If yes, attach a copy of each such written report to your answers to these interrogatories.

13. State the name and address or otherwise identify and locate any person or persons who, to your knowledge, or to the knowledge of your agents and attorneys, purport to have knowledge of facts relevant to the conduct described in these interrogatories.

14. Do you, your attorneys, or any person employed by you or your attorneys, have possession or know of the existence of any books, records, reports made in the ordinary course of business, other printed or documentary material, or photographs, drawings, or documents, or other tangible objects that are relevant to the conduct described in these interrogatories?

15. If yes, state:

(a) The name and description of each such item;

(b) The name and address of each person who made, prepared or took each such item;

(c) The name and address of the present custodian of each such item;

(d) The date, time and place where each such item was made, prepared or taken;

(e) The method by and purpose for which each such item was made, prepared or taken;

(f) The manner in which each such item is relevant to the conduct described in these interrogatories.

16. If the answer to question 14 is yes, do you have knowledge of any item mentioned there being altered in any manner, lost or destroyed?

(signatures)

Dated:

Prisoners' names and addresses
In Propria Personam

b. REQUEST FOR PRODUCTION

Prisoners' Names and Addresses
IN PROPRIA PERSONAM

IN THE UNITED STATES DISTRICT COURT
FOR THE   DISTRICT OF CALIFORNIA

NAME OF FIRST PRISONER LISTED IN COMPLAINT, et al.,
 	
        Plaintiffs,
 	
v.
 	
NAME OF FIRST DEFENDANT LISTED IN COMPLAINT, et al.,
        Defendants.
	REQUEST FOR PRODUCTION OF DOCUMENTS
	
	Civil Action No.

Plaintiffs request, pursuant to Rule 34 of the Federal Rules of Civil Procedure, that Defendants *[LAST NAMES OF DEFENDANTS WHO HAVE THE DOCUMENTS YOU WANT TO SEE]* produce for inspection and copying the following documents: *[These are suggestions only. Request whatever you need for your suit.]*

    1. The central file containing complete prison records of Plaintiffs

    2. All written statements, originals or copies, identifiables as reports of   made by prison and civilian employees of the Department of Corrections and prisoner witnesses.

    3. All medical reports of

    4. All interdepartmental memoranda regarding

    5. All rules, regulations and policy directives of the California Department of Corrections and the   Prison.

    PLEASE TAKE NOTICE that the above requested documents shall be produced for inspection and copying at the   Prison in   , California, on *[date],* at *[time].* Such documents shall be produced for inspection by Plaintiffs and shall be xeroxed or photo-copied by Defendants or their agents or employees and furnished to Plaintiffs.

(signatures)

Dated:

Prisoners' Names and Addresses

c. MOTION FOR AN ORDER COMPELLING DISCOVERY

Use this motion if a defendant does not answer your interrogatories fully or does not produce items you request. Use only the sections that apply to your situation.

Prisoners' Names and Addresses
IN PROPRIA PERSONAM

IN THE UNITED STATES DISTRICT COURT
FOR THE   DISTRICT OF CALIFORNIA

NAME OF FIRST PRISONER LISTED IN SUMMONS AND COMPLAINT, et al., Plaintiffs, v. *NAME OF FIRST DEFENDANT LISTED IN SUMMONS AND COMPLAINT,* et. al., Defendants.	MOTION FOR AN ORDER COMPELLING Civil Action No.

Plaintiffs move this court for an order pursuant to Rule 37(a) of the Federal Rules of Civil Procedure compelling Defendants *[LAST NAMES OF DEFENDANTS WHO FAILED TO FULLY ANSWER INTER-ROGATORIES OR REFUSED TO PRODUCE ITEMS YOU REQUESTED]* to answer fully interrogatories number   , copies of which are attached hereto *[or, "to produce for inspection and copying the following documents: ."]*. Plaintiffs submitted these interrogatories, pursuant to Rule 33 of the Federal Rules of Civil Procedure *[or "a written request for these documents, pursuant to Rule 34 of the Federal Rules of Civil Procedure"]* on *[date]*, but have not yet received the answers *[or "documents"]*.

Plaintiffs also move for an order pursuant to Rule 37(a)(4) requiring the aforesaid defendants to pay Plaintiffs the sum of $ as reasonable expenses in obtaining this order, on the ground that the Defendants' refusal to answer the interrogatories *[or "produce the documents upon request"]* had no substantial justification.

This motion is based upon the papers and files in this matter and the memorandum of law attached hereto *[if you submit a memo on your legal right to the answers or documents—you do not need to submit a memo]*.

(signatures)

Dated:

Prisoners' Names and Addresses
In Propria Personam

7. MOTION TO VACATE JUDGMENT

Prisoners' Names and Addresses
IN PROPRIA PERSONAM

IN THE UNITED STATES DISTRICT COURT
FOR THE   DISTRICT OF CALIFORNIA

NAME OF FIRST PRISONER LISTED IN COMPLAINT, et. al.,
 	
            Plaintiffs,
 	
            v.
 	
NAME OF FIRST DEFENDANT LISTED IN COMPLAINT, et al.,
 	
            Defendants.
	MOTION TO VACATE JUDGMENT
	
	Civil Action No.

Plaintiffs move in this court for an order pursuant to Rule 59(e) of the Federal Rules of Civil Procedure vacating the judgment of this court, entered on   , which *[dismissed Plaintiff's complaint, granted Defendants a summary judgment, or whatever]*. This motion is based on the papers and files in this matter and the memorandum of law attached hereto.

                              (signatures)

Dated:

                    Plaintiffs' Names and Addresses
                    In Propria Personam

8. NOTICE OF APPEAL

Prisoners' Full Names and Addresses
IN PROPRIA PERSONAM

IN THE UNITED STATES DISTRICT COURT
FOR THE   DISTRICT OF CALIFORNIA

NAMES OF FIRST
PRISONER LISTED IN
COMPLAINT, et al.,
          Plaintiffs,
 	
          v.
 	
NAME OF FIRST
DEFENDANT LISTED IN
COMPLAINT, et al.,
          Defendants.
	NOTICE OF APPEAL
	
	Civil Action No.

Notice is hereby given that Plaintiffs hereby appeal to the United States Court of Appeals for the Ninth Circuit from *[the order dismissing their complaint, the summary judgment, the final judgment, or whatever other order you are appealing]* entered in this action on *[Date]*.

(signature)

Dated:

Prisoners' Names and Addresses
In Propria Personam

9. AFFIDAVIT FOR AN EXTENSION OF TIME

Prisoners' Names and Addresses
IN PROPRIA PERSONAM

IN THE UNITED STATES DISTRICT COURT
FOR THE   DISTRICT OF CALIFORNIA

NAME OF FIRST
PRISONER LISTED IN
COMPLAINT, et al.,
         Plaintiffs,

      v.

NAME OF FIRST
DEFENDANT LISTED
IN COMPLAINT, et al.,
         Defendants.

AFFIDAVIT FOR
EXTENSION OF
TIME

Civil Action No.

STATE OF CALIFORNIA   ss.

COUNTY OF

[PRISONER'S FULL NAME], being duly sworn, deposes and says:
I am a plaintiff in this matter, representing myself in propria personam.

Due to *[reasons why you cannot file the particular legal paper within the time set by the court, such as injury, illness, denial of access to books or to other information you need]*, I have been unable to make the necessary investigations and research in order to prepare and file *[name of the legal paper you were supposed to file]* on or before the due date herein, *[date paper was due]*.

In view of the foregoing, I request an extension of   days from this date, to and including *[new deadline]* in which to file the *[name of legal paper]*.

                (signature)

                Prisoner's Name

Subscribed and sworn
to before me this   day
of   , 19   .

NOTARY PUBLIC

The note at the bottom of Form No. 2, "Affidavit," explains how to have a legal paper notarized and what to do if you have trouble getting it notarized.

10. DEFAULT JUDGMENT PAPERS

a. AFFIDAVIT FOR ENTRY OF DEFAULT

The note at the bottom of Form No. 2, "Affidavit," explains how to have an affidavit notarized and what to do if you have trouble getting it notarized.

Prisoners' Names and Addresses
IN PROPRIA PERSONAM

IN THE UNITED STATES DISTRICT COURT
FOR THE   DISTRICT OF CALIFORNIA

*NAME OF FIRST
PRISONER LISTED IN
COMPLAINT,* et al.,

Plaintiffs,

v.

*NAME OF FIRST
DEFENDANT LISTED
IN COMPLAINT,* et al.,

Defendants.

AFFIDAVIT FOR
ENTRY OF
DEFAULT

Civil Action No.

STATE OF CALIFORNIA

COUNTY OF

ss.

[PRISONER'S NAME], being duly sworn, deposes and says:

1. I am a plaintiff herein.

2. The complaint herein was filed on the   day of   , 19   .

3. The court files and record herein show that the Defendants were served by the United States Marshal with a copy of summons, together with a copy of Plaintiffs' complaint, on the   day of   , 19   .

4. More than 20 days have elapsed since the date on which the said Defendants herein were served with summons and a copy of the complaint, excluding the date thereof.

5. The Defendants herein have failed to answer or otherwise defend as to Plaintiff's complaint, or serve a copy of any answer or other defense which it might have had, upon affiant or any other Plaintiff herein.

6. This affidavit is executed in accordance with Rule No. 55(a) of the Federal Rules of Civil Procedure, for the purpose of enabling the Plaintiffs herein to obtain an entry of default against the Defendants

herein, for their failure to answer or otherwise defend as to the Plaintiffs' complaint.

(signature)

Name of Plaintiff

Subscribed and sworn to
before me this   day
of   , 19 .

NOTARY PUBLIC

b. MOTION FOR DEFAULT JUDGMENT
Submit this if the court clerk enters a default against the defendants.

Prisoners' Names and Addresses
IN PROPRIA PERSONAM

IN THE UNITED STATES DISTRICT COURT
FOR THE   DISTRICT OF CALIFORNIA

NAME OF FIRST PRISONER LISTED IN COMPLAINT, et al.,
      Plaintiffs,
 	
v.
 	
NAME OF FIRST DEFENDANT LISTED IN COMPLAINT, et al.,
      Defendants.
	MOTION FOR DEFAULT JUDGMENT
	
	Civil Action No.

Plaintiffs move this court for a judgment by default in this action, and show that the complaint in the above cause was filed in this court on the   day of   , 19   ; the summons and complaint were duly served on the Defendant,   , on the   day of   , 19   ; no answer or other defense has been filed by the Defendant; default was entered in the civil docket in the office of the clerk of this court on the   day of   , 19   ; no proceedings have been taken by the Defendant since default was entered; Defendant is not in military service and is not an infant or incompetent as appears in the affidavit of   submitted herewith.

Wherefore, plaintiff moves that this court make and enter a judgment that   *[same as prayer for relief in complaint].*

                                           (signatures)

Dated:

                           Plaintiffs' Names and Addresses
                           In Propria Personam

A-12

CONSTITUTIONAL ARGUMENTS AGAINST PRETRIAL DETENTION OF THE POOR: AN IN-DEPTH STUDY OF THE IMPACT OF THE BAIL SYSTEM ON THE OUTCOME OF A CRIMINAL CASE *

Bellamy v. Judges and Justices of New York, etc.

. . . .

The following, plaintiffs submit, are the constitutional requisites for any hearing at which bail may be set.

I. Presumption of Release on Recognizance

In every instance where the issue arises, the court must presume that the accused is entitled to pre-trial release on his own recognizance. This presumption is demanded by the presumption of innocence granted to an accused in our criminal justice system. Foote, *The Coming Constitutional Crisis in Bail,* 113 U. Pa. L. Rev. 1125, 1180, 1183 (1965); Ares, Rankin and Sturz, *The Manhattan Bail Project: An Interim Report on the Use of Pre-Trial Parole,* 38 N.Y.U. L. Rev. 67, 69 (1963); McCree, *Bail and the Indigent Defendant,* 1965 U. Ill. L. F. 1, 2; see also Tribe, *An Ounce of Detention: Preventive Justice in the World of John Mitchell,* 56 Va. L. Rev. 371, 403-405 (1970).[24]

The American Bar Association states unequivocally that "it should be presumed that the defendant is entitled to be released on order to appear or on his own recognizance." American Bar Association Project on Minimum Standards for Criminal Justice, *Standards Relating to Pre-Trial Release* §5.1(a) (hereafter cited as *"A.B.A. Release Standards").*[25] The A.B.A. report continues:

> The law favors the release of defendants pending determination of guilt or innocence. Deprivation of liberty pending trial is harsh and oppressive in that it subjects persons whose guilt

---

* The anterior portion of this brief is contained in Chapter 7 of this book.

[24] For a discussion of the analogous presumption of probation as opposed to confinement at sentencing, see American Bar Association Project on Minimum Standards for Criminal Justice, Standards Relating to Sentencing Alternatives and Procedures §2.3(c), at 72–73 (Approved Draft 1968).

[25] The federal government has, in enacting the Bail Reform Act of 1966, 18 U.S.C. §3146, et seq., recognized that the presumption of releasability on recognizance is inherent in the presumption of innocence. See S. Rep. No. 750, 89th Cong., 1st Sess. 10–11.

has not yet been judicially established to economic and psychological hardship, interferes with their ability to defend themselves and, in many cases, deprives their families of support. Moreover, the maintenance of jailed defendants and their families represents major public expense. *Id.* §1.1.

Thus, instead of recommending high money bail as a matter of course in every case,

[i]t should be the policy of prosecuting attorneys to encourage the release of defendants upon an order to appear or on their own recognizance. Special efforts should be made to enter into stipulations to that effect in order to avoid unnecessary pretrial release inquiries and to promote efficiency in the administration of justice. *Id.* §4.3(f).[26]

The statistical study has shown an "error rate" among detained persons of 38 per cent (see Table 5). In other words, 38 per cent of the people who are detained awaiting disposition of their case are either ultimately convicted and get no prison term (18 per cent) or else have their case dismissed (20 per cent). Thus, the present bail system makes a mockery of the presumption of innocence by punishing large numbers of people whose guilt the State is ultimately unable to prove. (According to official Department of Correction figures, in 1969 there were 6,200 such people citywide, a rise of over 1,000 over the previous year.) Furthermore, half of all people who secure pre-trial release are ultimately not convicted (see Table 4). Under these circumstances, the presumption of innocence must be regarded as more than an abstract principle. It demands a further presumption that the accused be released on his own recognizance.

Such an allocation of the burden of proof would not impose any extraordinary duty on the People. The District Attorney at present routinely exercises his prerogative to be heard on the question of bail or release on recognizance,[27] and it is he who has both the resources to investigate and access to information bearing on that decision.

The only legitimate interest the State can have in placing restrictions on an accused's right to liberty is the reasonable assurance that he will continue to appear in court. See *People ex rel. Lobell v. McDonnell,* 296 N.Y. 109 (1947). Without a showing that restrictions on an accused's liberty are necessary to assure his reappearance, such restrictions violate the constitutional guarantees of due process and equal protection of the laws. Since the study has shown that to deprive a man of his liberty determines the very outcome of his case, it must be presumed that a man's liberty cannot be curtailed unless the State

---

[26] In this regard, it is important to remember that "[t]he law requires reasonable assurance [of the accused's appearance when required] but does not demand absolute certainty, which would be only a disguised way of compelling commitment in advance of judgment." United States v. Alston, 420 F.2d 176, 178 (D.C. Cir. 1969).

[27] See CPL 530.20(2)(b)(i); 530.40(4).

can show by clear and convincing evidence that there is a serious risk that he will not appear unless some form of conditional release is imposed.

II. Non-financial Alternatives to Bail

Despite the presumption of the accused's innocence, and notwithstanding the likelihood in many cases that measures short of requiring a bail bond would reasonably assure the accused's reappearance, the defendant District Attorney does not recommend and the defendant Justices and Judges do not consider or impose non-financial alternatives to bail. The statistical study of bail described before reveals that in not one of the 857 cases studied did the court impose a non-financial alternative to bail.

Only thirteen per cent of all those for whom some amount of bail is set are able to post that bail in order to obtain their release from jail. An accused who secures his release is 2½ times as likely not to be convicted as a detained person and is about one-fourth as likely to receive a prison sentence as someone who is detained (Table 5). Such disparity of treatment, arising solely out of wealth or the lack thereof, dictates the need for defendant Justices and Judges to explore non-financial alternatives to bail in every instance and to impose non-financial conditions of release whenever such conditions will reasonably assure the appearance of the accused when required. Similarly, defendant District Attorney must be under a duty to investigate alternatives to bail in every case where bail might be set and must be required in good faith to recommend non-financial conditions of release whenever such conditions reasonably assure the accused's appearance. As the American Bar Association Project on Minimum Standards for Criminal Justice has recommended, consistently with due process a prosecutor may not recommend and a court may not require an accused to post money bail in order to obtain his release pending trial unless it is shown by clear and convicing evidence that no available non-monetary conditions of release will reasonably suffice to assure the accused's presence at trial. *A.B.A. Release Standards* §1.2(c). This alone would go a long way toward insuring that the determination of an accused's guilt or innocence and, if convicted, his proper sentence will cease to depend on whether he can afford to pay for his freedom.

Present practice is for the District Attorney automatically to recommend and the court automatically to require money bail whenever release on recognizance appears inappropriate. This all-or-nothing approach ignores the constitutional requirement that they recommend and impose the least onerous condition of release reasonably likely to assure the accused's appearance in court, a requirement which grows out of the gross discrimination between rich and poor inherent in the bail system. As the District of Columbia Circuit Court of Appeals said in *Pelletier v. United States*, 343 F.2d 322, 323 (D.C. Cir. 1965), criticizing the trial court's ordering of bail in an amount the accused could not meet:

> * * * if the court determined that high monetary bond would adequately deter flight, but that appellant could not provide this bond, then the court would be *constitutionally compelled* to inquire whether other assurances of appellant's presence would be adequate. It is an invidious discrimination to deny appellant release because of his poverty, when for example, his ties in the community or such devices as release to the supervision of the United States Probation Office, would adequately secure his presence. (Emphasis added)

Even if the accused has no roots in the community and no close family ties that would reasonably assure his appearance in court when required, the bail-setting court must attempt to fashion non-financial conditions of release. In *United States v. Bronson,* 433 F.2d 537 (D.C. Cir. 1970), the District of Columbia Circuit Court of Appeals reversed the District Court's imposition of money bail and remanded for consideration of non-financial conditions of release, stating:

> In our view, a lack of close family and community ties is not an insurmountable obstacle to pretrial release; it presents a problem which may be overcome by the imposition of carefully chosen conditions. *Id.* at 540.

Similarly, the American Bar Association Project on Minimum Standards for Criminal Justice states that:

> Upon a finding that release on order to appear or on defendant's own recognizance is unwarranted, the judicial officer should impose the least onerous condition reasonably likely to assure the defendant's appearance in court. *A.B.A. Release Standards* §5.2(a).

It has been held in similar contexts that before a trial judge may confine a person in custody, he must find and utilize the least burdensome alternative that would serve the purpose of the confinement. Applying "the principle of the least restrictive alternative" to a situation directly analogous to the bail-setting procedures, the court in *Covington v. Harris,* 419 F.2d 617, 623 (D.C. Cir. 1969), held that before a trial court can order civil commitment of a person to a mental institution, it must "satisfy itself that no less onerous disposition would serve the purpose of the commitment." See also *Hamilton v. Love,* 328 F. Supp. 1182, 1192–1193 (E.D. Ark. 1971) (applying the requirement of "the least restrictive alternative" to pretrial detainees who attacked the conditions of their confinement).

The Supreme Court likewise has long held that where fundamental personal liberties are involved, government must pursue its legitimate interest by the least restrictive means possible. *Aptheker v. Secretary of State,* 378 U.S. 500, 508 (1964); *Shelton v. Tucker,* 364 U.S. 479, 488 (1960). The reasoning in those First Amendment cases is directly applicable to the bail procedure at issue here. See Fabricant, *Bail as a Preferred Freedom and the Failure of New York's Revision,* 18 Buff. L. Rev. 303, 315 (1969). When the state makes classifications on the constitutionally suspect ground of wealth—as defendants do in the instant case by making an accused's likelihood of conviction and imprisonment depend on his ability to purchase his pretrial freedom— it is only fair "to require the state to accomplish its purpose by using a less onerous alternative where possible." Note, *Developments in the Law: Equal Protection,* 82 Harv. L. Rev. 1065, 1176 (1969), and cases cited therein. See also *Dean Milk Co. v. Madison,* 340 U.S. 349, 354 (1951) (state may not act discriminatorily in exercise of its legitimate powers where reasonable nondiscriminatory alternatives are available).

The non-financial conditions of release which defendant District Attorney must investigate and, whenever possible, recommend and which defendant Justices and Judges must require whenever possible include the following:

(1) Releasing the accused into the care of a person or organization responsible for assuring his continued appearance in court. See, *e.g., United States v. Bronson,* 433 F.2d 537 (D.C. Cir. 1970) (release to military police); *United States v. Alston,* 420 F.2d 176 (D.C. Cir. 1969) (employer to report accused's failure to appear at work); *United States v. Leathers,* 412 F.2d 169 (D.C. Cir. 1969) (*per curiam*) (supervision by employer).

(2) Placing the accused under the supervision of a probation officer or other appropriate public official. See, *e.g., Banks v. United States,* 414 F.2d 1150 (D.C. Cir. 1969) (supervision by offender rehabilitation agency); *White v. United States,* 412 F.2d 145 (D.C. Cir. 1968) (supervision by probation officer); *Ball v. United States,* 402 F.2d 206 (D.C. Cir. 1968) (report to Department of Recreation weekly); *Jones v. United States,* 358 F.2d 543 (D.C. Cir.), *cert. denied,* 385 U.S. 868 (1966) (report to probation officer); *McCoy v. United States,* 357 F.2d 272 (D.C. Cir. 1966) (supervision by probation officer). In Tulsa, Oklahoma, release in the custody of one's attorney has been successfully tried. Freed & Wald, Report to the National Conference on Bail and Criminal Justice, *Bail in the United States: 1964* (hereafter cited as *"Bail in the United States: 1964"*).

(3) Placing reasonable restrictions on the accused's activities, associations, movement or residence. See, *e.g., United States v. Alston, supra* (residence at halfway house with curfew and re-enrollment in alcoholic rehabilitation clinic); *Banks v. United States, supra* (residence at halfway house with curfew); *United States v. Leathers, supra* (residence in halfway house; restrictions on travel; accused must be employed); *White v. United States, supra* (accused not to leave city without court permission; must be employed); *Ball v. United States, supra* (residence with family; accused not to leave city without court permission); *McCoy v. United States, supra* (residence with member of family).

(4) Permitting day-time release or imposing other conditions requiring the accused to return to custody on weeknds or after specified hours. See, *e.g., United States v. Forrest,* 418 F.2d 1186 (D.C. Cir. 1969) (day-time work release); *Ball v. United States, supra* (day-time release until accused obtains employment; accused to appear in court with counsel monthly).

The American Bar Association Project on Minimum Standards for Criminal Justice, the National Conference on Bail and Criminal Justice, and legal commentators generally urge such use of non-financial conditions of release rather than automatic imposition of bail. In a leading article, for example, it has been stated that

> * * * if the accused is unable to provide security because he has no assets, other restrictions must be considered if imposition of bail is not to be used as a subterfuge for denial of release. These might include release in custody of a third party, such as the accused's employer, minister, attorney or a private organization; release subject to a duty to report periodically to the court or other public official, or even release subject to a duty to return to jail each night. Admittedly, the setting of individualized conditions poses a more difficult problem than the automatic imposition of bail. Yet if the risk of flight is not so great as to justify total subordination of the presumption of innocence, an attempt to find such conditions must be made. Note, *Bail: An Ancient Practice Reexamined,* 70 Yale L.J. 966, 975 (1961).

The use of non-financial conditions of release would bring the law more nearly in line with the presumption of innocence; would end the present, constitutionally impermissible system of making an accused's pre-trial release depend solely on his ability to pay for it; would end much of the *de facto* preventive detention of the poor; and would provide greater assurance of the accused's appearance than does a bail bond.

> The bail bond system conditions release on the payment of money * * * But this system breaks down when the accused is financially disabled. To condition his release on money may be to demand the impossible * * * Not only can [non-monetary] conditions "afford the opportunity of pretrial liberty to those presently unable to secure it, but in many cases provide greater assurance against forfeiture and flight." *Bail in the United States: 1964* at 73–74, citing *Report of the Attorney General's Committee on Poverty and the Administration of Criminal Justice* 78 (1964).

As noted in the Attorney General's Committee Report, the imposition of non-monetary conditions of release would not pose unduly difficult problems of supervision or administration:

> "The supervision of persons at liberty to guard against violation of the conditions upon which liberty was granted is a problem wholly familiar to the legal order. The rich fund of experience derived from decades of administration of parole and probation laws is highly relevant to the formulation of a sound policy of pre-trial release * * * Moreover, less formal procedures requiring persons to 'check in' periodically with the police and other official personnel are not unknown in many American and foreign jurisdictions." Examples include

release conditioned on remaining within the court's jurisdiction or at home, surrender of the accused's passport and periodic check-ins with the police, probation office or court. In the latter case, failure to report could be communicated promptly to the court so that efforts to recapture fleeing defendants could begin much sooner than they do now under the hit or miss checking arrangements of the bondsman. *Bail in the United States: 1964* at 75.

Moreover, conditional release would likely cost much less than pre-trial imprisonment. See *Bail in the United States: 1964* at 77 (cost of day-time release in North Carolina, for example, is one-twelfth the cost of imprisonment).

The American Bar Association Project on Minimum Standards for Criminal Justice also advocates the use of non-monetary conditions of release and states that money bail should be imposed, if at all, only as a last resort:

Upon a finding that release on order to appear or on defendant's own recognizance is unwarranted, the judicial officer should impose the least onerous condition reasonably likely to assure the defendant's appearance in court. *A.B.A. Release Standards* §5.2(a).

Money bail should be set only when it is found that no other conditions on release will reasonably assure the defendant's appearance in court. *Id.* §5.3(a).

Accord: LaFave, *Alternatives to the Present Bail System,* 1965 U. Ill. L.F. 8, 16 (recommending supervised or day-time release).

* * * *

The imposition of money bail only as a last resort would also tend to minimize the broad powers of bail bondsmen and return control over the pre-trial release process to the courts, where it belongs. Presently, the court conducts only the most cursory and general inquiry and then automatically proceeds to set bail (except in those few cases where an accused is released on his own recognizance). In effect, the court delegates the crucial decision of whether an accused will be released pending trial to a professional bondsman. The bondsman has the awesome and unreviewable power to refuse to write a bond for any person, however capricious his decision and however unrelated it may be to the concerns of the pre-trial release system.

The unlimited power granted to bail bondsmen frustrates the principle that the only legitimate purpose of bail is to insure the presence of the accused when required in court. It deprives the courts of control over the pre-trial release process, since

[i]n practice, the decision to release an accused may be over-ridden by the bondsman, a private individual subject to none of the responsibilities or restraints imposed on the judiciary.

In the final analysis the fulfillment of the constitutional proscription pertaining to bail reposes with the professional bail bondsman since he may refuse to write even the smallest bonds. The bondsman may act on whim or caprice and his decision is not reversible either in a court of law or by an administrative agency. The Supreme Court * * * cannot require that a bondsman write a bail bond, no matter how arbitrary the bondsman's refusal [citing the Report of the Third February, 1954 Grand Jury of New York County, New York to Hon. John A. Mullen, at 2–3].

The bondsman's reasons for denying bail may be unrelated to the likelihood of flight. Note, *Bail: An Ancient Practice Reexamined,* 70 Yale L.J. 966, 971 (1961).

The injustice of giving the bail bondsman such unlimited discretion to refuse to write a bond is compounded by the fact that there is no limitation on or supervision of the amount of collateral he may demand. Bondsmen decide *ad hoc* how much collateral to require. Because of the bondsman's usual requirement of such collateral, many relatively poor persons who can afford an ordinary bail premium are denied the services of a bondsman and therefore must remain in jail until their cases have been adjudicated. In addition to having the unfettered discretion to refuse to write a bond and to require any amount or type of collateral, a bondsman may withdraw the bond and send the accused back to jail (euphemistically called "exoneration") whenever he chooses—for any reason or for no reason at all, in his sole, unreviewed and unreviewable discretion. As Judge J. Skelly Wright succinctly stated in his concurring opinion in *Pannell v. United States,* 320 F.2d 698, 699 (D.C. Cir. 1963):

The effect of such a system is that the professional bondsmen hold the keys to the jail in their pockets. They determine for whom they will act as surety—who in their judgment is a good risk. The bad risks, in the bondsmen's judgment, *and the ones who are unable to pay the bondsmens fees,* remain in jail. The court and the commissioner are relegated to the relatively unimportant chore of fixing the amount of bail. (Emphasis in original.)

Mr. Justice Blackman, in *Schilb v. Kuebel,* 404 U.S. , (1971), described the "offensive" bail bondsman system in Illinois in terms fully applicable to the present practice in New York:

Prior to 1964 the professional bail bondsman system with all its abuses was in full and odorous bloom in Illinois. Under that system the bail bondsman customarily collected the maximum fee (10% of the amount of the bond) permitted by statute, and retained that entire amount even though the accused fully satisfied the conditions of the bond. Payment of this substantial "premium" was required of the good risk as well as of the bad. The results were that a heavy and irretrievable burden fell upon the accused, to the excellent profit of the bondsman, and that professional bondsmen, and not the courts, exercised significant control over the actual workings of the bail system. (Citations omitted.)

Judicial delegation to bondsmen of the power to control pre-trial release supports and nourishes what is already an invidious and arbitrary discrimination against the poor who cannot make bail. Thus, in *McCoy v. United States,* 357 F.2d 272 (D.C. Cir. 1966), where bail bondsmen had refused to write a bond even though the accused could afford to pay the required premium, the District of Columbia Circuit Court of Appeals set alternative conditions of release:

> It would be manifestly unjust to permit professional bondsmen to "hold the keys to the jail in their pockets" * * *
>
> [T]he injustice would be pyramided unconscionably if it should appear that a bondsman's unwillingness to take the risk [of writing a bond] is heightened where, as in this case, the appellant is young, is not "well known" to him through past involvements, and offers only modest opportunity for gain due to the low amount of bond. [$500] * * * We think it appropriate for the courts to avail themselves of their flexibility to vary terms and conditions as well as amounts of bail, and provide substitutes, in the case of indigent defendants, for conventional bonds of professional bondsmen. 357 F.2d at 273.

See also the concurring opinion of Chief Judge Bazelon in *United States v. Cook,* 442 F.2d 723, 725 (D.C. Cir. 1970); *Bail in the United States: 1964,* at 80.

Because of the importance of the bail decision to the outcome of the case it is essential that that decision remain within the control of the courts, rather than within the control of bondsmen. When non-financial alternatives to a bail bond will reasonably assure the appearance of the accused, the court must use them. Even if bail is imposed, the court may nonetheless remove the bail-or-jail decision from the bondsman by allowing the accused to post a partially secured or unsecured appearance or surety bond, CPL 520.10(1)(e)–(h), an alternative permitted by statute but never in fact employed at present. See *United States v. Cramer,* 451 F.2d 1198 (5th Cir. 1971). It is only by so doing that the court can avoid resorting to the imposition of money bail, which results in invidious discrimination against the poor.

III. Full and Fair Hearing

That a hearing must be held whenever bail determinations are made is, of course, basic. See *Ackies v. Purdy,* 322 F. Supp. 38 (S.D. Fla. 1970). The type of hearing which is required, however, depends on evolving notions of due process. *Bell v. Burson,* 402 U.S. 535 (1971); *People ex rel. Menechino v. Warden,* 27 N.Y.2d 376 (1971) (parolee faced with revocation of parole has right to hearing, including right to present evidence and witnesses); Foote, *The Coming Constitutional Crisis in Bail,* 113 U. Pa. L. Rev. 1125, 1175 (1965). The present bail-determination process, which takes a minute or two to resolve the most crucial question affecting the outcome of each case, obviously is neither fair nor full, nor even a hearing in any meaningful sense.

The right to a full and fair hearing must at minimum be held to encompass the right to have presented to the court accurate information bearing on the bail-or-release decision. At present, however, in large numbers of cases the accused comes before the court with either no ROR report or else one which is not verified. The usual response of the court in that event is to detain the accused. Once this happens, no further effort either to interview the accused or to verify his statements is made by the Probation Department, and consequently the initial decision based on inadequate information is perpetuated by the now-or-never nature of the bail hearing at the time of arraignment.

Proof of the rough and summary nature of the hearing may be found in both the brief duration of the entire arraignment process and in the formularized setting of bail in arbitrary multiples of $500. Furthermore, the undue emphasis at arraignment proceedings on disposing of a case by a guilty plea then and there has perverted the function of those proceedings by shifting the focus of arraignment from an initial to a terminal stage. Because of this, the setting of bail becomes either an annoyance to the court or a means of coercing a disposition.

The hearing to be held in the bail-setting process must include, at a minimum, the opportunity to present all material evidence, including the testimony of witnesses; to be confronted with information adversely bearing on the probability of the accused's release, and to cross-examine with respect to such information; and to have brought before the court all information pertinent to the release decision. Evidence must be presented with regard to non-financial release alternatives, *Banks v. United States,* 414 F.2d 1150 (D.C. Cir. 1969), and the financial status of the accused, *United States v. Cook,* 442 F.2d 723 (D.C. Cir. 1970); *Jones v. United States,* 358 F.2d 543 (D.C. Cir. 1966), before any bail decision can be made.

As to the requirement of a hearing on the accused's financial status, it is basic that

> * * * the sole purpose of money bail is to assure the defendant's appearance * * * [M]oney bail should be set no higher than that amount reasonably required to assure the defendant's appearance in court. *A.B.A. Release Standards* §§5.3(b) and 5.3(d). *Accord: People ex rel. Lobell v. McDonnell,* 296 N.Y. 109 (1947).

Any greater amount is excessive within the meaning of the Eighth Amendment. See *Stack v. Boyle,* 342 U.S. 1 (1942). Although this means that the bail determination must be individualized in each case, see *Ackies v. Purdy, supra,* present practice is to the contrary. Bail is set in a matter of moments, and no effort is made in advance to learn how much bail the accused can afford. The fact that bail is virtually always set in arbitrary multiples of $500 belies any claimed attempt to fix the minimum sum necessary for the declared purpose.

Unless bail is to be impermissibly used for preventive detention, a court in setting bail must first apprise itself of and then take into account the financial ability of the accused to make bail.

Special emphasis, of course, should be placed on "the financial ability of the defendant to give bail," because if the defendant cannot make the bail set, he is effectively denied bail. See *Bandy v. United States,* 81 S. Ct. 197, 5 L. Ed. 2d 218 (1960).

Pannell v. United States, 320 F.2d 698, 699 (D.C. Cir. 1963) (concurring opinion of J. Skelly Wright).

As Chief Judge Bazelon has observed in this connection, courts

* * * should recognize that an impecunious person who pledges a small amount of collateral constituting all or almost all of his property is likely to have a stake at least as great as that of a wealthy person who pledges a large amount constituting a modest part of his property. *Id.* at 702.

See also *People v. Rezek,* 25 Misc.2d 705, 707, 204 N.Y.S.2d 640, 643 (Sup. Ct. Kings Co. 1960) ("Being presumed innocent, [a defendant] is entitled to release on bail in a sum which he can furnish * * * The law requires the court to consider the economic circumstances of the defendant in fixing bail.")

IV. Statement of Reasons

It is an "elementary requirement" that where, as here, important rights are at stake, "the decision maker should state the reasons for his determination and indicate the evidence he relied on * * *." *Goldberg v. Kelly,* 397 U.S. 254, 271 (1970). Whenever the People sustain their burden of showing that release on recognizance will not assure an accused's appearance, due process requires the court to state on the record its reasons for so finding. *A.B.A. Release Standards* §5.1(d); Fabricant, *Bail as a Preferred Freedom and the Failure of New York's Revision,* 18 Buff. L. Rev. 303, 315 (1969). This statement must include the court's reasons why the terms of the securing order issued were found to be the least stringent necessary to assure such presence.

Several fundamental principles of due process compel the court to set forth a statement of reasons for the securing order decided upon by it. Such a requirement is essential to protect against careless or hasty action and serves to assure that the main facts to be adjudicated were indeed considered by the court. Davis, *Administrative Law Treatise* §16.00 (1970 Supp.) Concomitantly, there can be no meaningful right to judicial review of a bail determination unless reasons are given for the original finding. "Only when these reasons are spelled out can an appellant intelligently renew his motion before [the] court; and only then can [the reviewing] court fairly review the merits." *Weaver v. United States,* 405 F.2d 353, 354 (D.C. Cir. 1968); see also, *S.E.C. v. Chenery Corp.,* 318 U.S. 80, 94–95 (1943); Foote, *The Coming Constitutional Crisis in Bail,* 113 U. Pa. L. Rev. 1125, 1175 (1965). A statement of reasons prevents lengthy delays prejudicial to the accused caused by remanding a case to a lower court for a statement of the reasons why it has made a particular determination. See *People v. Sykes*, 22 N.Y.2d 159 (1968); *United States v. Seegers*, 433 F.2d 493 (D.C. Cir. 1970).

Moreover, the requirement of a statement of reasons safeguards against arbitrary action. "[T]he essence of due process is 'the protection of the individual against arbitrary action' * * *." *Housing Authority of Durham v. Thorpe*, 386 U.S. 670, 678 (1967) (concurring opinion of Douglas, J.). It is fundamental to basic notions of fairness and justice that a man may not be deprived of his liberty without being informed of the reasons therefor.[28]

A statement of reasons is an essential element of due process not only in the bail determination process, where the failure of a state court to give reasons for its denial of bail has been held to be in violation of the Eighth and Fourteenth Amendments, *United States ex rel. Keating v. Bensinger*, 322 F. Supp. 784 (N.D. Ill. 1971), but also in numerous other areas where hearings involving the adjudication of important rights are involved. Thus, unless one receives a statement of reasons:

—One may not be cut off from welfare benefits. *Goldberg v. Kelly, supra; Banner v. Smolenski*, 315 F. Supp. 1076 (D. Mass. 1970).

—One may not be evicted from a public housing project. *Thorpe v. Housing Authority of Durham*, 393 U.S. 268 (1969); *Caulder v. Durham Housing Authority*, 433 F.2d 998 (4th Cir. 1970), *cert. denied*, 401 U.S. 1003 (1971); *Escalera v. New York City Housing Authority*, 425 F.2d 853 (2d Cir.), *cert. denied*, 400 U.S. 853 (1970); *Williams v. White Plains Housing Authority*, 35 A.D. 2d 965, 317 N.Y.S. 2d 935 (2d Dept. 1970).

—One may not be denied conscientious objector status by a draft board. *United States v. Lenhard*, 437 F.2d 936 (2d Cir. 1970); *United States v. Speicher*, 439 F.2d 104 (3d Cir. 1971); *United States v. Lemmens*, 430 F.2d 619 (7th Cir. 1970); *United States v. Broyles*, 423 F.2d 1299 (4th Cir. 1970); cf. *Clay v. United States*, 403 U.S. 698 (1971).

—One may not be denied release on parole. *Monks v. New Jersey State Parole Bd.*, 58 N.J. 238, 277 A.2d 193 (1971); United States Parole Board Rule (effective July, 1972).

—One may not be dismissed as a school teacher. *Drown v. Portsmouth School District*, 435 F.2d 1182 (1st Cir. 1970), *cert. denied*, 402 U.S. 972 (1971).

—One may not be denied release from a hospital for mental patients, *United States v. McNeil*, 434 F.2d 502 (D.C. Cir.

---

[28] The requirement of a statement of reasons cannot be said to place an undue burden on the courts; since the judge "has already fully considered the merits, the additional task of articulating his reasons should pose no burden." *Weaver v. United States*, 405 F.2d 353, 354 (D.C. Cir. 1968).

1970) (*per curiam*), nor may one be transferred to a ward for the criminally insane, *Jones v. Robinson,* 440 F.2d 249 (D.C. Cir. 1971).

—One may not be institutionally confined. New York Mental Hygiene Law §307(2).

In other contexts, New York has recognized the essential nature of findings of fact and a statement of reasons whenever constitutional rights, CPL 710.60(6), or statutory rights, CPL 440.30(7), are being adjudicated.

Where so crucial a determination as pre-trial liberty is involved, it follows *a fortiori* from the above-cited authority that the court must state its reasons for its determination on bail.

V. Securing Order Supported by Clear and Convincing Evidence

(a) *Exclusion from scrutiny of any prior arrest where disposition is not indicated*

As shown in Appendix B, one of the most important factors in determining whether an accused will be released on recognizance or held in lieu of bail is his prior criminal record. Despite the importance of this factor, the record actually relied upon by the court in making a bail determination often contains incomplete, unverified or misleading information. No attempt is made to update with current information the arrest record ("yellow sheet") relied upon so heavily by the defendants in making bail determinations. Prior arrests which actually resulted in dismissal of the charges or acquittal at trial are noted on the yellow sheet merely as arrests, and the court is left with the misleading impression that the accused was found guilty of those past charges. If the accused attempts to tell the court that the arrests(s) did not result in a conviction, the court not only discounts this explanation but also may view the disclaimer as an indication of the accused's lack of veracity. Thus, since three of ten prosecutions end in dismissal of the charges (Table 5), it is crucial that the prior criminal record presented to the court at the time of arraignment not contain any reference to prior arrests unless it is also indicated what, if any, disposition occurred subsequent to that arrest.

At any bail hearing, the defendant District Attorney routinely places great emphasis on the prior criminal record of the accused. Of all those involved in the bail-setting process, it is he who has the most ready access to complete, up-to-date information about the disposition of those criminal charges, especially in the frequent instances where the prior charge was lodged in the same county. Nonetheless, in practice it is the District Attorney who, in support of his argument on bail, relies on the scantiness of information about disposition subsequent to arrest on the accused's prior criminal record. Contrary to this practice, it should be the responsibility of the District Attorney to produce current records accurately reflecting the posture of the prior charges, in default of which the prior charges ought not to be submitted for the court's examination.

(b) Complete and Verified Report by the Department of Probation

A second source of prejudice to the accused in the bail-setting process is the fact that a large number of the reports submitted by the Department of Probation's Bureau of Release on Recognizance concerning the accused's ties to the community have not been verified. As observed in the statistical study, 40 per cent of the people who were kept in jail in lieu of bail had given references to the Department of Probation which the Department failed to verify, either because the references could not be reached before arraignment (e.g., no phone) or because the Department had insufficient staff to verify the information. In many other cases, the Department of Probation was not able even to interview the accused at all because of insufficient staff.

In a 1969 report to the Mayor's Criminal Justice Coordinating Council, the Vera Institute of Justice observed that out of the total number of cases in which release was not recommended during the month of September 1968, 56 per cent were not recommended because of incomplete verification. The report indicated that the major reasons for lack of verification are that: (1) many references are not available when a staff member tries to contact them; (2) many references have no telephones; and (3) many of the accused fear giving the name of their employers as references. As noted in the report, second attempts are rarely made if a reference cannot initially be contacted. Schaffer, *The Problem of Overcrowding in Detention Institutions of New York City: An Analysis of Causes and Recommendations for Alleviation* (Vera Institute of Justice 1969).

It is evident that "the keynote to successful administration of any system of bail is the adequacy of the information upon which the decisions are based." *Pannell v. United States,* 320 F.2d 698, 702 (D.C. Cir. 1963); *A.B.A. Release Standards* §§1.2, 4.5. Since an accused's pre-trial status is determinative of the outcome of his case, as the study has shown, the right of all accused to have an adequate investigation of community ties is at least as important in most cases as the right of the accused to have an adequate investigation made of the merits of any defense he asserts to the charges against him. See *United States ex rel. Green v. Rundle,* 434 F.2d 1112 (3d Cir. 1970), *writ granted on remand,* 326 F. Supp. 456 (E.D. Pa. 1971); *Moore v. United States,* 432 F.2d 730, 739 (3d Cir. 1970) (*in banc*).

One fundamental requirement of equal treatment for all accused is that the court insist that they be interviewed prior to arraignment by the Department of Probation to ascertain their community ties. Beyond that, however, reasonable attempts to verify the information given by the accused must also be viewed as a prerequisite to the imposition of any conditions on his liberty. To detain one group of persons more frequently than another solely because of manpower shortages is a

plain denial of equal protection. See *United States v. Leathers,* 412 F.2d
169, 173 (D.C. Cir. 1969) (*per curiam*).

Equally important, the accused ought not to be penalized in those
instances where the information he gave has not been verified. Information may not be discredited solely because it has not yet been
checked.

Coupled with the lack of verified reports regarding pre-trial
release is the equally disturbing fact that the defendant Judges and
Justices often fail to follow recommendations for release made by the
Department of Probation in those instances where verification of an
accused's ties has been obtained. Stringent standards must be met
before the Probation Department will recommend that an accused be
released on recognizance. Great weight should be attached to the
recommendation of that Department, which attempts to present to the
court a balanced picture of the accused.

VI. Prompt, Automatic and *De Novo* Review of
All Bail Determinations; Expedited Appeal

Whenever money bail is set, and is set in an amount which the
accused proves unable to raise, it should be regarded as an indication
of a failure on the part of the defendants to discover the least onerous
means of assuring the accused's presence. That the accused remains
incarcerated ought to be viewed as a signal of the possibility that the
balance which in each case must be struck between the accused's right
to liberty and the State's interest in securing his continued appearance
has been weighted too heavily in the State's favor.

What this means in concrete terms is that whenever a person is
detained in lieu of bail, there must be

* * * prompt and periodic review * * * to determine whether
bail has been set too high or whether conditions have been
attached that are impossible for the accused to attain. [This]
also provides a check on the length and character of detention
between arrest and trial. *Bail in the United States: 1964* at 86;
accord, *A.B.A. Release Standards* §5.9(a).

It is important not only that there be provision for review but
also that there "be some avenue of *immediate* review." Note, *Bail: An
Ancient Practice Reexamined,* 70 Yale L.J. 966, 976 (1961) (emphasis
supplied). Furthermore, the review procedure ought to operate automatically whenever an accused is detained. Both promptness and automatic review are necessary because presently available review procedures (writ of habeas corpus or motion to reduce bail) are difficult to
institute and to have heard as expeditiously as necessary to prevent
prejudice to the accused. See *Bail in the United States: 1964* at 87.

Review at the lower court level must also be *de novo.* The purpose of such review is to guard against arbitrary action or abuse of the
institution of bail (*e.g.,* preventive detention or the "taste of jail") and to
insure that the securing order is no more stringent than needed to

assure the accused's presence. It can be meaningful only if the reviewing court may consider the current situation, possibly with new facts (such as a verified ROR report) at its disposal, without artificial constraints of judicial deference. *Cf. Baxstrom v. Herold,* 383 U.S. 107, 111 (1965) (*de novo* review by jury of commitment to mental hospital under New York Mental Hygiene Law §74).

The need for such review provisions to serve as a check on the bail-determination process is underscored by the study, which demonstrates the severe consequences that flow from the condition of being detained. Other studies, in fact, have shown that an accused who is initially detained but obtains his release prior to disposition is more likely to receive a favorable outcome than one who is detained the full time. Rankin, *op. cit. supra,* 39 N.Y.U. L. Rev. at 643 n.6.

The same reasons which compel prompt, automatic and *de novo* review in the trial court of all bail determinations also dictate the need for expedited appeal procedures whenever an accused is incarcerated in lieu of bail. *A.B.A. Release Standards* §5.9(b). All too frequently, problems concerning bail are kept from the scrutiny of appellate courts because of cumbersome procedures resulting in mootness of the bail issue. Prompt appellate review will help to insure that the lower courts are obeying constitutional and statutory directives. It will also provide a further check, by a body somewhat removed from the frenzied pace and high volume of the lower courts, against arbitrary action by those courts.

Conclusion

For all the reasons hereinbefore stated, plaintiffs respectfully request that the relief demanded in their Complaint be granted.

Respectfully submitted,

ROBERT KASANOF
The Legal Aid Society.
Attorney for Plaintiffs
100 Centre Street
New York, New York 10013
(212) 233-0250

Of Counsel:
SAMUEL H. DAWSON
ROBERT H. HERMANN
LINDA HUPP
HAROLD J. POKEL
Dated: New York, New York
March, 1972

. . . .

Appendix B

Determinants of the Bail-Setting Process

Of the 857 defendants in the study, 30 per cent were released on their own recognizance; 31 per cent had bail set at $500 or less; 15 per cent had bail set at $1000; and in 24 per cent of the cases, bail was set at over $1000. This appendix examines the determinants of whether an individual is released on recognizance and, if not, how his bail is set. Three sets of variables which have a bearing upon the bail process will be examined—the type of charge, the accused's prior record, and the accused's personal characteristics.

It will be shown that bail is decided by and large on the basis of the accused's prior criminal record and the type of charge. The accused's individual characteristics have little bearing on the bail decision.

As might be expected, those charged with misdemeanors were more often released on recognizance and had lower amounts of bail set than those who were charged with felonies. This can be seen in Table B-1.

Table B-1: Bail Determination By Whether Accused Charged
With Felony or Misdemeanor

	Felony	Misdemeanor
Released	24%	38%
Bail set at $500 or less	23	44
Bail set at $1000	19	11
Bail set at over $1000	35	7
	101%	100%
	(474)	(325)

The specific crime that the accused is charged with is related to bail determination in Table B-2 to see whether bail is set in high amounts according to the charge.

Those charged with sale of drugs or robbery, especially if a weapon was used in the robbery, were the least often released on recognizance and in the great majority of these cases bail was set at $1000 or more. In contrast, those charged with assault, burglary or other lesser crimes were more likely to be released or have low bail set.

Just as the charge is related to bail determination, so is the accused's prior record. The more severe his prior record, the less likely he will be released on recognizance and the greater the amount of bail. This can be seen from the data in Table B-3.*

---

* When a different indicator of how bad the accused's prior record—the number of prior arrests—is used, we find the same relationship. The greater the number of prior arrests, the less often is he released and the higher the bail amount.

Table B-2: Bail Determination By Specific Charge

	Robbery With a Weapon	Other Robbery	Sale of Drugs	Possession of Drugs	Assault	Burglary, Larceny, Possession of Stolen Property
Release on Recognizance	5%	12%	6%	30%	44%	30%
Bail:						
$500 or less	9	22	28	45	29	34
Bail: $1000	12	27	17	11	11	19
Bail: Over $1000	74	39	50	14	16	17
	100%	100%	101%	100%	100%	100%
	(57)	(41)	(54)	(183)	(91)	(294)

Table B-3: Bail Determination By Accused's Prior Criminal Record

	Felony Arrest Within Last 3 Years	Other Prior Arrest	No Prior Record
Released	12%	25%	61%
Bail: $500 or less	35	33	24
Bail: $1000	20	16	7
Bail: Over $1000	33	26	8
	100%	100%	100%
	(360)	(241)	(241)

It should be noted that fully forty per cent of those with no prior record were detained. Furthermore, the severity of the prior record is less significant than whether there was a record at all. The joint impact of prior record and type of charge upon bail is examined in Table B-4, presented on the following page.*

The data indicate that both type of charge and prior record bear upon the bail-setting process independently of each other. Regardless of the type of charge, those with a prior record are less frequently released and must post higher amounts of bail than those without a prior record. By the same token, when prior record is held constant, there remains a difference in amount of bail between those charged with robbery or sale of drugs and those charged with "lesser crimes."

---

* In Table B-4, type of charge has been collapsed into two categories: charges where bail is generally set high and charges where bail is set low. This gives larger bases upon which to percentage, yet retains the distinction between types of charges necessary for the purpose of the table.

Table B-4: Bail Determination By Type of Charge and Prior Record

	High Bail Charges: Robbery, Sale of Drugs		Low Bail Charges: Possession of Drugs, Assault, Burglary, Larceny	
	Prior Record	No Prior Record	Prior Record	No Prior Record
Released on Recognizance	3%	24%	19%	64%
Bail: $500 or Under	15	31	42	23
Bail: $1000	18	14	19	7
Bail: Over $1000	64	31	20	6
	100%	100%	100%	100%
	(113)	(29)	(392)	(154)

Taken together, prior record and type of charge account for much of the variance in bail determination. Accused with a prior record who are charged with the more serious offenses are rarely released on recognizance (3 per cent) and the great majority (64 per cent) must post bail over $1000, whereas those charged with less serious offenses are usually released on recognizance (64 per cent) and rarely have bail set at over $1000 (6 per cent).

Apart from the type of charge and the accused's prior record, there remains another set of variables which should relate to the bail-setting process, *viz.,* his personal characteristics such as community ties, employment status and family ties. Such information is collected by the Department of Probation's Bureau of Release on Recognizance, which submits a report with a recommendation to the judge at the arraignment.

In actuality, however, in only a minority of cases (27 per cent) is the Bureau able to verify its information. In 34 per cent of the cases, the accused has given complete information to the Bureau but the Bureau has not made a recommendation to the court because references could not be reached at that time since they were not at home or had no telephone. (Of the people in that group, the vast majority, 71 per cent, were not released on their own recognizance.) Some other accused (5 per cent) are not interviewed at all by the Bureau because of its insufficient staff; and of these people who were not interviewed, 76 per cent were denied release on their own recognizance. Even in those few cases where the Bureau is able to verify the information and its report recommends release (only 17 per cent of all cases), more than one-third of these accused were *not* released on their own recognizance.

Although in the majority of cases the accused's personal background information has not been verified, this information is nonetheless available to the judge on the report from the Bureau of Release on Recognizance. Thus, even if much of the information is unverified, it may still have a bearing upon the court's decision in the bail-setting process. In this section, the relationship between bail determination and the accused's ties to the community, his family ties and his employment status will be examined. The data will demonstrate that the accused's personal characteristics are given little consideration in the bail-setting process.

Although the accused's ties to the community, as measured by the length and stability of residence, ought to be a factor influencing the court in the bail-setting process, the data show that whether he lives in New York City and how long he has lived there is not an important criterion in bail determination, for neither is related to the amount of bail. The few accused not residing in New York were, if anything, more likely to be released than the New Yorkers (33 per cent compared to 31 per cent), and the bail amounts were similar for both New Yorkers and non-New Yorkers. As for the length of residence, the majority of persons who had lived in New York for five years or more were released in similar proportions to those residing in the city for less than five years, and the bail amounts were also similar for both groups.

Just as length of residence in New York City has little or no bearing upon the bail-setting process, the length of time the accused has lived at his present address also receives little consideration. This may be seen in Table B-5.

Table B-5: Bail Determination By Length of Residence at Present Address

	How Long Lived at Present Address:		
	Less Than 2 Years	3–5 Years	5 Years or More
Released on Recognizance	28%	37%	33%
Bail: $500 or Less	34	28	30
Bail: $1000	15	13	14
Bail: Over $1000	23	21	23
	100%	99%	100%
	(420)	(134)	(212)

Although those accused who have lived at their current address for less than two years are slightly less likely to be released on recognizance, the general pattern revealed in Table B-5 is that the length of residence has little bearing upon the bail decision. Indeed, the persons with the greatest residential stability (having lived at their current address for five years or more) are released less often and have higher bail set than those living at their present address for only three to five years.

At first glance, employment status appears to be a consideration in the bail-setting process. Those who were employed at the time of their arrest were somewhat more likely to be released on recognizance or be given bail of only $500 or less than the unemployed (70 per cent compared to 57 per cent). But, as can be seen from the data in Table B-6, the difference between the employed and unemployed with respect to the bail decision is greatly reduced when prior record is taken into account.

Table B-6: Per Cent Released on Recognizance or Given Bail of $500 or Less By Employment Status and Prior Criminal Record

	Employed	Unemployed
Prior Record	59% (217)	48% (294)
No Prior Record	87% (129)	84% (101)

Among those with a prior criminal record, the difference in favorable treatment in the bail-setting process between employed and unemployed accused is reduced to eleven percentage points, and among those with no prior record there is hardly any difference at all (only three percentage points). Thus, the slightly less favorable treatment given the unemployed persons is largely due to their being more likely to have a prior criminal record. That employment status is given little or no weight in the bail-setting process is further demonstrated by the fact that of the accused who were employed at the time of their arrest, the vast majority (58 per cent) were not released on their own recognizance.

Whereas community ties and employment status are largely overlooked in the bail-setting process, as has been shown, the accused's family ties might still be thought to have a bearing upon the bail decision. However, the data fail to bear out this hypothesis, for those defendants with strong family ties * are only slightly more likely to receive a favorable bail determination (ROR or bail of $500 or less) than those with weak or some family ties (65 per cent compared to 59 per cent).

In sum, the data clearly indicate that the individual characteristics of the accused, which by law should have a bearing upon the bail decision, in fact are given little consideration in the bail-setting process.

In the prior analysis of the correlates of bail determination, three sets of variables were examined with respect to their bearing upon the bail-setting process: type of charge, prior record and community ties. The relative importance of these factors in the bail-setting procedure is examined in Table B-7, which presents the relationship among four variables: bail determination, prior record, type of charge and community ties.**

---

* The index of family ties is derived from three items: whether the accused is married, whether he has children and whether he has any close relative other than his immediate family with whom he has regular contact. Those with none of these ties are scored "no ties," those with one of these are termed "some ties," and those with two or three such ties are termed "strong family ties."

** The format of Table B-7 is somewhat different from that of the other tables. For each combination of the three independent variables, the per cent who were released is presented in the right hand column. It should also be noted that all variables have been collapsed into dichotomies for the sake of clarity. The community ties index is constructed in the following way: the accused who are unemployed and have weak family ties are termed "weak ties" while all others are termed "some ties." Type of charge is dichotomized as in Table B-4.

Table B-7: Bail Determination By Type of Charge, Prior Record
and Community Ties

Prior Record	Type of Charge	Community Ties	% ROR or Bail of $500 or Less	(N)
1. Yes	High Bail Charge	Weak Ties	21%	(68)
2. Yes	High Bail Charge	Some Ties	16%	(45)
3. Yes	Low Bail Charge	Weak Ties	50%	(221)
4. Yes	Low Bail Charge	Some Ties	62%	(171)
5. None	High Bail Charge	Weak Ties	36%	(14)
6. None	High Bail Charge	Some Ties	73%	(15)
7. None	Low Bail Charge	Weak Ties	87%	(82)
8. None	Low Bail Charge	Some Ties	88%	(72)

Table B-8 below demonstrates the relative importance of the three determinants of bail charted in Table B-7. Holding two of the three determinants constant, the impact of the third factor is demonstrated.

For accused with comparably strong community ties facing the same type of charge, those with no prior records received more favorable bail decisions, on the average, 33.25 per cent more frequently than those with prior records. Among accused with comparably strong community ties and the same type of prior record, those with more severe charges against them received a favorable bail decision, on the average, 37.75 per cent more frequently than those with less severe charges. On the other hand, among accused with the same type of charge and prior record, those with strong community ties received favorable bail decisions, on the average, only 11.25 per cent more frequently than those with weaker community ties.

Table B-8: Average Percentage Difference For Each Factor in Bail
Decision When Other Factors Are Held Constant

Effect of:	Average % Difference in Favorable Bail Decision
No Prior Record	33.25%
Less Severe Type of Charge	37.75%
Strong Community Ties	11.25%

Type of charge and prior record are the most important factors affecting the bail-setting process. The impact of community ties is greatly reduced as a factor in bail determination when prior record and type of charge are taken into account. In other words, bail is largely decided on the basis of the accused's prior criminal record and the type of crime with which he is charged. His individual characteristics have little bearing on the bail determination.

MODEL REGULATIONS FOR CLASSIFICATION AND DISCIPLINE AT CORRECTIONAL INSTITUTIONS *

INTRODUCTION

Recognizing the difficulties of ordering a community of felons and misdemeanants, most penologists nevertheless agree that intra-prison discipline must be viewed in the light of the individual prisoner's long term rehabilitation and treatment. See *Manual of Correctional Standards,* American Correctional Association, 1966, at 10; President's Commission on Law Enforcement and Administration of Justice, *Task Force Report: Corrections* (1967), at 82. The goals for institutional regulations should not be merely to force conformity to the rules of the immediate prison community but rather to develop in a prisoner the self-respect and self-control that will help him adjust to society outside the prison. The *Task Force Report: Corrections* states:

> A first principle for any correctional institution is that staff control can be greatest and certainly inmate life will be most relevant to that in the free community, if rules regulating behavior are as close as possible to those which would be essential for law and order in any free community . . . at 50.

The same penologists have concluded that fair and impartial administration of disciplinary procedures is essential to achieving the above goals. "The disciplinary process . . . should contribute to an offender's general understanding of the nature of the rules and the need to abide by them." *Task Force Report: Corrections,* at 51. Arbitrary assertions of power by correctional authorities, absent any means for the offenders to challenge this authority or protect their rights, are clearly inconsistent with the goals of individual rehabilitation and in the long run are not in the ultimate interest of society. In fact the positive rehabilitative effect of fair disciplinary procedures has often been noted. *Task Force Report: Corrections,* at 82. Reflecting this same philosophy of fairness, the *Manual of Correctional Standards,* supra, adopts a statement which stresses the need for established rules and standardized disciplinary procedures. The guidelines insist that the rules should be "corrective" and "penalties shall not be cruel, inhumane, or degrading." Id. at 267–268.

Three Supreme Court decisions, *In re Gault,* 387 U.S. 1 (1967); *Specht v. Patterson,* 386 U.S. 605 (1967); and *Mempa v. Rhay,* 389 U.S. 128 (1967), suggest that any adjudicative proceeding that may result in

---

* These regulations have been prepared by the ACLU National Prison Project, Washington.

the imposition of restraints, or add restraints on a person's liberty must be surrounded with "minimal" due process safeguards. A most recent Supreme Court decision, *Argersinger v. Hamlin,* 407 U.S. 25 (1972) provides strong support for the proposition that any abridgement of liberty requires full due process protections. This principle, in the context of prison life, would require a fair and full due process hearing before revocation of any good time or other punishment jeopardizing liberty.

Recent cases in federal and state courts have made significant steps toward recognizing and implementing procedural due process guaranties in state prisons and jails by setting minimum standards for the imposition of intraprison discipline. See *Landman v. Royster,* 333 F. Supp. 621 (E.D. Va. 1971); *Krause v. Schmidt,* 341 F. Supp. 1001 (W.D. Wisc. 1972); *Collins v. Schoonfield,* 344 F. Supp. 257 (D. Md. 1972); *Bundy v. Cannon,* 328 F. Supp. 165 (D. Md. 1971); *Clutchette v. Procunier,* 328 F. Supp. 767 (N.D. Calif. 1971); *McCray v. Maryland,* Misc. Petitions 4363, et seq. (Circuit Court for Montgomery County, Maryland, 1971); *Wayne County Jail Inmates v. Wayne County Board of Commissioners,* 5 Clearinghouse L. Rev. 108, Civil Action No. 173–217 (Circuit Court for the County of Wayne, State of Michigan, 1971); *Meola v. Fitzpatrick,* 322 F. Supp. 878 (D. Mass. 1971); *Morris v. Travisono,* 310 F. Supp. 857 (D.R.I. 1970); *Urbano v. McCorkle,* 334 F. Supp. 161 (D.N.J. 1971). See also, *Goldberg v. Kelly,* 397 U.S. 254 (1970); *Bey v. Connecticut State Board of Parole,* 443 F.2d 1079 (2d Cir. 1971); *Jones v. Robinson,* 440 F.2d 249 (D.C. Cir. 1971); *Bearden v. State of South Carolina,* 443 F.2d 1090 (4th Cir. 1971).

Commentators have also recognized these basic principles. See Millemann, *Prison Disciplinary Hearings and Procedural Due Process,* 31 Md. L. Rev. 27 (1971); Jacob, *Prison Discipline and Inmate Rights,* 5 Harv. Civ. Lib. L. Rev. 227 (1970).

These decisions have clearly established as a constitutional mandate what most penologists recognize as an essential ingredient of the rehabilitative process; the right of prison inmates to receive a procedurally fair administrative hearing prior to the imposition of serious punishment for alleged misconduct. The following model regulations are suggested in order to assure compliance with constitutional requirements, guarantee basic administrative fairness and better implement the process of rehabilitation.[1]

---

[1] These regulations are drawn from several court opinions, see supra. In addition, the Model Act for the Rights of Prisoners developed by the National Council on Crime and Delinquency and the Administrative regulations of the Kansas and Delaware prison systems provide strong support for these regulations. Additional support for these regulations is gained from: Manual of Correctional Standards, American Correctional Association, 1966 (hereinafter "M.C.S."); A.L.I. Model Penal Code, §304.7 (May 1962) (hereinafter "M.P.C."); Task Force Report: Corrections, President's Commission on Law Enforcement and Administration of Justice (1967) (hereinafter "Task Force Report"); Federal Bureau of Prisons Policy Statement 7400.5 (hereinafter "Policy Statement"); Maryland Department of Correctional Service Administrative Directives, Nos. 11070, 12070, changes effective 6/1/70 (hereinafter "Maryland Directive").

I. Publication of Rules

All institutional rules and regulations defining and prohibiting inmate misconduct must be published and posted in prominent locations within the institution. All inmates shall receive copies of these rules and regulations upon admission to the institution. Prison rules must be as specific and precise as possible, giving all inmates actual notice of the conduct prohibited. Vague rules imposing punishment for "the good of the institution," prohibiting "agitation" or "disrespect" or punishing "trouble-makers," and other imprecise regulations forbidding other similar general behavior or conduct should not be allowed. Punishments must be standardized and a schedule of specific appropriate punishments for specific offenses must be published and posted.

II. Valid Forms of Discipline

The punishments enumerated herein are the only forms of discipline that may be administered. The punishments may only be imposed by the appropriate disciplinary board as established, infra.

A. Punishments May Include:

1. Reprimand and counselling;
2. suspended sentence;
3. temporary loss of privileges (movies, television, radio, etc.);
4. padlock "house arrest" or restricted confinement within general population;
5. loss of good time;
6. confinement in maximum-security quarters (whether designated "punitive" or "administrative" segregation);
7. interinstitutional transfers.

Solitary confinement cells (or "isolation," "meditation," etc., cells) shall not be used as punishment. See Maryland Department of Correctional Services Administrative Directive of 6/1/70.

B. Definitions and Limitation on Forms of Punishment

In those systems which maintain minimum-security camp centers as well as maximum- and medium-security institutions, a distinction must be made between the types of classification and discipline that may be used at each.

1. Minimum Security Units

(a) Reprimand and counselling is the ordinary disciplinary action that can be taken against a prisoner. *Manual of Correctional Standards,* supra at 411.

This is the only action that may be taken summarily by a custodial officer without a hearing before a disciplinary board, and such action may only be taken if approved by an officer of the rank of assistant superintendent or above.

The reprimand may consist of a written report in the prisoner's record and should be made available to the prisoner.

(b) Loss of privileges (movies, television, radio, etc.) may be imposed for a limited specific time no longer than ten days. *M.C.S.,* supra, at 412; *M.P.C.,* supra, at §304.7(3).

(c) Fines may *not* be imposed.

(d) Change of program assignments is not a proper method of punishment. Policy Statement 7400.5.

(e) Interinstitutional transfers to a higher security institution should be used as a punitive measure under exceptional circumstances only and if other disciplinary methods have been attempted and have failed.

(f) Punitive segregation is *not* valid punishment for prisoners at minimum-security prisons except under the most extraordinary circumstances.

(g) Good time may *never* be taken at a road camp.

2. Medium- and Maximum-Security Prisons

(a) Reprimand and counselling, supra, at 1(a).

(b) Suspended sentence should be used where feasible in disciplinary proceedings. *M.C.S.,* supra, at 412.

(c) Loss of privileges, 1(b), supra.

(d) House arrest, padlock or similar restrictions placed on inmates' liberty within general population may be imposed for a short period of time, *M.C.S.,* supra, at 414; at the most for ten days, *M.P.C.,* supra, at §303.6(2).

(e) Fines may not be imposed.

(f) Change of program assignments is not a proper punishment, 1(d), supra.

(g) Maximum-security segregation may be imposed only when there has been violence, a physical threat to a guard or prisoner, an attempt to escape or another violation of prison rules which is also a violation of state law. *M.C.S.,* supra, at 414; Policy Statement, supra, 7400.5A, 7/2/70; *M.P.C.,* supra, at §304.7(3.

i. The maximum time limit to such segregation should be no more than ten to fifteen days. (Mo. Ann. Stat. §216.455, Supp. 1968–69; *McCray v. Maryland,* supra.

ii. It should not be imposed on a prisoner found to be mentally incompetent.

iii. It requires reasonable privileges and conditions, see 2.d. (1), supra.

(h) Administrative segregation is a therapeutic status for that category of inmates who, because of their pattern of conduct or own protection require close, restricted movement and closer supervision than those in the general population. *M.C.S.,* at supra, at 413. This status:

i. may be initiated by recommendation from the disciplinary board (after a hearing in cases where the inmate does not wish to be placed in this status) to the classification board and approval my the latter;

ii. is subject to periodic review by the classification board;

iii. requires normal conditions and privileges. See 2d. (1), supra, and *Conklin v. Hancock,* 334 F. Supp. 1119 (D.N.H. 1971); *Nolan v. Smith,* — F. Supp. — (Nos. 6228, 6272, D. Vt. 7/1/71).

III. Administration

In accord with the theory requiring disciplinary rules and procedures to be administered in the interest of treatment and rehabilitation, due process requires a dual system of boards. A classification board will determine and oversee the long range treatment and rehabilitative program of every inmate using all medical, psychological, sociological, education and vocational resources available to the institution. The disciplinary board will be separate from the classification board and will administer disciplinary action to be taken against an inmate in light of the larger goals of treatment. For similar dual programs, see *M.P.C.,* supra, at §204; Policy Statement 7400.5A 7/2/70; *Maryland Directive* 6/1/70, supra.

A. Classification Board

1. The board may meet as a whole or in subgroups of not less than three. It shall consist of:

(a) custodial supervisor (assistant superintendent or above);

(b) correctional supervisor (vocational or educational);

(c) psychologist/psychiatrist (his written report);

(d) doctor consultant (or in his absence, his written report);

(e) any additional classification personnel.

2. Duties

(a) Determine each inmate's classification and rehabilitation program, review each inmate's progress and recommend changes in programs. (An inmate should be able to receive written report on his status periodically.)

(b) Review the status of every man in administrative segregation every 20 days and decide when an inmate should be released to the general population.

(c) Review, and where waranted, restore lost good time.

i. Initial review should be 30 days after good time is taken.

ii. Periodic review should be every 90 days thereafter.

iii. A man who is presently serving good time (e.g., if his good time had not been taken he would be free) should have immediate review upon forfeiture of good time by the disciplinary board and a periodic review thereafter every 20 days (Fla. Stat. Ann. §944.27–28, Supp. 1969; N.M. Stat. Ann. §42-1-57, 1964).

(d) Approve interinstitutional transfers from a medium- or minimum-security institution to a maximum-security institution in cases where the disciplinary board, after a hearing as provided, infra, recommends such a transfer.

(e) Approve intrainstitutional transfers to administrative

segregation status in cases where the disciplinary board, after hearing as provided, infra, recommends such a transfer.

(f) Make decisions on transfers of inmates to lesser-security institutions and acceptance of inmates in minimum-security assignments.

(g) Supply, periodically, every inmate with a statement of past achievements or failures, his prognosis for transfers to a lesser-security institution, his eligibility for participation in work, educational or other release programs and a statement of what must be done in the future to qualify for such programs or transfers.

B. Disciplinary Board

1. The board should be consttiuted of at least three members drawn from the following:

(a) hearing officer and chairman of the board provided by the central administrative office of the penal system;

(b) institutional employee to be drawn from the medical, counselling, treatment or chaplain's staff;

(c) person from outside the penal system chosen from membership of outside prisoner assistance groups if such groups exist. (See cases supra, particularly *Bundy v. Cannon,* supra, and *Collins v. Schoonfield,* supra.)

2. Duties

(a) Receive charges, Policy Statement 7400.5A, supra.

(b) Notify prisoner of charges.

(c) Cause investigation of charges.

(d) Hold hearings.

(e) Evaluate charges.

(f) Notify prisoner of decisions and evaluation.

(g) Decide disciplinary disposition of the inmate if guilty of an infraction of a written regulation.

(h) Recommend to the classification board:

i. change to administrative segregation status;

ii. transfer to another institution.

C. Regional Disciplinary Boards (Field Units)

The classification and disciplinary boards are only applicable to the larger maximum- and medium-security institutions. If a minimum-security inmate commits a serious infraction or requires reclassification he should be transferred to an institution with greater security and facilities to deal with disciplinary problems. Such dispositions do require hearings. In the interest of obtaining witnesses, testimony, etc., the hearing should be held within a reasonable proximity to the minimum-security unit. Considering these problems:

1. The board shall be constituted as B(1) with at least three members. Additional persons may be drawn from the local community, e.g., local lawyer, teacher, justice of the peace, minister, etc.

2. Duties, B(2), supra.

3. Only the following punishments may be imposed:

(a) reprimand and counselling;

(b) loss of privileges;

(c) transfer to another institution and imposition of the punishment to be administered at the receiving institution. (The recommendation for transfer must be approved by the classification board of the receiving institution.)

D. Minimum Guidelines

1. No guards may sit on disciplinary boards;

2. No prison personnel involved in the incident at issue may sit on the disciplinary board. Cases cited, supra; *Missouri State Penitentiary Personnel Information Pamphlet* 1967, at 3.

3. The only disposition of a prisoner that may be instituted without a hearing is reprimand and counselling.

4. Punishment may not be imposed until after a hearing has been held, *Task Force Report,* supra, at 84; *M.P.C.,* at §304.7; *M.C.S.,* supra, at 409; cases cited, supra.

5. If the prisoner is violent and poses an immediate and substantial threat to himself, or to other prisoners or guards and requires immediate restraint he may be held in padlock and if dangerous, in segregation, pending a hearing. See cases cited, supra, particularly *Wayne County Inmates v. Board of Commissioners,* supra. If a prisoner is so restrained, a hearing must be held within 72 hours.

6. A doctor or psychiatrist/psychologist must be present at hearings (or their written recommendation obtained) which confine inmates to any type of segregation (punitive or administrative) or must examine the inmate immediately after his confinement and make written recommendations to both the classification and disciplinary boards concerning the health and emotional stability of the inmate.

IV. Procedural Safeguards For Prison Discipline

Considering the substantial balance of personal liberty at stake and the rehabilitative effect of a fair disciplinary hearing, all punitive administrative dispositions of a prisoner (see II.A (1–7), supra), other than reprimand and counselling, require that a hearing with full procedural safeguards be held. See cases cited, supra; and other authorities cited in footnote 1, supra.

A. Written notice of charges shall be provided to the inmate within 24 hours of the alleged violation. Notice shall include:

1. the name of the officer or employee who observed and reported the violation and the names of any other known witnesses;

2. time, date, place of the violation;

3. specific rule violated (set out in full text);

4. summary of details describing the alleged incident;

5. a statement advising inmate of his constitutional right to remain silent if the alleged misconduct also constitutes a crime and criminal prosecution may be initiated.

6. A full and complete statement of all rights, listed infra, to which the accused inmate is entitled at his disciplinary hearing. See

Landman v. Royster, supra; Clutchette v. Procunier, supra; McCray v. Maryland, supra; Task Force Report, supra, at 13, M.P.C., supra, at §304.7.

B. Investigation and Review by Supervisor.

The supervisor may, after investigation and review, dismiss the charge, reprimand the inmate or refer the case to the disciplinary board. See cases cited, supra, particularly Bundy v. Cannon, supra, and Morris v. Travisono, supra; Missouri State Penitentiary Personnel Information Pamphlet Rules and Procedures, 1–6 (1967).

C. The inmate may not be interrogated by prison guards or officials while a hearing is pending. See Virginia Division of Correction, Reg. 800.

D. Notice of the hearing must be provided to the inmate sufficiently prior to the hearing to give him the opportunity to prepare his defense. See cases cited, supra.

E. The inmate has a right to be present at the hearing. See cases cited, supra.

F. The inmate may have the assistance of a representative and an opportunity to prepare before the hearing. See cases cited, supra; (Task Force Report, supra, at 13, 84, in limited circumstances).

    1. Representatives can be drawn from:

        (a) the counselling staff of the prison;

        (b) free men, e.g., teachers, doctors, psychologists, etc.;

        (c) fellow prisoners, see Johnson v. Avery, 393 U.S. 483 (1969).

    2. The prisoner shall have the right to request a representative of his choice.

    3. Where necessary the prisoner shall be allowed to make his defense through an interpreter.

    4. At hearings considering loss of good time or other severe punishment, the inmate may have the assistance of a lawyer or law student if available. See Landman v. Royster; Cluchette v. Procunier; McCray v. Maryland, supra; and Collins v. Schoonfield, supra. See also Model Act of National Council on Crime and Delinquency.

G. The accused shall have the opportunity to cross-examine and confront accusers and witnesses. See cases cited, supra.

H. The accused shall have the opportunity to call witnesses in his own behalf. See cases cited, supra; Washington Rev. Code Ann. §§995.070, 995.080 (1961).

I. The accused shall have the opportunity to present his case and discuss the incident. See cases cited, supra.

J. The accused or his representative shall have access to the inmate's file and any reports or records used or relied upon by the disciplinary board in reaching their determination.

K. The hearing shall be recorded. See *Wayne County Inmates v. Board of Commissioners,* supra, and *Collins v. Schoonfield,* supra. A written record shall be made and shall include:

 1. charges;

 2. summary of prodceedings and evidence presented;

 3. findings of fact;

 4. specific disciplinary action to be taken;

 5. evaluation and rationale for the decision that reflects a consideration of all the evidence and the inmate's previous record.

L. The superintendent may review the record and decision but he may not unilaterally increase punishment or reverse a finding of innocence. See cases, supra.

M. Where recommended by the disciplinary board, the classification board shall decide whether an interinstitutional transfer or transfer to administrative segregation quarters is appropriate. See cases, supra, particularly *Bundy v. Cannon,* and *Urbano v. McCorkle.*

N. A suspended sentence should be used whenever possible if punishment is to be imposed.

V. Conditions of Punishment

A. There must be a time limit set on every punishment imposed. See attached Kansas regulations; *Task Force Report,* supra, at 84.

 1. More particularly:

  (a) Padlock: maximum 10 to 15 days, *M.P.C.,* supra, at §303.6(2); *McCray v. Maryland,* supra.

  (b) Punitive segregation: 10 to 15 days, *M.P.C.,* supra, at 2g(1); *McCray v. Maryland,* supra.

B. Normal food portions, seconds, desserts, etc., must be served at all levels of segregation. See, Policy Statement, supra at App. 1.d.(4).

C. Normal health and sanity conditions shall be maintained at all levels of segregation, that is:

 1. All prisoners shall be provided with normal hygienic implements (e.g., toothbrush, soap, etc.), including a commode. All prisoners shall be also provided with the necessary materials to clean their cells twice a week.

 2. All prisoners shall be allowed to shower at least three times a week and shave and wash daily. Policy Statement, supra.

 3. All prisoners shall be provided with regular clothing and have the normal change of clothing.

 4. All prisoners shall be provided with normal bedding and change of linens.

D. None of the conditions listed in C, supra, shall be removed as punishment. Each may only be removed or restricted on the written recommendation of a psychiatrist or doctor, after a finding by him that the bedding or clothes, etc., constitute a substantial and immediate danger to the prisoner's health and safety.

E. Prisoners in punitive segregation shall be visited daily by a doctor or nurse, see cases, supra; *M.P.C.*, supra, at 304.7(3), who shall be required to sign in on a log book. A psychiatrist/psychologist as well as custodial supervisors shall also make daily checks of segregation units and sign the log. *M.C.S.*, supra, at 412.

F. All prisoners in punitive segregation or on padlock may request to see the following personnel:

1. the chaplain or minister of his faith;
2. a classification officer;
3. the prison doctor or dentist;
4. a psychologist or psychiatrist.

Requests shall be uncensored and shall be communicated immediately to the requested visitor. Medical emergencies shall be attended to immediately.

G. There shall be no restrictions on exercise at any level of segregation. Every prisoner shall have at least two hours of exercise per day. In case of inclement weather, an indoor exercise area shall be available.

H. There shall be no restriction on commissary privileges at any level of segregation.

I. There shall be no restrictions on reading materials, radio privileges or access to library facilities at any level of segregation. Industry and hobbies should be encouraged if the men are not permitted to work.

J. Full correspondence and visiting privileges shall be available at all levels of segregation. (*M.C.S.*, supra, at 412). These privileges may only be limited when there has been an abuse of these privileges. More specifically, mail to and from the courts, public officials, attorneys, and other bona fide public agencies and public interest groups shall never be opened or censored.

K. Prisoners at all levels of segregation shall be permitted to attend religious services unless a doctor or psychiatrist states in writing that he considers the prisoner to be too violent or dangerous. At no time shall a prisoner be deprived of religious counselling, books, pamphlets, etc.

L. There may be no corporal punishment, and that includes physical restraints such as handcuffing to bars, etc. See cases cited, supra (particularly *Landman v. Royster*), and *M.C.S.*, supra, at 417; *M.P.C.*, supra, at §304.17(4).

M. All cells at all levels of segregation must be well ventilated, heated, lighted and sanitary. A log shall be kept to register the temperature of every cell grouping every four hours. Policy Statement, supra, at App. 1.d.

N. Prisoners at all levels of segregation shall be permitted to converse in normal tones at reasonable hours.

O. Prisoners confined in administrative segregation for their own protection are entitled to all rights and privileges enjoyed by inmates in the general population. See *Conklin v. Hancock,* supra; *Nolan v. Smith,* supra.

P. In no case of discipline may an inmate be denied good time, as a result of his misconduct, if he is also (to be) indicted and tried for an alleged violation of criminal law, e.g., an inmate tried, convicted and sentenced for escape may not also have good time forfeited or revoked. See Kansas Penal System regulations attached hereto.

APPENDIX B

The following is The Fortune Society list of groupings to contact in the United States and in Canada.

Alabama

LINK Society
557 Dauphin St.
P.O. Box 684
Mobile, Alabama 36601

Arizona

7th Step Foundation
832 North Central Ave.
Phoenix, Ariz. 85004
　(602-258-7977)
(aim: remotivation of ex-cons, staffed by ex-cons; operation: in and out of prisons)

Society for the Advancement of
　Human Rights
P.O. Box 3341
College Station
Tucson, Ariz. 85720
(group of non-ex-cons, information to public)

Arkansas

Arkansas Release Guidance
　Foundation
P.O. Box 6155
Little Rock, Ark.
　(501-376-6525)

California

Abundant Living Foundation
P.O. Box 28028
San Diego, Cal. 92128
　Att: Jack Addington
(has classes in Folsom; religious group, non-sect.)

Citizens Committee for Parole
　and Prison Changes
1107 Ninth Ave.
Forum Bldg., Rm. 828
Sacramento, Cal. 95814
　Att: Laverne Brown

California (*cont'd*)

Committee for Prisoner Humanity
　and Justice
1029 Fourth Street, Rm. 37
San Rafael, Cal. 94901
　Att: Reba G. Mason
(correspondence with inmates)

Connections
3189 19th St.
San Francisco, Cal. 94103
　(415-673-0298)
(job-finding, info. service re prisons, counselling)

Delancey Street Foundation, Inc.
3001 Pacific Ave.
San Francisco, Cal. 94115
　Att: John Maher
(help ex-inmates)

ECO JUS, Inc.
P.O. Box 4381
Anaheim, Cal. 92803
(ex-cons and straights)

Ex-Squared
San Jose, Cal.
(helps ex-con find jobs, clothes, housing)

Friends Outside
2709 Buena Vista
Santa Barbara, Cal. 93103
　(805-323-1643)
(helps families of Cal. inmates, speaking engagements, jail counselling)

Home for Boys
Boy Because of Youth
P.O. Box 5081
San Jose, Cal. 95150
(for delinquent 16-18-year olds, center for treatment of county court wards)

California (*cont'd*)
Midway Center
4969 Sunset Boulevard
Los Angeles, Cal. 90027
(residential program for "no resource" adult male parolees)

NARCONON
833 Beacon Ave.
Los Angeles, Cal. 90017

Prison Law Project
5408 Claremont Ave.
Oakland, Cal. 94618

Project New Gate
1832 Barnett Rd.
Los Angeles, Cal. 90032
    Att: David Sandoval
(ed. prog. in prisons)

Recidivism Prevention
c/o Lee Halverson
2918 Florence Ave.
Huntington Park, Cal. 90255
(activities unknown)

7th Step of California
Vacaville Chapter
P.O. Box 1166
Sacramento, Cal. 95806
    Att: Pat Malone, Coordinator

Traveler's Aid Society
235 Broadway, Suite 505
San Diego, Cal. 92101
(helping find a residence; provides temporary food, shelter, and sometimes loans)

Colorado
PREP
(Prisoner Rehabilitation and Ed.)
University of Colorado
U.M.C., Rm. 420
Boulder, Colo. 80302

Marie H. Thomson, Clerk of the
    County Court
Golden, Colo. 80401
(work in courts in Colo.; volunteer courts; newsletter; Boulder Cty. Juvenile Ct.)

Connecticut
Citizens for Better Correctional
    Institutions
First Methodist Church
College and Elm Sts.
New Haven, Conn. 06511
(newsletter; pen pals; no ex-cons)

Connecticut Prison Assn.
92 Farmington Ave., Rm. 615
Hartford, Conn. 06115
    (203-527-6342, X 3320)
(working with inmates in prisons, after-care, job finding)

Federal Correctional Institution
Danbury, Conn. 06810
(inmates publish monthly magazine, "Grounded Eagle," c/o Educational Dept., Pembroke St., Danbury, Conn. 06810)

H.E.L.P., Inc.
(Helping Ex-Offenders Live Positively)
56 Union Place
Hartford, Conn. 06103
    (203-278-4920)

Imprisoned Citizens Assis.
18 Fairfield Ave.
P.O. Box 72
So. Norwalk, Conn. 06854
(working with people inside and with families outside)

National Council on Crime and
    Delinquency
Connecticut Council
975 Silas Deane Highway
Wethersfield, Conn. 06109
    (203-529-6835)

Revitalization Corps
1762 Main St.
Hartford, Conn. 06120
    (203-249-7523)
(provides rides for families to Enfield)

District of Columbia
ACLU Prisoners' Rights Project
1424 16th St. N.W.
Washington, D.C. 20036

Center for Government Studies
1701 K Street N.W. 906
Washington, D.C. 20006
(research on municipal gov't)

Federal Probation Quarterly
Supreme Court Building
Washington, D.C. 20544

Joint Commission on Correctional Manpower and Training (Publications)
1522 K. Street N.W.
Washington, D.C. 20005
(aim: rehabilitation of offenders
through correctional system)

National Center for Correctional
Law
1705 DeSales St. N.W.
Washington, D.C. 20036

National Legal Aid and Defender
Assoc.
National Law Office
1601 Connecticut Ave. N.W.
Washington, D.C. 20009

Newsletter-Visitors Services
Center
D.C. Jail
261 17th St. S.E.
Washington, D.C. 20003

Florida
AGAPE
P.O. Box 1377
Delray Beach, Fla. 33444
(for drug addicts: Sonny Pal-
mieri's group)

Alternative Vittles
1478 Gulf to Bay Blvd.
Clearwater, Fla. 33515

Florida (*cont'd*)
Convicts Anonymous
517 North "L" St.
Pensacola, Fla. 32501
(904-438-2840)
Att: Daniel D. Tibbett
(aims: about same as Fortune,
started 8/70)

Organization to Help Ex-Cons
c/o Marvin J. Ranzin
1150 S.W. 22nd St.
Miami, Fla. 33129

Georgia
Community Treatment Center
669 McDonough Blvd.
Atlanta, Ga. 30315
Att: Art Espinoza, Employment
Placement Officer
(jobs for ex-offenders)

Hugh Murray, Jr.
40 Marietta N.W.
First Federal Bldg.
Atlanta, Ga. 30303
(jobs of ex-off. in Ga.)

RINC
(Reclaim, Inc.)
Georgia State Prison
Reidsville, Ga. 30453
Att: W. James Foster, Chair-
man

Hawaii
Blue Moon Jaycees
Hawaii State Prison
2109 Kamehameha Hwy.
Honolulu, Hawaii 96819
Att: Roy Goss, External Vice-
Pres.

John Howard Assoc. of Hawaii
YWCA Bldg.
1040 Richards St.
Honolulu, Hawaii 96813
Att: Emmett A. Cohill, Exec.
Dir.

Illinois

Chance
9020 So. Bishop
Chicago, Ill. 60620

Chicago Connections
519 W. North Ave., Rm. 201
Chicago, Ill. 60610

CON/TACT
343 South Dearborn
Fisher Bldg., Suite 1114
Chicago, Ill. 60604
 (312-939-2925)
 (aid and assist. ex-offenders)

Correctional Programs
Stone Foundation
1439 S. Michigan Ave.
Chicago, Ill. 60605
(general information)

Defender Newsletter
Nat'l Legal Aid and Defender
 Association
American Bar Center
Chicago, Ill. 60637

Ray Elliott
Halfway House
P.O. Box 1263
Carbondale, Ill. 62901

The Illinois Jaycees
415 Woodruff Rd.
Joliet, Ill. 60434
(inmate organization inside institution)

John Howard Association
National Headquarters
608 So. Dearborn St.
Chicago, Ill. 60605
(group helping ex-offenders)

Office of Educ. Experimentation
6800 S. Stewart Ave.
Chicago, Ill. 60621
 Att: C. N. Somers, Dir. Corrections Counselling, Chicago State College

Indiana

P-A-C-E
(Public Action in Correctional
 Effort)
1803 N. Meridian St.
Indianapolis, Indiana 46202

Iowa

Project H.O.P.E.
P.O. Box 6177
Coralville, Iowa 52240
 Att: Samuel Hunt
(ex-inmate group, helping guys in and out of prison)

Scott County Corrections
Dept. of Counselling and Coordinating Services
418 Main St.
Davenport, Iowa 52801
 (319-324-1387)
 Att: Mr. Dan Warlop
(counselling and liaison between inmates and social agencies)

Kentucky

Don Beckhart
Rehabilitation Office
2210 Goldsmith Lane
Louisville, Ky. 40218
(jobs and rehabilitation)

Mr. Jack Feverly
Dept. of Justice
Bureau of Prisons
401 Federal Bldg.
Lexington, Ky. 40507

M. Michael Martin
Route #1, Brocklyn
Richmond, Ky. 40475
(works in volunteer project with ex-cons to stir community involvement in the field of corrections)

Louisiana

Community Service Center
4000 Magazine St.
New Orleans, La. 70130
 (504-897-6277)
 Att: Mr. Wm. Rucker

Louisiana (*cont'd*)
Insight House
1123 Prytania St.
New Orleans, La. 70130
   (504-523-1363)
   Att: Father Capel
(halfway house)

Maine
EXIT
(Ex-Offenders in Transition)
116 State Street
Augusta, Maine 04330
(job placement, counselling)

S.C.A.R.
158 Danforth St.
Portland, Maine 04103
   (207-772-3711)
   Att: Robbie Bothen

Maryland
American Friends Service
   Committee
319 E. 25th Street
Baltimore, Md. 21218

Community Reintegration Project
Division of Correction
Correctional Camp Center
Jessup, Md. 20794
   Att: Franklin D. Chesley,
   Program Dir.

The Joseph House
1823 Eutaw Place
Baltimore, Md. 21217
   Att: Rev. Martin Raumacher,
   Dir.
(in and out of prison program)

Nat'l Institute of Mental Health
   Support Programs
5454 Wisconsin Ave.
Chevy Chase, Md. 20203
(brochure on research, resources
   programs)

Massachusetts
Ditmas House
Deer Island House of Correction
Box 112
Winthrop, Mass. 02152
   Att: Norman R. E. Herr
(self-help, inmates)

Massachusetts Correctional
   Assoc.
(The Post-Conviction Legal
   Services Demonstration
   Project)
33 Mt. Vernon St.
Boston, Mass. 02108

Massachusetts Council on Crime
   and Correction
3 Jay Street
Boston, Mass. 02215
   (617-523-5527)

Massachusetts Half-Way Houses,
   Inc.
P.O. Box 348
Back Bay Annex
Boston, Mass. 02117
   (617-482-0787)
   Att: J. Bryan Riley

Massachusetts Law Reform
   Institute
2 Park Square
Boston, Mass. 02116

Massachusetts Rehabilitation
   Comm.
296 Boylston St.
Boston, Mass. 02116
(jobs in Mass.)

OUTLOOK
Self-Development Group
3 Joy Street
Boston, Mass. 02108
(ex-con group)

Project Re-Entry
YMCA
316 Huntington Ave.
Boston, Mass. 02115
(halfway house for ex-addict ex-
cons on parole or probation)

Michigan

The Mott Program of the Flint
    Bd. of Educ.
923 E. Kearsley St.
Flint, Mich. 48502
    Att: B. G. Hulsopple, Ph.D.
(helps ex-felony offenders in the
resocialization process)

Prison and Justice Subcommittee
State of Emergency Committee
8824 Fenkell St.
Detroit, Mich. 48238
    (313-322-8570)

Minnesota

Focus
439 Polk Street
Anoka, Minn. 55303
(publication)

Minnesota Connections
1427 Washington Ave. So.
Minneapolis, Minn. 55404
(helping visiting conditions with
families and inmates)

180 Degrees, Inc.
3332 Hennepin Ave.
Minneapolis, Minn. 55408
    Att: Mr. Robert Robinson
(reentry of ex-felons w/chemical
dependency and other problems)

OUTMATE
c/o Larry Wendinger
1107 8th Ave. South
St. Cloud, Minn. 56301
(trying to make public aware of
conditions in the St. Cloud State
Reformatory for Men; setting up
seminars; inmates speaking to
groups; letter-writing and visitation program with inmates)

Missouri

Charles H. Watts
Greater St. Louis Alliance for
    Shaping Safer Cities
5892 Delmar Blvd.
St. Louis, Mo. 63112

Nebraska

7th Step Foundation
3000 Farnam St. Suite 12
Omaha, Nebraska 68131
    Att: Mr. Don Bell, Exec. Dir.

New Hampshire

Michael Nichols, Rehabilitation
    Counselor
Dept. of Education
New Hampshire State Prison
Concord, New Hampshire 03301

New Jersey

Association of Black Law
    Students
180 University Pl.
Newark, N.J. 07112

Bayonne Outreach Center
2 West 22nd St.
Bayonne, N.J. 07002
    (201-823-2200)
    Att: Ann Magarelli

Black Inmates Protection Assoc.
827 So. 19th St.
Newark, N.J. 07108
    (c/o Watson)

Black Panther Party
355 University Pl.
Newark, N.J. 07111
    (201-242-9547)

The Bridge
75 Newark Turnpike
Route 23
Singac, N.J. 07424

Camden Legal Defense
    Committee
574 Benson St.
Camden, N.J. 08107

Center for Prisoners Aid
184 Kearney St.
Paterson, N.J. 07522

Citizens Employment Referral
    Assoc.
120 No. Oraton Pkwy.
E. Orange, N.J. 07017

New Jersey *(cont'd)*

Committee for Unified Newark
507 High Street
Newark, N.J. 07102

Community Information and
    Referral Service, Inc.
353 Springfield Ave.
Newark, N.J. 07103
    (201-824-3883)
    Att: Stanley Porteur,
    Coordination
(helps ex-offender, jobs, housing
adjustment)

High Impact Anti-Crime Program
38 Halsey St.
Newark, N.J. 07102
    (201-624-2922)
    Att: Mr. Michael McLaughlin
(citizens visit inmates)

Hudson County Pretrial
    Intervention Project
Health Services Bldg.,
Medical Center, 12th Fl.
30 Baldwin Ave.
Jersey City, N.J.
    (201-547-3361)

New Jersey Association of
    Correction
Central Office:
21 N. Clinton Ave.
Trenton, N.J. 08609
(special project: a citizen's assoc.
for correctional services)

New Jersey Assoc. of Correction
R.F.D. #4
Box 425
New Brunswick, N.J. 08902

New Jersey Coalition for
    Penal Reform
116 No. Oraton Pkwy.
East Orange, N.J. 07817

New Jersey Parents Federation
    for Child Care Development
819 Central Ave.
Asbury Park, N.J. 07712

New Jersey *(cont'd)*

O.Y.E. Solidarity
54 Spruce St.
Newark, N.J. 07102

Pathroad
c/o Mrs. Nel van Dijk
40 Bell Drive
Westfield, N.J. 07090
    (201-232-4070)
(civilian group for rehabilitation)

Princeton Students for Prison
    Reform
c/o Princeton University
Princeton, N.J. 08540

Prison Solidarity Committee
c/o Juanita Handon
504 Stuyvesant Ave.
Trenton, N.J. 08618

Prisoners' Rights Organized
    Defense
(P.R.O.D.)
45 Academy St.
Suite 209
Newark, N.J. 07102

Prisoners Service Committee
    of Southern N.J.
228 Kings Highway East
Haddonfield, N.J. 08033
(volunteer probation counselors)

United Ex-Convicts Union
c/o Ketter
33 12th Ave.
Paterson, N.J. 07502

Vantage House
1516 Atlantic Ave.
Atlantic City, N.J. 08401
    (201-348-4208)
    Att: Alfred Petrone
or:
35 So. Metropolitan Ave.
Atlantic City, N.J. 08401
(ex-cons and squares)

Woodrow Wilson School of
    Princeton
c/o Princeton University
Princeton, N.J. 08540

New Mexico

Project Justice
West Star Route
Box 2E
Portales, New Mexico 88130
(working with lawyers and judges
re justice system)

Project Newgate
P.O. Box 1059
Santa Fe, New Mexico 87501
(correctional ed. and rehab.)

New York

Ad-Hoc Comm. for the Survival
of Four Thousand
1010 Hagen St.
E. Elmhurst, New York 11373

Arbor House
100 Clinton Ave.
Albany, New York 12210
(halfway house)

The Avenue Program
75 Market Street
Poughkeepsie, New York 12601
(community group helping
parolees)

Black Africa
366 W. 125th St.
Manhattanville Station
P. O. Box 1022
New York, N.Y. 10029

BUILD
339 Genesee St.
Buffalo, New York 14204
(made public aware; jobs,
education)

Citizen Action Program of
Nat'l Council on Crime and
Delinquency
44 E. 23rd Street
New York, N.Y. 10010

Citizens Against Legalized
Murder, Inc.
P.O. Box 24
New York, N.Y. 10024
Att: Douglas Lyons,
Exec. Dir.

New York (cont'd)

Committee for Defense of
Political Prisoners
669 DeKalb Ave.
Brooklyn, New York 11206

Community Services Bureau
Coordinating Committee
96 Duane Street
New York, N.Y. 10007
Att: Peter Fairchild

Conquest
1301 E. 7th Street
New York, N.Y. 10009

Correctional Association of N.Y.
135 E. 15th St.
New York, N.Y. 10003
Att: Michael J. Smith

Dept. of Public Affairs
Community Service Society of
N.Y.
105 E. 22nd Street
New York, N.Y. 10010

Dutchess County Drug and
Alcohol Abuse Clinic
230 North Road
Poughkeepsie, New York 12601
Att: Ms. Rose Mary Hammerle

Erie County Jail
Buffalo, New York
Att: Bill Geller
(program in the jail)

Federation of Protestant Welfare
Agencies
281 Park Ave. So.
New York, N.Y. 10010

Harlem Hospital Center
National Alliance on Shaping
Safer Cities
165 E. 56th Street
New York, N.Y. 10022

Holy Apostle Center
300 9th Ave.
New York, N.Y. 10001
(residential house for ex-cons,
also tries to get jobs)

New York (*cont'd*)

Independence House
503 West 27th St.
New York, N.Y. 10001
(resident for youths from Rikers' Island)

Law Students Civil Rights
    Research Council
156 Fifth Ave.
New York, N.Y. 10010

Legal Aid Prisoners' Rights
    Project
119 Fifth Ave.
New York, N.Y. 10010

The Manhattan Court
    Employment Project
Criminal Justice Coordinating
    Council
City Hall
New York, N.Y. 10007

Mid-Hudson Crime Control
    Planning Board
Old Newburgh Courthouse
P.O. Box 1071
Newburgh, New York 12550
    Att: Robert Corlins, Dir.

New Horizon Rehab. Center
Lake Huntington, New York
    12752
    Att: Edward Davis
(for alcoholics)

NAACP Legal Defense Fund
10 Columbus Circle
New York, N.Y. 10019

NAACP
Project Rebound
2521 Broadway, Rm. 23
New York, N.Y. 10025
    (212-663-5771; 749-2323)
(helping ex-offenders; housing,
jobs; not staffed by ex-inmates)

National Committee for
    Prisoners' Rights
77 West Eagle St.
Buffalo, New York 14202

New York (*cont'd*)

National Council on Crime and
    Delinquency
44 E. 23rd St.
New York, N.Y. 10010

New York Comm. to Abolish
    Capital Punishment
2 W. 64th St.
New York, N.Y. 10023
    (212-874-2073)

New York State Division for
    Youth
155 Washington Ave.
Albany, New York 12210

Prison Action Group
105 Maxwell Ave.
Rochester, New York 14619
    Att: Emily Patall

Prison Task Force
c/o MICA-CV
330 West Church St.
Elmira, New York 14901

Project Deap
Junior High School 71
Ave. B. & 6th St.
New York, N.Y. 10009
    Att: Joyce McGrath,
    Elsa Gonzales

Project on Availability of
    Criminal Defense Counsel
    for the Indigent
N.Y.U. School of Law
33 Washington Sq. W.
New York, N.Y. 10011
    Att: Wm. R. Fry

Proposal to Set Up Pilot Prison
    Education Plan
c/o Susan Cantrell Smith
4609 Dickson Hall
Cornell University
Ithaca, New York 14850

Quaker Comm. on Social
    Rehabilitation, Inc.
135 Christopher St.
New York, N.Y. 10014

New York (*cont'd*)

QUERER
2801 Third Ave.
Bronx, New York 10455
(bilingual resocialization of
ex-offenders)

Phoenix House
205 W. 85th St.
New York, N.Y. 10024

Police and Community Theatre
1490 Franklin Ave.
Mineola, New York 11501
(development of short plays on
crime by the community)

Puerto Rican Ass'n for
    Community Affairs
1432 Lexington Ave.
New York, N.Y. 10028
    Att: Nicodemas Sanchez

Rochester Interfaith Jail Ministry
c/o Robert E. Bonn
670 South Avenue
Rochester, New York 14620

Settlement Houses Employment
    Development, Inc. (SHED)
114 E. 32nd St.
New York, N.Y. 10016
    Att: Rev. George E. Kandle,
    Dir.
        (Protestant Chaplain, Sing
        Sing)
(person-to-person program to relate the prison, the parolee and
the parish)

Shaping Safer Cities
American Jewish Committee
165 E. 56th St.
New York, N.Y. 10022

T.A.C.T.
51 Court St.
Buffalo, New York 14202
(help offender to return to
community)

United Black Coalition for Jobs
    in the Construction Industry
13 Astor Place
New York, N.Y. 10003

New York (*cont'd*)

Vera Foundation Report
The Manhattan Bail Project
30 E. 39th St.
New York, N.Y. 10016

The Vestibule
P.O. Box 352
Friendship, New York 14739
    (716-973-7135)
    Att: Mr. Tom Smith
(halfway house)

Volunteer Prison League
340 W. 85th St.
New York, N.Y. 10024
    Att: J. F. McMahon
(counselling, jobs, and help to
families)

Women in Prisons
c/o Ms. Susan Hesse
96 Main Street
Johnson City, New York 13790

Ohio

Citizens Aiding Public Offenders
3201 Stickney Ave.
Toledo, Ohio 43608
    Att: Sam Barbato, Coordinator
(general assistance)

Community Action Agency
110 Nelson Ave.
Lisbon, Ohio 44432
    (216-424-7369)
    Att: Alice L. Brooks

Concerned Convicts of America
1560 E. 21st St.
Cleveland, Ohio 44114
    Att: Donald M. Johnson,
    Chairman
(various programs)

Ex-Cons for a Better Society
213 N. Main St.
Dayton, Ohio 45402
    Att: George Alford
(ex-cons staff; jobs)

Man to Man Association
935 East Broad St.
Columbus, Ohio 43205

Ohio (cont'd)
Man to Man Assoc.
Ohio State University
1659 N. High
Columbus, Ohio 43210
    Att: Dr. White

Ohio Connections
P.O. Box 18560
Cleveland, Ohio 44118
(self-determination inside)

Ohio Connections
P.O. Box 424
Dayton, Ohio 45202

Operation PRIDE
359 Drew Ct.
Springfield, Ohio 45506
    (513-325-7391)
    Att: L. Kent or "Ed"

Prisoner Education
Mather Bldg.
Case Western Reserve University
Cleveland, Ohio 44106
(information center for prison
reform)

7th Step Foundation
133 E. Market Street
Akron, Ohio 44308
    Att: Roger A. Crial, Ass't
    Employment Dir.
(job counselling, parolee and
youth counselling, recreational
facilities, etc.)

7th Step Foundation
P.O. Box 788
Mansfield, Ohio 44901
(prerelease program inside
institution)

Violet J. Tarcai, Attorney
2929 East Overlook Road
Cleveland Heights, Ohio 44118
(postrelease rehabilitation)

Oklahoma
Freedom Center Inc.
Personal Incentive Involvement
    Program
2609 N. Eastern
Oklahoma City, Okla. 73111
    (405-424-5268)

On the Bricks, Inc.
c/o Jim
P.O. Box 3426
Tulsa, Okla. 74150
(halfway house for ex-cons)

Oklahoma State Employment
    Service
Correctional Program
    Coordinating Unit
824 South Boston Ave.
Tulsa, Okla. 74119
    Att: Mr. W.T. Hendren
(employment program for
ex-offenders)

State Employment Service
4th and Boston
500 Mid-Continent Bldg.
Tulsa, Okla. 74103
(jobs)

U.S. Jaycees
P.O. Box 7
Tulsa, Okla. 74101
    Att: Lloyd Bandy, Program
    Manager
(crime prevention programs)

Oregon
Con-tact Community, Inc.
215 S.E. 9th
Portland, Oregon 97214
    Att: Maurice Pellon
(live-in community; houses for
ex-cons)

Oregon Corrections Reform
    Information Center
University of Oregon School of
    Law
Eugene, Oregon 97403
    Att: Herbert W. Titus
(draft and direct reform
legislation)

Oregon (cont'd)

The Self-Help Program
2785 Hamilton Lane
Grants Pass, Oregon 97526
    Att: Meta M. Burke
(group of ex-inmates and
civilians)

State Street Jaycees
2605 State St.
Salem, Oregon 97301
    Att: Larry Schildan, Pres.
(Jaycee prison chapter at Oregon
State Pen.)

Pennsylvania

The American Foundation
    Institute of Correction
1532 Philadelphia Nat'l Bank
    Bldg.
Philadelphia, Pa. 19107
    (215-563-3236)
    Att: Frank Loveland, Dir.
(goal: improve prison conditions)

The Barbwire Society
Community Organization for
    Ex-Prisoners
Institute for Black Ministry Bldg.
1200 North Broad St.
Philadelphia, Pa. 19121
    (215-232-6876; 232-0824)
(nonprofit community organization; Bd. of Dirs. are ex-offenders;
employment assistance; housing;
transportation for families to visit
prison)

Big Brothers of Bucks County
95 North Broad St.
Doylestown, Pa. 18901
    (215-348-8385)
(citizen group; "big brothers" to
inmates in juvenile detention
home and prison)

J. Stephen Bremer, Chaplain
Susquehanna University
Selingsgrove, Pa. 17870
(holds group meeting for inmates
at Lewisburg Pen.)

Pennsylvania (cont'd)

Bucks County Assoc. for
    Correction and Rehabil.
Bucks County Prison
Doylestown, Pa. 18901
    Att: Warden John D. Case
(citizens' group working with
Bucks County Prison)

CRIME (Committee for Rehabili-
    tation of Inmates Through
    Meaningful Exchange)
Drawer R.
Huntingdon, Pa. 16652
(group of 6 inmates dedicated to
prison reform and rehab.; want
to go on speaking engagements
to inform public)

Grubstake, Inc.
2400 E. Carson St.
Pittsburgh, Pa. 15203
    Att: Rev. Dom T. Orsini,
    Exec. Dir.
(community treatment center for
the young adult offender)

Mr. William R. Hawthorne
c/o The Pittsburgh
    Experiment Employment
    Anon.
705 Benedum-Trees Bldg.
Pittsburgh, Pa. 15222
(helps parolees and acts as a
parolee sponsor)

The Pennsylvania Prison Society
311 South Juniper St.
Philadelphia, Pa. 19017
(service and referral agency interested in prison reform; publish
newsletter concerning various
programs for convicts and ex-
offenders)

Re-Entry Associates
c/o Rev. D.F. Howells
R.F.D. #6
Dover, Pa. 17315
(for ex-offenders; parolees,
probationers)

Pennsylvania (cont'd)

St. Joseph's House of Hospitality
61 Tannehill St.
Pittsburgh, Pa. 15219
    Att: Tom O'Brien

The X-Offenders' Program
1712 N. 22nd St.
Philadelphia, Pa. 19121
(ex-inmates making community aware; jobs; supportive services)

Rhode Island

Challenge House
359 Blackstone St.
Providence, R. I.
(halfway house)

The Jericho Society
P.O. Box 1095
Brown University
Providence, R.I. 02912
(changing conditions of local prisons in R.I.)

National Prisoners Reform Assoc.
135 Dodge St.
Providence, R.I. 02907
(ex-cons, squares, etc.)

Opportunities
1491 Broad St.
Providence, R.I. 02905
    Att: Rev. Harry W. McIntire,
    Exec. Dir.
(assistance to former offenders)

South Carolina

Alston Wilkes Society
1515 Richland St.
P.O. Box 363
Columbia, South Carolina 29201
    Att: H. Parker Evatt, Exec. Dir.
(helps ex-cons)

Manpower, Inc.
27 Broad St.
Charleston, South Carolina 29401
(jobs)

South Dakota

CONcerned
417 South Roosevelt Rd.
Trailer No. 1
Aberdeen, South Dakota 57401
    Att: Hal J. Henry
(trying to start something like Fortune in S.D.)

Tennessee

P.A.S.T.
P.O. Box 621
Oak Ridge, Tenn. 37830
    Att: Ms. Ruth G. Barton
(works with inmates in Brushy Mt. State Pen.)

7th Step Foundation Inc.
Middle Tennessee Chapter
Station A. West
Nashville, Tenn. 37203
    Att: Alfred Recor

Utah

Salt Lake Community Mental
    Health Center
837 East South Temple
Salt Lake City, Utah 84102
(help to inmate families)

Vermont

ADDICT
139 Main St.
Brattleboro, Vermont 05301
c/o John Schuchardt
(squares and ex-inmates; prison reform and help to ex-cons and families)

Project One
39 Central St.
Woodstock, Vermont 05091
    Att: George Kemon, Dir.
(parolees operating workshops for ex-cons; speaking)

Virginia

Concerned, Inc.
P.O. Box 111
Virginia Beach, Va. 23458
Att: Mrs. Willow T. Wilson
(halfway house; helping released
prisoners; jobs; housing)

Job Development Project
7 North 2nd St.
Richmond, Va. 23219

Penal Reform Institute
110 N. Royal
Alexandria, Va. 22314

Puddledock House
2056 Puddledock Rd.
Petersburg, Va. 23803
(place for friends and family
when visiting prisoners at Petersburg)

Richmond Offender Aid
    Restoration Program
The Mosque, Rm. 300
Laurel & Main Streets
Richmond, Va. 23220

Tazewell House
6235 Powhatan Ave.
Norfolk, Va. 23508
    Att: James A. Hayes

Total Action Against Poverty
Vista Project
702 Shenandoah Ave. N.W.
Roanoke, Va. 24016
(working with inmates inside
prior to release)

Virginia Employment Commission
318 East Cary St.
Richmond, Va. 23219
(job information)

Washington

Cons Unlimited
304 K Hub, Box 78
University of Washington
Seattle, Wash. 98195
(ex-cons on campus)

Washington (cont'd)

Inside-Out
Prisoner Support Group
314 Champion St.
P.O. Box 918
Steilacoom, Wash. 98388
or:
1821 E. Howell
Seattle, Wash. 98122

Jail and Prison Rehabilitation
600 9th Ave. #606
Seattle, Wash. 98104
    Att: Ron Hanna, Prison
    Inmates' Coalition

Jail and Prison Rehabilitation
    Project
Citizens for Prison Reform
National Prison Inmates Coalition
P.O. Box 5313 K Street Station
Tacoma, Wash. 98405

M-2 Job Therapy, Inc.
2210 North 45th St.
Seattle, Wash. 98103
    Att: Nell Dwyer Jones
(job program)

North Seattle Community College
Student Prisoners' Coalition
9600 Burke Ave. North,
Rm. 3459B
Seattle, Wash. 98103
(student group trying to form organizations for inmates, etc.)

S.I.G.
c/o Catholic Chaplain
Lock Box 500
Steilacoom, Wash. 98388
(inside inmate help to refer inmates to organizations)

West Virginia

Robert F. Kennedy Youth Center
Morgantown, W.Va. 26505
(part of federal prison system's
self-sufficient community: 4 cottages, housing 64 youths; all
levels of education, remedial
through high school provided;
health services; recreational facilities)

Wisconsin

Miss Ann Bass
1909 North 14th St.
Milwaukee, Wis. 53205
(organizing families of inmates
at Wisconsin State Prison)

Horace Harris
Office of the Governor
Room 116 East
State Capitol
Madison, Wis. 53702

International Prisoners' Aid
    Assoc.
526 West Wisconsin
Milwaukee, Wis. 53203
    Att: Mrs. Ruch Bakee;
        Mary Louise Cox

Northcott Neighborhood House
2442 North Third Street
Milwaukee, Wis. 53212
(working with juveniles prior to
institutions, but also with ex-
offenders)

Wisconsin (*cont'd*)

State of Wisconsin
Dept. of Ind. Labor and Human
    Relations
State Office Bldg.
1. W. Wilson & Sheboygan
Madison, Wis. 54302
    Att: Joseph C. Fagan
(ex-cons on state payroll job
training)

Wise Correctional Services
436 Wisconsin Ave.
Milwaukee, Wis. 53703
    Att: Bob Sayner, Exec. Dir.
(self-help; social action)

Canada

The John Howard Society of
    Alberta
1104 9th St. S.W.
Calgary, 3, Alta.
Alberta, Canada

St. Leonard Society of Canada
c/o Rev. T.N. Libby
491 Victoria Ave.
Windsor, Ontario, Canada
    (519-256-1878)
(community residential center for
released prisoners)

BIBLIOGRAPHY

Books

Acton, H.   The Philosophy of Punishment.   New York, St. Martin's Press, Inc., 1969.

American Friends' Service Committee.   Struggle for Justice: A Report on Crime and Punishment in America.   New York, Hill & Wang, 1971.

Badillo, H. and Haynes, M.   A Bill of No Rights: Attica and the American Prison System.   New York, Outerbridge & Lazard, 1972.

Bennett, J.   Of Prisons and Justice.   Prepared for the Subcommittee on National Penitentiaries of the Committee on the Judiciary, United States Senate.   Washington, D.C., Government Printing Off., 1967.

Chaneles, S.   The Open Prison: Saving Their Lives and Our Money.   New York, Dial Press, 1973.

Emerging Rights of the Confined.   S.C. Dept. of Correction, 1972.

Gaylin, W.   In the Service of Their County: War Resistors in Prison.   New York, Viking Press, 1970.

Goldfarb and Singer.   The Shame of Prisons.   New York, Simon & Schuster, 1972.

Griswold, H. et al.   An Eye for an Eye: Four Inmates on the Crime of American Prisons Today.   New York, Holt, Rinehart & Winston, 1970.

Haft, M. and Hermann, M.   Prisoners' Rights, 2 vols.   New York, Practising Law Institute, 1972.

Kassebaum, G.   Prison Treatment and Parole Survival.   New York, Wiley Press, 1970.

Manual of Correctional Standards.   American Correctional Assn., 133 E. 15 St., New York, 1966 ed.

Perlman, H. and Alington, T., editors.   The Task of Penology: A Symposium on Prisons and Correction Law.   Lincoln, U. of Neb. Press, 1969.

Preliminary Report of the Governor's Special Committee on Criminal Offenders.   State of New York, 100 Church St., New York, 1968.

Rudovsky, D.   The Rights of Prisoners: ACLU Handbook.   New York, Avon Books, 1973.

Singer, R.   Prisoners' Legal Rights: A Bibliography of Cases and Articles.   Boston, Warren, Gorham & Lamont; 1971.

The Jailhouse Lawyer's Manual: How to Bring a Federal Suit Against Abuses in Prison.   San Francisco, Prison Law Collective, 1973.

United States Bureau of Prisons.   The Jail: Its Operation and Management.   Washington, Gov't Printing Off., 1970.

Wolfgang, J.   The Sociology of Punishment and Correction.   New York, Wiley Press, 1962.

Articles

A jam in the revolving door: a prisoners' right to rehabilitation. 1971. 60 Geo. L.J. 225.

American Bar Association. Young Lawyers Section. Administration of Criminal Law and Prison Reform Comm. October 1971. 1 Prison Law Reporter No. 1.

An endorsement of due process reform in parole revocation. Morrissey v. Brewer, 408 U.S. 471 (1972); also, 6 Loyola A.A. L. Rev. 157.

Ashman, A. Rhetoric and reality of prison reform. 1972. 56 Judicature 7.

Bargaining in correctional institutions: restructuring the relation between the inmate and the prison authority. 1972. 81 Yale L.J. 726.

Besharov, D. J. and Mueller, G. O. W. The demands of the inmates of Attica State Prison and the United Nations standard minimum rules for the treatment of prisoners: a comparison. 1972. 21 Buff. L. Rev. 839.

Beyond the ken of the courts: a critique of judicial refusal to review the complaints of convicts. 1963. 72 Yale L.J. 506.

Brierly, J. The legal controversy as it relates to correctional institutions: a prison administrator's view. 1971. 16 Vill. L. Rev. 1070.

Censorship of prisoners' mail and the constitution. 1970. 56 A.B.A.J. 1051.

Civil death. Summer 1970. 11 Wm. & Mary L. Rev. 988.

Civil disabilities of felons. 1969. 53 Va. L. Rev. 403.

Civil disability: the forgotten punishment. June 1971. 35 Fed. Probation 19.

Clements, T. and Ferguson, T. Judicial responsibility for prisoners: the process that is due. 1970/71. 4 Creighton L. Rev. 47.

Cohen, F. Sentencing, probation and the rehabilitative ideal: the view from Mempa v. Rhay. 1968. 47 Texas L. Rev. 1.

Cohen, F. The discovery of prison reform. 1972. 81 Buff. L. Rev.. 854.

Cohen, W. Due Process, equal protection and state parole revocation proceedings. 1970. 42 U. Colo. L. Rev. 197.

Comment: prisoners' rights and equal protection. 1970. 20 Am. U. L. Rev. 482.

Conditioning and other technologies used to "treat?" "rehabilitate?" "demolish?" prisoners and mental patients. 1972. 45 S. Cal. L. Rev. 616.

Condon, J. Procedural due process in prison disciplinary actions. 1971. 2 Loyola U. L.J. 110.

Confining solitary confinement: constitutional arguments for a "new penology." 1971. 56 Iowa L. Rev. 1251.

Constitutional law: due process clause of fourteenth amendment may require elementary procedural standards for prisoners in administration of prison discipline. 1972. 25 Vand. L. Rev. 1079.

Constitutional law—jailhouse lawyering—judicial sanction in Wisconsin state prisons. 1972. Wis. L. Rev. 300.

Constitutional law: prison "no-assistance" regulations and the jailhouse lawyer. 1968. Duke L.J. 343.

Constitutional law: prison officials' opening of inmates' outgoing mail and incoming mail from attorneys, courts and public officials violates first amendment rights of free speech. 1971. 22 Syracuse L. Rev. 818.

Constitutional law—prisoners' rights—prisoners have first amendment right to mail unsealed letters to the mass media. 1972. 6 Vand. L. Rev. 132.

Constitutional law—rights of state prisoners—federal court intervention in state prison administration. 1972. 5 Akron L. Rev. 295.

Constitutional law: statute excluding jail time from the computation of good time held denial of equal protection. 1972. 17 N.Y.L.F. 1153.

Convicts: legal status. 1948. 34 Va. L. Rev. 463.

Courts, corrections and the eighth amendment: encouraging prison reform by releasing inmates. 1971. 44 S. Cal. L. Rev. 1060.

Crawford, J. Prisoners' rights: a prosecutor's view. 1971. 16 Vill. L. Rev. 1055.

Criminal law: court orders broad relief to inmates throughout the Virginia penal system where constitutional rights have been violated. 1972. 22 Buff. L. Rev. 347.

Criminal law—penal reform—habeas corpus available to challenge conditions of confinement. 1972. 3 Rutgers Camden L.J. 601.

Criminal procedure—pretrial detainment—the jailer has duty to provide jail inmates "reasonable protection" and facilities conforming to state and local housing codes. 1972. 18 Wayne L. Rev. 1601.

Criminal procedure: re-arrest of parolees. 1970. 46 Wash. L. Rev. 175.

Decency and fairness: an emerging judicial role in prison reform. 1971. 57 Va. L. Rev. 841.

Dell, S. Remands in Custody. May 11, 1972. 122 New L.J. 418.

Discretionary power and procedural rights in the granting and revoking of probation. 1969. 60 J. Crim. L.C. & P.S. 479.

Due process in California prison disciplinary hearings. 1972. 5 U. Cal. Davis L. Rev. 384.

Duress and the prison escape: a new use for an old defense. 1972. 45 S. Cal. L. Rev. 1062.

Edward, D. Constitutional law—cruel and unusual punishment—conditions in prison render confinement unconstitutional. 1971. 45 Tul. L. Rev. 403.

Enforcing prisoners' rights. Dec.–Feb. 1970/71. 73 West Va. L. Rev. 38.

Escape: the defenses of duress and necessity. 1972. 6 U. San Francisco L. Rev. 430.

Ex-convicts' right to vote. 1967. 40 S. Cal. L. Rev. 148.

Feldman, G. Legal rights of prisoners. 1972. 28 Mo. B.J. 293.

Flint, D. Judicial response to problems of prison administration: an introductory note. June/July 1971. 55 Judicature 24.

Forys, C. Constitutional rights of prisoners. 1972. 55 Military L. Rev. 1.

Freudberg, L. Administrative decisions in prisons: are prisoners entitled to procedural due process? 1971. 2 Memphis S.U. L. Rev. 85.

Garson, G. Disruption of prison administration: an investigation of alternative theories of the relationships among administrators, reformers, and involuntary social service clients. 1972. 6 L. & Soc'y Rev. 531.

Gelhaus, R. Prisoner assistance on federal habeas corpus petitions. 1967. 19 Stan. L. Rev. 887.

Gill, H. New prison discipline. June 1970. 34 Fed. Probation 29.

Goldart, I. Corrections: the plight of reform. Summer 1971. 1 U. Md. L.J. 27.

Goldberg, H. Civil rights: prisons and prisoners. 1970. 5 Suffolk U. L. Rev. 259.

Goldfarb, R. and Singer, L. Redressing prisoners' grievances. 1970. 39 Geo. Wash. L. Rev. 175.

Greenberg, D. F. and Stender, F. The prison as a lawless agency. 1972. 21 Buffalo L. Rev. 799.

Haynor, N. Attitudes toward conjugal visits for prisoners. 1972. 35 Fed. Probation 19.

Hirschkop, P. The rights of prisoners, in The Rights of Americans: What They Are—What They Should Be, 451 (N. Dorsen, ed. New York, Pantheon, 1970).

Hirschkop, P. and Millemann, M. The unconstitutionality of prison life. 1969. 55 Va. L. Rev. 795.

Hollen, C. Emerging prisoners' rights. 1972. 33 Ohio State L.J. 1.

Jablonski, J. Resolving civil problems of corrections inmates. 1969. Wis. L. Rev. 574.

Jacob, B. Prison discipline and inmates' rights. 1970. 5 Harv. Civ. Rights-Civ. Lib. L. Rev. 227.

Jacob, B. and Sharma, K. Justice after trial: prisoners' need for legal services in the criminal-correctional process. 1970. U. Kan. L. Rev. 493.

Jobson, K. Fair procedure in parole. 1972. 22 U. Toronto L.J. 267.

Judicial limitations upon discretionary authority in the penal process. 1972. 8 Calif. W. L. Rev. 505.

King, D. Religious freedom in the correctional institution. 1969. 60 J. Crim. L.C. & P.S. 299.

Krause, M. A lawyer looks at writ-writing. 1968. 56 Calif. L. Rev. 343.

Larsen, C. A prisoner looks at writ-writing. 1968. 56 Calif. L. Rev. 343.

Legal rights for prisoners. March 1972. 53 Chi. B. Rec. 273.

Margolis, E.   No more prison reform!   1972.   46 Conn. B.J. 448.

Marnell, G.   Comparative correctional systems: United States and Sweden.   1972.   8 Crim. L. Bull. 748.

Martinson, R.   Collective behavior at Attica.   1972.   36 Fed. Probation 3.

Mayhew, S.   Prisoners' rights: personal security.   1970.   42 Colo. L. Rev. 305.

Meyer, Jr., J.   Change and obstacles to change in Prison Management. 1972.   36 Fed. Probation 39.

Millemann, M.   Prison disciplinary hearings and procedural due process: the requirement of a full administrative hearing.   1971.   31 Md. L. Rev. 27.

Model act to provide for minimum standards for the protection of rights of prisoners.   Jan. 1972.   18 Crime and Delinquency 4.

Moore, B.   Prisoners are people.   1970.   10 Natural Resources J. 869.

Parole revocation in the federal system.   1968.   56 Geo. L. J. 705.

Paulsen, M.   Prison reform in the future: the trend toward expansion of prisoners' rights.   1971.   16 Vill. L. Rev. 1082.

Penal ombudsman: a step toward penal reform.   1972.   3 Pacific L.J. 166.

Pepper, C.   Judicial activism in prison reform.   1972.   22 Catholic U. L. Rev. 96.

Pirsig.   The constitutional validity of confining disruptive delinquencies in penal institutions.   1969.   54 Minn. L. Rev. 101.

Plotkin, R.   Enforcing prisoners' rights to medical treatment.   1973. 9 Crim. L. Bull. 159.

Prisoner classification and administrative decision making.   1972.   50 Tex. L. Rev. 1229.

Prisoners' constitutional rights: segregated confinement as cruel and unusual punishment.   1972.   Wash. U. L. Q. 347.

Prisoners' redress for deprivation of a constitutional right: federal habeas corpus and the civil rights act.   1972.   4 St. Mary's L.J. 315.

Prisoners' rights: federal jurisdiction, due process, indefinite solitary confinement, censorship of mail, inmate legal assistance, freedom of expression and damages.   1972.   21 Buff. L. Rev. 539.

Prisoners' rights find a friend.   1972.   58 A.B.A.J. 91.

Prisoners' rights—first amendment—state prison censorship procedures must include "rudimentary" elements of procedural due process for protection of prisoners' first amendment right to receive literature and magazines.   1972.   47 N.Y.U. L. Rev. 985.

Prisoners' rights: habeas corpus petitions of state prisoners stating claims cognizable under the civil rights act of 1871 to be read by the federal courts as civil rights actions thus circumventing the habeas exhaustion requirement.   1972.   17 Vill. L. Rev. 980.

Prisoners' rights: personal security.   1970.   42 U. Colo. L. Rev. 305.

Prisoners' rights under section 1983. 1969. 57 Geo. L.J. 1270. Also: 1970. 6 Crim. L. Bull. 237.

Prisons—escape—necessity as a defense. 1972. 37 Mo. L. Rev. 550.

Prisons: state must devise system ensuring indigent prisoners meaningful access to the court. 1972. 21 Buffalo L. Rev. 987.

Religious freedom in prison: free exercise vs. the need for prison security. 1972. 36 Albany L. Rev. 416.

Revolution in Corrections. 1973. 22 Drake L. Rev. 250.

Roth, R. Habeas corpus vs. prison regulations: a struggle in constitutional theory. 1971. 54 Marq. L. Rev. 50.

Rothman, D. Invention of the penitentiary. 1972. 8 Crim. L. Bull. 555.

Rubin, S. Man with a record: a civil rights problem. Sept. 1971. 35 Fed. Probation 3.

Saunders, H. Civil death: a new look at an ancient doctrine. 1970. 11 Wm. & Mary L. Rev. 988.

Schwartz, H. A comment on Sostre v. McGinnis. 1972. 21 Buffalo L. Rev. 775.

Schwartz, H. Prisoners' rights and the courts. June 10, 1971. 165 N.Y.L.J. 1, 4. Also: June 11, 1971. 165 N.Y.L.J. 1, 4.

Schwartz, et al. Due process in prison disciplinary proceedings. 1972. 29 Guild Practitioner 79.

Selected materials on prisoners' rights. 1972. 27 Record of N.Y.C. B.A. 188.

Singer, R. Bringing the constitution to prison: substantive due process and the eighth amendment. 1970. 39 U. Cin. L. Rev. 650.

Singer, R. Privacy, autonomy, and dignity in the prison: a preliminary inquiry concerning constitutional aspects of the degradation process in our prisons. 1972. 21 Buffalo L. Rev. 669.

Smith, J. Prison reform through the legislature. 1972. 29 Guild Practitioners 69.

Sneidman, B. Prisoners and medical treatment. 1968. 4 Am. L. Bull. 450.

Snowden, J. Statutory right to treatment for prisoners: society's right of self-defense. 1971. 50 Neb. L. Rev. 543.

Standard minimum rules for treatment of prisoners. 1969. 2 N.Y.U.J. Int'l L. & Pol. 314.

State liability to innocent prisoners in prison uprisings. 1972. 29 Wash. & Lee L. Rev. 119.

Symposium: court and prison reform. 1972. 6 Suffolk U. L. Rev. 775.

Symposium: prisoners' rights. 1972. 63 J. Crim. L. 154.

Symposium: sentencing and corrections. 1972. 11 Am. Crim. L. Rev. 1.

Symposium: the right to treatment. 1967. 57 Geo. L.J. 673.

Symposium: the right to treatment. 1969. 31 U. Chi. L. Rev. 742.

Tepper, J. and Fitch, T. Prison reform cases. Nov. 1971. 30 Nat'l Legal Aid & Defender Ass'n 54.

The cruel and unusual punishment clause and substantive criminal law. 1966. 79 Harv. L. Rev. 635.

The equal protection clause as a limitation on the state's power to disenfranchise those convicted of a crime. 1967. 21 Rutgers L. Rev. 299.

The right of counsel in parole release hearing. 1968. 54 Iowa L. Rev. 497.

The right of expression in prison. 1967. 40 S. Cal. L. Rev. 407.

The rights of the probationer: a legal limbo. 1967. 28 U. Pitt. L. Rev. 643.

The role of the eighth amendment in prison reform. 1971. 38 U. Chi. L. Rev. 647.

Tibbes, L. Ombudsman for American prisons. 1972. 48 N.D. L. Rev. 383.

"Turn 'em loose"—towards a flexible corrections system. 1969. 42 S. Cal. L. Rev. 682.

Turner, W. Establishing the rule of law in prisons: a manual for prisoners' rights litigation. 1971. 23 Stan. L. Rev. 473.

Turner, W. B. and Daniel, A. Miranda in prison: the dilemma of prison discipline and intramural crime. 1972. 21 Buff. L. Rev. 759.

42 U.S.C. Section 1983: an emerging vehicle of post-conviction relief for state prisoners. 1970. U. Fla. L. Rev. 305.

von Hirsch, A. Prediction of criminal conduct and preventive confinement of convicted persons. 1972. 21 Buff. L. Rev. 717.

Wagner, A. Sentence credit for "dead time." 1972. 8 Crim. L. Bull. 393.

Wexler, D. Jailhouse lawyer as a paraprofessional. Mar. 1971. 7 Crim. L. Bull. 139.

Yelich, S. The "hidden penalty"—criminal offenders' loss of rights. Dec. 18, 1970. 164 N.Y.L.J. 1, 4.

Zeigler, D. and Hermann, M. Invisible litigant: an inside view of pro se actions in the federal courts. 1972. 47 N.Y.U. L. Rev. 159.

TABLE OF CASES

References are to pages

A

Ackies v. Purdy, 322 F. Supp. 38 (S.D. Fla. 1970), 727; 728

Adams v. City of Park Ridge, 293 F.2d 585 (7th Cir. 1961), 294 n49

Advertising Specialty Nat'l Assn. v. Federal Trade Comm'n, 238 F.2d 108 (1st Cir. 1956), 292 n32

Alvarez v. Turner, 422 F.2d 214 (10th Cir. 1970), 86 n52

American Airlines, Inc. v. Transport Workers Union, 44 F.R.D. 47 (N.D. Okla. 1968), 292 n32

American Fidelity & Cas. Co. v. Owensboro Milling Co., 222 F.2d 109 (6th Cir. 1955), 294 n52

American Trading & Prod. Corp. v. Fischbach & Moore, Inc., 47 F.R.D. 155 (N.D. Ill. 1969), 293 n35

Anders v. California, 386 U.S. 738 (1967), 513 n20

Anderson v. Laird, 466 F.2d 283 (D.C. Cir. June 30, 1972), cert. denied — U.S. — (1972) No. 72-653, December 18, 1972, 367 n70

Anderson v. Nosser, 456 F.2d 835 (5th Cir. 1972), 115 n13; 126 n21; 170 n44; 172 n64; 295 n56; 524 n33

Antelope v. George, 211 F. Supp. 657 (D. Idaho 1962), 319 n11

Aptheker v. Secretary of State, 378 U.S. 500 (1964), 722

Arciniega v. Freeman, 404 U.S. 4 (1971), 67 n3; 207 n35; 586 n71

Arif v. McGrath (E.D.N.Y., Dec. 9, 1971), 297 n68; 300 n79; 301 n84

Arkadiele v. Markley, 186 F. Supp. 586 (S.D. Ind. 1960), 371 n99

Armstrong v. Cardwell, 457 F.2d 34 (6th Cir. 1972), 244 n8

Armstrong v. Manzo, 380 U.S. 545 (1965), 82 n25; 92 n94

Arthur v. Schoonfield, 315 F. Supp. 548 (D. Md. 1970), 256 n3

Askew v. Hargrave, 401 U.S. 476 (1971), 73 n44

B

Bailey v. Patterson, 323 F.2d 201 (5th Cir. 1963), 297 n66

Bailey v. Patterson, 369 U.S. 31 (1962), 263 n71

Bailey v. Richardson, 182 F.2d 46 (D.C. Cir. 1950), aff'd per curiam 341 U.S. 918 (1951), 89 n76

Baker v. Hamilton, 345 F. Supp. 345 (W.D. Ky. 1972), 359 n7

Baker v. Henderson, No. 16, 746 (N.D. Ga. Oct. 5, 1972), 70 n30

Ball v. United States, 402 F.2d 206 (D.C. Cir. 1968), 723

Bandy v. United States, 81 S. Ct. 197, 5 L. Ed. 2d 218 (1960), 729

Banks v. Norton, 346 F. Supp. 917 (D. Conn. 1972), 256 n1

Banks v. United States, 414 F.2d 1150 (D.C. Cir. 1969), 723; 728

Banner v. Smolenski, 315 F. Supp. 1076 (D. Mass. 1970), 730

Banning v. Looney, 213 F.2d 771 (10th Cir. 1954), 520 n10

Barnett v. Rodgers, 410 F.2d 995 (D.C. Cir. 1969), 67 n4; 71 n35; 126 n17

References are to pages

Barry v. Hall, 98 F.2d 222 (D.C. Cir. 1938), 87 n62

Barsky v. Board of Regents, 347 U.S. 442 (1954), 230 n88, n89

Barth v. Oswald, No. 72 Civ. 3775 (S.D.N.Y. Nov. 6, 1972), 69 n18

Basista v. Weir, 340 F.2d 74 (3d Cir. 1965), 262 n57; 323 n42

Batchelder v. Geary, 1 Prisoners' Rights Newsletter 39 (April 1972), —— F. Supp. ——, Civ. C-71-2017 (N.D. Cal. November 12, 1972), 175 n91

Baxstrom v. Herold, 383 U.S. 107 (1966), 87 n62; 362 n25; 405 n1; 407 n8; 409 n13, n14; 410 n15; 734

Bearden v. South Carolina, 443 F.2d 1090 (4th Cir. 1971), 96 n133; 742

Belknap v. Leary, 427 F.2d 496 (2d Cir. 1970), 297 n67; 303 n107

Bell v. Burson, 402 U.S. 535 (1971), 81 n21; 96 n137; 727

Bellamy v. Judges and Justices of New York, etc., 41 A.D.2d 196 (2d Dep't 1973), aff'd 32 N.Y.2d — (1973), 133; 719 (brief)

Berman v. Narragansett Racing Ass'n., Inc., 414 F.2d 311 (1st Cir. 1969), 293 n39, n41

Bethea v. Crouse, 417 F.2d 504 (10th Cir. 1969), 115 n12

Bey v. Connecticut State Board of Parole, 443 F.2d 1079 (2d Cir. 1971), 742

Biehunik v. Felicetta, 441 F.2d 228 (2d Cir. 1971), cert. denied 403 U.S. 932 (1971), 300 n81; 325 n57

Birdsong, In re, 39 F. 599 (S.D. Ga. 1889), 302 n101

Bivens v. Six Unknown Fed. Narc. Agents, 403 U.S. 388 (1971), 173 n76

Brenneman v. Madigan, 343 F. Supp. 128 (N.D. Cal. 1972), 115 n8; 127 n22; 323 n32

Brooks v. Florida, 389 U.S. 413 (1967), 116 n21; 117 n29; 125 n4

Brooks v. Moss, 242 F. Supp. 531 (W.D.S.C. 1965), 323 n42

Broughton v. Brewer, 298 F. Supp. 260 (S.D. Ala. 1969), 292 n34

Brown v. Bd. of Education, 347 U.S. 483 (1954), 44 n19; 256 n9

Brown v. Board of Education, 349 U.S. 294 (1955), 93 n108

Brown v. Kearney, 355 F.2d 199 (5th Cir. 1966) (dictum), 207 n30

Brown v. Peyton, 437 F.2d 1228 (4th Cir. 1971), 67 n4; 69 n19; 70 n26; 71 n35

Brown v. Wainwright, 464 F.2d 1034 (5th Cir. 1972), 521 n16

Bryant v. Hendrick, 7 Crim. L. Rep. 2463 (Ct. C.P. Phila., Pa., Aug. 17, 1971), aff'd sub nom. Pennsylvania v. Hendrick, 444 Pa. 83, 280 A.2d 110 (1971), 115 n8; 169 n36; 175 n89a; 256 n5; 271 n106; 288 n2

Bryant v. Wilkins, 45 Misc. 2d 923, 258 N.Y.S. 2d 455 (Sup. Ct. Wyo. County 1965), rev'd 24 A.D.2d 1077, 265 N.Y.S.2d 995 (4th Dept. 1965), 42 n14

BUILD of Buffalo v. Sedita, 441 F.2d 284 (2d Cir. 1971), 291 n20; 294 n47; 295 n57

Bundy v. Cannon, 328 F. Supp. 165 (D. Md. 1971), aff'd sub nom. Jones v. Metzger, 456 F.2d 854 (6th Cir. 1972), 79 n7; 80 n11, n13, n14, n15, n16; 84 n41, n43; 86 n53, n56; 90 n84; 91 n86, n89; 92 n97; 93 n105; 94 n111, n121, n123; 257 n16; 267 n93; 271 n106; 301 n94; 320 n17; 361 n24; 742; 746; 748; 749

Burnham v. Oswald, 342 F. Supp. 880 (W.D.N.Y. 1972), 69 n18; 471 n47

Burroughs v. Wainwright, 464 F.2d 1027 (5th Cir. 1972), 521 n16

Bush v. Babb, 23 Ill. App.2d 285, 162 N.E.2d 594 (1959), 170 n44

References are to pages

C

Cafeteria & Restaurant Workers Union v. McElroy, 367 U.S. 886 (1961), 81 n21; 89 n75

Campbell v. Beto, 460 F.2d 765 (5th Cir. 1972), 116 n18; 246 n23; 411 n17; 520 n13; 521 n15

Campbell v. Rodgers, Civil No. 1462-71 (D.D.C. Nov. 10, 1971), amended (D.D.C. Jan. 11, 1972), 257 n16

Canavari v. Richardson, 419 F.2d 1287 (9th Cir. 1969), 586 n72

Caperci v. Huntoon, 397 F.2d 799 (1st Cir. 1968), cert. denied 393 U.S. 940 (1968), 323 n42

Carothers v. Follette, 314 F. Supp. 1014 (S.D.N.Y. 1970), 68 n8, n11; 118 n32; 246 n20; 256 n6; 260 n46; 262 n61

Carrington v. Rash, 380 U.S. 89 (1965), 88 n67

Carter v. Carlson, 447 F.2d 358 (D.C. Cir. 1971), cert. granted sub nom. District of Columbia v. Carter, 404 U.S. 1014 (1972), 294 n51

Carter v. Gallagher, 452 F.2d 315 (8th Cir. 1971), 228 n78

Carter v. Stanton, 405 U.S. 669 (1972), 246 n20

Caulder v. Durham Housing Authority, 433 F.2d 998 (4th Cir. 1970), cert. denied 401 U.S. 1003 (1971), 730

Cender v. Lindsay (E.D.N.Y., Nov. 23, 1970), 287 n1; 290 n12; 295 n58; 296 n62; 303 n107

Checker Motors Corp. v. Chrysler Corp., 405 F.2d 319 (2d Cir. 1969), 297 n65

Choice v. Johnson, —— F. Supp. ——, 12 Crim L. Rep. 2298 (E.D. Pa. Dec. 28, 1972), 70 n24

Church v. Hegstrom, 416 F.2d 449 (2d Cir. 1969), 116 n19

City Line Center, Inc. v. Loews, Inc., 178 F.2d 267 (3d Cir. 1949), 297 n64

Clairol, Inc. v. Gillette Co., 389 F.2d 264 (2d Cir. 1968), 297 n65

Clay v. United States, 403 U.S. 698 (1971), 730

Close v. United States, 397 F.2d 686 (D.C. Cir. 1968), 323 n41

Clutchette v. Procunier, 328 F. Supp. 767 (N.D. Calif. 1971), 79 n7; 91 n86; 94 n111; 95 n127, n128; 246 n21; 256 n12; 300 n82; 301 n94; 320 n17; 465 n17; 466 n19; 609 (complaint); 742; 748

Coffin v. Reichard, 143 F.2d 443 (6th Cir. 1944), cert. denied 355 U.S. 887 (1945), 244 n3, n9; 260 n44; 299 n75; 363 n45

Coppinger v. Townsend, 398 F.2d 392 (10th Cir. 1968), 116 n17, 168 n28, n30

Coleman v. Johnson, 247 F.2d 273 (7th Cir. 1957), 167 n18

Colligan v. United States, 349 F. Supp. 1233 (E.D. Mich. 1972), 320 n20

Collins v. Schoonfield, 344 F. Supp. 257 (D. Md. 1972), 79 n7; 91 n86; 91 n90, n91; 92 n98, n99; 94 n111; 95 n124; 96 n131, n139; 127 n22; 261 n51; 265 n83, n84; 324 n51; 626 (notice of class action); 628 (interrogatories); 658 (request for production of documents); 661 (deposition of a friendly expert witness); 742; 746; 748; 749

Comings v. State Board of Education, 23 Cal. App.3d 94, 100 Cal. Reptr. 73 (1972), 231 n95

Commonwealth v. Daniel, 430 Pa. 642, 243 A.2d 400 (Sup. Ct. Pa. 1968), 342 n5

Commonwealth v. Page, 159 N.E. 2d 82 (Mass. 1959), 362 n26

Commonwealth ex rel. Bryant v. Hendrick, 444 Pa. 83, 280 A.2d 110 (1971
See: Bryant v. Hendrick

References are to pages

Commonwealth ex rel. Cole v. Tahash, 269 Minn. 1, 129 N.W.2d 903 (1964), 261 n52

Conklin v. Hancock, 334 F. Supp. 1119 (D.N.H. 1971), 745; 751

Conley v. Gibson, 355 U.S. 41 (1957), 246 n22; 521 n15

Cooper v. Pate, 382 F.2d 518 (7th Cir. 1967), 71 n35

Cooper v. Pate, 378 U.S. 546 (1964), 67 n1; 71 n34; 166 n9; 301 n97

Coppinger v. Townsend, 398 F.2d 392 (10th Cir. 1968), 116 n17; 168 n28, n30

Corby v. Conboy, 457 F.2d 251 (2d Cir. 1972), 116 n19

Coskery v. Roberts & Mander Corp., 97 F. Supp. 14 (E.D. Pa.), appeal dismissed, 189 F.2d 234 (3d Cir. 1951), 293 n41

Cotton v. United States, 355 F.2d 480 (10th Cir. 1966), 371 n95

Cotton v. United States, 446 F.2d 107 (8th Cir. 1971), 371 n93

Courtney v. Bishop, 409 F.2d 1185 (8th Cir. 1969), 116 n24

Covington v. Harris, 419 F.2d 617 (D.C. Cir. 1969), 87 n63, n64, n65; 362 n25; 411 n17; 722

Cruz v. Beto, 405 U.S. 319 (1972), 67 n2; 70 n28; 71 n34; 246 n22; 301 n97

Cruz v. Hauck, 404 U.S. 59 (1971), 520 n12

Curley v. Gonzales, Civ. Nos. 8372, 8373 (D. N.Mex. Feb. 13, 1970), 126 n15; 325 n59

D

Dailey v. City of Lawton, Okla., 425 F.2d 1037 (10th Cir. 1970), 294 n49

Dalrymple, Matter of, 5 Ed. Dep't Reps. 113 (1966), 365 n57

Daniels v. Brown, 349 F. Supp. 1288 (E.D. Va. 1972), 320 n19

Davis v. Lindsay, 321 F. Supp. 1134 (S.D.N.Y. 1970), 126 n12; 300 n82

Dawson v. Carberry, No. C-71-1916 (N.D. Calif., filed Sept. 1971), 347 n22; 348 n25

Dean Milk Co. v. Madison, 340 U.S. 349 (1951), 723

Dearman v. Woodson, 429 F.2d 1288 (10th Cir. 1970), 115 n14; 117 n30

Demarco v. Edens, 390 F.2d 836 (2d Cir. 1968), 292 n28

Dennson v. Tomkins, 464 F.2d 1033 (5th Cir. 1972), 521 n16

DeVeau v. Braisted, 363 U.S. 144 (1960), 229 n84, n85

Dewitt v. Wilkins, 335 F.2d 1 (2d Cir. 1964), 323 n41

Dierks v. Thompson, 414 F.2d 453 (1st Cir. 1969), 293 n41

Dino DeLaurentis Cinematografica, S.p.A. v. D-150, Inc., 366 F.2d 373 (2d Cir. 1966), 297 n65

Dioguardi v. Durning, 139 F.2d 774 (2d Cir. 1944), 504 n8

Director of Patuxent Institution v. Daniels, 243 Md. 16, 221 A.2d 397 (1966), 189 n2; 413 n23; 414 n26, n28

District of Columbia v. Carter, 404 U.S. 1014 (1972)
See: Carter v. Carlson

Dixon v. Alabama State Bd. of Education, 294 F.2d 150 (5th Cir. 1961), 94 n114

Doe v. Bell, 1 Prison L. Rep. 189 (N.D. Ohio Oct. 19, 1971), 69 n23

Dombrowski v. Pfister, 380 U.S. 479 (1965), 299 n76

Domingues v. Mosley, 431 F.2d 1376 (10th Cir. 1970), 168 n28, n30

Dorado v. Kerr, 454 F.2d 892 (9th Cir. 1972), 247 n26

Douglas v. California, 372 U.S. 353 (1963), 157

Douglas v. Siegler, 386 F.2d 684 (8th Cir. 1967), 82 n29; 85 n48; 92 n101

References are to pages

Dreyer v. Jalet, 349 F. Supp. 452 (S.D. Tex. 1972), 246 n23

Driver v. Hinnant, 356 F.2d 761 (4th Cir. 1966), 256 n3

Drown v. Portsmouth School District, 435 F.2d 1182 (1st Cir. 1970), cert. denied, 402 U.S. 972 (1971), 730

Duren v. Procunier, 1 Prison L. Rep. 279 (N.D. Cal. July 28, 1972), 69 n23

E

Edwards v. Duncan, 355 F.2d 993 (4th Cir. 1966), 168 n33

Edwards v. Sard, 250 F. Supp. 977 (D.D.C. 1966), 303 n106

Edwards v. Schmidt, 321 F. Supp. 68 (W.D. Wis. 1971), 246 n20

Eisen v. Carlisle & Jacquelin, 391 F.2d 555 (2d Cir. 1968), 292 n25, n32, n34; 293 n39

Elsberg v. Haynes, 257 F. Supp. 739 (W.D. Okla. 1966), 167 n19

Ernest v. Willingham, 406 F.2d 685 (10th Cir. 1971), 207 n33

Escalera v. New York City Housing Authority, 425 F.2d 853 (2d Cir.), cert. denied 400 U.S. 853 (1970), 94 n115; 730

Escobedo v. Illinois, 378 U.S. 478 (1964), 176 n97

F

Fagerstrom v. United States, 311 F.2d 717 (8th Cir. 1963), 371 n95

Fahey v. Mallonee, 332 U.S. 245 (1947), 96 n138

Fallis v. Toastmasters International, Inc., 467 F.2d 1389 (5th Cir. 1972), 521 n17

Faubus v. United States, 254 F.2d 797 (8th Cir. 1958), 263 n70

Ferguson v. Buchanan, Civil No. 64-107 (S.D. Fla., Mar. 12, 1965), 291 n22

Ferrell v. Huffman, C.A. No. 490-72-R (E.D. Va. 1972), 683 n2

Firkins v. Colorado, 434 F.2d 1232 (10th Cir. 1970), 586, n72

Fish v. United States, 254 F. Supp. 906 (D. Md. 1966), 371, n101, n106

Fitzgerald v. Jandreau, 16 F.R.D. 578 (S.D.N.Y. 1954), 293 n41

Flowers, In re, 292 F. Supp. 390 (E.D. Wis. 1968), 70 n24; 584, n54

Foote v. United States, 306 F. Supp. 627 (D. Nev. 1969), 191 n15

Ford v. Board of Managers, 407 F.2d 937 (3d Cir. 1969), 116 n24; 302 n104

Fortune Society v. McGinnis, 319 F. Supp. 901 (S.D.N.Y. 1970), 67 n4; 70 n26; 126 n16; 256 n7; 301 n96, n98; 320 n14

Foster v. City of Detroit, 405 F.2d 138 (6th Cir. 1968), 293 n35

F.P.C. v. Tennessee Gas Transmission Co., 371 U.S. 145 (1962), 96 n138

Freeley v. Henderson, 1 Prison L. Rep. 270 (N.D. Ga. June 29, 1972), 70 n29

French v. Bashful, 303 F. Supp. 1333 (E.D. La. 1969), 96 n133

Frierson v. Rogers, 289 F.2d 234 (5th Cir. 1961), 586 n72

Frontiero v. Richardson, —— U.S. ——, 41 L.W. 4609 (May 14, 1973), 348 n23

Frost v. Ciccone, 315 F. Supp. 899 (W.D. Mo. 1970), 191 n15

F.S. Royster Guano Co. v. Virginia, 253 U.S. 412 (1920), 156

Fuentes v. Shevin, 407 U.S. 67 (1972), 81 n21; 89 n78; 96 n137; 203 n9

Fulwood v. Clemmer, 206 F. Supp. 370 (D.D.C. 1962), 71 n35; 83 n32; 118 n32; 256 n10

Fulwood v. Stone, 394 F.2d 939 (D.C. Cir. 1967), 370 n89

References are to pages

Furman v. Georgia, 408 U.S. 238 (1972), 113 n1, n3, n4; 115 n10; 261 n49, n50; 523 n25; 525 n37

G

Gardner v. Thompkins, 464 F.2d 1031 (5th Cir. 1972), 521 n16

Garnes v. Taylor, Civ. No. 159-72 (D.D.C. filed January 25, 1972), 347 n22

Garren v. City of Winston-Salem, N.C., 439 F.2d 140 (4th Cir. 1971), 294 n49

Gates v. Collier, 349 F. Supp. 881 (N.D. Miss. 1972), 79 n1; 115 n7, n11; 322 n28; 324 n51; 325 n54

Gault, In re, 387 U.S. 1 (1967), 86 n60; 87 n61; 92 n94; 203 n12; 358 n2; 369 n79; 370 n91; 741

Gesicki v. Oswald, 336 F. Supp. 371 (S.D.N.Y. 1971), 343 n10; 359 n5

Gideon v. Wainwright, 372 U.S. 335 (1963), 203 n10

Gilmore v. Lynch, 319 F. Supp. 105 (N.D. Cal. 1970), aff'd sub nom. Younger v. Gilmore, 404 U.S. 15 (1971), 68 n11; 157; 244 n4; 245 n17; 246 n25; 247 n26; 260 n47; 262 n69; 301 n95

Gittlemacker v. Prasse, 428 F.2d 1 (3d Cir. 1970), 116 n20

Goble v. Bounds, 186 S.E.2d 638 (N.C. App. 1972), 369 n80

Goldberg v. Kelly, 397 U.S. 254 (1970), 81 n21, n23; 82 n24; 88 n68, n69, n70; 92 n94; 93 n102, n104, n109; 94 n116, n120; 96 n134, n137; 161; 209 n37; 210 n39; 227 n70; 729; 730; 742

Gomes v. Travisono, 353 F. Supp. 457 (D.R.I. 1973), 94 n113; 320 n16

Gonzales v. Maillard, —— F. Supp. —— (N.D. Cal. 1971), CCH Poverty L. Rep. ¶866, 359 n6

Goodchild v. Schmidt, 229 F. Supp. 149 (E.D. Wis. 1968), 168 n29, n30

Goodwin v. Oswald, 462 F.2d 1237, 1244 (2d Cir. 1972), 67 n4, n5; 68 n8; 72 n42; 291 n19

Goosby v. Osser, 409 U.S. 512 (1973), 72 n39

Graham v. Richardson, 403 U.S. 365 (1971), 85 n49; 227 n70

Gray v. Creamer, 465 F.2d 179 (3d Cir. 1972), 70 n31

Green v. Board of Elections, 380 F.2d 445 (2d Cir. 1967), 72 n37

Green v. McElroy, 360 U.S. 474 (1959), 82 n24; 93 n104, n107

Green v. Wolf Corp., 406 F.2d 291 (2d Cir. 1968), 293 n35

Gregory v. Litton Systems, Inc. 316 F. Supp. 401 (C.D. Calif. 1970), aff'd —— F.2d —— (9th Cir. 1972), 228 n75, n76, n77; 230 n91

Grene v. Britton, 455 F.2d 473 (5th Cir. 1972), 70 n30

Griffin v. Illinois, 351 U.S. 12 (1956), 157

Griggs v. Duke Power Company, 401 U.S. 424 (1971), 227 n72, n74

Griswold v. Connecticut, 381 U.S. 479 (1965), 82 n24; 366 n64

Gruzick v. Drebus, 431 F.2d 594 (6th Cir. 1970), cert. denied 401 U.S. 948, 365 n55

Guajardo v. McAdams, 349 F. Supp. 211 (S.D. Tex. 1972), 68 n12; 70 n27

H

Haas v. United States, 344 F.2d 56 (8th Cir. 1967), 69 n16

Hague v. CIO, 101 F.2d 774 (3d Cir. 1939), 319 n11

Haigh v. Sindow, 321 F. Supp. 324 (S.D. Cal. 1964), 167 n19

Haines v. Kerner, 404 U.S. 519 (1972), 176 n98; 246 n22; 301 n87

References are to pages

Hall v. Boslow, McCray v. Maryland, Clearinghouse No. 6493, 464 n8

Hamilton v. Love, 328 F. Supp. 1182 (E.D. Ark. 1971), 88 n71; 93 n109; 115 n8; 126 n13; 192 n16; 245 n14; 256 n5; 257 n16; 262 n58; 295 n59; 297 n68; 322 n27, n28; 722

Hamilton v. Schiro, 338 F. Supp. 1016 (E.D. La. 1970), 192 n16; 322 n30; 325 n56

Hancock v. Avery, 301 F. Supp. 786 (M.D. Tenn. 1969), 116 n21; 117 n29, n30; 302 n101

Hannah v. Larche, 363 U.S. 420 (1960), 81 n21

Hansberry v. Lee, 311 U.S. 32 (1940), 293 n37

Harkless v. Sweeny Indep. School Dist., 427 F.2d 319 (5th Cir. 1970), cert. denied 400 U.S. 991 (1971), 294 n49

Harman v. Forssennius, 380 U.S. 528 (1965), 88 n67

Harper v. Virginia Board of Elections, 383 U.S. 663 (1966), 157

Harrell, In re., 470 P.2d 640, 87 Cal. Rptr. 504 (Cal. 1970), 471 n43

Harris v. Nelson, 394 U.S. 286 (1969), 245 n13; 260 n40

Harvin v. United States, 445 F.2d 675 (D.C. 1971), 342 n5

Haskew v. Wainwright, 429 F.2d 525 (5th Cir. 1969), 168 n29, n30

Hatfield v. Bailleaux, 290 F.2d 632 (9th Cir. 1961), 247 n27; 262 n69

Hawker v. New York, 170 U.S. 189 (1898), 229 n86

Hawkins v. Board of Control, 253 F.2d 752 (5th Cir. 1958), 297 n64

Henderson v. Pate, 409 F.2d 407 (7th Cir. 1969), 168 n29, n30

Hewett v. North Carolina, 415 F.2d 1316 (4th Cir. 1969), 86 n59

Hickey v. Illinois Cent. R.R., 278 F.2d 529 (7th Cir. 1960), cert. denied 364 U.S. 918 (1960), 292 n28

Hirons v. Director, Patuxent Institution, 351 F.2d 614 (4th Cir. 1965), 168 n33

Hobbs v. Northeast Airlines, Inc., 50 F.R.D. 76 (E.D. Pa. 1970), 293 n35

Hobson v. Hansen, 269 F. Supp. 401 (D.C. Cir. 1967), appeal dismissed, 393 U.S. 801 (1969), 157; 158

Hodge v. Dodd, 1 Prison L. Rep. 263, Civ. A. No. 16171 (N.D. Ga. May 2, 1972), 126 n14; 323 n31

Hoggro v. Pontesso, 456 F.2d 917 (10th Cir. 1972), 67 n4; 70 n26

Holland v. Oliver, 350 F. Supp. 485 (E.D. Va. 1972), 320 n24

Holt v. Sarver, 309 F. Supp. 362 (E.D. Ark. 1970), aff'd 442 F.2d 304 (8th Cir. 1971), 79 n1; 88 n72, n73, n74; 93 n109; 114 n6; 116 n16, n21; 117 n29; 169 n37; 191 n15; 245 n17; 256 n5; 259 n33; 261 n50, n55; 271 n106; 289 n3; 291 n16; 292 n34; 301 n89, n93; 319 n4; 322 n28; 323 n34; 325 n58; 348 n24; 364 n51

Houghton v. Shafer, 392 U.S. 639 (1968), 246 n20; 301 n87; 521 n18

Housing Authority of Durham v. Thorpe, 386 U.S. 670 (1967), 730

Hudson v. Hardy, 424 F.2d 854 (D.C.C. 1970), 319 n12

Hugenot v. Wainwright, 464 F.2d 1077 (5th Cir. 1972), 521 n16

Hughes v. Noble, 295 F.2d 495 (5th Cir. 1961), 167 n21

Hull, Ex parte, 312 U.S. 546 (1941), 260 n47; 301 n95; 470 n40

Humphrey v. Cady, 405 U.S. 504 (1972), 195 n26; 245 n18

Hyland v. Procunier, 311 F. Supp. 749 (N.D. Cal. 1970), 72 n37; 206 n24

I

I.C.C. v. Louisville & N.R.R., 227 U.S. 88 (1913), 93 n104

References are to pages

Ilone I., Matter of, 64 Misc.2d 878, 316 N.Y.S.2d 356 (N.Y. 1970), 363 n35, n43

Indiana ex rel. Tyler v. Gobin, 94 F. 50 (C.C.D. Ind. 1899), 172 n60

Inmates of Attica Correctional Facility v. Rockefeller, 453 F.2d 12 (2d Cir. 1971), 115 n12; 245 n14; 287 n1; 289 n5; 291 n13, n15, n21, n23; 292 n34; 293 n38, n44; 295 n58; 297 n63, n65, n67; 298 n72; 300 n80; 301 n87, n88; 302 n99; 303 n107, n108, n109; 318 n3; 319 n4

Inmates of Cook County Jail v. Tierney, 4 Clearinghouse Rev. 388 (N.D. Ill. 1968), 169 n36; 175 n89a, n90; 291 n19, n22

Inmates of Greenhaven v. Zelker, Civil No. 71-4676 (E.D.N.Y., Nov. 15, 1971), 300 n82; 301 n84; 303 n105

Inmates of Rhode Island Boys Training School v. Affleck, 346 F. Supp. 1354 (D.R.I. 1972), 364 n47

Isenberg v. Prasse, 433 F.2d 449 (3d Cir. 1970), 168 n29, n30

Ivan v. City of New York, 407 U.S. 203 (1972), 373 n109

J

Jackson v. Bishop, 404 F.2d 571 (8th Cir. 1968), 83 n32; 115 n11; 118 n32; 246 n23; 291 n17; 292 n34; 301 n90; 302 n103

Jackson v. Godwin, 400 F.2d 529 (5th Cir. 1968), 67 n4; 83 n32; 260 n46; 522 n22

Jackson v. Hendrick, No. 71-2437 (Ct. C. P. Phila., Pa., April 7, 1972), 127 n22; 192 n16; 319 n6; 322 n28; 324 n53

Jackson v. Indiana, 406 U.S. 715 (1972), 195 n26; 405 n3; 407 n7; 408 n12; 412 n20

Jansson v. Grysen, 1 Prison L. Rep. 256 (W.D. Mich., June 1, 1972), 68 n12

Jeanette P., Matter of, 34 A.D.2d 661, 310 N.Y.S.2d 125 (2d Dep't 1970), lv. to app. denied 34 A.D.2d 657, 311 N.Y.S.2d 965 (N.Y. 1970), 363 n36

Jenkins, Ex parte, 25 Ind. App. 318 58 N.E. 560 (1906), 172 n60

Jenkins v. Averett, 424 F.2d 1228 (4th Cir. 1970), 319 n11

Jenkins v. United Gas Corp., 400 F.2d 28 (5th Cir. 1968), 291 n22

Johnson v. Avery, 393 U.S. 483 (1969), 68 n11; 83 n33; 95 n126; 260 n47; 301 n87, n95; 358 n1; 748

Johnson v. Georgia Highway Express, Inc., 417 F.2d 1122 (5th Cir. 1969), 292 n34

Johnson v. Rockefeller, —— F. Supp. ——, No. 1699 (S.D.N.Y. 1972), 173 n74

Joint Anti-Fascist Refugee Comm. v. McGrath, 341 U.S. 123 (1951), 81 n21; 82 n24; 97 n140

Jones v. Harris, 339 F.2d 585 (8th Cir. 1964), 191 n15

Jones v. Metzger, 456 F.2d 854 (6th Cir. 1972), 246 n20, n21 See: Bundy v. Cannon; Jones v. Wittenberg

Jones v. Robinson, 440 F.2d 249 (D.C. Cir. 1971), 87, n63; 411 n17; 731; 742

Jones v. Sharkey, —— F. Supp. ——, No. 4948 (D.R.I. June 12, 1972), 69 n23

Jones v. United States, 249 F.2d 864 (7th Cir. 1957), 172 n66

Jones v. United States, 358 F.2d 543 (D.C. Cir.), cert. denied 385 U.S. 868 (1966), 723; 728

Jones v. Wittenberg, 323 F. Supp. 93 (N.D. Ohio 1971), aff'd sub nom. Jones v. Metzger, 456 F.2d 854 (6th Cir. 1972), 115 n8, n9; 116 n16; 169 n36; 175 n89a; 192

References are to pages

n16, n17; 245 n14; 262 n58; 271 n106; 289 n3; 291 n19; 295 n59; 301 n93; 465 n17; 471 n46

Jones v. Wittenberg, 330 F. Supp. 707 (N.D. Ohio, 1971), 68 n12; 69 n23; 126 n12, n15; 127 n22; 192 n16; 245 n17; 323 n34, n35, n38, n40; 324, n47

Jordan, In re, 7 Cal. 3d 930, 500 P.2d 873 (1972), 68 n13

Jordan v. Fitzharris, 257 F. Supp. 674 (N.D. Cal. 1966), 116 n21; 117 n29, n30; 118 n32; 169 n37, n38; 171 n49; 256 n11; 261 n50; 262 n61; 271 n110; 301 n91; 302 n101; 324 n47

K

Kautter v. Reid, 183 F. Supp. 352 (D.D.C. 1960), 362 n29

Kendrick v. Adamson, 51 Ga. App. 402, 180 S.E. 647 (1935), 172 n60

Kennedy v. Mendoza-Martinez, 372 U.S. 144 (1963), 126 n10; 263 n71

Kent v. United States, 383 U.S. 541 (1966), 92 n94

Kirkland v. Hardy, 1 Prison L. Rep. 312 (D.D.C. June 22, 1972), 70 n32

Knauff v. Shaughnessy, 338 U.S. 537 (1950), 89 n76

Knights v. Auciello, 453 F.2d 852 (1st Cir. 1972), 258 n23

Knuckles v. Prasse, 302 F. Supp. 1036 (E.D. Pa. 1969), aff'd 435 F.2d 1255 (3d Cir. 1970), cert. denied 403 U.S. 936 (1971), 302 n104

Kostal v. Tinsley, 337 F.2d 845 (10th Cir. 1964), 82 n29

Krause v. Schmidt, 341 F. Supp. 1001 (W.D. Wisc. 1972), 79 n7; 91 n86; 94 n111; 96 n130; 742

L

Lack v. United States, 262 F.2d 167 (8th Cir. 1958), 172 n66

Lake Carriers Association v. Mac-Mullen, 406 U.S. 498 (1972), 246 n21

Lambert, In re, 134 Cal. 626, 66 P. 851 (1901), 87 n62

Lamont v. Postmaster General, 381 U.S. 301 (1965), 68 n6

Landman v. Peyton, 370 F.2d 135 (4th Cir. 1966), cert. denied 388 U.S. 920 (1967), 82 n30; 83 n31; 93 n107; 301 n87; 302 n104; 344 n9

Landman v. Royster, 333 F. Supp. 621 (E.D. Va. 1971), 12; 79 n1; 80 n11, n13, n14, n16, n17; 82 n24; 84 n43; 86 n56; 90 n84; 91 n86, n87, n89; 92 n100, n101; 93 n105; 94 n111; 95 n125; 96 n129, n132; 115 n13, n14, n15; 117 n30; 118 n32; 256 n12; 271 n108; 301 n94; 320 n17, n21, n22, n23; 324 n49; 361 n21, n23; 465 n17; 468 n26; 680 (contempt opinion); 742; 748; 750

Lankford v. Gelston, 364 F.2d 197 (4th Cir. 1966), 291 n20; 292 n34; 297 n67; 303 n111

LaReau v. MacDougall, —— F.2d —— (2d Cir. December 15, 1972), 524 n30

Lawrence v. Willingham, 373 F.2d 731 (10th Cir. 1967), 191 n15

Leather's Best, Inc. v. S.S. Mormaclynx, 451 F.2d 800 (2d Cir. 1971), 294 n52

Lee v. Southern Homes Sites Corp., 444 F.2d 143 (5th Cir. 1970), 258 n23

Lee v. Washington, 390 U.S. 333 (1968), 301 n87
See: Washington v. Lee

Lessard v. Schmidt, —— F. Supp. —— (E.D. Wisc. 1972), CCH Poverty Law Rep. ¶16,255, 87 n62

Lesser v. Humphrey, 89 F. Supp. 474 (M.D. Pa. 1950), 248 n39

LeVier v. Woodson, 443 F.2d 360 (10th Cir. 1971), 68 n8

References are to pages

Levy v. Louisiana, 391 U.S. 68 (1968), 82 n24

Liberti v. York, 28 Conn. Supp. 9, 246 A.2d 106 (1968), 342 n5

Lindsey v. Normet, 405 U.S. 56 (1972), 246 n21

Lloyd, Matter of, 33 A.D.2d 385, 308 N.Y.S.2d 419 (1st Dep't 1970), 363 n36

Logue v. United States, 459 F.2d 408 (5th Cir. 1972), reh. denied, 463 F.2d 1340 (5th Cir. 1972), 248 n37

Lollis and Pena v. Wyman, 322 F. Supp. 473 (S.D.N.Y. 1970), 359 n11; 361 n20; 363 n43; 364 n47

Londerholm v. Owens, 197 Kan. 212, 416 P.2d 259 (1966), 363 n36

Long v. Parker, 390 F.2d 816 (3d Cir. 1968), 67 n4; 70 n26; 71 n35; 247 n32; 256 n10; 320 n15

Long v. Robinson, 316 F. Supp. 22 (D. Md. 1970), 88 n71; 93 n109

Long v. Robinson, 436 F.2d 1116 (4th Cir. 1971), 256 n3; 259 n34

Lopez Tijerina v. Ciccone, 324 F. Supp. 1265 (W.D. Mo. 1970), 177 n100

Love v. Hughes, —— F. Supp. ——, No. C-72-1081 (N.D. Ohio Oct. 27, 1972), 72 n40

Loving v. Virginia, 388 U.S. 1 (1967), 82 n24

Lunch v. Kenston School Dist. Bd. of Educ., 229 F. Supp. 740 (N.D. Ohio 1964), 292 n28

Lynch v. Quinlan, 317 N.Y.S.2d 216 (Dutch Co. Sup. Ct. 1970), 173 n74

M

McArthur v. Pennington, 253 F. Supp. 420 (E.D. Tenn. 1963), 294 n51; 319 n11

McArthur v. Scott, 113 U.S. 340 (1884), 293 n37

McCarty v. Woodson, 465 F.2d 822 (10th Cir. 1972), 246 n25; 247 n29

McClain v. Manson, 343 F. Supp. 382 (D. Conn. 1972), 344 n10

McClelland v. Sigler, 456 F.2d 1266 (8th Cir. 1972), 246 n20

McCloskey v. Maryland, 337 F.2d 72 (4th Cir. 1964), 82 n27, n29; 83 n35

McCollum v. Mayfield, 130 F. Supp. 112 (N.D. Cal. 1955), 167 n19; 170 n39

McCoy v. United States, 357 F.2d 272 (D.C. Cir. 1966), 723; 727

McCray v. Fondre, —— F.2d —— (5th Cir. 1972), 521 n16

McCray v. Maryland, Clearinghouse No. 6493, see: Hall v. Boslow, McCray v. Maryland

McCray v. Maryland, Misc. Pet. 4363 et seq. (Cir. Ct. for Montgomery County, Maryland, Nov. 18, 1971), 10 Crim. L. Rep. 2132, 79 n7; 91 n86; 94 n111; 259 n33; 261 n52; 466 n22; 471 n43, n44, n46; 742; 744; 748; 749

McCrossen v. State, 277 App. Div. 1160, 101 N.Y.S.2d 591, lv. to app. denied 302 N.Y. 950, 98 N.E.2d 117 (1950), 170 n39, n44

McDonald v. Board of Election Commissioners, 394 U.S. 802 (1969), 72 n38

McDonough v. Director of Patuxent, 429 F.2d 1189 (4th Cir. 1970), 260 n47

McKeiver v. Pennsylvania, 403 U.S. 528 (1971), 358 n3; 364 n46; 371 n93

McMann v. Richardson, 397 U.S. 759 (1970), 519 n7

McNeil v. Director, 407 U.S. 245 (1972), 194 n23

McQuade, Matter of, 6 Ed. Dep't Reps. 36 (1966), 365 n57

Maddox, In re, 351 Mich. 358, 88 N.W.2d 470 (1958), 191 n12

References are to pages

Madera v. Board of Education, 267 F. Supp. 356 (S.D.N.Y. 1967) rev'd 386 F.2d 778 (1967), cert. denied 390 U.S. 1028 (1968), 96 n133

Mahaffey v. State, 87 Idaho 228, 392 P.2d 279 (1964), 261 n52

Maltex v. Nagle, 27 F.2d 835 (9th Cir. 1928), 96 n136

Mansell v. Saunders, 372 F.2d 573 (5th Cir. 1967), 319 n11

Mapp v. Ohio, 367 U.S. 643 (1961), 176 n96

Marsh v. Moore, 325 F. Supp. 392 (D. Mass. 1971), 68 n13; 260 n47; 264 n76

Martarella v. Kelley, 349 F. Supp. 575 (S.D.N.Y. 1972), 359 n8, n10; 362 n27; 363 n34; 364 n48, n52; 413 n21

Martin v. Martin, 308 N.Y. 136, 123 N.E.2d 812 (1954), 367 n71

Martinez v. Mancusi, 443 F.2d 921 (2d Cir. 1970), cert. denied 401 U.S. 983 (1971), 116 n19; 168 n31, n32; 169 n34; 177 n99

Martinez v. Procunier, —— F. Supp. ——, 12 Crim. L. Rep. 2420 (N.D. Cal. Feb. 2, 1973), 68 n10; 70 n27

Matthews v. Hardy, 420 F.2d 607 (D.C. Cir. 1969), 297 n67

Mayer v. Chicago, 404 U.S. 15 (1971), 157

Mead v. Parker, 464 F.2d 1108 (9th Cir. 1972), 245 n15; 247 n30; 248 n34

Medlock v. Burke, 285 F. Supp. 67 (E.D. Wis. 1968), 168 n29, n30

Mempa v. Rhay, 389 U.S. 128 (1967), 86 n59; 96 n135; 203 n8; 741

Menechino v. Oswald, 430 F.2d 403 (2d Cir. 1970), 86 n52; 202 n6; 203 n7

Menechino v. Warden, 27 N.Y.2d 376, 267 N.E.2d 238, 318 N.Y.S. 2d 449 (1971), 207 n32; 209 n38; 727

Meola v. Fitzpatrick, 322 F. Supp. 878 (D. Mass. 1971), 79 n7; 91 n86; 94 n111; 742

Mercer v. United States Medical Center, 312 F. Supp. 1077 (W.D. Mo. 1970), 191 n15

Merritt v. Johnson, —— F. Supp. —— (No. 38401 E.D. Mich. Nov. 30, 1972), 68 n13

Mersay v. First Repub. Corp. of America, 43 F.R.D. 465 (S.D.N.Y. 1968), 292 n32; 293 n37

Meyer v. Nebraska, 262 U.S. 390 (1922), 367 n65

Meyers v. Aldrich, Civil No. 72-132 (M.D. Pa. June 16, 1972), appeal docketed, No. 72-1819 (3d Cir. Sept. 5, 1972), 256 n1

Meyers v. Alldredge, 348 F. Supp. 807 (M.D. Pa. 1972), 80 n19; 318 n3

Millard v. Cameron, 373 F.2d 468 (D.C. Cir. 1966), 162; 362 n26

Miller v. D.C. Board of Appeals and Review, 294 A.2d 365 (D.C. App. 1972), 223 n50; 232 n101a, n102, n103

Miller v. Overholser, 206 F.2d 415 (D.C. Cir. 1953), 362 n26

Milwaukee Social Democratic Publishing Co. v. Burleson, 255 U.S. 407 (1921), 68 n6

Minnesota v. U.S. Steel Corp., 44 F.R.D. 559 (D. Minn. 1968), 291 n32

Miranda v. Arizona, 384 U.S. 436 (1966), 176 n97

Monks v. New Jersey State Parole Bd., 58 N.J. 238, 277 A.2d 193 (1971), 202 n6; 203 n7; 204 n17; 205 n18; 347 n21; 472 n59; 474 n75; 730

Monroe v. Pape, 365 U.S. 167 (1961), 166 n9; 173 n75; 294 n50; 301 n87; 319 n11; 504 n7; 521 n18

Montgomery v. Oakley Training School, 426 F.2d 269 (5th Cir. 1970), 256 n9

Moody v. Flowers, 387 U.S. 97 (1967), 246 n24

Moore v. Ciccone, 459 F.2d 574 (8th Cir. 1972), 68 n11

Moore v. United States, 432 F.2d 730 (3d Cir. 1970) (in banc), 732

Morales v. Schmidt, 340 F. Supp. 544 (W.D. Wisc. 1972), 79 n2; 244 n3, n4

Morales v. Schmidt, 12 Crim. L. Rep. 2378, —— F.2d —— (7th Cir. 1973), rev'g 340 F. Supp. 544 (W.D. Wis. 1972), 67 n4; 526 n40

Morales v. Turman, 326 F. Supp. 677 (E.D. Tex. 1971), 68 n11; 358 n1; 359 n12, n13; 522 n24

Morgan v. United States, 304 U.S. 1 (1938), 96 n137

Morris v. Travisono, 310 F. Supp. 857 (D.R.I. 1970), 79 n7; 91 n86; 94 n111; 94 n121; 117 n27; 245 n14; 256 n12; 259 n35; 267 n91; 271 n106, n108; 466 n20; 469 n36, n37; 470 n38; 742; 748

Morrison v. State Board of Education, 461 P.2d 375 (Calif. 1969), 231 n95

Morrissey v. Brewer, 408 U.S. 471 (1972), 68 n6; 79 n5; 80 n8; 81 n20; 83 n36; 85 n50; 87 n65a, n66; 90 n82; 91 n85; 93 n104, n108; 94 n110, n111, n120; 207 n31; 208 n36; 209 n37; 210 n40; 360 n17; 526 n43; 587 n74; 604 n14

Muhammad Ali v. Division of State Athletic Commission, 316 F. Supp. 1246 (S.D.N.Y. 1970), 230 n87

Mullane v. Central Hanover Trust Co., 339 U.S. 306 (1950), 292 n25

Murchison, In re, 349 U.S. 133 (1955), 94 n120

Murel v. Baltimore City Criminal Court, 407 U.S. 355 (1972) See: Tippett v. Maryland

Murel v. Director, 240 Md. 258, 213 A.2d 576 (1965), 413 n23; 414 n26

Murphy v. Benson, 151 F. Supp. 786 (E.D.N.Y. 1957), 263 n70

Murray v. Owens, 465 F.2d 289 (2d Cir. 1972), 359 n7

N

Nason v. Superintendent of Bridgewater State Hospital, 353 Mass. 604, 233 N.E.2d 908 (1968), 189 n2; 362 n27; 363 n34; 413 n21

N.A.A.C.P., Inc. v. Button, 371 U.S. 415 (1963), 259 n36

N.A.A.C.P. v. Thompson, 357 F.2d 831 (5th Cir. 1966), 297 n67

N.L.R.B. v. Raytheon Co., 398 U.S. 25 (1970), 297 n66

National Prisoners' Rights Association v. Sharkey, 347 F. Supp. 1234 (D.R.I. 1970), 69 n23

Newman v. Alabama, 349 F. Supp. 278 (M.D. Ala. 1972), citing Novak v. Beto, 453 F.2d 661 (5th Cir. 1971), 165 n6; 176 n93; 193 n19; 323 n36, n39; 324 n48; 411 n17; 512 n18

Newman v. Piggie Park Enterprises, Inc., 390 U.S. 400 (1968), 258 n23; 323 n46

Nieves v. Oswald (W.D.N.Y., filed Nov. 16, 1971), 300 n82

Nieves v. United States, 280 F. Supp. 994 (S.D.N.Y. 1968), 371 n92; 372 n103

Noble Co. Council v. State, 234 Ind. 172, 125 N.E.2d 709 (1955), 261 n54

Nolan v. Fitzpatrick, 326 F. Supp. 209 (D. Mass. 1971), 260 n46; 301 n96

Nolan v. Fitzpatrick, 451 F.2d 545 (1st Cir. 1971), 68 n7; 69 n17; 126 n18; 471 n46

Nolan v. Scafati, 430 F.2d 548 (1st Cir. 1970), 256 n6

References are to pages

Nolan v. Smith, —— F. Supp. ——
(Nos. 6228, 6272, D. Vt. 7/1/71),
745; 751

Norwalk Core v. Norwalk Redevelopment Agency, 395 F.2d 920
(2d Cir. 1968), 292 n34

Novak v. Beto, 453 F.2d 661 (5th
Cir. 1971), rehearing en banc
denied, 456 F.2d 1303 (5th Cir.
1972), cert. denied sub nom.
Sellars v. Beto 409 U.S. 968
(1972), 68 n11; 79 n3; 115 n14;
116 n22; 118 n32; 512 n18; 524
n32, n34; 525 n36
See also: Newman v. Alabama

Novak v. Beto, 456 F.2d 1303 (5th
Cir. 1972), 113 n2

Novak v. McCune, —— F. Supp.
—— Civ. 421-72-R (E.D. Va. July
1972), 204 n14; 205 n20

Numer v. Miller, 165 F.2d 986 (9th
Cir. 1940), 580 n23

O

O'Brien v. Blackwell, 421 F.2d 844
(5th Cir. 1970), 249 n40

Ojeda v. Hackney, 40 U.S.L.W.
2431 (U.S. Jan. 18, 1972), 258
n23

Olmstead v. United States, 227
U.S. 438 (1928), 366 n64

Olson v. Regents of the University
of Minnesota, 301 F. Supp. 1356
(D. Minn. 1969), 227 n71

Opinion of Justice Brandeis, 255
U.S. 427, 68 n6

Opp Cotton Mills v. Administrator,
312 U.S. 126 (1941), 96 n137

Oswald v. Rodriguez, No. 71-1369
(O.T. 1972), 246 n19
See: Rodriguez v. McGinnis

Oswald v. Sostre, 404 U.S. 1049
(1972)
See: Sostre v. McGinnis
See also: Sostre v. Rockefeller

Oswald v. Sostre, 405 U.S. 978
(1972)

See: Sostre v. Rockefeller
See also: Sostre v. McGinnis

Otsuka v. Hite, 64 Cal.2d 596, 51
Cal. Rptr. 284, 414 P.2d 412
(1966), 71 n36; 228 n79; n80; 256
n3; 474 n84

Owens, In re, 9 Crim. L. Rep. 2415,
CCH Pov. L. Rep. 5663, ¶4355.83
(Cir. Ct. Cook County, Ill. 1971),
194 n24; 361 n21, n23

Oyama v. California, 332 U.S. 633
(1948), 88 n67

P

Paden v. United States, 430 F.2d
882 (5th Cir. 1970), 249 n40

Palmigiano v. Travisono, 317 F.
Supp. 776 (D.R.I. 1970), 68 n11;
69 n15; 126 n12; 247 n28; 264
n76; 320 n13; 359 n13; 367 n73;
466 n21; 470 n42

Paniagua v. Moseley, 451 F.2d 228
(10th Cir. 1971), 168 n29, n30

Pannell v. United States, 320 F.2d
698 (D.C. Cir. 1963), 726; 729;
732

Paolella v. Phillips, 27 Misc.2d 763,
209 N.Y.S.2d 165 (Sup. Ct. Suffolk Co. 1960), 367 n71

Park v. Thompson, Civ. No. 72-
3605 (D. Hawaii, 1972), 345 n17;
347 n22

Patricia A., Matter of, 31 N.Y.2d 83,
286 N.E.2d 432, 335 N.Y.S.2d 33
(1972), 343 n11; 344 n12; 358
n4

Patrum v. City of Greensburg, Ky.,
419 F.2d 1300 (6th Cir. 1969),
cert. denied 397 U.S. 990 (1970),
294 n49

Payne v. District of Columbia, 253
F.2d 867 (D.C. Cir. 1958), 70 n24

Peek v. Ciccone, 288 F. Supp. 329
(W.D. Mo. 1968), 191 n15

Pelletier v. United States, 343 F.2d
322 (D.C. Cir. 1965), 721

References are to pages

Pennsylvania v. Brown, 260 F. Supp. 323 (E.D. Pa. 1966), modified other grounds, 373 F.2d 771 (3d Cir. 1967), 246 n23

Pennsylvania v. Hendrick, 444 Pa. 83, 280 A.2d 110 (1971), 261 n55
See: Bryant v. Hendrick

People v. Colozzo, 54 Misc.2d 687, 283 N.Y.S.2d 409 (Sup. Ct. Kings Co. 1967), aff'd mem., 32 A.D.2d 927, 303 N.Y.S.2d 348 (2d Dept. 1969), 160

People v. Hernandes, 229 Cal. App.2d 143, 40 Cal. Rptr. 100 (1964), cert. denied 381 U.S. 953 (1965), 206 n26

People v. Rezek, 25 Misc.2d 705, 204 N.Y.S.2d 640 (Sup. Ct. Kings Co. 1960), 729

People v. Sickler, 61 Misc.2d 571, 306 N.Y.S.2d 168 (Dutchess Co. Ct. 1969), 206 n27

People v. Sykes, 22 N.Y.2d 159 (1968), 730

People ex rel. Angell v. Lynch, 71 Misc. 2d 921, 337 N.Y.S.2d 556 (Sup. Ct. Westchester Co. 1972), 210 n41

People ex rel. Arthur F. v. Hill, 29 N.Y.2d 17, 271 N.E.2d 911, 323 N.Y.S.2d 426 (1971), 360 n19

People ex rel. Blunt v. Narcotic Addiction Control Comm., 58 Misc.2d 57, 295 N.Y.S.2d 276 (Spec. Term, Part J, 1968), 189 n2

People ex rel. Brown v. Johnson, 9 N.Y.2d 482, 174 N.E.2d 725, 215 N.Y.S.2d 44 (1961), 261 n52

People ex rel. Lobell v. McDonnell, 296 N.Y. 109 (1947), 720; 728

People ex rel. Menechino v. Warden, 27 N.Y.2d 376 (1971)
See: Menechino v. Warden

People ex rel. Silbert v. Cohen, 29 N.Y.2d 12, 271 N.E.2d 908, 323 N.Y.S.2d 422 (1971), 360 n16

Peoples v. Wainwright, 325 F. Supp. 402 (M.D. Fla. 1971), 68 n11; 264 n76

Perez v. Ledesma, 401 U.S. 82 (1971), 299 n76

Perrine v. Municipal Court, 488 P.2d 648, 97 Cal. Rptr. 320 (1971), 231 n94, n96, n97, n98, n99, n100; 232 n101; 474 n84

Perry v. Sindermann, 408 U.S. 593 (1972), 526 n42

Pierce v. LaVallee, 293 F.2d 233 (2d Cir. 1961), 42 n10; 367 n68

Pierce v. Society of Sisters, 268 U.S. 510 (1925), 367 n65

Pisacano v. State, 8 A.D.2d 335, 188 N.Y.S.2d 35 (4th Dep't 1959), 172 n64

Porth v. Templar, 453 F.2d 330 (10th Cir. 1971), 72 n37

Portland v. Sherill, No. M-47623 (Circuit Ct. Multonah County, Oregon, January 9, 1967, 342 n4.1

Portnoy v. Strasser, 303 N.Y. 539, 104 N.E.2d 895 (1952), 367 n65

Potts v. Flax, 313 F.2d 284 (5th Cir. 1963), 292 n34

Prewitt v. Arizona, 418 F.2d 572 (9th Cir. 1969), 168 n29, n30

Price v. Johnston, 334 U.S. 266 (1948), 244 n2

Price v. United Mine Workers, 336 F.2d 771 (6th Cir. 1964), 294 n52

Prisoners Labor Union at Jackson v. State of Michigan, 346 F. Supp. 697 (E.D. Mich. 1972), 72 n43

Puckett v. Cox, 456 F.2d 233 (6th Cir. 1972), 116 n20

R

Ragsdale v. Overholsen, 281 F.2d 943 (D.C. Cir. 1960), 413 n21, n24

Ramirez v. United States, 238 F. Supp. 763 (S.D.N.Y. 1965), 370 n83

Ramsey v. Ciccone, 310 F. Supp. 600 (W.D. Mo. 1970), 116 n17; 411 n17

References are to pages

Ready v. Kreiger, —— F. Supp. ——, No. C72-1192 (N.D. Ohio Nov. 7, 1972), 69 n23

Redding v. Pate, 220 F. Supp. 124 (N.D. Ill. 1963), 116 n19; 167 n20

Reed v. Reed, 404 U.S. 71 (1971), 348 n23

Reetz v. Bozanich, 397 U.S. 82 (1970), 73 n44

Regal Knitwear Co. v. N.L.R.B., 324 U.S. 9 (1944), 294 n48

Rhem v. McGrath, 326 F. Supp. 681 (S.D.N.Y. 1971), 69 n16; 92 n98, n99; 260 n47; 287 n1; 289 n3; 291 n19; 292 n25, n33; 293 n44; 301 n83, n85, n86; 303 n106; 361 n21, n23; 675 (deposition of a hostile witness)

Rhoads v. Horvat, 270 F. Supp. 307 (D. Colo. 1967), 319 n11

Richards v. Smith, 464 F.2d 1029 (5th Cir. 1972), 521 n16

Richards v. Thurston, 424 F.2d 1281 (1st Cir. 1970), 365 n56

Riddle, In re, 57 Cal.2d 848, 372 P.2d 304, 22 Cal. Rptr. 472, cert. denied 371 U.S. 914 (1962), 261 n52, n55

Rider, Ex parte, 50 Cal. App. 797, 195 P. 965 (1920), 260 n47; 359 n13

Riley v. Rhay, 407 F.2d 496 (9th Cir. 1969), 167 n23

Roberts v. Peperseck, 256 F. Supp. 415 (D. Md. 1966), 82 n27

Roberts v. Williams, 302 F. Supp. 972 (N.D. Miss. 1969), aff'd 456 F.2d 819 (5th Cir. 1971), cert. denied —— U.S. ——, 10 Crim. L. Rep. 4011 (Oct. 13, 1971), 115 n13; 173 n19; 262 n57; 294 n53; 295 n56

Robin R. v. Wyman, —— F. Supp. —— (S.D.N.Y. 1971), 70 Civ. 1402, May 26, 1971, 359 n10; 363 n33

Robinson v. Birzgales, 311 F. Supp. 908 (W.D. Mich. 1970), 256 n8

Robinson v. California, 370 U.S. 660 (1962), 115 n10; 118 n33; 166 n16; 261 n50; 359 n9; 362 n26, n27; 364 n52; 408 n9, n11; 413 n22; 523 n28

Rochin v. California, 342 U.S. 165 (1952), 166 n15

Rodriguez v. McGinnis, No. 34567 (2d Cir., Jan. 25, 1972), 301 n87

Rodriguez v. McGinnis, 307 F. Supp. 627 (N.D.N.Y. 1969), 92 n101; 94 n121

Rodriguez v. McGinnis, 451 F.2d 730 (2d Cir. 1971), 512 n17

Rodriguez v. McGinnis, 456 F.2d 79 (2d Cir. 1972), 246 n19
See: Oswald v. Rodriguez; United States ex rel. Katzoff v. McGinnis

Rodriguez v. Preiser, 41 L.W. 4555 (1973), 82 n28

Rohrer, Petition of, 353 Mass. 282, N.E.2d 915 (1967), 87 n62

Rose v. Haskins, 388 F.2d 91 (6th Cir. 1968), cert. denied 392 U.S. 946 (1968), 207 n34

Rouse v. Cameron, 373 F.2d 451 (D.C. Cir. 1966), 189 n1; 362 n27, n30; 373 n110; 413 n21; 414 n25, n31

Rowland v. Jones, 452 F.2d 1005 (8th Cir. 1971), 67 n4; 70 n26

Rowland v. Sigler, 327 F. Supp. 821 (D. Neb. 1971), aff'd 452 F.2d 1005 (8th Cir. 1971), 320 n14

Royster (F.S.) Guano Co. v. Virginia, 253 U.S. 412 (1920), 156

Ruark v. Schooley, 211 F. Supp. 921 (D. Colo. 1962), 82 n27

Rue v. Snyder, 249 F. Supp. 740 (E.D. Tenn. 1966), 319 n11

Ruffin v. Commonwealth, 62 Va. (21 Gratt.) 790 (1871), 83 n34; 520 n11

Rumbaugh v. Winifrede R.R. Co., 331 F.2d 530 (4th Cir. 1964), 294 n52

S

SaMarion v. McGinnis, 55 Misc.2d 59, 284 N.Y.S.2d 504 (Sup Ct. Erie County 1967), cert. denied 392 U.S. 944 (1968), 43 n15

SaMarion v. McGinnis, 35 A.D.2d 684, 314 N.Y.S.2d 715 (4th Dept. 1970), 43 n15

SaMarion v. McGinnis, 253 F. Supp. 738 (W.D.N.Y. 1966), 42 n13

Samuels v. Mackell, 401 U.S. 66 (1971), 299 n76

Sas v. Maryland, 295 F. Supp. 389 (D.C. Md. 1969), 413 n23; 414 n27, n28

Sawyer v. Sigler, 320 F. Supp. 690 (D. Neb. 1970), aff'd 445 F.2d 818 (8th Cir. 1971), 116 n16; 168 n33; 170 n40; 256 n4

Scarpa v. U.S. Board of Parole, 453 F.2d 891 (5th Cir. 1971), 205 n21

Scerbaty v. Oswald, 341 F. Supp. 571 (S.D.N.Y. 1972), 71 n33

Schack v. State of Florida, 391 F.2d 593 (5th Cir. 1968), 411 n17

Schilb v. Kuebel, 404 U.S. 357 (1971), 726

Schnell v. City of Chicago, 407 F.2d 1084 (7th Cir. 1969), 292 n34

School District of Abington Township, Pa. v. Schempp, 374 U.S. 203 (1963), 367 n70

Schware v. Board of Examiners of New Mexico, 353 U.S. 232 (1957), 227 n68, n69, n70; 228 n80a, n81; 474 n84

Schy v. Susquehanna Corp., 419 F.2d 1112 (7th Cir.), cert. denied 400 U.S. 826 (1970), 293 n37

Seale v. Manson, 326 F. Supp. 1375 (D. Conn. 1971), 69 n23; 70 n28; 126 n21; 246 n25; 365 n58

Sealy v. Dep't of Public Instruction, 252 F.2d 898 (3d Cir. 1958), 263 n70

S.E.C. v. Chenery Corp., 318 U.S. 80 (1943), 729

S.E.C. v. Frank, 388 F.2d 486 (2d Cir. 1968), 297 n64

Seidenberg v. McSorley's Old Ale House, 317 F. Supp. 593 (S.D. N.Y. 1970), 348 n27

Sellars v. Beto, 409 U.S. 968 (1972)
See: Novak v. Beto

Shaffer v. Jennings, 314 F. Supp. 588 (E.D. Pa. 1970), 168 n28, n30

Shapiro v. Thompson, 394 U.S. 618 (1969), 82 n24; 348 n28

Shelton v. Tucker, 364 U.S. 479 (1960), 722

Sheppard v. Maxwell, 384 U.S. 333 (1966), 261 n54

Shone v. Maine, 406 F.2d 844 (1st Cir. 1969), 94 n113

Siegal v. Ragen, 180 F.2d 785 (7th Cir. 1950), 82 n27

Sigafus v. Brown, 416 F.2d 105 (7th Cir. 1969), 256 n6; 323 n41

Simmons v. United States, 348 U.S. 397 (1959), 92 n94

Simon v. Wainwright, 464 F.2d 1038 (5th Cir. 1972), 521 n16

Sims v. Greene, 161 F.2d 87 (3d Cir. 1947), 297 n64

Sinclair v. Henderson, 441 F. Supp. 1123 (E.D. La. 1971), 320 n18

Singleton v. Board of Comm., 356 F.2d 771 (5th Cir. 1966), 259 n30

Skinner v. Oklahoma, 316 U.S. 535 (1942), 82 n24

Smith v. Miller, 241 Iowa 625, 40 N.W.2d 597 (1956), 172 n60, n61, n62, n63, n64

Smith v. Robbins, 328 F. Supp. 162 (D. Me. 1971), 264 n76

Smith v. Robbins, 454 F.2d 696 (1st Cir. 1972), 68 n11, n14; 126 n19

Smoake v. Fritz, 320 F. Supp. 609 (S.D.N.Y. 1970), 300 n82

Snaidach v. Family Finance Corp., 395 U.S. 337 (1969), 96 n137

Sobell v. Reed, 327 F. Supp. 1294 (S.D.N.Y. 1971), 72 n37; 204 n14; 206 n24; 465 n17; 472 n59

References are to pages

Sonnenberg v. Markley, 289 F.2d 126 (7th Cir. 1961), 371 n99

Sostre v. McGinnis, 334 F.2d 906 2d Cir. 1964), 38 n2; 42 n9, n11, n12

Sostre v. McGinnis, 442 F.2d 178 (2d Cir. 1971), cert. denied sub nom. Oswald v. Sostre, 404 U.S. 1049 (1971), 69 n18; 70 n30; 79 n4, n6; 80 n11, n14; 84 n43; 85 n50a, n51; 86 n56; 90 n80, n81, n83; 91 n92, n93; 93 n105; 116 n24; 117 n25, n26; 169 n38; 173 n77; 246 n20; 256 n7; 260 n46; 261 n50; 262 n57, n61; 294 n51, n53, n54; 295 n56; 301 n94, n97; 302 n100, n104; 323 n41, n43, n44, n45; 361 n22; 367 n68, n72; 523 n29; 526 n41

See also: Sostre v. Rockefeller

Sostre v. Otis, 330 F. Supp. 941 (S.D.N.Y. 1971), 38 n4, n6; 70 n27; 471 n43, n44

Sostre v. Rockefeller, 312 F. Supp. 863 (S.D.N.Y. 1970), cert. denied Oswald v. Sostre, 405 U.S. 978 (1972), 26 n5, n6; 38 n3, n5; 42 n7, n8; 43 n16, n17, n18; 92 n101; 256 n11; 262 n57, n61; 271 n109; 504 n6

See also: Sostre v. McGinnis

Spampinato v. City of New York, 311 F.2d 439 (2d Cir. 1962), cert. denied 372 U.S. 980 (1963), 294 n49

Specht v. Patterson, 386 U.S. 605 (1967), 86 n59; 94 n112; 405 n2; 741

Stack v. Boyle, 342 U.S. 1 (1942), 125 n7; 728

Stanley v. Georgia, 394 U.S. 557 (1969), 70 n25

Stanley v. Illinois, 405 U.S. 645 (1972), 81 n21; 96 n137

Startz v. Cullen, 468 F.2d 560 (2d Cir. 1972), 167 n25, n26; 168 n32

State v. Costello, 59 N.J. 334, 282 A.2d 748 (1971), 342 n5

State ex rel. Thomas v. State, 198 N.W.2d 675 (Wis. 1972), 68 n8

Stephens v. Yeomans, 327 F. Supp. 1182 (D. N.J. 1970), 228 n80; 474 n84

Stevenson v. United States, 250 F. Supp. 859 (W.D. Mich.), cert. denied 389 U.S. 884 (1966), 586 n72

Stewart v. Shanahan, 227 F.2d 233 (8th Cir. 1960), 294 n52

Stiltner v. Rhay, 371 F.2d 420 (9th Cir. 1969), cert. denied 386 U.S. 997 (1967), 167 n24

Stinnett v. Hegstrom, 178 F. Supp. 17 (D. Conn. 1959), 371 n100

Stinnie v. Gregory, Civ. No. 554-70-R (E.D. Va. filed Oct. 15, 1970), 259 n38; 642 (interrogatories)

Strasser v. Doorley, 309 F. Supp. 716 (D.R.I. 1970), 297 n67; 303 n110

Stringer v. Dilger, 313 F.2d 536 (10th Cir. 1963), 319 n11

Suarez v. Wilkinson, 133 F. Supp. 38 (M.D. Pa. 1955), 371 n99

Sullivan v. Houston Indep. School Dist., 307 F. Supp. 1328 (S.D. Tex. 1969), 292 n34

Sullivan v. Little Hunting Park, Inc., 396 U.S. 229 (1969), 166 n13

T

Talley v. Stephens, 247 F. Supp. 683 (E.D. Ark. 1965), 83 n32; 116 n18; 169 n37, n38; 170 n39; 174 n87; 175 n89; 177 n99; 256 n4

Tarlton v. Clarke, 441 F.2d 384 (5th Cir. 1971), 584 n53

Tarlton v. Henderson, 467 F.2d 200 (5th Cir. 1972), 521 n17

Tarlton v. United States, 430 F.2d 1351 (5th Cir. 1970), 369 n80

Tate v. Short, 401 U.S. 395 (1971), 158; 159; 356 n3

Taylor v. Blackwell, 418 F.2d 199 (5th Cir. 1969), 247 n32

Taylor v. New York City Transit Authority, 309 F. Supp. 785 (E.D.N.Y. 1970), 94 n120

References are to pages

Taylor v. Perini (N.D. Ohio 1972), 323 n37

Taylor v. Sterrett, 344 F. Supp. 411 (N.D. Tex. 1972), 257 n16

Technograph Printed Circuits, Ltd. v. Methode Electronics, Inc., 285 F. Supp. 714 (N.D. Ill. 1968), 293 n44

Theriault v. Carlson, 339 F. Supp. 375 (N.D. Ga. 1972), 71 n34; 195 n25

Thogmartin v. Moseley, 313 F. Supp. 158 (D. Kan. 1969), 191 n15

Thompson v. Blackwell, 374 F.2d 945 (5th Cir. 1967), 168 n29, n30

Thorpe v. Housing Authority of Durham, 393 U.S. 268 (1969), 730

Tinker v. Des Moines School District, 393 U.S. 503 (1969), 365 n54, n55

Tippett v. Maryland, 436 F.2d 1153 (4th Cir. 1971), cert. denied sub nom. Murel v. Baltimore City Criminal Court, 407 U.S. 355 (1972), 414 n29, n30

Tolbert v. Bragan, 451 F.2d 1020 (5th Cir. 1971), 115 n12

Tolbert v. Eyman, 434 F.2d 625 (9th Cir. 1970), 168 n33; 177 n101

Townsend v. Sain, 372 U.S. 293 (1963), 518 n5

Trimble v. Stone, 187 F. Supp. 483 (D.D.C. 1960), 370 n89

Trop v. Dulles, 356 U.S. 86 (1958), 114 n5; 166 n17; 261 n50; 523 n27; 524 n35

Trujillo v. Love, 322 F. Supp. 1266 (D. Colo. 1971), 70 n32

Tumey v. Ohio, 273 U.S. 510 (1927), 94 n120

U

United Mine Workers v. Gibbs, 383 U.S. 715 (1966), 294 n52

United States v. Alsbrook, 336 F. Supp. 973 (D.D.C. 1971), 191 n14; 371 n100

United States v. Alston, 420 F.2d 176 (D.C. Cir. 1969), 720 n26; 723

United States v. Becker, 444 F.2d 510 (4th Cir. 1971), 372 n107

United States v. Borders, 154 F. Supp. 214 (N.D. Ala. 1957), aff'd 256 F.2d 458 (5th Cir. 1958), 372 n103, n104

United States v. Bronson, 433 F.2d 537 (D.C. Cir. 1970), 722; 723

United States v. Broyles, 423 F.2d 1299 (4th Cir. 1970), 730

United States v. Cook, 442 F.2d 723 (D.C. Cir. 1970), 727; 728

United States v. Costanzo, 395 F.2d 441 (4th Cir. 1968), cert. denied 393 U.S. 883, 370 n91

United States v. Cramer, 451 F.2d 1198 (5th Cir. 1971), 727

United States v. Demko, 385 U.S. 149 (1966), 172 n71

United States v. Eramdjian, 155 F. Supp. 914 (S.D. Cal. 1957), 263 n71

United States v. Flowers, 227 F. Supp. 1014 (W.D. Tenn. 1963), aff'd 331 F.2d 604 (6th Cir. 1964), 371 n96

United States v. Forrest, 418 F.2d 1186 (D.C. Cir. 1969), 723

United States v. Fotto, 103 F. Supp. 430 (S.D.N.Y. 1952), 371 n95; 372 n104

United States v. Gaines, 449 F.2d 143 (2d Cir. 1971) (per curiam), 158; 159

United States v. Glover, 372 F.2d 43 (2d Cir. 1967), 370 n88

United States v. Hall, 306 F. Supp. 735 (E.D. Tenn. 1969), 371 n101, n106

United States v. Hoston, 353 F.2d 723 (7th Cir. 1965), 372 n104

United States v. Kinsman, 195 F. Supp. 271 (S.D. Cal. 1961), 372 n107

References are to pages

United States v. Leathers, 412 F.2d 169 (D.C. Cir. 1969) (per curiam), 723; 733

United States v. Lemmens, 430 F.2d 619 (7th Cir. 1970), 730

United States v. Lenhard, 437 F.2d 936 (2d Cir. 1970), 730

United States v. Lewis, 274 F. Supp. 184 (S.D.N.Y. 1967), 207 n30

United States v. McNeil, 434 F.2d 502 (D.C. Cir. 1970) (per curiam), 730

United States v. Morales, 233 F. Supp. 160 (D. Mont. 1964), 371 n94

United States v. Muniz, 305 F.2d 285 (2d Cir. 1962), 172 n67

United States v. Muniz, 374 U.S. 150 (1963), 248 n36; 323 n41

United States v. Preston, 352 F.2d 352 (9th Cir. 1965), 292 n28

United States v. Richberg, 398 F.2d 523 (5th Cir. 1968), 297 n67; 303 n109

United States v. Seegers, 433 F.2d 493 (D.C. Cir. 1970), 730

United States v. Speicher, 439 F.2d 104 (3d Cir. 1971), 730

United States v. Texas, 321 F. Supp. 1043 (E.D. Tex. 1970), 330 F. Supp. 235 (1971), aff'd with modifications 447 F.2d 441 (5th Cir. 1971), stay denied 404 U.S. 1206, cert. denied 404 U.S. 1016 (1972), 527 n45

United States v. Texas, 342 F. Supp. 24 (E.D. Tex. 1971), aff'd 466 F.2d 518 (5th Cir. 1972), 527 n45

United States v. Waters, 437 F.2d 722 (D.C. Cir. 1970), 191 n13

United States v. Webb, 112 F. Supp. 950 (W.D. Okl. 1953), 370 n83; 372 n104

United States v. W.T. Grant Co., 345 U.S. 629 (1953), 297 n66; 303 n107

United States ex rel. Bey v. Connecticut Board of Parole, 443 F.2d 1079 (2d Cir. 1971), 96 n133; 207 n32; 209 n38

United States ex rel. Campbell v. Pate, 401 F.2d 55 (7th Cir. 1968), 80 n12, n19; 84 n40; 256 n13

United States ex rel. Chubbs v. City of New York, 324 F. Supp. 1183 (1971), 512 n19

United States ex rel. Gabor v. Myers, 237 F. Supp. 852 (E.D. Pa. 1965), 68 n9

United States ex rel. Gittlemacker v. County of Philadelphia, 413 F.2d 84 (3d Cir. 1969), cert. denied 396 U.S. 1046 (1970), 294 n49

United States ex rel. Green v. Rundle, 434 F.2d 1112 (3d Cir. 1970), writ granted on remand, 326 F. Supp. 456 (E.D. Pa. 1971), 732

United States ex rel. Hyde v. McGinnis, 429 F.2d 864 (2d Cir. 1970), 116 n20; 168 n27, n30

United States ex rel. Katzoff v. McGinnis, No. 70 Civ. 272 (N.D. N.Y. 1970), aff'd sub nom. Rodriguez v. McGinnis, 456 F.2d 79 (2d Cir. 1972), 70 n29

United States ex rel. Keating v. Bensinger, 322 F. Supp. 784 (N.D. Ill. 1971), 730

United States ex rel. Lawrence v. Ragen, 323 F.2d 410 (7th Cir. 1963), 168 n29, n30; 261 n53

United States ex rel. Motley v. Rundle, 340 F. Supp. 807 (1972), 323 n41

United States ex rel. Neal v. Wolfe, 346 F. Supp. 569 (E.D. Pa. 1972), 79 n7; 80 n18; 84 n41; 91 n86; 94 n111

United States ex rel. Randazzo v. Follette, 282 F. Supp. 10 (S.D. N.Y. 1968), aff'd other grounds 418 F.2d 1319 (2d Cir. 1969),

References are to pages

cert. denied 402 U.S. 984 (1971), 206 n28

United States ex rel. Robinson v. York, 281 F. Supp. 8 (D. Conn. 1968), 342 n5

United States ex rel. Sabella v. Newsday, 315 F. Supp. 333 (E.D.N.Y. 1970), 504 n6

United States ex rel. Schuster v. Herold, 410 F.2d 1071 (2d Cir. 1969), 87 n62

United States ex rel. Schuster v. Herold, 440 F.2d 1334 (2d Cir. 1971), 411 n17

United States ex rel. Sperling v. Fitzpatrick, 426 F.2d 1161 (2d Cir. 1970), 206 n29

United States ex rel. Sumrell v. York, 288 F. Supp. 955 (D. Conn. 1968), 342 n5

United States ex rel. Wilson v. Coughlin, No. C-1793 (N.D. Ill. Nov. 22, 1971), CCH Poverty L. Rep. ¶4400.501, 359 n10; 364 n49

Upchurch v. Hawaii, 51 Hawaii 150, 454 P.2d 112 (1969) (dictum), 260 n44

Upshaw v. McNamara, 435 F.2d 1188 (1st Cir. 1970) 229 n83

Urbano v. McCorkle, 334 F. Supp. 161 (D. N.J. 1971), 79 n7; 91 n86; 94 n111; 742; 749

V

Valvano v. McGrath, 325 F. Supp. 408 (E.D.N.Y. 1970), 264 n74; 287 n1; 291 n15, n23; 292 n25, n26; 293 n40, n45; 294 n47; 295 n55, n58; 297 n67, n68; 298 n69, n74; 299 n75, n77; 300 n78, n80, n81; 303 n107

Van Erman v. Schmidt, 343 F. Supp. 377 (W.D. Wis. 1972), 70 n28

Van Geldern, In re, 14 Cal. App.3d 838, 92 Cal. Rptr. 592 (Cal. Ct. App. 3d Dist. 1971), 471 n43

Van Gemert v. Boeing Co., 259 F. Supp. 125 (S.D.N.Y. 1966), 293 n44

Vardinakis, In re, 160 Misc.13, 289 N.Y.S. 355 (Dom. Rel. Ct., N.Y. Co. 1936), 367 n71

Vartuli, Matter of, 10 Ed. Dep't Reps. —— No. 8297 (June 21, 1971), 365 n57

W

Walker v. Blackwell, 411 F.2d 23 (5th Cir. 1969), 71 n35; 256 n10; 320 n15

Wallach v. City of Pagedale, 359 F.2d 57 (8th Cir. 1966), 294 n49

Washington v. Lee, 263 F. Supp. 327 (M.D. Ala. 1966), aff'd Lee v. Washington, 390 U.S. 333 (1968), 27 n7; 83 n32; 245 n16; 246 n24; 291 n18, n22; 301 n92; 319 n4; 363 n45

Washington v. Official Court Stenographer, 251 F. Supp. 945 (E.D. Pa. 1966), 323 n42

Washington Post v. Kleindienst, 11 Crim. L. Rep. 2045 (D.D.C. April 4, 1972), 264 n75

Washington Post v. Kleindienst, 1 Prison L. Rep. 141 (D.D.C. April 5, 1972), stay granted pending appeal, 1 Prison L. Rep. 337 (D.C. Cir. Sept. 6, 1972), additional findings made, —— F. Supp. —— (D.D.C. Dec. 19, 1972), 69 n18

Wasson v. Trowbridge, 382 F.2d 807 (2d Cir. 1967), 96 n133

Wayne County Jail Inmates v. Wayne County Bd. Comm'rs, 5 Clearinghouse Rev. 108 (Cir. Ct., Wayne County, Mich. 1971), 115 n8; 127 n22; 169 n36; 175 n89a; 192 n16; 259 n33; 261 n54; 271 n106; 288 n2; 322 n28; 323 n33; 324 n51, n53; 742; 747; 749

References are to pages

Weaver v. Beto, 429 F.2d 505 (5th Cir. 1970), 168 n29, n30

Weaver v. United States, 405 F.2d 353 (D.C. Cir. 1968), 729; 730 n28

Weber v. Aetna Casualty & Surety Company, 406 U.S. 164 (1972), 526 n39

Weems v. United States, 217 U.S. 349 (1910), 113 n2; 114 n5; 117 n30; 118 n32; 261 n50; 523 n26

Weiss v. Tenney Corp., 47 F.R.D. 283 (S.D.N.Y. 1969), 293 n37

Whirl v. Kern, 407 F.2d 781 (5th Cir. 1969), 323 n41

White v. Reid, 125 F. Supp. 647 (D.D.C. 1954), 359 n7; 362 n28; 371 n100; 373 n110

White v. Reid, 126 F. Supp. 867 (D.D.C. 1954), 191 n10

White v. United States, 412 F.2d 145 (D.C. Cir. 1968), 723

Wieman v. Updegraff, 344 U.S. 183 (1952), 226 n66, n67

Wilkinson v. Skinner, 462 F.2d 670 (2d Cir. 1972), 68 n8, n11; 70 n26

Williams v. Illinois, 399 U.S. 235 (1970), 125 n5; 156; 157; 158; 159

Williams v. New York, 337 U.S. 241 (1949), 190 n7

Williams v. Robinson, 432 F.2d 637 (D.C. Cir. 1970), 411 n17

Williams v. White Plains Housing Authority, 35 A.D.2d 965, 317 N.Y.S.2d 935 (2d Dept. 1970), 730

Williams v. Zuckert, 371 U.S. 534 (1963), 96 n136

Willis v. White, 310 F. Supp. 205 (E.D. La. 1970), 168 n28, n30

Willner v. Committee on Character and Fitness, 373 U.S. 96 (1963), 81 n23; 82 n24; 92 n94; 93 n104; 94 n117

Wilson v. American Chain & Cable Co., 364 F.2d 558 (3d Cir. 1966), 294 n52

Wilson v. Kelley, 294 F. Supp. 1005 (N.D. Ga. 1968), 246 n24; 292 n34; 293 n37; 301 n92

Wilwording v. Swenson, 404 U.S. 249 (1971), 82 n28; 176 n98; 244 n10; 245 n12, n18; 301 n87; 521 n19

Winship, In re, 397 U.S. 358 (1970), 370 n91; 373 n108

Winston v. United States, 305 F.2d 253 (2d Cir. 1962), aff'd 374 U.S. 150 (1963), 172 n67, n68, n69

Winters v. Miller, 446 F.2d 65 (2d Cir. 1971), 411 n17

Wisconsin v. Constantineau, 400 U.S. 433 (1971), 301 n87

Wojnics v. Michigan Dep't of Corrections, 32 Mich. App. 121, 188 N.W.2d 251 (1971), 261 n55

Wong Yang Sung v. McGrath, 339 U.S. 33 (1950), 82 n25; 92 n94

Woolsey v. Beto, 450 F.2d 321 (5th Cir. 1971), 116 n18

Wright v. McMann, 387 F.2d 519 (2d Cir. 1967), on remand 321 F. Supp. 127 (N.D.N.Y. 1970), aff'd & rev'd in part, 460 F.2d 126 (2d Cir. 1971), 116 n21; 117 n29; 118 n32; 126 n20; 169 n37, n38; 171 n49; 173 n75, n78; 261 n50; 262 n61; 294 n53, n54; 295 n56; 301 n87, n91; 302 n102; 323 n41; 522 n21

Wyatt v. Stickney, Civ. Action No. 3195-N (April 13, 1972), 362 n32

Wyatt v. Stickney, 325 F. Supp. 781 (M.D. Ala. 1971), 334 F. Supp. 1341 (1971), 344 F. Supp. 373 (M.D. Ala. 1972), 189 n5; 190 n6; 322 n29; 323 n40; 325 n54; 362 n31, n32; 363 n35; 412 n19

Y

Yakov v. Board of Bar Examiners, 435 P.2d 553 (Calif. 1968), 231 n95

Yakus v. United States, 321 U.S. 414 (1944), 96 n138

References are to pages

Young v. Director, 367 F.2d 331
(D.C. Cir. 1966), 249 n43
Younger v. Gilmore, 404 U.S. 15
(1971), 256 n8; 387
See: Gilmore v. Lynch
Younger v. Harris, 401 U.S. 37
(1971), 246 n21; 299 n76

Z

Zangerle v. Court of Common
Pleas, 141 Ohio 70, 46 N.E.2d
865 (1943), 261 n54
Zwickler v. Koota, 389 U.S. 241
(1967), 246 n21

GENERAL INDEX

References are to pages

A

Association
prisoners' right, 69
Asylums
design and purpose, 7
Attica Prison Riot
prisoner's account of, 38
resemblance to Columbia student
riots, 15
Attorneys (*see:* **Counsel**)
Auburn Plan
model of regimentation, 8
nature and origin, 550

B

Bail
alternatives, 721
as denial of equal protection (Bellamy Brief), 133
determination of amount, 153, 159,
735
full and fair hearing, 727
impact on outcome of case, 719
mandatory factors for consideration, 140
movement for abolition, 604
relation to conviction rate, 134
Black Muslims
religious freedom for prisoners, 71
Black Prisoners
as victim, 25–31
indictment by, 35–46
Bonds (*see:* **Fidelity Bonds**)

C

Capital Punishment
frequency of use, 6

Civil Disabilities
former prisoners', 217
Class Actions
availability in seeking federal judicial review, 245
court's initiative, 512
prison crisis situations, 291
sample complaint, §1983 action,
609, 611
sample form of notice of commencement of §1983 action, 626
sample interrogatories, §1983 action, 628, 642, 652
Spanish-speaking prisoners, complaint form, 388
Clothing
right of juvenile offenders as to
appearance, 364
Complaint
crisis litigation, 291
non-crisis litigation, 260
samples, 388, 609, 611, 692, 697
specificity of pleading in crisis litigation, 295
Confessions
relation to making bail, 145
Confrontation
due-process right, 93
Consent Decrees
advantages for client, 267
Contempt Power
enforcement of judgments by
(opinion), 688
Convicts
arrest records in hiring decisions,
228
civil disabilities, 71
direct relationship test in hiring
decisions, 228
disabilities after release, 12, 217

Convicts (Cont'd)
Model Penal Code on convict hiring decisions, 232
programs to help upon release, 533–537
unemployment as "life sentence," 218
Coram Nobis Actions
timely exceptions to rulings, 54
Correspondence (*see:* **Mail**)
Costs
attorneys' fees in civil rights cases, 506
disadvantage of litigation, 332
due process budget, 88
fees of court-appointed attorneys, 510
imprisonment, 18, 26, 598
Counsel
access to prisoners, 264, 290
court appointment in advance of plea, 519
disadvantages to appointment of, 506
due process right to, 95
full-time presence in prison proposed, 508
juvenile offender's right, 359
juvenile offender's right at parole revocation hearing, 360
right of juvenile offender, 372
right of representation at parole hearing, 203
wrongs done to accused by, 52
Courts
modification of adversary system proposed, 503
reform role, 501
supervision and regulation of prisons, 527
Criminal Insanity
due process rights, 405
periodic review of adjudication, 408
right to treatment, 411
segregation of prisoners, 410
standards for release from commitment, 409

Cross-Examination
due-process right, 93
Cruel and Unusual Punishment
court guidelines, 525
enforced celibacy, 584
imprisonment, 113
Custody
theory of prison operation, 9

D

Damages
advisability of seeking in crisis litigation, 294
advisability of seeking in prisoner rights suit, 319
liability of government to prisoner suit, 248
Declaratory Judgments
action for challenging prison practices, 319
Defendants
choice, in crisis litigation, 293
Delinquents (*see:* **Juvenile Offenders**)
Depositions
discovery tool, 265
samples, 661, 675
Deviant Behavior
colonial American treatment, 6
Discovery
availability in prisoner rights action, 245
depositions as tool, 265
document production request, 265
inspection of facilities as tool, 266
interrogatories as tool, 265
medical examinations, 266
parole board procedures, 205
questionnaires and interviews, 266
Document Production
form of request for, 658
Due Process
administrative, before parole revocation, 79
criminally insane prisoners, 405
denial by refusal of bail, 137
direct relationship test in convict hiring decision, 230

References are to pages

Due Process (Cont'd)
economic cost of efficiency versus freedom, 88
in-prison disciplinary proceeding,
right as to time of hearing, 96
right to confrontation and cross-examination, 93
right to impartial tribunal, 94
right to present witnesses, 94
right to retained counsel or substitute, 95
right to written decision, 93
right to written rules and notice of charges, 92
juvenile offender commitment proceedings, 358
juvenile offender disciplinary proceedings, 361
juvenile offender's right to counsel, 372
mentally ill patients, 87
parole release hearings, 203
pre-trial punishment as violating, 126, 134
prison discipline procedures, 747
privilege-right distinction rejected, 85
recommended pretrial complaint theory, 260
requisites, 81
Spanish-speaking prisoners, 386

E

Equal Protection
bail system as violating, 133, 156
female offenders discriminated against, 342
Equitable Relief
availability in seeking federal judicial review, 245
Exhaustion of State Remedies
effect on prisoner rights suits, 521
federal deference to state courts, 509
limitation on federal habeas corpus petitions, 503
required before federal judicial review, 245, 249

Experts
sample deposition of friendly witness, 661

F

Fidelity Bonds
availability to convicts, 221
First Amendment
rights of prisoners, generally, 67–76
Force
excessive, as cruel and unusual punishment, 115
Forms
class action complaint, §1983 action, 609, 616
deposition of friendly expert witness, 661
interrogatories, §1983 class action, 628, 642, 652
notice to class of §1983 action, 626
pro se prisoner actions, 691–718
request for production of documents, 658
sample deposition of hostile witness, 675

G

Good Time
conflict with medical care needs, 170
defined, 12
forfeiture as punishment, 84
revocation as substantial punishment, 80
Guilty Pleas
constitutional infirmities, 519

H

Habeas Corpus
fees for court-appointed attorneys, 510
growing volume of petitions, 516
seeking federal judicial review by, 244, 247

References are to pages

Habeas Corpus (Cont'd)
way of challenging juvenile offender commitment, 358
Hearing
due process aspect of timing, 96
due process right to impartial tribunal, 94
full and fair on bail question, 727
grant or denial of parole, 202
prisoner's right to be heard, 520

I

Imprisonment
alternatives for juvenile offenders,
20
basis of criminal insanity, 405
breakup of family by, 346
civil death of felons, 173
continuing fact of life, 578
cruel and unusual punishment, 113
decline in inmate population, 5, 11
economic losses to prisoner, 161
female offenders, 341–352
future trends, 423–433
high cost, 18
longer sentences for female juveniles, 343
parole as alternative, 11
parole as source of frustration, 588
pretrial detention, 719
pretrial measure, 596
probation as alternative, 18
purposes, 599
rehabilitation as purpose, 190
retention of constitutional rights
during, 83
retribution as purpose, 20, 25
security of society as a basis, 424
Spanish-speaking prisoners, 385
treatment or punishment, 5
Incarceration (*see:* **Imprisonment**)
Injunction
action for challenging prison practices, 319
preliminary relief in crisis, 300
Insanity (*see:* **Criminal Insanity**)
Inspection of Facilities
discovery tool, 266

Insurance
against decarceration risks, 19
Interrogatories
discovery tool, 265
sample form, 628, 642, 652
Investigation
pretrial in prisoner rights cases,
258

J

Jailhouse Lawyers' Manual
forms for *pro se* prisoner actions,
691–718
Judgments
enforcement, 270, 318, 324
enforcement by contempt power
(opinion), 688
limits on judicial review, 522
review of bail determinations, 733
Jurisdiction
administrative agencies' action by
federal court, 248
basis in federal court, 262
civil suits seeking federal review,
244
federal courts over prisoner rights,
243
federal deference to state courts,
509
federal question basis in federal
court, 248
Juvenile Offenders
alternatives to imprisonment, 20
compensation for work, 369
confidentiality of training school
records, 369
discrimination against females,
342
federal offenses, 369
free expression and appearance in
training schools, 364
freedom from arbitrary transfers,
361
major role of probation, 11
right to coeducational activities,
366
right to hearing upon extension of
placement, 360

References are to pages

Juvenile Offenders (Cont'd)
right to medical treatment and rehabilitation, 362
right to sue civilly though confined,
360
right to vote, 368
right to worship or not worship,
366
solitary confinement, 12
training school confinement, 357–
375

K

Kerner Commission
racism findings, 27

L

Legal Aid Society
monopoly aspect, 55
nature and purpose, 59
Legislation (proposed laws)
Parole Act, 485
Prison Discipline Act, 476
Prisoners' Right of Communication
Act, 483
Letters
prisoners' right, 68
Libraries
inadequate in juvenile training
schools, 375
inadequate in prisons, 70
Licensing Boards
decisions on convicts' applications, 219
Litigation
alternatives, 331
class action advantages and disadvantages in crisis, 291
enforcement of judgments, 270,
318
function of the trial memorandum,
270
manual for non-crisis litigation,
255–272
particular parties to prisoner rights
suits, 259

Litigation (Cont'd)
pretrial goal planning, 256, 288,
318
principal interest of prisoner rights
groups, 463
prison crisis situations, 287–304
pro se special rules proposed, 511
reasons for choosing state forum
listed, 261
seeking publicity when filing suit,
263

M

Mail
attorney-prisoner, use in litigation,
266
juvenile offenders' right to receive
and send, 367
legislator receipt of prisoners' letters, 459
prisoner access, 470
prisoners' right, 68
problems of Spanish-speaking
prisoners, 387
role in preparing prisoner or release, 535
Mandamus
availability to federal prisoners,
248
Medical Care
barbarous and shocking, 512
damages question in breach of
duty, 172
cruel and unusual punishment by
withholding, 116
Federal Bureau of Prisons' guidelines, 171
forced work as injury cause, 169
liability of prison medics for denial
of orders, 168
Manual of Correctional Standards,
171
prison standards and prisoner
rights, 165
protection from involuntary treatments, 604
right to refuse treatment, 193
total denial or refusal of care, 167
U.N. Standard Minimum Rules, 171

References are to pages

Medical Examinations
discovery tool, 266
Mental Illness (*see:* **Criminal Insanity**)
Minorities
Black prisoners, 25–31, 35–46
  Black Vanguard liberation program, 45
criminal charges against, 52
prison population, 9–10, 26
Spanish-speaking prisoners, 385
Motions
crucial practice in crisis litigation, 296
preliminary, in non-crisis litigation, 263
recommended response to dismissal proposals, 264
responses to venue change proposals, 264

N

Norfolk Island
prison reform experiment, 542
Notice
class action §1983 form, 626

O

Ombudsman
legislators' service as, 459
proposed role in prison problems, 332

P

Parole
alternative to imprisonment, 11, 18
arbitrariness of decisions, 201
church attendance as condition, 206
due process before revocation, 79
jeopardy of, as punishment, 80
remedies for deprivation of hearing rights, 210
revocation, 206
right to counsel at hearing, 203
right to revocation hearing with counsel, 360

Parole (Cont'd)
sacred cow of prison system, 201
secret reasons for decisions, 204
source of added punishment, 585
standards for hearings, 202
unequal treatment of female offenders, 347
Petition for Redress of Grievances
prisoners' right, 69
Plea Bargaining
judges aligned with prosecution, 50
Political Views and Expression
prisoners' right, 71
Pre-trial Confinement
punishment without trial, 126, 134
Prison Administration
abandonment of rehabilitation theory, 20
court supervision and regulation, 527
disciplinary proceedings as adjudicatory, 89
disciplinary process, 467
distribution of budget, 26
due process to precede discipline, 80
expunging illegal actions from records, 320
immunity from judicial scrutiny, 243
inmate participation in government, 541–572
isolation of disruptive prisoners, 117
model regulations, 741
plenary disciplinary powers, 82
prisoners' rights, §1983 sample complaint, 616
private-sector operation, 19
rational basis of rules, 91
reasonableness of "First Amendment" regulations, 67
regimentation theory, 8
sample interrogatories, §1983 action on conditions, 642, 652
standards of medical care, 165
trusty system of operation, 114
Prison Crisis
techniques of disruption, 595

References are to pages

Prisoners' Rights Groups
list, 753
Prisons
alternatives, 601
Attica riot, 15
Black Vanguard liberation program, 45
challenging unlawful conditions, 321
changes in the foreseeable future, 579
conditions as cruel and unusual punishment, 113
coordination of sentencing with available facilities, 511
education programs, 580
elimination as rights movement goal, 13
future trends, 423–433
history of, 5–21
inadequate libraries, 70
inmate unionization, 72
inmates' ethnic and class status, 9–10
lack of equal facilities for women, 344
legislators' role in reform, 455
"prison crisis" defined, 287
proposals to eliminate, 17
reform methods, 257
reform proposals, 437–451
religious freedom in, 67
women inmates, 341–352
Privilege
attorney-client, 507
contrasted with "First Amendment" rights, 68
Protective Orders
recommended upon filing, 264
safety of witnesses in crisis litigation, 298
Publicity
daily prison life largely unchanged by, 465
prison reform by means of, 458
Punishment
alternatives to imprisonment, 595–606
corporal, outlawed, 115

Punishment (Cont'd)
cruel and unusual for juvenile offenders, 364
cruel and unusual in imprisonment, 113
cruel and unusual only in extreme cases, 302
due process to precede, 80
due process to precede juvenile prisoners', 361
effectiveness, 428
express authorization by legislature, 525
forbidden (examples), 12
insulation from constitutional attack, 302
parole as source of additional, 585
pre-trial, as due process violation, 126, 134
retribution as purpose, 601
"substantial," defined, 80
summary, unjustified as therapeutic, 87
withholding medical care, 116

R

Racism
Kerner Commission findings, 27
Reading
right of prisoners, 70
Receivership
enforcement and appeal of judgment, 271
Regimentation
theory of prison operation, 8
Rehabilitation
abandonment as prison theory, 20
absence as base to challenge juvenile offender case, 359
civil disability as barrier, 222
constitutional right, 189
employment as success factor, 223
goal of prisoner rights movement, 13
greater amenability of women, 342
incompatible with retribution or punishment, 577
lawyer's most difficult area, 473
punishment as therapy, 85

References are to pages

Rehabilitation (Cont'd)
purpose of regimentation, 8
right of juvenile offenders, 362
Religious Freedom
"preferred" right, 67
Remedies
choice of proper litigation goal,
    317
Retribution
purpose of punishment, 601
renounced as prison goal by U.S.
    Supreme Court, 190

S

Settlement
proper time for, 267
Sing Sing Prison (*see:* **Auburn
Plan**)
Solitary Confinement
cruel and unusual punishment, 116
juvenile offenders, 12
plausible in severe disciplinary in-
    fractions, 525
substantial punishment, 80
Spanish-Speaking
prison problems peculiar to, 385–
    387
"Strip Cells"
defined, 12

T

Three-Judge Courts
availability in prisoner rights
    cases, 248
election in prisoner rights cases,
    262
Torture
clearly violative of rights, 302
punishment by, 115
Trusty System
described, 114

U

Unemployment
civil disability of ex-convicts, 217
refusal to hire convict policeman
    as reasonable, 229

Unemployment (Cont'd)
right-privilege distinction in gov-
    ernment work, 224
Unionizing
prisoners' right, 72

V

Venue
prisoner rights action in federal
    court, 249
Victimless Crimes
decriminalization, 19
Visitation
conjugal, 583
female prisoners' children, 346
prisoners' right, 69
role in preparing prisoner for re-
    lease, 535
Voting
prisoners' right, 71
right of juvenile offender, 368

W

Witnesses
choice of credible prisoners, 259
due process right to present, 94
expert, 269
protective orders to shield prison-
    ers, 264
sample deposition of friendly ex-
    pert, 661
sample deposition of hostile, 675
selection and preparation for trial,
    268
Women
prison problems peculiar to, 341–
    352
Work-Release
defined, 11
designed for minimum-security in-
    stitutions, 84
programs in action, 582
rehabilitation purpose defeated by
    civil disability, 224
Writings
prisoners' right, 70